MOON HANDBOOKS®
NICARAGUA

© RANDY WOOD

Nicaragua's Pacific Coast

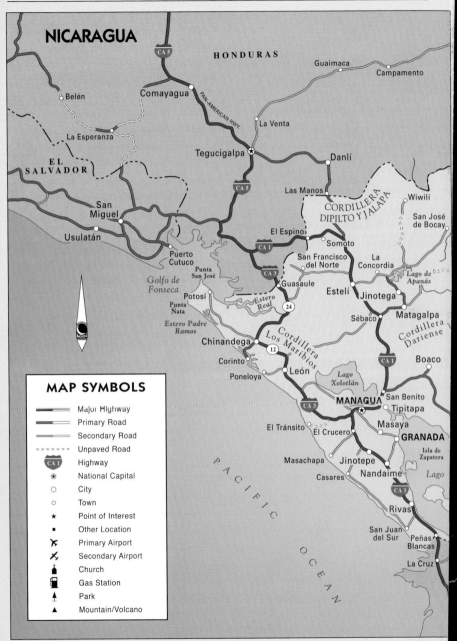

NICARAGUA

CA 5

HONDURAS

Guaimaca

Campamento

Belén

Comayagua

PAN-AMERICAN HWY.

La Venta

La Esperanza

Tegucigalpa ✪

Danlí

EL SALVADOR

CA 5

Las Manos

Wiwilí

CORDILLERA DIPILTO Y JALAPA

San José de Bocay

San Miguel

El Espino

Somoto

Usulatán

CA 1

San Francisco del Norte

La Concordia

Lago de Apanás

Puerto Cutuco

Punta San José

CA 3

Guasaule

Estelí

Jinotega

Golfo de Fonseca

Potosí

24

Esteró Real

Sébaco

Matagalpa

Punta Nata

Estero Padre Ramos

Cordillera Los Maribios

Chinandega

12

León

Corinto

Poneloya

Cordillera Dariense

Boaco

CA 1

Lago Xolotlán

San Benito

CA 4

MANAGUA ✪

Tipitapa

El Tránsito

El Crucero

Masaya

GRANADA

Masachapa

Jinotepe

Nandaime

Isla de Zapatera

Casares

Lago

CA 1

Rivas

San Juan del Sur

Peñas Blancas

La Cruz

PACIFIC OCEAN

MAP SYMBOLS

▬▬▬	Major Highway
▬▬▬	Primary Road
▬▬▬	Secondary Road
- - - -	Unpaved Road
CA 1	Highway
✪	National Capital
○	City
○	Town
★	Point of Interest
▪	Other Location
✕	Primary Airport
✕	Secondary Airport
▪	Church
▯	Gas Station
▲	Park
▲	Mountain/Volcano

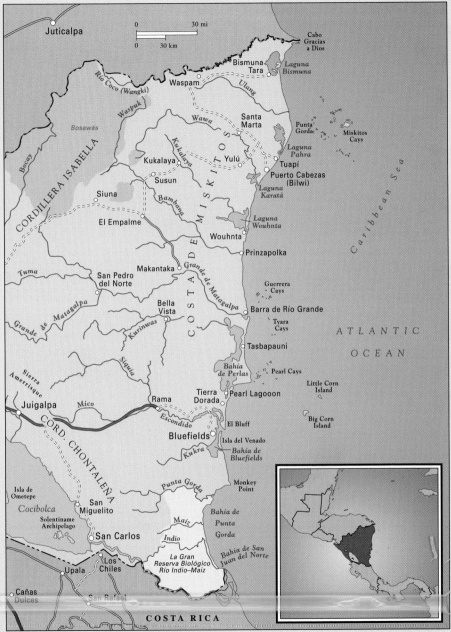

MOON HANDBOOKS®
NICARAGUA
FIRST EDITION

JOSHUA BERMAN & RANDY WOOD

AVALON
TRAVEL

Moon Handbooks: Nicaragua
First Edition

Joshua Berman & Randy Wood

Published by
Avalon Travel Publishing
1400 65th Street, Suite 250
Emeryville, CA 94608, USA

Please send all comments, corrections,
additions, amendments, and critiques to:

Moon Handbooks: Nicaragua
Avalon Travel Publishing
1400 65th Street, Suite 250
Emeryville, CA 94608, USA
email: atpfeedback@avalonpub.com
www.moon.com

Printing History
1st edition—January 2003
5 4 3 2 1

ISBN: 1-56691-481-7
ISSN: 1539-1019

Editor and Series Manager: Erin Van Rheenen
Copy Editor: Leslie Miller
Graphics Coordinator: Melissa Sherowski
Production: Jacob Goolkasian, Karen Heithecker
Cover Design: Kari Gim
Interior Design: Amber Pirker, Alvaro Villanueva, Kelly Pendragon
Map Editors: Olivia Solís, Naomi Adler Dancis
Cartographers: Mike Morgenfeld, Kat Kalamaras, Sheryle Veverka
Proofreader: Jeannie Trizzino
Indexer: Vera Gross
Front cover photo: © Joshua Berman

Distributed by Publishers Group West

Printed in USA by Worzalla

ABOUT THE AUTHOR
Joshua Berman

Randy Wood and Joshua Berman first joined forces as co-editors of Peace Corps Nicaragua's quarterly publication, *¡Va Pué!,* which they helped turn from an 18-page administrative newsletter into a 70-page volunteer magazine. Throughout their two-year tour, they continually grumbled that Nicaragua lacked a decent traveler's guidebook— so they wrote one.

Joshua Berman is a freelance writer and Outward Bound Instructor— and constantly figuring out how to support both habits. Born a Jewish hillbilly in Clarksburg, West Virginia, Joshua moved with his family to Long Island when he was 12 and quickly gained a New York attitude, a Grateful Dead tape collection, and eventually, a lot of facial hair. Despite New York, Joshua's favorite class during four years at Brown University was "Country, Bluegrass, and Old-Time Music." He graduated with a B.A. degree in Environmental Studies and went on to serve a year as an AmeriCorps volunteer in Northern California, where he swam with salmon and hooted at spotted owls. During the next two years, he found himself getting paid to sew backpacks in Maine, bounce rock concerts in Boulder, photograph Ozzy Osbourne in Denver, and write about inline skating and BASE jumping (neither of which he's ever tried). Some of the things he did *not* get paid to do were snowboard, hike, and serve as a rural EMT.

During his Peace Corps service in Nicaragua's misty mountains, Joshua—now known as Josué—started a listserv called NicaDayz that eventually served as the basis for an epistolary novel about his experience there. His articles have appeared in *Hooked On the Outdoors, Gravity, Backcountry, Transitions Abroad, Emergency Medical Services,* and *Brown Alumni Monthly* magazines.

Summertime finds Joshua leading wilderness expeditions for Outward Bound, teaching teenagers about things like fungus prevention and the "warrior spirit" while backpacking and canoeing through the northwoods of Maine and the wilds of New York City. Between trips, he plays guitar, banjo, and mandolin, and tries to read, write, and travel as much as possible. Joshua's website is www.stonegrooves.net.

ABOUT THE AUTHOR
Randy Wood

Born on the sandy shore of New York's Atlantic coast, Randy Wood spent his childhood in various small sailboats, developing a mariner's curiosity for what lies over the horizon. His first opportunity to find out was at the age of 11, when his family crossed the United States from New York to California in a beat-up Volkswagen bus.

After nearly 20 subsequent years of traveling, exploring, and switching jobs, Randy has crossed the United States several more times, traveled and worked his way through Pennsylvania's Amish country, Europe, Indonesia, Singapore, the Caribbean, and finally Central America, where he's resided since 1998. He's worked as a pizza chef, deep-sea salmon fisherman, teacher, surveyor, agronomist, and civil/environmental engineer. One of his most rewarding experiences was teaching English to refugees and immigrants in Boston; one of his least was pumping gas at Woody's.

Shortly after arriving in Nicaragua to teach soil conservation to rural Nicaraguan farmers, Randy experienced the devastation of Hurricane Mitch firsthand when he found himself trapped on the wrong side of a swollen, bridge-less river during the brunt of the storm. After the Peace Corps, he remained in Nicaragua as the in-country manager for the Army Corps of Engineers' Hurricane Mitch Reconstruction program, during which time he met and fell in love with the Nicaraguan woman he would later marry.

In his limited free time, Randy enjoys playing 12-string folk guitar, swimming and surfing, salsa, tango, and swing dancing, backpacking, making maps, and fiddling with Linux-based computers. He remains an insufferable gearhead whose challenge to find the perfect backpack and its contents continues unabated.

Randy's mother relates that when he was only three years old, he would surprise people asking him what he wanted to be when he grew up by replying not "a fireman" but "a writer." *Moon Handbooks: Nicaragua* is his first book. Randy's website is www.therandymon.com.

*A todos los Nicaragüenses que nos
han acogido como parte de sus familias.*

To all those Nicaraguans who have
taken us in as a part of their families.

Contents

SPECIAL TOPICS

MASAYA, CARAZO, AND THE PUEBLOS BLANCOS 145

MASAYA 145
Orientation and Getting Around; Sights and Attractions; Entertainment and
Events; Shopping; Accommodations; Food; Information; Services; Getting There
and Away
NEAR MASAYA 154
Coyotepe; Volcán Masaya National Park; Nindirí; Laguna de Apoyo
THE PUEBLOS BLANCOS 157
Orientation and Getting Around; Catarina; San Juan de Oriente; Diriá and
Diriomo; Niquinohomo; Masatepe; San Marcos
CARAZO AND THE PACIFIC BEACHES 160
Diriamba; Carazo Beaches; Jinotepe; Near Jinotepe

SPECIAL TOPICS

GRANADA 165

History; Orientation and Getting Around; Sights and Attractions; Nightlife and
Entertainment; Accommodations; Food; Shopping; Travel Information; Tour
Operators; Services; Getting There and Away
NEAR GRANADA 181
Las Isletas; Parque Nacional Archipiélago Zapatera

SPECIAL TOPICS

SOUTHWESTERN NICARAGUA: RIVAS, OMETEPE,
AND SAN JUAN DEL SUR 184

Nandaime
RIVAS 188
Attractions and Sights; Entertainment and Events; Sports and Recreation;
Accommodations; Food; Shopping; Services; Getting There and Away

SPECIAL TOPICS

BOACO, CHONTALES, AND THE ROAD TO EL RAMA 323

SPECIAL TOPIC

THE ATLANTIC COAST 347

WASPÁM AND THE RÍO COCO 384

The Land and the People; Entertainment; Accommodations; Food; Shopping;
Information and Services; Getting There and Away; River Trips from Waspám;
Trips by Land from Waspám

SPECIAL TOPICS

SOLENTINAME AND THE RÍO SAN JUAN 390

History; Climate and Seasons

SAN CARLOS 395

Orientation and Getting Around; Sights and Entertainment; Accommodations;
Food; Shopping; Information and Services; Getting There and Away

NEAR SAN CARLOS 400

Solentiname; Los Guatuzos Wildlife Refuge; Esperanza Verde; North of
San Carlos

DOWN THE RÍO SAN JUAN 407

Boca de Sábalos; El Castillo; Bartola; San Juan del Norte

SPECIAL TOPICS

RESOURCES 415

Maps

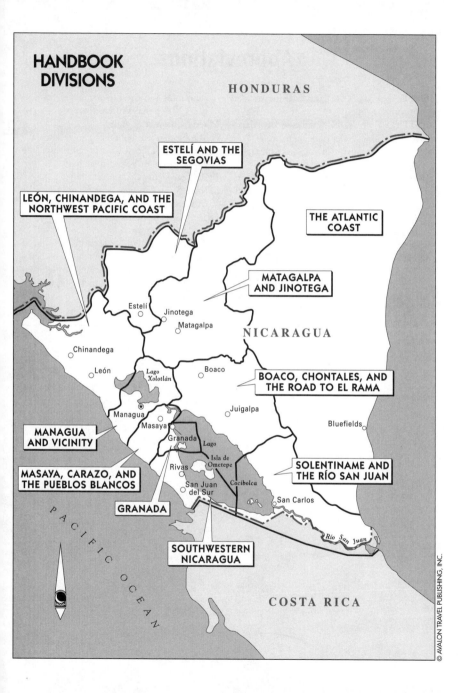

HANDBOOK DIVISIONS

HONDURAS

ESTELÍ AND THE SEGOVIAS

LEÓN, CHINANDEGA, AND THE NORTHWEST PACIFIC COAST

THE ATLANTIC COAST

MATAGALPA AND JINOTEGA

Estelí

Jinotega

Matagalpa

NICARAGUA

Chinandega

León

Lago Xolotlán

Boaco

BOACO, CHONTALES, AND THE ROAD TO EL RAMA

Managua

Masaya

Juigalpa

Bluefields

MANAGUA AND VICINITY

Granada

Lago

MASAYA, CARAZO, AND THE PUEBLOS BLANCOS

Rivas

Isla de Ometepe

SOLENTINAME AND THE RÍO SAN JUAN

GRANADA

San Juan del Sur

Cocibolca

San Carlos

SOUTHWESTERN NICARAGUA

PACIFIC OCEAN

Río San Juan

COSTA RICA

© AVALON TRAVEL PUBLISHING, INC.

Abbreviations

ENEL: Empresa Nicaragüense de Electricidad (electric company)

ENITEL: Empresa Nicaragüense de Telecomunicaciónes (telephone company)

FSLN: Frente Sandinista de Liberación Nacional (Sandinista party)

IFA: (EEH-fa) East German troop transport, used commonly in Nicaraguan public transportation system; it probably stands for something in German, but in Nicaragua, it means *imposible frenar atiempo* (impossible to brake on time).

INETER: Instituto Nicaragüense de Estudios Territoriales (government geography/geology institute)

MARENA: Ministerio del Ambiente y los Recursos Naturales (Ministry of Natural Resources and the Environment), administers Nicaragua's protected areas

MYA: Million Years Ago

NGO: Nongovernmental Organization

PLC: Partido Liberal Constitucionalista, the conservative anti-Sandinista party

PCV: Peace Corps Volunteer

SINAP: Sistema Nacional de Areas Protegidas (National System of Protected Areas)

UCA: Universidad de Centroamerica

UN: United Nations

UNAN: Universidad Nacional Autónoma de Nicaragua

USAID: United States Agency for International Development, channels congressionally approved foreign aid

Keeping Current

Writing a guidebook is very much like taking a snapshot: freezing the image of a place on a giant frame. But that snapshot ignores the fact that the subject was in motion. Progress, evolution, and change are inevitable, and although the authors have made a Herculean effort to ensure the facts are up-to-date, time and progress team up to ensure our information will never be perfect.

Since this book went to press, businesses have begun or failed, roads have been paved or been abandoned, and the *nacatamale* lady has moved up to selling burgers. Prices, naturally, have changed, and so the prices we quote in this book should be taken as general guidelines, as any good traveler knows.

If we've missed something noteworthy, or you find our advice off the mark, please let us know. This book will be stronger and more useful if you take the time to comment. Please address your letters to:

Moon Handbooks: Nicaragua
Avalon Travel Publishing
1400 65th Street, Suite 250
Emeryville, California 94608
atpfeedback@avalonpub.com

Preface

As we write, Nicaragua bursts loudly around our Managua apartment in hot colors and crude fireworks, the purpose of which are "to call the Lord's attention to our happiness." So explained our neighbor as we all sat in rocking chairs on the sidewalk in front of our building. Fireworks are everywhere here, punctuating religious events and fiestas throughout the year; they are maddeningly loud and easy to complain about. Tonight, however, we choose to celebrate — God, apparently, is watching.

Nicaragua, the black sheep of Central America, is sorely misunderstood in the world. Since disappearing from the headlines in the early 1990s, life in Nicaragua has moved steadily forward, leaving behind in the rest of the world's mind only the olive-clad images of the war-torn '80s. But this is not a nation of perpetual crisis! The revolution and ensuing civil war that ended in 1990 now make up one more chapter in the nation's tumultuous history, and their recent memory adds grit to the reality of being in Nicaragua.

Nicaraguans — five million of 'em (by the grace of God!) — survive amidst the day-to-day struggle that is life in the Developing World. They do so with an incredible vitality and with the ability to enjoy life in a way more prosperous societies have forgotten. Nicaragua is a place where a beat-up, rusted pickup truck that barely runs has shiny stickers across the back window that read: *Sonrie Porque La Vida es Maravilla* (Smile Because Life Is Wonderful).

This is a nation with much to teach. A friend recently wrote, "Nicaraguans help me become the best that I can be." While Nicaragua has never failed to attract visitors, the majority have been less than traditional — people from all over the world have come here to work, write, study, paint, and volunteer. Increasingly, they are also coming to relax on Nicaragua's beaches, hike her jungles, float her rivers, and explore her countryside. If you are only passing through Nicaragua, you may never know what you missed. But then, if you were merely passing through, you wouldn't be holding this book in your hands, preparing to immerse yourself deep within this geologically and culturally vibrant landscape.

Nicaragua's toddler tourism industry continues to stretch and improve, nourished by a recent investment boom and steady increase in visitors, and it is this freshness that makes touring Nicaragua such a powerful, rewarding, and challenging experience. Canned tourist programs are few and far between, and a trip to Nicaragua means spending time among Nicaraguans. Principal in your endeavors to understand this country is getting to know its people, whose charm, strong opinions, and casual hospitality are probably their nation's greatest attraction. They will show you that there is more to do and see in Nicaragua than you'll ever have time for—even if you make this your home for several years. If you let her, Nicaragua—and all her children—will take you in.

Moon Handbooks: Nicaragua features abundant destinations where it is entirely possible that the reader will be the *only* foreign traveler in town. This extraordinary opportunity carries unique cultural (and logistical) challenges. Consequently, this book will be most appreciated by travelers who find this lack of established infrastructure inspiring and exhilarating, rather than a shortcoming. Visitors who rise to Nicaragua's challenges find themselves changed by the experience.

In 1990, Alan Hulme, Steve Krekel, and Shannon O'Reilly self-published 1,000 precious copies of *Not Just Another Nicaragua Travel Guide.* More than a practical guidebook to a nation in the midst of its most critical moment, their book served as a celebration of a country they had grown to love during their time there in the 1980s. "How refreshing Nicaragua was," they wrote. "Revolution. Empty beaches. Lifelong friends and cheap rum. Priests, poets, and rocking chairs. Employment on movie sets and coffee cooperatives. Swedish nursing brigades. Reggae, Rumba, and Ragamuffin... daily doses of anger, laughter, irony, inflation, impassioned politics... a world in motion; a chance for spiritual redemption."

One decade and several governments later, *our* Nicaragua is a very different place than that of the 1980s. Nevertheless, we wholeheartedly believe that the "chance for spiritual redemption" endures today. This is your chance to find out for yourself.

A book has the capacity to express a country's heart, as long as it stays away from vacations, holidays, sightseeing, and the half-truths in official hand-outs; as long as it concentrates on people in their landscape, the dissonance as well as the melodies, the contradictions, and the vivid trivia.

Paul Theroux

Introduction

Fiery and molten under its shifting skin, peaceful and vast on the surface of its great lakes, Nicaragua is at once intensely inspiring, incredibly frustrating, and as deeply relaxing as a low-slung hammock. Here you'll find all manner of wild adventures, be they the kind with vines, monkeys, and machetes, or the type of unsought intercultural epiphanies that brand our souls for life.

Nicaraguans are fiercely proud of their heritage. Everything that makes them Nicaraguan—from the geology and history of their land to their poetry and music—distinguishes them from their Central American neighbors. Opening yourself to what makes Nicaragua Nicaragua—not least of which is the hospitality of your hosts—is the first step to really knowing this country.

Prepare to answer a lot of questions when you tell people about your visit to Nicaragua. In fact, the outdated jokes and curious (and often impressed) looks you'll get will provide perfect opportunities to spread a little-known truth: that, as the sign says in the airport in Managua, Nicaragua awaits you with *"Brazos Abiertos"* ("Open Arms"). Pack a little extra patience and the brightest color film you can find—and welcome to Nicaragua. The Land of Lakes and Volcanoes. The Heart of America.

©JOSHUA BERMAN

The old Spanish cross above La Trinidad, Estelí.

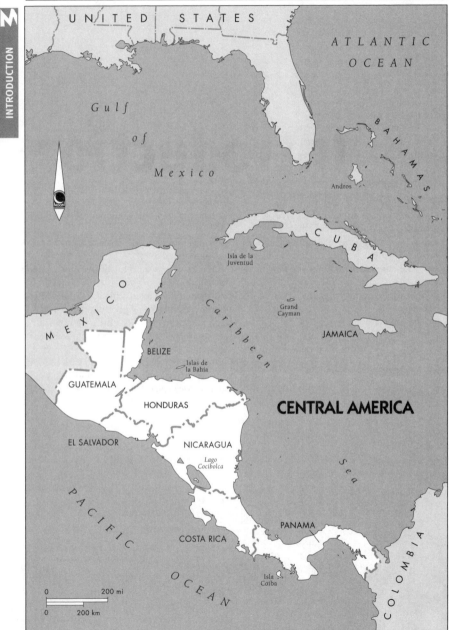

The Land

The largest and lowest Central American country, Nicaragua is a nation of geographical superlatives. Located at the elbow in the Central American isthmus where the land bends and then plummets southward to Panamá, Nicaragua is almost dead center between North and South America. It is part of a biological corridor that for millions of years has allowed plant and animal species from two continents to mingle, and the resulting blend of flora and fauna is fascinating.

In the 16th century, Nicaragua's geographical beauty enchanted the conquistadores, who reported, "The Nicaraguan plains are some of the most beautiful and pleasant lands that can be found in the Indies because they are very fertile with *mahicales* and vegetables, *fesoles* of diverse types, fruits of many kinds and much cacao."

Nicaragua is roughly triangular in shape and dominated by two large lakes in the southwest. The northern border with Honduras is 530 kilometers long, the longest transect across the Central American isthmus. To the south, the better part of the Nicaraguan–Costa Rican border is formed by the southern shore of the Río San Juan, with the river completely within Nicaraguan territory. (Costa Rica's attempts to navigate and patrol the river have been met aggressively by the Nicaraguan government and are the subject of current headlines; a compromise is yet to be reached.) To the east and west lie the Caribbean Sea and the Pacific Ocean, respectively. With 127,849 square kilometers of land area, Nicaragua is approximately the size of Greece or the state of New York. Nicaragua was once even larger, but in the last several centuries has lost some 50,000 square kilometers to her neighbors. When Nicaragua was still a colony of Spain, for example, the northern border included the eastern third of what is now Honduras, and the Costa Rican territories of Nicoya and Guanacaste.

Administratively, the nation is divided into 15 units called *departamentos,* and two vast autonomous regions on the Atlantic coast known as the North and South Atlantic Autonomous Regions (RAAN and RAAS). The departments, in turn, are divided into a total of 145 municipalities. The two autonomous regions elect their own officials, not necessarily on the same election schedule as the rest of the nation. Nicaragua's three largest cities are Managua, León, and Granada, followed by Estelí, Masaya, and the remaining department capitals.

GEOGRAPHY

Rivers run through me
Mountains rise in my body
And the geography of this country
Is taking shape in me
Turning me into lakes, chasms, ravines,
Earth to sow this love
—opening like a furrow—
Filling me with a longing to live
To see it free, beautiful,
Full of smiles
I want to explode with love ...

Gioconda Belli (**Nicaraguan writer**)

Nicaragua's favorite nickname for itself—the land of lakes and volcanoes—is indication enough of its geography, which is indeed dominated by two great lakes and a chain of striking volcanoes. Nicaragua's water and volcanic resources have had an enormous effect on its human history, from the day the first Nahuatl people concluded their migration south and settled on the forested shores of Lake Cocibolca (Lake Nicaragua), to the first Spanish settlements along the lakes, to the many as yet unrealized plans to build a trans-isthmus canal (see Canal Dreams special topic in Solentiname and the Río San Juan).

Geologic History and Formation

The earth that comprises Nicaragua, like all of Central America, took shape 60 million years ago (MYA) when the isthmus formed.

Geologically speaking, the land that makes up Nicaragua's northern third is the most ancient. In the area of Telpaneca and Quilalí, rocks dated at 200 million years old are thought to have once been part of a small Jurassic-Cretaceous continent that included the modern-day Yucatán Peninsula in Mexico and the Antilles Islands. To the south, what are now Costa Rica's Talamanca Mountains formed an archipelago of isolated volcanoes. During the Tertiary period (65–1.7 MYA), intense volcanic activity and erosion produced large amounts of sediment and volcanic flows that accumulated underwater.

There were at least two periods of intense volcanic activity: one in the Eocenic-Oligocenic period (55–25 MYA) when the lesser features of Nicaragua's central highlands were formed, and a second in the Miocene (25–13 MYA) that produced the larger mountains in Matagalpa and Jinotega. The Pacific region of Nicaragua was formed around two MYA, when shifting tectonic plates in the Pacific and Caribbean caused the seabed to be lifted. The main volcanic mountain range that runs northwest-southeast across the Pacific plains formed when the so-called Cocos plate slid under the Caribbean plate. Ocean water from the Atlantic rushed in along a broad sunken valley of the Pacific plate now known as the Nicaraguan Depression, and pooled to form the lakes. Some geologists believe the Atlantic and Pacific actually connected at this point in time and were later cut off by volcanic sedimentation. Erosion began pulling material from the landmass outward to the sea, building up Nicaragua's Pacific region and gradually forming the Atlantic coast.

Plate tectonics theory, in spite of being widely accepted since the 1960s, is most frequently criticized for its failure to adequately explain the geology and geography of several regions of the world, including Central America. It is highly probable that our concept of the geological events that formed Central America will change as geologic science progresses. Regardless of the mechanism, however, the convergence of the plates ensures crustal instability, which manifests itself in frequent volcanic and earthquake activity in all of Central America, and especially Nicaragua.

Volcanoes and Mountain Ranges

Nicaragua has some 40 volcanoes, six of which are active, and each of which is unique and climbable. Running roughly parallel to the Pacific shore, Nicaragua's volcanoes form part of the "Ring of Fire" that encompasses most of the western coast of the Americas and wraps around, by way of the Aleutian Islands of Alaska, into Japan and Indonesia. The Maribio (Nahuatl for the giant men) and Dirian mountain ranges stretch nearly 300 kilometers from the volcanic peaks of Concepción and Maderas in the middle of Lake Nicaragua (on Isla de Ometepe) to Cosigüina, which juts into the Gulf of Fonseca.

Volcanic activity is central to Nicaragua's history. The first volcanic event recorded in modern times was the eruption of Volcán Masaya in the early 1500s. The lava flow from this eruption helped form the present-day lagoon at the base of the mountain. Another great lava flow occurred in the year 1772, leaving behind a black, barren path still visible today where the Managua-Masaya highway crosses it. In 1609, the first Spanish settlers abandoned the city of León when Momotombo erupted. And in January of 1835, Volcán Cosigüina blew its top in a violent eruption that threw ash as far away as Jamaica and Mexico. The area for 250 kilometers around the volcano was covered in ash and burning pumice, and the entire devastated peninsula suffered three days of ash cloud–induced darkness. This volcanic activity is responsible for the exceptional fertility of Nicaragua's soils, most notably the agricultural plains on the Pacific coast near Chinandega and León.

Today, the most active volcanoes are Momotombo, San Cristóbal, and Telica, which seem to take turns trembling and throwing out plumes of gases, smoke, and occasionally lava. Don't let them put you off though—climbing these hills are reason enough to visit Nicaragua. San Cristóbal is the highest, at 1,745 meters. A smaller peak adjacent to San Cristóbal, "Casita," still bears the immense scar of the landslide that buried thousands in an avalanche of rock and mud during Hurricane Mitch (see Hurricane Mitch special topic), and that began shaking again in January of 2002.

Less prominent but more regularly violent, Volcán Telica, just north of León, erupts approximately every five years. At its base are several interesting gas vents that produce boiling mud and sulfur. Neighboring Cerro Negro is one of the youngest volcanoes on the planet, having pushed its way through a farmer's field in the middle of the 1800s. It has grown steadily and violently to the height of 400 meters in 150 years. Cerro Negro's last three eruptions have been increasingly powerful: in 1992 Cerro Negro belched up a cloud of burning gases and ash seven kilometers high, and buried the city of León under 15 centimeters of ash and dust. Eight thousand inhabitants were evacuated to prevent tragedy and with good reason—the weight of the ash caused several homes to collapse. Volcán Momotombo (Nahuatl for great burning peak) has a perfect conical peak and is visible from great distances across the Pacific plains from as far away as Matagalpa. One vantage point for a particularly striking view of the mountain is the Managua–Masaya highway. Momotombo is responsible for approximately 10 percent of Nicaragua's electricity via a geothermal plant located at its base. It hasn't erupted since 1905, but Momotombo's menace has in no way diminished. Increased seismic activity and rumbling in April 2000 caused Managua residents great concern until the mountain eventually quieted back down.

Volcán Masaya is the most easily accessed of Nicaragua's volcanoes, with a paved road leading right to the edge of the crater. Volcán Masaya is actually formed of three craters, the largest of which, Santiago, is the only crater in the Americas that contains a visible pool of incandescent liquid lava in its center. This lava was best seen from 1965 to 1979, as the quantity of visible lava appears to fluctuate on an approxiamtely 30-year cycle.

Ometepe and Zapatera are the two principal islands that occupy the center of Lake Cocibolca. Both are volcanic. Zapatera (625 meters), home to Nicaragua's first inhabitants, is the remnant of an ancient and collapsed volcano. Ometepe (Nahuatl for two peaks) is composed of the volcanoes Concepción (1,610 meters) and Maderas

(1,394 meters). While Concepción is still quite active and has erupted as recently as 1956, Maderas seems to be dormant and has a tough-to-reach mountain lake in its crater.

Also accessible and host to a protected cloud forest and system of coffee plantations, Volcán Mombacho (1,345 meters) is a dormant volcano whose explosion and self-destruction is thought to have formed the nearby archipelago of islets in Lake Cocibolca near the shore of Granada. Mombacho took its modern shape in 1570 when a major avalanche on the south slope buried an indigenous village of 400 inhabitants and left the crater open and exposed.

The central and northern areas of Nicaragua are dominated by three lesser mountain ranges: the Cordilleras Isabelia, Huapi, and Chontaleña. These three ranges radiate northeast, east, and southeast, respectively, from the center of the country, gradually melting into the lowland jungle and swamps of the Atlantic coast. These mountains include a half-dozen prominent peaks and were the scene of intense fighting during several conflicts in Nicaraguan history. Nicaragua's highest point, Cerro Mogotón, at 2,107 meters, is located along the Honduran border in Nueva Segovia.

Lakes and Lagoons

Nicaragua's geography is dominated by its two great lakes, Cocibolca (Lake Nicaragua) and Xolotlán (Lake Managua), which together occupy nearly 10 percent of the country's surface area.

Lake Xolotlán, although broad (1,025 square kilometers), is extremely shallow with an average depth of only seven meters. It reaches its deepest—26 meters—near the island of Momotombito. Unfortunately, Lake Managua is biologically dead, victim to a century of untreated human waste from the city of Managua and the extensive dumping of industrial wastes during the 1970s, including dangerous levels of lead, cyanide, benzene, mercury, and arsenic. Look out across the water from the shoreline in Managua and take note that no one is fishing. The tremendous opportunities for tourism, recreation, and potable water for human consumption that would be possible if Lake Managua were

INTRODUCTION

clean are the incentives of a plan backed by loans from Japan and the World Bank. The project entails collecting and treating Managua's sewage, as well as the daunting (and incredibly expensive) process of cleansing the lake itself in water treatment plants to be built on the lakeshore.

Before Hurricane Mitch, Lake Managua was a lake with no outflow, whose volume remained constant due to intense solar evaporation. Historically, the outlet at Tipitapa was naturally sealed by a low ridge that permitted water to cross the low divide between Lake Xolotlán and Lake Cocibolca only once every 15 years or so during severe storms. During Hurricane Mitch, however, Lake Cocibolca rose three meters in less than a week, and the Tipitapa River became a real river, and proceeded to flood most of the town of Tipitapa and the Pan-American Highway. For three years after Hurricane Mitch, the river flowed continuously, discharging the filthy waters of Lake Xolotlán into the relatively pristine Lake Cocibolca.

Lake Cocibolca is the larger of Nicaragua's two lakes and is easily one of Nicaragua's greatest natural treasures. At 8,264 square kilometers and 160 kilometers long along its axis, Lake Cocibolca is just smaller than the island of Puerto Rico and lies a scant 31 meters above sea level. It's also deep—up to 60 meters in some places, and relatively clean. The prevailing winds, which blow from the east across the farmlands of Chontales, make the eastern part of Cocibolca relatively calm, but the waters of the western half can often be choppy and rough. A massive pipe system is presently being designed, which, if built, would carry drinking water from Cocibolca to the city of Managua to meet the needs of the capital's rapidly growing population and industrial sector.

Lake Cocibolca and Río San Juan are well known in scientific circles for the presence of the world's only known freshwater shark (*Carcharhinus leucas*), sawfish, and tarpon. The bull shark was once thought to be an ancient species that was trapped in Lake Cocibolca when, in prehistoric times, the land mass shifted, leaving it trapped in a lake that gradually lost its salinity. It has since been proven that the sharks actually travel between the Caribbean Sea and Lake Cocibolca (via the Río San Juan), adjusting for the change in the water's salinity as they go. Unfortunately, these sharks have not been seen in nearly 10 years, and it's presumed they've been forced into extinction by overfishing and habitat loss.

Nicaragua is home to nearly a dozen stunning lagoons, most of which are volcanic in origin and occupy ancient volcanic craters. Around Managua alone are the Nejapa, Tiscapa, and Asososca lagoons. West of Managua on the Chiltepe peninsula are the beautiful twin craters of Xiloá and Apoyeque. Xiloá was a popular swimming hole for the Managua crowd before Hurricane Mitch inundated most of the tourist facilities there. The water is still clean, but the structures—gazebos and concrete platforms—remain underwater. Near Masaya, the 200-meter-deep Laguna de Apoyo was formed sometime in the Quaternary period (1.6 MYA) by what is thought to be the most violent volcanic event in Nicaragua's prehistory. Not far away is Laguna de Masaya, at the base of the volcano of the same name. Other lagoons can be found on the western flank of Volcán Momotombo, and in the craters of the volcanoes Maderas and Cosigüina.

Rivers

To the original Spanish settlers in Granada, the Río San Juan was the elusive "drain" of Lake Cocibolca; after its "discovery," it became the shining star in many a trans-isthmus canal-builder's fantasies. The possibility of traveling up the Río San Juan, across Lake Cocibolca, and then by land to the Pacific Ocean, has made the San Juan the most historically important river in Nicaragua. In the years of the gold rush, many thousands of prospectors navigated up the Río San Juan en route to California; some made the return trip laden with riches, others with nothing. These days it isn't navigable by large ships due to several sets of rapids and decades of sedimentation exacerbated by shifts in the riverbed from occasional earthquakes. Along the shores are cattle ranches and small farms that primarily produce basic grains.

There's only one way to float: downstream on the Río San Juan.

The Río Escondido is a principal link in the transportation corridor from Managua to Bluefields and the Atlantic coast. Trucks of produce and merchandise (and busloads of travelers) are driven to El Rama and then shipped down the Escondido. The Río Escondido is formed by the convergence of three major rivers: the Siquia, Mico, and Rama. The Escondido and its tributaries are important to the cattle industry in Chontales, but massive deforestation along its banks have provoked frequent floods that have adversely affected the river port of El Rama.

The Río Coco, 680 kilometers long, is the longest river in Central America, fed by one headwater in Nicaragua and one in Honduras. Also known as the Río Segovia or by its indigenous name Wanki, the Coco passes through many types of terrain, including several minor canyons and vast stretches of virgin forest. Its shores are home to many small communities of the indigenous Miskito people, to whom the river bears great spiritual significance.

The Estero Real (The Royal Estuary), at 137 kilometers in length, is the most consequential body of water on the Pacific coast. It drains most of northwestern Nicaragua through extensive mangroves and wetlands to the Gulf of Fonseca. It is also home to extensive shrimp farming operations and is one of Nicaragua's best places to spot waterfowl.

Sea Islands

Corn Island and Little Corn Island are located in the Caribbean Sea, only 70 kilometers from the mainland. Their reefs are home to several diverse species of tropical fish, lobster, crab, shark, and more. Several sets of keys and reefs north of the islands are used extensively for fishing. These keys also provide an invaluable breeding ground for the green and carey turtles (*Chelonia mydas* and *Eretmochelys imbricata,* respectively) but, being relatively unlit and unpoliced, are also increasingly invaluable stopovers in the drug trade from Colombia.

Soils

In the Pacific region, the soils are typically of volcanic origin, highly fertile, and high in minerals.

HURRICANE MITCH

It was late October 1998, and in northern Nicaragua the rainy season had all but ended. The first harvest of the year had been lost to drought, and all hopes were on the second harvest, only one month away. From day to day there was sporadic drizzle, just right for the fields of red beans that were slowly gathering strength.

Then, quickly and determinedly, from a leaden sky, the rains began to fall. It was a loud, steady rain, the likes of which Nicaraguans had never experienced before, and in some parts of the country, it fell for seven straight days. The newspapers had mentioned a hurricane forming off the Atlantic coast, but Nicaraguans hadn't given much thought to the storm, named "Mitch," which had shifted course to the north, barely grazing the coast.

But Mitch was enormous and robust, with thick gray arms of clouds that swept in long spirals across the entire Central American isthmus, greedily gathering strength from both the Atlantic and Pacific Oceans. Off the north coast of Honduras, where Mitch had all but parked, winds around the eye of the hurricane had reached 290 kilometers per hour, making it a deadly class five storm, and Nicaragua would not escape its force. Hurricane Mitch was lethal to a degree never seen in the Western Hemisphere in recorded history, and even though it didn't pass directly over Nicaragua, the rains that fell there were so devastating—physically and psychological-ly—that many Nicaraguans will be measuring life "before and after Mitch" for generations to come.

The rains fell day and night, scarcely letting up for an hour at a time. On Thursday, October 29, the electricity failed in most of the north as power lines fell and poles were swept away. The country roads of red earth turned muddy, then became dangerous rivers of coffee-colored water coursing through the center of towns. Cattle that had been left in the fields found high ground under trees or were drowned and swept away. The rivers rose quickly and mercilessly, as the waters swelled into violent masses, tearing out the trees along their banks, snatching away thousands of homes, and spilling far beyond their banks. The debris carried away by the waters became deadly ballast, as enormous tree trunks, boulders, and mud came roaring down out of the mountains, carrying away bridges, buildings, and bodies.

Along the Pacific coast, in Chinandega, the rains were particularly ruthless, dumping the equivalent of a full year's rainfall in under four days. By October 29, the rivers of northern Nicaragua had risen to 10 times their normal size, overtopping, cutting around, or simply mangling and carrying away every bridge in their path. In Sébaco, the Río Viejo and the Río Grande de Matagalpa, which normally pass within a kilometer of each other, rose and combined, unleashing a wall of water on Ciudad Darío. Nicaragua's three principal hydropower reservoirs overflowed, unleashing torrents of water through their spillways and causing erosion damage that all but carried the dams away.

Just outside of Managua, the waters of Lake Xolotlán rose three meters (that's 3,300,000,000 cubic meters of water) over three days. Rising up and flowing out of the lake basin, the waters barreled through the old, dry

channel of the once-intermittent Río Tipitapa, raising the level of Lake Cocibolca and the Río San Juan as the waters traveled out to the Atlantic Ocean. Tipitapa, a lowland city built in the saddle between the two lakes, was half submerged by the river. On the Pan-American Highway, the enormous bridge that crossed over the Tipitapa River was damaged, then destroyed, and finally carried away completely. The entire northern half of the country was cut off from Managua. Major bridges were missing in Sébaco and Tipitapa, and every bridge without exception between León and Managua had been destroyed.

Meanwhile, near Chinandega, the crater of Volcán Casita had been filling with rainwater and at 2 P.M. on October 30, the southwest edge of the crater lip liquefied and broke off, descending in a torrent of mud, water, and rock 1.5 kilometers wide and three meters high, completely consuming several communities that inhabited the volcano's slopes, and killing thousands in a single moment. The mudflow poured southwest for a distance of over four kilometers to the highway, crossed it, and continued southwest into the town of Posoltega. In the aftermath there was no hope of recovering or even identifying victims. Teams were sent out to collect and burn the bodies before their advanced state of decomposition caused further health problems for the living.

Across Nicaragua, the losses continued even after the rains stopped. Campesinos who hadn't lost their homes lost much of what little they had. Cattle drowned or died from exposure, and the harvest was completely lost. Outbreaks of mosquito-borne diseases like dengue fever ensued, not to mention thousands of cases of pink eye and skin fungus caused from the moisture. In Condega, Mitch washed the town's three factories away, leaving the entire town without industry. This scenario was repeated in small towns throughout the country. The nation as a whole found itself at a standstill. Refugees occupied the schools and churches, and some communities waited nearly three months before electricity was restored to them.

The national economy fared no better—it is estimated that Hurricane Mitch reduced Nicaragua's gross domestic product by half, and decimated over 70 percent of the physical infrastructure of the country. Hundreds of health clinics were destroyed, as well as over 20,000 homes. Arable farmland was reduced by 11,550 hectares due to erosion, sand deposits, or flooding. Overall, economic losses sustained by this already suffering country were around $1.5 billion.

Hurricane Mitch also opened up scars less obvious than those of the deforested hillsides. Rather than increasing the sense of Nicaraguan solidarity in the process of rebuilding, political divisions were opened like raw wounds as the aid money poured in and politicians struggled to divert it to their own—and their constituents'—interests. President Alemán, never one to pass up an opportunity to further himself politically at the cost of a tragedy, fed fuel to this noxious fire. When the Sandinista mayor of Posoltega reported to Managua the tragedy that had occurred there, Alemán called her crazy and stalled the relief. The first day after the rains diminished, a planeload of Cuban doctors bearing crates of medical supplies landed on the tarmac in Managua and Alemán sent them away, saying his country had many starving people and couldn't afford to be sharing the limited supplies of food with additional visitors. A day later, Alemán greeted an aircraft of gringos by strutting across the tarmac with his arms outstretched in an open embrace.

Though the press called Mitch "the storm of the century," scientists estimate it was much more severe even than that, declaring it the most deadly storm event in at least 200 years. Mitch has given Nicaragua the chance to rebuild itself, to grow, and to learn. Hundreds of millions of dollars of aid money poured into Nicaragua in its aftermath, and the destroyed bridges were replaced with new, better-quality ones. Campesinos who lost their little homes were given new ones of concrete with corrugated steel roofs. Schools were rebuilt, new clinics constructed. Above all, in the post-Mitch years, much effort has gone into ensuring the Nicaraguan government and people are better prepared to deal with future disasters: training programs, flood warning detection systems, computer models, and more have been installed. They are all important steps, given that Hurricane Mitch will surely not be the last storm to wreak havoc in Nicaragua.

The north and central regions of Nicaragua are less fertile and consist of land with steeper slopes that encourage erosion and soil degradation. These soils are the result of the breakdown of basalt, andesite, and granite rock. The better soils are usually found alongside rivers. However, deforestation and fierce storms such as Hurricane Mitch have carried much of Nicaragua's best soil away, stripped it of its nutrient value, or buried it under thick layers of sand. In the north and northeast of Nicaragua, the soils were formed as a result of the breakdown of quartz and are far less fertile for agricultural purposes, though they are good for the production of forest, particularly the white pine and other pine species. The Sébaco Valley, home to Nicaragua's rice industry, is thought to have once been the bed of an immense lake. The clay-like black soils there are difficult to farm corn or beans on due to their ability to retain water and form marshland, qualities that are perfect for rice growing.

CLIMATE

Seasons

Nicaragua has two seasons, *invierno* (winter), which refers to the rainy season from approximately May to October, and *verano* (summer), or the dry season, lasting from November to April. However, the seasons vary from region to region and are inconsistent from one year to the next. The Río San Juan and much of the Atlantic coast, for example, have significantly longer, wetter rainy seasons, often stretching into January and sometimes even longer. In nearly all of Nicaragua, April and May are the hottest, driest months, prone to intense dust and clouds of smoke from farmers burning their fields in preparation for planting. In 1998 the smoke and dust were so intense the international airport at Managua was forced to close for nearly a full week.

Precipitation

Nicaragua's rainfall patterns are characterized by a six-month drought considered the single most serious limiting factor for Nicaragua's economic growth. The rainy season traditionally starts

WHEN TO GO

December and January are the coolest months and easily comprise the most refreshing and greenest time to visit Nicaragua. Daytime temperatures are pleasant, and the nights are marked by cool air and clear, starry skies. The temperature gradually climbs and the humidity increases from February until the first rains in May or early June. April and early May can be oppressively hot, dry, and dusty, especially in the lowland cities of Managua, León, and Granada. The temperature drops when the rainy season begins. Be aware that unpaved roads become unmanageable during the peak of the wet season, becoming completely unusable in some regions until things dry out. After extreme rainfalls, some streams will grow in size so suddenly that vehicles will be unable to cross. Have patience (a good mantra for traveling in Nicaragua anyway): most streams will drop back down within six hours of a heavy rainfall.

around May 15 and is typically marked by clear blue skies in the morning and then clouds that gather until around midday, when the rain begins to fall. The rainy season continues through November or December depending on the region, except for an Indian summer known as the *canícula,* which traditionally occurs from July 15 to August 15, during which time the rains temporarily cease. Most Nicaraguan farmers take advantage of the dry spell to harvest the corn and plant red beans in anticipation of the second half of the rainy season.

September and October are hurricane season in the Caribbean and the rainiest months in Nicaragua, when sustained, intense storms are common. However, the uncertainties of the global climate, and specifically the effects of El Niño and La Niña have considerably destabilized traditional rainfall patterns. In 2001, Nicaragua and most of Central America experienced a record drought, resulting in failed harvests and communities obliged to take food aid to survive in the Matagalpa countryside. On the Atlantic coast the dry season is unnoticeable—you can expect rain showers just about any time of year, while certain valleys in northern Nicaragua experience locally reduced rainy seasons.

Temperatures
Nicaragua, located between 11 and 15 degrees north latitude, is squarely in the tropics. The climate, while generally warm to hot, presents considerable variation from region to region and as you climb in altitude. Temperatures generally range from 27°C to 32°C (81°F to 90°F) during the rainy season, and from 30°C to 35°C (86°F to 95°F) in the dry season. In the mountains of Matagalpa and Jinotega, temperatures are significantly cooler (15°C–20°C, 59°F–68°F). The temperature rises noticeably as you travel from Managua northwest to León and Chinandega, and south into the Pueblos Blancos.

Hurricanes and Tropical Storms
August through November is the traditional hurricane season for all of the Caribbean basin, of which Nicaragua is a part. If traveling during these months, pay close attention to the newspaper and radio broadcasts, which will warn you if trouble is coming your way. If it looks like you are in the path of destruction, your best bet in most cases is to stay put. Find a room somewhere on high ground, buy some bottled water and flashlight batteries, and sit tight until it blows over.

Flora and Fauna

Nicaragua's position at the biological crossroads between North and South America and between the Atlantic and Pacific Oceans has blessed it with an astonishingly broad assortment of wildlife. Nicaragua's wide-ranging geography has also been a primary factor in the diversity and complexity of its ecosystems and their denizens.

FLORA
Of the world's 250,000 species of flowering plants, an estimated 15,000 to 17,000 are found in Central America. It is estimated Nicaragua is home to some 9,000 species of vascular plants, many of which are thought to be of medicinal value. Little has been done in the way of conservation of Nicaragua's plant species. A few areas are relatively well protected, but the majority of the land set aside by the government continues to experience intense pressure from the agricultural frontier (the farthest limits of deforestation and cultivation) and the scattered human settlements within the confines of the reserves.

Trees
The *madroño (Calycophyllum candidissimum)* is the national tree of Nicaragua. The hills south of Sébaco form the southern limit of the pine family found on the continent; south of Nicaragua the pines are outcompeted by other species. As of 2002, Nicaragua has a forest area of 5.5 million hectares, the majority of which is broadleaf forest, followed by pine forest *(Pinus caribea* and *P. oocarpa)*. At altitudes greater than 1,200 meters the forests also include *P. maximinoi* and *P. tecunumanii.* A full 2.5 million hectares of forest are considered commercial timber forest. Though the land and forests are often privately owned, the exploitation of forest products is under the control of the Nicaraguan government.

Principal Ecosystems
Nicaragua's varied topography and uneven rainfall distribution, not to mention a wide variety of tropical reefs, volcanoes, and volcanic crater lakes, translate into a phenomenal diversity of terrain and ecosystems. This can be easily appreciated during any road trip through Nicaragua, as you watch prairie grasslands melt into rolling hills into near-desert into craggy mountain ranges whose peaks are draped in cloud forest. You can burn your feet on an active volcano's peak and cool your heels in ocean surf the same day. Nicaragua's higher peaks are isolated ecosystems in their own right and home to several endangered as well as endemic species, and the streams, rivers, and two very different coastlines provide the settings for other distinct

ecosystems. In general, the land can be divided into the following ecological zones:

Pacific Dry Forest: The lowlands of the Pacific coast, specifically the broad, flat strip that borders the Pacific Ocean from sea level to approximately 800 meters in altitude, are a rain-stressed region dominated by thorny, rubbery species. The region typically receives less than 2,000 mm of rain per year. Both trees and non-cactus-like plants in this ecosystem shed their leaves in the middle of the dry season in preparation for the rain to come, and often burst into flower in April or May.

Upland Pine Forest: With the exception of the slopes of several Pacific mountains, namely San Cristóbal and Las Casitas in Chinandega, and Gùisisíl in Matagalpa, the majority of Nicaragua's pine forests are found in the north near Jalapa and Ocotal. Pines particularly thrive on poor, acidic soils, which are easily eroded if the area is logged.

Lower Mountainous Broadleaf Forest: Nicaragua's higher peaks are cloud covered for most of the year and home to a cool, moist biosphere rich in flora and fauna. Most of these areas are the more remote peaks of Matagalpa and Jinotega like Kilambé, Peñas Blancas, Saslaya, and Musún. But the beautiful and easily visited peaks of Volcán Mombacho near Granada, and Volcán Maderas on Ometepe are also home to this cloud forest.

Caribbean Rainy Zone: The Atlantic coast experiences rain throughout nearly 10 months of the year and the humidity hovers around 90 percent year-round. Most of the Atlantic coast is covered with tropical forest or even lowland rainforest, with trees that often reach 30 or 40 meters in height. In the north along the Río Coco are the remains of Nicaragua's last extensive pine forests *(Pinus caribaea)*, presently subject to intensive logging by national and international concessions.

FAUNA

Nicaragua is home to a great deal of exotic wildlife, much of which—unfortunately—you'll see for sale on the sides of the highways and at intersections in Managua, where barefoot merchants are seen hawking toucans, reptiles, ocelots, parrots, and macaws. This is a huge, largely unchecked problem, made more disturbing by the fact that of the animals that are captured for sale or export in Nicaragua, four out of every five die before reaching their final destination. To view fauna in their natural habitat involves getting out there and looking. Most critters are shy and many are nocturnal, but they're out there. To date, 1,804 vertebrate species, including 21 species endemic to Nicaragua, and approximately 14,000 invertebrate species have been defined. However, Nicaragua remains the least-studied country in the region, and it is thought that excursions into the relatively unexplored reserves of the north and northeast will confirm the existence of many additional new species.

Mammals

There are 176 mammal species (including sealife) known to exist in Nicaragua, over half of which are bats or small mammals, including rodents. Nicaragua has at least three endemic mammal species, two of which are associated with the Caribbean town of El Rama—the Rama squirrel *(Sciurus richmondi),* considered the tropical world's most endangered squirrel due to reduced habitat, and the Rama rice mouse *(Oryzomis dimidiatus).*

Nicaragua is also home to six big cat species, but there's no guarantee they'll be around for long. All six are listed as endangered, most seriously of all the jaguar and puma. Both were once common, but require extensive amounts of land on which to hunt. The Pacific region of Nicaragua, home to extensive agriculture for so many consecutive years now, is most likely devoid of big felines, with the possible exception of isolated communities on the higher slopes of some forested volcanoes like Mombacho. In the Atlantic region, small communities of cats eke out their survival in the dense forests of the southeast side of the Bosawás reserve. These species are unstudied and untracked, and are presumably preyed upon by local communities. Better off than the pumas and jaguars are smaller felines like ocelots and *tigrillos* trapped in the central forests, the latter of which are notorious chicken killers in rural farming communities.

Pizotes are playful and curious.

The agouti paca (a large, forest-dwelling rodent known in Nicaragua as the painted rabbit), the white-tailed deer *(Odocoileus virginianus),* and the collared peccary *(Tayassu tajacu,* a stocky piglike creature with coarse, spiky fur), though abundant, are under much pressure from hunters all through the north and east of Nicaragua. You may still see an agouti or peccary in Jinotega and to the east, if you're lucky.

Aquatic Life

Nicaragua is home to a wide variety of both saltwater and freshwater species of fish, due to the presence of two large lakes, two ocean coastlines, and numerous isolated crater lakes. Among Nicaragua's many saltwater species are flat needlefish *(Ablennes hians),* wahoo *(Acanthocybium solandri),* three kinds of sole, spotted eagle rays *(Aetobatus narinari),* the Gill's sand lance *(Ammodytoides gilli),* two kinds of moray *(Anarchias* sp.*),* croakers *(Bairdiella* sp.*),* triggerfish *(Balistes* sp.*),* hogfish *(Bodianus* sp.*),* eight kinds of perch *(Diplectrum* sp.*),* sea bass *(Diplectrum* sp.*),* and a dozen kinds of shark, including blacktip *(Carcharias. limbatus),* great white *(C. carcharias),* silky *(C. falciformis),* and spinner *(C. brevipinna).*

There are three primate species in Nicaragua: the mantled howler monkey *(Alouata palliata),* known popularly in Nicaragua as the *mono congo;* the Central American spider monkey *(Ateles geoffroyii);* and the white-faced capuchin *(Cebus capucinus).* Of the monkeys, the *congo* is the most common. On the slopes of Mombacho alone there are an estimated 1,000 individuals. You can also find them (or at least hear their throaty, haunting cries) on the slopes of Volcán Maderas (on the island of Ometepe), and the mountains of Matagalpa, particularly Selva Negra. Howler monkeys are able to project their voices an incredible distance; you can easily hear them several kilometers away. They eat fruits and leaves and spend most of their time in high tree branches. The white-faced capuchin is most frequently found in the forests in southeastern Nicaragua and parts of the Atlantic coast. It is a threatened species, but more so is the spider monkey, which is close to disappearing from Nicaragua.

The Baird's tapir is present in very small numbers in eastern Nicaragua; it is estimated that there are several communities of this three-toed ungulate in Bosawás. Nevertheless, this species is severely threatened with extinction.

Among the freshwater species are needlefish *(Strongylura* sp.*),* grunts *(Pomadasys* sp.*),* introduced tilapia *(Oreochromis aureus),* catfish *(Hexanematichthys* sp.*),* mojarra *(Eucinostomus* sp.*),* and snook *(Centropomus* sp.*).* The crater lakes in Nicaragua are thought to be home to some species of cichlid *(Amphilophus* sp.*)* found nowhere else in the world.

At least 58 different types of marine corals have been identified in the Atlantic, specifically in the Miskito Cays, Corn Island, and the Pearl Cays. Nicaragua's most common coral species include *Acropora pamata, A. cervicornis,* and *Montastrea anularis.* Brain coral *(Colypophylia natans)* and black coral *(Antipathes pennacea)* are common. Studied for the first time in 1977 and 1978, the shallow reefs of the Pearl Cays contain the best coral formations in the nation, but are currently in danger due to the enormous sediment load discharged by the Río Grande de Matagalpa.

The manatee *(Trichechus manatus)* is an important species currently protected by international statutes. In Nicaragua it can occasionally be found in the Caribbean in the mouth of the Río San Juan and in the coastal lagoons, and notably in Bluefields Bay. In 1993 the freshwater dolphin *(Sotalia fluviatilis)* was first spotted in Nicaragua and is most commonly sighted in Laguna de Wounta. The northern range for the freshwater dolphin was previously thought to be limited to Panamá.

Birds

Nicaragua has been blessed with abundant birdlife, owing partially to its location along the Central American biosphere corridor, along which many thousands of species migrate annually with the seasons. To date 676 species of birds in 56 families have been observed here, the more exotic of which you'll find in the mountains of the north and east, and along the Atlantic shore. Nicaragua has no endemic bird species of its own, but hosts 87 percent of all bird species known. The most exotic species known to reside in Nicaragua is also its most elusive, the quetzal *(Pharomacrus mocinno),* known to inhabit highlands in Bosawás, Jinotega, and Mata-galpa, especially along the slopes of Mt. Kilambé, and in Miraflor in Estelí.

Nicaragua's elegant and colorful national bird, the *guardabarranco (Momotus momota),* is more easily found than you'd think. The "Guardian of the Stream" (as its Spanish name translates) can be found catching small insects in urban gardens in the capital. It is distinguished by its long, odd-shaped, iridescent tail, which it carefully preens to catch the eye of the opposite sex. The *urraca* is a bigger, meaner version of the North American blue jay, with a dangly black crest on the top of its head. It's one of the larger of the common birds in Nicaragua and can frequently be found in treetops scolding the humans below. Though the *urraca* are everywhere, there's a particularly big population living along the slopes of Ometepe's volcanoes. Also at Lake Cocibolca, *oropendolas (Psarocolius wagleri)* build elaborate nests that hang suspended from the treetops around the lakeshore.

Reptiles

Of the 172 reptile species that make their homes in Nicaragua, nearly half are North American species, found in Nicaragua at the southern limit of their habitat, while 15 species are found only

crocodile

in Central America. Five species are endemic to Nicaragua, including the recently discovered *Norops wermuthi* and *Rhadinea* sp.

Also found in Nicaragua are several species of marine turtles, all of which are in danger of extinction. The paslama turtle *(Lepidochelys olivacea)* in the Pacific and the carey turtle *(Eretmochelys imbricata)* and green turtle *(Chelonia mydas)* in the Atlantic are protected species, and much effort has gone into setting aside habitat for them, particularly nesting beaches. However, the struggle is fierce between those who aim to conserve the turtles and those who'd like to harvest their eggs and meat (green and paslama) and shells (carey). There are approximately 20 beaches in the Pacific that present adequate conditions for the nesting of these turtle species, most of which play host to only occasional nesting events. Two beaches, Chacocente and La Flor on the Pacific coast, are the nesting grounds of the paslama turtle. Massive annual egg-laying events between July and January (primarily during the first and third quarters of the moon) involve between 57,000 and 100,000 turtles, which crawl up on the moist sand at night to lay eggs. It's a safety-in-numbers approach to survival—only one out of 100 hatchlings makes it to adulthood.

Frequently seen along the Río San Juan and some larger rivers of Jinotega are alligators, crocodiles *(Crocodilus acutus),* caimans *(Caiman crocodilus),* and the ñoca turtle *(Trachemys scripta).*

Garrobos are a kind of bush lizard that you're more likely to see suspended by its tail on the side of the road than in the wild. It is hunted by poor campesino children and then sold to passing motorists who take it home and make an aphrodisiac soup from the meat.

Amphibians

Nicaragua's humid forests and riversides are inhabited by 64 known species of amphibians, four of which are endemic, including the Mombacho salamander *(Bolitoglossa mombachoensis),* the miadis frog, the Cerro Saslaya frog *(Plectrohyla* sp.*),* and the Saslaya salamander *(Nolitron* sp.*).*

Insects

Each of Nicaragua's different ecosystems has a distinct insect population. Estimates of the total number of species reach as high as 250,000, only 1 percent of which have been identified. Notable species to seek out are several gigantic species of beetles, including *Dynastes hercules* (found in cloud forests, including Hotel Selva Negra if you're lucky); several species of brilliant green and golden *Plusiotis,* (found in Cerro Saslaya and Cerro Kilambé); the iridescent blue butterfly *Morpho peleides,* common all over the country, and its less common cousin, *M. amathonte,* found at altitudes of 300–700 meters, especially in the forests of Bosawás. Nocturnal moths like the *Rothschildia, Eacles,* and others are common. For more information about bug hunting in Nicaragua, you'll want to contact Belgian entomologist Jean-Michel Maes, who, with nearly 20 years of research experience in Nicaragua, knows his stuff. He runs the entomological museum in León (normally closed to the public), and has a CD-ROM for sale, entitled *Butterflies of Nicaragua* ($30). Email: jmmaes@ibw.com.ni. There is an increasing number of *mariposarios,* (butterfly farms) in Nicaragua, notably in Los Guatuzos Papaturro, El Castillo, and San Ramón in Matagalpa.

National Parks and Reserves

Nicaragua has an extensive system of more than two million hectares of protected areas. The Sistema Nacional de Areas Protegidas (SINAP) is made up of 76 parks, reserves, and refuges classified as "protected" by the Ministerio del Ambiente y los Recursos Naturales (Ministry of the Environment and Natural Resources, or MARENA). Of these, many are composed of privately owned land, making enforcement of their protected status difficult. That, combined with MARENA's paltry resource base and budget, has led an increasing number of international NGOs to step in and offer their services. This so-called "comanagement" is very much a novel, ongoing experiment, and while it has been surprisingly successful in some areas, the great majority of protected lands in Nicaragua remain unmanaged, unguarded, and completely undeveloped for tourism. They are sometimes referred to as "paper parks," existing only in legislation and studies, not in reality. An example is the Río Estero Real, a wetlands preserve in the northwest corner of the country, where half of the "protected" territory has been granted to private shrimp farmers who have eliminated most of the mangrove swamps and lagoons where shrimp once bred naturally, replacing them with artificial breeding pools.

Occasionally, being left alone results in untouched, virgin forests and wetlands protected by their own remoteness and natural tropical hostility. More commonly however, it means that some of Nicaragua's richest treasures continue to be plundered by foreign and national cattle, logging, and mining interests, as well as destructively managed by campesino populations who are given little incentive or education to do otherwise. In the latter case, a typical example is the government's declaring "protected" an area where people have been living traditionally for generations, and who are suddenly expected to drastically alter their fishing, hunting, and planting patterns to protect a "park" that is and always has been their homeland. A prime example is Bosawás, where Mayangna and Miskito people

were not consulted during the planning of the reserve and have consequently fought against the new regulations which interfere with their traditional lifestyle. Conversely, Fundación Cocibolca, in management of La Flor, has relied its heavily on local residents, both for staffing the reserve and for ideas on how to run it. The appreciation and interest shown by tourists in discovering these areas—and money they leave behind in doing so—can go a long way toward bolstering local incentive to protect—rather than consume—their natural world.

Following is a selection of some of the more accessible (or just spectacular) of Nicaragua's protected areas.

NATIONAL PARKS

Volcán Masaya

Nicaragua's best-organized and most easily accessed park, with a paved road leading to the crater, a museum, interpretive center, and paid guides to take you through more than 20 kilometers of nature trails. Declaring the 5,100 hectares that surround Volcán Masaya a national park was one of the last things President Anastasio García Somoza did before the revolution took him from power in 1979. The park's extensive lava fields are home to coyotes, *garrobo* lizards, white-tailed deer, and *cusucos.* There is also a rare variety of sulfur-tolerant parakeets that inhabit the inside of the crater's walls.

Zapatera Archipelago

Made up of the Zapatera Volcano and the eight islets that surround it, the park is located in Lake Cocibolca between the Isla de Ometepe and the city of Granada, 34 kilometers to the north. Although owned by private landholders, the islands were given national park status in the 1980s in recognition of their immense natural, cultural, and historical value. The government subsequently took control over much of the land. The islands still contain virgin forests, lovely shorelines, and are perhaps most famous for the pre-

© RANDY WOOD

Volcán Masaya

Columbian statuary found there. Many of the statues are observable today in the Convento San Francisco in Granada. Many others were sold or plundered, to be spirited off to the far corners of the world. The park and adjacent mainland peninsula served as a massive burial ground for the indigenous people here. Zapatera rises 629 meters above sea level and still contains primary forest and impressive wildlife.

BIOLOGICAL RESERVES

Río Indio Maíz

Composed of the nearly 264,000 hectares of jungle pressed between the Indio and Maíz Rivers, *"La Gran Reserva,"* as it is known, is adjacent to two additional protected areas, the Punta Gorda Nature Reserve to the north, and the Río San Juan Wildlife Reserve to the south. Together the reserves are part of the Biósfera del Sureste de Nicaragua, an immense chunk of southeastern Nicaragua dedicated to the preservation of animal and plant species along with their natural ecosystems in the Río San Juan wa-

tershed. The reserve is one of the few areas remaining in the Americas where you can experience virgin tropical humid forest as it was 200 years ago (and all the rain, insects, and heat that goes with it). The extent of the wildlife in the reserve has still not been completely determined, but it is, at the very least, one of the last refuges in Nicaragua for ocelots and other big cats.

Cayos Miskitos

Defined as all the cays and small islands found in a 40-kilometer radius from the center of Isla Grande in the Atlantic Ocean off Puerto Cabezas, plus a 20-kilometer swath of shoreline from Cabo Gracias a Dios to the south, the Reserva Biológica Cayos Miskitos has important economic and cultural significance to the Miskito people, who depend on it for the fish and shellfish they catch there. The Cayos Miskitos are an ecological treasure whose impenetrable lagoons, reefs, and mangrove forests and swamps are home to marine turtles, manatees, dolphins, and several types of endangered coral species. The mangrove forests give shelter to bird species such as *pancho galán,*

PROTECTED AREAS

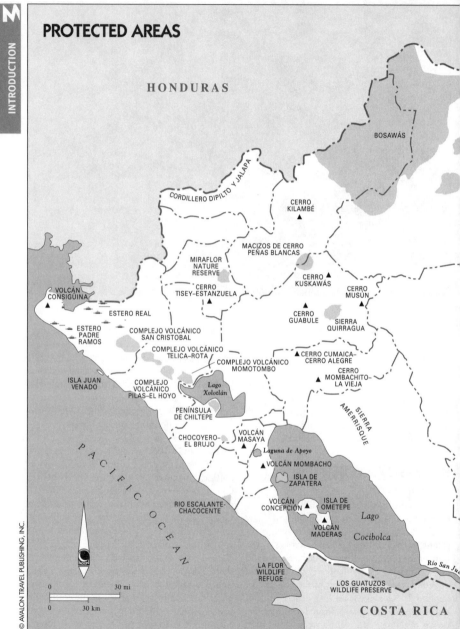

HONDURAS

BOSAWÁS

CORDILLERO DIPILTO Y JALAPA

CERRO KILAMBÉ

MACIZOS DE CERRO PEÑAS BLANCAS

MIRAFLOR NATURE RESERVE

CERRO TISEY–ESTANZUELA

CERRO KUSKAWÁS

CERRO MUSÚN

VOLCÁN CONSIGUINA

ESTERO REAL

CERRO GUABULE

SIERRA QUIRRAGUA

ESTERO PADRE RAMOS

COMPLEJO VOLCÁNICO SAN CRISTOBAL

COMPLEJO VOLCÁNICO TELICA–ROTA

COMPLEJO VOLCÁNICO MOMOTOMBO

CERRO CUMAICA–CERRO ALEGRE

CERRO MOMBACHITO–LA VIEJA

ISLA JUAN VENADO

COMPLEJO VOLCÁNICO PILAS–EL HOYO

Lago Xolotlán

SIERRA AMERRISQUE

PENÍNSULA DE CHILTEPE

CHOCOYERO–EL BRUJO

VOLCÁN MASAYA

Laguna de Apoyo

VOLCÁN MOMBACHO

ISLA DE ZAPATERA

PACIFIC OCEAN

RIO ESCALANTE–CHACOCENTE

VOLCÁN CONCEPCIÓN

ISLA DE OMETEPE

Lago Cocibolca

VOLCÁN MADERAS

Río San Ju

LA FLOR WILDLIFE REFUGE

LOS GUATUZOS WILDLIFE PRESERVE

COSTA RICA

0   30 mi

0   30 km

© AVALON TRAVEL PUBLISHING, INC.

NICARAGUA

CABO VIEJO AND
LAGUNA BISMUNA

CAYOS
MISKITOS

C a r i b b e a n   S e a

WAWASHÁN

*Bahía de
Perlas*

RESERVA

DE BIOSFERA

SURESTE

DE NICARAGUA

garza rosada, and the brown pelican. It is believed substantial deposits of petroleum lie below the continental shelf in the Cayos Miskitos area, so the management of the region will warrant much caution and a careful balance. In the meantime the cays' most immediate threat is human and involves their use by drug traffickers.

WILDLIFE RESERVES

Río Escalante/Chacocente

Named for the peculiar smell of *"choco"* (rotting turtle eggs after a hatching), the Refugio de Vida Silvestre Río Escalante/Chacocente consists of 4,800 hectares of dry tropical forest along the edge of the Pacific Ocean. The area was declared a reserve primarily because of its importance as the nesting grounds of the endangered tora and paslama turtles, incredible multitudes of which crawl up on the beach each year to lay eggs in the sand. Chacocente (as the reserve is commonly referred to) is also home to exotic orchids like the *flor de niño* and *huele noche* that fill the nocturnal air with a sweet, romantic fragrance. Chacocente is also home to important forest species, mangrove systems, and the "salt tree." Check the treetops for howler and white-faced monkeys, and keep an eye peeled for the many reptiles, pelicans, white-tailed deer, and *guardabarrancos* that linger in the forest edges.

La Flor

This southern Pacific beach is one of the most beautiful beaches in Nicaragua, a gorgeous white sandy crescent at the edge of a broad strip of tropical dry forest. The entire reserve is 800 hectares, where each year between July and January, thousands of paslama turtles beach themselves to nest and lay eggs. It's one of just a handful of beaches in the world that witness such a spectacle. Also in La Flor are many *garrobo negro, iguana verde, lagartijas,* monkeys, coyotes, raccoons, and skunks, some of which prey on the turtle eggs. The skies at La Flor are full of bird species that make their homes in the relatively intact dry forest: *urracas, gavilanes caracoleros, chocoyos, querques, garzas, and sonchiches.*

INTRODUCTION

Los Guatuzos Wildlife Preserve

Named for one of the indigenous tribes that once lived here, this is a strip of 43,000 hectares of protected wetlands between the southern shore of Lake Cocibolca and the Costa Rican border. Los Guatuzos is home to several small border communities and an impressive quantity of all kinds of wild animals.

NATURAL RESERVES

Volcán Cosigüina

In the farthest northwestern corner of Nicaragua, over 12,000 hectares of the Cosigüina peninsula have been declared a natural reserve. The area has been quietly revegetating itself since the volcano's massive eruption in 1835, predominantly as dry tropical forests of *genícero, tempisque,* and *guanacaste* trees. Its nearly inaccessible crater has become the home to spider monkeys, coyotes, black iguanas, white-tailed deer, and coatis, but more obvious to the naked eye are the hundreds of bird species, notably the scarlet macaw. Climbing the volcano offers a phenomenal view of the crater lake (which began filling after the eruption 150 years ago), the Gulf of Fonseca, and beyond.

Isla Juan Venado

Much more than a sandy barrier beach island, Isla Juan Venado contains 4,600 hectares of estuary and coastline along the Pacific coast west of León. Its vegetation is successional, going from mangroves at the water's edge to inland dry tropical forest. Isla Juan Venado is rife with bird species due to the estuary system—its mangroves are home to the nests of thousands of parrots and herons—as well as crabs, mollusks, and over 50 species of mammals and reptiles.

Volcán Mombacho

A scant 41 kilometers from the lowland heat of Managua is an otherworldly island of cloud forest atop an ancient and dormant volcano. Volcán Mombacho's lower slopes are dedicated to agriculture, cattle raising, and coffee production, but its upper third—above 800 meters—is a spectacular, misty wildlife and cloud forest reserve. Mombacho is managed by the Fundación Cocibolca, which has done an admirable job of constructing trails and low-impact guest and research facilities. Mombacho is home both to several endemic species of butterflies and the endemic Mombacho salamander.

Chocoyero-El Brujo

The closest natural reserve to Managua, Chocoyero-El Brujo makes up for its small size with the sheer quantity of *chocoyos* (parakeets) that inhabit its cliff caves. There's no excuse for not exploring Chocoyero-El Brujo some lazy afternoon at sundown when the skies fill with the ruckus of thousands of squawking green *chocoyos.* Chocoyero is set in a semihumid forest of stately *pochote, tigüilote,* and cedar trees, and, in addition to its famous birds, provides habitat for several types of owls, monkeys, and squirrels.

Other Reserves

There are many more nature reserves, typically small and designated as such in an attempt to protect a very specific resource. In addition to those mentioned above, there are 11 reserves that protect

MIRAFLOR

Draped with Spanish moss and carpeted with orchids and lush vegetation, the more than 5,600 hectares of the Reserva Natural Miraflor is a cloud forest, considered one of the most important natural reserves of its type in Nicaragua. The area is privately owned in its entirety, and is managed by several different groups of farmers and campesino cooperatives. This is one of the few places in Nicaragua to spot the exotic (and elusive) quetzal, and up to a third of the total number of bird species observed in Nicaragua. Miraflor is relatively easy to access, if you have a few days to spare while passing through Estelí, and has a limited number of rustic lodging opportunities, including sleeping in the humble homes of one of several dozen small-scale organic vegetable farmers.

© RANDY WOOD

Volcán Mombacho

volcanic or coastal lagoons, 16 that protect specific peaks such as Kilambé and Pancasán, six that protect volcanic complexes such as San Cristóbal or Pilas–El Hoyo, plus dozens of others.

BIOSPHERE RESERVES

Nicaragua's two biosphere reserves were indirectly based on a model proposed for protecting several vast areas in the southeast United States. The strategy is to create a central "nucleus zone," with wilderness status totally preventing human activity. The nucleus is then surrounded by various levels of buffer zones with increasing, but still regulated, resource exploitation allowed as the distance increases from the center. That's how it looks on paper anyway. The virgin lands of Bosawás and the Río San Juan areas have long served as "safety valves" for Nicaragua's expanding population, accommodating campesinos as they look for new forestland to clear and farm. Several hundred campesino families currently inhabit the Bosawás reserve, and in the absence of regulation, more will surely follow.

Bosawás

You heard it here first: the largest continuous expanse of virgin cloud forest in Central America is found in Nicaragua. Located 350 kilometers north of Managua, the 730,000 hectares of forest, mountains, and rivers are located within the municipalities of Waspám, Bonanza, Siuna, El Cuá-Bocay, Wiwilí, and Waslala. Although inhabited by some 40,000 widely dispersed people (more than half of which are Mayangna and Miskito), most of Bosawás remains unexplored, unmapped, and untamed. Its name is derived from the region's three most salient features: the Río Bocay (BO), Cerro Saslaya (SA) and the Río Waspuk (WAS). Besides unequaled stretches of cloud forest, Bosawás contains tropical humid forest, rainforest, and a wealth of disparate ecosystems that vary in altitude from 30 meters above sea level at the mouth of the Waspuk River to the 1,650-meter peak of Cerro Saslaya. Bosawás is a Central American treasure, an immense genetic reserve of species that have vanished elsewhere in Mesoamerica, including jaguars, rare small mammals, 12 kinds of poisonous snakes, and many bird species, including the gorgeous scarlet macaw and 34 boreal migratory species.

SI-A-PAZ

A play on the words, "Yes to Peace," the Sistema de Áreas Protegidas (System of Protected Areas) was a late 1980s effort led by former minister of natural resources Jaime Incer to protect the Río San Juan watershed in a joint operation with Costa Rica. The program was abandoned in 1990 with the change in government administration. The river itself, which belongs to Nicaragua, has been severely affected by sedimentation caused by converting forest to pastureland on the Costa Rican side of the border. Los Guatuzos Wildlife Preserve is now located on the land once incorporated into the SI-A-PAZ reserve.

Río San Juan

Located in the extreme southeast of Nicaragua, the Refugio de Vida Silvestre Río San Juan stretches from El Castillo southeast to the Atlantic Ocean along the north edge of the Río San Juan. In addition to the river itself, an important part of the reserve are the four interconnected lagoons at the river's mouth and their related pools, all of which are important habitat for manatees and several other mammals.

PRIVATE RESERVES

Nicaragua's newest category of protected areas are called Reservas Silvestres Privadas (Wild Private Reserves). These are entirely private landholdings whose owners have applied to MARENA to become officially declared as part of SINAP. The landowners must meet a number of criteria as well as present a management plan to be classified as protected. At present there are a handful of approved private reserves, and more pending. The areas are usually near other parks or reserves, contain substantial vegetation and wildlife, and are often a part of some biological corridor. At this early point in the game, they are in varying stages of developing their tourism infrastructures. The original six private reserves are Montibelli near Chocoyero, Domitila outside Nandaime, La Maquina on the road to the coast from Diriamba, Toromixcal in San Juan del Sur, César Augusto in Jinotega, and Greenfields near Pearl Lagoon. Look for them in the appropriate regional chapters.

Environmental Issues

Nicaragua's ability to resolve its environmental issues will almost certainly determine the course of its immediate economic growth and social well-being. However, those environmental issues are complex and entangled in a rat's nest of bigger issues, including politics, land rights issues, population pressure, war, and frequent natural disasters. The remedies are anything but simple.

Chief among Nicaragua's immediate environmental problems is the rapid loss of its once-extensive forests at the rate of 150,000 hectares harvested per year. Some analyses indicate Nicaragua's timber reserves will be completely depleted by the year 2015. The full extent of the problem is not entirely clear, as the calculations of remaining forest are based on figures collected in the 1970s.

The great majority of families in the countryside use firewood *(leña)* as their prime fuel source for cooking, which has put tremendous pressure

"ECO"-RESPONSIBILITY

The word "ecotourism" was created in the 1980s with the best of intentions—ostensibly, to describe "travel to natural habitats which creates an understanding of the cultural and natural history pertaining to the environment, emphasizing care not to alter the integrity of the ecosystem, while producing economic benefits that encourage the preservation of the inherent resources of the environment" (as defined by the Ecotourism Society). The success of the concept and its accompanying marketing label led directly to a worldwide boom in the usage of that warm, fuzzy prefix that we know so well, even if its actual practice has sometimes fallen short of the original intentions.

"Eco" has been used, abused, prostituted, and bastardized all over the world, and Nicaragua is not exempt. Surely, anything "eco" has something to do with the outdoors, but that's about all we can promise you. We've limited our eco-writing, not because we don't believe in its precepts, but because we're wary of what it means in this day, age, and place. Some word-savvy tourism marketers have tried to freshen things up by using "alternative" or "adventure tourism," but, when trying to describe an operation that practices the original definition of ecotourism mentioned above, we prefer "sustainable," "responsible," or "ethical." There is power in words, but there is more power in your critical intelligence, which you should always use when confronted with so many eco-options.

Semantics aside, as a visitor, you should never forget how incredibly important and vital your role is in helping to protect Nicaraguan natural areas. The concept of protected areas is new in Nicaragua and viewed with great skepticism, especially by the rural folk who live near (or sometimes actually within) these areas. Left to their own devices, the desperately poor, sometimes even starving campesinos use the wilderness to supplement their paltry incomes, by chopping wood for fuel, cutting out badly needed farmland, or hunting wild game. MARENA, the government ministry charged with protecting Nicaragua's vast system of parks and refuges, has scant enforcement resources to prevent such activities.

That's where you come in. By contributing some form of economic benefit to the people who live nearby, foreigners can help encourage locals to view a natural area as a resource worth protecting, as it can attract tourists. This economic benefit can mean hiring a local guide, buying a meal from a family, or paying a few cordobas to pitch a tent or hang a hammock outside a farmer's hut. Those going on a trip with a tour company are not exempt from this—you must be sure that the company you go with leaves some money behind, rather than using their own guides, transportation, food, etc. Just imagine how a self-sufficient trip must look to the locals—here come these unfathomably wealthy foreigners out enjoying themselves in our forest that we are no longer supposed to touch, and they don't leave us a single cordoba! And after that, they really expect us *not* to go hunting to feed our families?

Collecting *leña* (firewood) is a part of the day for most campesinos.

break of the pine bark beetle that began in October 1999 in Teotecacinte, Nueva Segovia. By March 2001 an estimated 6,000 hectares were destroyed in the seven departments that make up north and northwest Nicaragua, with the area around Jalapa being the most hard hit. The beetle attacks both young and mature pine forests weakened by fires, resin harvesting, and poor management, boring through the bark of the tree to feed on the resin that lies between the wood and the bark. At the start of each rainy season, young beetles disperse and fly longer distances. The infestation can spread up to 20 meters per day, spreading a full kilometer in distance in just under two months. As of 2002 the outbreak had still not been completely contained.

By whatever mechanism, deforestation leaves the fragile tropical soils exposed to rainfall and the ensuing erosion leads directly to the contamination and elimination of water sources, and even outright microclimate changes. This is the case in much of Nicaragua, where within one human generation, rivers and streams that were once perennial now flow only sporadically, if at all. On the Pacific coast, several decades of intensive agriculture and wind erosion have caused the loss of once-rich volcanic soils as well. In general, the entire Pacific, central, and northern regions of the country are at immediate risk of sustained soil erosion.

Massive efforts are underway to attack the problem from all sides, from environmental education of the youngest children in order to change cultural habits, to the active replanting of hillsides via tree nursery projects, to the teaching and implementation of less-destructive agricultural techniques. Much of the effort is coming through international funding and expertise, since the beleaguered government ministries have traditionally lacked even the most basic of resources.

on forest resources as Nicaragua's increasing population expands into previously unsettled lands. Population pressure and the swelling cattle industry have led to a progression of the agricultural frontier from both the Atlantic and Pacific sides of the country, reducing Nicaragua's forests by 4.6 million hectares from 1950 to 1995. On the Atlantic coast, much of the hardwood logging is happening at the hands of U.S., Canadian, and Asian companies that have weaseled fat timber concessions out of Nicaragua's successive cash-strapped governments.

As if forest depletion due to humans hasn't been enough, the remaining pine forests in Nueva Segovia were further devastated by a massive out-

History

For the past 135 years, Nicaragua has been a kind of geopolitical mind-altering substance. American politicians and journalists go there, sample the local politics, and immediately start babbling in tongues. It began with William Walker, the nineteenth-century adventurer who declared himself president of Nicaragua, and it continues right up through this morning's newspaper.

Glenn Garvin,
Everybody Had His Own Gringo, *1992*

PRE-COLONIAL YEARS

Even older than the famous footprints baked into the 6,000-year-old mud in a quiet corner of Managua are the remnants of a Caribbean people known as "*Los Concheros*" (the shell collectors), who inhabited—or frequently visited—the Atlantic coast around 8,000 years ago. Deposits of shells from their fishing and collecting forays have been discovered in several locations on the Atlantic coast, but except for the fact that they liked clams, little else is known about Nicaragua's first inhabitants. Agriculture began around 5,000 years ago with the cultivation of corn. Pottery making followed 2,000 years later.

Sometime in the 13th century, the Chorotega and Nicarao people, under pressure from the aggressive Aztecs in Mexico, fled south through the Central American isthmus. Their legends relate that they were led by a vision of a land dominated by a great lake. They settled on the shores of Lake Cocibolca and in points farther south. When the Spanish conquistadores first set foot in Nicaragua in the late 15th century, they found numerous Chorotega settlements occupying the lands around the Masaya and Apoyo volcanic craters while the Nicaraos inhabited points farther south.

© JOSHUA BERMAN

Nicas love a parade; Independence Day (Sept. 15) is celebrated in even the smallest towns.

INTRODUCTION

AUGUSTO CÉSAR SANDINO (1893–1934)

The term "Sandinista" is easily related to Nicaragua, but less well known is the story of the man, who, through his long struggle against imperialism, became a legend in Nicaragua and the world, a cultural icon recognized today by just the merest rendering of his famous broad-brimmed hat.

Augusto C. Sandino was born in Niquinohomo (Nahuatl for "Valley of Warriors"), the bastard son of a wealthy, landed judge and one of his servant women. The judge lived a respectable life with his legal wife and children while Sandino's mother worked in his fields outside of town, so poor she often resorted to stealing crops from other fields to eat. When Sandino was a young boy, his mother was jailed for failure to repay a debt, and young Augusto, caring for her in prison, was disgusted and horrified at a Nicaraguan society that allowed such brutal inequity. He began questioning civil society and the Catholic religion, which he believed was doing little more than maintaining the aristocratic hierarchy of landed and poor classes.

At the age of 17, Sandino witnessed the U.S. Marines' invasion of Nicaragua to prop up Adolfo Díaz's failing Conservative presidency. The ensuing Liberal rebellion, led by General Benjamin Zeledón, was crushed brutally near Masaya—practically in Sandino's backyard. The young man's rage grew, fueled by the memory of U.S. Marines parading Zeledón's dead body through the streets of Masaya. At 26, Sandino left Nicaragua after shooting his friend in the leg during a quarrel in

General Augusto César Sandino

© JOSHUA BERMAN

COLONIALISM

Christopher Columbus, known in the Spanish world as Cristóbal Colón, first set eyes on the land of lakes and volcanoes in July of 1502, on his fourth and final trip to the Americas. Searching for a navigable passage through the land mass, Columbus skirted Nicaragua's Mosquito Coast without noticing the outlet of the San Juan, and ended up in South America. Seventeen years later the conquistador Pedro Arias Dávila returned under orders from the Spanish crown to explore the land bridge of Nicaragua. During his brief foray, González encountered the caciques (tribal leaders) Nicarao and Diriangén, who engaged González's men in a brief battle. This gave the Spanish a hint of the warrior spirit of the original Nicaragüenses—a warning that went unheeded amongst the Europeans who would face the same rebelliousness often over the next few centuries.

Francisco Hernández de Córdoba arrived not long after González, entrusted with the duty of establishing Spain's first settlements in the new land. Córdoba settled Granada alongside the Chorotega communities on the banks of Lake Cocibolca, and, pushing farther inland and up the Tipitapa River, the settlement of León on the western shores of Lake Xolotlán. Nicaragua remained a part of Spain's overseas possessions for the next 300 years under the governance of the colonial capital in Guatemala.

church. In Mexico he was inspired by Tampico laborers struggling to unionize in spite of resistance from the U.S.-owned oil companies. These were the years surrounding World War I, and anarchy, socialism, and communism were all growing in popularity, no doubt having a profound influence on a man searching for an alternative worldview. Sandino returned to Nicaragua with a new sense of purpose and a strong self-identity.

He became a renegade general for the Liberals, setting up camp in the rugged mountains of the north, where he attracted mine workers to his cause from the area around San Albino. San Rafael del Norte, Jinotega, became Sandino's central hideout, where he became one of the first to practice guerrilla (Spanish for "small war") warfare, staging effective hit-and-run raids over the next few years against U.S. Marine installations in Ocotal and the north. Sandino's men, who grew to number nearly 1,800 by 1933, also attacked U.S. mining and lumber companies with enough force to drive some of them away from the Atlantic coast.

Sandino and his men were brutal—they sometimes killed prisoners of war and were known to slit the throats of the dead and pull the tongue out and down through the gash, like a necktie. They earned the wrath of the U.S. military, which struggled diligently but fruitlessly for seven years to flush Sandino out of the hills and be done with him. In Sandino's advantage was a complete and profound knowledge of the land, the support of the people, the willingness to live poor, and a stunning ability to vanish into thin air.

Among his enemies, Sandino was unsurprisingly portrayed as anything but a Nicaraguan nationalist: in the words of one U.S. Army lieutenant, "Sandino poses as the George Washington of Nicaragua but he is only a cut-throat and a bandit, preying upon foreigners and the law-abiding citizens of his country."

While Sandino's struggle was ostensibly to force the U.S. military and business interests out of Nicaragua, he represented much more than brute nationalism. In the Segovias, where Sandino

(continues on next page)

INDEPENDENCE

Central America won its independence from Spain in 1821, and for a short time remained united as the five provinces of the Central American Federation. The belief that Europe would act militarily to return the former colonies to Spain led to the proclamation of the Monroe Doctrine by the United States in 1823, declaring the New World off limits to further European colonization and interference. When Nicaragua withdrew from the federation in 1838, the remaining states opted to become individual republics as well and the federation dissolved.

The Birth of a Rivalry

After gaining independence, the nation of Nicaragua suffered several years of complete anarchy. The two primary cities, León and Granada, operated as independent city-states until a national government was finally agreed upon in 1845.

The conflict between León and Granada in the 1800s is noteworthy because it established political rivalries that endure to this day. In the early 19th century, Nicaragua's principal exports were cacao, indigo, and cattle, the sale of which allowed the landed and merchant classes to accumulate considerable wealth—with the help of the Native Americans and landless farmers who worked the farms and ranches essentially as indentured servants. At the same time, the aspiring bourgeoisie, influenced by the Liberal teachings of the universities in León and by the American and French Revolutions, sought to liberate the poor working classes of their feudal labor obligations, thus making their labor available to all at market prices. The landed class, mostly based in Granada and loyal to the aristocratic system that favored them, resisted. The León Liberals–Granada Conservatives split was responsible for over 100 years of civil war and exists even today: León has always been a staunch supporter

AUGUSTO CÉSAR SANDINO (1893–1934)
(continued)

enjoyed massive popular support, he formed agricultural cooperatives of landless peasants, imposing taxes on wealthy ranchers and businessmen to support them. He also fought in support of the exploited timber, banana plantation, and mine workers.

The marines finally left in the midst of the Great Depression, and the new president of Nicaragua, Anastasio Somoza García, had Sandino shot in February 1934. Sandino's body was never found, and, à la Jimmy Hoffa, rumors abound that Sandino lies buried under the floor of the Managua Palacio de Comunicaciones (now the central post office).

Thirty years after Sandino's death, a young idealistic student named Carlos Fonseca Amador resurrected Sandino's image and ideals as the basis of a new political and guerrilla movement which he called the Frente Sandinista de Liberación Nacional (FSLN)—the Sandinista Front for National Liberation.

Sandino's ideals—and the FSLN's interpretation of them—are subject to discussion and debate even today. There is no doubt the FSLN greatly enhanced Sandino's reputation as a "poor, repressed peasant who fought righteously against the imperialistic designs of the United States," because it suited them to do so. But despite Fonseca's and the FSLN's claims, Sandino was no communist. His ideology was a mix of his own peculiar leftism with a curious indigenous mysticism. He changed his middle name from Calderón to César in honor of the Roman emperor, claimed he could give orders to his troops using silent mental communication, and predicted Nicaragua would be the site of Armageddon, where "armies of angels would do battle alongside more temporal troops."

It is also argued that the FSLN distorted Sandino's anti-U.S. sentiments by playing down his primary hatred of the bourgeois Nicaraguan Conservatives. Because of this class division, Sandino never represented Nicaraguans as a whole.

Nevertheless, to this day, Sandino remains a hero to Nicaraguans and the world leftist community. In that regard, Sandino inadvertently came to spearhead a movement that fought for drastic social and political change and sought to make up for centuries of class discontent that dated back to the earliest days of European colonization.

of leftist Sandinismo, while Granada has traditionally voted conservatively.

THE CANAL, WILLIAM WALKER, AND THE U.S. MARINES

Nicaragua's unique geography has resulted in a long history of unrealized transcontinental canal plans, which continue even in the present day. During the California gold rush (1849–1856), the Central American isthmus served as the route for many a prospector bound for the West Coast—and not a few impoverished ones headed back east. Steamship baron and businessman Cornelius Vanderbilt established a cross-isthmus transport company to challenge the Pacific Steamship Company then operating in Panamá. Travelers bound for California sailed up the Río San Juan and across Lake Nicaragua to the small port at San Jorge, where they were taken by horse cart 18 kilometers across the narrow isthmus through Rivas to the bay of San Juan del Sur. Ships waiting in the harbor then carried the travelers north along the Pacific coastline to California. Vanderbilt dredged the channel of the Río San Juan and built roads, railroads, and docks on both coasts to accommodate the traffic.

In 1853, American adventurer, white supremacist, and filibuster William Walker, the self-proclaimed "Grey-eyed Man of Destiny" from Nashville, Tennessee, arrived in Nicaragua at the invitation of the Liberals of León, whose dispute with the Conservatives had recently grown bitter. With the help of Walker and his mercenaries—an army of some 300 thugs recruited from the tough neighborhoods of San Francisco and elsewhere—the Liberals promptly conquered Granada. Two years later, Walker usurped power, declared himself president of Nicaragua via a rigged election, and put in motion his plan to make Nicaragua, and later all of Central America, slavery states loyal to the southern United States.

The United States, at the brink of the Civil War, officially recognized Walker as president of Nicaragua. Walker reinstituted slavery and declared English the official language of Nicaragua, and the Liberals realized they'd made a deal with the devil. In a rare moment of solidarity, the Nicaraguans temporarily forgot their differences, and with the help of the other Central American nations and some financing from Cornelius Vanderbilt (who had lost his steamship company to Walker), defeated Walker at the Battle of San Jacinto on September 14, 1856, which is now a national holiday. The Liberals fell into disgrace, and the Conservatives effectively ruled the nation for the next 30 years. Thus ended the first direct intervention by the United States in Nicaraguan affairs. The gringos, however, would return over a dozen more times over the next 150 years, always with the pretext of "protecting American interests."

Though the relative peace of the Conservative period fostered many advances in infrastructure and technology—including the train from Granada to Corinto and the introduction of the telegraph—the famous "Thirty Years" were also a time of economic stagnation, when spiteful legislation prevented the Liberals from opening up new lands to coffee production. In 1893, Nicaragua was already several decades behind its neighboring countries in coffee exportation, most notably Costa Rica. Under the leadership of Liberal general José Santos Zelaya, the bourgeoisie rebelled, and Zelaya was made president. Zelaya was a fierce nationalist who, among other things, marched troops to the Atlantic coast in order to end Britain's territorial claims and officially incorporate the Atlantic region into the nation (the two administrative units of the Atlantic coast bore Zelaya's name until the 1990s). He was also a staunch opponent to foreign intervention and thus promptly made himself an enemy of the United States. His manipulated downfall was sealed the moment he rejected Washington's proposals to build a cross-isthmus canal through Nicaraguan territory while at the same time courting Great Britain to finance the construction of a transcontinental railway. The United States, which had already commenced the construction of the Panama Canal in 1904, was threatened by the idea of a competing transport mechanism. Washington, frustrated with Zelaya, perceived him as a dangerously nationalist dictator, and in 1909, forced him out with pressure from the U.S. Marines, who landed in Bluefields in a show of force.

The U.S. intervention reestablished the Conservatives in power, but in 1912, a rebellion led by the Liberal and nationalist Benjamin Zeledón provoked the United States to step in again. This time the invasion was on a much larger scale; 2,700 marines landed at Corinto and took immediate control of the railways, ports, and major cities.

Military aggression aside, the U.S. government was subtly gaining control over Nicaragua in other ways as well. Following the 1912 attack, U.S. financial institutions began to quietly gain control of the coffee export business and the railway and steamship companies, forcing Nicaragua into a credit noose. Under the watchful eye of the marines, governmental control was handed over to the Conservatives, whom Washington thought would more faithfully represent U.S. interests. But the Liberals resisted, staging 10 uprisings between 1913 and 1924, all of which were quelled by the U.S. military presence.

In 1924, Conservative president Bartolomé Martínez instituted a novel form of government—a power-sharing arrangement between the Liberals and the Conservatives at the local level. The United States withdrew the marines in 1925 but they were back within the year. No sooner had power sharing begun than ambitious Conservative Emilio Chamorro staged a coup d'etat, seized power, and sparked the Constitutional War. The United States stepped in to prevent the imminent takeover by the Liberals, but because the Conservatives had discredited themselves, the United States was unable to simply hand the power back to them. The deal they worked out was known as the Espino Negro Pact (named after the town where it was signed, Spanish for Black Thorn), and represented a crucial moment for the Liberals. One of their generals, Augusto C. Sandino, was opposed to the pact, and fled to the northern mountains to start a guerrilla war in opposition of the continued presence of the United States in Nicaragua. The leader of the Constitutional Army was forced to declare, "All my men surrender except one."

The U.S. military was unable to roust Sandino from the mountains in spite of drastic measures which included the aerial bombing of the city of Ocotal, so in 1933, Washington tried a new approach. Withdrawing U.S. troops from Nicaragua, the United States formed a new military unit called the National Guard, placed a young Anastasio Somoza García at its head, and handed the power over to them and the new president, Juan Bautista Sacasa. At this point, Sandino had achieved two of his goals—the removal of the U.S. armed forces and the Conservative oligarchy from power. The rest of the world was too concerned with the fascist government Franco was forming in Spain to pay much attention to Nicaragua, and Sandino lost the support of Mexican Communist Party. But Sandino represented a major threat to Somoza's political and military ambitions. He had already come down once from the mountains to negotiate with President Sacasa, achieving several of his aims. In February of 1934, Sandino returned to Managua at Sacasa's invitation to continue the negotiations. When Sandino left the presidential palace that night, several National Guard members ambushed and assassinated him on the streets of Managua. Sandino's assassination was quickly followed by a government-sponsored reign of terror in the northern countryside, destroying cooperatives, returning lands to their previous owners, and hunting down Sandino's supporters who were imprisoned, exiled, or killed.

THE SOMOZA ERA

The formation of the National Guard paved the way for its leader, General Anastasio Somoza García, to seize control of Nicaragua in 1937 and begin a family dynasty of enormous wealth and power that would permanently reorient and completely control Nicaraguan politics for more

than 42 years. So formidable was the rule of the Somoza family that many Nicaraguans and foreigners alike refer to the succession of three Somoza presidents as one all-powerful "Somoza." The Somozas were wily politicians with a near-genius for using existing political conflicts to their personal advantage. Anastasio Somoza García successfully created a split in the political opposition that enabled him and his successors to always have a token, but powerless, opposition against which to run in elections.

The Somoza family also maintained power using a favorite trick of Latin American dictators, *continuismo*, which entailed the election of a puppet leader who would resign shortly afterward, handing the power back to the Somozas. Five such "presidents" were elected during the 42-year reign of the Somozas, but not one of them lasted longer than three years in power. The Somozas maintained a strong foothold in the national commercial markets as well (much to the dismay of merchants in Granada) by manipulating the government licensing mechanisms and importing contraband for local markets with the complicity of the National Guard. If there was money to be made anywhere in Nicaragua, the Somozas took notice and squeezed something out, if not taking over the operation entirely. They extracted personal income from public utilities such as the railroad, water, and electric companies, and even public sector individual incomes. Once they had control of one financial sector, they turned their sights elsewhere, capitalizing on and controlling the cotton industry when it surged in the 1950s and, later, meat, shrimp, and lobster export in the 1960s and 1970s. In addition to their other endeavors, the Somoza family was earning good money in food processing industries, sugar refining, cement production, cardboard, tobacco, the recording industry, and sea and air transport. By the late 1970s, it is said, the Somoza family owned everything in Nicaragua worth owning.

The upper echelons of the National Guard turned a tidy profit as well during the Somoza years, primarily by allowing landowners who paid the right bribes to take control of the properties held by poorer farmers who had no legal titles. While the expropriation of poor or indigenous farmers' lands was nothing new—in practice ever since the Spanish in the 1500s—the number of landless farmers increased dramatically on Somoza's watch.

Anastasio Somoza García (Presidencies: January 1, 1937–May 1, 1947; May 6, 1950–September 21, 1956)

By the time a coup landed him in the presidency, Somoza García had gained control of the government, the military, the Liberal party, and a piece of the opposition party as well. He began building his financial empire and the longest-running and most corrupt dictatorship in Latin American history. Born in San Marcos, Carazo, and educated at the Pierce School of Business Administration in Philadelphia, Somoza García was able to use his command of the English language and his sharp business sense to ascend rapidly through his military and political career. One of the first things he did upon taking power was build a mansion on a hill overlooking Managua and make a gift of it to the U.S. ambassador for his home (today it's called the Casa Grande, and it still belongs to the U.S. Embassy); in 1939 Somoza García made an official visit to Washington, D.C., where President Franklin D. Roosevelt received him like royalty. Such was the relationship Somoza García enjoyed with the United States, which saw in Somoza a good businessman and a source of stability for the country, overlooking his rapacious greed, questionable politics, and strong-handed military tactics in exchange for a Central American leader they could rely on to protect their own political and financial interests.

World War II prevented Nicaragua from exporting to any nation except the United States, and coffee prices remained low, as they had since the Great Depression of the 1930s. So Somoza opened up a new market—the exportation of gold from mines in Nicaragua's central mountains. This was a resource that had gone unexplored since the days of the Spanish, and Somoza was able to monopolize it without stepping on the coffee producers' and cattle ranchers' toes.

He did so by offering the gold to U.S. and Canadian companies under advantageous conditions, in exchange for which he received lucrative and undocumented kickbacks. Nicaragua was also a reliable provider of raw goods like cotton, timber, minerals, and rubber to feed the U.S. war machine during World War II. Without any thought to a conservation strategy, these boom years had a devastating effect on the country's natural resources and environmental cleanliness. World War II proved to be an economic windfall for Somoza in other ways as well: taking advantage of the political situation, he declared formal war on Germany and Japan, then confiscated the lands of most German citizens living in Nicaragua. Those properties, prime coffee land, were some of the most valuable in the nation.

In spite of Somoza García's rapid accumulation of personal wealth during the approximately 19 years of his presidency, he is remembered fondly for several public works projects, including the railway from Chinandega to Puerto Morazán, which began service in 1939; the construction of several public buildings and Managua's city water system; the construction of the Managua International Airport in 1942, which was originally named Aeropuerto Las Mercedes; and perhaps most importantly, the construction of the Pan-American Highway, which began in 1942 (and which not coincidentally happened to pass along the edge of several of his personal farms). Under increasing political pressure to step down from the presidency, Somoza García handed power over to a series of puppet governments that many foreign nations refused to recognize due to the manner in which elections had been manipulated. He stepped back into power in 1951 and maintained his position as president through a series of constitutional reforms that eliminated the need for elections. In 1956, while attending a celebratory ball in the Social Club of León, he was assassinated by the poet, political idealist, and frustrated nationalist Rigoberto López Pérez.

Luís Somoza Debayle (President September 21, 1956–May 1, 1963)

The son of Anastasio Somoza García, "Tacho," as Somoza Debayle was known, assumed the presidency upon his father's assassination. An agronomist by training, he showed great political skill at keeping the nation stable in spite of the political agitation that filled the years of his presidency. Some of the tension was due to the political aspirations of his younger brother Anastasio Somoza Debayle, and there were several attempts on Tacho's life as well, including one in 1959 when 100 young men, inspired by Fidel Castro's success in Cuba, attempted to spark a popular uprising. The operation was a military failure, and they were forced to surrender after only two weeks. Meanwhile, Tacho continued his father's legacy of large public works projects, including the hydropower plant and reservoir of Lake Apanás in Jinotega; the improved port facilities at Corinto; the highway from San Benito to El Rama, which helped unite the Atlantic and Pacific coasts; and the first social security system (INSS) in the nation's history. The United States continued to support the Somoza political dynasty, and in return, Luís Somoza Debayle allowed the gringos to stage their disastrous Bay of Pigs operation from Nicaragua's Atlantic coast. In 1963, Tacho lost in popular elections to the Liberal candidate Renée Schick. Somoza never sought another political office but dedicated himself instead to his many businesses until he died in 1967 of a massive heart attack, setting the stage for the return of the dynasty.

Anastasio Somoza Debayle (Presidencies: May 1, 1967–May 1, 1972; December 1, 1974–July 16, 1979)

"Tachito" was the third and most avaricious president of the Somoza dynasty. Like his father, Tachito was a military man and a graduate of the West Point Military Academy (1946). Although he was ostensibly elected over Lorenzo Guerrero, the heated and violent elections of 1967 were never resolved to everyone's satisfaction. At the same time, the nascent Sandinista (FSLN) movement was gaining attention through attacks and kidnappings in the north. The FSLN would, over the next decade, prod Tachito into becoming the most relentless and cruel president the nation had ever seen. In early

1972, Somoza resumed his former post as head of the National Guard, and handed the presidency over to a triumvirate government whose purpose was to reform the constitution. The earthquake of December 1972 provided Tachito a new opportunity to fill his pockets. Appointing himself head of the Emergency Committee, he did little more to rebuild the country than funnel aid money into his own bank accounts, after which he was reelected to the presidency in 1974. In the United States, the Democratic government of Jimmy Carter, elected in 1977, began to pressure Tachito to be more sensitive to human rights issues. His failure to do so, the assassination of journalist Pedro Joaquín Chamorro, and his increasingly violent responses to FSLN attacks earned Tachito the animosity of the Carter administration and much of the international community. Tachito surrendered the government to the victorious FSLN on July 16, 1979, and fled to Miami, and then to Paraguay, where on September 17, 1980, an antitank rocket slammed into his limousine, killing him. The Sandinista government denied all responsibility for the attack, but it was clear at that point the Somoza dynasty had finally come to an end.

THE SANDINISTA REVOLUTION

The FSLN got its start in the late 1950s, when Nicaraguan guerrilla groups inspired by Fidel Castro's success in Cuba began training in clandestine camps in the northern mountains. In July 1962, Carlos Fonseca Amador, Silvio Mayorga, and Tomás Borge formed the Frente Sandinista de Liberación Nacional (FSLN). The seeds of the Sandinista revolution were sown on the basic principal that a dictatorship could never be reformed—only overthrown.

Fonseca had studied law in León and was captivated by the Marxist theory, which he was able to experience firsthand during a trip to Moscow in 1958 and a meeting with Che Guevara in 1962. In many ways, the Sandinista movement owes its ideological roots to Fonseca, whose inspired combination of Marxism and the nationalist, anti-imperialist beliefs of Augusto Sandino formed the basis for the revolu-

© JOSHUA BERMAN

Sandinista guitar to gun mural in Estelí

tion and the economic and social reforms that followed thereafter.

Early insurrections in the Ríos Coco and Bocay (1963) and Pancasán (1967) regions were quickly crushed but legitimized the FSLN among radical university students and city-dwellers, indicating, among other things, how much support the movement was gaining among the disenfranchised campesino population. The Sandinistas' military strength and daring escalated rapidly in the countryside, in spite of several bitter blows at the hands of the National Guard in the 1970s.

In January 1978, Pedro Joaquín Chamorro, who at the time was the editor for the national newspaper, *La Prensa,* and who was seen by many as a potential presidential candidate, was assassinated in the streets of Managua on his way to work. This was likely the backlash of months of unfavorable press that even Somoza's mounting censorship of the media was unable to stifle. One month later in response the largely indigenous population of the Masaya neighborhood of Monimbó rose up. The protest lasted five days, after which the National Guard massacred hundreds of Nicaraguans in a fit of unprecedented rage.

The FSLN gained more and more strength as increasing numbers of trade unions, student organizations, and popular movements, both private and religious, joined its ranks. By May 1979, the Sandinista command offensive, encouraged by an increasingly militant attitude among the people, was strong and well organized enough to carry out the final military strikes to overthrow the dictatorship. The final insurrection lasted 52 days. Combat erupted almost spontaneously and simultaneously around Chinandega, León, and Chichigalpa in the Pacific, and in the mining triangle in the northeast. At the same time, Sandinista troops began pressing north from the border with Costa Rica. They entered León, capturing the city after a two-day battle, and at the same time, a massive general labor strike commenced.

On June 8, 1979, the insurrection began in Carazo, just south of Managua, and quickly flowed into the capital itself. Foreigners began evacuating the city immediately as the National Guard began shelling Managua. Most of the fighting in Managua took place in the lower-middle-class neighborhoods of Bello Horizonte and El Dorado in the eastern half of the city.

INTRODUCTION

There, an extensive network of concrete drainage ditches made easy battle trenches. On the streets, concrete barricades were erected by tearing up the concrete *adoquines* (paving stones) with which Nicaraguan streets are lined. The fact that the *adoquines* were products of Somoza's monopoly is a much-loved irony to this day. The insurrection in Managua was worldwide news, and viewers and readers were appalled by the images of Somoza's aircraft machine gunning and bombing the capital city indiscriminately.

Meanwhile, in the north, Matagalpa fell to the FSLN on July 2, 1979, and the strategic town of Sébaco fell the day after. The Sandinistas controlled the entire north of Nicaragua. The military barracks at Estelí fell on July 16th. It was the last—and most important—barracks outside of Managua to crumble. Managua had been surrounded by Sandinista forces since July 10th. Their all-out attack on the capital was held back because Somoza's surrender was inevitable. Somoza fled Nicaragua in the predawn hours of July 17th, leaving Francisco Urcuyo Malianos behind as interim president with the single responsibility of handing power over to the Sandinistas. Instead, he decided he'd hang on as Nicaragua's new president, serving out the rest of Somoza's term. This brilliant idea lasted two days, and Urcuyo fled Nicaragua when the National Guard disintegrated around him. The Sandinistas had won.

THE FSLN GOVERNMENT

Throughout history, every single revolutionary has discovered winning a war is simpler than running a nation, and the exuberance of having overthrown the dictator quickly wore off as the new leaders struggled to convert the revolutionary fervor into support for the new nation they wanted to build. They were starting from scratch: Somoza had run the nation as his own personal farm, and overthrowing him

As I rode through the countryside, I began to realize that contradictions were probably all I was ever going to find in Nicaragua. My search for the truth of what was happening there would never fully be successful, because in such a place there is always more than one truth.

Stephen Kinzer

had meant obliterating the entire institutional infrastructure of a nation—including the economic, financial, and legislative bodies. The sweeping economic, political, and social reforms of the Sandinista revolution made Nicaragua a real-world experiment; the entire world—particularly the United States—watched with fascination and fear.

Politically, *Nicaragua Libre* (Free Nicaragua) in its infancy was a battleground of competing interests of the social classes and foreign powers, all squeezed by the need to raise immediate currency to reactivate the economy. The Conservative alliance that had been promised a role in the new government found itself nudged off the ruling platform, as the "Group of Nine" fatigue-clad FSLN *comandantes* took full control of the government and began displaying their Marxist-Leninist tendencies.

True to their word, the Sandinistas began their land reform policy almost immediately. Two million acres of Somoza's holdings were confiscated and nationalized with the aim of distributing the land among the poor. This was a first in Central America, socially significant, but also environmentally harmful, opening up previously unexploited and sensitive lands such as hillsides that farmers soon cleared and planted, unleashing massive deforestation and erosion problems. Worse, in the years after the revolution, critics point out that many of the best pieces of land were distributed not to the needy but rather to the Sandinista elite.

Another of the FSLN's initial acts was their massive and world-acclaimed literacy campaign to combat Nicaragua's abominably high illiteracy rate. The year 1980 was proclaimed "The Year of Literacy" and thousands of volunteers—typically zealous university students—marched out to the rural corners of Nicaragua to teach reading, writing, and basic math skills. Even now, the most fervent opponents of the Sandinista government admit the literacy campaign was a triumph of the revolution. But it was not without its criticisms, most notable of which was the Cuban-style incorporation of Sandinista propaganda into the teaching materials. Often the first phrases a campesino learned to read was a revolutionary slogan, and the math exercises frequently involved counting items like rifles and tanks. Still, teaching otherwise unlearned campesinos how to read was no small accomplishment, and the literacy campaign encouraged young idealistic urbanites to go out into the countryside and learn about the nation. An unprecedented nationalism grew that can still be felt today.

The Sandinistas' legendary "Plan 80" was developed during their first year in power. It defined Nicaragua's economy as a balance between private ownership and state control, but with a plan to gradually tighten state control over time. This did not sit well with the commercial sector, and many private industries balked at joining the new economy. Their refusal to cooperate in the mixed economy eventually contributed in no small way to its failure.

OPPOSITION TO THE FSLN

In their zeal to "defend the revolution at all costs," the Sandinista leaders ran into opposition from all sides—from the business community (represented by the business organization COSEP); from Somoza's former cronies who missed their days of wealth and privilege and were enraged by the policy of confiscation; from the former members of the National Guard, many of whom regrouped outside of Nicaragua and became the nucleus of the military *contrarevolucionarios* (Contras); and lastly, from the United States. President Ronald Reagan, upon taking office in 1981, immediately seized on the Communist tendencies of the Sandinista leadership and launched a political, economic, and military program designed to strangle the Sandinistas out of power and replace them with something more amenable to the economic interests of North America.

Reagan's concern was not primarily economic. Central America in the 1980s was a hotbed of civil and political unrest, and the Sandinistas were not only openly collaborating with Cuba and the Soviet Union but also openly supporting the FMLN, a revolutionary group in El Salvador who violently opposed the murderous, U.S.-backed dictator there. Sensing a shift in the geopolitical balance of the hemisphere, the United States stopped all aid to Nicaragua in 1981, and later imposed an economic embargo in 1985. But the desire and the ambition to remove the Sandinistas was not North America's alone—many moderate Nicaraguans felt betrayed by the Sandinistas, who, they felt, had forced a Marxist-Leninist regime on the nation at the expense of the private sector and right-wing interests. Thus the U.S.-financed Contras became just the military expression of a multi-faceted movement that led to yet another Nicaraguan regime's downfall.

Under state-led Sandinismo, all sectors of the economy plummeted due largely to gross economic mismanagement and the effect of the economic embargo. By 1985, export earnings had dropped violently to half their prerevolution figures, and much of the confiscated agricultural land turned into cooperatives remained unproductive and was administered at great expense. The business class, in fear of further expropriations, lacked the financial incentives to invest, and many of Nicaragua's skilled laborers fled the country in search of profitable employment elsewhere. The increasing military pressure put on the Sandinistas by the Contras forced them to increase military spending at the cost of social programs, and tied up much of the country's productive labor force in battle. Austerity measures didn't earn the Sandinista government many friends either, as previously common goods like toothpaste and rice were parsimoniously rationed, and shoddy Eastern-bloc goods replaced imports from the United States.

Chief of all the Sandinista government's hated policies was the military draft. While a necessary measure in light of the increasingly violent Contra attacks in Matagalpa, Jinotega, and much of the east, Nicaraguans were in no way willing to send their sons and brothers off to be cannon fodder in order to defend a revolution in which

OF BEANS AND BULLETS: WHO WERE THE CONTRAS?

"Freedom fighters," "bandits," "heroes," "outlaws": by any name, the Contras were one of the most powerful, divisive, and enigmatic elements of Nicaragua's recent history. Decades later, they're still one of the most elusive to understand. Nicaraguan society is still sharply divided between those who supported and those who opposed the Sandinistas, and mention of the Contras can simultaneously evoke a sense of fear, pride, anger, and triumph, all from Nicaraguans sitting at the same table. They owe their name to the Sandinista leaders who christened them *"contra-revolucionarios"* (against the revolution); the Contras preferred to call themselves *"La Resistencia."*

Not long after the Sandinistas took power in 1979 and long before the Contra movement even had a name, discontent was already swelling among some groups of campesinos, who sensed the Sandinista revolution had gone wrong: small farmers were being forced to join collectives, and those who resisted lost their land or went to jail. There were regular political meetings, an air of government-sponsored atheism (or at least dubious support for the Catholic Church), and a rapid saturation of Cuban advisers in the government. Price controls were making it hard to turn a profit in agriculture, and a lot of people were incarcerated, including many indigenous Miskito people, who had never wanted much more than to be left alone. The revolution was supposed to have made the lives of the poor farmers easier, not harder. As the first campesinos picked up arms and slipped across the northern border into Honduras, they encountered another group eager to see the Sandinistas return to where they had come from: former members of Somoza's National Guard, professional military personnel who longed for their former positions of power and prestige and thirsted for one more battle.

Though they received some early training and organizational help from Argentine military advisers, the Contras weren't an organized force per se until late in the game. Even then, they were composed of numerous factions rife with internal divisions, petty grudges, and ambition among and within their units. Many were simple farm boys looking for fame and fortune at the end of a rifle; others were would-be warlords who used the armed

maneuvers to settle old civil disputes or have some vengeance on former drinking buddies in town. The Contras survived on limited supplies, donations from sympathizers in Miami, and whatever they could take at gunpoint.

The only thing that united the various Contra groups was the feeling that the Sandinista revolution had been a step in the wrong direction. That group included U.S. president Ronald Reagan, who in March 1986 claimed to be a Contra himself, with these words: "I guess in a way they are counter-revolutionary, and God bless them for being that way. And I guess that makes them Contras, and so it makes me a Contra, too." At various points in the 1980s, the U.S. government played a critical part in the financing and arming of the Contras, in violation of its own laws and without the knowledge of the public.

Based out of camps along the Honduran border, the Fuerza Democrática Nicaragüense (FDN) staged raids in Jinotega, Matagalpa, and Chinandega, and was led primarily by ex-National Guard officers and groups of farmers that called themselves Milicia Popular Anti-Somoza (MILPA, a play on the Spanish word for corn patch). Fighting a completely separate battle along the Río San Juan from camps over the Costa Rican border was the Alianza Revolucionaria Democrática (ARDE), led by the infamous Edén Pastora, a.k.a. Comandante Cero (Zero), former Sandinista militant turned Contra. ARDE was a military disaster from the start, so thoroughly riddled with Sandinista spies it never had any hope of victory. Pastora was a would-be caudillo that hated organization, refused to delegate authority, and kept his own men divided to prevent any claims to his throne. His macho posturing and reputation for womanizing made him an easy target for sexy female Sandinista spies, a half dozen of which coaxed him to pillow-talk away just about every military secret he had. Pastora's own men feared he was really a Sandinista sympathizer sent to lead them into military devastation.

Though the Sandinista military committed its share of mistakes and atrocities, the Contras' propensity for brutality and terror is well documented and undeniable. Militarily, they were best at short, sharp raids and random ambushes of military and civilian vehicles. Complicated operations that required timing or planning nearly always went awry, and communication and coordination problems plagued them throughout the war. What they were best at was seeding terror in the hillsides. Their tactics were barbaric: Contras regularly disemboweled victims, chopped their limbs off, and tore bones out of bodies which they shook at the victims' family members. Columns of hungry Contra troops didn't think twice about taking at gunpoint anything they needed from local campesinos, from cattle to liquor to boots. On the way, many young women and girls were taken away to be raped and killed, sometimes by decapitation. Young boys and men were routinely castrated and mutilated before being killed.

The Contras commonly targeted suspected Sandinista sympathizers, including government workers in nonmilitary organizations. They brutalized and killed mayors, doctors, nurses, judges, schoolteachers, clergy, policemen, even the staff of utility offices and wealthy townspeople suspected of supporting the new government. Often, those victims who escaped death at the hands of the Contras were forced into the mountains at gunpoint to become soldiers. Intent on derailing the Sandinista economy by preventing the harvest, Contras frequently burned the installations of agricultural cooperatives and massacred anyone who stayed to defend them.

The Contras never had the satisfaction of a military victory. Rather, when the Sandinistas lost public elections and handed power over to the Chamorro government, the incentive to be a Contra vanished. Though some Contras rejected the peace accords and slipped back into the mountains to continue fighting (these so-called *"recontras"* cause occasional trouble in the backwoods of Nicaragua even today), most disarmed and went back to farming their beans and corn. In the end, though foreign powers had helped the Nicaraguans to nearly destroy themselves over ideology and geopolitics, the Contras who returned to the land knew the struggle to defeat the Sandinista government had been about the simplest things all along—the right to a piece of land, to be left alone to work it, and to sell their crops at market value.

they were rapidly losing faith. *Servicio militar patriotico* (patriotic military service), or SMP, was parodied by young men as *"Seremos Muertos Prontos"* (soon we will be dead).

Elections were called in 1984, and the Sandinistas won easily. Most of the world conceded the elections had been fair and transparent, but Washington claimed to be unconvinced. Contra financing increased, though the U.S. Congress placed limits on the aid, such as declaring it for nonmilitary purposes only (a trick made possible by labeling the Contra soldiers as "refugees").

By the close of the 1980s the Contra war and the Sandinista government had degenerated simultaneously and finally collapsed altogether. The Sandinista economy was ruined and could no longer support a prolonged war of attrition, while overseas the Soviet Union had collapsed and could no longer prop up the Sandinistas. The Contras had suffered severe military setbacks, mixed messages from their patrons, and had little hope of a military victory. In the political carnage of the Iran-Contra scandal (in which Ronald Reagan and senior government officials had secretly and illegally raised funds for the Contra forces by selling arms to Iran), funding for the Contras dried up, and their biggest supporter, former CIA director William Casey, died in May 1987.

Both sides of the conflict were suffering and inflicting great losses, and Nicaragua's young men were being killed at the rate of 50 per day. The moment was propitious for a peace initiative, and it was Costa Rican president Oscar Arias who supplied it. In 1987, five Central American presidents attended talks at Esquipulas, Guatemala, and emerged with a radical peace accord (which was opposed by the United States). The five governments pledged to permit full freedom for political parties, hold periodic elections monitored by external agencies, and commence healing dialogues with opposition groups. The United States and other extraregional governments were told, in no uncertain terms, to stop open or covert aid to insurrection movements, which in turn were declared illegitimate and obstacles to the peace process.

THE NEW DEMOCRACY: THE 1990S

Doña Violeta

The year 1990 saw another radical shift of power in Nicaragua—this time a quiet one. With the Reagan administration gone and the Contras largely abandoned, the Sandinistas organized elections to show the world that their government was committed to democratic principles and to give Nicaraguans the chance to reaffirm their support for the FSLN. To their surprise, the Nicaraguan people overwhelmingly voted them out of office. To their credit, the Sandinistas abided by the results and stepped down from power. The new president of Nicaragua became Violeta Barrios de Chamorro, widow of the slain journalist Pedro Joaquín Chamorro and center of a ragtag coalition of a Sandinista opposition known as the Unión Nacional Opositora (UNO).

Doña Violeta (as she is affectionately known) had no formal political affiliations or training, yet it was her ability to reconcile and unite that ushered Nicaragua into its new era. She attempted to rebuild the nation as though it were a shattered family, which to some degree, it was. In a sense, she was more symbolic than political, yet Nicaragua's progress was anything but symbolic in the time she was in office. Her administration made great gains in reestablishing the country in the world diplomatic and economic community. The draft was stopped immediately, and the army was subsequently reduced to more manageable levels. The new administration put both the army and the police force under civil control, and then began the lengthy and arduous process of demobilizing and disarming the Contras. As a peace offering, Doña Violeta offered them 1,600 square kilometers of land, including much of the Río San Juan area, to resettle and enter the agrarian labor force. Other Contra communities can be found in Jinotega and Matagalpa. Her administration also initiated a new protocol of agrarian reform, which aimed to reassign formerly expropriated lands. Over 12 years later, the issue of who owns land in Nicaragua remains incompletely resolved and often hotly disputed.

In the first few years of her government, Doña Violeta was able to successfully woo the international aid community back to Nicaragua to help with the reconstruction. Unfortunately, the aid did not arrive in the quantity that the government had hoped for. Notably stingy was the U.S. government, which, once assured the Sandinistas would fall from power, seemed to forget about Nicaragua entirely. Much of the effort of the Nicaraguan administrations of the 1990s has been to reinvigorate the failing economy, which was still in a free fall in the early 1990s. The 1991 economic stabilization plan pegged the cordoba to the dollar and established a slow devaluation program that would offset inflation. The banking market was opened to private banks, legislation was authored that encouraged foreign investment, and much of the accumulated international debt was pardoned, largely due to Doña Violeta's remarkable diplomacy. An unfortunate result of economic streamlining, the mass privatization or sale of economically disadvantageous state-run businesses like the railroad system led to widespread unemployment that has lasted to the present.

Sandinistas in the 1990s

The Sandinistas reinvented themselves as a legitimate political party after their defeat in 1990, and have been strong participants in municipal and presidential elections ever since. However, in spite of their continued support, particularly among their traditional base—the poor and disenfranchised—they have been unable to retake the presidency. Most Nicaraguans still remember all too well the civil war, chronic shortages of basic commercial goods, and the military draft that plagued the 1980s. Also unforgivable for many was an event now known as *"la piñata,"* in which a lame-duck Ortega administration looted the state of everything it could, from office equipment to fancy Managua homes, keeping the best of it for themselves. FSLN party heads privatized many state companies under anonymous cooperatives, and passed a series of decrees ensuring they would retain some power. In the eyes of many Nicaraguans, it was the final abandonment of every ideal the revolution had ever claimed to stand for.

VISITORS FROM THE NORTH: A BRIEF HISTORY OF U.S. INTERVENTION IN NICARAGUA

In President Teddy Roosevelt's addition to the Monroe Doctrine of regional dominance, he proclaimed that the United States, by virtue of its status as a "civilized nation," had the right to stop "chronic wrongdoing" throughout the Western Hemisphere. Subsequently, the so-called Roosevelt Corollary was used to justify troop deployment to Latin America 32 times between the end of the Spanish-American War and the years of the Great Depression. President William Howard Taft provided further rationalization for aggressively dominating Latin America with his "Dollar Diplomacy," an unabashed strategy to advance and protect U.S. businesses in other countries. Nicaragua, which had been host to U.S. fruit, mining, and transportation interests since the 1850s, was a frequent recipient of such foreign policy.

U.S. Marines landed at least seven times during the aforementioned period, and spent a total of 21 years occupying Nicaragua. Official reasons for these visits included "pacification of Nicaragua," "prevention of rebellion," and, of course, "protection of U.S. interests and property." It would be unfair to call these visits "uninvited," since nearly all were ostensibly serving the purpose of one or more Nicaraguan parties, usually the Conservatives.

The following is a more detailed list of gringo interventions:

1853: Washington sends U.S. Navy commander George H. Hollins to Greytown to extract an apology from local British officials for having insulted U.S. diplomat Solon Borland. Those responsible were nowhere to be found, so, reports a U.S. Marine Corps historical website, Hollins's "only alternative was to bombard the town, and this he tried to do in the most humane manner possible." Hollins allowed 24 hours for evacuation, then commenced firing. "At 0900 on 13 July, 177 shells plowed into Greytown. That afternoon a landing party of Marines and seamen completed the destruction of the town." Humanely, of course.

1853–1856: U.S. citizen William Walker usurps power and declares himself president of Nicaragua;

he is briefly recognized by Washington before the other Central American nations briefly unite, drive him out, and eventually execute him by firing squad.

1894: Monthlong occupation of Bluefields by U.S. Marines under Lieutenant Franklin J. Moses.

1896: From May 2–4, when fighting near Corinto "endangers American holdings," 15 marines, under 1st Sergeant Frederick W. M. Poppe, and 19 seamen land in Corinto and stand guard in a "show of force."

1898: As President Zelaya extends his tenure for still another term, the local U.S. consular agent requests the U.S.S. *Alert*, at anchor in the harbor of Bluefields, to stand by in case of an attack on the city. On the morning of February 7, the U.S. flag on shore rises "union downward" over the consulate, signaling a force of 14 marines and 19 seamen to land, who withdraw the following day.

1899: Another display of force lands, this time with a Colt automatic gun to "prevent both rebels and government troops from destroying American property."

1910: Marines and navy vessels concentrate in Nicaraguan waters and land in Bluefields and Corinto on May 19 to "guard American property."

1912: Nicaraguan president Adolfo Díaz requests the support of U.S. forces. The United States complies when the U.S.S. *Annapolis* arrives in Corinto, deploying a contingent of naval officers to Managua on August 4. Three companies of marine infantry also land and are transported to Managua by train.

1927–1933: President Coolidge sends marines to find Sandino and "gun the bandit down."

1981–1990: The CIA runs a secret command operation directing and financing Contra forces in their contra-revolution. They carry out supply and intelligence activities, train commanders and soldiers, plant harbor mines, and sabotage Sandinista holdings.

Arnoldo Alemán

The elections of 1996, run without the massive international funding that characterized the elections of 1990, were rife with abnormalities, near-riots, and chronic disorder. Polling places opened hours late, bags of discarded ballots turned up afterward in the houses of officials paid to count them, and the difficulties of the communication network all laid the groundwork for dispute, charges of vote-rigging, and fraud. Even so, the record number of voters that turned out to cast their ballots elected to the presidency Managua's slippery Liberal mayor, Arnoldo Alemán, in lieu of Daniel Ortega, by a margin of 49 percent to 38 percent. At the heart of the controversy was the Consejo Supremo Electoral (CSE), whose responsibility was to run the elections and tally the results. Thus was the scandalous beginning to a scandalous presidency.

A lawyer by training, Alemán was a political conservative and hard-core capitalist with a sworn aversion to all things Sandinista. He was also an outspoken fan of Somoza, whose proclivity for political manipulation and capacity to accumulate personal fortune Alemán admired and imitated deftly. His economic program courted foreign investment and promoted exports at the expense of a social safety net. The Alemán years saw the continued growth of the economy, boosted by the establishment of *zonas francas* (free trade zones), and the resulting construction of *maquiladoras* (export clothing assembly plants, a.k.a. sweatshops).

Nicaraguans were infuriated time and time again by the endless scandals of kickbacks, back-room deals, and pocket filling. After reportedly selling cars in Miami during the 1980s, Alemán is said to have been worth $20,000 when elected as mayor of Managua in 1990. In May 2001 the Nicaraguan newspaper *El Nuevo Diaro* reported Alemán's personal wealth at $250 million, stashed in Swiss, Miami, and Canary Island bank accounts. In the same article, Alemán claims his net worth is $2 million. His political and personal cronies didn't do too poorly either.

Hurricane Mitch

On October 28, 1998, the worst storm in recorded history struck Nicaragua (see Hurricane Mitch

special topic). Nicaragua's already wimpy physical infrastructure was devastated, thousands lost their homes and migrated to urban centers to look for work or beg on street corners, and the harvest was almost completely lost. Yet even in the wake of the hurricane, politics played a role: many criticized the Alemán administration for administering aid to Liberal communities first, while Sandinista communities like the landslide-devastated Posoltega were allowed to suffer.

The nation has struggled to recover ever since, with the added problems of poor harvests in the three years that followed Hurricane Mitch and a severe drought in all of Central America that—yet again—all but destroyed the year's harvest of beans and corn.

The 2001 Elections

Many believed that Alemán's abuses would engender enough popular opposition to reelect the FSLN to power in 2001. To combat this possibility, the campaign of Liberal candidate Enrique Bolaños, the 73-year-old vice president under Alemán, focused almost exclusively on reminding Nicaragua of the long lines, rations, and hardships of the 1980s. FSLN candidate Daniel Ortega's campaign called for "Peace, Love, and the Promised Land," and he substituted the color pink (called *chicha rosada,* for the beverage of the same tint) for the harsh *rojinegra* (red and black) of the revolution. He managed to form a broad-based alliance, *La Convergencia,* that included several of his former enemies. Tensions were high; foreign investment and construction projects ground to a halt while investors held their breath, straining the fragile economy just as a drought and coffee crisis added to the unease. The terrorist attacks of September 11 shook the world and entered into the campaign as attempts were made to vilify Ortega as a friend of terrorists. The country braced itself for the worst on the weekend of November 4: the army was put on high alert, the sale of alcohol was completely banned, and commerce essentially shut down until the polls closed. In the end, Bolaños won by a 53–44 percent margin, in an election scrupulously observed by a posse of some 12,000 foreign and national observers. All the while,

U.S. officials have made no pretense or excuses concerning their unabashed backing of (and even campaigning for) non-Sandinista candidates in the 1990, 1996, and 2001 elections.

Government

You will learn more about Nicaraguan government on the streets and in the countryside by engaging the vivacious Nicaraguans in conversation than any book can hope to teach you, including this one. The history of government and politics in Nicaragua is lengthy and convoluted, and made more enticing by Nicaragua's rare distinction of having experienced three radically different systems of government in as many decades. In 1979 the dictatorship fell to Marxism/Leninism, which was itself later replaced by capitalism and an open market. The ramifications of the changes are still being discussed.

The revolution of 1979 gave the Nicaraguan people unparalleled freedom of expression by Latin American standards. Discussions that would have resulted in searches by the death squads in El Salvador or Guatemala flow freely and unmolested throughout Nicaragua. Nicaraguans take advantage of their freedom and you should too. Encourage the people to share their beliefs, opinions, and ideas with you— starting with your taxi driver on the way from the airport. Politics are central to the lives of most Nicaraguans, and everyone has an opinion— and a solution. It is not uncommon to see Nicaraguan friends, neighbors, and family members engaged in heated, and often alcohol-fueled, political debate. But regardless of the ferocity of the discussion, instead of degenerating into fistfights, Nicaraguans almost always leave the session with smiles, toasts, and handshakes.

ORGANIZATION

The Republic of Nicaragua is a constitutional democracy which gained its independence from Spain in 1821. In addition to the national government, there is a parallel government responsible for the administration of the two autonomous regions of the Atlantic coast. The government of the autonomous regions elects its own leaders separately from the rest of the nation.

Branches of Government

Nicaragua's government is divided into four branches. The executive branch consists of the president and vice president. The judicial branch includes the Supreme Court, subordinate appeals courts, district courts, and local courts, plus separate labor and administrative tribunals. The Supreme Court oversees the entire judicial system, and consists of 12 justices elected by the National Assembly for seven-year terms. Many consider the judicial system ineffective and plagued by party interests and manipulations by the rich, but it does have some points in its favor, including an approach that attempts to reduce crowding in jails by having the aggressor and the aggrieved meet to strike a deal. For minor offenses, this is an effective tactic. There is no capital punishment in Nicaragua, the maximum sentence being 30 years (though the abominable conditions of Nicaraguan prisons makes one wonder if the sentence isn't equally harsh).

The legislative branch consists of the *Asamblea Nacional* (National Assembly), a chamber in which 90 *diputados* (deputies) representing Nicaragua's different geographical regions vote on policy. The *diputados* are elected from party lists provided by the major political parties, though defeated presidential candidates that earn a minimum requirement of votes automatically become lifetime members, and by law, former presidents are also guaranteed a seat.

Elections

The Nicaraguan people vote for their president and *diputados* every five years. The president cannot run for consecutive terms, though once stepping down from power is eligible to run again as a candidate in the following elections.

The *Consejo Supremo Electoral* (Supreme Electoral Council, or CSE) consists of seven magistrates elected by the National Assembly for five-year terms. The CSE has the responsibility of organizing, running, and declaring the winners of elections, referendums, and plebiscites. Electoral reforms put in place in 2000 allowed the FSLN and the Partido Liberal Constitucionalista (PLC) the new ability to name political appointees to the Council, politicizing the CSE to the extreme. The international community decried the fact that the entire process of recognizing new political parties, declaring candidates, and managing the mechanics of holding elections could be so easily subverted to ensure the two strongest parties—the PLC and the FSLN—divide the spoils of government between themselves. These "reforms" have led to a perceived reduction in the transparency of the Nicaraguan government as a whole.

It is interesting to note that nearly every Nicaraguan presidential candidate (with the exception of Doña Violeta), has been, at one time or another, jailed by a previous administration. Daniel Ortega was jailed by Somoza, Arnoldo Alemán by Ortega, and Enrique Bolaños by Ortega as well. Agustín Jarquín, former comptroller-general and FSLN vice-presidential candidate in 2001, was jailed by both the Sandinistas and by Alemán… and the cycle of vengeance continues.

THE CONSTITUTION

The present constitution, written in 1987 by the FSLN administration, was amended in 1995 to balance the distribution of power more evenly between the legislative and executive branches. The National Assembly's ability to veto was bolstered and the president's ability to veto reduced. It was revised again in 2000 to increase the power of the Supreme Court and the comptroller-general's office.

Civil Liberties

Among Latin American societies the people of Nicaragua enjoy unequaled freedom. Most notable is their nearly unparalleled freedom of speech, a right guaranteed by the constitution and exercised with great vigor by Nicaraguans of all persuasions. The repression, censorship, and brutality of Somoza's dictatorship ended within the recent memory of many Nicaraguans, and they do not take the freedom they enjoy in the 21st century for granted. There is no official state censorship of the media in Nicaragua, though there have been occasional governmental attempts to exert influence through subtler means, such as the embargo of government-sponsored ad revenue of newspapers that seem overly critical.

The constitution additionally guarantees freedom of religion, freedom of movement within the country, the freedom of foreign travel, emigration and repatriation, and the right to peacefully assemble and associate. Domestic and international human rights monitors are permitted to operate freely and interview whomever they wish.

The Nicaraguan constitution prohibits discrimination in all forms, including discrimination by birth, nationality, political belief, race, gender, language, religion, opinion, national origin, or economic or social condition. In practice, however, there are many social forms of discrimination, from former president Alemán's public derision of Managua mayor Herty Lewites as *el Judío* (the Jew) to the day-to-day behavior of a *machista* society that additionally associates lighter-skinned people with the aristocracy and darker-skinned people with the labor force, regardless of whether that's the case. As a popular graffito in Managua exhorts, *"No hay democracia posible en una sociedad de clases."* (Democracy is not possible in a society of classes.)

Nicaraguans are permitted to form labor unions. Nearly half of the workforce, including much of the agricultural labor, is unionized. The trade unions receive much international support from labor groups overseas, who stepped in on behalf of Nicaraguan laborers in disputes in the free trade zones in 2000 and 2001. Alemán's administration earned some bad press by preventing one group of union officials from the United States from entering the country.

POLITICAL PARTIES

It's easy to believe the concept that the political party in Nicaragua is more for organizational convenience than for conviction of principles. Nicaraguan politicians change from one political party to another as necessary to suit their own ambitions. At the same time, smaller parties continuously coalesce into alliances that later fracture into new arrangements. Infighting and division have been an integral part of the Nicaraguan political scene for well over a century, starting with the split between the Conservatives and Liberals in the 1800s that defined political disputes for a century. No other major political party came onto the scene until the FSLN took power in the 1980s. By 1990, no fewer than 20 political parties had risen in opposition to the FSLN; Doña Violeta's UNO coalition was formed from 14 of them.

By 1996, the number of parties swelled to 35, all of which participated in the elections on their own or as one of five coalitions. In 2000, new legislation was enacted to prohibit such a free-for-all at the polls and to make entry more difficult for the smaller political parties. The requirements a political party had to meet to become eligible to run in elections were made prohibitively stringent, which prevented many political parties from participating in the national elections. Popular perception was that it was more of the same political maneuvering in an effort to exclude any newcomers from taking a piece of the government pie.

Three parties were represented in the presidential election of 2001: the FSLN, the PLC, and the Partido Conservador Nicaragüense (PCN), the latter being the moderate-right representatives of the Conservative party. The FSLN, which many considered usurped by the egotistical ambitions of its longtime caudillo (Latin American strongman) Daniel Ortega, was a stronger contender than many thought possible. Ortega's campaign downplayed the use of the word "Sandinista" and concentrated on his own personality instead: banners read not "FSLN!" but "Daniel!" The Sandinistas (and their anti-Liberal coalition, La Convergencia) battled the PLC-dominated Alianza Liberal (Liberal Alliance), which ultimately won the election.

The Pact

Chief among the factors thought to be crucial to the political future of Nicaragua is *El Pacto,* (the pact), a set of constitutional reforms harshly criticized by the majority of Nicaraguans. Developed by Arnoldo Alemán and Daniel Ortega in 2000, when the FSLN was politically weak and Alemán was struggling to find a way to retain some form of political power after handing over the presidency to his successor in the upcoming 2001 elections, the pact gave the FSLN and PLC parties a virtual monopoly on government. By raising the requirements necessary for new or small political parties to participate in elections, essentially forcing them off the ballot, the reforms allow candidates to win the presidency with as little as 35 percent of the vote. The pact was also personally beneficial to both Alemán and Ortega, who granted themselves political immunity and guaranteed lifetime seats in the National Assembly. The immunity was providential for Ortega, who was facing charges regarding the alleged sexual abuse of stepdaughter Zoilamerica during the 1980s.

Economy

Nicaragua's economy has been essentially jump-started from a complete standstill twice now, once when the Sandinistas took power in 1979, and once when they handed it over to Doña Violeta's administration at the end of a failed decade of economic reform. In its present incarnation, the economy of Nicaragua has been developing and fighting to strengthen itself since 1991. By some economic measuring sticks it has made dramatic progress in reducing the foreign debt by over half, slashing inflation from 13,500 percent to 12 percent, and privatizing several hundred state-run businesses. The new economy began to expand in 1994 and reached a 5 percent growth rate in 2000, despite several major catastrophes, including Hurricane Mitch in 1998, and extended drought periods from 1997 through 2001.

Nevertheless, in the year 2000, Nicaragua dropped from the status of second poorest nation in the Western Hemisphere to the poorest. It is a nation heavily dependent on foreign aid, which in the year 2000 made up 45 percent of its government revenue. After 10 years of civil war and another decade of slow recovery, Nicaragua's per capita GDP stands at $495, lower than it was in 1979. Three-fourths of the population now lives on less than $2 per day. The minimum wage requirement is ignored, especially in the countryside, where agricultural laborers typically earn as little as $1 a day with no provision made for food, insufficient for survival even by Nicaraguan standards. Nearly 600,000 people face severe malnutrition.

Nicaragua has an economy almost entirely based on agricultural export of primary material, though in recent years tourism and several nontraditional exports have gained in importance. Export earnings are $700 million and rising: agricultural programs in 2000 and 2001 that helped increase Nicaragua's ability to export beef and milk give hope that exports will rise in the latter part of the decade. Traditional export products include coffee, beef, and sugar, followed by bananas, shellfish (especially lobster tails and shrimp), and tobacco. New nontraditional exports are on the rise as well, including sesame, onions, melons, and tropical fruit.

DEBT, FOREIGN AID, AND THE HIPC

For years, Nicaragua has been one of the most highly indebted nations of the world. When Somoza fled the country, he took the capital reserves of the banks with him, leaving behind $1.6 billion of debt. The armed conflict in Nicaragua during the 1980s combined with economic mismanagement, extensive borrowing (primarily from Eastern bloc nations), the U.S. economic embargo, and high defense expenditures meant that the Sandinistas left behind a debt that had grown by a factor of 10. In 1990, 40 percent of that debt was in arrears. By 1994 Nicaragua had the highest ratio of debt to GDP in the world. Working for the pardoning or restructuring of that debt has been an extreme challenge for the administrations of the 1990s and beyond. Among the nations that forgave Nicaragua its debt were Germany, Russia, and Mexico.

Since 1990 Nicaragua's fragile economy has been bolstered by massive amounts of foreign aid—nearly $500 million per year (22 percent of the GDP), much of which is returned to the same countries that lent it in the form of debt servicing. Even so, Nicaragua is unable to meet its repayment obligations.

Propitious to Nicaragua's future economic growth was its inclusion in the Highly Indebted Poor Countries (HIPC) debt relief initiative in 2000. Inclusion in the initiative means Nicaragua will be exonerated from the majority of its international debt upon compliance with an International Monetary Fund (IMF) and World Bank program that mandates austerity programs, debt restructuring, and the opening of its economy to foreign markets. Central to the HIPC initiative is Nicaragua's continued effort toward macroeconomic adjustment and structural and social policy reforms (with additional assurances for social sector programs, primarily basic health and education).

AGRICULTURE

Nicaragua is, above all, an agricultural nation—a third of its gross domestic product is agriculture-based, and agriculture represents the fastest growing economic sector, at 8 percent growth per year. However, much of the new land put into agricultural production is opened at the expense of the forests, the indiscriminate harvesting of which has had a negative effect overall on the environment and water supply. Agriculture employs 45 percent of the workforce. Outside of the small, upscale producers who export to international markets, the majority of Nicaraguan agriculture is for domestic consumption, and much of that is subsistence farming. Drought years from 1997 through 2001 prompted the importing of basic grains.

Subsistence farmers typically grow yellow corn and red beans. The choice of red beans over black and yellow corn over white is cultural and presents additional challenges to farmers, as red beans are more susceptible to drought (and less nutritious) than black beans. The Sébaco Valley is an agriculturally productive area and the primary source of wet rice for local consumption; it's also widely planted with onions. Extensive irrigation of rice plantations has caused the water table in the Sébaco Valley to drop over three meters in the 1990s. Jinotega, with its cool climate, is a major source of fruit and vegetable production, including cabbage, peppers, onions, melons, watermelons, squash, and tomatoes.

THE COFFEE ECONOMY

There's no underestimating the importance of coffee to the Nicaraguan economy. Coffee is produced on over 100,000 hectares of Nicaraguan land, contributes an average of $140 million dollars per year to the economy, and employs over 200,000 people, nearly a third of the agricultural workforce (13 percent of the national workforce). Nicaragua exports its beans primarily to Europe, North America, and Japan—to the tune of 105 million 100-pound burlap sacks every year. These beans are roasted and ground (usually abroad) to produce 11 billion pounds of java.

The Coffee Crisis

But producing and selling Nicaraguan coffee, challenging even in good times, has been dealt a staggering blow since 1997, when coffee producers in Vietnam began to flood the market with cheap robusta beans, driving world prices downward to 25 percent of 1994 prices, a 100-year low. Analysts have declared it one of the most dramatic moments in the past hundred years of worldwide coffee history. With market prices well below the costs of production, the effect on rural Nicaraguan coffee workers has been severe—September of 2001 saw, for the first time, hundreds of Nicaragua's poorest coffee workers camped out in the city of Matagalpa asking for food and money to survive on.

Revitalizing and protecting Nicaragua's coffee crop has become a national priority. Fortunately, Nicaragua has several advantages over other similarly struggling coffee producing nations. First of all, nearly 95 percent of Nicaraguan coffee is shade grown, in conditions similar to natural forest. It can thus be classified as "bird friendly," since the forest canopy that maintains the coffee bushes in shade also provides habitat for migratory birds. Secondly, many Nicaragua growers produce full-bodied arabica beans, which earn a higher market price than other beans.

Escaping the current coffee crisis will require a government-level effort to address several factors, including investment in the environment (especially in the areas of soil fertility and water contamination), modernization of the processing methods, and perhaps most crucially, the resolution of severe microcredit and marketing issues. Addressing the coffee crisis may provide the framework for addressing the social ills inherent in modern coffee production. Paul Katzeff, CEO of the California-based Thanksgiving Coffee Company and two-time president of the Specialty Coffee Association of America, the largest coffee trade organization in the world, says that the future of coffee is in farmer-run cooperatives in which small-scale farmers, rather than a single, super-rich hacienda owner, possess the power to control their product. At present, nearly 10 percent of Nicaraguan coffee is produced by such cooperatives and as much as 80 percent of their coffee can be marketed as specialty coffee for the gourmet and organic market, making them less vulnerable to the extreme oscillations of the conventional coffee market.

Katzeff further maintains that the quality of coffee is inextricably tied to the quality of life of those that produce it, as well as the quality of the environment in which they live. He and several covisionaries are actively involved in empowering small-scale farmers to recognize and judge the quality of their product and eliminate the middlemen, called *coyotes,* that traditionally take the lion's share of the profits. This vision for Nicaraguan coffee involves empowering the cooperative growers by providing them with the tools to assess the quality of their beans. The chief tool to do this is something called a "cupping lab," which is a specially equipped kitchen where trained Nicaraguan cooperative members can grind, brew, and rate their own coffee using internationally recognized criteria. Such a facility is standard with U.S.-based coffee roasters and importers, but until September 2001, was unknown in Nicaragua. Not only does a cupping lab enable members of a cooperative to control quality, it gives them the ability to speak the world coffee trade language and invite buyers to travel directly to their *beneficios* (processing mills). Today, tourists and coffee merchants alike can travel a circuit of small coffee cooperatives scattered throughout the spectacular mountains of Jinotega, Matagalpa, and the Segovias.

INDUSTRY

Industrial production in Nicaragua reached its zenith in 1978 under Anastasio Somoza, who encouraged industrial expansion in Managua at the expense of the environment, especially Lake Xolotlán. Investment policies of the time exonerated industries from the need to worry about environmental protection. Industry—even agro-industry—has been underdeveloped in the years following the revolution. There is a small amount of production for domestic and regional markets, including cement processing, petroleum refining, and a small amount of production of plastic goods. Another aspect of Nicaragua's export industry is the steadily increasing number of *Zonas Francas* (free trade zones) near Managua, Sebaco, Masaya, and Granada, where tens of thousands of Nicaraguans are employed in foreign-owned sweatshops.

TOURISM

The so-called "industry without smokestacks" is widely hoped to be a panacea to Nicaragua's economic ills, although Nicaragua's tourism policies are often without any balanced vision. At present, tourism represents the third-largest source of foreign exchange. Public Law 306 provides a 10-year tax break to newly constructed tourist facilities that meet certain criteria. Certainly, legislation of this type will help to foster economic growth in this sector. More beneficial still are travelers like you, who spend a little money and hopefully take home a good impression of Nicaragua. The second half of the 1990s saw a rapid increase in construction of hotels and restaurants; the boom is especially evident in Managua, Granada, and San Juan del Sur. During his campaign, President Enrique Bolaños pledged to augment tourism with luxury cruise ships and large international hotel and resort chains up and down the Pacific coast. If realized, the plan would turn low-key beach towns like El Velero, Pochomíl, and San Juan del Sur into five-star resort centers much like Montelimar, symbolically and physically constructing new walls between rich foreigners and Nicaraguan tourists and residents. Time will tell.

The People

Population

As of 2000, Nicaragua is a country of 4.8 million inhabitants, a full third of which live in Managua. Nicaragua is paradoxically the least populous Central American nation and the fastest growing, at just over 3 percent annually. At this rate, Nicaragua's strained resources will have to support a population of between nine and 12 million by the year 2030. The pressure is already being felt, and as many as one million Nicaraguans have migrated to other countries, especially Costa Rica and the United States.

ETHNIC GROUPS

While Nicaraguans can trace their ancestry back to many sources, most of the population is a blend of Spanish, Native American, and other European nation stock. Indigenous blood is most easily noticed in the northeast of the nation,

where the Spanish had less presence, and on the mid-Atlantic coast, where English and African influences are prominent.

In the Pacific region, the native population thinned from nearly 800,000 when the Spanish arrived to less than 60,000 after only a couple centuries of conquistador policy and influence, including war, forced slavery, all-out genocide, and introduced European diseases. The native peoples of the northeast, including Matagalpa and Jinotega, were less affected, and thus retain larger populations today.

Mestizos

The term *mestizo* refers to any mixture of Spanish blood with native populations and thus refers to the majority of Nicaraguan citizens, whose Spanish colonial ancestors began intermingling with the locals about as soon as they got off the boat. A second wave of mixing occurred in the

Miskito girls along the Río Bocay

CORN CULTURE

Corn is ancient and majestic and its planting cycle has governed the life of Nicaraguans since centuries before Columbus, when Nicaragua's indigenous peoples selected the first yellow kernels from endemic plants and laid them in the dark volcanic soil. *El maíz* is central to the Nicaraguan (and Central American) diet much the way white rice is to the peoples of southeast Asia. Beans are just as critical a staple (and a nutritionally necessary complement to provide complete protein), but in Nicaragua, corn is prepared with more variety than beans can dream of.

Corn is prepared and consumed in over a hundred different ways, and the rich vocabulary of words related to corn reflect this variety. In Nicaragua you'll find corn hot, cold, cooked, ground, liquefied, and loved. You'll find it in food and in beverages. The only place you'll find a flour tortilla here is in a Mexican restaurant in Managua; Nica corn tortillas are thick, heavy, and (hopefully) hot off the wood stove and slightly toasted.

Tortillas are, of course, flat cakes of corn dough softened with water and cooked on a slightly rounded clay pan known as a *comal.* When the same dough is fortified with sugar and lard, then rolled into small lumps and boiled while wrapped in yellow corn husks, the result is called a *tamal.* Market women balance steaming, heavy bowls of tamales on their heads and loudly hawk their goods up and down the street. *Nacatamales,* a Nicaraguan classic, are similar but with meat—often spiced pork—in the middle. *Atol* is corn pudding, and *güirila* is a sweet tortilla of young corn, always served with a hunk of salty white cheese called *cuajada. Elote* is corn on the cob, especially tasty when roasted directly over open coals until the grains are dry, hot, and a little chewy. When harvested young, the ears of corn are called *chilotes* and are served in soup or with fresh cream. Corn is also oven-baked into hard, molasses-sweetened cookie rings called *rosquillas,* flat cookies called *ojaldras,* and many other shapes. Corn dough is also combined with cheese, lard, and spices to produce dozens more items including *perrerreques, cosas de horno,* and *gofios.*

What do you wash it down with? More corn, of course. *Pinol,* drunk so frequently in Nicaragua the Nicaraguans proudly call themselves *pinoleros,* is toasted and ground cornmeal mixed with water. *Pinolillo* is *pinol* mixed with cacao, pepper, and cloves; *tiste* is similar. *Pozol* is a ground cornmeal drink prepared from a different variety of corn that has a pinkish hue. Ultrasweet, pink baggies of *chicha* are made from slightly fermented cornmeal; especially strong batches are called *"chicha brava."* Then, of course, there is crystal-clear, Nicaraguan corn tequila: *la cususa.* Corn: it's what's for breakfast, lunch, and dinner.

© JOSHUA BERMAN

1860s–1890s during the wave of rubber and banana production that occurred along the Atlantic coast, and again in the 1950s as Pacific farmers moved eastward in search of new agricultural lands at the expense of the Sumu-Ulúa and Miskito peoples.

Note: Mestizo Nicaraguans sometimes use the term *Indio* as a pejorative label for anyone with any Native American features, which include high cheekbones, straight black hair, short eyelashes, and dark brown skin.

Creoles

After decimating the indigenous peoples of the New World, the Spanish soon found they had reduced the available labor force to critical levels, and were forced to import African slaves to their colonies in the Americas. Beginning in 1562, English slave traders, and later Dutch, Spanish, and others, supplied the colonies with their human cargo. Along the Atlantic coast of Nicaragua, African slaves intermingled with Miskito Indians, giving birth to the Zambo (or Sambo) people. They also bred with the Spanish and English, forming the Creoles, primarily found today in Bluefields and San Juan del Norte. Creoles speak a form of English which still bears traces of 19th-century Queen's English, as well as Caribbean and Spanish traits. Their culture, while considered primarily influenced by the English, includes distinct African elements, including the belief in a form of African witchcraft once called Obeah and now called *sontín,* a corruption of the English "something," or "something special."

Miskitos

The modern-day Miskitos are really a mixture of several other races, and include traces of English and African blood. The Native American Bawihka people, whose territory extended from the Río Coco (Wangki) at Cabo Gracias a Dios south to Prinzapolka, mixed with African slave refugees of a Portuguese ship that wrecked on the Miskito Cays in 1642, and then with the English during their long occupation of the Atlantic coast. Over the centuries, the word "Miskito" has been written many other ways, including "Mosquito," "Mosca," "Mískitu," and

POPULAR SAYINGS (*REFRANES*)

Nicaraguans in general, and campesinos in particular, love to speak in refrains. They're an easy way to make a point, and both the way they are phrased and the points they make say much about the country folks' way of thinking. If you learn a refrain or two and throw one out once in a while in casual conversation, you are sure to earn broad smiles.

Hay más tiempo que vida.—"There is more time than life." This is why there's no need to rush things.

Él que a buen árbol se arrima, buena sombra le cobija.—"He who seeks protection will find it."

Perro que ladra no muerde.—"Dogs who bark don't bite."

No hay peor sordo, que él que no quiere escuchar.—"There's no deaf person worse than he who doesn't want to hear."

A todo chancho se le llega su sábado.—"Every pig gets his Saturday." Everyone eventually gets what he deserves.

Indio comido, puesto al camino.—"An Indian who has eaten, gets up immediately from the table." A way of pointing out someone ready to leave as soon as he/she gets what he/she wants.

Quien da pan a un perro ajeno, pierde el pan y pierde el perro.—"If you give bread to someone else's dog, you'll lose the bread and lose the dog."

Él que madruga come pechuga, él que tarda, come albarda.—"He who gets up early eats the best piece of chicken, he who gets up late eats the saddle."

Él que no llora no mama.—If you don't complain, you'll never get any attention. (The literal translation is "He that does not cry does not suckle.")

Él que anda con lobos, aullar aprende.—"He who walks with wolves, learns to howl." A warning about the company you keep.

Barriga llena, corazón contento.—"Full belly, happy heart." Lean back and use this one after a big meal.

Él que tiene más galillo, siempre traga más pinol.—"He who has a bigger throat, drinks more pinol." He who is more aggressive goes farther.

OLD WIVES' TALES: NICARAGUAN CREENCIAS

Like any society with a long tradition of rural folk culture, Nicaraguans have hundreds of unique beliefs, or *creencias,* that explain mysteries, offer advice, and dictate practices that prevent or cure common health ailments. In general, most behaviors are associated with causing harm to oneself, and Nicaraguan mothers can be heard admonishing their children *"le va a hacer daño!"* (it will cause you harm!).

Nicaraguans are sensitive to subtle differences in temperature, and many of the *creencias* involve avoiding hot things when you are cold, or vice versa. Intense bodily harm can come from drinking a cold beverage after eating something hot, bathing in the evening after a hot day in the sun (or bathing with a fever), and ironing with wet hair. If you come in from the fields on a hot day and you're sweaty, drinking a cold glass of fruit juice could cause you irreparable physical harm, especially to your kidneys. Better is a cup of hot coffee. If you want to walk outside at night after drinking coffee, however, you should protect yourself by draping a cloth over the top of your head, being careful to cover the ears. Dietary rules tie into the same theme and other worries as well: no fish, eggs, or beans while menstruating, no citrus when sick, and no fish soup when *agitado* (worked up or sweaty).

The "evil eye" *creencia* is common in many Developing World countries: the Nicaraguan version states that a drunkard who looks directly into an infant's eye can kill the child, or make it evil. A person well versed in the art of applying the evil eye can cause birth defects in newborn babies, stroke, paralysis among the living, and other woes like the loss

---

others. The word is seemingly derived not from the insect, but from the Spanish word *mosquete,* referring to the Miskitos' possession of muskets, a firearm provided to them by the British that gave them a tactical advantage over their neighbors.

The Miskitos' warlike nature—combined with English firearms—helped them to subdue nearly 20 other Native American tribes along the Atlantic coast of Central America, and they were valuable allies of the English, who used them in raids against inland Spanish settlements. The Miskitos also absorbed the Prinsu tribe (located along the Bambana and Prinzapolka Rivers) and the Kukra tribe.

Today the Miskitos inhabit much of the Atlantic coast of Nicaragua from Bluefields northward and all along the Río Coco, which they consider their spiritual home. There are additional Miskito settlements on both Corn Islands, but their two principal centers are Puerto Cabezas and Waspám. Their language, Miskito, is the old indigenous Tawira language enriched with English and African vocabulary.

The Kukra

The Kukra people were assimilated by the Miskitos over the last two centuries and no longer exist as a tribe. Of an unknown but reportedly cannibalistic Caribbean origin, they once inhabited Bluefields, the Corn Islands, and the area around Pearl Lagoon. Today the only remaining trace of them is the name of the small Pearl Lagoon community of Kukra Hill.

The Garífuna (Black Caribs)

The Garífuna, as a race, are relative newcomers to the world. They came to exist on the Lesser Antillean island of San Vicente (Saint Vincent), which in the 1700s had become a refuge for escaped slaves from the sugar plantations of the Caribbean and Jamaica. These displaced Africans were accepted by the native Carib islanders, with whom they freely intermingled. The new island community vehemently denied their African origins and proclaimed themselves Native Americans. As the French and English began to settle the island, the Garífunas (as they had become known), established a worldwide reputation as expert canoe navigators and fierce warriors as they resisted the newcomers. The English finally got the upper hand in the conflict after tricking and killing the Garífuna leader, and in 1797, they forcefully evacuated the Garífunas from San Vicente to the Honduran Bay Island of Roatán.

of a job or just plain bad luck. You'll frequently see children wearing a red bracelet with two small gray beads—this is to protect the child from *mal de ojo* (the evil eye). Similarly, if a sweaty man looks at a baby, the only cure is to wrap the baby up in the man's sweaty clothes. To guard against the risk, many babies are kept well covered when out of the house. Allowing dew to fall on a baby's brow will stunt its growth (look for women holding umbrellas over their children on a clear night), and letting a baby look in a mirror will cause his or her eyes to cross permanently.

If you have trouble with bats, you can keep them away by hanging a red cloth from the rafters. To keep flies off of your food, suspend a bag of water over the table. To avoid family fights, don't cook with a knife in the pan.

Some Nica *creencias* coincide with North American and European practices even if the reasoning is different. As an example, Nicaraguans recommend you don't walk around barefoot, but not because you run the risk of contracting ringworm; rather, walking barefoot, they claim, is an unhealthy temperature combination (hot feet on cold floor). Foreigners tempted to make fun of the "crazy" Nicaraguan beliefs will do well to remember even "modern" societies have *creencias*. North American parents, for example, have long insisted that giving children sugar will cause them to be hyperactive in spite of overwhelming scientific evidence to the contrary. Nicaraguan *creencias* are popularly believed because they have been passed from generation to generation, and should be given proper regard.

From there, many of the Garífunas migrated to mainland Central America at Trujillo. Today, they exist up and down most of the Central American Caribbean coast, with a small but distinct presence in Nicaragua, primarily around Pearl Lagoon. Orinoco (originally Urunugu) is the largest settlement of Garífunas in Nicaragua, established in 1912 by the Garífuna John Sambola. The communities of San Vicente and Justo Point are both Garífuna as well. During the 1980s the Contra war forced many Garífunas out of their communities and into Bluefields, Puerto Limón (Costa Rica), and Honduras.

The Mayangna (Sumu)

"Sumu" is a derogatory word the Miskito people used to describe all other peoples of Ulúa descent and as such the word has fallen out of favor. (It means stupid; the Mayangna name for the Miskito people was *Wayas,* stinky.) The Mayangna people, as the new generation has decided to call themselves, are really a combination of several Ulúa tribes, including the Twahka, Panamka, and Ulwa, which once settled the Kurinwas, Siquia, Mico, Rama, and Grande Rivers of the Atlantic coast. Mayangna tradition has it that they were the original inhabitants of the Atlantic coast and Río Coco, and

their territory extended to the Pacific, but they were forced off the Atlantic coastal lands by the more aggressive and warring Miskito people and out of the Pacific by the Nahuatls, Maribios, and Chorotegas in the 9th and 10th centuries. The Mayangna people are now centered around the mining triangle and the massive forest reserve of Bosawás.

The Rama

The Rama are the least numerous indigenous people in Nicaragua, numbering only several hundred. Their language is distinct from Miskito and Sumu and is closely related to the ancient tribal languages of Native American tribes of Panamá and Colombia. Today only several dozen people can still speak Rama and anthropologists are scrambling to document what they can of the language before it disappears entirely. The Rama people inhabit the pleasant bay island of Rama Cay in the Bay of Bluefields, where they fish and collect oysters. They also grow grains and traditional crops on small plots of land on the mainland of Bluefields Bay and along the Kukra River. The Rama people are reserved and keep mostly to their traditional ways, even using traditional tools and implements. They are excellent navigators and fishermen.

COMMUNICATION

Language

Spanish is, according to the Nicaraguan constitution, the official language of the republic, though indigenous languages are respected and even used officially in certain areas of the Atlantic coast. Ninety-six percent of Nicaraguans speak Spanish as their first language, 3 percent speak indigenous languages (Miskito, Mayangna and Rama), and 1 percent speak languages of African origin (Criollo and Garífuna). To hear pure Miskito, travel north from Bluefields or visit Puerto Cabezas or any village along the Río Coco; in some villages Spanish is completely unknown.

Nicaraguan Spanish is probably unlike any Spanish you've ever come across. The chameleon-like ability of the Spanish language to adapt to new areas of the world is strong in Nicaragua, where it is spoken rapidly and liquidly, the words flowing smoothly together and eating each other's tails. The ends of words, especially those ending in an "s," are often implied, similar to the Cuban accent. Central Americans enjoy making fun of how their Latin neighbors talk, and the Honduran nickname for Nicaraguans, *mucos* (bulls with their horns chopped off), is actually a reference to the Nicaraguans' habit of chopping the "s" off the ends of spoken words.

Backcountry campesino Nicaraguan is inevitably less intelligible to the untrained ear than its urban counterpart, but it is also distinctly more melodic. The words "cadence" and "rhythm" come to mind, a fact not lost on many Nicaraguan songwriters who cherish and showcase the vernacular. These same singers love to pronounce the wonderful place-names of their country as well— Chichigalpa, Yalagùina, Diriamba—names which are Spanish but strongly shaped by the people's Nahuatl past.

Nicaraguans are proud of their regional brand of Spanish. So much so, in fact, that most areas of the country have developed their own particular *regionalismos* (local expressions) that you'll come across as you move through Nicaragua if you pay close attention to the language. Even neighboring towns may have different nicknames for animals, fruits, and liquor.

And then, of course, there are the vulgarities. Ernest Hemingway wrote, "There is no language

A FEW NICARAGUANISMOS

The textbook Spanish you learned back home will be understood without trouble, but Nicaraguans take pride in the fact that their version of the old country Castilian is decidedly unique. When you try to look up some of the new words you're hearing and realize they're not in the dictionary, you'll see what we mean.

Blame it on campesino creativity and the Nicas' propensity for inventing words they need; blame the centuries of educational starvation, during which language evolved on its own; blame the linguistic mishmash of pre-Columbian Central America and the words left behind. Or just get out your pencil and paper and try to write down some of the unique vocabulary and phrases you hear, because you won't hear it anywhere else. Nicaraguan Spanish uses some old, proper Spanish no longer used in the Old World, and has assimilated pre-Columbian words from Nahuatl and Chorotega tongues as well

(especially local plant and animal names). Still other words are pure onomatopoeia. Those interested in pursuing the topic further will be interested in Joaquim Rabella and Chantal Pallais's *Vocabulario Popular Nicaragüense,* available in many bookstores in Managua. Here's an incomplete sampling (with the Castilian in parentheses when possible).

arrecho: extremely angry (*enfurecido*)
bochinche: a fistfight among several people
boludo: lazy, unmotivated (*haragán*)
bullaranga: loud noises, ruckus (*tumulto, alboroto*)
curutaca: diarrhea (*diarrea*)
cususa: country moonshine (*aguardiente*)
chapa: earring (*arete*)
chigüin: little kid (*bebé*)
chinela: sandal (*sandalía*)

so filthy as Spanish. There are words for all the vile words in English and there are other words and expressions that are used only in countries where blasphemy keeps pace with the austerity of religion." In Nicaragua, many fruit and vegetable names can cause a room to break out in wild laughter if said in the right tone and context (and if accompanied by the appropriate hand gesture). As with any language, be careful—the degree to which most *vulgaridades* are considered offensive varies depending on the gender of your company, their age, your relationship with them, and a variety of other factors. Swearing can be a fun, complex, and subtle game if you have the patience to learn … *y los huevos!*

Body Language

Limber up your wrist and stretch out those lips. You'll need 'em both if you want to communicate like a true native. Watch people interact on the buses, in the markets, and on the streets, and see if you can spot any of the following gestures in action—then try some out yourself.

Probably the single most practical gesture is a rapid side to side wagging of the index finger. It means "no," and increases in strength as you increase the intensity of the wagging and the amount of hand and arm you use in the motion. In some cases, a verbal "no" in the absence of the **Finger Wag** is disregarded as not serious enough. Use this one liberally with pushy vendors, beggars, and would-be Romeos.

To pull off the **Nicaraguan Wrist Snap,** simply join the tips of your thumb and middle finger and let your index finger dangle loosely. Then with a series of rapid wrist flicks, repeatedly let your index finger slap against the middle one, exactly as you would do with a round tin of tobacco dip. The resulting snapping noise serves to either emphasize whatever it is you're saying, refer to how hard you've been working, or, when combined with a nod and a smile, infer something like, "Damn that's good!"

You can ask "what?" (or "what do you want?") with a quick **Cheek Scrunch,** occasionally performed with a subtle upward chin tilt. Rather than point to things with your finger, use the **Lip Point** by puckering up as if for a kiss and aiming where you want. Or, if you are listening to a friend's dumb story, point to the speaker with

chingaste: the granular residue of a drink like coffee (*poso, resíduo*)

chunche: any small, nameless object (*cosita*)

chusmón: mediocre

guaro: general term for booze or alcoholic beverages

hamaquear: to rock something rhythmically (*mecer rítmicamente*)

moclín: perverted old man

ñaña: excrement (*excremento*)

panzona: big bellied, implies pregnant (*embarazada*)

pinche: cheap (*tacaño*)

pipilacha: small airplane (*avioneta*)

salvaje: awesome; literally, "savage," fun response to "*¿como estas?*"

timba: big belly (*barriga*)

Exclamations

chocho!: Holy cow! Dude!

a la puchica!: Wow!

ideay? (eedee-EYE?): What was that all about? What do you mean?

va pué: OK then, see you, I agree, or whatever (short for "*va pués*")

dalepué: OK, I agree, let's do that.

¡Qué barbaridad!: What a barbarity! How rude! What a shame!

¡Sí hombre!: Yeah man!

hijueputa, jueputa: extremely common, short for the vulgarity "hijo de puta" (son of a whore), pronounced hwayPOOtah and at times inserted between every sentence.

tranquilo como Camilo: "Chillin' like Dylan"; fun response to "*¿como estas?*"

your lips while looking at everyone else to say "this guy's crazy or drunk."

The gesture North Americans would normally use to shoo something away—the outstretched, waving down-turned hand—means just the opposite in Nicaragua, where the **Downward Wave** (occasionally combined with the whole arm for emphasis) means "Come here." This one is a favorite with drunks in the park who love to talk at foreigners for as long as they are allowed. The North American "come here," i.e., the upturned and beckoning index finger, is a vulgar, possibly offensive gesture here. Speaking of vulgar, a closed fist atop a rigid forearm indicates the male sex organ, and an upturned, slightly cupped hand with the fingertips pressed together into a point is its female counterpart. Here's one more for the road: make a fist, lock your elbow into the side of your body, and move your hand up and down; combined with a dramatic grimace, the **Plunger Pump** tells the whole world you have diarrhea.

RELIGION

Officially, the Republic of Nicaragua endorses no religion. In practice, Nicaragua is around 90 percent Catholic, with evangelical Protestant religions (120 different kinds!) at around 9 to 15 percent and increasing annually. Beginning in the early 1970s and continuing through the revolution, Nicaragua was the setting for the fascinating phenomenon of Liberation Theology, in which Christianity was taught as essentially a poor people's movement in which Jesus' teachings were equated with Marxism. The degree to which biblical parables were equated to the Marxist struggle varied, and the most radical versions placed Sandino as Jesus or Moses, Somoza as the Pharaoh, and the Nicaraguan masses as the Israelites searching for their promised land through revolutionary struggle.

A tiny percentage of Nicaraguans are descended from one of several Jewish families that were allowed to escape here during World War II. Some of them still identify themselves as Jewish, but there is no real practicing community, the only synagogue having been dismantled and sold during the 1980s. Their numbers are small, and the vast majority of Nicaraguans have no concept of Judaism as a modern religion, relating the word *Judios* only to the race of Hebrews they read about in the Old Testament.

CONDUCT AND CUSTOMS

Nicaraguans are generally open, talkative, and extremely hospitable. They will be curious about you, and they won't be discreet about it. Expect blunt questions right off the bat about your age, marriage status, and your opinions about Nicaragua. Most Nicaraguans are easily approached and excited to talk to foreigners—sometimes if the foreigner in question welcomes the attention or not (see section on alcohol below).

Despite their directness, Nicaraguans are prone to circuitous and indirect behavior associated with the cultural concept of "saving face." For example, when asked something they don't know, people will create or fudge an answer so that nei-

Virgin Mary

ther party has to suffer *pena* (embarrassment). Other examples can be found in the unspoken and implied details of business contracts. To prevent the discomfort brought on by discussing payment details and clarifying the work to be done, Nicaraguans may opt to keep things to a casual handshake, both sides hoping they are not taken advantage of. Travelers, in general, ought not to do the same.

Significant differences in societal behavior are observed between the city and *campo* (countryside). The urban/rural differences one would expect are generally observed, such as country folk having simpler worldviews and more traditional family lives. City dwellers have a greater connection to the rest of the world and, if they have the means to do so, live a relatively modern life. But many urbanites, especially in Managua, are in fact recently immigrated campesinos, and they bring their country ways with them to town—observable, for example, in the casually roaming livestock in a city park. The poorest of these people live in sprawling shantytowns outside most cities, with the exception of Managua, where the shanties are spread throughout the city limits among better neighborhoods.

Family

The Nicaraguan family is the most basic and strongest support structure of society, and, like in most Developing World nations, it is big—rural women have an average of four to six children, and families of a dozen or more aren't uncommon. Urban couples, particularly in Managua, typically have no more than three or four children. In addition, extended families—cousins, in-laws, and fictitious kin (a.k.a. godparents)—are all kept in close contact and relied upon during hard times (which, for some, is their whole lives). Families live close together, often in small quarters, and the North American and European concepts of independence and privacy are not well understood, let alone practiced.

Nicaraguans' traditional dependence on large family structures mandates that they take care of stragglers, even foreign visitors. If, for example, you were stranded in a strange country town in the pouring rain, someone would most

PERCEPTION OF THE UNITED STATES

In most areas of the country, Nicaraguans are accustomed to seeing foreigners, and the reaction is nearly always one of curiosity, hospitality, and friendliness. Nicaraguans are particularly adept at distinguishing between a nation's people and its government's policy—arguably more so than most travelers—so those travelers from the United States should not expect to receive any rancor regarding recent history from Sandinista supporters. In addition, because most Nicaraguan families adore cable TV and have at least one relative sending money back from Miami, Houston, or Los Angeles, many are quite fond of the United States and maintain the dream of traveling there one day. The word "gringo" is used often, but as a descriptive, casual term, almost never with negative connotations. Likewise for *chele, chela,* and their diminutives, *chelito* and *chelita,* all of which simply mean, "pale" or "light-skinned," and are in no way disrespectful. In fact, many cries of, "*Oye, chele!*" (Hey whitey!) are directed at light-skinned Nicaraguans in addition to foreigners.

likely take pity on you and invite you into their home for coffee and *rosquillas* (hard-baked cornmeal rings).

Clothing and Neatness

Nicaraguans place a great deal of importance on cleanliness and order. The initial comic nature of a woman sweeping dirt in front of her house may turn into respect when you realize the sense of pride that drives her actions. Even the poorest campesino with the most threadbare and patched clothing takes great care to tuck his shirt in and keep his clothes clean and wrinkle-free. City folk are just as conscientious about looking good and smelling clean. Nicaraguans only wear shorts for playing sports or lounging around the house. Nicaraguan women dress the spectrum from long, conservative dresses to unbelievably bright, tight, and revealing outfits.

Unshaven international travelers wearing stained shorts, ripped t-shirts, and natty dreads stand out like sore, malodorous thumbs, even without their trademark backpacks. If you plan on being taken seriously in any kind of day-to-day business activities, we highly recommend you put a little effort into your wardrobe and appearance: deodorant, ironed clothing, and a clean appearance will open a lot of doors for you (and do away with the question, "Is it true people in your country don't bathe because it's too cold?"). If, however, you prefer to remain true to your filth, seek out the hip, bohemian population of young Managuans who take well to carefully unkempt foreigners, especially ones wearing Che Guevara t-shirts.

Concept of Time

Hay más tiempo que vida. (There is more time than life.) So why hurry? The day-to-day approach to living life in Nicaragua may come from the necessity of survival, or it may just be an effect of the hot sun. Probably both. Nicaraguan life, in general, goes according to *La Hora Nica* (Nica Time), which means a meeting scheduled for 2:30 won't start until at least 3 in Managua, and later in the countryside. Foreign travelers accustomed to *La Hora Gringa,* in which everything starts and stops exactly when planned, will spend their days

in Nicaragua endlessly frustrated (and consistently early for meetings). Appointments and meetings are loose, and excuses are easy to come by and universally accepted. Gradually, as you experience Nicaragua, this concept of time will win you over; just be careful when you go home.

Alcohol

For better or worse, alcohol plays an important role in Nicaraguan society. Both plague and pastime, alcohol is everywhere and is increasingly acknowledged as a problem. Most towns have an Alcoholics Anonymous chapter, and many churches forbid their members to drink. Nevertheless, many otherwise religious holidays (including Sundays)—in addition to all nonreligious events—are often used as excuses to get passed-out-in-your-own-piss-and-puke drunk. Just about all men drink, and are firm believers in the famous expression *"Una es ninguna"* (one is nothing). Their benders often start before breakfast and end when the liquor does. In small towns, women are socially discouraged from drinking, though they sometimes do so in the privacy of their own homes or with close friends. Bigger towns and cities, of course, are more modern in this regard.

On The Road

"In the tropics one must before everything keep calm."

Joseph Conrad

Highlights and Sample Itineraries

The first rule of planning your trip in Nicaragua is flexibility. This country has amazing powers to lead you to places and experiences you never could have arranged, even with this book in your hands. In addition, sticking to a tightly planned itinerary means you'll allow things like lost luggage, flat tires, and other common unavoidables to wear you down. Do not be afraid to wander, linger, and be drawn deep into the countryside.

Following, we've outlined some regional routes to serve as general launching pads for your own adventures. You can choose to explore just a portion of a route or combine several routes, with little trouble. Be creative.

the daily commute in the mountains of Estelí

© JOSHUA BERMAN

HEADING SOUTH

The Southwest Backpacker Trail

Like other countries in the region, Nicaragua has its own carved out tourist route (a.k.a. gringo trail) through its principal attractions, offering the chance to travel in the company of fellow vagabonds. The **Granada–Ometepe–San Juan del Sur circuit** can be done in about one week. Granada is a good place to ease into things, with colorful surroundings, wonderful cuisine, and more creature comforts than elsewhere in the country. Ometepe is chief among Nicaragua's riches, with beaches, rigorous volcano hikes, and pre-Columbian artifacts, all bathed in the island lifestyle (allow two or three days there, as getting around the island can be slow). San Juan del Sur's picturesque bay, lively beach bars, and calm atmosphere make a good getaway, as well as a base for fishing and surfing excursions up and down the coast—including visits to **Bahía Majagual** and up-and-coming **Playa El Coco.**

Common side trips along this route (also possible day trips from Managua) include the active and awe-inspiring **Volcán Masaya** with caves, hiking trails, and the famous sulfur-resistant crater parakeets. Speaking of birds, make a point to visit **El Chocoyero,** a unique wildlife spectacle, newly accessible and less than an hour from the capital. It's worth spending half a day in **Masaya's crafts market,** but there's more than meets the eye in this merchant city and the surrounding **Pueblos Blancos.**

The Río San Juan

The watery "Golden Route" through southern Lake Cocibolca and down the Río San Juan is easier to access than you may think, but you'll need a minimum of a week or two to get there and get around. Once you reach San Carlos, public boat transportation is regular and cheap, but limited to only two days a week to get to **Solentiname, Los Guatuzos,** and **San Juan del Norte** (unless you're ready to spend major bucks on hiring a private boat, which considerably streamlines logistics and lightens your wallet at the same time). As a result, you may

SPEAKING SPANISH

You can certainly get along in Nicaragua with a survival level of Spanish, but it should go without saying that the more you know, the more profound an experience you will have. English-speaking Nicaraguans are few and far between, even in Managua, and almost nonexistent elsewhere. Much of this guidebook is written with the assumption of a basic conversational proficiency of Spanish. We believe that in spite of the astonishing natural beauty of Nicaragua, its greatest charm is its friendly and interesting people. If you don't speak at least some Spanish you will be missing out on one of the best reasons to visit Nicaragua. Combining your travels with a few weeks—or months—of Spanish school is a great idea and a totally viable option (see Spanish Schools section in this chapter).

find yourself stranded on one of 36 Solentiname islands for three days, with nothing to do but go fishing or bird/crocodile watching in a dugout canoe—we can think of worse things. The Río San Juan is unquestionably worth a visit, but allow some time.

TO THE NORTH

Northwest

León is one of Nicaragua's more beautiful cities, worth at least a day or two of your time. Tour the churches, enjoy the colonial architecture, pop out to **Poneloya** for a swim and a beer, then continue northwest with the **Maribio Volcano** chain, all the way through **Chinandega** and into the remote northwest thumb of the **Cosigüina Peninsula.** You can experience the whole region in four or five days (more if you lose yourself on one of Chinandega's deserted beaches), and then you'll be ready to head east and upward, out of the heat and into the mountains.

The Highlands Trail

After touring **Estelí's revolutionary murals and cigar factories,** it's time to go deeper. This is where you can really get creative, constructing any number of loop routes through the countryside pueblos, each one with a unique local hike, waterfall, or swimming hole. An alternative way to enter the region is to pass from León through El Sauce, and then board a bus to make the slow, lazy climb up one of several spectacular valleys. Allow a day or two in Estelí, two or three in the organic wonder world of **Miraflor,** and two or three in and around **Ocotal,** exploring the pine forests, colonial ruins, hot springs, and indigenous communities. Or use that week in the **Jinotegan and Matagalpan coffee country cloud forests;** connect Estelí with the trip to Jinotega via **San Rafael del Norte** for a mountain adventure.

TO THE EAST
The Atlantic Coast

As incredibly remote as they are, the **Corn Islands** can be reached from Managua in one hour in the comfort of a small aircraft, after which your concept of time and the rest of the world will fade completely away. The full mid-Atlantic coast trip requires at least a week though, especially if you are making the heroic overland journey to Bluefields via El Rama and the Río Escondido, a two-day ordeal if you include the day-after recovery time. Spend a night in **Bluefields,** one or two in **Pearl Lagoon,** then reach the Corn Islands, cut open a fresh coconut, and relax.

Outdoor Recreation

HIKING

Walking Nicaragua is an extraordinary experience, and not just because of the scenery. There is no system of cut, well-blazed trails as there is in the National Parks of more developed countries (except in some newly constructed protected areas). Hiking Nicaragua means turning off the pavement, taking a poor dirt road to an even poorer one, and then entering the country's vast network of mule and footpaths that have connected rural communities of campesinos for centuries. If you are conversant in Spanish and have some minimal equipment, you can spend days or even weeks trekking between the pueblos. You'll share the road with horses, cattle, and families of campesinos walking to and from their fields. You'll pass through myriad small farming and ranching communities, rest by the side of streams, and discover small adobe chapels, hidden shrines to the Virgin Mary, and cool watering holes. Above all, you'll experience Nicaragua from eye level, and learn about the country in a way no one gazing from behind the glass of the bus window could ever hope to.

Throughout this book we include particularly interesting country walks, and enough information to get you where you're going, although you should always take advantage of the opportunity to use local knowledge, or even hire a guide for a few cordobas. If you plan on doing a great deal of

hiking Momotombo

© TOMÁS STARGARDTER

hiking, prepare well before leaving Managua. Pick up an appropriate INETER topo map at their office and don't set out into the backwoods of Nicaragua without a small compass (and the knowledge to use it), an idea of where you are and where you're going, and a bit of food and water, plus some way to purify more water if you need to (like iodine drops or pills). For any hiking or exploring east of the city of Jinotega, always notify your embassy in Nicaragua before departing, and be sure to obtain up-to-date security reports from both U.S. and Nicaraguan officials.

WILDLIFE VIEWING
Bird-Watching

You'll start checking species off your list in the courtyard of your hotel. Even in Managua, with its extensive urban tree canopy, you can expect to see a variety of wrens, hummingbirds, and the not-so-elusive national bird, the *guardabarranco*. In the farmlands of the Pacific coast you won't find as many exotic species as you will in the more forested regions of the country. One of the best areas for birding is Miraflor (in Estelí), where more than a third of the **644 species** identified in Nicaragua have been observed. The mountains of Jinotega and Matagalpa are excellent as well (home of the **quetzal**), including Selva Negra, where 200 species have been identified. Additionally as impressive are the Solentiname islands and the Los Guatuzos Wildlife Reserve along the south shore of Lake Cocibolca. Floating the Río San Juan takes you through lush jungle and along the Río Indio–Maíz Reserve, where there are large stretches of prime bird habitat. Waterfowl are also abundant around Ometepe and in the mangrove estuaries on the northwestern Pacific coast, including Isla Juan Venado and the Estero Real. If you're serious about your birding, consider visiting Jeffrey McCrary, a professor who works at the Proyecto Ecológico in Laguna de Apoyo, and who is publishing a book on birds in Nicaragua, due out soon.

Orchids

Nicaragua is home to hundreds of orchids, some of them endemic. Look for them in any damp forest; they are especially accessible at the top of Volcán Mombacho, in the Miraflor Reserve in Estelí, and at the Papaturro research lodge in Los Guatuzos. At least one guidebook specifically for Nicaragua's orchids is available in the Hispamer bookstore in Managua.

BOATING
Kayaking and Canoeing

Someday, somebody's going to make a lot of money selling canoes, kayaks, and rafts in Nicaragua. There are already limited opportunities to rent plastic boats at many of the newer resorts, and in Granada, there are sea kayak classes and rentals. For the most part though, you'll have to be creative to find ways to float the endless lakes, rivers, estuaries, archipelagos, and coastlines of Nicaragua that gave the country its name. Any water-bordering community will likely have small boats the owners use for fishing or transport. Ask for a *canoa, panga,* or *botecita,* and see what shows up. Dugouts are common, as are makeshift rafts and box-floats that you'll want to inspect carefully before boarding.

For the glory-seeking paddler, Nicaragua is a place to make the cover of an extreme sports rag: the 700-kilometer stretch of the Río Coco from Wiwilí to the Caribbean at Cabo Gracias a Dios has (as far as we know) only been navigated end to end by pirates and indigenous boaters. There may be a few hairy portages around some of the legendary waterfalls, and rumor has it that no one has ever even published a photograph of the falls between Raiti and San Carlos.

Yachts and Cruises

Many port towns in Nicaragua offer luxury (or semi-luxury—it's all relative, really) yacht trips, including the *Cosiguina II* in Puerto Morazán, *Pelican Eyes* in San Juan del Sur, and the *Crucero Solentiname* out of Granada. The Holland America Cruise Line has been using San Juan del Sur as a port of call on several of its trips, unloading passengers on the dock to spend a couple of days riding tour buses to Granada and Masaya.

SNORKELING AND SCUBA

Snorkeling is widely available in Nicaragua, but diving is new, and once again, if you take advantage of the sport here, you'll be riding the very first wave of a phenomenon that is surely going to grow.

There are only two existing dive shops currently operating in Nicaragua, one on each of the **Corn Islands.** They share a combined 12 kilometers of reef. The shop on Little Corn (website: www.divelittlecorn.com) has newer equipment, and the reef there was less affected by recent hurricanes. Both islands' reef systems feature a stunning diversity of wildlife, including rays, eels, angels, groupers, sharks, and enormous pools of African pompano. Both shops offer PADI certifications for about $250, plus a range of packages for all skill levels. Although the diving off the Corn Islands is impressive, the most spectacular and undoubtedly world-class site is found nearly 25 kilometers farther out to sea around a sea mount called **Blowing Rock.**

Nicaragua's Pacific side offers excellent diving as well, particularly in the south near San Juan del Sur, but there are no standard dive shops and conditions are predictably unpredictable (visibility can change from 1 to 20 meters from day to day). Equipment and guides can be found through one of several tour operators,

---

SURFING

*You fight for democracy and the "American Way"
But you're not in your country,
"What am I doing here?" you say
But now it's too late,
you're entering Managua
If you had brought your surfboard
you could surf Nicaragua!*

*The Sacred Reich
[thrash song from the 1980s]*

Surfing is a personal and spiritual pursuit considered more an art form than a sport by its true followers. Nevertheless, the modern world is one in which 17-year-old kids are paid $70,000 to surf, and magazines cover their lives as though they were rock stars. There is ferocious competition worldwide for the best waves and Nicaragua is one of the last countries on the planet to be overrun by this phenomenon.

Nicaragua has its share of waves—some would say better waves than elsewhere, perhaps because they're so completely unpopulated. Those who have been living and surfing in Nicaragua for some time now feel very strongly about how these vacant waves are presented to the world. Nicaragua is one of the few places left where a surfer can find his or her own wave and surf it without jockeying for position amongst dozens of other surfers. In an already overcrowded world, this is too special a thing to take away. There are several articles and publications that go into the details about where to surf in Nicaragua (the *Surf Report Nicaragua 19.9* is the most comprehensive, available for $7 at www.surfermag.com/travel).

Surfers, in general, come from fantastically rich and powerful countries, and should be careful to tread lightly—as should all travelers—in the remaining pristine places of the world. As you travel Nicaragua in search of the perfect tube, be very aware of your interactions with the locals. This is your chance to be an ambassador—or an embarrassment.

In general, the Caribbean coast is vast and empty, and probably gets incredible swells during hurricane season, but there are also sharks, drug runners, and who knows what else. More accessible (relatively, anyway) are the breaks up and down the entire Pacific coast, with the most-surfed spots closer to the San Juan del Sur community. If you have the time, spend a few weeks in one of the many small coastal towns up or down the coast; you'll be far away from the bar scene of San Juan, but who cares, when you're spending your days walking the beaches and looking for your own precious break… it's out there.

including **Eco Expedition Tours.** There are rock reefs here (no coral formations) inhabited by large fish, including colorful wrasses, parrotfish, snappers, and huge surgeonfish. Once abundant, sharks have been overfished and their populations have thinned severely. The best Pacific diving in Nicaragua is between December and April during periods of clear, cold water upwelling associated with the strong offshore winds. Visibility is significantly poorer during the rainy season (June–November) due to sediment from the rivers enriching coastal water and provoking algal blooms.

An organization called Sub Ocean Safety has managed to get two decompression chambers into Nicaragua—currently both in Puerto Cabezas (for commercial lobstermen and navy tech divers). Arrangements are currently underway to install one of the tanks on Corn Island.

For freshwater diving, Nicaragua offers the volcanic crater lakes of **Apoyo** (near Masaya) and **Xiloá** (near Managua). The diving in both lakes is part of ongoing biological research of the endemic cichlid species of fish, and experienced divers can rent tanks from the folks at the **Proyecto Ecológico** in Laguna de Apoyo. Apoyo has better visibility, but Xiloá has more colorful fish, and is especially interesting during the peak breeding season in November and December. There are still at least 10 undescribed fish species in the freshwater crater lakes.

PARASAILING

Also known as paragliding or *parapente* in Spanish, the sport of jumping off a high, windy point with a deployed parachute and then riding the air currents has a handful of devotees in Nicaragua. According to Frenchman Silvan Depury, who first brought the sport to Nicaragua and helped form the Asociación Nicaragüense de Anivuelo Libre (winner of the best acronym award), Nicaragua has incredible sites to practice this pastime. First and foremost of these sites is the Laguna de Apoyo. The *laguna* is easily accessible (close to Managua) and has strong, rideable winds from May to December (after January, the wind is too strong and dangerous to ride). Less accessible

sites can be found all over the country. The current contact is Alejandro Murillo for information on trips, classes, and gear rental, tel. 776-6428.

HORSEBACK RIDING

Depending on how far off the beaten track you get, horses may be your preferred means of travel. We're not talking well-groomed stallions though; the reality is more likely to be renting someone's work horse to get where you're going. Any country town will be full of horses—you can see them "parked" outside stores and bars in country villages in most northern and central Nicaraguan towns. Estelí, Boaco, and Chontales areas are pure cowboy country. There, you'll find some truly well taken care of show horses in addition to the standard scrawny campesino beasts of burden.

There are lots of opportunities to rent horses for expeditions up the Pacific volcanoes, especially Cosigüina and San Cristóbal. There is also an honest-to-goodness stable on the road between Managua and Montelimar, where you can actually wear a funny helmet and take riding classes with Managua's elite: **Fatima Riding Club,** located at kilometer 51.2 on the paved road to Montelimar. From the highway, follow the orange signs, tel. 276-2158 or 886-8213.

FISHING

Sportfishing trips are available out of San Juan del Sur, the Corn Islands, and an increasing number of Pacific beach towns. Saltwater sportfishing on the Pacific coast is focused primarily on jacks (*hurel*), snapper (*pargo*), and roosterfish (*pez gallo*) in inshore waters and bonito, sailfish (*pez vela*), and mahimahi (*dorado*) in offshore areas. All commonly reach sizes in excess of 50 pounds.

In addition to casting for kingfish, amber jack, red snapper, and barracuda off the Corn Islands, **bonefishing** in the flats around Little Corn Island is reportedly among the best in the world, but you'll have to have some idea of what you are doing, as experienced guides are limited.

There are freshwater fish to be caught in Lake Apanás and El Dorado in Jinotega, and of course, in Lake Cocibolca and down the Río San Juan.

countryside sluggers

The giant freshwater bull sharks and sawfish are all but gone, but mammoth **sábalos** (tarpon), bigger than your mother and carrying up to 25 kilograms of meat, are still abundant, as are robalos, *guapote,* and the basin's newest resident, tilapia. The introduction of the tilapia has had a disastrous effect: one study shows that diseases introduced by tilapia have resulted in a 50 percent decline in Lake Cocibolca's total biomass and another reports that the foreign fish have eliminated all aquatic vegetation in the Laguna de Apoyo.

HUNTING

Killing animals—both for meat and for no reason at all—has always been popular in Nicaragua, visible today in most small towns where every *chavalo* (boy) and his brother have a slingshot that they use to shoot sharp rocks at all living things smaller than themselves. As for more "civilized" sport, quail and duck hunting is rumored to be world-class in Nicaragua. There are bigger creatures out there too, just waiting to be shot and eaten. Guerrilla soldiers surviving in the jungles

did a good job wiping out the monkey populations in many parts of the country. There are still pockets of white-tailed deer in Nicaragua, though population pressure and habitat reduction will probably ensure they won't be around much longer. Better stick to the birds.

BASEBALL

Unlike other Central American countries, decades of Cuban and North American influence have engendered a nation of baseball fanatics. Though soccer is followed as well (especially in the Carazo region, the one place where it dominates), there is no doubt that baseball is king.

There are municipal leagues, town leagues, little leagues, competitions between universities, and even between government ministries. The national league consists of six teams, with squads in Estelí, León, Chinandega, Masaya, Granada, and Managua (the Managua team is referred to as "El Boer," Masaya as "San Fernando," and Granada as "Los Tiburones"—the sharks). Matagalpa and Rivas used to be in the league, but had to drop out recently for financial reasons. The league is administered by the **Federación Nicaragüense de Beisból Asociado** (with offices in the national stadium in Managua, tel. 222-2021). The 60-game regular season begins officially in early January and is followed by 24 playoff games and a seven-game championship series at the end of May. Fans from the United States are sure to find the simplicity and honesty of Nicaraguan baseball refreshing; it is played as a sport and a pastime, not a mega-marketed six-figure salary circus.

One of Nicaragua's supreme national heroes is Denis Martínez, the local Nica who made it big in "the show" as one of the U.S. major league's greatest pitchers. His name graces the stadium in Managua, as well as several foundations. There's always a handful of young Nica players in the majors up north, and their seasons are followed passionately in the local sports pages.

No matter where you are in Nicaragua you only need to ask around to find the town ball field. Most cities and pueblos also have basketball (and occasionally volleyball) leagues, with regular pickup games if you need to get your ball on. Courts are typically near the central park, and every town still has a soccer field as well. Out in the countryside the passion for sport is no less diminished, and you'll be amazed at the creative improvisation of equipment—bats of tree branches for swinging at rocks and homemade balls of rope and twine.

Entertainment and Events

THE ARTS

Nicaraguans are, by nature, a creative people, and the many countries and cultures that have taken part in its history have each left an unmistakable mark on dance, sculpture, painting, writing, and music. There are many opportunities to experience traditional dance and song, but equally vibrant are the artisans, writers, and performers who are creating in the present, helping to form an artistic environment that's very much Nicaragua's own.

Literature

"Nicaragua," wrote the poet Pablo Neruda, "where the highest song of the tongue is raised." José Miguel Oviedo called the writing of Nicaragua "the richest and most tragic national literary tradition on the continent." Most start the story of Nicaraguan literature with the groundbreaking words of Rubén Darío; it continues with the vanguardists of the 1950s and 1960s, the generation of revolutionary poets and novelists, and the current wave of soul-searchers.

Though poverty has placed books out of the economic reach of most Nicaraguans, the **Casa de los Tres Mundos** art gallery in Managua doubles as ground zero for the **Society of Nicaraguan Writers,** and is a good place to start if you have questions about readings, book releases, or other events. There are a few bookstores in Managua that carry Nicaraguan and Latin American selections, as well as Spanish translations of foreign works; Estelí and León also boast interesting bookstores to explore.

Poet and author Gioconda Belli was called one of the 100 most important poets of the 20th century. Her work deals with the themes of feminism, mystical realism, and history, all mixed with a breath of sensuality. Her books **Wiwilí, Sofía de los Presagios,** and **El País Bajo Mi Piel** (*The Country Under My Skin*) are acclaimed. The writing of Ricardo Pasos Marciacq reflects not only his appreciation for the long and tumultuous history of Nicaragua but for the richness of its society. His book **Maria Manuela Piel de Luna** is considered a modern classic, and describes the years when British-armed Miskito Indians were wreaking havoc on the Spanish settlements of the Pacific. Rubén Darío is loved throughout the world of Latin American literature and is considered the father of modernism in Spanish literature. A few of the many other books by Nicaraguan writers worth reading if you have the time and the facility of the language include **El Nicaragüense** by Pablo Antonio

Cuadra, *Nicaragua, Teatro de lo Grandioso* by Carlos A. Bravo, and *El Estrecho Dudoso* by Ernesto Cardenal.

Dance and Theater

There's plenty of traditional and folk dance—often mixed with a form of theater—to appreciate. There are several dance institutions in Managua that teach folk classics alongside modern dance and ballet, and sponsor frequent performances. The presence of dance schools outside the capital is on the rise, which means fortunate travelers have a good chance of seeing a presentation outside of Managua, especially in Masaya, Diriamba, Matagalpa, León, and Granada. *El Gùegùense*, for example, is a 19th-century dance of costumed dancers in wooden masks that satirically represents the impression Nicaragua's indigenous peoples first had of the Spanish and their horses. This dance and others are often featured at *fiesta patronales* (patron saint celebrations), notably in the Masaya and Carazo regions. *El Viejo y La Vieja* (*The Old Man and Woman*) pokes ribald fun at old age and sexuality. One dancer, dressed up as an old gentleman with cane and top hat, and the other, dressed up as a buxom old woman, perform a sexy dance that usually involves the old man trying to dance with young female members of the audience while his wife chases him, beating him with her handkerchief. *Aquella Indita* is a celebration of the Nicaraguan woman, and her reputation for being graceful and hardworking. *El Solar de Monimbó* (*Monimbó's Backyard*) is a traditional dance from the indigenous neighborhood of Masaya which captures the spirit of community and celebration.

Besides the traditional folk pieces, Nicaraguans love to dance. Period. And there is no occasion (except maybe a funeral) at which it is inappropriate to pump up the music and take to your feet. The ultrasuave, loose-hipped movements associated with merengue, salsa, *cumbia,* and reggae are most commonly seen at discos, street parties, or in living rooms around the nation. The **Palo de Mayo** is an ultrapopular, modern Caribbean dance form featuring flamboyant costumes, vibrating chests, and not-so-subtle sexual simulations. When you see mothers rocking their babies to loud Latin rhythms, and two-year-old girls receiving hip-gyrating lessons, you'll understand

© JOSHUA BERMAN

Music runs deep within the Nicaraguan countryside.

THE POET IS THE HIGH PRIEST

Throughout Nicaraguan culture, the poet is the high priest. The prophet. The maker of visions. The singer of songs. The one who knows and can say it for others the way others feel it but cannot say it for themselves.

Margaret Randall wrote this in her collection of interviews with Nicaraguan writers entitled *Risking a Somersault in the Air,* commenting on the extraordinary role that poetry has played in Nicaraguan society. Salman Rushdie was equally impressed when, during his tour of Nicaragua and the Sandinista government in the mid-1980s, he found himself surrounded by young warrior-poets at all levels of society.

Indeed, an inordinate number of the revolution's leaders were published writers—including minister of the interior and head of state security, Tomás Borge, and President Daniel Ortega, both of whom published poems from Somoza's prisons in the 1970s (Somoza's forces found and destroyed the only manuscript of the book Ortega wrote during the same time period). Ortega once told Rushdie, "In Nicaragua, everybody is considered to be a poet until he proves to the contrary."

Literature (and painting, pottery, theater, music, and crafts) was strongly supported by the Sandinista government, whose Ministry of Culture stayed busy instituting poetry workshops and publishing magazines and books. The man in charge of this effort was Father Ernesto Cardenal, whose poetry is internationally acclaimed and widely translated into English. Gioconda Belli, whose work evokes the sensuality of her country's land and people, was named one of the 100 most important poets of the 20th century. But Nicaraguan poetry, no matter how entwined with the revolution, goes way back, even before the life of Sandino.

Invariably, one must turn to Nicaragua's literary giant, Rubén Darío, who 100 years ago set the stage for his nation's love affair with poetry by producing a style that was revolutionary and unprecedented in Spanish literature. Poet, journalist, diplomat, and favorite son of Nicaragua, Rubén Darío has become the icon for all that is artistic or cultural in Nicaragua. Today his portrait graces the front of the 100 cordoba bill, his name is on most of the nation's libraries and bookstores, and his sculpted likeness presides throughout the land.

why Nicaraguans are able to move so much more fluidly on the dance floor than you are.

Visual Arts

There are a number of Nicaraguan sculptors and painters whose work is displayed at numerous galleries in Managua, Granada, León, and other places. Though the primitivist painters of Solentiname have gotten the lion's share of the press, there is much more in Nicaragua to be seen. In Managua there are frequent expos of art, often accompanied by buffets or musical performances. More detail is provided in the Managua chapter.

Music

Music, in an infinite variety of forms, is incredibly important in Nicaraguan society. Expect to find loud, blaring radios in most restaurants, bars, vehicles, and homes. It may seem strange at first to find yourself listening to fast, pulsing merengue beats at six in the morning on a rural chicken bus, or in your hotel lobby at midnight for that matter, when the only people listening are sitting calmly in their rocking chairs. Realize, however, that this behavior is seen as a way to inject *alegría* (happiness) into the environment, or alternately, to get rid of the "sadness" that some Nicaraguans associate with silence. Radio mixes are eclectic, featuring the latest Dominican merengues, Mexican and Miami pop, cheesy *romanticas,* plus a bizarre U.S. mélange of Backstreet Boys (*"Los Back"* for those in the know), Air Supply, and Guns N' Roses. Another wildly popular genre is the *ranchera,* featuring slow, drippy, lost-love, mariachi tearjerkers, performed by one of a handful of super-celebrity Mexican crooners. Old, rootsy, U.S. country music is extremely popular on the Atlantic coast, and in northern Nicaragua, Kenny Rogers (pronounced Royers)

ON THE ROAD

His legacy is incredible, and Randall asks if today's poets owe everything to him, or to the fact that they, like their hero, glean their inspiration "from that violent expanse of volcanic strength called Nicaragua."

Darío is called the father of the modernist movement in Spanish poetry, a literary style which shed long, grammatically intricate Spanish phrases for simplicity and directness. His experimentation with verse and rhythm made him one of the most acclaimed Latin American writers of all time. Darío's legacy stands firm, and stories about his drinking bouts and international exploits still abound. A hundred years later, the Sandinistas pointed to his anti-imperialist references, including a passage written at the time of the Spanish-American War in which he denounces the North Americans as "buffaloes with silver teeth," and a poem in which he issues a directed warning to the U.S. president:

O men with Saxon eyes and
barbarous souls,
our America lives. And dreams.
And loves.

And it is the daughter of the Sun.
Be careful.
Long live Spanish America!
A thousand cubs of the Spanish lion
are roaming free.
Roosevelt, you must become,
by God's own will,
the deadly Rifleman and the
dreadful Hunter
before you can clutch us in your
iron claws.
And though you have everything,
you are lacking one thing:
God!

The muse still reigns in today's generation. *Rubén's Orphans* is an anthology of contemporary Nicaraguan poets, with English translations by Marco Morelli, published in 2001 by Painted Rooster Press (website: www.NicaPoets.org). Also, seek out Steven F. White's book, *Poets of Nicaragua, a Bilingual Anthology,* which covers the poets following Darío up to the revolution (published in 1983 by Unicorn Press).

is recognized as the undisputed king of *La Música Country.*

Managua is host to a small, exciting scene of young bands and solo musicians, most of whom are direct descendants—children, nephews, cousins—of the generation of musicians that brought Nicaraguan folk music to the world (see El Son Nica special topic in Managua and Vicinity). Their acts range from quiet acoustic solo sets to the head-banging throaty screams of a couple of angry, politically minded metal bands. Common venues to catch live music are Café Amatl, Bar La Cavanga, and Guantanamera.

Live music is found at most *fiestas patronales,* performed by one of several Nicaraguan commercial party bands whose sets imitate the radio mixes of the day. Among the most popular bands is Los Mokuanes (named after the enchanted hill and witch in La Trinidad, Estelí), who have been around in one form or another for more

than three decades. During the war, they were conscripted by the government to don fatigues and perform at army bases throughout the country. Other favorite bands are Macolla and, representing the Palo de Mayo side of things, Sir Anthony and his Dimensión Costeño.

CRAFTS

Nicaraguan culture is rich in handicrafts, partly due to natural creativity and partly due to necessity. Much of the *artesanía* (crafts) for sale in Nicaragua was produced because there was a household need for it, and contain as much function as form.

Nicaraguans are big fans of their **hammocks,** and with good reason. They're gorgeous, well made, and very reasonably priced. *Hamacas* are probably the number one souvenir shipped out of Nicaragua. Masaya is the heart of Nicaragua's home-crafted hammock industry, and visiting the many family "factories" is as easy as walking up to the porch and saying *"Buenas días."* The most economical places to purchase hammocks, besides from the source, are at Masaya's two markets, and in Managua's Roberto Huembes market.

The artisans of San Juan de Limay produce beautiful **soapstone carvings** of animals and big-bodied women. You can purchase lovely pieces small enough to fit in your backpack if you want to take something home with you, or ship larger pieces in well-padded boxes. Iguanas, parrots, frogs, oxen, wagons, and more are the subjects of some of the carvings, though you can also find ornately carved nativity scenes and chess sets, all in the naturally subtle gray and pink color schemes.

Nicaraguan **pottery** is where artisans have truly shone. Nicaraguan potters produce all sorts of vases, bowls, urns, pots, and more, some delicately etched, some left crude, some in the patterns of the indigenous Nahuatl designs. You can also find fantastic mobiles and wind chimes consisting of clay birds, bells, or ornamental shapes like stars and planets.

The small towns around Masaya have many skilled woodworkers, and because most Nicaraguans can't afford expensive imported furniture, they create their own. It is not uncommon to see a dirt-poor campesino shack graced with a set of beautifully crafted **rocking chairs** of stained wood and woven rattan. Rocking chairs are called *abuelitas* (grandmothers) or *mecedoras,* and are constructed in pieces that are easily packed down and carried or shipped home.

You'll find **basketwork** around the country as well, usually of bamboo and cane, or pine needles in Nueva Segovia and the northeast of Nicaragua. The needles are first bound into long coils, then wrapped and stitched to form the basket and lid.

Nicaragua's brilliant **primitivist painting** has existed as an art form for less than four decades, originating in the late 1960s as part of a social movement on the Solentiname Islands in southern Lake Cocibolca. The paintings, sold all over the world, are made on canvases of all sizes, and make excellent gifts that are totally unique to Nicaragua.

Other sinful keepsakes sure to impress your friends back home include **fine rum, superb cigars,** and **world-class coffee.** While in Nicaragua, look for Selva Negra, El Supremo, or San Sebastian brand coffee, which are considered the highest quality gourmet coffees. In the States, try the Mendocino, California–based **Thanksgiving Coffee Company** (website: www.thanksgivingcoffee.com), which promotes and sells fair-trade and organic Nica beans.

Cuban-seed, Nicaraguan grown and rolled cigars are easy to come by, especially in the Estelí area. Fat Cuban Cohibas are widely available as

BARGAINING

Bargaining is a sport—half social, half business, and is expected with most outdoor market vendors and taxi drivers. But be warned: bargaining is *al suave!* Aggressive, prolonged haggling is not cool, won't affect the price, and may leave ill feelings. To start off the process, after you are given the initial price, act surprised and use one of the following phrases: *¿Cuánto es lo menos?* (What is your lowest price?) or *¿Nada menos?* (No less?)

Remember these guidelines when bargaining:

You can't bargain for everything; this includes small items for under $1, all bus fares, and most lodging expenses.

Bargaining is social and friendly, or at least courteous. Keep your temper under wraps and always smile.

Go back and forth a maximum of two or three times, and then either agree or walk away. Remember that some Nicaraguans, to save face, may lose a profit.

Once you make a deal, it's done. If you think you've been ripped off, remember the $5 you got overcharged is still less than you'd pay for a double-tall mocha latte back home. Keep it in perspective and be a good sport.

When bargaining with taxi drivers in Managua, bargain hard, and agree on a price before you enter the cab—once the vehicle is moving, your leverage has vanished in a puff of acrid, black exhaust.

well, for a tenth of the black-market price in the United States. As for the Flor de Caña rum, airport customs will limit you to six liter-size bottles.

SHOPPING

Born-and-bred First World consumers will find plenty of opportunities to practice their number one passion of buying stuff in Nicaragua. Despite Managua's attempt to recreate the slick, safe, and spendy U.S. mall experience, you'll still no doubt find shopping in Nicaragua to be its own extreme sport.

Markets

This, of course, is where the action is—crowded aisles, tin roofs, stifling heat, and a thousand intense smells, ranging from fresh citrus and coffee to raw meat and buckets of gizzards. Wherever you are in Nicaragua, the town market is where you'll find the widest variety and the cheapest of whatever it is you're looking for. Some markets are exceptionally clean and organized, and many more are filthy and chaotic. Put your money in your shoes, backpack on your chest, and prepare to have all five senses violently assaulted.

Supermarkets

Every major Nicaraguan city has at least one supermarket, complete with air-conditioning, elevator music (substituted by bumpin' merengue to advertise a sale), and strategic product placement. Towns too small for a *super* are sure to have at least one *distribuidora,* or *centro comercial* where basic foodstuffs are sold in bulk.

Pulperías

These are the ubiquitous corner stores, present on nearly every block in the country, and immediately identifiable by the collage of free advertising randomly nailed to their walls. In addition to the rusted metal Tabcin and Alka-Seltzer signs, many *pulpería* owners have jumped at the opportunity to have a free Coca-Cola or Pepsi billboard painted across their storefronts (which are usually their homes as well). Inside, you'll find strings of cheap chips, batteries, coolers of sugary drinks, and a selection of groceries, vegetables,

Boaco market

and basic needs, often sold out of the owner's dark living room.

Secondhand Clothes

Thrift shop lovers rejoice! All the bulk second through fifth generation clothing from the United States that makes it to Nicaragua ends up in one of the innumerable used clothing stores. Selections are phenomenal, clothes are cheap, and priceless polyester treasures are waiting to be found.

NIGHTLIFE

Discos

Nicaraguans are never too far from the dance floor, and there is always an opportunity to get down to loud Latin (and cheesy U.S.) music. From the swankest clubs and *discotecas* in Managua to the dingiest dance huts of the Atlantic coast, you are guaranteed to find somewhere to shake it, even in the countryside.

Bars

Bars are often casual affairs consisting of a few plastic tables in somebody's cleared-out living

REGIONAL FIESTAS

Every community's *fiestas patronales* revolve around one particular Saint's Day, but the actual party may begin weeks before that day and continue for days after. This partial list should help you catch (or avoid) regional parties as you travel. Be aware that all year long, Thursdays in Masaya are Jueves de Verbena, Fridays in Granada are Noches de Serenata, and Sundays in León are Tertulias Leonesas.

January

1: New Year's Day

18: Fiestas Patronales, El Sauce

Third Sunday: Señor de Esquipulas, El Sauce (León)

Third weekend: Viva León Festival, León

Third weekend: San Sebastían, Acoyapa (Chontales), Diriamba, Carazo (San Sebastián)

Last weekend: La Virgen de Candelaria, La Trinidad (Estelí)

February

Second weekend: Music and Youth Festival, Managua

March

Third weekend: Folklore, Gastronomy, and Handicraft Festival, Granada

April

Semana Santa

First week: Religious Ash Paintings in León

19–21: Fiestas Patronales in San Jorge (Rivas)

May

1: Labor Day

1: Fiestas Patronales, Jinotega

15: San Isidro Labrador, Condega (Estelí)

30: Mother's Day

Third weekend: Palo de Mayo Festival, Bluefields

June

16: Virgen del Carmen, San Juan del Sur (Rivas)

24: St. John the Baptist, San Juan de Oriente (Carazo), San Juan del Sur (Rivas), San Juan de Jinotega (Jinotega)

29: St. Peter the Apostle, Diriá (Masaya)

July

Second Saturday: Carnival, Somoto

15–25: Fiestas Patronales, Somoto

19: National Liberation Day

25: Santiago, Boaco, Jinotepe (Carazo)

26: St. Ana, Nandaime (Granada), Chinandega, Ometepe

August

1–10: Santo Domingo ("Noches Agostinas"), Managua

10: St. Lorenzo, Somotillo (Chinandega)

14: Gritería Chiquita, León

15: The Assumption, Granada

15: The Assumption and Fiesta del Hijo Ausente, Juigalpa

Third weekend: Mariachis and Mazurcas Festival, Estelí

September

10: San Nicolás de Tolentino, La Paz Centro (León)

14: The Battle of San Jacinto

15: Independence Day

14 and 15: Fishing Fair, San Carlos (Río San Juan)

15: Patron Saint Festival of Villa Nueva, Chinandega

20: San Jerónimo, Masaya

24: La Merced, León and Matagalpa

Fourth weekend: Polkas, Mazurcas and Jamaquellos, Matagalpa; Festival of Corn, Jalapa

October

12: San Diego (Estelí)

Second weekend: Norteño Music Festival in Jinotega

24: San Rafael Arcángel, Pueblo Nuevo

Last Sunday: Toro Venado, Masaya

November

2: All Souls' Day

3–5: Equestrian Rally in Ometepe

12–18: San Diego de Alcalá, Altagracias (Ometepe)

4: San Carlos Borromeo, San Carlos (Río San Juan)

Fourth Sunday: Folkloric Festival, Masaya

December

First Sunday: Procesión de San Jerónimo, Masaya

6: Lavado de La Plata, Virgen del Trono, El Viejo (Chinandega)

7: Purísimas (Immaculate Conception Celebrations) in Managua, Granada, Masaya, and León

© JOSHUA BERMAN

Diriamba's fiestas are totally unique in Nicaragua.

room, adorned with bikini beer babe posters and a jury-rigged stereo system blasting *ranchera* music. Often instead of tallying your bottle consumption on a check, your host will allow your empties to accumulate on the table, counting them up when you're ready to leave. Of course these establishments vary considerably, and in places like Managua, Granada, and San Juan del Sur there is an ever-increasing eclectic collection of pubs, bars, and clubs with different nationality themes.

Gambling

This is a relatively new part of Nicaraguan nightlife, mostly found in Managua, but with a few clusters of slots popping up around the country. Ubiquitous around the country are the scratch-off lottery tickets, hawked by vendors waving handfuls of them in bus terminals and street corners.

FESTIVALS AND HOLIDAYS

Just like most Latin American countries, each town and city in Nicaragua has their own patron saint whom the residents honor each year with a prolonged party, lasting from one to three weeks in length. These *fiestas patronales* combine holy religious fervor with a fierce celebration of sin that features alcohol consumption of biblical proportions. Highlights of the fiestas are Virgin and Saint processions, special masses, fireworks, cockfighting, rodeos, concerts, gambling, and show horse parades. Many towns have additional annual parties to celebrate particular events in their history. On the eve of Valentine's Day (February 14) and Mother's Day (May 30), look for roving bands of musicians delivering *serenatas* to their girlfriends and mothers outside their windows.

Official Holidays

Expect all public offices to be closed on the following days. Also remember that Nicaraguan holidays are subject to decree, shutting the banks down without warning to suit some politician's inclination.

January 1: New Year's Day
Late March/early April: Semana Santa, including Holy Thursday, Good Friday, and Easter
May 1: Labor Day
May 30: Mother's Day
July 19: National Liberation Day
August 1: Fiesta Day
September 14: Battle of San Jacinto
September 15: Independence Day
November 2: Día de los Muertes (All Souls' Day)
December 8: La Purísima (Immaculate Conception)
December 25: Christmas Day

ON THE ROAD

Accommodations

Despite a recent boom in luxury hotels, overall, Nicaragua is still a very affordable place to sleep, provided you are willing to sacrifice some of the amenities of home. Most cities and towns offer a range of options, encompassing several of the following types of accommodations.

Hospedajes

Also called *casas de huespedes* (guesthouses) or *pensiones,* low-end lodging establishments cater to two principal groups of people: working-day

Nicaraguans, and foreign travelers on a budget (or just cheap—you know who you are). Don't expect much in the way of creature comforts, but if all you want is a cheap bed in a simple room, with a shared bath and shower, you won't be lacking for options. Prices range from $2 – 8 per person per night. Many *hospedajes* are charming, clean, and well run, often by a family. In turn, every town has at least a few unbelievably filthy roach-fests. In this book we only mention examples of the latter variety when we feel the traveler should be warned against staying there, usually because the dump in question appears deceivingly safe and clean from the outside. When choosing a *hospedaje,* pay attention to the cleanliness of the sheets and bathrooms, and more importantly, the lock on the door and the kind of people hanging around. *Hospedajes* near (or containing) bars or discos are not recommended.

Midrange Hotels

The growing business class and tourist trade demands a step above basic, and Nicaragua is struggling to provide that. In many major cities and tourist areas you'll find better-quality establishments for $15–30, typically including air-conditioning, cable TV, and hot water (where it's necessary), as well as enclosed parking for your vehicle—a big advantage if driving.

High-end Hotels

As of recently, Managua is home to nearly a half-dozen upscale, internationally known hotel brands, all in the $100 and above range. That kind of pampering is rarely found anywhere else in the country.

Auto-Hotels, Motels

Though ostensibly for the traveling motorist looking for a roadside bed, auto-hotels are almost exclusively for the use of clandestine romantic getaways, and should not be considered a viable lodging option for travelers looking for a good night's sleep. These "no-tell motels" usu-

ON THE ROAD

GETTING IN HOT WATER

In the cooler parts of the country, namely Matagalpa and Jinotega, some hotels and *hospedajes* offer hot water by means of electric water heating canisters attached to the end of the shower head. Cold water passing through the coils is warmed before falling through the holes of the spout. The seemingly obvious drawback to the system is the presence of electric wires in and around a wet (i.e., conductive) environment. While not necessarily the electric deathtraps they appear to be, the prudent traveler will approach them with caution. Before you step into the shower, check for frayed or exposed wires (or the burned carcasses of former hotel occupants on the shower floor). Set the control knob to "II" and, very carefully, turn the water on. Once you're wet and water is flowing through the apparatus it's in your best interest not to mess with the heater again.

To save you many cold showers trying to figure out how the darned thing works, we'll let you in on the secret: if the water pressure is too low, the heater isn't triggered on, and the water will not be heated, but if the water pressure is too high, it will be forced through the nozzle before it's had sufficient contact with the coils, and the water will not be heated. Open the faucet to a moderate setting, and rub-a-dub-dub, you're taking a hot shower. When you've finished, turn the water off first and dry off, then turn the little knob back to "off."

ally offer bar service in your room, curtained-off parking spots (so nobody can get your license plate number), and total anonymity. Names like **Hotel El Amor Eterno** (Hotel Eternal Love) and **Hotel El Escape** are great sources of amusement, and one, on the road to Matagalpa wins the authors' vote for best Spanish pun in the nation: **5 Mentarios** (Get it? *"Cinco," "Sin comentarios,"* which means no comment). Incidentally, the Spanish term *un rato* translates into a moment or a short while; auto-hotels charge by the *rato,* which in most cases is about two hours.

Homestay Programs

Spanish schools throughout Nicaragua typically have combined forces with a network of local families. These homestay programs ensure you are speaking Spanish day and night—an incredibly effective (and intense) tactic in learning a new language. Generally, seven days of room and board costs well under $100.

Rural Nicaragua

It's worth mentioning that *if* you're in the backwoods of Nicaragua, and *if* you get in trouble/miss your bus/have an emergency, the typical Nicaraguan campesino would not think twice before extending his hospitality to you, sometimes insisting that you sleep in his own bed while he sleeps on the floor or in a hammock. If the family is reluctant to take cash because they have offered you their home out of kindness, you should certainly offer and, if that fails, make a trip to the market and provide some groceries. This is an incidence where the transaction is more of a *suave* gift exchange than a business deal. In an effort to promote local, grassroots tourism, some areas of Nicaragua have trained residents in how to host a foreign guest. Miraflor, Estelí is a prime example, offering a range of rural experiences living with kindhearted campesino families.

Camping

Camping is rare in Nicaragua and there are few advertised campgrounds. More common are rustic natural compounds that allow camping on their property if you have the gear. These

---

¿DONDE ESTÁ EL BAÑO? A GUIDE TO NICARAGUA'S TOILETS

Nicaragua boasts an enormous diversity of bathrooms, from dark, infested *letrinas* (outhouses) to various forms of the common toilet *(inodoro* or *trono).* There is a widespread shortage of toilet seats, so having to squat over the bowl is common, and in many cases, a manual flush is required. This is an important technique to master, useful any time the normal pump mechanism breaks down or when the city water pressure drops: just dump three gallons or more of water into the bowl at once, forcefully and from high up.

With any flush toilet, always throw used toilet paper in the basket next to the toilet, not in the bowl, so as not to clog up the weak plumbing. You'll get used to it. The most commonly encountered toilet paper is pink and made of recycled paper in a plant in Granada. It's not so soft—you'll get used to that too. Or if not, pick up some luxury rolls to travel with, available in most supermarkets. Toilet paper in Spanish, by the way, is *papel higienico,* or just *papel,* as in, *"Fijase señor que no hay papel."* (You see, sir, we're out of paper). If you'd rather avoid having that particular bit of news ruin your evening, remember to always carry a roll with you, protected in a plastic bag and easily accessible.

---

include **Derek's** on Corn Island, the **El Chocoyero** and **Montibelli Private Reserves** near Managua, the **APDS** compound in Solentiname, the **Biological Station** on Mombacho, and the **Centro Ecológico** at Los Guatuzos. There are surely a number of beaches where you can set a tent up as well, notably La Flor and any of the isolated spots on the Cosigüina Peninsula in Chinandega. Without a tent, feel free to make like a guerrilla soldier—string up a cheap hammock and mosquito net in the trees and add a plastic tarp during the wet season.

Elsewhere, your interest in sleeping on the ground will be viewed with much suspicion, even in the Nicaraguan countryside. Out in the campo, poor farmers are so busy trying to make

ON THE ROAD

their own lives more comfortable they can't imagine why you'd want to make yours less, and may feel obliged to offer you a place to stay in their own home. Should you desire to pitch a tent in the campo, remember all land belongs to somebody—it's in your best interest to find out if you're on somebody's cornfield, and to ask permission to spend the night. The landowner will also be able to inform you about latent dangers you should be aware of, for example uncleared minefields (see Land Mines in Nicaragua special topic).

Also, expect to hear all kinds of stories in the countryside regarding the danger in sleeping outside. Some have a basis in reality and some don't, involving fantastic nocturnal creatures—ghosts, *chupacabras* (legendary "goat-sucking" creatures), dwarves, armed bandits, and more. When determining a possible campsite's safety, ask around (but be careful about advertising your whereabouts to the wrong people). Tales about "the headless man on the black horse who rides through town at midnight" can probably safely be discarded; warnings of *rearmados* (rearmed men) should be taken more seriously. Local police and army posts are good for current information.

Food and Drink

Nicaraguan cuisine is simple, honest, and unsubtle. Those expecting Mexican fare will find similar base ingredients—beans, rice, cheese, and tortillas—but without the spice and diversity. In fact, going out to a Mexican restaurant in Managua is just as exotic an experience as going out for Italian or Chinese. However, what Nicaraguan food lacks in renown and variety is made up for in *cariño* (affection). Remember that in most of the family-run *comedores,* you will be offered a heapin' plate of love by somebody's mom—probably the same food she just served her own kids. It should be noted that vegetarians shouldn't have a problem at all, especially in the campo, where meat is a luxury item anyway.

Where to Eat

The cheapest, most basic unit of eating out in Nicaragua is the **comedor,** sometimes called a **cafetín,** several of which are found in every market and most town parks. They serve a fixed plate of *comida corriente,* which includes *gallo pinto* (rice and beans), cabbage salad, white cheese, and your choice of a fried egg or piece of meat; served with coffee, juice, or a *gaseosa* (soda/pop/soft drink) for under $2 or $3.

The next step up is the **fritanga,** best defined as backyard barbecue meets the deep fryer. Beef, chicken, pork, potatoes, and tortillas: all of it deep-fried, flame-roasted, cheap, and delicious. Stop worrying about those pesky arteries and

enjoy Nica street food the way it was made to be eaten—off a steamy square of banana leaf. About $3 a plate, depending on how much you eat. Every town has a *fritanga,* and most set up right there on the sidewalk, surrounded by plastic tables and chairs that often creep back into someone's

© JOSHUA BERMAN

Fritanga: backyard barbecue meets the deep fryer.

living room. Smell the cooking meat as it drips salty juices onto the open flames, right next to a giant, smoke-blackened pot of oil in which sizzles breaded treats like enchiladas (stuffed with rice and shredded beef) and *papas rellenas,* a deep-fried, cheese-filled potato. Order a bag of cold, corn-based beverage or fruit drink, walk over to the park, and discover what "finger-licking good" is all about.

Many cities have an upscale, indoor version of the *fritanga,* with a huge variety of food, served buffet-style behind a sneeze guard. The more reputable buffets attract long lines and usually offer lots of bang for your buck.

More elegant Nicaraguan restaurants usually offer more in the way of environment and high prices than they do in fine cuisine. You'll find them everywhere, often under a large, open-air, thatched-roof *rancho,* with bright fluorescent lights, loud music, and meals for $5–11. They may offer seafood, steak, and fancy soups. They are at their best on weekend nights, when they can be lively places to drink. Off nights are not as exciting.

Managua abounds with foreign cuisine, and most cities have at least one attempt at a Chinese, Italian, and Mexican restaurant. Of course, "American" food is everywhere, and although you probably won't be writing home about the burgers and pizza you encounter, at least you can appreciate a salty,

A SAMPLE MENU

RESTAURANTE TRES BOBOS
Serving Nicaraguan *Traditional Cuisine* since the 1980s
Chefs and Founders O'Reilly, Krekel, and Hulme

DESAYUNO	**BREAKFAST**
Huevos	Eggs
Enteros, Revueltos, Volteados	Hardboiled, scrambled, over-easy

ALMUERZO Y CENA	**LUNCH AND DINNER**
Carne/res	**Beef**
Desmenuzada	Shredded and stewed
A la plancha	Served on a hot plate
Churrasco	Grilled steak
Filete jalapeño	Steak in a creamy pepper sauce
Puerco/chancho	**Pork**
Chuleta	Porkchop
Pollo	**Chicken**
Empanizado	Breaded
Frito	Fried
Al vino	Wine sauce
Rostizado	Rotisserie
Valenciano	A chicken and rice dish
Mariscos	**Seafood**
Pescado entero	The whole fish
Langosta al ajillo	Lobster in garlic sauce
Camarones al vapor	Steamed shrimp
Sopa de conchas	Conch soup
Huevos de paslama	Endangered turtle eggs
Platos Tradicionales	**Traditional Dishes**
Baho	Plantain and beef stew
Nacatamales	Meat-filled corn *tamal,* wrapped and boiled in banana leaves
Indio viejo	Beef, veggie, and cornmeal mush
Caballo bayo	A sampler's plate of traditional dishes

(continues on next page)

ON THE ROAD

A SAMPLE MENU (cont'd)

Gallo pinto	Red beans and rice, generously doused in oil and salt
Cuajada	White farmer's cheese
Leche agria	A sour cream–yogurt combo
Vigorón	Pork rinds with yucca and coleslaw, served on a banana leaf

Bocadillas	**Appetizers**
Tostones	Thick, fried, green plantain chips
Tajadas	Crunchy, thin strips of green plantain
Maduro	Ripe, sweet plantains fried in their own sugar
Ensalada	Shredded cabbage, tomatoes, and a dash of lime
Tortilla	Heavy, floppy discs of toasted white corn

Bebidas y (Re)frescos	**Drinks and Fruit Juices**
Tiste	Toasted cooked corn with cacao, pepper, and cloves
Pinol	Toasted, milled corn
Pinolillo	Pinol with pepper, cloves, and cacao
Horchata	Toasted and milled rice with spices
Chicha	Rough milled corn with vanilla and banana flavors, sometimes fermented

Postres	**Desserts**
Flan	Flan
Sorbete, Helado	Sherbet, Ice cream

greasy plate of *papas fritas* (French fries), even if they come soaked in salt and mayonnaise.

Alcohol

> *So he sipped the drink, which was cold and clean-tasting, and he watched the broken line of the keys straight ahead and to the westward... But over half of the drink was still in the paper-wrapped glass and there was still ice in it... I wonder where she is now... I could think about her all night. But I won't.*
>
> **Ernest Hemingway**

Forget the girl, think about the drink: it goes largely undisputed that Nicaragua makes the best rum in all of Central America. Rum is the drink of choice among Nicaraguans and it is more often than not served up in a rocks glass with Coca-Cola and spurt of lime, called a **Nica Libre** (a clear shout out to the comrades in Cuba). Of all the rum produced in Nicaragua, **Flor de Caña** is considered the best, of which the caramel-colored, seven-year-old **Gran Reserva** is the best of the best (except, of course, their 12-year **Centenario,** which is twice as expensive). Flor de Caña produces a half-dozen varieties of rum, which increase in price and quality as they age. A *media* (half-liter) of seven-year, bucket of ice, bottle of Coke, and plate of limes (called *un servicio completo*) will set you back only $4 or so. Reach, however, for the plastic bottle of **Ron Plata,** and take a giant step down in price, quality, and social class. Enormously popular in the campo, "Rrrrron Plata!" is the proud sponsor of most baseball games and not a few bar brawls.

But wait—you can get drunk for even less! Most street corners and town parks are the backdrop for many a grimacing shot of **Tayacán,** or its homemade, corn-mash equivalent, often served in clear plastic baggies that look like they should have a goldfish swimming in them. West Virginians call this stuff "that good 'ole mountain dew"; Nicaraguans call it *la cususa, el guaro,* or *la lija* brought down from the hills by the moonshine man and his mule. *La cususa* is gasoline-clear, potent in smell (including when you sweat it out the next day), and will bore a hole through your liver quicker than a 9-millimeter. It's sold by the gallon for about $4, often in a stained, sloshing, plastic container that used to contain some automobile-related product, and then resold in baggie-size portions.

The national beers—**Victoria** and **Toña**—are both light tasting pilsners and, well, you can't really say anything bad about an ice-cold beer in the tropics. Expect to pay anywhere from $.60 to $1 a beer (if you're paying anything more than that, you are either in the Hotel Inter or a strip club). A recent addition to the national beer market is the slightly higher-priced Premium, as well as liter-sized bottles of both Toña and Victoria—an excellent bargain at under $2. Together, Victoria, Toña, and Flor de Caña are known affectionately by those who care as **Vickie, Toni,** and **Flo.**

Should you decide to partake in this part of the culture and get drunk *(borracho, bolo, picado, hasta el culo),* be sure you have a decent understanding of your environment and feel good about your company. Remember that many a traveler's disaster story begins with "Man, I was so wasted. . . ." Always take it slow when drinking in a new place, and remember that your hydration level has an enormous impact on how drunk you get. And oh, by the way, rum does not make you a better dancer, but it may improve your Spanish; and if you are drinking it alone, staring straight ahead over the broken line of the keys, try not to think about the girl.

ON THE ROAD

Health

BEFORE YOU GO

Resources
Staying Healthy in Asia, Africa, and Latin America, by Dirk G. Schroeder, is an excellent and concise guide to preventative medicine in the Developing World and is small enough to fit in your pack. Consult the "Mexico and Central America" page of the U.S. Centers for Disease Control (CDC) website for up-to-date health recommendations and advice (website: www.cdc.gov/travel/camerica.htm), or call the Nicaraguan Embassy in your country for up-to-date information about outbreaks or other problems. Or check the CDC International Travelers Hotline: 404/332-4559 and 877/FYI-TRIP (394-8747).

Vaccinations
Required: A certificate of vaccination against yellow fever is required for all travelers over one year of age and arriving from affected areas.
Recommended: Before traveling to Nicaragua, be sure your tetanus, diphtheria, measles, mumps, rubella, and polio vaccines are up-to-date. Protection against hepatitis A and typhoid fever is also recommended for all travelers.

STAYING HEALTHY

Ultimately your health is dependent on the choices you make, and chief among these is what you decide to put in your mouth. One long-time resident says staying healthy in the tropics is more than just possible—it is an "art form." Nevertheless, as you master the art, expect your digestive system to take some time getting accustomed to the new food and microorganisms in the Nicaraguan diet. During this time (and after), use common sense: Wash or sanitize your hands often. Eat food that is well cooked and still hot when served. Avoid dairy products if you're not sure whether they are pasteurized; be wary of uncooked foods, including shellfish (like the cold seafood salad ceviche) and salads. Use the finger wag to turn down food from street vendors and be aware that pork carries the extra danger of trichinosis, not to mention the disgusting garbage diet (and worse) most country pigs are raised on.

Most importantly, be aware of flies, the single worst transmitter of food-borne illnesses. Prevent flies from landing on your food, glass, or table setting. You'll notice Nicaraguans are meticulous about this, and you should be too. If you have to leave the table, cover your food with a napkin or have someone else wave their hand over it slowly. You can fold your drinking straw over and put the mouth end into the neck of the bottle to prevent flies from landing on it, and put napkins on top of the bottle neck and your glass, too. Have the waiter clear the table when you've finished with a dish to keep the task of guarding your dishes simpler. You'll notice if a Nicaraguan sees a fly has landed on her straw, she'll stop using the straw. Follow suit.

"Don't Drink the Water!"

At least one well-meaning friend or relative told you this before you shipped off to Central America, and we agree. Even though most municipal water systems are well treated and probably safe, there is not much reason to take the chance, especially when purified, bottled water is so widely available and relatively cheap. Even Nicas buy bottled water. Avoid ice cubes unless you're confident they were made with boiled or purified water. Canned and bottled drinks without ice, including beer, are usually safe, but should never be used as a substitute for water when trying to stay hydrated, say during a bout of diarrhea or when out in the sun.

If you plan on staying awhile in a rural area of Nicaragua, check out camping catalogs for water filters that remove chemical as well as biological contamination. Alternately, six drops of liquid iodine (or three of bleach) will kill everything that needs to be killed in a liter of water, good if you're in a pinch, but not something you'll find yourself practicing on a daily basis.

Oral Rehydration Salts

Probably the single most effective preventative and curative medicine you can carry are the packets of powdered salt and sugar known in Spanish as *suero orál.* One packet of *suero* mixed with a liter of water, drunk in small sips, is the best immediate treatment for dehydration due to diarrhea, sun exposure, fever, infection, or—say some—a hangover. Particularly in the case of diarrhea, rehydration salts are essential to your recovery. They replace the salts and minerals your body has lost due to liquid evacuation (be it from sweating, puking, or urinating), and they're essential to

your body's most basic cellular transfer functions. Whether or not you like the taste (odds are you won't), consuming enough *suero* and water is very often the difference between being just a little sick and feeling really, really awful.

Sport drinks like Gatorade are super-concentrated *suero* mixtures and should be diluted 3:1 with water to make the most of the active ingredients. If you don't, you'll urinate out the majority of the electrolytes. Gatorade is common in most new gas stations and supermarkets but *suero* packets are more widely available and much much cheaper, available from any drugstore or health clinic for about $.50 a packet. It can be improvised even more cheaply, according to the following recipe: mix one-half teaspoon of salt, one-half teaspoon baking soda, and four tablespoons of sugar in one quart of boiled or carbonated water. Drink a full glass of the stuff after each time you use the bathroom. Add a few drops of lemon to make it more palatable.

Sun Exposure

> *Theo, I want the sun. I want it in its most terrific heat and power. I've been feeling it pull me southward all winter, like a huge magnet …*
>
> *Vincent van Gogh*

Nicaragua is located a scant 12 degrees of latitude from the equator, so the sun's rays strike the Earth's surface at a more direct angle than in northern countries. The result is that you will burn faster and sweat up to twice as much as you are used to. Did we mention that you should drink lots of water?

Ideally, do like the majority of the locals do, and stay out of the sun between 10 A.M. and 2 P.M. It's a great time to take a nap anyway. Use sunscreen of at least SPF 30 (Bullfrog's alcohol-based SPF 36 is the authors' choice), and wear a hat and pants. Should you overdo it in the sun, make sure to drink lots of fluids—that means water, not beer—and try not to strain any muscles as you kick yourself for being so stupid. Treat sunburns with aloe gel, or better yet—find a fresh *sábila* (aloe) plant to break open and rub over your skin.

DISEASE AND COMMON AILMENTS

Diarrhea and Dysentery

Diarrhea is one symptom of amoebic (parasitic) and bacillic (bacterial) dysentery, both caused by some form of fecal-oral contamination. Often accompanied by nausea, vomiting, and a mild fever, dysentery is easily confused with other diseases so don't try to self-diagnose. Stool sample examinations *(examenes de heces)* can be performed at most clinics and hospitals and are your first step to getting better (cost is $2–8). Bacillic dysentery is treatable with antibiotics; amoebic is treated with one of a variety of drugs that kill off all the flora in your intestinal tract. Of these, Flagyl is the best known, but other non-FDA approved treatments like Tinedazol are commonly available, cheap, and effective. Do not drink alcohol with these drugs, but do eat something like yogurt or acidophilus pills to refoliate your tummy.

Generally, simple cases of diarrhea in the absence of other symptoms are nothing more serious than "traveler's diarrhea." If you do get a case of **Diriangén's Revenge** (see History section in Introduction), your best bet is to let it pass naturally. Diarrhea is your body's way of flushing out the bad stuff, so constipating medicines like Imodium-AD are not recommended, as they keep the bacteria (or whatever is causing your intestinal distress) within your system. Save the Imodium (or any other liquid glue) for emergency situations like long bus rides or a date with Miss Nicaragua. Most importantly, drink water! Not replacing the fluids and electrolytes you are losing will make you feel much worse than you need to. If the diarrhea persists for more than 48 hours, is bloody, or is accompanied by a fever, see a health professional immediately. That said, know that all bodies react differently to the changes in diet, schedule, and stress that go along with traveling, and many visitors to Nicaragua stay entirely regular throughout their trip. Some have recommended "lining" your stomach with Pepto-Bismol each day as a preventative measure, but we have no clinical results to be able to recommend this practice.

Malaria

Malaria is present in Nicaragua, and to date, the newer chloroquine-resistant strains of the disease have not been detected in Nicaragua. Though the risk is higher in rural areas, especially those alongside rivers or marshes, malaria-infected mosquitoes breed anywhere stagnant pools of water (of any size, even in an empty bottle cap) are found, including urban settings.

Malaria works by setting up shop in your liver and then blasting you with attacks of fever, headaches, chills, and fatigue. The onslaughts occur on a 24-hour-sick, 24-hour-feeling-better cycle. If you observe this cycle, seek medical attention. They'll most likely take a blood test and if positive, prescribe you a huge dose of chloroquine that will kill the bug. Allow time to recover your strength. Weekly prophylaxis of chloroquine or an equivalent is recommended, and the CDC specifically recommends travelers to Nicaragua use brand name Aralen pills (500 mg for adults). Begin taking the pills two weeks before you arrive and continue taking them four weeks after leaving the country. A small percentage of people have negative reactions to chloroquine, including nightmares, rashes, or hair loss. Alternative treatments are available, but the best method of all is to not get bit (see section on mosquitoes below).

Dengue Fever

Dengue, or "bone-breaking," fever, will put a stop to your fun in Central America like a baseball bat to the head. The symptoms may include any or all of the following: sudden high fever, severe headache (akin to nails in the back of your eyes), muscle and back pain, nausea or vomiting, and a full-bodied skin rash, which may appear 3–4 days after the onset of the fever. Although the initial pain and fever may only last a few days, you may be out of commission for up to several weeks, possibly bedridden, depressed, and too weak to move. There is no vaccine, but dengue's effects can be successfully minimized with plenty of rest, Tylenol (for the fever and aches), and as much water and *suero* as you can possibly manage. Dengue itself is undetectable in a blood test, but a low platelet *(plaquetas)* count indicates its presence. If you believe you have dengue, you should get a blood test as soon as possible to make sure it's not the hemorrhagic variety, which can be fatal if untreated.

AIDS

Although large numbers of HIV cases have not yet appeared in Nicaragua, health organizations claim that geography, as well as cultural, political, and social factors may all contribute to an AIDS explosion in Nicaragua in the near future. Exacerbating the spread of AIDS is the promiscuous behavior of many married males, an active sexworker trade, less than ideal condom-using habits, and growing drug trouble. AIDS is most prevalent in urban populations, mainly Managua and Chinandega, and is primarily transmitted sexually, not through needles or contaminated blood.

Blood transfusions are not recommended. Travelers should avoid sexual contact with persons whose HIV status is unknown. If you intend to be sexually active, use a fresh latex condom for every sexual act: oral, vaginal, and anal. Condoms are inexpensive and readily available in just about any local pharmacy; in Spanish, a condom is called *condón,* or *preservativo.*

Other Diseases

Cholera is present in Nicaragua, with frequent outbreaks, especially in rural areas with contaminated water supplies. Vaccines are not required because they offer incomplete protection. You are better off watching what you put in your mouth. In case you contract cholera (the symptoms are profuse diarrhea the color of rice water accompanied by sharp intestinal cramps, vomiting, and body weakness), see a doctor immediately and drink your *suero.* Cholera kills—by dehydrating you.

Leptospirosis is caused by a bacteria found in water contaminated with the urine of infected animals, especially rodents. Symptoms include high fever and headache, chills, muscle aches, vomiting, and possibly jaundice. Humans become infected through contact with infected food, water, or soil. It is not known to spread from person

to person and can be treated with antibiotics in its early stages.

There is moderate incidence of hepatitis B in Nicaragua. Avoid contact with bodily fluids or bodily waste. Get vaccinated if you anticipate close contact with the local population or plan to reside in Nicaragua for an extended period of time.

Most towns in Nicaragua, even rural ones, conduct a yearly rabies vaccination campaign for dogs, but you should still be careful. Get a rabies vaccination if you intend to spend a long time in Nicaragua. Should you be bitten, immediately cleanse the wound with lots of soap, and get prompt medical attention.

Tuberculosis is spread by sneezing or coughing, and the infected person may not know he or she is a carrier. If you are planning to spend more than four weeks in Nicaragua (or plan on spending time in a Nicaraguan jail), consider having a tuberculin skin test performed before and after visiting. Tuberculosis is a serious and possibly fatal disease but can be treated with several medications.

BITES AND STINGS
Mosquitoes

Mosquitoes are most active during the rainy season (June–November) and in areas near stagnant water, like marshes, puddles, or rice fields. They are much more common in the lower, flatter regions of Nicaragua than they are in mountains, though even in the highlands, old tires, cans, and roadside puddles can provide the habitat necessary to produce swarms of *zancudos* (mosquitoes). The mosquito that carries malaria bites during the night and evening hours, and the dengue fever courier is active during the day, from dawn to dusk. They are both relatively simple to combat, and ensuring you don't get bitten is the best prophylaxis for preventing the diseases.

First and foremost, limit the amount of skin you expose—long sleeves, pants, and socks will do more to prevent bites than the strongest chemical repellent. Choose lodging accommodations with good screens and if this is not possible, use a fan to blow airborne insects away from your body as you sleep. Avoid being outside or un-protected in the hour before sunset when mos-quito activity is heaviest, and use a *mosquitero* (mosquito net) tucked underneath your mat-tress when you sleep. Several lightweight back-packers' nets are available, either freestanding or hangable. Consider purchasing one before you come south. Once in Nicaragua, you can pur-chase *tela de mosquitero* anywhere they sell fabric and have a mosquito net made by a seamstress. Also, many *pulperías* sell *espirales* (mosquito coils), which burn slowly, releasing a mosquito-repelling smoke; they're cheap and convenient, but some brands use DDT as an active ingredient.

Chagas' Disease

This is a rare ailment passed by the Chagas bug *(Trypanosoma cruzi)* to unsuspecting, often sleep-ing, humans. The Chagas bug bites the victim (usually on the face, close to the lips), sucks its fill of blood, and, for the coup de grâce, defecates on the newly created wound. The Chagas bug is a large, recognizable insect, also called the kiss-ing bug, assassin bug, and cone-nose. In Spanish it's known as *chinche,* but this word is also used for many other types of beetlelike creatures. Chagas bugs are present in Nicaragua, found mostly in poor campesino structures of crum-bling adobe. Besides the downright insult of being bitten, sucked, and pooped on, the Chagas bug's biggest menace is the disease it carries of the same name, which manifests itself in 2 percent of its victims. The first symptoms include swollen glands and a fever that appear 1–2 weeks after the bite. The disease then goes into a five- to 30-year remission phase. If and when it reap-pears, Chagas' disease causes the lining of the heart to swell, sometimes resulting in death. There is no cure.

Scorpions, Spiders, and Snakes

Scorpions, or *alacránes,* are common in Nicaragua, especially in dark corners, beaches, and piles of wood. Nicaraguan scorpions look nasty—black and big—but their sting is no more harmful than that of a bee and is described by some as what a cigarette burn feels like. Your lips and tongue may feel a little numb, but the venom is nothing compared to their smaller, translucent cousins in Mexico. Needless to say, for people who are prone to anaphylactic shock, it can be a more serious or life-threatening experience. Be aware, in Nicaragua the Spanish word *escorpión* usually refers not to scorpions but to the harmless little geckos (also called *perros zompopos*) that scur-ry around walls eating small insects . And in spite of what your campesino friends might insist, those little geckos are neither malevolent nor deadly and would never, as you will often hear, inten-tionally try to kill you by urinating on you.

Arachnophobics, upon arriving in country, should run to the nearest pharmacy, pick up some Valium (Diazepám), and chill out. The spiders of Nicaragua are dark, hairy, and occa-sionally attain the size of a small puppy. Of note is the *picacaballo* tarantula, whose name, "horse-biter," refers to the power of its flesh-rotting venom (similar to that of the brown recluse) to destroy a horse's hoof. Don't worry, though; spi-ders do not aggressively seek out people to bite, and do way more good than harm by eating things like Chagas bugs. If you'd rather the spiders didn't share your personal space, shake out your bedclothes before going to sleep and check your shoes before putting your feet in them.

There are several kinds of poisonous snakes in Nicaragua; of these, the coral snake is the most frequently encountered. There are other nonven-omous snakes that are nearly identical to the coral, but their stripe pattern gives them away. Remem-ber the expressions "Red next to yellow, kills a fel-low," and "Red next to black, friend to Jack."

MEDICAL ATTENTION

Medical care is in short supply outside of Man-agua, and even in the capital city, doctors in pub-lic hospitals are underpaid (earning about $200 a month) and brutally overworked. Though there are qualified medical professionals in Nicaragua, there are also many practicing doctors and med-ical staff that have less-than-adequate creden-tials. Use your best judgment. Hospitals and medical facilities typically expect immediate pay-ment for services rendered. Larger facilities accept credit cards and everyone else demands cash.

Government-run health clinics, called *Centros de Salud,* exist in most towns throughout the country, usually near the central plaza. They are free—even to you—but often poorly supplied and inadequately staffed.

If you are feeling adventurous, nonserious medical situations can be an opportunity to experience Nicaraguan country medicine. Many campesinos have excellent practical knowledge of herbal remedies that involve teas, tree barks, herbs, and fruits. The first medicines came from the earth, and the Nicaraguans haven't lost that connection. Try *apazote* or coconut milk for intestinal parasites, *manzanilla* (chamomile) for stress or menstrual discomfort, or *tamarindo* or papaya for constipation. A popular cold remedy involves hot tea mixed with two squeezed limes, *miel de jicote* (honey from the jicote bee), and a large shot of cheap rum, drunk right before you go to bed so that you sweat out the fever as you sleep.

Medications and Prescriptions

Many modern medicines, produced in Mexico or El Salvador, are available in Nicaragua, though they're often prohibitively expensive. Because of a struggling economy and plenty of competition, some pharmacies may sell you medicine without a prescription. For simple travelers' ailments, like stomach upsets, diarrhea, or analgesics, it's worth going to the local pharmacy and asking what they recommend. Even relatively strong medications like codeine can be purchased over the counter (in Alka-Seltzer tablet form).

Birth Control: Condoms are cheap and easy to find. Any corner pharmacy will have them, even in small towns of just a few thousand people; a three-pack of Trojans costs under $2. Female travelers taking contraceptives should know the chemical name for what they use. Birth control pills *(pastillas anticonceptativas)* are easily obtained in pharmacies in Managua and in larger cities like León, Granada, and Estelí. No prescription is needed. Other forms of birth control and sexual protection devices such as IUDs, dental dams, and diaphragms are nonexistent in Nicaragua.

Safety

CRIME

Believe it or not, Nicaragua is considered one of the safest countries in all of Latin America. If you're traveling south from El Salvador or Guatemala, you should feel your anxiety level drop noticeably. You're more likely to be harassed than attacked in Nicaragua, and most physical assaults involve alcohol, so pay special attention to the situations you get into while out on the town. Avoid traveling alone at night or while intoxicated, and pay the extra dollar or two for better-quality cabs. Women should not take cabs when the driver has a friend riding up front.

Pickpocketing (or hat/watch/bag snatching) occurs occasionally in Nicaragua, but again, this is a situation that can usually be avoided by reducing your desirability as a target and paying attention when in crowds. Try to avoid urban buses in Managua and, when visiting the markets, don't wear flashy jewelry, watches, or sunglasses. Keep your cash divided up and hidden in a money belt, sock, bra, or underwear.

If you are the victim of a crime, report it to the local police department immediately. Remember, if you've insured any of your possessions, you won't be reimbursed without a copy of the official police report. Nicaraguan police have good intentions but few resources, lacking even gasoline for the few patrol cars or motorcycles they have—don't be surprised if you are asked to help fill up a vehicle with gas. This is not uncommon, and remember a full tank of gas should cost no more than $30. Travelers are often shocked to find that the police occasionally do recover stolen merchandise. While police corruption does exist—Nicaraguan policemen earn a pitiful $55–60 per month—the Nicaraguan police force is notably more honest and helpful than in some Central American nations.

Bigger cities, like Estelí and Chinandega, have their shady neighborhoods to avoid, and, because of its size and sprawl, Managua is the most dangerous of Nicaraguan cities. Still, it's a pretty simple task to avoid the unsafe barrios. Worsening poverty, desperation, and unemployment in the 1990s have led to a surge in gang membership and violence in the poorer neighborhoods, and drug use—including crack—is also on the rise. Still, by not entering unknown areas, not walking at night, and sticking with other people, you can reduce the chances of anything bad happening.

Rural Violence and Armed Groups

Possibly the most dangerous region of the entire nation is *El Triangulo Minero,* the area around the northeastern Jinotega mining towns of La Rosita, Bonanza, and Siuna. The area is poorly policed and home to a number of armed groups of ex-soldiers that have become infatuated with the bandit lifestyle. FUAC *(Frente Unido Andrés Castro)* is the most prolific and visible armed group. When the Chamorro government failed to come through with promises of land and technical support for the thousands of former soldiers and Contras who laid down their arms, many took to the hills to live a life of banditry. Their political agenda has largely been forgotten, not to mention tainted by a number of psychopathic *comandantes* who lurk around the edges of civilization, living off the campesinos. You'll see the word FUAC spray-painted on some buildings in Managua, Matagalpa, and Jinotega, but little else of the armed band itself.

In 2001, however, major gun battles broke out between FUAC and the Nicaraguan police and army in the mining triangle. FUAC staged several ambushes on Nicaraguan police forces, in which officers were killed. The police and army responded quickly and with great force, killing the legendary FUAC commander Marenco. His partner in crime Tiniebla and other paramilitaries still roam the area. Their exploits—typically the robbing and kidnapping of wealthy Nicaraguans in Matagalpa and Jinotega—are the stuff of modern Nicaragua legends.

There have been no attacks on foreigners with the 1999 exception of Manley Guarducci, a Canadian mining engineer who was kidnapped and held for ransom. He was released five weeks later, unharmed and unshaken in his desire to remain in Nicaragua.

Always check the latest crime and U.S. State Department reports. In general, avoid the wilds outside Quilalí, Waslala, and the entire *Triangulo Minero.*

Drugs

All travelers in Nicaragua are subject to local drug possession and use laws. Penalties include stiff fines and prison sentences of up to 30 years. Nicaragua is part of the underground highway that transports cocaine and heroin from South America to North America and as such, is under a lot of pressure from the United States to crack down on drug traffickers passing through in vehicles or in boats off the Atlantic coast. Drug-related crime is rapidly increasing on the Atlantic coast, particularly in Bluefields and Puerto Cabezas.

Marijuana *(mota* or *monte)* is grown in a few northern areas of Nicaragua. Although rare and always on the sly, some Nicaraguans do smoke pot and may try to sell you some, especially on the Atlantic coast and in San Juan del Sur or Corinto. Never would they—or should you—conduct business or sample any goods out in the open. Canine and bag searches along the Atlantic coast, and at the Honduran and Costa Rican border crossings are the norm, not the exception. Be smart.

In a highly publicized case, a Canadian farmer and his Nicaraguan partner were jailed for growing industrial hemp (called *cáñamo)* on a farm near Managua, the seeds of which had been previously approved by both U.S. and Nicaraguan officials. The incident was interesting for the public debate it sparked about the difference between marijuana and hemp.

Prostitution

Sex is for sale in Nicaragua and the world's oldest business is one facet of Nicaragua's economy that has more than tripled in recent years, especially among young girls in Managua, Granada, Corinto, and border/trucking towns like Somotillo.

LAND MINES IN NICARAGUA

"By the way, how do you know when there's a mine in the road?"
"There's a big bang," came the straightforward reply.

My breakfast of rice and beans— "gayo [sic] pinto," it was called, "painted rooster"—began to crow noisily in my stomach.

Salman Rushdie, The Jaguar's Smile

Nicaragua has the ignominious honor of having more land mines—over 135,000 in place and another 136,000 stockpiled in the wilds of the northeast—than any other country in the Western Hemisphere. This is one of the most brutal and pernicious legacies of the conflicts of the 1980s, and the focus of a major de-mining cleanup effort by the Nicaraguan Army and the Organization of American States (OAS).

The Chamorro government initiated the process of removing Nicaragua's land mines with a request to the OAS in 1991. An international team of Hondurans, Brazilians, and Chileans, among others, commenced de-mining operations in 1993 under the jurisdiction of the Junta Interamericano de Defensa (JID) but was forced to stop the same year for budget reasons. De-mining efforts commenced again in 1996 and continue through the present, this time sponsored by the OAS. The JID provides technical support and the Nicaraguan military provides troops and logistical support. Both Sweden and Norway have been active contributors and financiers of the endeavor.

The de-mining process, though still incomplete, can largely be considered a success: in the year 2000 alone, 6,155 land mines, 16,172 "explosive artifacts," and 20,000 antipersonnel mines were uncovered and destroyed by the joint team effort. Worldwide, no country is making as great an effort as Nicaragua to clear the land of mines. The demining effort takes place in six-month modules. At the end of each module, after having combed a region thoroughly with specially trained troops,

and dogs trained to sniff out explosives, the region is "certified" mine-free. The weapons, when uncovered in the field, are detonated on-site. Stockpiles are transferred to one of two special detonating zones for destruction at the Escuela de Sargentos Andres Castro outside of Managua, or at the ENABI army base a few kilometers south of Condega, Estelí.

The locations of mined areas are generally known due to information divulged (postwar) by the Sandinista military and the Contra forces. There are five areas where OAS troops are actively searching for and destroying land mines: (1) the Honduran border near San Pedro, (2) San Carlos area on the Río San Juan (especially near San Francisco), (3) Boaco/Chontales/RAAS, including sites in Muhan, Muy Muy, Bopal Piedra Colorada, and Murra, (4) the area around Siuna, and (5) the area around Nueva Segovia. Nueva Segovia, in particular, due to the repeated confrontations between the Sandinista military and Contra troops, was a heavily mined area, and the de-mining effort there is particularly intense. OAS troops have been combing the Honduran border from Las Sabanas (Madriz, just south of Somoto) through Jalapa to Wamblán, Jinotega, a distance of nearly 150 km. The department of Chinandega and the border with Costa Rica were declared free of mines in late 2001.

Parallel to the actual physical detection and removal of land mines is an intensive education campaign aimed at the campesinos in the affected areas. OAS distributes Superman and Wonder Woman comic books with a story line that discusses the danger of land mines and what to do if you suspect you've found one. But it's impossible to reach everyone with the message before it's too late. Nicaragua has over 800 residents handicapped by land mines, and countless more injured. Each year, an average of 20 people are injured. More frequent still are losses of cattle, which go unreported but are the subject of many a campesino story.

Unfortunately Hurricane Mitch added further to the difficulty of extracting Nicaragua's land mines. The intense floods, landslides, and erosion that occurred during the storm is thought to have uncovered previously buried land mines in river banks, swept known mines downstream to unknown locations, and buried other minefields under a layer of sediment and sand.

What does the presence of land mines mean to the traveler? In a word, that you should ask a lot of questions as you go off the beaten trail, and particularly in the north: Nueva Segovia, Jinotega, Matagalpa, and Jalapa, as well as eastern parts of Boaco. The locals know where the minefields are. Loose mines don't lie scattered randomly in the hillsides, they were placed at strategic locations like radio towers, bridges, and known Contra border crossings. The locals are your best sources of information. They'll be able to tell you if there were battles or heavy Contra presence in the area, if there are known minefields, and if the OAS teams have passed through to de-mine. In general, in the regions mentioned above you should not go snooping around under bridges or around radio towers, hike river beds, or go bushwhacking without asking first, particularly along the Honduran border (which isn't a good idea anyway). In towns like El Cuá and Bocay you'll find parcels of land in chest-high weeds even though the land on both sides is intensely farmed. Ask around, and look for the yellow *Area Minada* signs, then move on.

Puterías (whorehouses), barely disguised as "beauty salons" or "massage parlors," operate with virtual impunity, and every strip club in Managua has a bank of rooms behind the stage, some with an actual cashier stationed at the door. Then there are the street girls (and transvestites) on Carretera Masaya and around the Plaza Inter, and the nation's numerous auto-hotels, with rooms for rent by the hour. The situation is nowhere near as developed as the sex tourism industries of places like Cuba, but it is undeniable that foreigners have contributed in no small way to Nicaragua's sex economy. Travelers considering indulging should think seriously about the social impacts that result from perpetuating this institution, and should start by reading the section on AIDS above.

BEGGING

Inevitably, foreigners in Nicaragua are assumed to have lots and lots of money. You can definitely expect to have poor children and adults ask you for spare change wherever you travel in Nicaragua. The universal gesture is either a single outstretched index finger or a cupped, empty hand, both accompanied with an insistent, *"Chele, deme un peso."* It's low-key, nothing like the aggressive beggars in countries like India, so don't be worried or afraid. If you are against giving such handouts, employ the finger wag and keep walking. If you want to contribute, one cordoba is the traditional amount, and oftentimes the transaction is a great way to initiate a conversation.

Another poignant sight, encountered at sidewalk restaurants and market eateries, are hungry children waiting silently as you eat, watching you place food into your mouth just as eagerly as the skeletal dogs standing behind them. Your leftovers will

Many desperate Managuan families send their children to work at the city's traffic lights.

not go to waste here as they would at home—a small concession.

In many cities, increasing numbers of adolescents asking for money are glue sniffers, and your money will only go to buy them more of H. B. Fuller's finest. These *huele-pegas* are identified by glazed-over eyes, unkempt appearances, and sometimes a jar of glue tucked under a dirty shirt. Do not give them money, but feel free to give them some time, attention, and maybe a little food.

Visas and Officialdom

Passport and Visa Requirements

Every traveler to Nicaragua must have a passport valid for at least six months following the date of entry. A visa is required only for citizens of the following countries: Afghanistan, Albania, Bosnia-Herzegovina, Colombia, Cuba, Haiti, India, Iran, Iraq, Jordan, Lebanon, Libya, Nepal, Pakistan, People's Republic of China, People's Republic of Korea, Somalia, Sri Lanka, Vietnam, and Yugoslavia. Everyone else is automatically given a visa good for three months, which can be extended by going to the Office of Immigration (Dirección General de Migración y Extranjería, located in Managua across from Catastro and INETER, office hours 7 A.M.–4:30 P.M. Monday to Friday, tel. 249-2981), or by leaving and reentering the country. Additional requirements exist for those who intend to work, study, reside for an extended period, or engage in nontourist activities. Contact your nearest Nicaraguan embassy for details about the requirements.

Customs and Immigration

Upon entering Nicaragua, tourists are required to pay a $7 entrance fee. You also must be in possession of an onward/return ticket, a valid passport, and have evidence of sufficient funds. When leaving Nicaragua by plane, you must pay an airport tax of $20. Light-skinned travelers don't frequently experience luggage searches, as the customs agents are more interested in nailing rich Miami Nicas bearing loot for their

NICARAGUAN EMBASSIES ABROAD

North and South America

Argentina: Embajada de Nicaragua, Avenida Corrientes No. 2548, Piso 4, Oficina "I" (1046), Capital Federal, Buenos Aires, tel. 4951-3463, fax 4952-7557.

Brazil: Embajada de Nicaragua, Shis qi 03, conj. 1, No. 6, Lago Sul, Brasilia, D.F., CEP: 71605-210, tel. 365-2463, fax 365-2562.

Canada: Enquiries from Canada must be addressed to the embassy in Washington, DC, tel. 202/939-6570.

Chile: Embajada de Nicaragua, El Bosque Norte 0140, Dpto. No. 33, Los Condes, Santiago de Chile, tel. 234-1808, fax 231-2034.

Colombia: Embajada de Nicaragua, Carrera 19 No. 106-91, Santafé de Bogotá, tel. 612-8777, fax 215-7911.

Costa Rica: Embajada de Nicaragua, Avenida Central No. 2440, Barrio La California, (frente al Pizza Hut), San Jose, tel. 222-2373, fax 221-5481.

Cuba: Embajada de Nicaragua, Calle 20 No. 709, entre 7ma. y 9na. Avenidas, Miramar, Plana, tel. 331-380.

Dominican Republic: Embajada de Nicaragua, Av. México, No. 152, Condominio Elsa María, Apto. 1, La Esperilla, tel. 562-2311, fax 565-7961.

Ecuador: Embajada de Nicaragua, Av. 12 de octubre 1942 y Cordero, Edif. World Trade Center, Piso 4, No. 405, Quito, tel. 230-810, fax 228-957, email: embnicec@uio.satnet.net.

El Salvador: Embajada de Nicaragua, 71 Avenida Norte y Primera Calle Poniente No. 164, Colonia Escalon, San Salvador, tel. 298-6549, fax 223-7201.

Guatemala: 10 Avenida, 14–72, Zona 10, Guatemala, tel. 268-0785, fax 337-4264.

Honduras: Embajada de Nicaragua, Colonia Tepeyac, Bloque M-1, No. 1130, Tegucigalpa, tel. 232-7224, fax 239-5225.

Mexico: Embajada de Nicaragua, Prado Norte No. 470, Colonia Lomas de Chapultepec, Esquina con explanada y monte alti, Delegación Miguel Hidalgo, Código Postal 11000, México D.F., tel. 540-5625, fax 520-6960.

Panamá: Embajada de Nicaragua, Intersección de Avenida Federico Boyd y calle 50, Apartado 772 - Zona 1, Corregimiento Bella Vista, Ciudad de Panamá, tel. 223-0981, fax 211-2080.

Paraguay: Enquiries from Paraguay must be addressed to the embassy in Brazil, tel. 365-2463, fax 365-2562.

Peru: Embajada de Nicaragua, Calle Uno, No. 1064, Dpto. 202, Urbanización Corpac, San Isidro, Lima, tel. 474-797.

United States and Canada: Embajada de Nicaragua, 1627 New Hampshire Ave. N.W., Washington, DC 20009; 202/939-6531, fax 202/939-6532.

Consulado General de Nicaragua, 8370 West Flagler St., #220, Miami, FL 33144; 305/220-6900, fax 305/220-8794.

Oficina Consular de Nicaragua, 820 2nd Avenue, Suite 802, New York, NY 10017; 212/983-1981.

Consulado General de Nicaragua, World Trade Center N2, Canal Street, Suite 1937, New Orleans, LA 70130 ; 504/523-1507, fax 504/523-2359.

Consulado General de Nicaragua, 6300 Hillcroft, Suite 250, Houston, TX 77081 ; 713/272-9628, 713/272-7131.

Consulado General de Nicaragua, 3303 Wilshire Blvd. # 410, Los Angeles, CA 90010; 213/252-1178.

Consulado General de Nicaragua, 870 Market Street, Suite 1050, San Francisco, CA 94102; 415/765-6825, fax 415/765-6826.

Uruguay: Enquiries from Uruguay must be addressed to the embassy in Argentina, tel. 4951-3463, fax 4952-7557.

Venezuela: Calle el Cerezo, Quinta Candilejas, Urbanización Prados del Este, Caracas, tel. 977-4284, fax 979-9167, email: embnicve@mail1.lat.net.

Asia

Japan: Embajada de Nicaragua, Kowa Bldg. 38, Rm. 903, 4–12-24, Nishi-Azabu, Minato-ku, Tokyo, 106, tel. 3499-0400, fax 3499-3800.

(continues on next page)

ON THE ROAD

NICARAGUAN EMBASSIES ABROAD (cont'd)

South Korea: Enquiries from Korea must be addressed to the embassy in Japan, tel. 3499-0400, fax 3499-3800.

Taiwan: Embajada de Nicaragua, IF. 110 Chung Cheng Road, Sec. 2, Shih Lin District, Taipei, tel. 8281-4513, fax 2873-0908.

Thailand: Enquiries from Thailand must be addressed to the embassy in Japan, tel. 3499-0400, fax 3499-3800.

Europe

Austria: Embajada de Nicaragua, Ebendorferstrasse, 10–3-12, 1010 Vienna, tel. 403-1839, fax 403-2752; email: 113350.2341@compuserve.com.

Belgium: Embajada de Nicaragua, 55 Av. de Wolvendael, 1180 Brussels, tel. 375-6500, fax 375-7188.

Denmark: Enquiries from Denmark must be addressed to the embassy in Sweden, tel. 468/667-1857, fax 468/662-4160.

Finland: Enquiries from Finland must be addressed to the embassy in Sweden, tel. 468/667-1857, fax 468/662-4160.

France: Embajada de Nicaragua, 34 Avenue Bugeaud, 75116, Paris, tel. 450-04-102, fax 450-09-681.

Germany: Embajada de Nicaragua, Konstan-

tinstrasse 41, D-53159 Bonn/2, tel. 362-505, fax 354-001.

Great Britain: Consulado de Nicaragua, Vicarage House, Suite #12, 58–60 Kensington Church Street, London W84DB, tel. 171/938-2373, fax 171/937-0952.

Italy: Embajada de Nicaragua, Via Brescia 16, Scala 1, Int. 7–700198, Roma, tel. 841-4693, fax 884-1695.

Netherlands: Embajada de Nicaragua, Sumatrastraat 336, 2585 CZ, The Hague, Holland, tel. 306-1742, fax 306-1743.

Norway: Enquiries from Norway must be addressed to the embassy in Sweden, tel. 468/667-1857, fax 468/662-4160.

Russia: Embajada de Nicaragua, Mosfilmovoskaya 50, Korpus 1 Moscu, tel. 938-2064, fax 938-2701.

Spain: Embajada de Nicaragua, Paseo La Castellana, 127, 10-B, 28046, Madrid, tel. 555-5510, fax 555-5737.

Sweden: Embajada de Nicaragua, Sandhamnasgatan 40–6 tr, 11528, Estocolmo, tel. 468/667-1857, fax 468/662-4160.

Switzerland: Enquiries from Switzerland must be addressed to the embassy in Germany, tel. 362-505, fax 354-001.

---

friends. Should they go through your luggage you can expect to be taxed for carrying items you obviously don't intend to use yourself, especially electronics, jewelry, and perfume. If your Walkman, camera, or laptop computer isn't in its original box or accompanied by several more of the same, you will pass through customs in a flash.

Foreign Embassies and Consulates in Nicaragua

All diplomatic missions in Nicaragua are located in Managua, mostly along Carretera Masaya or Carretera Sur. The city of Chinandega additionally hosts consulates from El Salvador, Honduras, and Costa Rica, and the city of Rivas hosts a consulate from Costa Rica.

North and South America

Argentina: Las Colinas, primera entrada 1 cuadra al este, tel. 276-0857.

Canada: De Los Pipitos, Calle Nogal No. 25, Bolonia, tel. 268-0433 or 268-3323, fax 268-0437, email: mngua@dfait-maeci.gc.ca. The Canadian Embassy in San José has jurisdiction over affairs in Nicaragua.

Colombia: Planes de Altamira, de donde fue Motorama 1 cuadra al sur, 1.5 cuadras abajo, casa #82, tel. 278-4405.

Costa Rica: one-half block east of Estatua Montoya along Calle 27 de Mayo, tel. 268-7460.

Cuba: Carretera Masaya from the 3rd entrance to Las Colinas, 2 blocks east, 75 varas to the south, tel. 276-2285.

The Dominican Republic: Las Colinas, 3 blocks east of the Spanish Embassy, tel. 276-0654.

El Salvador: Las Colinas, Ave. El Campo Pasaje Los Cerros no. 142, tel. 276-0160.

Guatemala: Carretera Masaya km 11, tel. 279-9834.

Honduras: Carretera Masaya km 12, 100m hacía Cainsa, tel. 279-8231.

Panamá: Carretera Masaya 3ra entrada de Las Colinas 2 cuadras al este, 75 varas al Sur, tel. 276-0212.

United States: Carretera Sur km 4, Barrio Batahola Sur, tel. 266-6010, after-hours phone 266-6038.

Venezuela: Carretera Masaya km 10, tel. 276-0267.

Europe

Austria: From the Rotonda El Gùegùense, 1 block north, tel. 266-0171 or 268-3756.

Belgium: Consulado de Bélica, Reparto El Carmen across from the Esso station, Calle 27 de Mayo, tel. 228-2068.

Denmark: Plaza España 1 block west, 2 blocks north, one-half block west, tel. 268-0253.

Finland: Bolonia, 1 block north, 1.5 blocks west of the Hospital Militar, tel. 266-3415.

France: Reparto El Carmen, 1.5 blocks west of the church, tel. 222-6210.

Germany: 1.5 blocks north of the Rotonda El Gùegùense, tel. 266-3917.

Great Britain: Los Robles, del Sandy's Carretera Masaya 1 cuadra al sur, .5 cuadra abajo, tel. 278-0014 or 278-0887.

Italy: 1 block north and one-half block west of the Rotonda El Gùegùense, tel. 266-6486.

The Netherlands (Holland): Bolonia canal 2, one-half block north, 1 block west, tel. 266-4392.

Norway: 1 block west of Plaza España, tel. 266-4199.

Russia: Las Colinas, Calle Vista Alegre #214, tel. 276-0131.

Spain: Las Colinas Avenida Central No. 13, tel. 276-0968.

Sweden: 1 block west, 2 blocks north, and one-half block west of the Rotonda Plaza España, tel. 266-8097.

Switzerland: Consulado de Suiza, 1 block west of the Las Palmas Clinic, tel. 266-5719.

Asia

Republic of China: Planes de Altamira, from the Copa office 200 varas south across from the tennis courts, tel. 267-4024

Japan: Bolonia, from the Rotonda El Gùegùense 1 block west 1 block north, tel. 266-1773.

Special Interest Traveling

VOLUNTEERING

Nicaragua, because of its history of poverty and social experimentation, has always attracted non-traditional "tourists." Shortly after 1979, hordes of would-be revolutionaries poured in from all over the world to participate in the great experiment—they picked coffee, taught in schools, wrote poetry and editorials of solidarity, put themselves in the line of fire, and protested in front of the U.S. Embassy (the less ardent, Birkenstock-clad were called "Sandalistas"). Though the waves of idealist volunteers trickled off about the same time the FSLN government lost power, Nicaragua is still very much a needy country, and thousands of *internacionalistas* come

here to work, study, and volunteer every year. Anyone with an independent head on their shoulders and a couple hundred dollars a month for living expenses can create their own volunteer opportunity. Grants and awards abound for such individuals.

Many groups (both faith-based and secular) come to Nicaragua to complete short-term construction projects. Some of these charge the participants (or help them raise donations to fund the trip), and some are funded by other sources.

Habitat for Humanity is active in Nicaragua (website: www.habitat.org). **Global Exchange** is a human rights organization "dedicated to promoting environmental, political, and social justice around the world"; they have a series of "Reality

PEACE CORPS IN NICARAGUA

The Peace Corps *(El Cuerpo de Paz)* is a U.S. government program created by John F. Kennedy in 1961. Its original goal was to improve the image of the United States in the Third World (and thus decrease the temptation for the world's poor to turn to Communism) by sending young, idealistic volunteers deep into the countryside of developing countries. Participants sign up to receive an intensive three-month training in their host country's language and culture, as well as in technical aspects of their assignment. They then serve a two-year tour, receiving a bare-bones living allowance. After four decades, 165,000 Americans have served as Peace Corps Volunteers (PCVs) worldwide; there are currently some 7,000 volun-teers serving in more than 90 countries around the world.

The first Peace Corps Volunteers arrived in Nicaragua in 1969. PC-Nica took a hiatus during Sandinista control and was invited back in 1991. About 150 volunteers are currently serving in Nicaragua, situated in some of the most remote corners of the country, as well as nearly every major town and city (except Managua). They work in one of five sectors: Environment, Agriculture, Small Business Development, Youth at Risk, and Community Health. If you're interested in learning more, seek out a PCV in his or her site by asking *¿Donde vive el gringo?* or by visiting the main website at www.peacecorps.gov.

Peace Corps volunteers are found in the country's most remote corners, where they live for two years.

© IOSHUA BERMAN

Tours" in which participants can tour fair-trade coffee cooperatives, monitor elections, and have other unique experiences in Nicaragua (website: www.globalexchange.org). **Witness for Peace** is a politically independent grassroots organization "committed to nonviolence and led by faith and conscience." Based in Managua, Witness for Peace has maintained a permanent presence in this Central American country since 1983; they "examine and challenge unjust U.S. policies and corporate practices that hurt the poor majority in Nicaragua" (website: www.witnessforpeace.org). The **American Jewish World Service** has a program called the Jewish Volunteer Corps, which provides support for professionals looking to volunteer in Nicaragua and other countries (website: www.ajws.org).

If you are interested in setting up a work trip to Nicaragua for a group, several organizations exist to help plan the project and facilitate logistics: **Bridges to Community** works with small Nicaraguan communities on construction, health, and environmental projects (in the United States, 914/923-2200; email: brdgs2comm@aol.com; website: bridgestocommunity.org). **Educandonos**, or Learning in the Community, is an organization based in Managua that places groups and individuals in work and service projects around the country (tel. 268-0801, email: learningic @hotmail.com).

STUDYING

There are many possibilities for spending a summer, semester, or extended internship in Nicaragua. Programs range from biological fieldwork at remote research stations to language training to social justice programs like the School for International Training's semester program in Managua entitled "Revolution, Transformation, and Civil Society" (in the United States, 888/272-

7881). You'll find a complete listing of all the possibilities at www.studyabroad.com.

SPANISH SCHOOLS IN NICARAGUA

Nicaragua has a strong system of Spanish schools for travelers looking to learn some *Español*. Most follow the same basic structure of cultural immersion: four hours of class in the morning, community activities or field trips in the afternoon, and optional homestays with Nicaraguan families—for a fraction of what it costs in Costa Rica. **How to choose:** It goes without saying that some programs are better than others, and to a certain extent, choosing a school is as much a question of geographical preference as anything else. It is, however, a good idea to come down and personally look into a few options before making any commitments. Get a feel for the teachers, the professionalism of the business, and the activity plan. Do not trust everything you see on the websites.

NSS

Nicaragua Spanish Schools is a network of four schools, one each in León, Granada, San Juan del Sur, and Managua. Some find NSS attractive because it offers the option of studying and living in different cities and because the popularity of NSS virtually assures that you'll have classmates. Instructors are generally young and less demanding than other programs—great if you're the kind of student who takes charge, but not if you need a lot of discipline. The schools are independent and not of equal caliber—Granada was said by several students to have the strongest of the programs, and León delivered the least-impressive excursions. All four NSS schools start at $195 a week, and the price goes down the more weeks you study. Subtract $60 a week for no homestay. They can all be contacted in Managua at tel. 244-4512, email: nssmga@ibw.com.ni, website: www.pages.prodigy.net/nss-pmc.

Estelí

Estelí has the most schools, the lowest prices, and the coolest climate. **Escuela Horizonte**

Nica has one of the longest track records in town, and proffers the lofty vision of "promoting peace and social justice for those living in poverty, those struggling against class, race, and gender prejudices, and those fighting for political freedom." It donates part of its profits to local organizations and has an afternoon activity program that includes visits to local cooperatives and community development programs. One week of class, with 20 hours of intensive study, afternoon activities, and homestay with a family costs $150, discounts for groups of six or more; with large groups, some students can do one activity while others do another. Located 2 blocks east and one-half block south of Supermarket El Hogar, tel. 713-4117, email: horizont@ibw.com.ni, website: www.ibw.com.ni/~horzont/escuela.htm.

The **CENAC Spanish School** has also been around since 1990. Room and board plus 20 hours of class for $130 a week. Located on the west side of the Pan-American Highway, 150 meters north of the Shell Esquipulas (near the police station), tel. 713-2025, email: cenac@ibw.com.ni, website: www.ibw.com.ni/~cenac.

Run by a Belgian expat and his Nicaraguan wife, **The Language School** will set you up in the house of a local family, and provide 20 hours of private Spanish (or French or English) instruction per week. Class, room, and board will cost you $125 per week; discounts offered for longer stays. Registration is $35, and trips into the surrounding mountains can be arranged for a minimal extra cost, tel. 713-3835, email: tschool@ibw.com.ni.

The Association of Mothers of Heroes and Martyrs, contacted at its Galería in the Casa de Cultura, offers courses for $140, weekly; including class, room, and board; $70 for just class, tel. 713-3753, email: emayorga70@yahoo.com.

Spanish School Gueguense has seven years of experience and is located 250 meters east of the Shell Esquipulas. Its afternoon activities include trips to Jinotega, Quilalí, San Juan del Río Coco, and local Estelí attractions. Class and homestay cost $120 per week, tel. 713-7172. It also has an office next door to the Super El Hogar, tel. 713-4260.

Granada

Roger Ramírez's Spanish Tutoring Academy is reportedly the single most effective Spanish school in Granada. Roger is a fully certified and extremely demanding teacher who offers two-hour sessions, either once or twice daily. Class costs $80 a week, plus $60 a week for room and board with a family. Custom, group, and cultural activities can also be arranged, tel. 552-6771.

The **Escuela Palacio de Cultura** is home to the Granada chapter of the NSS. Located in a grand building on the west side of Granada's main plaza, it can be contacted through the central NSS office. **Casa Xalteva** offers the same package, tel. 552-2436.

San Juan del Sur

Escuela San Juan del Sur is located in the Casa de Cultura, across the street from the beach. The 15 teachers are all university-trained and relatively young, and classes are small: one-on-one, or two students maximum. They also offer a free hour-long sample class every Thursday at 3 P.M., tel. 458-2115, or at NSS in Managua.

María Dolores Silva was one of the founders of the original school above and now runs her own **Spanish Lesson Nicaragua,** tel. 458-2388, offering one-on-one class and homestays. **Vicente Lira** offers three hours of class a day for $40 a week, plus homestays for $50 a week, tel. 458-2237.

Laguna de Apoyo

If you prefer to study outside the city, the **Proyecto Ecológico** is the only Spanish school in Nicaragua in a purely natural setting—the lakeside lodge is in the crater of an ancient volcano. The spot is incredible, only an hour from Managua, yet still tucked away in its own green world. Lodging and food are excellent (homestays are possible too), and the organization is not-for-profit. One week costs $185, four weeks $685, five-day instruction only, $125, tel. 0882-3992 or 265-7225, email: eco-nic@guegue.com.ni, website: www.guegue.com.ni/eco-nic.

León

Escuela Leonesa (NSS), is located 1.5 blocks west of the Iglesia La Merced.

Managua

Located two blocks south of the Rotonda Bello Horizonte, **Escuela Hermanos** is also the NSS main office. Prices start at $195 a week, and go down the more weeks you study. Subtract $60 a week for no homestay. In the United States, call 805/687-9941. In Managua, tel. 244-4512, email: nssmga@ibw.com.ni, website: www.pages.prodigy.net/nss-pmc. Private lessons and tutoring are offered by **Raúl Gavarrette,** tel. 233-1298, cellular 776-5702, email: aige@tmx.com.ni.

WORKING

In light of Nicaragua's exceeding poverty and sky-high unemployment rate, you'll have a tough time finding paying work. Additionally, immigration laws force you to prove your job couldn't have otherwise gone to a Nicaraguan. Your best bet is to start your job search with your embassy and the many NGOs that work in Nicaragua, including CARE, Save the Children, ADRA, Project Concern International, and Catholic Relief Services. If you are a licensed English teacher you might also try the universities in Managua, though your salary will be the same as a Nicaraguan's (i.e., you'll be able to sustain yourself from day to day but you'll wish you had a cousin in Miami sending you checks). Universidad Centroamericana (UCA), Universidad Nacional Autónoma (UNAN), and Universidad Americana (UAM) all have English departments that may be looking for staff. For more ideas, check out the book, *Work Abroad,* edited by Clay Hubbs, available at website: www.transitionsabroad.com.

RESORT VACATIONS

For the more sedentary traveler content to stay put and be served, Nicaragua has a handful of resort-type destinations. **Montelimar,** on the Pacific coast, is an all-inclusive beach compound for a fraction of what you'd pay for the same experience elsewhere. The **Río Indio Lodge** in San Juan del Norte is a new installment of plushness, and in the mountains, **Selva Negra** offers a more rustic, honeymoon-style getaway on a German coffee farm and private wildlife reserve.

TOUR OPERATORS

Nicaragua's independent tour companies offer a huge variety of trips, from afternoon city tours to weeklong pirate cruises in the farthest reaches of the country, the logistics of which would be next to impossible for the solo traveler. These adventures cost money, and of course, as part of a group, you lose some independence; but then again, you are provided with security, freedom from making plans, and with some companies, luxury. For a full list of active tour operators in Nicaragua, see Tour Operators special topic, or go to www.intur.gob.ni.

Tour operators in Nicaragua are numerous enough to undoubtedly cover a wide range in their levels of responsibility—surely, in large part, a result of the range of responsible behavior demanded from their clients. Before choosing a tour company, research it well and ask lots of questions. Will you interact with the communities through which you'll be traveling? If so, are the people of those communities benefiting in some way other than the opportunity to watch you pass through their homes? Will your tour operator create an environment that allows you to practice the tenets of ethical tourism as listed in this section?

ALTERNATIVE TOUR PROVIDERS

There are several organizations in Nicaragua that work exclusively to promote low-impact, ground-up tourism, using infrastructures and programs designed to benefit campesinos living in and near Nicaragua's overlooked, undertraveled destinations. **COMARCA TURS Nicaragua,** initiated by a Canadian NGO, is attempting "to diversify and increase incomes of Nicaraguan families and communities through the development, training, and marketing of sustainable tourism micro-businesses, thus contributing to an enhanced standard of living throughout the country." Their programs are aimed at open-minded, unrushed foreign travelers, or in their words, "Sustainable Tourists who appreciate the time spent with a local family more than the night slept in the bed of a luxury hotel, or the thrill and treasures found in local transportation more than an all-in-one bus tour." COMARCA TURS Nicaragua has created a website geared specifically to backpackers, including an online map and guide to their menu of tourism opportunities, which range from horseback rides and hikes with campesino guides to multiday trip-planning

ON THE ROAD

ETHICAL TOURISM

The North American Center for Responsible Tourism suggests that travelers keep the following guidelines in mind on their trip:

• Travel with a spirit of humility and a genuine desire to meet and talk with local people.
• Be aware of the feelings of others. Act respectfully and avoid offensive behavior, particularly when taking photographs.
• Cultivate the habit of actively listening and observing rather than merely hearing and seeing. Avoid the temptation to "know all the answers."
• Realize that others may have concepts of time and attitudes that are different from—not inferior to—those you inherited from your own culture.
• Instead of looking only for the exotic, discover the richness of another culture and way of life.

• Learn local customs and respect them.
• Remember that you are only one of many visitors. Do not expect special privileges.
• When bargaining with merchants, remember that the poorest one may give up a profit rather than his or her personal dignity. Don't take advantage of the desperately poor. Pay a fair price.
• Keep your promises to people you meet. If you cannot, do not make the promise.
• Spend time each day reflecting on your experiences in order to deepen your understanding. Is your enrichment beneficial for all involved?
• Be aware of why you are traveling in the first place. If you truly want a "home away from home," why travel?

TOUR OPERATORS

EINSA

Ecotourism International of Nicaragua offers science-based trips to some of the least-traveled and most biologically diverse areas in Latin America. Trips include multilingual, highly trained staff; personalized service; and expert, on-site explanations and interpretations of the tropical ecosystem by world-renowned biologists and ecologists. Whether your interest is bird-watching, marine biology, butterflies, or just experiencing nature, Ecotourism International can provide a rewarding, educational, and unforgettable trip; call 276-0821 in Nicaragua, toll-free 877/867-6540 in the United States, or email: info@eco-nica.com, website: www.adventuresports.com/travel /econica/welcome.htm.

NICARAGUA ADVENTURES

Run by a Frenchman named Pierre Gédéon with an interesting penchant for skiing the scree inside active volcano craters. Trips are focused mostly on mountain biking and hiking expeditions, especially around the Pacific volcano chain, and include standard Granada-area tours. Offers two dozen full packages, many of which are combined with Costa Rica trips, tel. 883-7161, email: info@nica-adventures.com, website: www.nica -adventures.com.

ORO TRAVEL

Based in Granada (half a block west of the Convento San Francisco), Oro Travel has a standard list of classic tours, or it can design any trip you can imagine. Trips begin in Granada, Managua, or Peñas Blancas (for those arriving from Costa Rican adventures), Tel. 552-4568, fax 552-6512, email: pascal@orotravel.com, website: www.oro-travel.com.

NICARAO LAKE TOURS

Nicarao will make you a custom trip anywhere in the country; its specialty, however, is in the "Golden Corridor for Tourism," as it refers to the southern part of the country. Adventure, historical, natural, and fishing expeditions. Special events for groups and businesses. Located in Managua, from the Bancentro Bolonia, 120 meters east, tel. 266-1694, fax 266-0704, email: nlr@nicaraolake.com.ni, website: www.nicaraolake.com.ni.

ECO EXPEDITION TOURS

Wide range of theme tours including agriculture, adventure, cultural, and fishing. Also scuba diving in El Ostional and jungle trips to Bosawás and Reserva Indio-Maiz. In Managua, located near the Galería, tel. 278-1319, fax 270-5430, email: turismo@cablenet.com.ni, website: www.eco -expedition-tours.com.

services. Visit www.comarcaturs.com, or contact its office in Managua, tel. 248-6155, fax 249-2679, email: medanic@ibw.com.ni.

Run by a Californian who has been working with Nicaragua's street children for years, **Chela Personalized Destinations** "promotes global awareness through exploration" in the form of seven- or nine-night tours to Nicaragua. The cost is $1,150 and $1,350 per person, respectively, and includes everything except airfare. Chela's owner, Birgit Cory, assures that a portion of all tour profits goes to projects dedicated to keeping children off the streets of Nicaragua. In the United States, call 415/333-4104; website: www.chelatravel.com.

SPECIAL CONCERNS

Travel with Children

There's no reason you can't travel with your children. The family unit is strong in Nicaragua and children everywhere are cherished and adored, not seen as a burden. You may find traveling with your children helps form a new connection between you and the Nicaraguans you meet. That said, be aware your children will have to endure the same lack of creature comforts, change in diet, and long bumpy bus rides you do.

Nicaraguan children generally grow up with cloth diapers, which are painstakingly washed out and hung to dry in the sun. Disposable dia-

ON THE ROAD

CARELI TOURS

This is a full-service, all-inclusive tour company owned by the Chamorro family, complete with air-conditioned buses and 4X4s, offering guides, hotel reservations, conventions, charters and cruises, as well as car rentals and more. In Managua, located two blocks east of the old Sandy's and one block south. Tel. 278-2572, fax 278-2574, email: info@carelitours.com, website: www.carelitours.com.

NTUR

Group or individual tour packages, custom fit to your budget, and including free shuttle to and from the airport (they have a *hospedaje* in Managua as well). Del Canal 2 TV, 3 c Oeste, 75 varas Sur; tel. 268-6692, fax 266-2081, email: ntur@alfanumeric.com.ni, website: www.angelfire.com/ns/posadita.

TURAVIA

Tours throughout Pacific Nicaragua, specializing in Montelimar resort packages with airport pickups. Located 1.5 blocks west of the Mexican Embassy; tel. 270-0550, fax 270-0438, email: turavia.rep @ibw.com.ni.

SOLTOURS NICARAGUA

Bilingual staff, offering all the standard Nicaragua packages, including conventions, luxury hotels, plane reservations, and airport shuttles. 15 years experience. Located in the Edificio Policlínica Nicaragüense, tel. 266-7164, fax 266-1591, email: soltours@cablenet.com.ni, website: www.soltoursnicaragua.com.

SERVITOURS

In addition to the standard repertoire of fishing, hunting, cruises, and business meetings, Servitours has a small fleet of private planes and will fly you anywhere, anytime. Located in the airport in Managua; tel./fax 233-1624, ext. 2446-2498, email: stours@ibw.com.ni, website: www.servitoursnicaragua.com.

TOURS NICARAGUA

"Friendly, personalized trips" to all the major cities, plus volcano treks, jungle river safaris, beaches, and islands. Can also focus on archaeology, history, and rustic artisan villages. In Managua, located one block south of the Plaza Inter, tel. 228-7063, fax 228-7064, email: nicatour@nic.gbm.net, website: www.toursnicaragua.com.

SOLENTINAME TOURS

This is a German-Nicaraguan family-run business with a wide range of products, including volcano trekking, camping trips, city tours, and pirate trips from the Corn Islands up the Río San Juan (sacking and burning of Granada costs extra, we presume). They can also hook you up with windsurfing and parasailing equipment, tel./fax 265-2716, email: zerger@ibw.com.ni, website: www.solentiname.com.ni.

---

pers are available in most supermarkets, but they're imported from elsewhere, so they're not cheap. If the nature of your trip permits it, consider taking a supply of diapers along, or purchasing the cloth diapers (which are infinitely cheaper). Other necessities available in Nicaragua include powdered milk for formula, rubber pacifiers (*pacificadores* or *chupetas*), and bottles (*pachas*).

Women Travelers

In Nicaragua, as in all of Latin America, women are both adored and harassed to their wits' end by "gentlemen" hoping for attention. Catcalls and whistles are everywhere, often accompanied with an *"Adios, amorrrr,"* or a sleazy, *"Tss-tss!"* More often than not, the perpetrators are harmless, immature young men with struggling moustaches. It will either comfort or disgust you to know that Nicaraguan women are forced to endure the same treatment every day and you should note how they react—most ignore the comments and blown kisses entirely, and some are flattered and smile confidently as they walk by. Acknowledging the comment further is probably ill-advised, as it will only feed the fire. Be prepared for this part of the culture, and decide ahead of time how you plan to react.

Physical harassment, assault, and rape are much less common in Nicaragua than elsewhere

stereotypical ideal of a woman: decal on bus

in Central America, but certainly not unheard of, especially when alcohol is involved. Take the same precautions you would anywhere else to avoid dangerous situations. The Canadian Department of Foreign Affairs has an excellent online publication with specific advice for women travelers in Latin America, at website: www.voyage.gc.ca/consular-e/publications/her_own_way-e.htm.

As for feminine products, tampons can be difficult to find, as almost all Nicaraguan women use pads *(toallas sanitarias).* They are carried in most pharmacies and *pulperías,* and are usually referred to by the brand name Kotex, regardless of the actual brand. Nicaraguan women favor pads over tampons due to custom as well as social stigma, as tampons are sometimes associated with sexually active or aggressive women.

Gay and Lesbian Travelers

Nicaragua has a significant gay population, despite the fact that homosexuality is officially forbidden by the Catholic Church and the state. Lesbianism is rarely spoken of and never seen displayed publicly, while men who identify themselves as gay are typically associated with the transvestite prostitutes of Managua or the open cross-dressers in some rural towns. Nicaraguan society considers the submissive men in homosexual relationships as gay *(maricón),* and the dominant men as straight *(macho).* Homosexuals are sometimes socially accepted and sometimes chastised; discretion is advised.

There is one openly gay club in Managua, with a reputation for some of the best music in town; it is referred to as "El Bistro," or simply, "La disco," one block north and half a block west of the Estatua Montoya. Elsewhere, there are few publicly accepted opportunities for gay travelers to be open about their sexuality.

Disabled Travelers

Owing to bullets, land mines, and poor health care, Nicaragua has a significant population of *descapacitados* (disabled) who get around with much difficulty because of ruined sidewalks, dirt roads, aggressive crowds, and open manholes. While Nicaraguans agree the disabled have equal rights, no attempt is made to accommodate them, and the foreign traveler with limited mobility will certainly struggle.

The Los Pipitos organization, based in Managua with 24 chapters around the country, is devoted to providing support, materials, and physical therapy to Nicaragua's disabled children and their families. Los Pipitos is always looking for volunteers and support. The Managua office is located half a block east of the Bolonia Agfa, tel. 266-8033.

Money and Measurements

MONEY

Currency

Since 1912, Nicaragua's currency has been the cordoba, named after Francisco Hernández de Córdoba, the Spanish founder of the colony of Nicaragua. It is divided into 100 centavos or 10 reales. In common usage the cordoba is also referred to as the peso. The U.S. dollar is also an official currency in Nicaragua and the only foreign currency you can hope to exchange (although many communities along the Río San Juan also use Costa Rican colones). Travelers from nations other than the United States should bring their money to Nicaragua in U.S. dollars. The currencies of neighboring Central American nations can only be exchanged on the borders. Even in Managua, trying to exchange Central American currency is nearly impossible. As of January 2001, one bank—Bancentro—exchanges the euro, but the exchange rate is not favorable.

The runaway inflation of the Sandinista years (as much as 30,000 percent) is now a mere memory, and the currency these days is relatively stable. However, to offset inflation, the cordoba has been steadily devalued since its inception at the rate of approximately $0.37 every six months. That is, the exchange rate on June 30, 2000, was C$12.68 per dollar; on December 31 of the same year it was C$13.05. You can do the arithmetic yourself before arriving in Nicaragua, or check the Central Bank of Nicaragua's website: www.bcn.gob.ni.

Costs

Nicaragua is a budget traveler's paradise, as prices for lodging and food are lower than other Central American nations, notably Costa Rica. You can comfortably exist in Nicaragua on $20 per day, less if you're not traveling. Because there's more to do in Managua and taxi costs add up, budget a little more ($25–30) per day while in the capital. Needless to say, you can travel for less by eating the way the locals do and forgoing the jalapeño steak and beer, but why would you want to? Budget travelers interested in stretching their hard-earned dollars to the maximum should stick to *fritangas* and *comedores*, and avoid prolonged stays in the major cities.

Bank Machines

Known in Spanish as *cajeras automáticas,* ATMs are no longer a novelty to Nicaragua—since 1999 they've appeared in over 25 gas stations all over Managua. Any bank card affiliated with the Cirrus logo will work. You will receive your cash in cordobas, and you won't get a good exchange rate.

Wiring Money

There's a branch of Western Union in just about every midsize and large city in Nicaragua. Western Union is the most convenient way for someone to wire you cash, but the transaction fee is steep.

Bank Hours

Unless noted otherwise in this book, all bank hours are Monday–Friday 8:30 A.M.–4 P.M. and Saturday 8:30–noon. Nicaraguans receive their pay on the 15th and 30th or 31st of every month. Should you need to go to a bank on those days you can expect the lines to be extra long. Bide your time by watching businesspeople carry away large sums of cash in brown paper lunch bags.

Traveler's Checks

Traveler's checks for U.S. dollars are accepted in some banks, notably Bancentro branches. Although Bancentro accepts traveler's checks other than American Express, other banks do not. Checks for currencies other than U.S. dollars will not be cashed. You will need to show your passport to cash traveler's checks, and be sure that your signature matches your previous one or you'll convert your precious dollars into a worthless piece of paper.

Credit Cards

Nicaragua is largely a cash society, but in the last couple of years (thanks to a company called Credomatic), credit cards (Visa, MasterCard, American Express, or Diners Club) have been usable in Managua and better establishments throughout Nicaragua. This is not to say you can get far on your credit card in the countryside. In most major cities, an increasing number of hotels and restaurants will accept plastic, but in most of the country, your credit card is still more useful for prying open your hotel door; in budget establishments and open air markets, it's not even good for that.

Sales Tax

Nicaragua's sales tax (IGV or Impuesto General de Valor) is a whopping 15 percent—the highest in Central America. You'll find it automatically applied to the bill at nicer restaurants, fancy hotels, and upscale shops in major cities. Elsewhere, sales tax is casually dismissed. Should you decide to splurge on a fancy upscale restaurant (places where you'd expect to spend more than $6–10 a meal), expect to pay 25 percent of your

bill for tax and tip. Prices in this book do not include the IGV.

Tipping

In better restaurants a 10–15 percent *propina* (tip) will be graciously added on to your bill, even if the food was undercooked, the beer flat, and the service atrocious. You are under no obligation to pay it if it is unmerited. You might want to give a little something after getting your hair cut: 10 percent is appropriate. Skycaps at the International Airport in Managua will jostle to carry your luggage out to a waiting taxi. Remember their daily wage is around $5, so if you decide to tip them it shouldn't be any more than $1, and never accept the services of someone not wearing an official airport identity badge. Taxi drivers and bartenders are rarely tipped and don't expect to be unless they are exceptionally friendly or go out of their way for you. If you accept the offer of children trying to carry your bags, find you a hotel, or anything else, you have entered into an unspoken agreement to give them a peso or two.

TIME

Nicaragua is in standard time zone GMT-6, i.e., six hours earlier than London. Daylight saving time is not observed. That means during standard time, Nicaragua is in Chicago's time zone, and during daylight saving time, it is one hour behind Chicago. Don't forget, no matter what your watch says, you're always on "Nica Time"—everything starts late, and your whining can't change it.

ELECTRICITY

Nicaragua uses the same electrical standards as the United States and Canada: 110V, 60 Hz. The shape of the electrical socket is the same as well. Travelers from Europe and Asia should consider bringing a power adapter if they want to make extensive use of electrical appliances brought from home. Laptop computer users should bring a portable surge protector with them, as the electrical current in Nicaragua is highly variable. Spikes, brownouts, and outages are commonplace.

THE METRIC SYSTEM

Distances are almost exclusively in kilometers, although for smaller lengths, you'll occasionally hear feet, inches, yards, and the colonial Spanish *vara* (about a meter). Gasoline is measured in gallons. The most commonly used land area term is the *manzana,* another old measure, equal to 1.74 acres.

Communications and Media

MAIL

Post Offices

The national postal system is called **Correos de Nicaragua,** and it is surprisingly effective and reliable. Every city has at least one post office, often near the central plaza and adjacent to the telephone service (but not always). Legal-size letters and postcards cost about $.50 to the United States, and a little more to Europe. Post offices in many cities have a gorgeous selection of stamps. *Correo* is open standard business hours (with some variations), almost always closed during lunch, and open until noon on Saturday.

Receiving Packages

Always have the sender use a padded envelope instead of a box, even if the shipment must be split into several pieces; keep the package as unassuming as possible, and try writing *Dios Te Ama* (God Loves You) on the envelope for a little help from above. In general, mail service to Nicaragua is excellent and reliable, even to remote areas, provided you use envelopes and keep packages relatively small. Boxes, on the other hand, of whatever size, are routed through the *aduana* (customs). This means schlepping to their office at the airport in Managua, where you will wait on long, meaningless lines to have uncaring, ineffective (sniveling,

Go postal: every town has a *correos*

weasel-like) bureaucrats invent some exorbitant fee based on how much money they think you have in your pocket (yes, we have been burned there and we are bitter). Alternately, most major international courier services have offices all over Nicaragua, including DHL and Federal Express, but even these services don't obviate your obligatory pass through the customs office.

TELEPHONES

The national phone company is **ENITEL** (Empresa Nicaragüense de Telecomunicaciónes), but it is just as commonly referred to by its old name, TELCOR. Every major city has an ENITEL, as do most small towns. In some towns like Puerto Momotombo (León), there is no ENITEL office but one local family will let you pay to make calls on their own private phone. Calls within Nicaragua are not typically too expensive—$.50 for a five-minute call. If you don't see an ENITEL office around, try asking the locals if anyone nearby has a phone you can use.

When you enter the ENITEL building go to the front desk and tell the operator where you'd like to call. The operator will place the call for you, and if it goes through, will then send you to one of several private booths to receive it. When you complete the call, go back up to the front desk to pay. Alternately, look around town for **Publitel** phones. These phones are typically located on street corners in larger cities and operate by means of a prepaid calling card you can purchase in Nicaragua. Oftentimes the store nearest the Publitel phone will sell the calling cards regardless of whether it's a pharmacy, meat market, or hair salon. The cards come in several denominations and are a handy thing to carry around if you frequently call ahead to make reservations, etc.

Remember when making calls within Nicaragua, that you must prefix your number with a "0" when dialing out of your municipality or to any cell phone. Cell numbers begin with "88," "86," and "77," and cost extra to call. Satellite phones are wickedly expensive to call, begin with "892," and do not require a "0" beforehand.

International Calls

There are several ways to call home. If you intend to pay for it locally, follow the procedure above. However, the operator will ask you how many minutes you want to pay for, and that time amount will be the predetermined length of your phone call. No going over the limit; your call will automatically be cut off at the bell. If you have an international calling card account with a company like AT&T or MCI, tell the operator to connect you with the international operator for that company, or if they're not familiar with the process, ask them to dial one of the following three digit codes: **USA:** AT&T 164, MCI 166, Sprint 171; **Canada:** 168; **UK:** BTI 175; **Germany:** 169; **Spain:** 162. Once you connect with the international operator, place your call. In many larger cities the ENITEL offices will have specially marked booths with direct hookups to international companies like MCI or AT&T, circumventing the need to use an operator.

Fax

Most ENITEL offices have fax machines as well. A two-page international fax may cost you $4–5 to send, a local fax will cost about $1. Also check in copy shops, Internet providers, and post offices.

INTERNET

The information superhighway came to Nicaragua as early as 1993 but wasn't widely accessible until 1999, when makeshift Internet cafés began appearing in Managua. To date, there are some 60 Internet service providers in the country, servicing most populated regions of the country, usually for around $2–4 an hour. Nicaragua's telecommunications system is connected to the rest of the world by satellite, which is cheaper and more reliable than cable.

If you are staying a significant time in Nicaragua, have your own computer, and would rather not use webmail (web-based email accounts like Yahoo or Hotmail), there are several options for opening your own account, which you can then access by dial-up anywhere in the country. **IBW Communications** has reasonable monthly rates, including options with or without

Internet access ($10 a month for an email account). For your own ibw.com.ni address, visit the Managua office (200 meters north of the Semaforos ENITEL Villa Fontana), any of its regional offices around the country, or contact them at tel. 278-6328 or website: www.ibw.com.ni. It will install the necessary software and configure your computer, as well as provide reliable tech support as long as you are a customer. Other options are **IFX** (tel. 278-5528, email: info@ifxnw.com.ni) and **Cablenet** (tel. 277-0999, email: acliente@cablenet.com.ni).

Macintosh

Most of Nicaragua is PC, but for Mac addicts and those traveling with an iBook, the **iMac Center,** located in Managua one block east and half-block south of the Semáforo UCA, provides all kinds of Macintosh-related services, repairs, and products, plus cheap Internet service, tel. 277-2189, website: www.imaccenter.com.ni. Nicaragua's largest Mac distributor is **Desarollo Digital,** which can also be relied on for service and parts, tel. 278-3021.

NEWSPAPERS AND MAGAZINES

Local newspapers are hawked by street vendors before 6 A.M. every day and are also found in most corner stores. *La Prensa* offers fairly conservative coverage and the front page contains a list of events for the week; the Mosaico section on Saturdays features a particular region of Nicaragua as a destination. *La Prensa* was so anti-Somoza in the 1970s, the dictator allegedly had the editor, Pedro Joaquín Chamorro, bumped off. Needless to say, it didn't help his press. Not long after the revolution, *La Prensa* turned anti-Sandinista as well and has remained so to this day. During the course of the 2001 presidential election campaign, *La Prensa* ran a regular series of "flashback" articles recalling the atrocities of the Contra war in the 1980s and dredging up every unresolved Sandinista scandal available. *El Nuevo Diario* is more blue-collar and sensationalist—its coverage of popular scandals is often hilarious.

La Barricada was the Sandinista state paper that continued printing through 1998, when it folded due to economic insolvency and reduced readership. During its heyday, *La Barricada* was printed on the most modern printing press in Central America, courtesy of East Germany. It was subsequently sold for parts and scrap metal.

International papers and magazines are sold in Managua at the Casa de Café, a kiosk on the first floor of the MetroCentro mall, and in the lobbies of the major hotels.

Maps and Tourist Information

MAPS

The best Nicaraguan maps are not available in country (with the exception of the INETER topographic maps, which are sold for very specific regions and aren't suitable for large-scale travel in Nicaragua). They should be hunted down before your trip.

The overall champion map of Nicaragua is published by **International Travel Map (ITM),** scaled at 1:750,000, colored to show relief, and with good road and river detail. They also offer an excellent Central America regional map. International Travel Map, 345 West Broadway, Vancouver, BC, Canada V5Y 1P8, 604/687-3320, website: www.itmb.com. It's easily found in many bookstores and travel stores as well.

Nelles Maps' Central America map (1:1,750,000) offers a quality overview of the region (plus more detail on Costa Rica) and is good if you are traveling the whole area and don't intend to venture too far off the beaten track.

Guía Mananíc, produced by the Nicaraguan government, contains basic facts about Nicaragua and maps of the major cities. In the back is a two-sided foldout map of Managua and Nicaragua, dotted with numerous advertisements. The country map lacks detail, and the city maps are out of date, but the street map of Managua is invaluable for anyone spending more than a few days in the capital (and for anyone who needs convincing the roads truly have no names).

INETER, the Nicaraguan Institute of Territorial Studies, produces the only complete series of 1:50,000 maps of Nicaragua. Produced in the 1960s and photo-revised in the 1980s with Soviet help, these are the most detailed topographical maps of Nicaragua that exist. They can be purchased from the INETER office in Managua (and occasionally at regional offices) for $3 each. The Managua (main) office is located across from Policlinica Oriental and the Immigration office, tel. 249-2768; open Monday–Friday 8 A.M.–4:30 P.M.

Tactical Pilotage Charts TPC K-25B and TPC K-25C cover North and South Nicaragua, respectively, with some coverage of Costa Rica, Panamá, and Honduras at 1:500,000 scale. Designed for pilots, these maps have good representation of topography and are useful if you do any adventuring in the eastern parts of the country (far easier than carrying a stack of topo maps). Many smaller towns are shown, but only major roads.

TOURISM OFFICES

The Instituto Nicaragüense de Turismo (INTUR), an institution of the national government, is based in Managua and, since 1999, has been opening regional offices around the country. How useful INTUR is to you depends on your agenda in Nicaragua. Most INTUR offices can give you a list of the year's upcoming festivals and help arrange tours with trusted (and expensive) operators. INTUR's regional offices are small and underbudgeted (with the notable exception of Granada and Ocotal), and there is zero coordination with local governments in Sandinista-run cities. INTUR Managua produces and sells maps and the Guía Mananíc.

Nicaragua's Best Guide is a free, bilingual, quarterly magazine available in the airport, bookstores, and hotels (and distributed on TACA flights and in Miami). Each issue spotlights a geographical region with beautiful photography.

What to Take

"Take everything," her colleagues had advised Margaret Kochamma in concerned voices, "you never know," which was their way of saying to a colleague traveling to the Heart of Darkness that: (a) Anything Can Happen To Anyone. So (b) It's Best to be Prepared.

Arundhati Roy

Everyone has their perfect backpack that balances practicality with weight, and everyone has their own bag of traveling tricks (like bringing duct tape by wrapping it around your water bottle). While you obviously can't take everything with you, some items will be more useful than others. Use your own system when preparing for your journey, and consider the following suggestions:

LUGGAGE

Everything you take to Nicaragua should be sturdy and, ideally, water-resistant, especially if you intend to explore the Atlantic coast or any part of Nicaragua in the rainy season. Make sure you're comfortable carrying it for long distances or when running after your bus. The best kind of travel backpack is constructed with dual zippers that can be secured with a small padlock. Remember, most buses you ride in Nicaragua are retired, worn-out yellow school buses, refitted with an overhead rack and another long luggage rack on the roof. For rain and theft concerns it's preferable to have your luggage inside the vehicle with you and this will be harder to ensure if you bring a monster backpack. Paying for an additional seat may help, but even then you may be forced to carry that bloated rucksack on your lap so an additional passenger can sit down. If your pack is not water-resistant, a simple plastic garbage bag can serve as a pack liner. Take small padlocks to secure the zippers shut and "keep honest people honest." Many travelers take a small day pack or shoulder bag in addition to their backpack for hiking volcanoes or walking city streets.

CLOTHING

There's an old saying: "There's no such thing as bad weather—only improper clothing." Nicaragua is a low, tropical country, and your clothing should be light and breathable. If you plan on visiting the northern mountainous areas, something a bit warmer will be necessary, like a flannel shirt or lightweight sweater. Don't forget a shade hat that preferably covers the back of your neck. You'll use it during the entire trip to keep the sun off. In general, for typical backpack travel in Nicaragua you should take two or three changes of clothing, which you can wash and dry as you go.

Dressing for Success

It's not necessary to come to Nicaragua dressed for safari or wilderness (although Managuans laugh themselves silly watching gringos get off the plane dressed to hunt elephants). It is, however, very important to look clean. Having a neat personal appearance is important to Nicaraguans, as it is for all Latin Americans. Most travelers to Nicaragua are surprised to see how well-dressed even the poorest Nicaraguans are. Old, faded, or torn clothing is tolerated, but you'll find being well-groomed will open a lot more doors. In the countryside, Nicaraguan men don't typically wear shorts. Women concerned about receiving too much negative attention should make an effort to wear conservative clothing. Jeans travel well, but you will probably find them hot in places like León and Chinandega. Khakis are lighter and dry faster.

Footwear is also abundant, but you'll be hard-pressed to find shoes larger than a men's 10.5 (European 42). In the country, walking shoes with adequate ankle support are important, and a pair of sandals is useful everywhere you go. Also, if you plan on going out dancing or making any official-type visits, pack some appropriately nice shoes. You can get them polished and shined in any town park for well under a dollar. Take a pair of shower-sandals with you, or better yet, buy a pair of rubber *chinelas* anywhere in Nicaragua for about $1.

Laundry Facilities

See that cement-ridged square contraption in the corner of your *hospedaje?* That's your laundromat. Get a local to teach you the technique; then, when your arms get tired, pay your instructor $2 to finish the job. Be prepared to abandon most of the clothes you take, as extended laundering on concrete washboards, followed by drying on barbed-wire fences under the tropical sun, will devastate most of what you take. Dry cleaning is expensive but available in major cities.

PAPERWORK

Make a photocopy of the pages in your passport that have your photo and information. When you get the passport stamped in the airport, it's a good idea to make a photocopy of that page as well, and store the copies somewhere other than in your passport. This will facilitate things greatly if your passport ever gets lost or stolen. Also consider taking a small address book, credit cards, traveler's checks, your insurance policy, an international phone card for calling home, and a small dictionary and phrase book. Also bring a couple of photos of home, to show Nica hosts and friends, who will invariably be interested in your life "over there."

TRAVEL UTILITY ITEMS

A lightweight, breathable raincoat and/or umbrella will serve you well. Also pick up some cheap sunglasses, a toiletry kit, and a light line and clothespins for drying clothes on the road. A pocket knife or utility tool can be worth its weight in gold. If you intend to do any serious wildlife watching, pack binoculars.

Even travelers who don't plan on leaving the tourist trail should take a water bottle, though you can easily purchase a bottle as you travel, and then just refill it. Traveling with a small compass can be useful for orienting yourself in cities and on buses—the smallest, cheapest one you can find would be more than sufficient. A small flashlight is indispensable for walking at night on uneven streets, and for those late-night potty runs in your *hospedaje.* An alarm clock will facilitate catching those early-morning buses, and you might want a repair kit with a needle, thread, duct tape, spare buttons, and eyeglass repair kit, as well as small scissors, and earplugs (for snoring roommates and those damn roosters).

GADGETS AND GEAR

Most travelers like to carry a cassette player or Discman with their favorite music from home. Also consider a shortwave radio. Don't forget your camera and film, pen and journal, and art supplies and sketchpads. Use a small tape recorder to record the sounds of Nicaragua, otherwise indescribable back home—from the monkeys and roosters to the street vendors melodically hawking *quesillo.* Frisbees and Hacky Sacks are great for downtime, especially if you enjoy being mobbed by children wanting to play.

FIRST AID KIT

At the very minimum, your first aid kit should contain the following: rehydration salt packets, bandages/gauze, moleskin for blister prevention (although duct tape is a fantastic substitute and sticks better), tweezers, antiseptic cream, strong sunblock (SPF 30), aloe gel for sunburns, sulfur pills or other antibiotic for intestinal trouble, acetaminophen (Tylenol) for pain/fevers, eye drops (for dust), birth control pills, condoms, and antifungal cream (clotrimazole).

BEDDING

Any *hospedaje* you call home for the night will provide linens for the bed, but you may prefer to carry your own sheet with you—many travel gear companies sell silk and cotton sleep sacks that pack down to the size of a grapefruit and weigh next to nothing. You can sleep on top of it in questionable hotels, or wrap up in it in the cool early hours of the morning. In colder mountainous areas of the country, like Matagalpa and Jinotega, your *hospedaje* will provide you with a blanket.

CAMPING GEAR

If you plan to get very far off the beaten track, or spend a night sleeping on the ground, pack a lightweight tent and a small kerosene stove. Remember, if flying into Nicaragua, you will not be permitted to carry fuel for your stove. White gas is unavailable, but kerosene is easily found even in the smallest town; locals use it for small lanterns. Finally, don't leave the highway without a good compass, or a GPS unit. Take a small shovel for burying waste. In almost no conditions will you want a heavy sleeping bag, even in the mountains. A good summer-weight bag should be more than enough, or even just a cotton sack or sheet.

FILM AND PHOTOGRAPHY
Film Processing and Supplies

Quality film and basic camera supplies are widely available in Nicaragua, and there are modern camera shops in most cities. Film processing is considerably more expensive (up to $20 a roll with no doubles) and often of lower quality than back home. The biggest company is Kodak Express (sometimes known by taxi drivers as the chain's owner, Roberto Teranm), of which there are 18 shops in Managua alone, as well as one in nearly every major city in Nicaragua. Other chains include Fuji-Clinica, Agfa, and Konica. Black-and-white film is available in many photo shops but only a handful of private studios can process it; they do so by hand, and the cost can reach $40 a roll! Slide film *(película diapositiva)* and processing is just becoming available in Nicaragua, but supplies are limited and expensive. See the photography supplies section in the Managua chapter for more detailed information.

Photo Tips and Etiquette

Cameras are by no means foreign objects in Nicaragua, but in many towns and neighborhoods, they are owned only by a few local entrepreneurs who take pictures at weddings, baptisms, graduations, etc. and then sell the print to the subject. Because of this, some Nicaraguans may

© JOSHUA BERMAN

Photo tip: Always sneak up on your subjects.

expect that the photo you are taking is for *them,* and that you will either charge them for the photo, or that you are going to send them a free copy. In general, people love getting their pictures taken, but often insist on dressing up, stiffening their bodies, and wiping all traces of emotion from their faces. The only way to avoid this (apart from making monkey noises to get them to laugh) is to take candid, unsolicited photos, something adults may perceive as bizarre, and possibly rude. A solution is to ask first, concede to a few serious poses, and then snap away later when they are more unsuspecting but accustomed to your happy trigger finger. If you promise to send a copy, take down their address and actually do it.

Getting Around

AIRPLANES

Nicaragua's two local carriers, **La Costeña** and **Atlantic Airlines,** are both based at the International Airport in Managua and between them, offer daily public flights to Puerto Cabezas, Waspám, and Siuna in the northeast, Bluefields and Corn Island in the east, and San Carlos in the south. Flights are in single- and double-prop planes and may be a little bouncy at times. Don't be surprised if your pilots (who you'll practically be sitting next to) kick back and take a nap or read the morning paper after they gain altitude and throw on the cruise control (we're not kidding).

BUSES

Physical discomfort is important only when the mood is wrong. Then you fasten on to whatever thing is uncomfortable and call that the cause. But if the mood is right, then physical discomfort doesn't mean much.

Robert Pirsig

Nicaragua has a massive fleet of old yellow school buses, retired from the First World and custom fitted to transport Nicaraguans to and from the farthest reaches of their country. Each major

puddle jumper

© JOSHUA BERMAN

population center has one or two bus hubs, with regular and express service to the capital and nearby cities, plus rural routes to the surrounding communities. Generally speaking, Nicaragua's bus system is safe, cheap, and sure to be one of the most memorable parts of your travels. Enjoy being a part of the chatting, smiling, sweating crowd, even when you are packed so tightly into the mass of real-life Nicaragua that you confuse your limbs with someone else's.

In theory, *expresos* are buses that do not stop to pick up extra passengers en route to their destination. This is usually, but not always true. They are almost always faster than the *ordinarios,* or *ruteados,* which take their sweet time and pick up every Tom, Dick, or Pedro who waves his hand from the side of the highway. Microbuses, sometimes called *interlocales,* are minivans or short buses, and are a great deal if you can grab one.

Regardless of which type of bus you choose, in some terminals, you'll purchase your ticket before boarding, especially for *expresos.* In these cases, you may actually have an assigned seat. More often than not though, you'll board the bus, find a seat, and then wait for the *ayudante* (driver's helper) to come around and collect your *pasaje* (fare). Asking the Nica sitting next to you how much the ride should cost will help you avoid being ripped off (very rare). In some cases, if the *ayudante* doesn't have change, he'll write the amount owed to you on your ticket, returning later in the trip to pay you. This is normal. Most buses have overhead racks inside where you can stow your bags. Less desirable, but common, is for the *ayudante* to insist you put your pack up on the roof or in some cargo space in the back of the bus. It is obviously safer to keep your stuff on your lap or at least within sight.

Urbanos

We advise against using the Managua urban bus system unless you are with a Nicaraguan or another traveler who has experience with it. The routes are long and confusing and you and your fancy backpack are obvious targets for thieves. *Urbanos* are, of course, much cheaper than taxis, but it only comes down to a couple dollars—or less; you can decide how much it's

worth to not feel a knifepoint in your side. Actually, urban buses probably aren't too dangerous during the day, but during rush hour and nighttime, the risk shoots up. Most other major cities have a basic *urbano* bus loop and are much safer than Managua.

BOATS

In several regions of Nicaragua—notably Solentiname, Río San Juan, Río Coco, and the entire Atlantic coast—boat travel is the only viable means of transportation. Because gas prices are as high as $3–4 a gallon in these areas, locals get around in public boat taxis called *colectivos* that help cut costs. The areas mentioned above have different kinds of water travel and we've provided a boat vocabulary list for each region.

TAXIS

There are new Japanese models slowly joining Nicaragua's taxi fleet, but the vast majority remain the same tin-can Russian Ladas that were imported during the 1980s and, miraculously, are still chugging along. Granted, many windows don't open, windshields are shattered, and the seats are shot—but who cares when the engine works and there's a sound system more powerful than the one you had in your freshman dorm. In every city except Managua, urban taxis operate on a fixed zone rate, usually no more than $.35 within the central city area. In the capital, however, it's a different story, and you should never get into a cab before settling on a price (see Taxis in the Managua chapter). Strangely, most old Nicaraguan taxis have no handle with which to roll the windows down. If you can't stand the heat, ask the driver for the *manigueta de la ventanilla;* he's probably got it stashed up front.

TWO WHEELS

If you intend to ride a motorcycle or bicycle in Nicaragua be sure to bring your own helmet. The use of helmets is largely ignored by Nicaraguans—even when baby, junior, and

Custom ride: "El Chopper"

grandma are all crammed onto the motorcycle or bike, with dad pedaling. Helmets are quite difficult to find and are frequently poor-quality, lightweight models that offer little real protection.

HITCHHIKING

The Zen of walking out to the highway, sticking out your thumb, and ending up in the back of a breezy pickup truck as it speeds through the mountains and past smoking volcanoes is one of the most wonderful experiences to be had in Nicaragua. In general, hitchhiking (in Spanish, *pedir* ride, with the English cognate), is common in Nicaragua and, provided you are smart, is relatively safe. In most cities, setting yourself up is as easy as taking a taxi or bus to the *salida* (exit) and waiting a couple of minutes. We've tried to provide region-specific tips for hitching to and from individual cities. The farther into the countryside you get, the easier it is to score a ride, especially when you get off the paved road and folks start feeling more responsible for each other.

Obvious things to watch out for are drunk drivers, sketchy vehicles, and dangerous cargo.

Women should use extra caution; traveling alone is probably ill-advised. Hitchhiking is a main mode of transportation for soldiers and police officers, and standing next to them may be a good way to get a ride (actually, they may do the same to you, thinking that your foreign appearance is more of a ride magnet than their uniform and gun).

Nicaraguan drivers, true to their culture's desire to save face, may pass you by in a cloud of dust, but they nearly always make some attempt to exonerate themselves, usually in the form of an apologetic face and a hand signal. An upraised, rotating index finger signifies they are turning around soon, and a thumb and forefinger measuring out about an inch shows they are only traveling a short distance. Some drivers will use their entire hand to indicate an impending left or right turn, and others will bunch their fingers and thumb together and point the tips upward to tell you their vehicle is full. Some, flustered at how to respond to your request, may point forward or give some incomprehensible sign. Making eye contact, or catching them pulling out of a gas station, may give them enough *pena* (embarrassment) that they will feel obliged to let you in.

Payment for a ride is not expected, but you should certainly offer, especially if they have taken you a long way, or carried a large group of your friends. Gas is expensive, and your weight on a long trip costs money. If they turn you down, fine—if not, the experience is well worth a couple of dollars.

DRIVING
Rental Car Agencies, Car Insurance

Car rental services (including Avis, Budget, Hertz, Econo, and Hyundai) are easily found in Managua at the airport, the fancier hotels, and a number of agency offices and lots. In terms of price, renting a car here is comparable to just about anywhere else, so for Nicaraguan standards, it will be a huge chunk of your travel budget. However, if you have a group of five people or so, it can be a reasonable way to make a road trip to see the turtles, or to go anywhere else with limited public transportation.

Vehicular Safety

The most dangerous thing you can do in Nicaragua, without a doubt, is travel on its highways. Outside the cities, roads are poorly lit, narrow, lacking shoulders, and are often full of axle-breaking potholes, unannounced speed bumps, fallen rocks, and countless other obstacles. Even in Managua, you can expect to find ox-carts, abandoned vehicles, and grazing horses wandering the streets. Because there are no shoulders for taxis to use when boarding passengers, they stop in the right lane and let traffic swerve around them. Also expect macho, testosterone-crazed bus drivers trying to pass everything they can on blind, uphill curves. The fact that beer and rum are sold at most gas stations should give you an idea of how many drivers are intoxicated, especially late at night.

When possible, avoid traveling during peak rush hours in the cities, and after dark anywhere. New highway projects since 2000 have improved the situation in many parts of the country, but road and vehicle conditions are still hazardous and many drivers even more so, occasionally taking advantage of the newly repaved straightaways to speed like bats out of hell. Everywhere you drive, keep an eye out for dogs crossing the road. Experienced drivers suspect they are specially trained and then released on the roads to test driver reactions.

Getting Pulled Over

So how's that Spanish coming along? This is where your language skills will really pay off—literally. Police in Nicaragua are well known to be fairer and less corrupt than elsewhere in Central America. They are commonly called *la pesca* (a reference to fishing). They are often seen in groups at intersections and traffic circles, surrounded by construction cones, wearing orange gloves, and pulling over everything in sight—especially light-skinned drivers without diplomatic plates. Foreigners complain that the cops' definition of *mala maniobra* (moving violation, literally "bad driving") is just about any movement of your vehicle within their sight. Have your papers ready when the officer approaches your window, and know that calling him *compañero* is likely to double the bribe. Speaking of bribes, slick talking and some quick cash will get you out of some situations; however, honest Nicaraguan cops who not only won't accept your 50 cordobas, but will ticket you for the attempt, are known to exist. Also, paying off the police only serves to encourage and perpetuate corruption. You (and your soul) are better off playing by the rules.

In Case of a Traffic Accident

Do not move your vehicle from the scene of the crime until authorized by a police officer, even if it is blocking traffic. For lack of high-tech crime scene equipment, the Nicaraguan police force will try to understand how the accident occurred based on what they see at the site. Drivers who move their vehicle at the scene of the accident are held legally liable for the incident—even if you just move your vehicle to the side of the road. Any driver in Nicaragua who is party to an accident where injuries are sustained will be taken into custody, even if the driver has insurance and does not seem to be at fault. This custody will be maintained until a judicial decision is reached (sometimes weeks later) or until the injured party signs a waiver releasing the driver of liability. In many cases, to avoid a lengthy court proceeding and horrifying jail stay, it may be worth your while to plead guilty and pay a fine (which will probably not exceed $1,000, even in the case of a death).

Getting There and Away

BY AIR

All air traffic to Nicaragua (and the rest of Central America) is routed through the cities of Houston, Texas, or Miami, Florida. American Airlines has two flights a day to Nicaragua via Miami, and Continental Airlines has one flight every evening via Houston. Latin American airlines TACA, LACSA, and Sansa have service between Miami and Nicaragua, as well as to other Central American destinations. Iberia has one flight per day to Miami with connections to European destinations. Be aware of the $25 cash-only exit fee when flying out of Nicaragua (they're serious about the fee: in one incident, the tenacious taxman ran out across the runway to collect from a critically injured young woman being evacuated on a stretcher after a severe car accident).

BY LAND

The three legal northern border posts are (from west to east): Guasale (in Chinandega), El Espino (near Somoto), and Las Manos (near Somoto). While crossing into Honduras north of Puerto Cabezas may be technically possible, it is a guaranteed lengthy series of risky and expensive challenges and is not recommended. On the southern border, the legal border crossings are Peñas Blancas on the Pan-American Highway, and Los Chiles, reached via an hour-long boat ride from San Carlos. The feasibility of crossing into Costa Rica via the Río Colorado to Tortuguero is undetermined, but would most likely involve convincing the migration officer in San Juan del Norte that you are not trafficking drugs or jaguar pelts.

Crossings by foot, boat, or bus are pretty standard at both the Honduran and Costa Rican borders. Sometimes you breeze right through, sometimes there are multiple bag and document checks. Always remember that you always need an exit and an entrance stamp—at some of the borders, when leaving Nicaragua, it is possible to walk into the neighboring country with your Nicaraguan exit stamp, and then continue right past the other country's customs. You'll have a lot of explaining to do at your next encounter with customs.

Driving Across the Border

If you are driving your own vehicle, the process to enter Nicaragua is lengthy, but usually not difficult. You must present the vehicle's title, as well as your own driver's license and passport. You will be given a temporary (30-day) permit to drive in Nicaragua which will cost $10—should you lose the permit, you will be fined $100.

Managua and Vicinity

Introduction

Nestled in the ashes of ancient volcanic eruptions, pockmarked by crater lakes, and riven with tectonic faults, Managua's very geology speaks of destruction and rebirth. This is a city grown out of rubble and shaped indelibly by the desperation and tragedy of the past 25 years. Like the rest of Nicaragua, Managua is a place of contradictions and challenges. Once a quiet tropical village of

fishermen, in recent history Managua has been broken, burned, and bombed a half-dozen times, suffering just as often at the hands of nature as the hands of humankind. To this day, Managua continues to shake off the dust and recreate herself.

Less a city that "is" than a city that "was," there is history around every corner. Less an urban center than an enormous patchwork of neighborhoods, modern-day Managua is what a city looks like when everything has gone wrong. Managua is sun-baked and sweltering and not an easy place to get to know, but you will

Rebuilding statue, Managua

© JOSHUA BERMAN

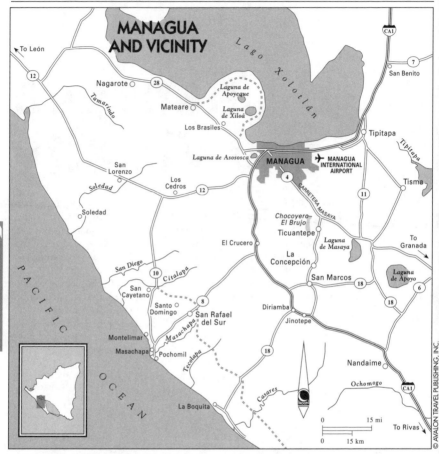

MANAGUA AND VICINITY

To León
San Benito
CA1
7
12
Nagarote
28
Mateare
Laguna de Apoyeque
Laguna de Xiloá
Tipitapa
Tamarindo
Los Brasiles
Lago Xolotlán
Laguna de Asososca
MANAGUA
MANAGUA INTERNATIONAL AIRPORT
Tisma
Tipitapa
San Lorenzo
Los Cedros
12
4
11
CARRETERA MASAYA
Soledad
Soledad
Chocoyero-El Brujo
Ticuantepe
Laguna de Masaya
To Granada
El Crucero
La Concepción
San Diego
10
Citalapa
San Marcos
18
Laguna de Apoyo
6
San Cayetano
8
Santo Domingo
San Rafael del Sur
Diriamba
Jinotepe
18
Montelimar
Masachapa
Pochomil
Masachapa
Tecolapa
18
Nandaime
Ochomogo
CA1
Casares
La Boquita
To Rivas
PACIFIC OCEAN

© AVALON TRAVEL PUBLISHING, INC.

0   15 mi
0   15 km

be rewarded for the time you spend trying. There is much to experience in this intense, loud, colorful noncity, and being among its 1.5 million inhabitants (nearly 25 percent of Nicaragua's population) is essential for anyone who hopes to understand the country.

THE LAND AND ENVIRONMENT

Both the lake and city of Managua lie in a broad rift valley. Managua sits precariously atop a loose bed of volcanic debris and ash, which shifts noticeably during tremors. Unlike other Central American capitals, Managua's geography serves well to disperse air pollution. However, the waters of the lake are completely defiled. Lago de Xolotlán (a Nahuatl reference to water), also known as Lago de Managua, is over a thousand square kilometers in area, only eight meters deep, and has been polluted since 1927 when the newly constructed Managuan sewer system dumped its first untreated load into the water. Still, the lake's edges are breezy and open to spectacular vistas: crater lakes and volcanoes to the west and north, and the Meseta de Estrada mountain range to the northeast.

Though Managua struggles with a mounting solid waste problem that has resulted in streets that are often trash-ridden and filthy, it remains a surprisingly green city: even the poorest neighborhoods are shaded by lush, diverse canopies of trees far older than the dwellings beneath them and often chock-full of squawking birds. Managuans care very much about their trees and several movements are underway to plant more trees along newly constructed roads.

THE PEOPLE

Upon entering Managua for the first time in the 1500s, the conquering Spaniards were confronted by a fierce people who defended their community to the last warrior. Managuans of the 21st century live with the same kind of intensity. Managuans, who refer to themselves as *Capitalinos,* have been challenged repeatedly by nature, politics, and adversity, yet never backed down. The pride and longing they feel for the Managua of old is as palpable as their disappointment in the Managua of today.

Nicaraguans are a resilient people and Managuans more so: the sweating taxi driver negotiating his Russian-made cab down unnamed streets; the university student clamoring for a bigger education budget; the seamstresses in the free trade zone demanding fair treatment; these are the people struggling to shape the new Managua into a more livable environment. Even the poorest *Capitalinos* helped gather relief supplies for their compatriots affected by Hurricane Mitch, when grassroots food and clothing drives successfully raised many tons of aid to be delivered around Nicaragua. These people are the reason that Managua, after so much disaster and bad luck, refuses to be beaten. Taking the time to get to know them will enrich your capital city stay immeasurably.

HISTORY
Precolonial through the early 1900s
Archaeological evidence uncovered in the Barrio Acahualinca shows that Managua has been inhabited since 4,000 B.C. More recently, the Nahuatl people that gave the city her modern name (*Mana-huac,* for "the big water vessel") developed a civilization at about the time of Christ. The Spanish encountered intense indigenous resistance in Managua and retaliated by razing the town and then leaving it abandoned for some 300 years. Under colonial rule, Managua remained an indigenous village subject to León's municipal government, located geographically (and politically) between Granada and León, whose rivalry has torn Nicaragua in half for most of its history. In a move to ease these tensions, Managua was declared Nicaragua's capital in the mid-19th century, shortly after independence from Spain and in blissful ignorance of the seismic faults underlying it. Managua, under the thumbscrew of the United States since investment began in the mid-1800s, was occupied by U.S. Marines twice in the early 1900s.

Earthquake and Disaster
In 1931, an earthquake of 5.6 on the Richter scale devastated Managua, still a small municipality of approximately 10 square city blocks. Over 1,000 people perished. For five years, Managuans rebuilt their city, only to see it consumed by flames in the fire of 1936. Again, they rebuilt. By 1972, Managua had been developed into a progressive, orderly city of nearly 500,000 inhabitants and had a modern center with two skyscrapers. But at 12:27 A.M. on December 23rd, an earthquake of 6.3 on the Richter scale instantly and completely leveled five square miles of the city. In the aftermath, Christmas decorations still hung in tatters from the rubble. Ten thousand people lost their lives, 50,000 homes were destroyed, and the city's entire infrastructure lay shattered in the rubble. Managua was without water, sewers, and electricity, hospitals lay in ruins, and the roads were choked with debris. This was a disaster from which Managua has never quite recovered, and the ruins of the old city center are still visible, home to poor squatting families.

Latin American nations rushed to the rescue with food and supplies, and U.S. president Richard Nixon deployed the U.S. military to help with relief efforts. But little of the material aid arrived at its intended destination. President Anastasio Somoza Debayle, consumed by avarice, saw to it that most of the aid money channeled through the "emergency committee" under his control ended up in his personal bank accounts. For Nicaraguans who'd lost everything, being forced to purchase donated relief items from the National Guard was the last straw: the revolution would fully erupt only seven years later.

The Revolution and Contra Years

The streets of Managua were again stained with blood during the widespread insurrection that finally overthrew Somoza in 1979. In *Blood of Brothers, New York Times* correspondent Stephen Kinzer writes of sitting with other journalists atop a hill in Managua and watching Somoza's planes drop bombs on his own people. This was after the FSLN had gained control of a number of Managua barrios like El Dorado and Riguera, but before they had forced Somoza and his guardsmen out of the country. Tens of thousands of Managuans died in the violence, many of whom are memorialized in shrines and monuments found throughout the city today. With the fall of the dictatorship, Managua fell stagnant, as the Sandinista government was forced to devote its precious resources to fighting the Contras, rather than rebuilding the city.

Managua Today

Managua is still very much the economic, political, academic, and transportation heart of Nicaragua and it is being rebuilt and reshaped more rapidly than ever. In 1997, the pace of new construction began to overtake the decay and blight: tens of kilometers of roads have been repaved, several luxury hotels completed, and a new cross-city bypass built. Spearheading this investment is the wave of nouveau riche Managuans (a.k.a. Nicas Ricas) returning from Miami who, after years of self-imposed exile, are arriving with a new vision for Nicaragua's capital (and a new social scene). Managua is home to nearly a quarter of the nation's population, and it has tripled in size in the last 30 years, primarily because throughout Nicaraguan history, any hardship affecting the countryside—be it war or natural disaster—has inevitably spurred a new wave of Managua-bound refugees.

Managua was not as affected as other cities during Hurricane Mitch in October of 1998; most of the rain fell north of the city. But that same rain rushed into Lake Xolotlán, bearing tons of sediment torn out of northern hillsides, and caused the lake to rise over three meters in four days. The waterfront was severely flooded, electric towers stood a meter deep in water, and the residents of poorer lakeside barrios had to move inland. The Río Tipitapa that connects Lake Xolotlán to Lake Cocibolca and, traditionally, only bore water once every 20 years, became an active waterway for two full years.

SAFETY

Compared to other Latin American capitals, Managua is safe, even more so than San José, Costa Rica. Crime exists, to be sure, and the best way to stay out of trouble is to avoid areas where you'll find it. Questionable barrios include Renée Schick, Jorgé Dimitrov, La Fuente, San Judas, Villa Venezuela, Batahola, Las Americas, Bello Amanecer, Vida Nueva, Los Pescadores, Domitila Lugo, Santana, and Hialeah. In addition, the walk between the *hospedajes* of Barrio Martha Quezada and the Plaza Inter should be avoided after dark (if this latter point gets repeated in this book, it is with good reason, as this small and seemingly peaceful section of town is increasingly home to braver and braver knife-bearing teenagers). Also, watch yourself in crowds, particularly those of the Mercado Oriental, urban buses, and sporting, music, or political events.

Be smart if you decide to brave Managua's *rutas* (city buses). Avoid buses that are so overly crowded you can't keep your hands on your belongings. Keep your bags in your hands and in front of you, and if you've got a small padlock, use it to keep the bag shut. One technique of bus thieves is to slice open your bag or pocket and remove the contents without your noticing—and if you do notice, they've got a knife. Avoid *rutas* during rush hours (6–8:30 A.M. and 4:30–7:30 P.M.) and after sundown. Stay near the front of the bus within sight of the driver, who will often keep an eye on you.

ADDRESSES IN MANAGUA

Locating addresses in Managua is unlike any system you've ever seen, but with a few tips, some basic vocabulary, and a couple of examples, you'll master it in no time. Street names and house numbers are few and far between, and where they do exist, they are universally ignored. Addresses in Managua begin with a landmark (either existing or historical) that is then followed by a listing of how many *cuadras* (blocks) should be traveled and in which direction. Remember this: north is *al lago* (toward the lake); east is *arriba* (up, referring to the sunrise); south is *al sur* (to the south); and west is *abajo* (down, where the sun sets).

Some other key phrases to know are *contiguo a* (next door to), *frente a* (across from), *casa esquinera* (corner house), and *a mano derecha/izquierda* (on the right/left-hand side). Also note that *varas* are often used to measure distances of less than one block; this is an old colonial measurement nearly equivalent to a meter. Directions throughout this chapter are given in English for consistency's sake, but always beginning with the landmark exactly as it is referred to in Spanish. By studying the following examples, you should be able to find your way around with few hassles.

De la Plaza España, tres cuadras abajo, tres c. al lago, casa esquinera.
From the Plaza España, three blocks west, three north, corner house.

De donde fue el Sandy's, 200 varas arriba, frente al gran hotel.
From where Sandy's used to be, 200 meters to the east, across from the big hotel.

De los semáforos El Dorado, dos c. al sur, una c. arriba, casa lila.
From the El Dorado traffic light, two blocks south, one east, purple house.

Reparto San Juan, de la UNIVAL, 50 varitas al lago, edificio de cinco pisos.
In the San Juan neighborhood, just 50 meters north of the UNIVAL, five-story building.

ORIENTATION

Most budget travelers choose a *hospedaje* within Barrio Martha Quezada, a neighborhood with most services and a long history of hosting *internacionalistas* and Peace Corps Volunteers. From there, one can easily walk to the Plaza de la Revolución to visit the lakefront and many of the sights listed below (always take a cab in the late afternoon or at night). Carretera Masaya is the main drag for *discotecas* (discos), casinos, and restaurants; and the Rotonda Bello Horizonte is another nightlife hot spot with outdoor cafés and strolling bands of mariachis. The safest, most upscale central Managua neighborhoods are Los Robles, Altamira, San Juan, and Bolonia.

GETTING AROUND

Managua's sprawling layout is devoid of a true city center, and its congested streets and perplexing system of directions make exploration a challenging endeavor. The addresses given in this book provide enough information for a taxi driver (use Directions in Managua special topic to help you translate). If you plan on staying for a more extended period, learning the *ruta* bus system will save you a lot of coin, as taxi fares add up quickly. When walking Managua's rutted streets, be extra careful that you don't fall into one of the thousands of uncovered, ankle-breaking manholes, sometimes up to three meters deep and alternately known as "gringo traps." It is rumored that victims who break through the initial layer of trash and sludge will find themselves in the very depths of hell—or, even worse, washed into the waters of Lake Xolotlán. Watch your step.

Taxis

Managua's 14,000 taxis are easier to find than avoid—odds are if you even approach the edge of the street, you'll have taxis driving circles around you and beeping for your attention. Taxis won't take you anywhere in Managua for less than about $1, but you should never have to pay more than $5 to go from one end of Managua to the other (i.e., from the airport to Barrio Martha Quezada).

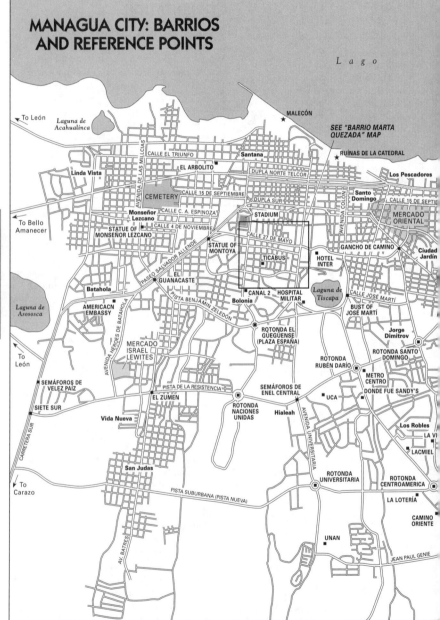

MANAGUA CITY: BARRIOS AND REFERENCE POINTS

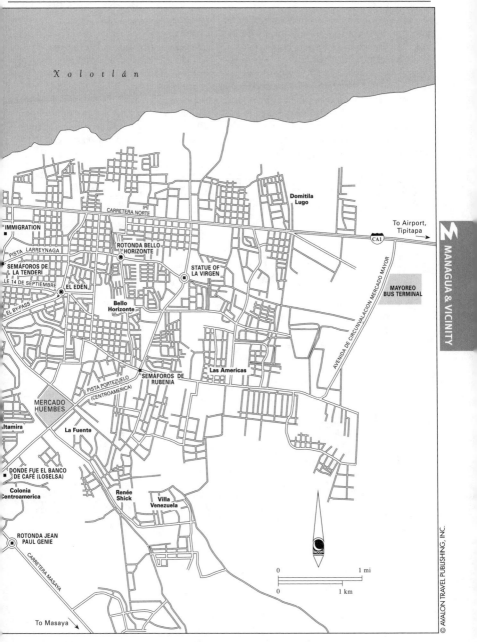

X o l o t l á n

CARRETERA NORTE

Domitila
Lugo

IMMIGRATION

To Airport,
Tipitapa

CA1

ROTONDA BELLO
HORIZONTE

PISTA LARREYNAGA

SEMÁFOROS DE
LA TENDERÍ

STATUE OF
LA VIRGEN

LE 14 DE SEPTIEMBRE

EL EDÉN

MAYOREO
BUS TERMINAL

EL BY-PASS

Bello
Horizonte

AVENIDA DE CIRCUNVALACIÓN MERCADO MAYOR

SEMÁFOROS DE
RUBENIA

Las Americas

MERCADO
HUEMBES

PISTA PORTEZUELO
(CENTROAMERICA)

ltamira

La Fuente

DONDE FUE EL BANCO
DE CAFÉ (LOSELSA)

Colonia
Centroamerica

Renée
Shick

Villa
Venezuela

ROTONDA JEAN
PAUL GENIE

MOON

CARRETERA MASAYA

0   1 mi

0   1 km

To Masaya

MANAGUA & VICINITY

© AVALON TRAVEL PUBLISHING, INC.

Taxis do not have meters in Managua, so be sure to settle on a price—before getting in the vehicle! This is a subtle art: begin by leaning into the passenger seat window and reading your directions to the *taxista*. After he responds with an offer, know that the negotiations never go back and forth more than two or three times, and once you've accepted a price, be prepared not to gripe about it (remember as you argue over the equivalent of a couple pennies that these guys scrape by to support their families by driving 12 hours a day, six or seven days a week). Each additional person raises the fare, and what you pay depends ultimately on how well you bargain.

Taxis with red plates are officially registered and belong to cooperatives. They're more professional and typically safer, but their prices are a tad higher. Some newer fleets have air-conditioning and radio service, and can be telephoned to pick you up anywhere in town (check the phone book for taxi *cooperativas*). White-plated taxis are *piratas* (unregistered and illegal), and though less expensive, you get what you pay for. In April of 2001, a government operation began to remove the nearly 4,000 *piratas* from circulation.

SIGHTS AND ATTRACTIONS

Most of Managua's historical buildings and sights can be visited in a single morning's walk. In most

cases, the relevance of the city's monuments and buildings is understated. To appreciate what Managua's sights mean to its inhabitants, make an effort to talk with them. Try striking up conversations with your taxi driver or anyone on the street about old-time Managua, what happened during the revolution, the 1980s, and how the city has changed and continues changing.

Plaza de la Revolución and the Old City Center

In pre-Sandinista days, **Plaza de la Revolución** was known as Plaza de la República. Today, it still forms a "city center" of sorts, around which are located many of the historical sights of Managua, and is best visited early in the morning, when the breeze off the lake is cool, the trees are full of birds, and the streets are safer.

Catedral Santiago de los Caballeros had barely been completed when the earthquake of 1931 struck. It survived that one, but was significantly weakened in 1972, still standing, but unusable. *Las Ruinas de la Catedrál* (as they're known now) have remained a standing testament to the earthquake and are Managua's most captivating tourist attraction. If INTUR hasn't closed it for safety reasons (which it does whenever Managua experiences tremors), its ravaged and sunlit interior can be a cool, quiet refuge in which to contemplate the Managua of old. Open daily, 9 A.M.–5 P.M., entrance $1, tel. 222-4820. Bring a sketchbook and pencils.

The president doesn't live in the **Casa Presidencial,** but he does his work there. The postmodern, eclectic-looking building, built just after Hurricane Mitch, was funded largely by foreign donors.

The **Palacio Nacional de Cultura** was recently restored and painted a vivid yellow, and is home to Nicaragua's **National Museum** (see below). At various times, it has also housed the Ministry of Housing, the National Congress (Sandinista commandos raided the building in 1978 and held the entire Congress hostage, winning international recognition and the liberation of several political prisoners), the treasury, and the comptroller-general. The *palacio* is also home to the national library, several murals, and the Institute of Culture. The parking garage–looking framework tucked behind it is a building that was under construction when the 1972 earthquake hit.

El Centro Cultural de Managua is housed in the first two floors of what was once a much taller Gran Hotel, Managua's principal lodging before 1972. It is now a green two-story building with murals on the outside whose first floor is home to continually updated art exhibits, concerts, puppet shows, and dances. In addition to a pair of public bathrooms, the second floor hosts studios of prominent Nicaraguan artists. The centro's hallways are lined with striking black-and-white photographs of old Managua, pre- and post-earthquake, and are a must-see to understand how radically Managua was rebuilt. Handicraft fairs are held here the first Saturday of each month and carved into the southeast corner of the building is **La Cavanga,** a bar built in the style of 1950s Managua, where you can catch live acoustic music on weekend nights. It's also worth sneaking up to the roof to see how the upper floors of the old hotel were never replaced, yet another monument to the earthquake. At the building's western end is the old **Cinema Gonzalez,** reincarnated as a Coca-Cola–sponsored evangelical church.

President Alemán received much international criticism for building the **Fuente Audiovisual** while Nicaragua was still recovering from Hurricane Mitch. The sound-and-light show happens twice every evening to the dancing of the fountain waters, 6–7:15 P.M. and 9–10 P.M.

Set in the small green space of the **Parque Central** are several monuments of historical significance. The **Tomb of Comandante Carlos Fonseca,** father of the revolution, is guarded by an eternal flame. Buried across from him is **Santos Lopez,** a member of General Sandino's "crazy little army" in the 1930s who helped train latter-day Sandinistas in Sandino's theology and the art of guerrilla warfare. In the center of the park is a gazebo called **El Templo de la Música** whose historical frieze highlights the arrival of Columbus, Rafael Herrera fighting pirates, independence from Spain, Andrés Castro fighting William Walker, and more. It's just as interesting for the antics of the sparrows that inhabit its arches.

The **Plaza de la Cultura República de Guatemala** is a small park dedicated to Guatemalan author Miguel Angel Asturias Rosales. Asturias received the Nobel Prize in literature in 1967 for his colorful writings, rooted in national individuality and Native American traditions. He wrote frequently of the tyranny of dictators, the beauty and hostility of nature, and the struggle against domination by U.S. trusts, themes with which the Sandinista government felt much empathy.

West of the Parque Central is the immense **Palacio de Telecomunicaciones** (ENITEL), and across the street, two colonial-style homes that also withstood the earthquake—not much else did in this neighborhood, including a *discoteca* on the same block that collapsed and killed nearly everyone inside.

Parque Rubén Darío is adjacent to the Parque Central and dominated by a marble statue to Nicaragua's beloved poet. Built in 1933, it was restored in 1998 with the help of the Texaco Corporation (whose logo is displayed a little too prominently on the statue's base). The **Teatro Rubén Darío** was designed by the same architects that created New York's Metropolitan Opera House and also survived the earthquake. Filled with marble and brass, this is a classy place to take in a performance of dance, theater, or music. Not a cheap night out, but the second-floor balcony offers a wonderful view of the lake, and the crowds give you a glimpse of Managua's upper crust. Check the newspaper for performances or call 266-3630 or 228-4021.

Across the street is a decrepit park in memory of **Samora Moises Machel,** leader of the guerrilla movement that brought independence to Mozambique, a nation whose history of attempted socialism, counterrevolution, and democracy parallels Nicaragua's.

The **Plaza de la Fé** (Plaza of Faith) was built during Alemán's administration in tribute to Pope John Paul II's second visit to Nicaragua in 1996. Spartan, clean, and ringed with white cast-iron benches, it boasts the only public trash cans in the city (just to the west, hungry gangs of children pick through uncontained piles of garbage in empty lots). Managua's northern limit is defined by the blustery shoreline of Lake Xolotlán, and the **Malecón** is a public walkway along the water's edge lined with food and drink stands. Between the Malecón and the monument to the pope, a large blue-and-white **grandstand** provides a good place from which to check out the city skyline and watch people along the Malecón. To the east is a brass statue of **Simón Bolívar,** hero of the Latin American liberation movement.

Los Escombros are the grass-lined ruins of old downtown Managua, where no one dares build, and where families squat in the standing hulks of what the earthquake didn't pull completely to the ground. Not a safe area after dark.

You might be surprised to find a lighthouse in the middle of an inland city, but rather than guide ship traffic through downtown traffic, the **Monumento de la Paz** is meant to lead Nicaragua toward a new era of peace. Beneath the concrete are buried the destroyed remains of thousands and thousands of weapons from the Contra war, many of which—including a tank—can be seen protruding through the concrete. Inaugurated by Doña Violeta in the early days of her presidency, the concrete park surrounding the monument is disturbingly apocalyptic.

The striking statue **El Guerrillero sin Nombre** (The Nameless Guerrilla Soldier) is an imposing, gold-painted, and powerful looking (and well-endowed) man, clutching a pick-axe in his right hand and an AK-47 in his upraised, hulklike left hand. This is an important city landmark and a symbol of the revolution's aspirations, inscribed with the words of Sandino that translate: "Only the laborers and farmers will go to the end." Across the street is another photogenic **statue honoring the worker,** put up by the Liberal government to counter the monster soldier.

Across from the new *cancillería* building where the old Iglesia de San Antonio used to stand, is **the monument to victims of the earthquake of 1972.** This touching statue was the brainchild of journalist Aldo Palacios in 1994. It shows a man standing amidst the wreckage of his home and is inscribed with the poem *Requiem a una Ciudad Muerta* by Pedro Rafael Gutierrez.

La Avenida Bolívar

One of the few Managua streets known by name, Bolívar runs south from the Nameless Guerrilla statue, past several noteworthy sites. One block south of the Guerrillero sin Nombre, the southwest corner with a lone wooden telephone pole marks **the site of journalist Pedro Joaquin Chamorro's assassination** as he drove to his office on January 10, 1978. Whether the drive-by was paid for by Tachito or his business partner in the infamous blood bank business was never determined, and Chamorro's death was the spark that finally brought fire to the revolution. Directly behind the telephone pole is a concrete monument. Continuing south, you'll pass some government buildings and basketball courts before coming to the **National Arboretum** on your left, home to over 180 species of trees found in Nicaragua. It is practically unvisited except by local school groups and is especially attractive in March, when the fragrant *sacuanjoche* (Nicaragua's national flower) blooms brightly; the scarlet flowers of the *malinche* tree come out from May through August. The trees are planted atop the remnants of Somoza's **Hormiguero** (Anthill), a military base belonging to the National Guard and destroyed in 1972 by the earthquake. This is the site where popular legend has it that on February 21, 1934, after meeting with President Sacasa at his home on the Tiscapa Crater, General Sandino was ambushed and assassinated. Beware the ghosts. Foreigners pay $.50 entrance fee. It's open Monday–Saturday, 8 A.M.–5 P.M.

Passing the Plaza Inter mall and cinema, turn left behind the Hotel Intercontinental to access the Tiscapa Crater. The twin-towered monument halfway up the road is the **Monumento Roosevelt,** which once delineated the southern terminus of the city, pre-earthquake. Twenty meters farther up the hill is the **decapitated statue of justice.** Continuing upward, you'll enter the **Parque de la Paz** on the lip of the Tiscapa crater. Here you'll find an enormous Nicaraguan flag and **the famous silhouette of Sandino** that accompanies it, always guarded by an armed soldier. The statue of Sandino was erected atop the wreckage of Somoza's presidential mansion, and just down the hill from his infamous jail for political prisoners—**Las Masmorras** (inaccessible). Daniel Ortega and many other FSLN leaders were held here at one point, and during the 1980s, these same men held the dungeon keys. Today, this is a Peace Park open during daylight hours, and with a fantastic view of the city and the crater lake of Tiscapa.

The **Laguna de Tiscapa** is one of several crater lakes in Managua. In the 1980s a sewage line was diverted to dump raw effluent into the crater and now, needless to say, the water is contaminated, to the disgust of local residents who fondly recall swimming there in their childhood. Inside the confines of the crater, at the edge of the lagoon, is an **abandoned amphitheater** once popular for concerts. On the northeast side of Laguna Tiscapa, just two blocks from the Ministerio de Gobernación, is the site of the **old U.S. Embassy,** destroyed during the earthquake.

Other Sights of Natural and Historical Interest

At the center of an immense field of young coconut trees along the Carretera Masaya is the new cathedral, **Catedral de la Inmaculadá Concepción de María,** constructed just two years after the conclusion of the civil war. Commissioned by American Thomas Monahan and designed by Mexican architect Ricardo Legorretta, this is the successor to Managua's original cathedral. Dynamic and open, it houses the Dutch bells of the old cathedral. Playing on the soaring forms of Spanish colonial architecture and using colors and materials of the Latin culture, the new cathedral is home to the pulpit of Nicaragua's famous and controversial Cardinal Miguel Obando y Bravo. Mass is celebrated Tuesday – Saturday at noon and 6 P.M., and Sunday at 11 A.M. and 6 P.M., tel. 278-4232.

The **Laguna de Asososca** is an important source of Managua's drinking water, so it is well protected. You can get a good view of it from the Parque las Piedrecitas on Carretera Sur. The name *piedrecitas* refers to the nearby volcanic rock outcroppings, testament to what's cooking below the Earth's surface.

In the quiet residential barrio of San Cristóbal is a **monument to Bill Stewart,** the U.S. journalist

© TOMÁS STARGARDTER

MANAGUA & VICINITY

Unfortunately, you'll find a diverse array of wildlife for sale at Managua's traffic lights.

for ABC-TV whose death at the hands of the National Guard was captured by his cameraman. The resulting news footage, when released the following day to television audiences, was the blow that broke U.S. support of Somoza's faltering regime. Located one block west and two blocks south of the semáforo de El Dorado.

On the south side of the street a block east of the Plaza Inter is an old pavilion known as **La Tribuna.** In the pre-Somoza days it was used by Presidents Chamorro and Zelaya for grand ceremonies; it was damaged in the earthquake of 1972 and never repaired. Check it out on your way next door to La Barracuda for a swim (see Public Swimming Pools below).

Just west of the petroleum refinery on the road leading west out of town is **La Cuesta del Plomo,** the ravine where Somoza was allegedly fond of making folks "disappear." Families whose loved ones didn't come home after a few days would go to this hillside to search for their bodies. The monument is in their memory. Accessible from *ruta* bus 183. Off in the distance in Lake Managua is **La Isla del Amor** (Island of Love), the small island where the dictator used to take his lovers to a personal cottage in the days before auto-hotels proliferated throughout the country.

Museums

Las Huellas de Acahualinca is a modest and recently remodeled museum at the northwest end of the city, showcasing the traces of a civilization 6,000 years old. The prehistoric footprints were found in the last century, four meters below the ground surface. Debate rages as to whether they represent humans fleeing a volcanic eruption or just heading to the lake to fish. The neighborhood around the museum is wretchedly poor, the lake has been contaminated, and the threat of volcanic activity remains. Visit the museum and glimpse another world (open Mon.–Sat. 8 A.M.–5 P.M., tel. 266-5774). Charter a taxi to take you there and back (about $5 for an hour), or take buses 102, 106, or 159 (102 runs past Barrio Martha Quezada). Entrance fee is $1.

El Museo Gemologico de la Concha y el Caracol is an intriguing collection of fossils with particular attention to snails, shells, circular corals, and precious stones (open Mon.–Sat. 8 A.M.–7 P.M.; located one block east and 120 meters south of the semáforos de Rubenia, tel. 289-2912).

Located in the Palacio de Cultura, **El Museo Nacional de Nicaragua** highlights natural history, as well as pre-Columbian ceramics and statues from all over Nicaragua's territories. Open every day but Saturday 8 A.M.–5 P.M.; entrance fee $1, tel. 222-2905.

El Museo Geologico de la UNAN-Managua is a small museum in the national university that houses rocks, fossils, and mineral finds gathered by students both in Nicaragua and abroad. Open Monday–Friday, 8 A.M.–4:30 P.M. but call before arriving to make sure someone's there to show you around. Located at Colonia Miguel Bonilla #258, tel. 270-3983.

Art Galleries

More a cultural center than a museum, **Códice** displays changing exhibitions of sculpture, paintings, and ceramics, all set around a lovely courtyard. There are often musical performances here in the evenings, and the patio is a peaceful corner in which to enjoy a light lunch and a drink (possibly the only place in town with hummus). Open Monday–Saturday 9 A.M.–8 P.M. or later if there is a special presentation. Located in Colonial Los Robles segundada etapa, house #15, tel. 267-2635.

Galería de Los Tres Mundos is the home base for Padre Ernesto Cardenal, displaying not only many of his sculptures, but also a wonderful selection of paintings and balsa work from the Solentiname Islands. This is also the center for Nicaragua's writers association, and some of the country's most famed poets and authors can be found bustling around the gallery and few offices. Los Tres Mundos is run by a foundation of the same name that offers painting classes and has a small library and bookstore (located in Los Robles, two blocks north of the French restaurant Marseilles, open Mon.–Fri. 8 A.M.–5 P.M.).

Galería Añil boasts works from over 40 Latin American painters and sculptors. Located in Bolonia, from Canal 2 TV, one block west, 10 meters south, tel. 266-5445. **El Museo Galería Genesis** specializes in contemporary and primitivist art (open Mon.–Sat. 9 A.M.–7 P.M.; located one block east and 75 meters south of the old Sandy's, #22, tel. 277-2480). Visit **Galería Epikentro** for more contemporary and primitivist Nicaraguan art, sculpture, and frequent book readings by local authors (located from the Plaza España, four blocks north, 75 meters west;

open Mon.–Fri. 9 A.M.–6 P.M., Sat. 9 A.M.–4 P.M., tel. 268-5953).

Galería Praxis has drawings, paintings, sculpture, and a small café; located from the Bolonia Optica Nicaragüense one block west, one block north, tel. 266-3563. **Galería Pléyades** is actually a private home that displays several genres of Nicaraguan art set around a graceful patio; open Monday–Friday 8:30 A.M.–6 P.M., Saturday 9 A.M.–1 P.M., on the Blvd. Villa Fontana #40, tel. 278-1350.

El Águila is the home and studio of celebrated artist Hugo Palma, who will gladly show you his works Monday–Saturday 9 A.M.–5:30 P.M. Located at km 6 on the Carretera Sur, tel. 265-0524. **Galería Plaza Inter** has occasional displays next to the food court on the top floor of the Plaza Inter mall.

Galería Solentiname is set in the home of Doña Elena Pineda, a native Solentinameña who has done a great job of promoting the works of painters from the famous archipelago. Open Monday–Saturday 9 A.M.–5 P.M. Located in Barrio Edgard Munguía Transfer, 600 meters south of the UNAN, tel. 277-0939.

The **Central Bank** exhibits paintings by local primitivist artists such as Marina Ortega and Manuel García. Located in the Banco Central, 100 meters east of the intersection Siete Sur.

UNIVERSITIES

M anagua has no fewer than 27 universities, the three biggest of which are La Universidad de Centroamerica (or La UCA, pronounced la OOHka), La Universidad Nacional Autónoma de Nicaragua (La UNAN), and La Universidad Nicaragüense de Ingeniería (La UNI), all of which have courtyards, soda shops, cafés, and bars on campus where you can mingle with up-and-coming revolutionaries. Find out about the latest student strike, sit-in, or tire-burning session in the fight for 6 percent of the national budget, cheaper tuition, and of course, a classless society without corruption or war. The intersection in front of the UCA and UNI is particularly happening during the day, with plenty of cheap Internet cafés, leftist bookstores, and people-watching.

ENTERTAINMENT AND EVENTS

Although there are innumerable pool halls and cheap dives littering every corner of the city, you'll most likely want to stick to three main areas for your Managua entertainment needs. The first exists all along the **Carretera Masaya,** from the new cathedral south to the city limits. This area is known as Managua's *zona rosa* (or hot spot) for the multitude of restaurants, clubs, and casinos that line it. It's an active, lively area, with numerous destinations worth your time— but note that this is no pedestrian promenade (except for the multitude of prostitutes who occupy several major stretches at night).

The region immediately around the old Hotel Intercontinental and the neighboring **Plaza Inter** mall has several decent bars (Amatl and La Curva) and upscale restaurants (the Shannon Irish Pub and *hospedajes* of Barrio Martha Quezada are only about eight blocks west of here, but always take a cab). Third in the list of Managua nightlife centers is the **Rotonda Bello Horizonte,** a middle-class residential community with a movie theater, pizzerias, and most famously, roving bands of big-hatted, deep crooning mariachis.

Discotecas

Nicaraguans love to dance and there is no shortage of venues, which range from enormous and open to intimate and mysterious. In the list of top five things to do in Managua, dancing is at least two of them. Make sure to coordinate your stay in Managua to include a weekend, so you can experience this scene. "I don't know how to dance" is no excuse, as you've got plenty of friendly instructors at hand; if you'd still rather not partake, go out and nurse a beer while watching Managuans of all ages dressed to the nines and acting their exuberant best. Thursdays and Fridays are both all right, but Saturday is where it's at. **Along Carretera Masaya: Amnésia,** is tucked off the main drag, just south of the Metrocentro traffic circle; an attractive disco with small, romantic tables converging around an intimate dance floor. Cover charge depends on the evening and is often free (open Wed.–Sun. 7 P.M.–7 A.M.). **Insomnia** has dancing both inside and outdoors on the second story; lots of space and a well-dressed, often under-21 crowd. Located on Plaza San Ramón, tel. 278-7112. **X/S** has a slick, modern dance floor, sandwiched between Subway and Bongó (open Wed.–Sat., tel. 277-3086).

El Quetzál is a time-tested favorite in Managua and is more family-friendly than smaller, newer clubs. Open air, with fans instead of a/c, but that lets the cigarette smoke out. Never a cover charge, rum served by the bottle at your table (and to move the way Managuans do you'll probably need a drink or two). Just east of the Rotonda Centroamerica, tel. 277-0890.

Ignore the cheesy American Indian theme of **El Chamán** and focus on the walled-off dance floor in the middle of the room. Right next door to Metrocentro and close to many Carretera Masaya restaurants, this is a good place to finish your evening and it goes pretty late. El Chamán also hosts live music on Thursday nights; if it's still this popular with the college crowd after four years, they must be doing something right, tel. 278-6111.

Stratos Disco-Bar is small but popular with 20- and 30-somethings. Salsa, merengue, reggae, and *bachata music,* cover charge $3.50. Located two blocks west of the Vicky in Altamira, tel. 278-4013. The upscale disco most frequented by the older crowd (and sometimes their younger lovers) is **Moonlight,** with a/c, bar. Km 5 Carretera Masaya in the Delta building, tel. 278-1944. **El Cartel** is an open frat party, usually packed with karaoke lovers. Dinner menu and wide selection of drinks, across from Metrocentro, tel. 277-2619.

Near the Plaza Inter: KTV is a popular, high-end disco on the bottom floor of the mall, with a $7 cover charge. Located two blocks east of the Antiguo Cine Cabrera in the Edificio La Merced, tel. 222-5960. A large, open-air disco with an immense dance floor, **El Mirador de Tiscapa** is a cheap (no cover) way to enjoy good dancing and the occasional live salsa/merengue band. They offer a full dinner menu as well. Located on the Paseo Tiscapa, tel. 222-5945.

Caribbean Grinding: Managua's Costeño crowd is at home in **Island Taste.** Go on a Thursday, when there's enough elbow room to enjoy the Garífuna, *soka,* and reggae vibes—Fridays and Saturdays the place is typically too full to turn around, much less dance. Km 6 Carretera Norte, tel. 240-0010.

Bars and Clubs
Along Carretera Masaya

Nearly at the northern terminus of the Carretera Masaya, **La Rumba** is a relaxed salsa bar with indoor and outdoor candlelit seating, tight dance space, and well-mixed, nontraditional Latin tunes. La Rumba's uncomplicated atmosphere has made it ragingly popular with international expats during the week and mobs of Managua *salseros* on the weekends.

Sports Rock Café is just what it sounds like. Best place in Managua to watch a game on 17 big-screen TVs, but a little loud for casual

EL SON NICA

Marimbas, Carlos Mejía Godoy, and Nicaraguan Folk Music

Interestingly, in the wide, vast—and incredibly loud—sea of music flowing through Nicaragua's living rooms, bars, vehicles, and airwaves, music of true Nicaraguan roots is not the easiest to hear. In fact, to the casual listener, Nicaraguan music must be sought out. However, once you get to know the distinctive 6/8 rhythms, the sound of the marimba, and the melodies that every single Nicaraguan knows by heart, you'll realize just how much Nicaraguan music is woven into its society.

Of Nicaragua's indigenous societies, only a few musical remnants survived the conquistadores; these precious acts of dance, costume, and distinctive melodies are observed today in the *fiestas patronales* of Masaya and Diriamba—and all the towns in between. Inevitably, even these fragments have been enriched by the different cultures that have encountered them. Of course, much of this influence was European, and at some point, an African marimba traveled up the Río San Juan, landed in Granada, and found its home among the *folkloricos* of Carazo and Masaya.

Things are different in the northern hills of Nicaragua, where Carlos Mejía Godoy was born in 1943. The music there, he explains, is composed of campesino versions of the waltz, polka, and mazurka. Born and taught to play the accordion and guitar in Somoto, Carlos Mejía is neither the "father" nor "inventor" of Nicaraguan folk music, as some would have it. In fact, he is only one in a line of multiple generations of songwriting Nicaraguans. However, his love and passion for Nicaraguan culture, combined with his sheer talent as a musician, songwriter, and performer, have made Carlos Mejía and his long catalog of songs a central figure in any discussion (or jam session) involving Nicaraguan music.

Carlos Mejía says he wishes he had two lives: one to learn all there is to be learned about Nicaraguan culture and a second to perform and use that knowledge. To most observers (and fans), it would appear he has done an adequate job at squeezing both into the one life he was given. Not only did he join the revolution in 1973 and proceed to compose its soundtrack, but throughout his life, Carlos Mejía has delved deeply into the campo, always in search of the regionally distinct riches of his country's cultural fabric. His songs are vibrant, colorful celebrations of everything Nicaraguan—from its geography, food, and wildlife, to praise for the town gossip and shoe-shine boy.

When asked about the Nicaraguita flower that inspired him to write the most famous song in the country's history ("Nicaragua, Nicaraguita"), Carlos Mejía quotes a passage entitled "La Flor Escogida" (The Chosen Flower) by Profesor Carlos A. Bravo, in which the rare variety of *sacuanjoche* (Nicaragua's national flower) is described as *"roja incendida, un clarinazo, listada de oro"* (burning red, a trumpet blast, with golden rays). Carlos Mejía calls this "such a beautiful thing," and one is not sure if he speaking of the flower or the lyrical words describing it—perhaps for him, there is no distinction between the two.

Look for Carlos Mejía's music and lyrics but don't stop there. His brother Luis Enrique is a world-renowned salsa king, and they can both be found performing at their club in Managua, La Casa de los Mejía Godoy. Nandaimeño Camilo Zapata is the granddaddy of them all; also seek out Tino Lopez, Justo Santos, Otto de la Rocha, Norma Elena Madea, and the duo Guardabarranco. In addition, every town in Nicaragua has multiple generations of pluckers and crooners, many of whom are a wealth of knowledge and all too willing to sing (or teach) you some songs.

An excellent guide (in Spanish) to Nicaraguan music can be found at www.musicanica.com.

conversation. Next door to the Shell Centroamérica, tel. 267-0424. **Hipa-Hipa** is a flashy scene, whose tiny dance floor and cramped outdoor terrace mean you're guaranteed to bump elbows with cell phone–toting Miami Boys and *fresas* (strawberries), as Managua's young glamour girls are called (in the Plaza Coconut Grove, tel. 278-8504).

Bongó features Cuban cuisine, local musicians, and karaoke; Thursday is Cuban night (located in the Centro Comercial Behrmann, tel. 277-4375). Nearby, **Siboney** is a candlelit, more intimate bar, named after a Cuban TV brand and featuring a small menu and Cuban *mojitos* (a mint and rum drink). **Guantanamera** is yet another Cuban-themed bar with occasional live music, tucked off the west side of the highway, near the Metrocentro Rotonda.

Near Plaza Inter: Located right in Barrio Martha Quezada, The **Shannon Pub** is quite possibly the most acclaimed bar on the expatriat scene, being the only spot in the country where you can drink a tall, dark Guinness (imported draught cans). Owned by—surprise—an Irish expat, the Shannon offers a respectable selection of bar food, national beers, and Irish whiskey; also darts, live acoustic music, and a mixed Nicaraguan and international crowd. From TicaBus, one block east, half-block south, open 6 A.M.–10 A.M. (breakfast), 3 P.M.–closing, tel. 222-6683.

Café Amatl has a scruffy, bohemian atmosphere and medium sized, open-air dance floor that is used sometimes for dancing, sometimes for staging local rock bands. Great music (everything from James Brown to Bob Marley to salsa) and a relaxed international and Nica crowd. Pay $2.25 or $4.50 cover charge depending on the night (closed Sunday), which covers a couple rounds of drinks. Tasty appetizers. Thursday night is live music; expect anything from Nica Speed Metal or folk to Brazilian, jazz, and African. Two blocks south and 15 meters west of the Hotel Inter, tel. 266-2485.

In a 1950s-style reminiscent of old Managua in the Centro Cultural, **La Cavanga** (the heartbreak) provides mellow, live music Thursdays–Saturdays, closed Sundays. One of the most atmospheric bars in the city. Located in the south-

east corner of the Centro Cultural Managua, tel. 228-1098.

Bar La Loma is discretely hidden behind Escuela de Manejo la Profesional, one block south of the Plaza Inter, and is a big hit with the young 20s crowd. Same goes for **La Curva** just downhill. Chill atmosphere, cheap beers, and friendly Nicas. **Licorería La Chocoya,** half a block west of Amatl, is a recent addition to the bar scene, most popular on Friday nights; good service and best of all, open 24 hours a day.

If you're feeling culturally adventurous, go dancing and drinking at the **Sandinista Union Club,** located next to the Shell station around the corner from Santos. It's only happening on Sundays from 2 P.M. to the early evening, but the liquor is cheap and the hardworking crowd is incredibly friendly.

Rotonda Bello Horizonte: The south side of the Rotonda has several eating and drinking establishments, whose mainstay is Pizzería Los Vidolos. The Rotonda is the lively base camp for hordes of roving mariachi bands that (for a small fee) serenade you with all the best of Vicente Fernández, Guadalupe Esparza, and Pepe Aguílar. **Dexter's Club,** just south of the Rotonda, is another Caribbean culture hangout, but much more low-key than Island Taste. From the Rotonda, walk down the road between the supermarket and Vidolos 1.5 blocks south.

Live Music

Although small and inbred, Managua's music scene is alive and well—as long as you know where to look. Many of the bars and clubs listed above have live shows once or twice a week, listed in this book whenever possible. In addition, the following nightclubs specialize in live performances.

Casa de los Mejía Godoy: Instead of trying to book themselves gigs around town, the legendary Mejía Godoy brothers (Carlos and Luis Enrique) simply built their own club. Actually, Casa de los Mejía Godoy is a foundation, sponsoring projects around the country to help battered women and youth at risk. Both brothers perform here regularly, Carlos on Thursday and Saturday, with or without his band, Los de

RADIO

Managuan radio stations have a wide range of cultural programming, if you know when to listen. Tune in for traditional music and folk tunes, the weekly presidential address, horrible pop imports from the United States, and the strong opinions of just about everybody.

Radio El Güegüense (FM 101.1): Traditional Nicaraguan music 6–7:30 A.M. every day.

Radio Corporacion (FM 97.5, AM 540): Political and economic commentary courtesy of the Liberal Party. News programs approximately once an hour. National music Sundays from 5–6 A.M. and 3:30–4 P.M.

Radio Mujer (FM 94.7): Marimba music every day from 8:30–9 A.M. and 9:30–10 P.M., folk tunes Saturdays from 9–11 A.M., and feminist political commentary Sundays from 7–10 A.M.

Radio Universidad (FM 102.3): Traditional music programs Mon.–Fri. 8–9 P.M., Sundays 8–9 A.M., and the shining star of cultural programming, *"Radio con sabor a pinól,"* Wednesdays 8–9 P.M.

Radio Nicaragua (FM 88.7, AM 620): The presidential address Mondays from 6–7:30 P.M. (sometimes a few minutes late), Carlos Mejía Godoy, Mon.–Fri. 6:30–7 P.M., traditional music Mon.–Fri. 8–8:30 P.M., and traditional favorites from the countryside Saturdays 7:45–8:30 P.M.

Radio Pirata (FM 99.9): It's safe to say that nowhere else in Nicaragua will you hear programming this eclectic—Bob Marley, Black Sabbath, Beatles, classic rock, speed metal, and Nicaraguan traditional and rock music—spun by a robot named Henry. Check out "La Onda Barbara," also streaming live at www.pirata.com.ni; make a request at tel. 270-2819.

Palacagüina. Friday is Latin rhythm night with salsa king Luis Enrique, and Sunday features other Nicaraguan or international performers. Both brothers are born showmen, and the shows are a theatrical mix of stories, bawdy jokes, and famous songs. The club is expensive by Nica standards, but well worth it. Buy tickets the afternoon of the performance for $8–15; shows start around 9 P.M., tel. 270-4928.

La Ruta Maya: Featuring an outdoor terrace with live music by a variety of performers, La Ruta Maya is open Thursday–Saturday. Entrance $4–6. Located 150 meters east of the Estatua de Montoya, tel. 268-0698.

Hard Rock Café Managua: Located on the top floor of the Legends Hotel (under the giant guitar), the Hard Rock offers an upscale menu of chicken, beef, fish ($8 a meal) and all the rock 'n' roll you'd expect Friday and Saturday. If the leather jacket signed by the Backstreet Boys doesn't impress, enjoy the views from a table on the breezy terrace, tel. 270-0061.

Casinos

Pharaoh Casino is the latest and greatest in government-sponsored tourist attractions. Poker,

roulette, slots. Glassy and gaudy and everything you look for in a casino. Look for the big sphinx on Carretera Masaya; open 24 hours, tel. 278-6383. **Montecarlo** is a smaller, more relaxed casino next to Emiliano's Mexican restaurant. The **Casino Fiesta** is in the Hotel Intercontinental—upscale and very professional, high rollers welcome (open every day 2 P.M.–6 A.M., tel. 222-2762).

Cinemas

Managua's movie theaters are modern, viciously air-conditioned, and show most new Hollywood releases only months or weeks after they come out in the States. English movies are typically presented in English with Spanish subtitles. If you need to get away from it all, check the newspaper or the *Revista Cinematográfica* (a weekly bulletin distributed at most gas stations and some hotels and restaurants) for show times. Shows change every Thursday.

Alhambra and **Cinemas One and Two** and are on the south edge of town, right off the Carretera Masaya, and are surrounded by a complex of restaurants, ice cream parlors, bars, and a bowling alley. Cinemas One and Two, tel. 267-0964; Alhambra, tel. 270-3842. Located in the

Metrocentro Mall, **Cinemark** is a six-plex right above the food court, tel. 271-9037 or 271-9000.

The **Cinema Plaza Inter** is on the third floor of the mall with the same name. Although conveniently located just east of Barrio Martha Quezada, the neighborhood between the two places is sketchy. Take a cab after dark, tel. 222-5090 or 222-5122. **Cine América** is located on the lively Bello Horizonte traffic circle, near a number of happening restaurants and bars, tel. 244-1889.

Theater and Dance

Managua's finest theater, **El Teatro Nacional Rubén Darío** hosts top-name international acts. Check the newspaper for performances or call 266-3630 or 228-4021. **La Escuela Nacional de Teatro** is primarily a teaching facility that presents performances on weekends by students and visiting groups; call for a list of events, as they're not always published.

Sala De Teatro Justo Rufino Garay is a small, air-conditioned theater where you can find dance and drama performed by small professional troupes from all over Latin America; weekends only, calendar of events often available at supermarkets and Texaco stations, From the Estatua Montoya three blocks west and 20 meters north, next to Parque Las Palmas, tel. 266-3714.

Located in front of the UCA, **La Academia de Danza** has frequent performances and concerts. The students deliver professional and talented renditions of traditional, folk, modern jazz, Brazilian, and ballet; call or drop by for a schedule of events, or if you're in town for the long haul, consider taking one of their dance classes to prepare you for the club scene, tel. 277-5557.

SPECIAL EVENTS

Las Fiestas Patronales are the biggest and most sustained parties in the city. Managua celebrates its patron saint Santo Domingo every August. On the first of the month, the Saint is brought down from a small church in the hilly neighborhood of Santo Domingo and on the 10th he is returned. On both those dates, and for much of the

Waiting for the saint: a youngster paints himself in motor oil for the arrival of Managua's Santo Domingo.

time in between, Managua celebrates. Expect parades, horse shows, unlimited quantities of beer and rum, and a lot of fun and colors. The festivities are accompanied by a series of events sponsored by INTUR like **Las Noches Agostinas,** featuring cultural presentations and live music throughout the capital.

In celebration of the final victory against Somoza of the Sandinista revolution in 1979, **July 19th** is a holiday throughout the country and is especially exciting in Managua, with parades and presentations in Plaza de la Fé. The parades used to take place in Plaza de la Revolución, until the musical fountain was built.

SPORTS AND RECREATION
Billiards, Bowling, and Batting
Located across from the once-legendary Lobo Jack's disco mentioned in Carlos Mejía Godoy's song "Pobre la María," **Bolerama** has video games, a mediocre skating rink, a dozen bowling lanes, air hockey, and several good billiards tables, and everything is cheap (open Mon.–Fri. 1 P.M.–midnight, weekends 10 A.M.–midnight; Camino de Oriente, tel. 277-2260). A standby hole-in-the-wall pool hall is **Topacio,** with quality tables and a wild crowd (open 4 P.M.–midnight every day, located from the Estatua de Montoya three blocks west, tel. 266-3428). **Denis Martínez Sport** is a popular batting range located just west of the UCA, open six days a week. There are special events every July 28th on the anniversary of Martínez's perfect game.

Public Swimming Pools
Escuela Club de Natación La Barracuda is a clean swimming school that opens its facilities to the public for about $1 per visit, or $10 for a monthlong membership. Located one block east of the semáforo Plaza Inter, tel. 222-7044 or 222-4610. The UNI has a medium-size pool open to the public ($1.50 per hour, tel. 267-0274). **Hotel Best Western Las Mercedes,** across from the airport, has the best swimming pool in the city and it's spotless; they charge $10 to get in and use the facilities, but your admission can be applied to club sandwiches and beers (open 9 A.M.–5 P.M.

every day, tel. 263-1011 or 263-1028). **Hotel Camino Real** is a five-star hotel with a beautiful pool; admission $10 any day of the week, poolside barbecues on Sundays ($18 more), tel. 263-1381. The pool at the Hotel Intercontinental is only open to the public on Sundays 10 A.M. to 5 P.M., and you pay $12, tel. 228-3530.

Spectator Sports and Other Sports Facilities
El Estadio Nacional, a.k.a. the Denis Martínez Baseball Stadium, is a proper metaphor for Managua: partially destroyed and rebuilt after the earthquake to something less than its original grandeur, originally named after Anastasio Somoza García, then renamed by the Sandinistas after his assassin, and then renamed again, this time after Nicaragua's native son baseball hero. Catch Managuans at their baseball-lovin' finest as you help them root for the home team: Boer, with its logo blatantly ripped off from the Cleveland Indians. Seats behind home plate cost less than $2.

ACCOMMODATIONS
Under $10
Barrio Martha Quezada isn't called *Gringolandia* for nothing. The streets around the TicaBus terminal are thick with an ever-changing buffet of cheap places to stay. The hands-down favorite among backpackers and the budget crowd is **Guesthouse Santos** with 30 quasi-secure rooms, no right angles, and sheets occasionally damp from the previous guest; $3.50 per person, simple breakfasts available. Ask the owner, Don Uriel Santos, about the time Daniel Ortega and Yasser Arafat met in his *salón.* A block away, **La Quintana** is known for its cleanliness and safety. The proprietress shuts the door at 11 P.M. and doesn't open it until morning (argue with her and see what happens); $4 per person; try to get a front room with a window for ventilation, tel. 222-6918. Laundry service available. **Anexo de la Quintana Los Mangos** provides the same services right across the street, tel. 228-6090.

Catering to a largely Central American clientele, **Hospedaje Meza** has 10 rooms, some with private bath, from $3.50. Ask to see several rooms before choosing; knock on the gate late at night to be let in. One door south of Sala de Belleza Marcia, on the same side of the street, is a woman who rents out one room to groups of travelers. Knock on the door and ask; you'll probably pay about $8–10 per person for cable TV, hot water, and a very safe environment. Not recommended if you're going out partying, as you have to wake her up to get back in at night.

The proprietress of **Hospedaje El Dorado** chooses her guests very carefully, so it's among the safest places—if you make the cut, that is. You are given a key to the gate for late-night entry (eight rooms, laundry, under $5 per person, tel. 222-6012). **La Casa Castillo** has six rooms with private baths, $5 per person, tel. 222-2265. It's cleaner than most but sometimes hot; real boxspring mattresses. **El Viajero** also has six rooms set alongside the proprietor's house, all of which have private bath, towel, and soap for $6 per person, tel. 228-1280.

A small *hospedaje* with a lot of character, **El Molinito** has 14 simple rooms for $6 per person, all with private bath and fan, tel. 222-2073. Ask for a room toward the front. Doors close at 10 P.M., but you can knock to get in later. **La Casa Azul** is convenient if you're off to the TicaBus station early in the morning; doors close at 10 P.M. and don't open until morning; pleasant TV room and mixed crowd. Clean, spartan rooms cost $4 per person; the back rooms have more privacy, tel. 222-3713. The **TicaBus station** has its own *hospedaje* to accommodate travelers simply stopping over in Managua. Slightly cramped but awfully convenient, $6 per person.

You'll walk right past **Hospedaje El Molinito 2** if you don't ask. One block east of the TicaBus on the south side (look for the small, tiled footstep), Molinito 2 looks like a private house. Inside are four rooms with a/c and private bathrooms; knock on the front door to be let in at night. Simpler rooms with fan instead of a/c cost $6 per person, tel. 222-5100.

$10–25

A necessary and much welcomed addition to Barrio Martha Quezada, **Hotel Los Felipe** offers accommodations a step above basic but still reasonably priced. Rooms are clean and safe, parking is available, cable TV, coin-operated phone, Internet, patio area under a thatched roof, swimming pool, laundry service, private baths. They'll open the door for you any time of the night; $15 per person with TV, $12 without, doubles $15/$18, tel. 222-6501. **Jardín de Italia** is a relatively upscale, quaint affair, with five rooms and quality mattresses, $20 for a double, tel. 222-7967.

$25–50

Located not far away in La Bolonia, **Hotel Europeo** is clean, quiet, and beautifully furnished. Eleven rooms at $45–55 include hot water, breakfast, a small pool, laundry service, a/c, and cable TV; 75 meters west of Canal 2, tel. 268-5999 or 268-2130.

Hotel El Ritzo is in the central Altamira neighborhood (from the Lacmiel, three blocks east, 25 meters south), with 10 rooms for $40 s, $50 d, tax and breakfast included; ask for group rates (tel. 277-5616, email: hotelritzo@alianza.com.ni, website: www.hritzo.com.ni).

Back in Los Robles, **Hotel Sol y Luna** has six rooms with hot water, TV, a/c; breakfast and tax included, $40 s, $50 d; located on the same block as the Restaurante Marseilles, tel. 277-1009, email: solyluna@ibw.com.ni. **Casa de Huespedes Familiar** is a humble bed-and-breakfast with two rooms in a family setting, $35 single or couple (located three blocks east of the Funeraria Don Bosco, tel. 278-0149, email: drivera@ibw.com.ni).

$50–100

This is generally the range in which you'll find Managua's bed-and-breakfasts, most of which are immaculate and situated in some of the safest, nicest, most central parts of the city. **Hotel El Almendro** provides a fridge, fully equipped kitchen, microwave, a/c, hot water, cable, telephone, fax, and Internet for $55, special discount for weekly and monthly rates; located near the UCA, two blocks west and one south of the Rotonda Rubén Darío (tel. 270-1260 or 277-2476, email: informacion@el-almendro.com, website: www.al-almendro.com). Another good quality bed-and-breakfast in a safe, central neighborhood is **Hotel Brandt,** with excellent, top-notch facilities (hot water, a/c, phone, minibar, TV) for $60 s, $80 d, includes breakfast, Internet, and tax, tel. 270-2114/5/6, fax 278-8128, email: bbbho@cablenet.com.ni, website: www.brandt-shotel.com.ni.

A convenient place to stay if you have an early flight, the **Hotel Best Western Las Mercedes** is directly across from the airport. Great restaurant and a mixed bag of travelers and diplomats lounging by the pool, from $52 d, tel. 263-1011.

Hotel Real Bolonia is like staying in a museum; 14 rooms with antiques, paintings, and sculpture, all set around a large garden; $75 includes breakfast, from Plaza España 1.5 blocks north, across from the German Embassy (tel. 266-8133, email: hotelreal@hotelreal.com.ni, website: www.hotelreal.com.ni). **La Posada del Angel** has a long-standing reputation for excellent customer service; rooms with hot water, minibar, laundry service, cable TV, and strongbox for $55 and up (from the Hospital Militar three blocks west, 20 meters north, across from the Iglesia San Francisco, tel. 266-1347 or 266-1483).

Posada de Maria La Gorda is accustomed to the international set; hot water, a/c, Internet, laundry, cable TV; $35 – $60 plus special group rates, Reparto El Carmen, tel. 268-2455/6. **Maracas Inn** has 30 clean, well-kept rooms; a/c, private bath, breakfast, fax, laundry service, taxi service to airport, parking; $55–80. One block north and one west of the Hospital Militar, tel. 266-8612 or 266-8982.

Over $100

In general, all of Managua's high-class hotels offer the same basic services: airport shuttle, five-star service, pool, dry cleaning, concierge, business center, top-notch restaurants, hundreds of rooms, etc. Catering largely to business travelers, there is presently much more supply than demand for these rooms.

The distinct faux-Mayan shape of **Hotel Intercontinental** has been a Managuan landmark since way before the big earthquake, and its bar and lobby have witnessed many an important scene throughout Nicaraguan history, tel. 228-3530, email: managua@interconti.com. The baby brother to the Inter, the **Intercontinental Metrocentro** was one of several high-rise buildings built in the late 1990s. Just south of the Metrocentro mall, tel. 271-9483. The **Hotel Princess** is located on Carretera Masaya, tel. 270-5045.

The **Holiday Inn** makes up for its less than central location by offering the quality service you'd expect. Pista Juan Paul II, tel. 270-4515, email: holidayinn@tmx.com.ni. **Hotel Legends,** home to the Hard Rock Café, has 94 rooms, plus live music, tel. 270-0061.

Long-Term Accommodations

If you don't mind the grunge, you can surely work out some kind of long-term rate at any of the cheap *hospedajes* for around $150 a month. That's about the least you'd pay for your own safe apartment in Managua, and entire houses can be found for rent for as low as $300.

For a fully serviced guesthouse, $500 per month is the going rate. **Los Cedros** has 30 furnished rooms with bath, terrace, kitchen, and pool. Plenty of green space. Km 13, Carretera Sur, across from the Iglesia Monte Tabor, tel. 265-8340. Next to Las Cazuelas restaurant and across from Guesthouse Santos, **Hotel/Apartamentos Los Cisneros** rents small apartments fully furnished including refrigerator, private phone, and parking facilities, tel. 222-3535. If you've got a fat expense account, **Los Robles** has 12 safe rooms at $1,300 per month with maid service, cable TV, fridge, kitchen, a/c, located one block west, two blocks south of the Hotel Inter Metrocentro, tel. 278-6334.

FOOD

The late 1990s witnessed a major restaurant boom in Managua—some would argue to the point of saturation. *Buen provecho.*

Street Food, a.k.a. *Fritangas*

La Racachaca is easily the most famous *fritanga* in Managua. A little out of the way but worth the trip (from the Plaza España, 1.5 km west).

MANAGUA & VICINITY

Anyone staying in Barrio Martha Quezada must eat at least one meal at the *fritanga* on the east of side of the street, just north of El Viajero hostel—only open from about 6–9 P.M.

Breakfast

Cafetín Tonalli is a unique women's bakery cooperative that produces extraordinarily good breads and cakes, and sells juices, cheese, coffee, and more (Swiss training!). Take out or eat in their enclosed outdoor patio; 2.5 blocks south of Cine Cabrera, tel. 222-2678. **Café Myrnas** offers up the best pancakes in town (North American fans of the International House of Pancakes call it affectionately "MIHOP"), *huevos rancheros,* fresh coffee, and delicious fruit drinks. Open 6 A.M. for breakfast, stays open through lunch. About $2 for a full meal.

Cafés and Coffee Shops

Managua's premier classy coffee shop is **La Casa de Café,** with pricey meals, key lime pie, strawberry muffins, juice drinks, and first-class coffee on a patio overlooking the street. If you're a big breakfast person and miss your bacon and eggs, this is your place (there's also a branch in Metrocentro). Newer and more low-key, **Indigo & Café** looks like it came out of your old college town and they work hard for the money. Lattes, espressos, chocolate truffles, tiramisu, and more. Across from Valenti's Pizza, tel. 270-6470. **Don Pan** offers great coffee, sandwiches, and fantastic baked goods (Calle Principal Los Robles, tel. 278-4091).

Spanish

El Figón Español can be described as "sidewalk bistro meets delicatessen." A nice place to sit on the sidewalk and drink wine (one block west, one south of the Rotonda Metrocentro, tel. 270-0582). **El Mesón Español y Barra La Tasca** boasts fantastic paella and shellfish for about $20 (Bolonia Mansión Teodolinda 350 meters south, tel. 266-8561).

Mexican

La Hora del Taco serves traditional, reasonably priced Mexican food; the fajitas are a favorite, dishes run from $3.50 (Monte de los Olivos,

one block north, tel. 277-5074). **Tacos Charros** is the cheapest place to eat tacos, enchiladas, and the like, all for around $3, located in the Colonia Centroamérica, tel. 278-2337. **Emiliano's** has an impressive booze menu, plus roast pig for $6 (one block south and 30 meters west of Rotonda de Metrocentro, tel. 278-5689). **María Bonita** offers dinner in an open, romantic atmosphere for about $6, and a traditional and European breakfast bar Monday–Saturday 6:45–10 A.M. for $3 (1.5 blocks west of Distribuidora Vicky, tel. 270-4326). **Tacos al Pastor**

VEGETARIAN

Naturaleza is the only holistic, new age, organic food store in the city. It's small but packed with soy products, healthy foods, vitamins, natural body care and medicines, candles, and incense. Located two blocks west, one north from the Hospital Bautista, tel. 222-6944, email: natural@tmx.com.ni.

Take a traditional Nica food kiosk, substitute tofu for fried meat and soymilk for Coca-Cola, and you've got **Casa Nutrem Food,** the best budget veggie option in the city. Located in a little roadside park at the UCA (200 meters west of the main UCA gates), Nutrem serves tofu "cho shuey" (chop suey), bulgur rice and lentils, and the plate of the day. Food and a tall glass of soy milk costs $1.50; open Monday–Saturday 7 A.M.–5 P.M. Both Naturaleza and Nutrem, by the way, are distributors of **SOYNICA** products, an organization that promotes all things soy and has many excellent programs; located 4.5 blocks south of the semáforo Roberto Huembes, tel. 289-4941.

Bufete Casero is on Carretera Sur km 8, serves lunch only, and delivers mountains of veggie pastas, etc. **Ananda** is the most upscale of Managua's veggie joints, with whole foods and fresh fruit juices, open 7 A.M.–9 P.M., half a block east of the Estatua Montoya (close to Barrio Martha Quezada), tel. 228-4140. You can get fresh fruit and smoothies at the place across from Valenti's Pizza, and two long blocks north of there, look for **Healthy Foods, Inc.,** serving breakfast, lunch, and early dinner, open 7 A.M.–7 P.M.

is a small but charming restaurant that also sells beautiful pottery; dishes run about $3 (just south of the Rotonda Centroamerica, tel. 278-2650).

Seafood

Las Anclas is conveniently located in Barrio Martha Quezada and has cold beer, basic fresh fish, and no atmosphere whatsoever (unless you're really into fluorescent lighting); meals $4 with beer. Step things up a notch at **El Muelle,** one block east of the Hotel Intercontinental Metrocentro; easily some of the best seafood in Managua at around $6–8 a dish, tel. 278-0056.

Asian

Antojitos Chinos is an unassuming place in Barrio Martha Quezada on the Calle 27 de Mayo; the food is good and prepared cleanly, and the kitchen and bar are open 24 hours; $5–7. **The Wok,** in the Carretera Masaya area, is very good. Dishes start at $5. Top of the line is **Ming Court,** adjacent to the Plaza Inter, and easily the best and most expensive Chinese food in the country. Dishes start at $8.

Italian

Seems like there's a new fancy spaghetti and wine joint every day but the following few are the faithful standbys that have been around a while and will probably be around a while to come. **La Casa del Pomodoro** is a big favorite, serving large portions of quality food; their $4.50 calzones will fill you up for two days (Carretera Masaya km 4, tel. 270-9966). Top-notch food and service are found at **Mágica Roma;** the owner was a photo-journalist during the war, and has remarkable albums of his work for you to enjoy while you work on your focaccia and *vino tinto;* about $8 per plate, located a half-block west of the Plaza Inter, tel. 222-7560. Managua old-timer **Pasta Fresca** has famous *canelones* and lasagna; expect to pay at least $8–10 a person (two blocks east of the Hotel Inter Metrocentro, tel. 267-5206). **Valenti's Pizza** serves inexpensive pizza and beer, festive atmosphere (Colonial Los Robles, two blocks east of Lacmiel, tel. 277-5744). **La Piazzetta** has nice ambience and good, high-priced food at $9 per plate; km 4,

Carretera Masaya, tel. 267-3313. **Bella Napoli Pizzeria** is the closest to the *hospedajes* of Barrio Martha Quezada; pizzas, burgers, and sandwiches for about $2.

French

La Marseillaise is one of the most expensive—and best—restaurants in town, serving classic French cuisine in a gorgeous building; delicious fillets of meat and fish, and stunning desserts (Calle Principal Los Robles, tel. 277-0224).

Typical or Traditional

Mi Pueblo is slightly more expensive than most, but this open-air restaurant on a hill overlooking the city is worth the trip; located on Carretera Sur km 9. **La Cocina de Doña Haydee** serves Nicaragua's best specialties in a clean, quiet atmosphere; you could get the same food at a good *fritanga* for a fourth of the price, but if you'd rather avoid street food, this is your place. Specialties include *vaho, indio viejo,* and *nacatamales* (one block west of Optica Matamoros, tel. 270-6100).

Steak and Burgers

La Plancha is home to some of the best meat in town. Ask for the *parrillada* or just go *a la plancha,* about $10–12 a plate; from the Semáforos Plaza del Café 150 meters to the east, tel. 278-2999. Right on Carretera Masaya km 5, **T.G.I.Fridays** is just like in the States with burgers, chicken, sandwiches, pasta dishes, and bouncy waiters in dippy costumes; about $10 a person by the time you've ordered drinks, tel. 277-2762. Perhaps the best-known steak place in the city, **El Churrasco** is located right on the Rotonda El Gùegùense, tel. 266-6661. **Texas Steak House** has burgers, Mexican specialties, and plenty of hot sauce. **Los Ranchos** isn't cheap (about $15), but they've served a solid *steak au poivre* since the days of Somoza (open noon–3 P.M., 6–11 P.M., Carretera Sur km 3, tel. 266-0526). **Eskimo** serves a varied menu of meats, fish, and shellfish, all in the $6–9 range; the *pollo en vino* is a solid choice; located next door to the Fábrica Eskimo, tel. 266-9701. If the Nica beef isn't cuttin' it for ya, **Hippo's Bar and Grill** sells $5 burgers made of USDA-approved, genetically enhanced, imported gringo ground beef—plus a polished bar with all kinds of treats; located from the old Sandy's, one block west.

Fried Chicken and Fast Food

Pollo Campero and **Tip-Top** chicken chains are all over the city and offer decent fried chicken, sandwiches, and more, for about $3–4. If you just can't leave it behind, there's fast food in Managua too. **McDonald's** is back after a hiatus during the 1980s (in Plaza de España, mall food courts, and La Rotonda Bello Horizonte), as is **Pizza Hut, Domino's** (yes, they both deliver), and **Subway** (on Carretera Masaya). Also, burger stands like **Hamburlooca** and **Quickburger** are scattered around the city wherever university students hang out; burger combos for under $3.

SHOPPING
Markets

Mercado Huembes (Mercado Central) is full of the exuberance, color, and life that so typifies Nicaragua. Huembes is the most tourist-friendly of the markets in Managua. Cavernous and cacophonous, Huembes offers fruits, vegetables, meat, cheese, flowers, cigars, clothes, shoes, and the best arts and crafts section this side of Masaya. Open every day from around 7:30 A.M. to around 5 P.M. Huembes is also a major bus terminal (see Getting There By Bus below).

　Mercado Oriental and **La Calle de los Árabes:** It is said that in the war years you could find contraband firearms and aircraft parts in the Mercado Oriental, if you knew where to ask. It's still the wildest ride in the city, and it's true that if you can't find it here, you can't find it in Nicaragua. However, it's not for the faint of heart: someone gets robbed here every seven minutes. If you venture in, do so very carefully and keep your money in your sock. Adjacent to Mercado Oriental is a street that sells nothing but fabric by the yard. Wondering where Nicas get their beautiful clothing? It starts here. To get to Calle de los Árabes ask your taxi driver to take you to the electronics store **El Gallo Más Gallo.** If you are in Managua during the first

few weeks of December, be sure to catch the massive IMPYME crafts fair on Avenida Bolívar—arts, crafts, and food from all over the country, plus a two-week carnival.

Malls

You'll notice two things while "malling" in Managua: (1) that there really is no commercial center in the city, and (2) how deeply divided are the country's economic classes. In addition to the two U.S.-style malls built in 1998 and 1999 (**Plaza Inter** and **Metrocentro**), Managua has a pleasant shopping area built in the years of the dictator called **Centro Comercial de Managua,** an open-air strip mall with bookstores, clothing, fabric, banks, an Internet café, sporting goods, and a post office. **La Galería** is another high-end shopping complex, just north of the National Cathedral (the DISNISA there has a great selection of imported wine and booze).

Supermarkets

La Colonial, right off the Plaza España and about a 12-minute walk from Barrio Martha Quezada, has all the prepackaged goodies and fresh veggies you could want (open Mon.–Fri. 8 A.M.–7 P.M., Sat. 8 A.M.–5 P.M., Sun. 9 A.M.–3 P.M.). Of special note is the **Costco Familiar,** located across the street from Valenti's Pizza, and offering all kinds of gourmet goodies, alcohol, and imported bulk items, including dark European beers (and crappy U.S. ones), shiitake mushrooms, chewing tobacco, and specialty olive oils and cheeses (Mon.–Sat. 9 A.M.–10 P.M., Sun. 9 A.M.–3 P.M.). There is another Colonial off Rotonda Centroamerica, plus other supermarkets and smaller "mini-supers" scattered around the city.

Bookstores

Hispamer is the largest bookstore in the city, though not necessarily the best stocked or organized (although it does have air-conditioning); Reparto Tiscapa, just east of the UCA, tel. 278-1210. **El Parnaso,** right across from the UCA gates, caters to a leftist-thinking crowd, with a café and sometimes live music (open Mon.–Fri. 9 A.M.–6 P.M., Sat. 9 A.M.–3 P.M., tel. 270-5178).

Libros Internacionales is a little bookstore two doors down from the coffee shop Indigo & Café (just east of Lacmiel), tel. 278-5508. Two stores in the Centro Comercial: **Librería El Gùegùense** is one of the better choices for books about Nicaragua and foreign-language dictionaries, tel. 278-7399 or 278-5285; and, named for the poet that, for love of his country, assassinated Anastasio Somoza García, **Librería Rigoberto López Pérez,** tel. 277-2240.

Photography Supplies

In addition to all the major supermarkets, film can be bought and processed at the **Fuji Foto Clinic** next to the Holiday Inn, or at one of 18 **Kodak Expresses** (a.k.a. Roberto Teran); the biggest, most complete Kodak branch is its central store, located behind CompuMax in the Colónia Centroamérica, and distinguished as **Kodak Express Profesional.** Ektachrome slide film can be purchased, processed, and mounted here. **Konica,** across from the McDonald's at Plaza España, has the cheapest slide film and processing, but it's their own Konica brand. For expensive black-and-white processing by hand, go to the **Galería Mexico,** located in Altamira, across from María Bonita, tel. 278-1058. As mentioned earlier, the quality of film processing in Nicaragua ranges from barely adequate to downright horrible; try it out if you don't believe us, or just save your film for home.

Musical Instruments

Instruments, guitar strings, and accessories are available at two stalls in the artisan section of the Roberto Huembes Market. Or one of two modern music stories in **Altamira;** they are practically across the street from each other, located just north of the Farmacía Quinta Avenida.

INFORMATION AND SERVICES

The budget of Nicaragua's official Instituto de Turismo has grown, and INTUR is now able to offer more than ever before (relatively speaking, of course). The main office is located one block west of the Plaza Inter (open Mon.–Fri. 8:30 A.M.–2 P.M., tel. 222-3333, website:

EMERGENCIES

Police: dial 118. There are several hospitals in Managua; the best is Hospital Bautista, tel. 249-7070; in an emergency dial 164 or 211. Ambulance: 265-1761. Fire Department: 265-0162, or dial 115.

www.intur.gob.ni). You can purchase various tourism magazines, maps, posters, and guidebooks, including *La Guía Facil* (now in English and Spanish). The Guía Telefonica (phone book) is a good information source, and you can always dial free directory service at 112.

Managua Guides and Maps

The best source of information for events occurring in Managua is the daily newspaper. The *Guía Mananic,* available at the airport, all major hotels, and INTUR, costs $5 and contains a large pull-out road map of Managua.

Libraries

Managua's public library, Biblioteca Dr. Roberto Incer Barquero, was built in 1999, courtesy of the Central Bank, and located behind the bank at km 7 Carretera Sur. Notable is its collection of newspapers from the war years (open Mon.–Fri. 8:30 A.M.–4:30 P.M., tel. 265-0500, ext. 408). The old national library is located in the Palacio de Cultura down by the waterfront. The UCA has an excellent library of historical and cultural resources (INHCA). You can acquire a library card valid for six months by getting permission from the director and paying a $10 fee.

Banks

So many banks went down in the corruption and financial scandals of 2000–2001 that it's difficult to present an up-to-date list. Banking hours in Managua are 8 A.M.–4 P.M. Monday–Friday, and 8 A.M.–noon on Saturday. Along Carretera Masaya you'll find the Banco de América Central (BAC, owned by the wealthy Pellas family), Banco Caley Dagnal, Banco de Finanzas (BDF), and Banic. For travelers staying in Barrio Martha Quezada the nearest bank is the Banco de

Nicaragua (Banic) Sucursal Bolonia. Several other banks are clustered around Plaza España, including Bancentro (a solid, proven bank with heavy foreign investment backing it), BAC, and Banexpo. An underused (i.e., shorter lines to wait on) facility for currency exchange is Multicambios, on the east side of the street across from McDonald's. Additionally there's a BDF conveniently located in front of the Hotel Inter.

Mail and Phone

The Palacio de Comunicaciones, located across the plaza near the ruins of the old cathedral, contains the central office of both Correos de Nicaragua and ENITEL, with full mail, fax, telex, express courier, and phone services. In the palacio, the *oficina de filatelía* sells stamps from previous editions beginning in 1991 (Nicaragua is well known among philatelists for having the most beautiful postage stamps in Central America), plus postcards and greeting cards (the palacio is open Mon.–Fri. 8 A.M.–5 P.M., Sat. 8 A.M.–1 P.M.). More compact, easier post offices to deal with are found in the Centro Comercial, Altamira, and the airport.

For packages, DHL is located in front of the Hotel Intercontinental, and on Carretera Masaya near the Hotel Princess, tel. 228-4081. On the second floor of the Malaga building in Plaza España shopping center (modulo A-3-B), IML is the local representative for the UPS package service, offering 24-hour shipping to the United States, 72 hours to Europe. Open Monday–Friday 7:30 A.M.–6 P.M., Saturday 8 A.M.–noon, tel. 266-4289. Federal Express has been operating in Nicaragua since 2000 and has various locations, including Carretera Masaya near Subway, and Ofiplaza El Retiro Ste. 515 (150 meters south of Rotonda Los Periodistas), tel. 278-4500.

Phone Cards

Buy a prepaid Publitel phone card in most post offices, *pulperías*, drugstores, and small shops; the card is usable in public phones around the country and is the best way to make calls within the country (as opposed to waiting on long lines in the phone offices). The pay phone most con-

venient to Barrio Martha Quezada is located in front of the TicaBus station. Otherwise visit the Palacio de Comunicaciones or any of the other ENITEL offices, such as those in the Centro Comercial and Barrio Los Robles, where you can use your international calling card by connecting to an operator, or just pay the cashier after making your call.

Fax Services

The Correos de Nicaragua office in the Palacio de Communicaciones offers international fax services for the price of the phone call (see information above for hours and location). Many *librerías* (office supply shops) will also send faxes within Nicaragua.

Internet

There's certainly no shortage of choices; Internet is everywhere and costs from $1.50 an hour near the universities, to over $6 an hour in the malls. If you'd rather not budget in a taxi ride from Barrio Martha Quezada, Cyber Center Banisa, located two blocks south of the stadium, is your best bet, tel. 222-5383. Punto.com is right in the Palacio de Correos and charges $1.50 per half hour (open Mon.–Sat. 7 A.M.–8 P.M., Sun. 7 A.M.–6 P.M.).

The original Cyber Café is located underneath Hipa-Hipa in the Plaza Coconut Grove; $3.50 per hour (open Mon.–Sat. 8 A.M.–10 P.M., Sun. 8 A.M.–6 P.M., tel. 278-8526). The Kafé Internet, $2.50 for the first hour, $1.50 each additional hour, has a scanner and CD burner; half block north of Cybercenter Banisa and adjacent to Farmacia Anteka (open Mon.–Sat. 8 A.M.–8 P.M., Sun. 9 A.M.–6 P.M., tel. 886-8253). The Cybershack in Centro Comercial charges $3.50 for two hours, $2 for one hour (open Mon.–Fri. 8 A.M.–7:30 P.M., Sat. 9 A.M.–3 P.M.).

Near the UCA: There are probably half a dozen choices within a stone's throw of the university, all of which are cheaper than anywhere else in the city. The SuperCyber Café, right under the pedestrian bridge, has 44 new computers, scanner, CD burner, and free (instant) coffee (open Mon.–Thurs. 8 A.M.–9 P.M., till 7 P.M. Fri., 2 P.M. Sat.). One block east of there, and one south, the Internet Café/iMac Center is open daily, 8 A.M.–8 P.M., tel. 277-2195 or 278-2180.

Laundry and Dry Cleaning

Try one of Dryclean USA's several locations, or Lavandería Dry Cleaning, in Barrio Monseñor (one block south of Lezcano ENITEL, tel. 266-1228). If you're traveling out of a backpack, most *hospedajes* have someone who will wash and iron your disgusting travel clothes for a reasonable fee, or pay the $.30 for a bar of laundry soap at the nearest *pulpería*, roll up your sleeves, and scrub away just like everyone else.

Haircuts

For a cheap, old-fashioned barbershop cut, ask your taxi driver or *hospedaje* owner for advice. If you're looking to step things up a notch, Danilo is a renowned hairstylist; both he and his staff speak some English. In Plaza España across from the supermarket, tel. 266-6144.

Travel Agents

The city is littered with travel agents, particularly around the Plaza España (a short walk from Barrio Martha Quezada). Agencia de Viajes La Frontera is accustomed to foreign travelers; located in the Edificio Malaga, room B-16, tel. 268-3639 or 268-3581. Viajes Atlantida is a renowned travel agency and the official representative for American Express in Nicaragua; one block east and a half block north of Plaza España, tel. 266-4050 or 266-8720.

Immigration Office

If you need to renew your visa, visit the Dirección General de Migración y Extranjería—at least four days in advance—with your passport, current visa, and $25. Extensions are not automatic; when given, they are for one month at a time. Remember to look presentable. Open Monday–Friday 8:30 A.M.–noon, 2–4:30 P.M. Located 1.5 blocks north of the semaforos Tenderí, tel. 244-0741/1320/3960.

Classes/Studying Opportunities

Dance: You can join in for classes in Latin dancing any time at La Academia Nicaragüense de la Danza, 50 meters north of the UCA gates, tel. 277-5557.

Sewing: How's this for random—the Libyan Embassy offers a short course in *sastrería* (tailoring) from time to time; one block south of the Mansión Teodolina, tel. 266-8541.

Horseback Riding: Technically, this one's outside of town, but you can learn horseback riding on the beautiful facilities at Escuela de Equitación Haras de Albanta, km 13 Carretera Vieja a León, 500 meters north of the Entrada Chiquilistagua, tel. 883-8899 or 882-0369.

Getting There and Away

All air traffic to Managua is routed through the cities of Houston, Texas, or Miami, Florida. For more detailed information, please see the Getting There and Away section in the On the Road chapter.

BY BUS

Buses bound for every corner of Nicaragua leave from and arrive at one of three terminals. In general, buses leave for major cities every hour, beginning at 5 A.M. and running through 5 P.M. Buses fill up and leave early, or wait extra time for more passengers. *Expreso* tickets are sold in advance, cost about 25 percent more than *ordinarios,* and you are given a reserved seat. *Expresos*

BUS SCHEDULE

San José, Costa Rica (continuing to Panamá City, Panamá)

TicaBus *	6 A.M., 7 A.M.
Nica Bus	6 A.M.
Transnica	5:30 A.M., 7 A.M., 10 A.M.
Panaline *	1 P.M.

To Tegucigalpa, Honduras

TicaBus	4:45 A.M.
Cruceros del Golfo	4:30 A.M.

To Guatemala City, Guatemala

TicaBus	4:45 A.M.
Cruceros del Golfo	4:30 A.M.

To San Salvador, El Salvador

TicaBus	4:45 A.M.
Transnica	5 A.M.
Cruceros del Golfo	4:30 A.M.

---

to farther cities like Estelí or Ocotal can save you an hour's travel or more and are well worth the extra money. To points west and south, there is an especially large number of express microbuses (minivans) that leave every 20 minutes—or whenever they fill up. See regional chapters for more specific information.

To Points North and East

Buses to Estelí, Matagalpa, Ocotal, Jinotega, Boaco, Juigalpa, El Rama, and San Carlos operate out of the Mayoreo bus terminal on the eastern edge of town. From the other end of Managua (i.e., Barrio Martha Quezada), you can take the 102 *ruta* but plan up to an additional hour's travel through Managua's heart; a taxi is much quicker and should cost around $3 for a solo traveler.

The entire northern mountain region is serviced by Expresos del Norte, easily one of the best-organized and punctual of Nicaragua's bus companies. Their *expreso* fleet includes Scania luxury buses (a rare treat), and they have a posted schedule, ticket window, and office where you can call to check on times (tel. 233-4729).

Buses to El Rama–Bluefields leave from both Mayoreo (Transporte Aguilar, tel. 248-3005 or 244-2255) and Mercado Ivan Montenegro in the center of town (Transporte Vargas, tel. 280-4561). Another bus leaves the Terminal Coatlantico (a block away from Mayoreo) at midnight (see the Atlantic Coast section for details).

To Points West and Northwest

Buses to León, Chinandega, and Carazo depart from the Israel Lewites terminal on the west side of Managua, named after a Jewish-Nicaraguan martyr of the revolution (occasionally referred to by its non-Sandinista name, El Boer). The terminal is in the center of a chaotic fruit market by the same name; watch your stuff and expect a slightly more aggressive crowd. The microbus *expresos* to Carazo towns leave from *el portón rojo* (the big red door), a specially named corner of the Israel Lewites terminal.

To Points South

Buses to Carazo, Masaya, Granada, Rivas, Ometepe, the border at Peñas Blancas, and San Juan del Sur depart from Mercado Roberto Huembes in south-central Managua. The ride from Barrio Martha Quezada should cost no more than $2 a person, less in one of several *rutas* that pass through the area. Before you get to Huembes, be sure to specify *parada de los buses* (bus stop) to your driver, as opposed to *el mercado de artesanía* (crafts market), also at Roberto Huembes, but on the other side of the market complex and approached differently when driving. This is a very busy terminal, serving thousands of commuters from points south. Keep your guard up.

Additional Carazo/Masaya/Granada Expresses

A once-makeshift bus lot across from the UCA has become a permanent and very convenient resource for anyone looking for fast, cheap, regular express service to Carazo (Jinotepe, Diriamba), Masaya, and Granada. Commute with the college kids for less than $1 each way; service starts around 6 A.M. and runs as late as 9 P.M.

International (Long-Distance) Buses

There are five carriers that pass through Managua with service to and from the rest of Central America. They all have very similar schedules (see Bus Schedule special topic), and most have regional offices around the country, with their Managua terminals in or near Barrio Martha Quezada.

TicaBus is the oldest and best-established Central American international bus company, servicing all of Central America with connections to Mexico. Its prices are a good measuring stick for the other companies; its one-way rates (in 2002) are as follows: Panamá City $35, San José $10, Tegucigalpa $20, San Salvador $25 (plus $30 visa for U.S. citizens), and Guatemala City $33. Located two blocks east of the Antiguo Cine Dorado, tel. 222-6094 or 222-3031.

Across the street, **Cruceros del Golfo** (a.k.a. King Quality) provides more services (like breakfast and a drink cart), and costs more than anyone else (over $50 to Guatemala); travels to points north only, tel. 228-1454 or 222-3065.

NicaBus travels to Costa Rica only ($20 round-trip) and is located three blocks east of the Cine Cabrera, tel. 228-1383 or 228-1373. **TransNica** makes its home in the Centro Comercial Lucila (Módulo #8), tel. 278-2090. **Panaline** serves Panama and Costa Rica; located on Calle 27 de Mayo, tel. 266-9559 or 778-2487.

HITCHHIKING

Hitching out of Managua is difficult and not advised because the *salidas* are harder to access, and it is less obvious where you are going; some are also in less-than-desirable neighborhoods.

Near Managua

CHOCOYERO–EL BRUJO NATURE RESERVE

Only 28 kilometers away from Managua is a little pocket of wilderness so vibrant with wildlife you'll forget the capital is just over the horizon. **Chocoyero–El Brujo** is close enough to Managua to be an easy day trip, and interesting enough that you'll want to spend the night. Chocoyero (as the area is also known) is also one of very few places in Nicaragua that encourages tent camping, making it a great place to spend an evening in the wild.

Chocoyero–El Brujo is a 41-square kilometer protected area within one of Managua's most important water supplies (nearly 20 million gallons of water per day—20 percent of the city's consumption). In the midst of moist hardwood forest and pineapple farms are two 25-meter waterfalls separated by a rocky knife-edge. One of the falls dumps all of its water straight into the ground, magically disappearing into the earth instead of forming a river—or so thought the natives. For this, they assumed the waters were enchanted and named the cascade *El Brujo* (the warlock). The other fall, Chocoyero, was named because of the incredible number of *chocoyos* (parakeets) that inhabit the adjacent cliff walls.

Chocoyero–El Brujo is a bird-watcher's paradise, though you'll likely bump into some other creatures as well. In addition to the five kinds of *chocoyo* that inhabit the valley, there are 113 other bird species (including several owls), 49 species of mammals, and 21 species of reptiles and amphibians. Sharp-eyed travelers may even spot small cat species like *tigrillos* and *gatos de monte*, and though you might not see them, you'll hear the monkeys in the treetops—both howlers and capuchins.

Getting There

Take any bus leaving Managua's Huembes terminal bound for La Concepción (called "La Concha" for short); buses leave Managua every 15 minutes. Get off at kilometer 21.5, where you'll see a wooden sign for the park entrance, then stretch out for a good, long walk. The dirt road that travels seven kilometers southwest to the reserve will lead you down a series of volcanic ridges and across a broad valley to the falls. It's an easy two-hour walk, passing through fields of pineapples, bananas, and coffee. Halfway down the road you'll find a small community where you can rent bikes or horses to take you the rest of the way in (horses $1 per hour, guide $1 per hour, bicycles $.50 per hour).

Chocoyero–El Brujo's infrastructure consists of a rustic, wooden base camp where guides will meet you and walk you the remaining way to the falls; entrance fee is $1. The best time to see the *chocoyos* is at around 4 P.M., when the flocks are returning to their cliff nests after a long day at the office… er, forest. They leave the nests at around 5:30 A.M., so to witness it you'll need to arrive the previous day and spend the night. You can rent two-person tents on the premises for $10.75 each, or set up your own.

Montibelli Wildlife Reserve

A 162-hectare private reserve on the road to Chocoyero–El Brujo, Montibelli offers a campground set within the biological corridor between Chocoyero–El Brujo, Montibelli, and Volcán Masaya National Park; this will eventually be the site of a mountain hotel and fully developed mini-park system as well. Montibelli already has a two-hour loop trail, views of the Masaya Volcano, tent areas, a small restaurant with Sunday barbecues, guided tours, bird-watching, and recurrent butterfly festivals. It is accessed by turning off the Ticuantepe–La Concha Highway at km 19; from there, it's a 2.5-km walk to the facilities, known locally as the "Casa Blanca"; take any bus or *expreso* to La Concha and get off at the dirt road at km 19 on the north side of the highway—or better yet, arrange for transport by contacting Claudia Belli in Managua, tel. 270-4287, fax 270-4289, email: rsp-montibelli@hotmail.com.

THE LAGUNAS OF XILOA AND APOYEQUE

Less than a half hour from the capital on the highway to León, the Peninsula de Chiltepe bulges into the southwestern shore of Lake Xolotlán, breaking up the otherwise uniform shoreline. The peninsula is formed by two ancient volcanic cones, their fiery insides long extinguished and drowned in clean rainwater. A part of the same line of fire that forms the rest of the Maribios volcanoes, these two are known as the twin crater lagoons of Xiloá and Apoyeque.

Legend says the Xiloá lagoon was formed when an Indian princess of the same name, spurned by her Spanish lover, went down to the lake's edge to cry. She cried so much that the valley begin to fill with tears, and the lagoon formed around her. Broader and more easily accessed, Xiloá was a popular swimming hole for daytrippers from Managua for decades, but former Minister of Tourism Herty Lewites took the initiative to develop the site more completely, with thatched-roof *ranchónes,* concrete pads, parking areas, and lunch stands. In 1998 Hurricane Mitch raised the water level of Xiloá nearly a meter, and the facilities remain partially submerged, the straw roofs casting their reflections on the still waters of the lagoon. The level should go back down as the water slowly evaporates. Very slowly. You can still cool your heels in Xiloá, though you have to be careful where you jump in to avoid bumping your head on a picnic bench. You'll probably have the lagoon all to yourself except for the occasional marine biologist, scuba diving to study the endemic species in the crater lake.

Apoyeque still bears much of its original cone shape—the lagoon is enclosed in steep crater walls that form the highest part of the Chiltepe Peninsula. The Nicaraguan military occasionally uses it for training special forces in the art of rappelling, and there's a radio tower on the southwest lip of the crater. In 2001, Apoyeque was the epicenter of a series of seismic tremors. Around the rest of the peninsula and the lower slopes of the two volcanic peaks are lush cattle farms, many owned by the Seminole tribe of Florida, which is heavily invested in the area.

There are frequent buses from Managua along the dirt road that will take you right to the water at Xiloá. Getting to Apoyeque is more of an undertaking and should be treated more like a challenging hike than a casual trip to the local swimmin' hole. Take the road from Mateare, which you can walk or hitch down until you reach the access road for the radio antenna. That road will lead you to the ridge, from where you'll have to painstakingly and carefully make your way into the crater.

If you're not into swimming, the entire region makes a great place for hiking if you ever need a quick break from Managua. From Xiloá, there is a well-marked but little-used dirt road that circles the entire peninsula (28 km), coming out in Mateare. The road passes by several cattle ranches as you circumnavigate the two craters. The view from the northeastern side of the peninsula is particularly beautiful in the late afternoon when the sky fills with colors.

EL CRUCERO

The Pan-American Highway heads out of Managua at its western edge, leading toward points south and known locally as Carretera Sur. As the kilometer numbers increase, so does the altitude, as the highway takes you up to beautiful, exposed ridgelines and the community of El Crucero (home to former President Alemán). From there the road runs southeast toward Carazo and Costa Rica, and has several branches that run west down the plains to the ocean.

Restaurants on the Carretera Sur

The corridor between Managua and El Crucero is affluent, housing many upscale residential neighborhoods, private schools, coffee farms, and several elegant restaurants to boot. Of these, the **Al Di La** in El Crucero is the most notable, with 360-degree windswept views, thick plantations of African violets, and top-notch cuisine for $10 a plate. **La Cueva del Buzo** (the diver's cave) is rumored to have the best seafood in all of Nicaragua, caught fresh every day by the scuba-diving Italian owner. **Rancho de Pepe** serves

MANAGUA & VICINITY

skyline at El Crucero

seafood and French cuisine, with tango and jazz music as a backdrop.

PACIFIC BEACHES

Roughly 65 kilometers due west of the capital are a handful of easy-to-reach beaches, with facilities ranging from low-key *hospedajes* to all-out resort.

Pochomíl

Pochomíl is one town whose name does not originate from the original Nahuatl settlers. In the early 20th century, farmers used the word *pocho* to mean money. At the time, the lands now known as Pochomíl were called *La Quijada,* (the jaw). A farmer from a few kilometers south, Felipe Gutierrez, moved in and started an ambitious farm on which he raised ducks and goats, among other things. Gutierrez named his farm Pocho-Mil, in reference to the thousands of cordobas he hoped to earn on the farm.

Pochomíl's gorgeous sandy coastline is quickly being bought up by wealthy Managua politicians constructing their beach homes, making competition among hotel and restaurant owners particularly fierce. As you get off the bus expect to be assaulted by employees of a dozen restaurants all trying to drag you into their establishments to eat and drink. No one place is any better than another—you can expect palm thatch huts built on the sand, and a menu of fried fish and cold beer no matter where you go—so shake off the restaurant lackeys, take a deep breath, and choose whichever establishment you want. Travelers driving their own vehicles will pay a $1 entrance fee.

Accommodations

Hotel and restaurant rates fluctuate wildly according to the calendar, Semana Santa and Christmas being the most expensive time of year to visit, followed by random peaks during the dry season. In the wet season, prices become significantly more flexible. Any month of the year, traveling with a group gives you significant leverage to bargain for a good deal.

One of the longest established places on the beach, **Hotel Altamar** (tel. 269-9204) has 15 rooms along a long corridor that leads down to the patio restaurant and beach. Five rooms with private bath cost $11, and 10 rooms with shared bath cost $9 or so; rooms generally hold three travelers. Its restaurant, situated at the top of a long stairway to the beach, is good, if a bit slow, and has a great view of the Pacific; it's also got shady huts and hammocks down on the beach.

All the way down the road at the north end of the beach is the luxury **Hotel Villa del Mar.** Originally one of Herty Lewites's creations, the government let it deteriorate until by the mid-1990s it was practically abandoned. The Universidad Americana (UAM) bought and renovated it, and now uses the hotel as part of the curriculum for students studying tourism and business administration; 30 double-occupancy rooms cost $35 with private bath and air-conditioning. Besides the beautiful beach, there is a swimming pool, kiddie pool, a wood-paneled conference room, palm thatch huts set on a grassy lawn, and a fancy open-air restaurant serving three meals a day. Credit cards are accepted, call 269-0426 for reservations. You can visit Villa del Mar for the day; the $7 entrance fee can be applied to meals and beverages served on the premises.

Next door to Villa del Mar is the more humble **Hotel Cabañas del Mar,** with 8 rooms trimmed in bamboo. Four clean rooms with private bath and a/c run $18 d or $25 t. One six-person room is available for $43. Knock $7 off the price for one the room that doesn't have a/c, tel. 269-0433. It also has a full menu of traditional food and some vegetarian dishes.

Hotel Mar Azul is accessed by going straight over the dune at the traffic circle, and then down 20 meters of dirt road. This is the establishment with which you'll most likely be able to work out a bargain, but the asking price for five bleak, concrete rooms is $17 per room, tel. 885-9539.

Getting There and Away

Buses leave Managua for Pochomíl every 30 minutes all day until about 5 P.M. The last bus from Pochomíl back to Managua departs at 5:30 P.M. from the cul-de-sac.

Pacific beach resort

Montelimar

Montelimar

Somoza knew what he was doing when he picked this spot to build his personal beach paradise, and Barceló Resorts knew what they were doing when they turned it into Nicaragua's premier resort. In between, the Sandinistas used it as a military base. Open to anyone with $112–144 a couple; before you balk at the prices, realize that this is an all-inclusive, five-star facility, and the rates include 24 hours of feasting, drinking, swimming, and playing. The Montelimar compound is enormous, with multiple beachside bars, sports, and a co-ed, spunky crew of "animators" to help you have a good time. The 290 rooms (includes 56 beachside bungalows) are first rate, with private bath, a/c, TV, strongbox, and minibar. Facilities for groups and conventions, plus airport shuttles, shopping, travel agency, etc. (tel. 269-6769 or 269-6752, fax 269-7669 or 269-7757, email: playamontelimar @barcelo.com). Any bus to Pochomíl will also get you to Montelimar, and there are various tour operators that arrange for pickups from Managua airport or your hotel.

Masaya, Carazo, and the Pueblos Blancos

Masaya

The "City of Flowers," as Rubén Darío christened Masaya a century ago (reportedly in praise of its *muchachas*—girls), has been marketed as Nicaragua's folk culture and *artesanía* center. Tourism officials have, throughout the latter 1990s, attempted to solidify this image by concentrating all that is Masaya into the refurbished Old Market. They've done an admirable job, and a visit to the market within its castlelike walls is a safe, colorful, pleasant experience, especially when there is folk dancing and music on one of the stages. In fact, the Old Market is so pleasant, many visitors choose not to stray from the one square block comprising it—while the rest of the city vibrantly rambles on, virtually unnoticed by the hordes of tourists who go there to shop.

The Gate of Hell, a.k.a. Volcán Santiago

MASAYA, CARAZO, AND THE PUEBLOS BLANCOS

Masaya is not as prettily painted as Granada, and the faces of many of its buildings are still cracked from the earthquake of 2000, exposing the old adobe construction; but because Masaya's economy is based on trade rather than ritzy tourism, you may find a journey through the city to be a very real and tangibly cultural experience. Take a horse-drawn carriage to the breezy *malecón,* 100 meters above the crater lake; go to a ball game with 8,000 cheering Masayan fans; tour the family-run hammock factories; sit in the shade of one of 11 parks—or stay and relax amidst the sights and smells of the market all day.

Land and History

Masaya is a hot, tropical plains city, only 234 meters above sea level, and virtually on the slopes of the volcano with the same name. On its western edge is a steep drop-off to the Laguna de Masaya, with paths first carved out by the inhabitants of 20 Chorotega villages that originally occupied the Laguna's shores. These people were referred to as Darianes by the first Spaniards that encountered them in 1529, and they were ruled by the cacique Tenderí. Masaya was officially founded as a city in 1819.

LAGUNA DE MASAYA

The old crater of the adjacent volcano has been filled with water since long before the first humans arrived. It is most easily appreciated from the vantage points atop the 100-meter-high cliffs on its eastern side, which are accessible at the *malecón* next to the baseball stadium, and from several restaurants along the highway to Managua. It has a surface area of 8.5 square kilometers and a maximum depth of 73 meters. Its shores are reached by numerous trails that date back to the Chorotegans who maintained some 20 villages along its shores. One trail runs straight down from the *malecón,* but the water has been contaminated since the old hospital first starting dumping waste in 1936 (followed shortly thereafter by municipal sewage). Its waters are additionally sullied by the wastes from the coffee processing operations on the opposite shores from the city of Masaya.

The People

Present-day Masayans, a population of around 85,000, are proudly connected to their Chorotegan roots. They earned a reputation as fighters after several centuries of rebellious history—first against the original Spaniards, and later against William Walker's forces in 1856, the U.S. Marines in 1912, and in a number of fierce battles against the National Guard during the revolution. This was a strong Sandinista town until the Liberals won the city seat in the 2000 municipal elections. Masayans are a creative, festive people with many unique customs, including their solemn, mysterious funeral processions, where the coffin is slowly paraded from the deceased's home to the church, and then to one of 15 cemeteries—drawn by a pair of white, elegantly costumed horses, and surrounded by slow-walking crowds of mourners.

ORIENTATION AND GETTING AROUND

Masaya is situated south of the Managua-Granada Carretera, from which branch several entrances to the city, two of which run all the way to Masaya's central plaza. The street that runs north along the plaza's east side is the Calle Central, and as you travel it toward the Carretera, it becomes increasingly commercial, essentially making up Masaya's main drag. One block east of the southeast corner of the park, you'll find the stone walls of the Mercado Viejo (Old Market). Walking six blocks west of the central park will take you to the hammock factories, baseball stadium, and *malecón;* traveling due south leads you to Barrio Monimbó; going five blocks north will put you in the heart of the Barrio San Jerónimo around the church of the same name, situated at the famous *siete esquinas* intersection. As for getting around, if you get tired of walking, the mayor's office claims there are 270 units of urban transportation, made up of buses, minivans, taxis, and horse carriages.

SIGHTS AND ATTRACTIONS

Plazas and Parks

The central plaza is officially called **Parque 17 de Octubre,** named for a battle against the *Guardia* in 1977. Look around—there are plenty of bullet holes to prove it, plus two imposing command towers immediately to the west. The church in the northeast corner is **La Parroquia La Asunción.**

The **Plaza de Monimbó** is a small, unremarkable triangular park in front of the enormous Don Bosco private school on the southern side of Masaya; but starting around 3 P.M., the space comes to life as the throbbing social and commercial heart of the Barrio Monimbó, a particularly indigenous-rooted, Sandinista neighborhood. It's an inspiring scene, with lots of food, smiles, and action, and the photo opportunities are endless.

High above the blue waters of Laguna de Masaya, the *malecón* is a beautiful promenade with long views to the north and west. It shares its space with the baseball stadium parking lot, making for the most scenic tailgate party you'll ever experience.

Museum

The **Museo y Galería Héroes y Mártires,** located within the Alcaldía (Mayor's Office), 1.5 blocks north of the park, is a tribute to those Masayans who fought against the National Guard during the many street battles of the revolution. An interesting collection of guns, photos of the fallen (and some of their personal effects), and an unexploded napalm bomb dropped on the people by Somoza's forces. Open Monday–Friday 8 A.M.–5 P.M., donation requested.

ENTERTAINMENT AND EVENTS

Jueves de Verbena is the weekly show offered in the Old Market on one of several stages. Every Thursday from about 5–11 P.M., you'll find dance, theater, art expos, music, and more.

Bars

The most famous Nicaraguan scene is found across from the Central Park at **La Rhonda,** with beer, lots of space, good appetizers—in the words of one Masayan native, "All for the three Bs: *bueno, bonito, y barato*" (good, nice, and cheap). The **Coconut Sport Bar** boasts lots of beer, TVs, and a mellow place to hang. If you're into dives, check out the **Bar Confianza,** two blocks north and one east of the Old Market.

Baseball

If you're here on a weekend during the season (January–May), be sure to catch Team Masaya, a.k.a. San Fernando, play ball in the **Estadio Roberto Clemente** (named for the Puerto Rico–born Pittsburgh Pirate who died in a plane crash delivering aid to Nicaraguan earthquake victims in 1973). Start with a tailgating party in the parking lot overlooking the Laguna de Masaya.

Clubs and Nightlife

Although a decent trek from the city center, **Cocojambo** is easily the most obvious spot to drink and dance. It may cost a few dollars to get in, but this slick joint is one of Nicaragua's better discos and provides a solid night out. In the same area, the private **Club Social** occasionally books

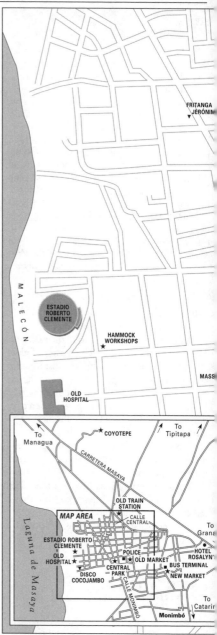

MASAYA, CARAZO, & THE PUEBLOS BLANCOS

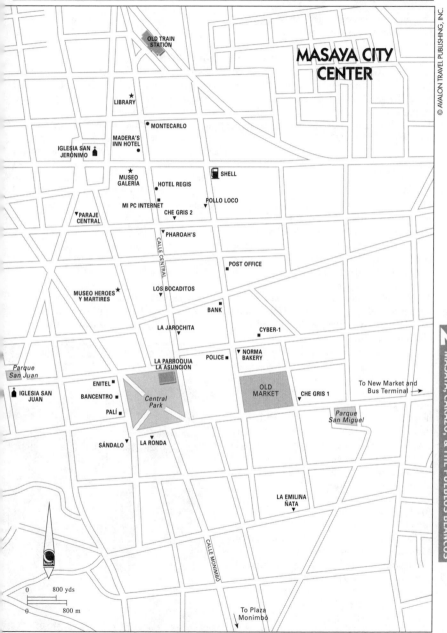

OLD TRAIN STATION

MASAYA CITY CENTER

★ LIBRARY

● MONTECARLO

MADERA'S INN HOTEL

IGLESIA SAN JERÓNIMO ♦

★ MUSEO GALERÍA

● HOTEL REGIS

⛽ SHELL

MI PC INTERNET

POLLO LOCO

▼ PARAJE CENTRAL

CHE GRIS 2 ▼

▼ PHAROAH'S

CALLE CENTRAL

POST OFFICE

MUSEO HEROES Y MARTIRES ★

LOS BOCADITOS ▼

BANK ■

LA JAROCHITA

CYBER-1 ■

LA PARROQUIA LA ASUNCIÓN

POLICE ■

▼ NORMA BAKERY

Parque San Juan

ENITEL ■

OLD MARKET

CHE GRIS 1 ■

To New Market and Bus Terminal →

♦ IGLESIA SAN JUAN

BANCENTRO ■

Central Park

PALÍ ■

Parque San Miguel

SÁNDALO ▼

▼ LA RONDA

LA EMILINA ÑATA ▼

N Moon

0   800 yds
0   800 m

To Plaza Monimbó ↓

MASAYA, CARAZO, & THE PUEBLOS BLANCOS

a big music act and opens its doors to the public. The **Delfín Azul** is the most centrally located disco, in the "Hotel" Montecarlo on the main drag; open every night and it fills up on Saturdays (soon to have six expensive, air-conditioned, "very private" rooms—hubba hubba). Managua-based **Pharaoh Casino** has a branch in Masaya, on the main drag with a clean, cool room of slots, roulette, and cards (open 11 A.M.–3 A.M. every day, tel. 522-5222).

SHOPPING

Markets

This is, ostensibly, the reason anyone comes to Masaya. As mentioned, all roads lead first to the **Mercado Viejo**, built in 1891, destroyed by fires in 1966 and 1978, and most recently refurbished in 1997—this time in a successful attempt to convert it into a destination for foreign tourists rather than a center for local trade. Also known as the **Mercado Nacionál de Artesanías,** the Old Market is safe, open, and comfortable—as opposed to the new market, or the **Mercado Municipal,** located at the main bus station about a half kilometer to the east. This is the real deal, with a low, hot, tin roof, cramped aisles, and everything for sale, from hammocks to raw beef livers. The new market has a decent *artesanía* section as well, but there are noticeably more flies and pickpockets. Prices are slightly lower there, and if your Spanish skills are up to it, you've got more bargaining power. Some cordoba-pinchers choose to browse at the new market, and then walk east to find the same item in the old one for a lower price.

Art Gallery

Just off the main street and right behind the Iglesia San Jerónimo, seek out the **Museo Galería Motivación Sevilla,** a small, varied exhibit of Nicaraguan painters, including primitivist works, volcanic rocks, and a beautiful selection of greeting cards. The proprietress, Esperanza Sevilla (*"Esperanza,"* she explains poetically, "Hope—the last thing we lose in life."), opens her gallery's doors in the afternoons, but if they are closed, feel free to knock, tel. 860-4466, email: espsevilla@yahoo.com.

Hammocks

Masaya **hammocks** are handmade by the thousands, for sale in local markets and for export alike. The most obvious place to purchase one is in either of the markets. However, if you'd like to get closer to the source, you'd do well to visit one of the many *fábricas de hamacas* (hammock factories) in Masaya, most of which are clustered on the same block near the southwest edge of town, across from the old hospital on the road to the *malecón* and baseball stadium. There you'll find at least a half-dozen family businesses, with Mom, Dad, Grandpa, and Junior, all casually weaving and working away on their front porches. Many of these factories have casual shops that accept credit cards, and they will gladly show you how their wares are produced. It takes roughly two full days for three people to make a single hammock, which in turn, sells for around $30. Prices vary widely though, according to style, size, and quality. Happy hangin'.

© JOSHUA BERMAN

PARTY TOWN

Masayans party all year long, celebrating various religious, historical, and indigenous rites with a wild collage of marimba music, traditional dance and costume, poetry, painting, food, drink, legends, and age-old customs. Many of the specific dances you see are family traditions, in which a certain role—and its accompanying mask and costume—is passed down from generation to generation. The costumes are a key element of the festivals and are often elaborate and gorgeous.

The Festival of the Cross, in which the people exchange thousands of palm-thatch crosses in honor of La Señora de la Asunción, is celebrated in May. The virgin icon is carried to Monimbó in remembrance of the miracle that occurred there during the last eruption of Volcán Masaya's Santiago Crater, in which the virgin saved the city from the hot ashes.

September, October, November, and December are the peak fiesta months in Masaya, when nearly every weekend is colored by festivities. Things get started with the official *fiestas patronales* on September 20, in honor of the Patron Saint Jerónimo.

The Festival of San Sebastian boasts a dance unique in all of Nicaragua, and within Masaya, only occurring in the indigenous Monimbó barrio. This is the **Baile de Chinegro de Mozote y Verga,** in which participants have a mock battle, hitting each other with big sticks, and finally coming together in a peace ritual. The music is marked by the *tunkún* drum (a Mayan instrument), and a whistle called a *pífano.* At the end of the ritual, everybody screams together:

¡Viva San Sebastian!
¡Viva el Mayordomo (Master of the Parade)!
¡Viva Santa Marta Vencedera (Saint Martha the Conqueror)!

Perhaps the most stunning of Masaya's fiestas is the **Procesión de San Jerónimo** on the first Sunday of December, when the statue of the city's patron saint is paraded through the streets amidst a sea of flowers. It is marked by the Baile de las Inditas (Dance of the Little Indian Girls), Baile de Negras (Dance of the Black Women), and the Baile de Fantasía (Dance of Fantasy).

A week before Semana Santa, the celebration of **San Lázaro** is equally interesting, when believers turn out with ornately costumed pets, in thanks to the patron saint for maintaining the household animals in good health.

La Novena del Niño Dios is an interesting December ritual in which small children are given pots, pans, whistles, and firecrackers and are sent into the streets at 5 A.M. to noisily call all the other children together for the 6 A.M. mass, in celebration of the Christ-child's birth.

Sundays throughout the months of September, October, November, and December it's possible to find dancers that go from house to house performing short dances to marimba music.

Guitars

Sergio is a third-generation luthier at Guitarras Zepeda, making quality guitars in the same home and workshop as his grandfather did, 200 meters west of the ENEL Central. His cedar guitars go for about $55, *caoba* (mahogany) for $90, and *granadillo* guitars fetch $125, tel. 883-0260.

ACCOMMODATIONS

Apart from the clients of the 17(!) sex hotels along the highway that passes through Masaya, most visitors have traditionally based themselves in nearby Managua or Granada; thus, the demand for a wide variety of accommodations has yet to arrive here. Nevertheless, there are a handful of adequate options if you choose to stay the night in Masaya.

Under $10

Hotel Regis, on Calle Central, 3.5 blocks north of the church on the main plaza, has a dozen neat, clean rooms (including some for groups and families), with shared bath and fan for $5 a person; breakfast for $2. The couple that runs the place is very friendly, knowledgeable about things to do in the area, and speaks some English—however, they are strict about running a clean shop, look down on partying, and close their doors at 10 P.M., tel. 522-2300.

MASAYA, CARAZO, & THE PUEBLOS BLANCOS

Right up the block, **Madera's Inn Hotel** has another dozen rooms on two floors, ranging from a $10 double with fan and shared bath to $25 with private bath and a/c. Happily open 24 hours with a beautifully furnished common room, Internet, and friendly service, tel./fax 522-5825, email: hmaderas@ibw.com.ni.

$10–25

Rosalyn's is a good step up in quality and space, located on the highway to Granada next to the Pepsi distributor, tel. 522-7328. There are 10 rooms, ranging from $15 single or double (with fan), to $30 with a/c and TV. The best deal is two rooms with five beds each for $40, with a/c and TV. **Hotel Volcán Masaya,** on the Carretera Masaya (km 23) next to the national park entrance, has 14 rooms starting at $10 a couple with shared bath ($20–25 with private bath), tel./fax 522-5825.

FOOD

Comida Típica

Hot 'n' juicy street food is found at **Fritanga Alvarez,** across from la entrada Santa Rosa, or at the **Fritanga San Jerónimo,** a few blocks west of the church of the same name. The most famous *carne asada* (grilled beef) in Masaya is found at "Flat-nose Emilina's in the Crazy Neighborhood." In local speak, that's *"La Emilina Ñata en el Barrio Loco."* Open every day from 5 P.M. till the meat runs out.

Los Bocaditos on the Calle Central has a wide range of cheap sandwiches, soups, and more. Open 10 A.M.–10 P.M. For juicy roast chicken and keg beer, try the **Rosticería Pollo Loco,** just south of the Shell San Jerónimo.

For overpriced but safe and tasty Nica food, try one of the two **Che Gris** locations (a.k.a. Chema Canoso, which means gray-haired Jose-María). One is located across from the east side of the Old Market; the other, about four blocks north. Similar fare can be had at **El Paraje Centro,** just south of the Iglesia San Jerónimo.

Bakeries

On the corner half a block north of the Old Market and across from the police, find **Norma's bakery,** with an excellent selection of baked goods, sandwiches, and burgers; open every day 8 A.M.–9 P.M. Or follow your nose to a hole-in-the-wall bakery just south of the central park.

Gringo Fare

Plenty of burger joints, including **Hamberlooca** near the Old Market (delivery service, tel. 522-5661), and **Burguer-Mania** two blocks north on the same street. **Pizza Hot** is okay, and the **Esso Tiger Market** delivers pies to your hotel, tel. 522-7005.

Mexican

La Jarochita Taquería Mexicana is clean and safe, with a decent burrito for $3 and taco dishes for less than that. Also plenty of meat and seafood, open 10 A.M.–11 P.M., tel. 522-4831.

Chinese

Across from the central park is the enormous ballroomlike **Sándalo,** with the standard Nica-Chinese selection of chop sueys. Across town is the **Bamboo Chino,** on the main street, three blocks north of the plaza, closed Tuesdays.

INFORMATION

The INTUR office is located within the Old Market, open business hours (closed for lunch), tel. 522-7615. They might be able to answer specific questions about the area or current activities.

SERVICES

Emergency

Hospital Hilario Sanchez Vásquez, located on the highway toward Granada, is the biggest facility in town, tel. 522-2778. The central police station is half a block north of the Old Market, occupying a large corner across from Norma's bakery, tel. 522-4222 or 522-2521.

Money

There are a number of banks in town, including a Bancentro across from the central plaza, and several banks just north of the Old Market. There are now multiple ATMs within the Old Market, plus a Western Union on the north end of Masaya near the old train station.

Internet

Across from the giant Don Bosco school, about five blocks south of the central plaza, Monimbo.Net charges under $3 an hour, open Monday–Friday 8 A.M.–8 P.M. (closed 1–2 P.M.), Saturday until 6:30 P.M. Mi PC a Colores is on the main drag, 3.5 blocks north of the church in the main plaza, $2 an hour, open Monday–Friday 8 A.M.–6 P.M., Saturday until noon. Diagonally across from the police station, Cyber-1 has Internet access for $2.50 an hour and free coffee.

Massage and Natural Medicine

For stress therapy by a certified acupressure and reflexologist, spend an hour with Patricia Cuadra, located a half block west of the Iglesia San Juan. She will open up your body's energy paths and magically relieve muscular tension, and all for under $5! Reiki Tibetan chakra alignment costs the same for an extra hour, tel. 522-2893.

Offering herbal meds and a treatment called the "Bio-energetic Method," Medicina Natural is located half a block southwest of the Plaza de Monimbó, tel. 522-3122.

Phones and Mail

There is both a Correos de Nicaragua and a DHL Worldwide Express within the Old Market compound to facilitate sending gifts immediately. There is another Correos located 2.5 blocks north of the Old Market.

Photos

The Kodak Express, half a block west of the police station, sends all film to be processed in Managua (open Mon.–Fri. 8 A.M.–6 P.M., Sat. till 2 P.M.).

Other Services

Feel like getting pumped up after a long day of shopping? Try the Gimnasio Zeus, one block south of the Old Market, and just before Masaya's only dry cleaning operation. Get a pro haircut half a block east of the northeast corner of the Old Market—for under $2, even cheaper at one of the stalls in the new market.

GETTING THERE AND AWAY

"Masaya! Masaya! Masaya!" It's almost difficult *not* to travel to Masaya, as nearly every southbound bus leaving Managua from Roberto Huembes passes the city, which is right on the highway, only 27 kilometers from Managua. The most efficient way to go is to take any of the Masaya- or Granada-bound *expresos* from the UCA. They leave regularly from 7 A.M.–9:30 P.M., arriving in Masaya's Parque San Miguel; from there, they depart for Managua from 6 A.M.–8 P.M. The ride costs under $1. There is also *expreso* service between Masaya's Plaza de Monimbó and Mercado Oriental in Managua, first leaving Masaya at 3 A.M., and running through 7 P.M. Ordinary bus service leaves and arrives at the main terminal in the parking lot of the Mercado Nuevo.

Near Masaya

COYOTEPE

The battlements of the Coyotepe fort are visible atop an isolated hill on the opposite side of the highway from Masaya. Take a cab, or hike up the road—the diversion is worth it just for the view of Masaya, its lagoon and volcano, both great lakes, and the far-reaching surrounding countryside; in addition, you can go on a freaky tour of this underground prison-fort. Built at the turn of the 20th century, Coyotepe was once the site of a battle between the national troops and U.S. Marines in 1912. It saw action again during the overthrow of Somoza. Today it is run by the Nicaraguan Boy Scouts as a tourist destination (for special attention—or at least a smile— greet your guide with the three-finger Scout salute and their motto in Spanish: *Siempre Listo* — Always Prepared). Take a flashlight with you to tour the underground prison, as the complex has absolutely zero light.

VOLCÁN MASAYA NATIONAL PARK

Easily accessible as a day trip from Managua, Masaya, or Granada, Volcán Masaya is one of the most visibly active volcanoes in the country, featuring several bare, gaping craters and a constant stream of sulfurous gas, visible from as far away as the airport in Managua. From one of its craters, you can glimpse incandescent rock and magma— but at only 632 meters above sea level, Volcán Masaya looks more like a vulgar wound in the earth's surface than the traditional image most of us have of a volcano (for that, just glance north toward Momotombo). The crater and its unique environs have been successfully set aside and managed as a national park, complete with a visitor center, nature museum, hiking trails, and a road all the way to the dramatic abyss which the Spaniards declared to be the very gates of hell.

© RANDY WOOD

Coyotepe

Volcán Masaya was called *Popogatepe* (mountain that burns) by the Chorotegas, who feared it and explained eruptions as displays of anger to be appeased with sacrifices, often human. In the early 1500s, Father Francisco Bobadilla placed a cross at the crater lip hoping to exorcise the devil within. Not long afterwards though, it occurred to the Spanish that the volcano might contain gold instead of the devil, and—hell forgotten—both Friar Blas del Castillo and Gonzalo Fernandez de Oviedo lowered themselves into the crater on ropes in order to begin tentative excavations of the molten lava. Neither the devil nor gold was found.

The park is composed of several volcanoes and craters, including Volcán Nindirí, which last erupted in 1670, and Volcán Masaya, which blew its hole in 1772 (actually, in April 2000, Masaya burped up a single boulder which crushed an Italian tourist's car in the parking lot).

The relatively new Santiago Crater was formed between the other two in 1852. It is inhabited by a curious species of parakeet that lives contentedly in the crater walls, oblivious to the toxic gases and in defiance of what science says should be inhospitable conditions. You might see these *chocoyos del cráter* (crater parakeets) from the parking area along the crater's edge.

Information and Services

The Visitor's Interpretation Center and museum boast continually improving exhibits, including three-dimensional dioramas of Nicaragua and Central America, models of active volcanoes, and remnants of indigenous sacrifice urns and musical instruments found deep in the volcano's caves; there is also a display of old lithographs and paintings of the volcano as the Spaniards saw it.

There are several guided tours worth considering, none of which cost more than $2 and all of which support the protection of the park and will surely open a new perspective of the volcano for you, especially if you speak some Spanish. Of special interest is the walk to the Tzinancanostoc Bat Cave, a passageway melted out of solid rock. The park also contains several hiking trails through a veritable moonscape of

lava formations and scrubby vegetation. Consider spending a day here, as the hikes are well worth the time and offer a good chance to encounter some of the park's wildlife, including coyotes, deer, iguanas, and monkeys. The Coyote Trail will lead you east to the shore of the Laguna de Masaya. If planning to hike, bring plenty of water and adequate protection from the sun, as there are no shade trees.

The park is open seven days a week 9 A.M.–5 P.M., and its headquarters can be reached at tel. 522-5415. Admission is $5 for foreigners; make sure to buy tickets for any guided tours you want to take while you're at the visitor center before proceeding up to the crater's edge. Tours leave from the lip of the Santiago crater, not the visitor center, and you can't purchase tickets from the guides.

Getting There and Away

Any southbound bus from Roberto Huembes in Managua will drop you off at the turnoff to the park; the ride takes about a half hour. From there, hitch or hike up to the visitor center (a half-hour's walk). If driving, the entrance is hard to miss, with a big wooden sign on the west side of the highway, a few kilometers south of the city of Masaya. The guard up at the crater will strongly suggest that you back into your spot, to ensure an easy getaway in case things start a-shakin'.

NINDIRÍ

Situated just north of the highway between the entrance to the national park and the city of Masaya, Nindirí was the most important and densely populated of the indigenous settlements in the area—up to 1,500 years before the arrival of the Spanish. In Chorotega, its name means "Hill of the Small Pig," and its principal attraction is a museum celebrating pre-Columbian life in the area. **Museo Tenderí,** named after an important cacique, is home to more than 1,000 archaeological pieces. Also, ask around about the **Cailagua site,** with petroglyphs overlooking the Laguna de Masaya. In celebrating their patron saint, Santa Ana, during the last week of July, residents of Nindirí employ many of the ancient dance, costume, and music rituals popular to the whole Masaya and Carazo region.

LAGUNA DE APOYO

The *laguna* is a spectacular, incredibly blue body of water trapped inside the crater of the Apoyo Volcano. The water is cool, clean, and wonderful, and the deepest *measured* point (200 meters) is the lowest point in all of Central America. Its shores are easily accessible, and a cluster of tourist facilities (as well as luxurious private homes) have been constructed at the water's edge, inside the crater. The volcano still has some underwater thermal vents and experiences the occasional seismic tremor, but for the most part, it's considered dormant and its walls are thickly vegetated with green forest and a chaotic network of trails. The earthquake in 2000 originated under the town of Catarina and actually caused the water of the lake to slosh from side to side, starting a rumor that it was boiling. There are several fish species endemic to the lake—products of the forces of evolution in an isolated habitat. Scientists at the Proyecto Ecologico are at work describing some of the remaining "undiscovered" species here, and offer scuba tours to view their subjects.

Hiking in the forests of the crater walls, you may observe species of toucans, hummingbirds, blue jays, howler and white-face monkeys, and rare butterflies. To find the monkeys, continue to the right when the road into the bottom of the crater turns from pavement into dirt; follow it two kilometers and start looking (and listening) for the monkeys on your left-hand side (toward the water). After five or six kilometers, you'll pass the Quinta El Nono, and the road turns into a trail; the first creek you come to is home to several troops of monkeys. Be sure to wave a friendly greeting when passing the Lugareños (as the local residents are known). To fit in, pronounce your "Adios" as a long, drawn out, "Adiooooh." No need to be as cordial to the monkeys, who will probably fling their feces at you.

Food and Accommodations

Apart from the food at each of the *hospedajes*, **Los Ranchitos** offers simple Nica food, served by the humble Doña Chepita; located right at the bottom of the road as it approaches the lagoon. The **Monkey Hut** is quickly gaining comparable popularity to its nearby urban cousin in Granada. This is a relaxing spot set at the water's edge among lush gardens and palm trees, with a fully equipped kitchen for your use. Soft drinks, water, and beer can be purchased at the hut—all other supplies need to be packed in. Dorm beds and hammocks go for $7 a person, $15 s, $19 d. Or come on a day trip and use the facilities for less than $3 a person. For reservations and weekly/monthly rates, contact the Bearded Monkey in Granada at tel. 552-4028.

Los Clarineros Hospedaje has four rooms with balconies facing the water: two singles for $13 a night, and two for couples at $15, or rent a cabin for $30; credit cards accepted, tel. 522-6215 or 887-5952.

Norome is the local Ritz, with seven bungalows along the water's edge where you can spend your day swimming, sailing, kayaking, hiking, and then finish by soaking in the hot tub and ordering something from the restaurant/bar. Transportation from Managua, Granada, or San Juan del Sur can be arranged. Rooms have a range of facilities, and prices range from $38 with fan, $48 with a/c, tel. 883-9093 or 886-7123, fax 278-7120, email: edulat@yahoo.com.

Proyecto Ecologico

This is a not-for-profit research station with ties to the governmental natural resource ministry (MARENA). It is also a Spanish school (since 1992), an organic garden project, and a *hospedaje* and backpacker getaway. For the Spanish school, you can stay with local families, or in the Proyecto's dormitory (see the sectin on Spanish Schools in On the Road). The director, Jeffrey McCrary, is developing a birding book for the area (144 species in the *laguna* alone), and studying the endemic fish species in the lake. Not only will he tell you all about his project, he can take you diving—$20 a tank for certified, card-carrying divers. The Proyecto also has a *hospedaje* for $12 a night, and home-cooked meals served on a *tranquilo* (shady wooden deck.) Also offered:

fishing and motorboat trips, kayaks, and the chance to participate in one of several volunteer reforestation brigades each year.

Services

There's not much in the way of public services once you are down in the crater; best to do some shopping in your base city and come prepared. As for tours, low-key, locally guided "Eco Excursions" can be arranged by calling Bismarck in Masaya at tel. 862-0777; ask about bird-watching, hiking, biking, swimming, horseback riding, and camping trips.

Getting There and Away

There is a new paved road branching south off of the Carretera Masaya a few kilometers beyond the turnoff for Catarina (km 37.5); it passes through the small town of Valle de Laguna where you turn right at the T if coming from Masaya

(turning left takes you toward Granada). The road continues left into the crater (pay a $1 entrance fee if driving), and winds downward, ending exactly at the gate to former president Alemán's vacation home (hmm). Buses cost $.50 and leave the main Masaya market terminal at 10:30 A.M. and 3:10 P.M. for the bottom of the *laguna (baja al plan);* buses leave for Valle de Laguna (the town) hourly 5:30 A.M.–6 P.M. (from Valle, it's about a half-hour walk to the bottom of the crater). A taxi from Masaya will cost $5–9, a good deal if you have a group. Leaving Laguna de Apoyo, there are three buses: 6 A.M., 11:10 A.M., and 4:40 P.M.

From Granada: Transportation is provided from the Bearded Monkey, Tuesday at noon and Friday at 10 A.M., returning from the Monkey Hut Wednesday at 11 A.M. and Friday at 2 P.M.—the ride costs about $1 each way and can be arranged for other times as well. Taxis from Granada cost $7.

The Pueblos Blancos

Escaping the heat of the lakeside lowlands is as easy as a 40-minute bus ride to the Pueblos Blancos and Carazo. A dozen curious towns cluster together in the coolness of the hills just south of Managua. The "White Villages" are named for the purity and color of their churches, each of which, when placed against an azure sky, makes for a photograph you can brag about. The towns are spread throughout the Meseta de los Pueblos, a cool plateau 500 meters above sea level that stays green all year long and is surrounded on the north by the Sierras de Managua, the east by the slopes of Volcán Masaya, the south by the Laguna de Apoyo and Volcán Mombacho, and to the west by the dry, desolate decline toward the Pacific Ocean.

The names of the different villages sound best when sung out consecutively by bus *ayudantes* hanging out the open doors as they trawl the terminal at Huembes: "Masatepe!Catarina! Niquinohomo!Nandasmo!Piodoce!Masatepe!" Each town proudly claims some unique treasure to set it apart from the rest—bamboo craftwork, black magic, folk dances, Sandino's birthplace, crater lakes, wicker chairs, beaches,

and renowned festivals. The area was a little shaken by an earthquake in June 2000, but such is life on the ring of fire.

Visiting the pueblos makes an easy day trip, but to really take advantage, book a room in San Marcos, Catarina, or Jinotepe, and take some time. Whether you are touring furniture workshops, coffee plantations, or hiking down for a dip in the Laguna de Apoyo, there's plenty to do.

ORIENTATION AND GETTING AROUND

Getting around is easy—both in a car, and in the *expreso* minivan system. The distance between towns is never more than 10 or 12 kilometers, and you'll need to pay attention to your map to stay on top of the spiderweb of roads. The towns are all easily and quickly accessible from Masaya and Granada as well as Managua—if you should decide to start or end your trip in either of those cities.

Buses to the Pueblos Blancos leave from Huembes, continue south on the Carretera

MASAYA, CARAZO, & THE PUEBLOS BLANCOS

in front of the Church in Catarina

Granada, Lake Nicaragua, and the double cones of Ometepe in the distance. The view at the Mirador is only one reason people visit Catarina; the town also has dozens of lush, ornamental plant nurseries and local crafts like basket and pottery making, all of which you'll find for sale along the roadside.

The *laguna* is 200 meters deep and beautiful to swim in, despite the requisite monster legends. It is reachable by either a network of trails that descend from Catarina and Diriá, or by a road that splits off the Masaya-Granada highway. The road winds partway around the lagoon, built to provide access to several homes of the rich and famous. At the bottom, you'll find restaurants, hotels, and a Spanish school (see the section above on Laguna de Apoyo).

The Catarina shopping spree begins before you even turn into the entrance to the town, and continues up past the church and along the final hill to the entrance of the Mirador. There you'll only be asked to pay an *entrada* if you have a vehicle (ciclo-taxis—three-wheeled bicycle taxis—and their drivers that get out and push you up the hill don't count); the fee is $.75 for unlimited parking, 8 A.M.–10 P.M.

The only accommodations are found in **Hotel Jaaris,** with four nice rooms, private bath, TV, and fan, starting at $6 s. Meal service is also available, and a beautiful airy, enclosed porch with a hammock, tel. 558-0020.

Catarina is home to one of the new AOL/Peace Corps–sponsored Internet businesses, called Cyber Center Catarina and located in the Alcaldía, open Monday–Friday 8 A.M.–5 P.M. (with an hour lunch break at noon); $3 an hour, plus CD burner and scanner, tel. 558-0428, email: catarina@ibw.com.ni.

Masaya, and then turn west into the hills at various points, depending on the route. Be sure to tell your *ayudante* the town where you'd like to get off and have him tell you when you are there. The Carazo buses—to Jinotepe and Diriamba—leave from the Mercado Israel and from a lot across from the UCA, and they take the Carretera Sur. The many microbuses are nice for zipping to and from Managua, but the ordinary big yellows are the most interesting way to get between the towns, especially since the ride is never long (although it can get packed around rush hour).

CATARINA

This hillside pueblo ascends the slope of an ancient volcano all the way to the lip of the old crater, which has been developed into a tourist attraction called the **Mirador.** Enjoy the stiff breeze as you look out over the Laguna de Apoyo, and

SAN JUAN DE ORIENTE

The sign at the entrance boasts San Juan as the Cuna de Artesanía Precolombiana, only true if Columbus arrived here after 1973, when local residents began turning out the pottery that has made the town famous. Despite the false advertising, San Juan pots, vases, and plates are attractive and, in fact, they do an excellent job celebrating pre-Columbian styles (as well as their own inventions). Shop at one of the small co-operatives along the entrance to town, or in the many tiny displays in people's homes as you walk through the narrow, brick streets.

DIRIÁ AND DIRIOMO

These across-the-street neighbors are two of many towns in Nicaragua named for the indigenous Dirian people and their leader, Diriangén, the famed rebel cacique and martyr whose spilled blood (at the hands of the conquistadores) is immortalized in Carlos Mejía Godoy's anthem, "Nicaragua Nicaragüita." Both towns are known for their unique celebrations throughout the year, mixing elements of pre-Columbian, Catholic, and bizarre regional customs (like smacking each other with dried-out bull penises). Diriá, on the east side of the road, is a lesser-known gateway for hiking down to the Laguna de Apoyo, or simply accessing a beautiful mirador that is much less developed and crowded than the traditional one in Catarina. Across the highway, Diriomo is famous for its sorcery, and the intrepid traveler looking for a love potion or revenge should seek out one of the pueblo's *brujos*.

NIQUINOHOMO

Birthplace of Augusto César Sandino, Niquinohomo also boasts a 320-year-old church with an impressive red tile roof. Sandino's childhood home (off the northwest corner of the park) was severely damaged in the latest earthquake, but is being restored as a library and Sandino museum (with the help of a $60,000 gift from the Japanese). Another memorial to the general is found at the main entrance to Niquinohomo: a 4,000-pound, solid bronze statue of the man, with the famous hat and bandolier of bullets around his waist, standing proudly on his own pedestal. The cemetery on the opposite end of town is worth a look, with many brightly painted tombs and ornaments. Although the town is famous for its *brujas* (witches), the mayor's office denies that such things still exist. "Go to Diriomo," they advise.

MASATEPE

Masatepe (Nahuatl for "place of the deer") is a quiet pueblo of about 12,000. The view of the Volcán Masaya crater is deceptive as you drive into town—it appears close, but is actually 30 kilometers away. The naked rawness of the volcano juxtaposes with the beauty of the pastel-colored church, a photo of which is worth the quick diversion. There are no hotels in Masatepe, but there is a movie theater and a few places to eat, including **Restaurant/Bar Ulisses** on the main drag between the highway and town (Masatepe's culinary claim to fame is *sopa de mondongo*—tripe soup). The **Fiesta Patronales de la Santísima Trinidad** is a grand, three-week affair at the end of May and beginning of June, honoring a black Christ icon found ages ago in the trunk of a tree by an indigenous person.

SAN MARCOS

San Marcos is home to the Ave Maria College of the Americas, a Catholic, bilingual, four-year liberal arts university with about 400 students and a sister campus in Ann Arbor, Michigan. The facilities are modern and were built as the campus of the University of Mobile (Alabama) until Ave Maria took over in 1998. To learn more about studying there, look up its website: www.avemaria.edu.ni.

True to any college town, San Marcos has several Internet options to cater to the students who decide not to use the free services provided to them on campus. One block east of the plaza, the **Chat House Internet and Restaurant** has four computers, a nice dining room with a cheap sandwich and lunch menu, and a pool table, all dispersed throughout an elegant home (open 8 A.M.–noon, 2–7 P.M., $4 an hour, tel. 432-2276). Five blocks south of the park, on the road to Masatepe, is another Internet service, next door to the **Spaghetti Restaurant.**

The **Casa Blanca**, located about five blocks south of the park, and one block away from the highway, has 16 spiffy, simple rooms with private bath ($35 s or d, $46 t, $56 junior, which has four beds), tel. 432-2717 or 432-2720. The other option is the **Hotel Castillo.**

Carazo and the Pacific Beaches

The Pan-American Highway runs along the western edge of the Pueblos plateau, through the towns of Diriamba, Dolores, Jinotepe, and Nandaime before continuing south through Rivas to the border. The towns are referred to collectively as "Carazo" (after the department name), and a road at Diriamba (a couple blocks north of the clock tower) leads west to a handful of beach towns. The area is notable for the costumes, dancing, and music of its festivals, unique in Nicaragua for its preservation of precolonial Nicaraguan culture. Carazo is also considered the soccer capital in a country where baseball is king. Diriamba is home of the Nicaraguan national soccer team, and it is a great place to see a game on the weekend.

DIRIAMBA

The map suggests that this pueblo is no more than a small suburb of Jinotepe, a place to drive through on your way to the beach. But Diriamba is most definitely a town with its own flavor. Its primary fame is the **Fiesta of San Sebastian** in the third week of January, a long tradition involving religion, theatrical dance, and folk art. You'll find an interesting selection of architecture in Diriamba any time of the year, and as for orientation, everything revolves around the central and prominent *reloj* (clock tower), slowly losing its paint in flakes. Of note is the **Museo Ecológico de Tropico Seco,** which boasts displays of the region's natural history, open Monday–Friday, tel. 422-2129. The MARENA office here ministers some of the local turtle nesting refuges, tel. 422-2142.

Diriamba's **Teatro Gonzalez** (more run-down than Jinotepe's but half the price) shows recent Managua runs Friday–Monday, and porn from Tuesday–Thursday. The posters outside let you know what is coming in both categories.

Accommodations

Things get tight around the fiestas in January so plan ahead. **Hospedaje Diriangén,** one block east of the Shell and a half block south, has 12 rooms with private bath and fan, $7, tel. 422-2428. The **Casa Hotel** is within spitting distance of the clock tower, with about a dozen rooms with private bath; $7 s, $11 d, tel. 442-2523. Out on the boulevard heading out of town, **Jardín and Vivero Tortuga Verde** is reinventing itself as a bed-and-breakfast. There are very few rooms but they're clean and set amidst a beautiful garden filled with statues. A room costs about $20 but the price will increase when cable TV gets installed sometime in 2003, tel. 422-2948, email: rodalsa@ibw.com.ni.

Food

For **baked goods,** walk five blocks west from the Teatro Gonzalez, to a place with no name but great breads—go late afternoon if you want something warm out of the oven. Also try the **thatched-roof restaurant** near the museum, or **Restaurante Mi Bojía. Comedor Flamboli** on the highway is a good bet, as is the old standby, **Pizza to Go,** located within two blocks of the *reloj.*

Getting There and Away

Right next to the clock tower, a fleet of *interlocales* run to and from Jinotepe for about a quarter, daily from 6 A.M.–9 P.M. Walk east and take your first left to find microbus *expresos* to Managua's Israel Market for $1, 5 A.M.–7 P.M. A little farther east, the first *caseta* (booth) on the left is home to a guy that knows about all the buses that pass from Jinotepe (Managua: 4:30 A.M.–6 P.M.; Masaya: 5 A.M.–6 P.M.).

CARAZO BEACHES

La Boquita and **Casares** aren't the most glorious beaches in the country, but there is no denying the grandeur of the Pacific Ocean, and this stretch of coastline is home to several small fishing communities, ready to serve you fresh seafood and a bottle of cold Victoria which turns golden in the setting sun (or the rising sun, depending on what

THE FIESTA OF DIRIAMBA

Every pueblo's *fiesta patronales* has something that makes it unique, but Diriamba's celebration of the Holy Martyr San Sebastian stands above the rest as Nicaragua's most authentic connection to its people's indigenous roots. Many of the dances, songs, and costumes are true to traditions that predate the arrival of the Spanish by hundreds of years. But this is no nostalgia act—indeed, the integration of pre-Columbian ritual with Catholicism and the telling of modern history is as fascinating as the colors, costumes, and music.

This is actually three fiestas for the price of one, since icons of San Santiago of Jinotepe and San Marcos (of San Marcos) have been celebrated together since the three of them first traveled from Spain, landing at nearby Casares beach. The three are still believed to have the special bond they formed during their journey, and they get together to celebrate this three times a year during the fiesta of each of their towns. Santiago and Marcos meet up at the *tope* (end of the road) in Dolores on (or around) January 19, where they are danced around the village to a bombardment of cheers and homemade fireworks. The next day they reunite with their pal, Sebastian, in Diriamba, where the town has been partying for four days in preparation.

the snake charmer of Diriamba

The following day is the peak of activities, the actual Día de Santo, marked by special masses and (increasingly) groups of tourists that come to view the long, raucous procession, famous for its theatrical dances and costumes. The following are the most important acts: The **Dance of Toro Huaco** is entirely of indigenous ancestry, and features peacock feather hats and a multigeneration snake dance, with the youngest children bringing up the rear and an old man with a special tambourine and whistle up front. **El Gùegùense,** also called the Macho Ratón, is marked by its intricate masks and costumes depicting burdened-down donkeys and the faces of Spanish conquistadores. The Gùegùense (from the old word *gùegùe,* which means something like "an old grumpy man") is a hardhanded social satire with cleverly vulgar undertones that depicts the indigenous peoples' first impression of the Spanish—it has been called the oldest comedy act on the continent. The biblical story of David and Goliath is depicted in **El Gigante,** and **La Danza de las Inditas** is a group dance, recognized by the white cotton costumes and the sound of the marimba. Most of the dancers are carrying out a family tradition that has been kept for dozens of generations, and each usually has a grandma-led support team on the sidelines to make sure their costumes and performances are kept in order.

A true believer will tell you that Diriamba's fiesta begins not on January 19, but on February 2 of the previous year, when the official *fiesteros* apply for roles in the upcoming celebration; they then begin more than 11 months of preparation, all of which is seen as a display of faith and thanks to their beloved San Sebastian. Those that don't show their devotion by dancing or playing music do so by carrying the icons or fulfilling promises to walk a certain number of blocks on their knees, sometimes until bloody.

Bring plenty of film, and be sure to try the official beverage of the festival: *chicha con genibre,* a ginger-tinted, slightly fermented cornmeal drink. Most of the masks and costumes in the productions are also for sale, as are action figures depicting the various dance characters.

kind of night you have in mind). On a big swell, the surf is up at both places. Located within a few kilometers of each other, La Boquita and Casares also boast interesting rock formations and beachcombing. Note that this area is very popular during Semana Santa, New Year's Day, and several other national holidays. Make reservations at the hotels, or at the very least, expect a drunken mob scene, especially at La Boquita.

La Boquita

Easily accessed by public transport all day long, La Boquita is a beach complex specifically for tourists, the vast majority of whom are Nicaraguans on family outings. There is a $1 entrance fee to enter with your own vehicle, and you can expect representatives of the dozen or so *rancho* restaurants to try to corner your business right there in the parking lot. Take a gander before making a commitment; you may very well wish to rent some shade under one of the *rancho* roofs, where you can also order drinks and food.

To make a night of it (highly recommended if you're into drawn-out, beautiful sunsets), the **Hotel Palmas del Mar** is the mainstay of the town. The creation of a Frenchman, Palmas del Mar is a fancy place with swimming pools and good restaurant service, and 22 rooms (a/c, cable TV, and private bath, at $40), tel. 552-8715/6 or 887-1336, email: pglo@tmx.com.ni. Special package deal: $40 per person includes three meals and room—a good deal, given that most dishes on the menu run about $12 each.

Immediately adjacent to Palmas del Mar is **Hospedaje El Pelícano,** a dilapidated dive of bare, wooden rooms for $11 each. If you continue walking down to the estuary past a row of several restaurants, you'll find **Hospedaje Suleyka,** $14 for six small, bare rooms at the side of the restaurant, tel. 552-8717. Better than the *hospedaje* is the restaurant and store, where you can buy bathing suits, suntan lotion, sandals, and more.

Casares

More oriented toward catching and selling fish than hosting beachgoers, Casares is uncomfort-

the Diriamba Clocktower rendered in beachshells

ably short on shade. However, it's also short on crowds, and its long, wide beach is great for watching the boats coming in and out. On the drive between La Boquita and Casares, seek out **El Pozo del Padre,** a self-contained rocky bathtub that's loads of fun at high tide. The only place to stay in Casares is **Hotel Lupita,** offering 16 rooms with private bath and a/c, and small pool for $40.

La Maquina

This is one of the "private wild reserves" protected by MARENA and managed by the landowners—it is located on the north side of the road between Diriamba and the coast, identifiable by a rather inconspicuous sign. The main attraction is a popular waterfall and shallow bathing area on the river when you first enter, but there is much more to the park than that, including forested areas and short hiking trails, and picnic facilities.

Río Escalante – Chacocente

Río Escalante – Chacocente is one of two Pacific shore beaches where the paslama turtle lays its eggs (La Flor in Rivas is the other), and as such is a protected wildlife area. The beach provides habitat for numerous other species as well, including white-tailed deer, reptile species, and several types of flora. Getting to Chacocente isn't easy, which, for the sake of the turtles, is just as well. There's one bus a day from Diriamba, and one bus back. There's no way to make a day trip out of it, as both buses leave at the crack of dawn, and Chacocente has no facilities for travelers. The ecological importance of the beach obviously dictates that camping is not a viable option during the nesting season (see Flora and Fauna section in the Introduction).

Getting There and Away

La Boquita and Casares are about 35 kilometers due west of Diriamba. Public transportation leaves from the main market, on the highway east of the clock tower. Express microbuses leave every 20 minutes for the 40-minute, $.75 ride to La Boquita from 6:20 A.M.–6 P.M. Regular buses take 1.5 hours and leave between 6:40 A.M.–6:30 P.M.—they like to turn off their engines and coast the last part. From La Boquita the first bus leaves at 5 A.M., the last one back from the beach at 6 P.M.

JINOTEPE

Jinotepe is a sometimes-sleepy, sometimes-bustling villa of 27,000. Home to a campus of the UNAN-Managua, Jinotepe's student population serves to keep things youthful and relatively lively. There is good food here, a fun outdoor market, and a wonderfully shady park, whose church, **La Iglesia Parroquial de Santiago,** was built in 1860. The village of Xilotepetl (Field of Baby Corn), as Jinotepe was first named, was built atop ash from Volcán Masaya and is surrounded on three sides by tectonic faults. The attraction of Jinotepe is the town itself. Walk around and be sure to view the beautiful **two-block-long mural** on the nursing school, three blocks west of the park.

Accommodations

It's a simple choice: $3 at the **Hospedaje Masaya** (a half-block north of the northwest corner of the park), or $4 at **Hospedaje San Carlos** (1.5 blocks south of the Palí); the latter should be used only out of desperation. Otherwise, it's the **Hotel Casa Grande,** where you'll pay $35 s or d, $45 t, $55 suite, which includes in-room telephone, TV, private bath, hot water, and fan; laundry and ironing service, guard for your car, restaurant and bar, Internet. They can also organize a trip to their facilities at Huehuete Beach and are experienced at dealing with large groups and conferences, tel. 412-2741 or 412-3284, fax 412-3512, email: casagrande@nicarao.org.ni.

Food

The **kiosk** in the park serves a delicious, chocolaty *cacao con leche* and offers a basic menu in a cool, shady, and green eating area. Solid lunches are found at **Buen Provecho** (a buffet, 1.5 blocks north of the cathedral), and at the **Buffet Santa Ana** (two blocks north, half-block west of the cathedral). Next door to Buen Provecho is the **Pizzería Coliseo,** a legitimate Italian restaurant. Its got authentic pizza, garlic bread, spaghetti, and lasagna, and top it off with tiramisu and cappuccino; meals for about $5 and up; open Tuesday–Sunday 12:30–9 P.M., accepts credit cards, tel. 412-2150.

On the same street, 2.5 blocks north of the cathedral, you'll find **Pizza To Go** right next door to **Pollos del Parque.** Combining these two establishments—cheap 'za which you can bring next door to eat with pitchers at Pollos, or vice versa—makes for a traditionally raging Jinotepe evening. Pollos also has a full menu and stunning murals by a local artist depicting Don Quixote's journeys. Pizza To Go, served out of someone's garage, is decent and half the price of the Coliseo. Try the massive calzones, an incredible deal at $1.50. Around the corner, the **Café Arte** is a small, funky bar/café with a huge drink menu, good food, but sometimes cranky service, tel. 412-2974.

One block south of the cathedral and a half-block west is **Royal Burguer,** offering a subway sandwich menu (real hero bread), empanadas (sometimes), and of course, "burguers." **Restaurante Casa Blanca** has an impressive and varied menu (including chop suey), with meals for $4–10, open 11 A.M.–10 P.M., accepts credit cards, tel. 412-2379. The spendiest eats are in the **Hotel Casa Grande**, or, upon paying $200 to join, in the "Social Club" on the east end of town (provided the members vote to accept you). Better stick with the cheap pizza.

Services

Enitel, Correos, and the *Alcaldía* (mayor's office, note Sandino paintings inside and out) are all on the north side of the main plaza. Bancentro and Banco de Finanzas are on the block north of the cathedral, and there is a Western Union, tel. 412-0301. Street money changers are found on the corner outside the Restaurante Casa Blanca. There are two supermarkets: Super Santiago and Palí (open 8 A.M.–8 P.M.). Film is widely available—check the Kodak Express across from the Palí.

Bookstores: This being a university town, there are loads of dinky bookstores and copy shops, but the most well stocked seems to be the Librería Santiago, two blocks north of the cathedral with a decent variety of books, international magazines, and mainstream American porn; open 8 A.M.–6 P.M.

Gym: The Olympus Master is a fully equipped gym, complete with massage service, sauna, and aerobics classes, open 5 A.M.–9 P.M. every day; membership is only $1.50 a week, or $6 a month. One block north of the Laboratorio Shell, tel. 412-2591 or 889-1788.

Internet: The Cyber Café CIENGI has four computers, a CD burner, and scanner; Internet access is $4 per hour. They also charge $25 to "call free" to the United States or Canada. Open Monday–Saturday 7 A.M.–9 P.M. (closed noon–1 P.M.), tel. 412-0459. Also check the Hotel Casa Grande.

Getting There and Away

Jinotepe is easy to get to—go to Managua's Mercados Israel, Huembes, or to the lot across from the main UCA (last bus to Jinotepe leaves there at 10 P.M.). Figuring out how to leave the city is a

decidedly more complicated task. The main bus terminal is known as the **Terminal COOTRAUS Principal** and is located on a dirt square on a curve of the Pan-American Highway directly in front of the police station. Ordinary school buses leave there regularly: for Managua (4:30 A.M.–6 P.M.), Masaya (5 A.M.–6 P.M.), Nandaime (6 A.M.–6 P.M.), and Rivas (5:40 A.M.–3 P.M.). From Rivas, you can travel to either Ometepe, San Juan del Sur, or the border. These *ordinario* routes are barely cheaper than the endless fleet of microbus *expresos,* which leave from at least three different parts of Jinotepe, mostly for Managua, Masaya, or local destinations.

Sapasmapa is the name of the unofficial terminal on the south side of the Instituto Alejandro, with microbuses that go to Managua from 4:45 A.M.–7:30 P.M., cost $.75, and take about an hour. They're convenient and cheap enough you may never have reason to take a slow bus. Check the streets around the other side of the Instituto for more options.

At any one time, about half of the people hanging out in the park are minivan drivers to Managua, and they will let you know this by chanting the word "Managua" quickly and mantralike (you try it); they run from 5:45 A.M.–7:30 P.M. to and from the UCA in Managua. *Interlocales* to Diriamba and San Marcos line up on the street in front of the Super Santiago—only the front one will load passengers, departing when the van is full.

If you are traveling to Costa Rica, TicaBus coaches pass by the local office bound for San José every morning at 8 A.M.; purchase tickets in advance.

NEAR JINOTEPE

Hertylandia

Just one or two kilometers outside Jinotepe, on the road to San Marcos, you'll find a big castlelike entrance to Nicaragua's only amusement park: **Hertylandia,** created in the 1990s as a private venture by old-school Sandinista and Managua's current mayor, Herty Lewites. Water rides, bumper boats, video arcades, and a motocross track, $12 to get in and play, tel. 412-3081.

Granada

Granada is at once both the oldest city on the continent and the most developed tourist destination in Nicaragua. Some consider this "colonial jewel" to be the future of Nicaraguan tourism, the vanguard of what could be; true, if one is holding up Antigua, Guatemala as the archetype—i.e., the backpacker mecca model, where there are more foreign-run Internet cafés and hostels than actual native residents. But most agree that the city's charm will never be taken over—too many of the distinctive buildings are private homes of well-off, proud Nicaraguans who wouldn't think of giving up their piece of Granada. And there is good reason for Granada's recent boom. It is a fascinating city—full of bright colors, violent history, lake breezes, and the sounds (and smells) of horse-drawn carriages.

Granada is the place to meet other vagabonds with whom you'll swap stories over a few liters of Victoria in the tropical shadow of Volcán Mombacho. This is also your base camp for boat trips through the Isletas and canopy tours in the Mombacho cloud forest. There's even a ship to Ometepe and the Río San Juan—but hold your horses, bucko, and check into one of the funky *hospedajes* for a couple of nights. Take in some Granada before going back to the wilds of Nicaragua. Nowhere else in the country will you find such an array of excellent restaurants set against a rainbow of architecture. This is less a "city" than a large, relaxed colonial town, where most evenings find the people out on the sidewalks, talking and laughing. Walk the streets, tour the churches, then enjoy a free concert in the park; there is much to love about Granada.

the streets of Granada

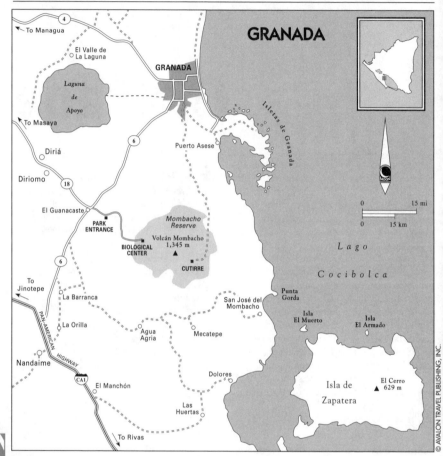

© AVALON TRAVEL PUBLISHING, INC.

HISTORY

Granada's history is as long as the history of colonial Nicaragua itself. Granada was founded by Francisco Hernández de Córdoba on the edge of the warm waters of Lake Cocibolca, nestled against the indigenous community of Xalteva, and despite its tradition of being repeatedly destroyed and rebuilt, if Córdoba were to rise from the grave today and walk the streets of his city, he would find it relatively familiar. A trade city, Granada soon became the home of an affluent Spanish merchant class, largely of Veracruz, Cartagena, and La Habana origin. From its be-

ginnings, Granada was a symbol of Spanish opulence, an unsubtle show of mercantile success in the New World. Combined with its vulnerability as a port town, this made Granada a popular target for other powers. The English especially enjoyed sending their fiercest buccaneers up the Río San Juan to sack and burn the city, humiliating the Spaniards before returning to their homeland with gold and treasures.

Because of its population of old-money, landowning families, Granada has always been the seat of the Conservative Party (and still is, even though they only won 3 percent of the vote in the last presidential election). As such, Granada was the capital of Nicaragua several times, always vying with the Liberals of León for control of Nicaragua.

It was the Liberals who first called upon United States filibuster William Walker to launch what was perhaps the worst attack against Granada, even by pirate standards. Walker was eventually driven from the area, but not before burning it to the ground and burying a symbolic coffin in the central plaza under a wooden sign that read *Aquí fue Granada* (Here was Granada).

Since then (in true Nicaraguan form), Granada has risen from its own ashes, existing today as both a "living museum" and a modern, industry- and tourism-based city.

ORIENTATION AND GETTING AROUND

Granada has several easy landmarks, starting with the central, tree-lined plaza (known alternately as the **Parque Central** and the Parque Colón) and the **cathedral** on its east side. Calle Calzado extends east along the north side of the cathedral

and runs straight to the municipal dock. A number of *hospedajes* and hotels are clustered along this street. You can also orient yourself to the ever-glowering peak of Volcán Mombacho, rising to the south of the city. Walking west from the main plaza, you'll come to the Xalteva neighborhood and eventually the cemetery and road to Nandaime. There are many services and a number of attractions along the Calle Atravesada, which runs north-south, one block west of the plaza. Taxis are numerous and cheap, and of course, there are the horse carriages, which you can always find on the western side of the plaza (prices vary).

SIGHTS AND ATTRACTIONS

Lace up your comfy shoes, fill up a water bottle, and slip on your shades—this town was made for walkin'. There's really no other way to get a feel for Granada than to strut its varied streets, ideally early or late in the day with a camera in hand. You'll want to use color film, as there are more shades of yellow and orange paint here

VOLUNTEERING IN GRANADA

There are numerous opportunities in Granada to reach out and get involved—both short- and long-term. If you're serious about finding somewhere to volunteer, you'll want to seek out Donna Tabor at her guesthouse, **Another Night in Paradise.** Donna first came to Granada in the mid-1990s as a Peace Corps volunteer, and although she's got her own business now, she never lost her commitment to her adopted community. Her upcoming book talks about the street kid and glue-sniffing problem in Granada, issues with which she has spent considerable amounts of time. She'll tell you more about each of the following organizations, help figure out how you can help, and she even offers a discount to volunteers staying in her guesthouse (email: ugogirl@tmx.com.ni). Another good resource, whom you can contact before your trip, is volunteer Birgit Cory, who lives in San Francisco in-between her frequent expeditions to Nicaragua, primarily to work with the street

kids of Granada (415/333-4104, email: birgitlein@hotmail.com).

Cristo Sana a los Niños is located near the park, and is a home for boys from dysfunctional families. Residents agree to leave their glue jar outside, and in exchange, receive room, board, and schooling, including a computer project and art class. Talk to Sister María Mercedes about volunteering here in the afternoon—having a special skill helps.

Hogar Madre Albertina is a desperately underfunded orphanage for girls where residents typically have nothing to do except watch *novelas* on television all day. Volunteers are welcome to read to the girls, play games with them, or take them on day trips; while in Granada, ask around for a copy of an activity guide to help you with ideas.

Harmonía is an Italian-run organization for disabled children around the corner from the Casa de los Leones. If your Spanish is good, visiting medical missionaries are always looking for translators.

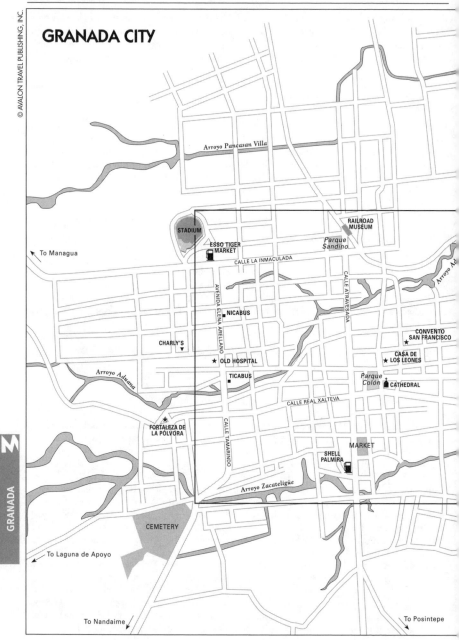

GRANADA CITY

Arroyo Pancasan Villa

To Managua

STADIUM

RAILROAD MUSEUM

ESSO TIGER MARKET

Parque Sandino

CALLE LA INMACULADA

CALLE ATRAVESADA

Arroyo A...

AVENIDA ELENA ARELLANO

NICABUS

CHARLY'S

OLD HOSPITAL

CONVENTO SAN FRANCISCO

CASA DE LOS LEONES

Arroyo Aduana

TICABUS

Parque Colon

CATHEDRAL

CALLE REAL XALTEVA

FORTALEZA DE LA PÓLVORA

CALLE TAMARINDO

MARKET

SHELL PALMIRA

Arroyo Zacateligüe

CEMETERY

To Laguna de Apoyo

To Nandaime

To Posintepe

GRANADA

© AVALON TRAVEL PUBLISHING, INC.

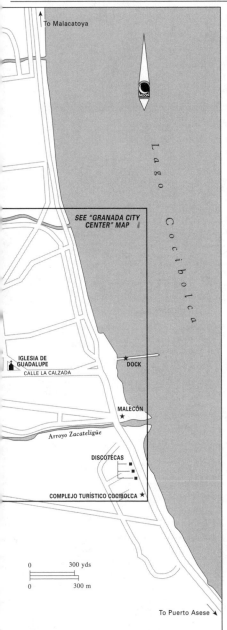

To Malacatoya

Lago Cocibolca

SEE "GRANADA CITY CENTER" MAP

IGLESIA DE GUADALUPE
CALLE LA CALZADA

DOCK

MALECÓN

Arroyo Zacateligüe

DISCOTECAS

COMPLEJO TURÍSTICO COCIBOLCA

0   300 yds

0   300 m

To Puerto Asese

than Vincent van Gogh ever dreamed of. Be sure to break away from the main plaza and its environs, as the twisting, narrow streets to the north and west are chock full of Granada.

Museums

Perhaps the most impressive museum in all of Nicaragua, the **Antiguo Convento San Francisco** is recognized by its towering, sky-blue facade two blocks north and one east of the main cathedral. First built by Franciscan monks in 1529, the building was razed by Henry Morgan 150 years later, rebuilt, and in the early 1800s, served as the National University. Soon after, William Walker quartered his troops here (some of whom are reportedly buried in the basement catacombs) before burning it down when he left the city in ruins. Rebuilt again, the Convento housed U.S. Marines in the 1920s, and then U.S. Army Engineers studying a possible canal in the 1930s. Today's museum and ongoing restoration of the structure is due in large part to donations from the Swiss government.

For an entrance fee of $1, you can access an archaeological exhibit showing the daily life of lakeside indigenous tribes, as well as an open-air display of 30 Chorotega stone carvings, collected from Isla de Zapatera. The rooftop views of Granada, the lake, and Mombacho from here are stunning. Afterwards, walk across the plaza to see the photography and primitivist painting displays. The Convento also has a small bookstore and *cafetín*, so plan lunch into your visit. Open seven days, 9 A.M.–6 P.M., tel. 552-5535.

The pedestrian space guarded by the cannon off the northeast corner of the main plaza is the **Plaza de la Independencia,** and **La Plazuela de los Leones.** This is where Henry Morgan placed 18 cannons during his sacking of the city, and a century later, where William Walker was sworn in as president of Nicaragua. On the plazuela's eastern side, you'll find the famous **International Cultural Center,** housed in the **Casa de los Leones.** The stately building was first constructed in 1720 by Don Diego de Montiel, governor of Costa Rica. All but the portal bearing the Montiel family crest (still visible) was destroyed by

GRANADA

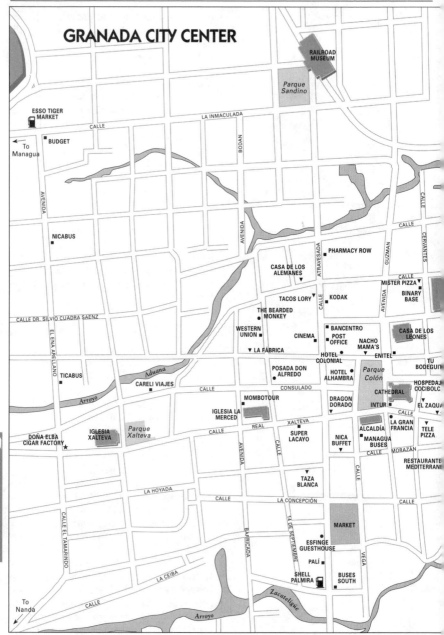

GRANADA CITY CENTER

RAILROAD MUSEUM

Parque Sandino

ESSO TIGER MARKET

LA INMACULADA

CALLE

BODAN

← To Managua

BUDGET

AVENIDA

NICABUS

PHARMACY ROW

CASA DE LOS ALEMANES

GUZMAN

CERVANTES

CALLE

CALLE

MISTER PIZZA

ATRAVESADA

TACOS LORY

KODAK

CALLE

AVENIDA

BINARY BASE

CALLE DR. SILVIO CUADRA SAENZ

THE BEARDED MONKEY

WESTERN UNION

CINEMA

BANCENTRO
POST OFFICE

CASA DE LOS LEONES

EL ENA ARELLANO

LA FÁBRICA

NACHO MAMA'S

HOTEL COLONIAL

ENITEL

TÚ BODEGUIT

POSADA DON ALFREDO

HOTEL ALHAMBRA

Parque Colón

TICABUS

Aduana

CARELI VIAJES

CONSULADO

DRAGON DORADO

CATHEDRAL

HOSPEDAJ COCIBOLC

Arroyo

CALLE

MOMBOTOUR

INTUR

EL ZAQUA

IGLESIA LA MERCED

XALTEVA

LA GRAN FRANCIA

CALLE

TELE PIZZA

DOÑA ELBA CIGAR FACTORY

IGLESIA XALTEVA

Parque Xalteva

REAL

CALLE

SUPER LACAYO

NICA BUFFET

ALCALDÍA

MANAGUA BUSES

AVENIDA

MORAZÁN

RESTAURANTE MEDITERRANE

CALLE

CALLE EL TAMARINDO

LA HOYADA

CALLE

TAZA BLANCA

CALLE

BARRICADA

LA CONCEPCIÓN

CALLE

11 DE SEPTIEMBRE

MARKET

VEGA

CALLE

ESFINGE GUESTHOUSE

PALÍ

SHELL PALMIRA

BUSES SOUTH

To Nanda

CALLE

LA CEIBA

Zacatelíguse

Arroyo

GRANADA

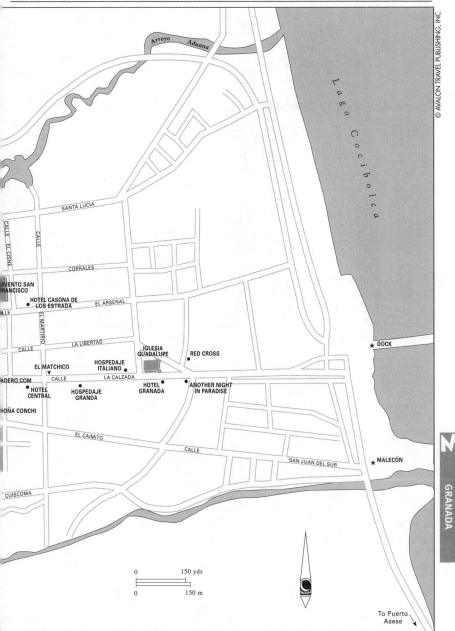

Lago Cocibolca

Arroyo Aduana

SANTA LUCIA

CALLE

EL CISNE

CALLE

CORRALES

VENTO SAN
RANCISCO

HOTEL CASONA DE
LOS ESTRADA

EL ARSENAL

LLE

EL MARTIRIO

LA LIBERTAD

CALLE

IGLESIA
GUADALUPE

RED CROSS

DOCK

EL MATCHICO

HOSPEDAJE
ITALIANO

ADERO.COM

CALLE

LA CALZADA

HOTEL
CENTRAL

HOSPEDAJE
GRANDA

HOTEL
GRANADA

ANOTHER NIGHT
IN PARADISE

OÑA CONCHI

EL CAIMITO

CALLE

SAN JUAN DEL SUR

MALECÓN

CUISCOMA

0   150 yds

0   150 m

To Puerto
Asese

GRANADA

© JOSHUA BERMAN

the Cathedral in Granada

At the terminus of Calle Xalteva, next to a deep gully, you'll find the **Fortaleza de la Pólvora.** The fort was built in 1748 to secure Granada's gunpowder supply from invading pirates. Its medieval architecture speaks of simplicity and strength: five squat towers and one heavily guarded gate with two oaken doors. In the 1900s La Pólvora was used as a military garrison, and later, a jail, both by the city and by the National Guard. These days it's a museum of arms. Climb the towers for a breath of wind and a good perspective of the skyline.

Walking Tours

Design your own excursion by trekking the lengths of the following streets.

La Calle Atravesada is one of Granada's original streets, which runs north-south from the old train station to the tin-roofed, bustling chaos of the **municipal market.** The railroad station was built in 1886 and was recently renovated by young Nicaraguans participating in a Spanish-funded trade school, which is now moving on to make way for a **Railroad Museum.** Walking south, you'll pass a number of grandiose, **aristocratic homes,** representative of the lifestyle of Granada's wealthy—past and present.

Calle Real la Xalteva is the second principal street of the city. Walking west from the south side of the plaza, you'll come across the **Iglesia la Merced,** which served as a source of poetic inspiration in the 1940s for renowned Nicaraguan poets like Pablo Antonio Cuadra, Joaquín Cuadra, and Ernesto Cardenal. A few blocks farther west brings you to the **Iglesia Xalteva** and the stone-tower park across the street. At its western end, **Los Muros de Xalteva** are a series of 10-meter-high arched stone walls erected by the Spaniards in the mid-1700s to separate them from the indigenous communities.

William Walker, and later rebuilt with a unique, neoclassical colonnade facade. In 1987, the historical monument became the headquarters of the **Casa de los Tres Mundos Foundation,** whose lofty mission is "to foster an understanding of universal and human values among people of all religions and political persuasions, as well as providing new economic opportunities for the Nicaraguan People." As such, the Casa houses an art and music school, museum, historical archive, library, concert hall, literary café, bookstore, exhibition space, and regularly hosts resident artists from around the world. Visiting artists exhibit their work, teach classes, and donate a piece of art created during their stay. The initial vision of the Casa de los Tres Mundos project was shared by Nicaraguan poet-padre Ernesto Cardenal and Austrian film director and actor Dietmar Schoenherr. It is still going strong today, open every day 7 A.M.–6 P.M., tel. 552-4176 or 552-6437, email: c3mundos@tmx.com.ni, website: www.tmx.com .ni/~c3mundos/index.html.

If, for some cosmic reason, you're not convinced of Granada's historical wealth, visit the cemetery on the southwest corner of the city grid. Enormous marble tombs—bigger than the homes of most Nicaraguans elsewhere—house half a millennium of very rich (and, as things go, very dead) bodies. Note the column-lined **Capilla de Animas** and the replica of

GRANADA

the **Magdalena de Paris,** built between 1876 and 1922.

Back at the central plaza, note the grand, yellow building along its west side, home to the **Pellas,** Nicaragua's wealthiest family. Across the way, next to the cathedral, is the **Cruz del Siglo** (Century Cross), inaugurated January 1, 1900; frozen in its cement are coins, pieces of art, and a gilded bottle from the 19th century. From there, head east along the Calle la Calzada, which takes you to the castlelike **Iglesia de Guadalupe,** first built in 1626, and most recently refurbished in 1945. Continuing along the palm-lined straightaway, you'll reach the *muelle* and *malecón* (dock and quay) on the water's edge. Turn right to enter the **Complejo Turístico Cocibolca,** where the afternoon breeze is fresh and clean, and the sidewalks are filled with hot dog and *chicharrón* vendors. The entranceway consists of a pair of towers reminiscent of a pair of rooks, and an archway, the construction of which you'll help pay for with a nominal entrance fee. It's less a tourist complex than a long, green park with nothing to do except stare out over the lake—not necessarily a bad option during languid tropical afternoons when it's too hot to breathe.

Cigars

Estelí may be the biggest producer of *puros* (cigars), but Granada rolls its share of fine smokes as well, primarily from tobacco grown in the cool hills around Masatepe, and often blended with northern Nicaraguan leaves. Don Silvio loves to receive visitors in his **Doña Elba Cigar Factory** (named after his mother), located a couple blocks west of the Iglesia Xalteva. He has a wide variety of cigars for sale in his showroom (right under a photo of him smoking a *maduro* with Arnold Schwarzenegger). Come see the rolling factory where some 3,000 *puros* are produced daily, open 7 A.M.–7 P.M. Also, there is a tiny cigar shop with a decent selection next to the post office on Calle Atravesada.

NIGHTLIFE AND ENTERTAINMENT

Don't miss **Noches de Serenatas,** free outdoor music on the plaza in front of the Casa de Leones every Friday night. Also, be sure to keep an eye on the Casa's events listing for other concerts, often by visiting international musicians, and ranging from jazz to strings to ambient jungle sounds. One block west of the plaza, El Teatro Karawala shows relatively recent Hollywood flicks and porn.

Bars

Tu Bodeguita is a mellow, comfortable hangout—Cuban/Nica-style, good music, great service, and a cool loft; open every night, located on Calle Calzado just east of the plaza. **La Fábrica** has built up quite a buzz among Nicas and foreigners alike, who come from as far as León, Managua, and Masaya just to drink here. The charm is in the run-down building, open courtyard, and lively, mixed crowd. Unique mixed drinks and great food, located 1.5 blocks west of the northwest corner of the plaza. Another mellow option is in the **Casa de los Alemanes,** across from the fire department.

Discos

The only city center disco is the Chinese restaurant, the **Dragon Dorado,** open every night. The rest are located down by the lake — and of the countless options, only three are worth your time. **Cesar's,** just past the gate, is one of the most popular, attracting a more mature crowd. **Centauro's** is a younger scene, with the bonus of air-conditioning, and **Pantera** is another good bet. Do not walk to or from the disco strip at night, even in a group, and especially when drunk—the stretch of road between the water's edge and the city center is a notorious hangout for young, nervous, and knife-wielding would-be crooks.

ACCOMMODATIONS

Under $10

Airy dorm-style rooms centered around a wooden bar and open colonial courtyard give the **Bearded Monkey** the kind of friendly, communal space that makes such places automatic backpacker gathering spots. Of course it doesn't hurt to have a delicious kitchen, a solid movie and book collection (you won't find six copies of *The*

Firm in this library), fantastic music, Internet, footlocker and bike rentals, and a popular happy hour (4–7 P.M.). One of 28 dorm beds cost under $3, the two singles are $5, and the romantic loft is $6 a couple. There is a $4 corkage fee if you want to bring in your own liquor, coffee is always available, and the water is safe to drink. They also offer international call service, laundry facilities, and will change dollars and traveler's checks, tel. 552-4028, email: thebeardedmonkey@yahoo.com, website: www.thebeardedmonkey.com.

Don Alfredo's Esfinge Guesthouse is a large building of 22 rooms (capacity for 70 people!) right on Calle Atravesada across from the market. Dorm beds cost $3 a person, $5 s, $7 d, $14 with private bath. There is also parking, ping-pong, a patio, restaurant, and conference room. Contact the Don at tel. 552-4826 or at his colonial hotel, Posada Don Alfredo (see below), tel. 552-4455, email: alfredpaulbaganz@hotmail.com. Down the block, across from the Palí, is **Adela's House,** with seven basic rooms from $4, with some more expensive options, tel. 552-7961.

Hospedaje Row on the Calle la Calzada begins 1.5 blocks east of the plaza with **Hotel Central**; garishly overdecorated, the constant happy hour scene at the bar may warrant the celebratory feel. This is one of the first places gringos and Europeans alike head to stay, eat, or kill a hot afternoon over coffee and cigarettes. Its 20 rooms with shared bath start at $7 per couple or $5 per person. Laundry service, books to read or trade, and a well-liked menu of gringo food (French toast, fruit shakes, salads, sandwiches), tel. 552-7044.

If the Central scene is a little much, the family-run **Hospedaje Cocibolca,** just down the block, is a good alternative—clean, private bath, and a common kitchen; 13 rooms starting at $5 s, $10 d. Three computers in the dining area/TV room have Internet for $3.50 an hour. Breakfast is served 7–11 A.M.

Hospedaje and Cafetín la Calzada has been around longer than most; seven rooms with shared bath cost $3 per person; a better deal is the three nicer rooms upstairs with private bath and a view, $5.50 per person. Breakfast is available,

plus laundry service, TV, and a ping-pong table, tel. 552-6736.

Hospedaje Granada has 11 spartan, concrete rooms set around a nice pool. Despite the cell-like quality of the rooms, the place is clean, safe, and quiet and, of course, has a pool. Five rooms with shared bath start at $6; the other six rooms have private bath and run for $7 s, $11 d. Breakfast and lunch for $2. The outside doors shut at 10 P.M., tel. 552-3716.

$10–25

Not ready to leave Granada after serving there as a small business development Peace Corps volunteer, Donna Tabor snatched up the corner house next to Hotel Granada and opened a quaint, rainbow-colored guesthouse which she boldly named **Another Night in Paradise.** She charges $11 s, $16 d to stay in one of five bright, clean rooms, with communal bath and use of a fully equipped kitchen, TV room, and a volcano-facing, second-story veranda with cable TV; discounts offered for guests volunteering in the community (see Volunteering in Granada special topic). English spoken, tel. 552-7113, email: ugogirl@tmx.com.ni.

$25–50

Located in a beautiful 176-year-old home, **Posada Don Alfredo** boasts seven enormous, airy rooms around a lush, open-air garden and patio. There are plenty of beds, with capacity (and special rates) for groups of up to 32 people. Prices run $25–35 (depending on how many people) and include private bath, hot water, and TV, plus bike and kayak rental. Says Don Alfredo: "I am German so hotel is very clean." Located two blocks west of the plaza, tel. 552-4455, email: alfredpaulbaganz@hotmail.com.

Located on Calle Calzada, just before the Convento de Guadalupe, **Hospedaje Italiano** is spotless, well run, and caters to a more upscale crowd. If you'd rather not laze around common areas sucking down clove cigarettes and humming Dylan tunes all day, try one of 10 rooms, all with remote-controlled a/c, private bath, and TV for $25 s, $30 couple, $35 d, and $40 t. Breakfast is served every morning for $2.50 per person. Credit cards accepted, and discounts are given for group stays, tel. 552-7047.

Right on the west side of the plaza, and built around a grand lobby and patio, **Hotel Alhambra** is a plush choice with reasonable prices, $33 s, $42 d, up to a suite for $65. All 56 rooms include a/c, TV, private bath, telephone, hot water, and access to the pool, tel. 552-4486, fax 552-2035, email: hotalam@tmx.com.ni.

Pleasant and professional with lots of room, **Hotel Granada** has 27 rooms with private bath, hot water, a/c, and TV, starting at $29 s, $37 couple, and $39 d. Breakfast and light lunches served in its sidewalk café, tel. 552-2178 or 552-2974, fax 552-4128.

Over $50

Live large in four-star *Granadino* luxury: **Hotel Colonial,** just 20 meters west of the northwest corner of the park, has capacity for 50 guests in rooms surrounding an outdoor patio, pool, and bar; also laundry, bilingual staff, business services, local tours, and conference room. Rooms range from $50 s, $65 d, up to a $90-a-night suite for two, tel. 552-7299, tel./fax 552-7581, email: hotel-colonial@nicaragua-vacations.com, website: www.nicaragua-vacations.com.

Hotel Casona de los Estrada is another high-budget *hostal y ristorante,* located one block east of the Convento San Francisco. Their six rooms have private bath, hot water, telephones, TV, a/c and fan, and alarm clocks (just in case you've got an appointment). If you plan ahead, they'll run you out to their miniresort on Zacatolosa Island, where you can relax, play tennis, jog, and swim—or stay on the island in one of four rooms (reserve rooms one month in advance). Rooms cost $57 s, $86 d (after tax), tel. 552-7393/4, fax 552-7395, email: gensa@munditel.com.ni, website: www.casonalosestrada.com.ni.

Over 150 years old, La Gran Francia is an impressive colonial home that has been delicately restored to house **La Gran Francia Hotel & Restaurant.** Located on the southwestern corner of the park, La Gran Francia is an architectural and historic jewel: its four-foot thick adobe walls once imprisoned Nicaragua's infamous would-be conqueror, William Walker, and then sur-

vived the great fire he started in 1856. The hotel has 19 spacious luxury suites with a/c, cable TV, minibar, etc., priced at $75, and one presidential suite with all amenities for $125 a night; also pool, room service, and laundry.

FOOD
Breakfast

There are countless options, including most hotels, but if you really want to treat yourself, check out the **Nica Buffet's** huge menu, which includes pancakes, biscuits and gravy, eggs and bacon, and huge omelets; also a chance to talk to Ceffie about her native Miskito Coast (or to her husband Steve about his native Brooklyn). Open every day 6–11:30 A.M. Competing for the claim of "best breakfast in Granada" is Don Alfredo's five-course German buffet, served in his Posada hotel 7–11:30 A.M.

Corriente

Forget variety—out of the many vendors and kiosks in the main plaza, they serve only *vigorón* and *chancho con yuca* (pig with yuca); cheap, salty, and served on a green banana leaf, you can actually fill up on just the yuca and salad if you decide to order it vegetarian-style. The best *fritangas* set up evenings on Calle Calzada, all the way to the lake. For a solid *comedor* with meals for under $2, try the **Taza Blanca,** one block north of the market, and a half-block west.

Mexican

On the northwest corner of the plaza, check out the popular outdoor tables of **Nacho Mama's,** under the shade of a gorgeous ficus tree; serving breakfast, burritos, burgers, sandwiches, and fronting a realty shop with Che Guevara coffee souvenirs (Café Che); Nacho Mama's is open 7 A.M.–4 P.M. **Tacos Lory** is on Calle Atravesada, just past Bancentro, and the burritos at **La Fábrica** are reportedly some of the fattest in town.

Vegetarian

Asadero.com is not an Internet café, a fact surmised by the lack of computers and the woman grilling juicy cuts of chicken on the sidewalk of Calle la Calzada. Never mind the meat—Don Chepe (who is multilingual and has traveled the world) has created an impressive, Indian-influenced menu of grilled veggie masterpieces, including gingered greens, Middle Eastern eggplant, curries, and Asian dishes. They're open for business Monday–Saturday 4 P.M.–10 P.M. Also check the **Bearded Monkey** and **Hotel Central** for veggie chili and other options.

Pizza

Tele Pizza has excellent, hand-tossed, U.S.-style 'za, located a half-block east of the southeast corner of the plaza, delivery service, tel. 552-4219. **Don Luca's Pizzería** is another good choice, with thin-crust pizza baked in a traditional Italian stone hearth. **Mister Pizza** is another option, across from Convento San Francisco, and if you're in a pinch, the **Esso Station Tiger Market** delivers pizza 9 A.M.–9 P.M., tel. 552-4189.

Chinese

Choose from 60 plates of Chinese and vegetarian fare at the **Dragon Dorado,** which also houses a minimall and *discoteca,* tel. 552-5428, one block west of the plaza.

Nica

La Tequila, located on Calle Nueva, is old-school, funky Nicaragua, right out of the 1950s; great prices for giant bowls of soup—black bean, crab, and fish—plus freshly squeezed orange juice served ice cold in individual glass pitchers. And, of course, cold, cold beer. **El Zaquan,** in a converted garage on the back side of the cathedral, is an excellent and classy dinner option. They cook a beautiful plate of meat right in front of you on a juice-soaked *parrilla* (grill), in a converted garage. Service is top-notch; plates start at $6.

Housed in the Gran Francia Hotel off the southeastern corner of the park, **El Arcángel** features Nicaraguan food "presented in a contemporary style," as well as a variety of international dishes; prices average $6.50 a plate. The bar on the second floor of the old home has a "Gold Fever" theme, featuring Goldschlager cocktails.

European Cuisine

This is one of Granada's principal attractions, especially after all the *gallo pinto* you've been eating elsewhere in Nicaragua. Of course you'll pay a little more at any of the following restaurants than you would at the local *fritanga,* but nearly everyone offers at least a few cheaper plates, and most places accept credit cards.

How 'bout starting with some schnitzel, sauerkraut, and draft beer served in a big, crystal boot? **Charly's Bar and Restaurant** is a German-style *rancho* located four blocks west of the old hospital mansion on the edge of town—don't worry, they'll pay for your taxi if you eat there (open Mon.–Fri. 11 A.M.–3 P.M. and 6–11 P.M., Sat. and Sun. 11 A.M.–11 P.M., closed Tues., tel. 552-2942, email: charlyst@tmx.com.ni).

Art, music, poetry, and chess are on order at the **Galería Café la Diferencia,** just south of the cathedral and serving Greek food, baguette sandwiches, salads, and cappuccino. Open Wednesday–Sunday 3–9 P.M. **Ristorante Il Portico,** in front of the Hotel Alhambra on the main plaza, has a fancy Italian menu, with an even fancier rack of wine, tel. 552-4486.

Doña Conchi offers a taste of her native Spain in the most intimate atmosphere in Granada; dinner by candlelight under the stars, surrounded by a dramatically lit, lush garden patio. Everything is delicious, especially the large, fresh dinner salads and pitchers of sangria. If you're lucky, Doña Conchi will even play her castanets for you. Closed Tuesdays, tel. 552-7376, located two blocks east of the cathedral on Calle Caimito. Nearby **El Mediterraneo** is another elegant Spanish restaurant set in an airy garden patio adorned with colorful artwork. This is the only place in town to taste authentic paella (for two); closed Mondays, tel. 552-6764.

El Matchico is a French-owned, French cuisine restaurant in a "very trendy, uptown New York loft atmosphere," as one longtime U.S. resident described it. They serve a variety of dinner and dessert crepes (orange/chocolate with chantilly sauce), interesting salads, cappuccino, and a menu of moderately priced dishes far from the standard Nicaraguan fare.

SHOPPING

Granada was founded on the exchange of goods. The **municipal market** is located one block south of the plaza, and the chaotic bustle spills out onto the shops and sidewalks of Calle Atravesada. Less-frantic crafts shopping is found in a number of places surrounding the main plaza, including **Souvenir Dalia,** on the west side, with a wide range of local crafts, postcards, etc. (open 8 A.M.–6:30 P.M. Mon.–Fri., to 5 P.M. on weekends, tel. 552-6732.) Another *artesanía* shop is around the corner from the Casa de Leones, directly across from Gimnasio Zeus. **Coco Loco** is a unique clothing boutique and crafts store attached to Doña Conchi's restaurant. Also, this is *guayabera* country, and there are several places to buy the elegant Latin shirts, including **Guayabera Nora,** right around the corner from the Bearded Monkey.

The two major supermarkets are the **Palí,** on Calle Atravesada just south of the market and **Lacayo,** west of the park on Calle Xalteva (with an ATM and great wine selection).

TRAVEL INFORMATION

The local INTUR office is located on the southeast corner of the plaza, open Monday–Friday 8 A.M.–noon, 2–5 P.M., tel. 552-6858. It has a good selection of local brochures and maps. There is also a good deal of information at Granada's well-crafted homepage: www.granada.com.ni.

MARENA has jurisdiction over the three protected areas in the area—Volcán Mombacho, Isla de Zapatera, and the Laguna de Apoyo. Its office on the north side of Granada is open Monday–Friday 7 A.M.–2 P.M., tel. 552-4560.

TOUR OPERATORS

Just about all of the major tour companies based in Managua offer packages involving Granada. In addition, there are a handful of operators located in Granada. Oro Travel is a Nicaragua-wide tour service half a block west of the San Francisco Convent; it offers information, tour packages, weekend Mombacho trips, multilingual tour guides and translation service, car rental, and other travel ser-

© MARILYN WOOD

Plazuela de los Leones, Granada

VOLCÁN MOMBACHO NATURE RESERVE

Every bit of cool, misty, Volcán Mombacho cloud forest higher than 850 meters above sea level is officially protected as a nature reserve. This equals about 700 hectares of park, rising to a peak elevation of 1,345 meters, and comprising an incredibly rich, concentrated island of flora and fauna. Thanks to the **Fundación Cocibolca,** the reserve is accessible and boasts the most well designed hiking trails in the country. Mombacho is home to hundreds of orchid and bromeliad species, tree ferns, and old-growth cloud and dwarf forests. There are also three species of monkeys, 168 observed birds (49 of which are migratory), 30 species of reptiles, 60 mammals (including at least one very secretive big cat), and 10 amphibians. The flanks of the volcano are composed of privately owned coffee plantations and cattle ranches, 21 percent of which remains forested; maintaining this cover is another crucial objective of the foundation, since this is where over 90 percent of Mombacho's 1,000 howler monkeys reside (the monkeys travel in 100 different troops, and venture into the actual reserve only to forage).

Your admission fee to the reserve includes free guide service (tips optional) on one of two trails. The standard trail is the **Sendero el Cráter,** which encircles the forest-lined crater, and features a moss-lined gorge, several lookout points, and a spur trail to the fumaroles, which are holes in the ground venting hot sulfurous air; the fumaroles area is an open, grassy part of the volcano with blazing wildflowers and an incredible view of Granada and her Isletas. The whole loop, including the spur, is 1.5 kilometers, mostly flat, and takes a casual hour to walk. The **Sendero la Puma** is considerably more challenging—it is a four-kilometer loop with several difficult climbs that lead to breathtaking viewpoints; it begins at a turnoff from the fumaroles trail, and you should allow a minimum of three hours to complete it.

The reserve is closed on Mondays (for maintenance), and usually restricts Tuesdays and Wednesdays to organized groups, but if you call in advance concerning one of these days, you can probably squeeze your way in. From Thursday to Sunday, all are welcome. The entrance fee ($6 for foreigners, $4 for Nicas and residents, $3 students and children) includes admission to the reserve, transport to and from the parking lot, and insurance. Call the Biological Station at tel. 552-5858, or Fundación Cocibolca (in Managua) at tel. 278-3224 or 277-1681, or email: fcocibol@ibw.com.ni.

Volcán Mombacho Biological Center

Located at the base of one of Mombacho's 14 communications antennas, on a small plateau called Plan de las Flores at 1,150 meters, the research station is also a *hospedaje, cafetín,* ranger station, and conference center. The center was completed in 2000 and is still growing. As of press time, there are 10 dormitory beds in a loft above the interpretive center; sleeping here costs $25 a person, a package deal which includes dinner, a guided night hike (on which you can search for the famous red-eyed frog and Mombacho salamander), and breakfast; or pitch a tent for $8 and buy meals on the side.

vices, tel. 552-4568, email: orotravl@tmx.com.ni, website: www.orotravel.com.

Servitur is connected to the Hotel Alhambra, offering travel agent services, and a variety of local trips in the Granada area, tel. 552-2955 or 552-4390, email: servitur@ibw.com.ni. Nicaragua Adventures has an office in the lobby of the Hotel Colonial around the corner. It offers half-day trips to Masaya, Los Pueblos Blancos, Mombacho, and San Juan del Sur, starting at $25 a person; city tours of Granada cost $10.

Walk through the lobby of the Palacio de Cultura on the west side of the plaza to find JB Fun Tours. It has a huge selection of guided tours all over the country, including Granada and Isletas trips. JB Fun has bilingual guides, will make your hotel and plane reservations before you come down, and offers information on real estate and translation services. Office is open 8 A.M.–8 P.M. Monday–Saturday, tel. 552-6732, email: jbtravel1228@aol.com, website: www.jbtour.com.

Getting There

Although the majority of Mombacho's visitors arrive as part of a tour package, it is entirely possible to visit the reserve on your own, and—if you'd rather not spend the night—it makes a perfect day trip from Managua, Granada, or Masaya. You'll start by taking a bus (or express minivan) headed for Nandaime or Rivas (or, from Granada, to Carazo as well), and getting off at the Empalme el Guanacaste. This is a large intersection, and the road up to the parking lot and official reserve entrance is located 1.5 kilometers up the brick volcano road—look for the signs. The walk to the parking lot is a solid half-hour trek, mostly uphill and in the sun. Water and snacks are available at the parking lot—be sure to hydrate yourself before and during this first leg of your journey. Once you arrive at the parking lot, you'll pay the entrance fee and then board one of the foundation's vehicles to make the half-hour, six-kilometer climb up to the Biological Station. Thursday–Sunday, the "*Ecomovil*" departs at 8:30 A.M., 10 A.M., 1 P.M., and 3 P.M., and returns shortly after each climb up the hill. In your own 4WD vehicle, you'll be asked to pay $11 in addition to your entrance fee.

Canopy Tours

Canopy Tours Mombacho is located up the road from the parking lot, just before the road passes through the El Progreso coffee mill. They've got a 1,700-meter course involving 16 platforms and a 25-meter-long hanging bridge, all for $20 a person ($15 for Nicas), tel. 267-8256 or 888-2567. Many tour operators offer a full-day Mombacho package that involves a visit to the reserve followed by a canopy tour on the way down (Oro Travel, based in Granada, charges $40 a person for this trip).

On the opposite (east) face of Volcán Mombacho, cloud forest coffee farm meets canopy tour at the Cutirre Farm. **Mombotour** offers a range of half-day trips, involving some combination of high-ropes canopy tour, horseback ride, bird-watching hike, and coffee farm tour. Trips cost $15–30 a person, and all include transportation to and from Granada, plus an optional lunch buffet for $7.50. The 15-kilometer ride to the Cutirre Farm takes longer than you'd expect, and the road turns into a river during the wet season, but the trip is worth it, and once you arrive, the views from the lodge are spectacular, looking straight out at Isla de Zapatera, and behind it, the cone of Volcán Concepción. There is also a small but attractive insect museum, with a full butterfly farm in the works. Bird-watchers can take a walk through the plantation with guides experienced in spotting any of the 43 species observed here.

The canopy tour, suspended from 14 of the giant shade trees on the coffee farm, is a professional, safe system of 17 platforms, a hanging bridge, and 13 horizontal zip lines, ending with a 23-meter rappel from a massive ceiba tree. Mombotour's office is located on the west side of the Iglesia La Mercéd in Granada. Show up to arrange your trip, which leaves at either 10 A.M. or 2 P.M. (arrive one hour prior), returning you to Granada about three hours later, tel. 552-4548 or 860-2890, email: mombotur@tmx.com.ni.

SERVICES

Emergency

The biggest hospital (Bernardino Díaz Ochoa) is a few kilometers out of town, on the road toward Managua, tel. 552-2207 or 552-2719. On the same highway, a bit closer to town is the Hospital Privado Cocibolca, tel. 552-2907 or 552-4092. For minor treatments, the section of Calle Atravesada just south of the bridge is occupied by over a dozen clinics, blood labs, and pharmacies. The National Police station is located on the highway to Nandaime, tel. 552-4712, and 75 meters west of the cinema, tel. 552-2977 or 552-2929.

Phones and Mail

The main ENITEL building is right off the northeast corner of the plaza, and the post office is on Calle Atravesada across from the cinema (beautiful stamp selection).

HAIRCUTS

Granada has particularly famous old-style barber shops, all clustered together on the block running west off the plaza. Try one of the two "007" salons, where skilled craftsmen—all wearing bleached white *guayaberas*—will give you the perfect cut for barely more than a buck. Splurge a couple cordobas extra for a straight-edged shave, nose-hair cut, and face massage.

Internet

Where to begin? Most local residents will tell you without hesitation: the Binary Base, across from the Convento San Francisco. Lots of space, lots of air, mellow tunes, a speedy satellite connection, used bookstore, Web design service, and fresh-squeezed lemonade, tel. 552-7914. The café in the Casa de Leones also has a nice environment, plus a full bar and cheap Internet 8 A.M.–10 P.M. every day, tel. 552-6847.

Just off the northwest corner of the plaza, Inter Café packs a bunch of services into a cramped room: satellite Internet, scanner, CD burner, international Internet phone service (about $2.50 a minute to the United States, $6 to Europe). Internet is $3 an hour, open 8 A.M.–9 P.M., Sunday 10:30 A.M.–7 P.M., tel. 552-7284.

Granada has many other Internet options, and more cyber-joints are popping up every day. Ask around, or start at the place on the southeast corner of the park ($3.25 an hour) and head toward the lake.

Banks

Banco de America Central is on the southwest corner of the plaza, and Banpro and Bancentro are on Calle Atravesada, just a few blocks away. There are street money changers out in full force along this same section of Atravesada, a Western Union over by the Bearded Monkey, and two ATMs: one in the Supermercado Lacayo, the other in the Esso Tiger Market.

Car Rental

The Budget office is in the Shell Guapinol gas station at the *salida* to Managua. Open seven days a week 8 A.M.–6:30 P.M.; cars rent from $19–100 a day, and you can throw in a cell phone for $1 a week, tel. 552-2323.

Film

The Kodak shop is on Calle Atravesada, just north of the Bancentro; open every day 8 A.M.–6 P.M., tel. 552-5455.

GETTING THERE AND AWAY

By Bus to Other Points in Nicaragua

There are four places to catch a bus out of town. Managua-bound *expresos* (COGRAN, tel. 552-2954) leave every 15–20 minutes from a lot 1.5 blocks south of the southwest corner of the plaza, 5:45 A.M.–8 P.M. Monday–Friday, until 7 P.M. Saturday, and until 6 P.M. Sunday. Another fleet of minivans leaves from the Parque Sandino, on the north side of Granada near the old railroad station, leaving regularly from 5 A.M.–7:30 P.M. Both services travel to la UCA in Managua. From there, the same vehicles leave for Granada every 15 minutes, from 5:50 A.M.–9:30 P.M.

Yellow bus service to Rivas, Nandaime, and Jinotepe works out of the Shell Palmira, on Granada's south side, just past the Palí supermarket. The first bus to Rivas leaves at 5:45 A.M. and takes 1.5 hours; service continues at random intervals until the last one at 3:10 P.M. Nandaime buses leave every 20 minutes. Jinotepe *expresos* take a mere 45 minutes compared to the nearly two-hour *ordinario* trip through the pueblos. Around the corner, behind the Palí, is the bus terminal with service to Masaya (although any Managua-bound *expreso* will let you off in Masaya as well).

By Bus to Costa Rica and Panamá

Avenida Arrellano, on the west end of Granada, is part of the San José and Panama City–bound routes for all three Central American bus lines. The three offices are all located on the east side of the street, and reservations should be made at least two days in advance. The TicaBus terminal is half a block south of the Old Hospital, tel.

552-4301; be there at 6:15 A.M. for the 7 A.M. bus. NicaBus is three blocks north of there, tel. 552-5299, same schedule as above. TransNica is three long blocks south of the Old Hospital, on the corner of Calle Xalteva, tel. 552-6619; three daily southbounders leave at 6:30 A.M., 8 A.M., and 11 A.M.; be there a half-hour before departure.

By Boat

The old ferry departs Granada's municipal dock Monday and Thursday at 2 P.M., arriving in San Carlos around 3 A.M. When weather permits, the boat stops at Altagracia before cutting across to the eastern lakeshore and a port call in San Miguelito. The trip costs about $4 each way, and returns from San Carlos at 2 P.M. on Tuesday and Friday. The boat can get crowded and uncomfortable at times, especially around Semana Santa when the lake turns *bravo* (rough) and the weather is hot. Get to the port early and be aggressive to stake your territory. During the rest of the year, the ride is usually *tranquilo,* and you may even be able to get some sleep on the deck.

The M/N *Mozorola* makes the four-hour cruise to Altagracia, Ometepe (depending on the wind) twice a week, leaving Granada every Wednesday and Saturday at 11 A.M. (returns from Altagracia Tuesday and Friday at 11 A.M.). Adverse weather conditions can cause the cancellation of the trip, but it's otherwise a great ride past the Isletas and the Island of Zapatera, tel. 552-8764 or 884-9548.

The *Crucero Solentiname* offers coach and first-class accommodations on its cross-lake trip. Leaves the dock at Granada Friday at 7 A.M., arrives in Moyogalpa, Ometepe 10 A.M., Solentiname at 5:30 P.M., and San Carlos at 8 P.M. Returns Sunday, arriving in Granada at 6:30 P.M. Pricey tour packages are available that include pickup in Managua; call 552-4313 in Granada, or Solentiname Tours in Managua at tel. 265-2716, email: zerger@ibw.com.ni. Note: as of press time, due to lack of demand, the *Crucero* was running every 15 days, sometimes less—you should definitely contact them beforehand to make reservations and be sure that it is traveling when you are.

Near Granada

Hike to the Laguna de Apoyo

All that's separating you and a dip in the deep waters of the Laguna de Apoyo is an easy 2.5-hour round-trip hike due west from Granada's cemetery. Simply go to the northeast corner of the cemetery and start walking the dirt road that borders it on the north side. Keep walking as straight as possible whenever there is a fork in the road, and feel free to ask the Nicas living along the road if you are on the right track. They all know the trail, using it to water their cattle or sometimes to do laundry. Eventually, the rutted road will curve to the south and you will come to a crossroads. Turn right across a fenced-in field, which you will cross until you hit the lip of the crater. The descent is pretty obvious but treacherous after a rain, since it is torn up by the cows. At the bottom you'll find a beach (of sorts) directly across from Catarina and the lakeside services. There are no services here—just

cool swimming and a bunch of birds. The walk is mostly level, but not very shaded until you hit the crater.

LAS ISLETAS

This 365-island archipelago was formed when Volcán Mombacho erupted some 20,000 years ago, hurling its top half into the nearby lake in giant masses of rock, ash, and lava. Today, the islands are inhabited by a few hundred campesinos and an ever-increasing number of wealthy Nicaraguans and foreigners who continue to buy up the *isletas* for their garish vacation homes. Apart from the natural beauty of the *isletas,* the **Fortín de San Pablo** is a Spanish fort that was largely unsuccessful in preventing pirate attacks on Granada. The islanders themselves are interesting and friendly, maintaining a rural life unique in Nicaragua. The children paddle dugout canoes or rowboats to school from an early age, and their folks get along by fishing and subsistence farming.

Visiting the Isletas

Your trip begins at Puerto Asese, a short ride south of town at the end of the waterfront road (about $1 via taxi). At the dock, you'll find a restaurant, snack bars, and a whole bunch of boats looking for your business; choose a *lanchero* (boatman) and don't expect to haggle over prices, as gasoline is expensive. You'll pay about $8 a person for a half-hour tour. Beef up your visit by asking to visit an island where a family can serve you lunch—or pull up and "refuel" at one of the mellow island bars before continuing your tour. You can also take a dip in the lake water or have your *lanchero* bring you to the island cemetery or old fort. A better deal is to be dropped off at one of the deserted islets and then picked up later in the afternoon. Take along provisions and make a lazy afternoon of it.

If you're not into noisy motors in your wilderness experience and prefer only the sound of the birds singing as your paddle cuts through the water, sign up for a **kayak tour** in the Mombotour office in Granada, located on the west side of Iglesia La Merced, tel. 552-4548 (ask for Mister Andy). Learn how to sea kayak (intro, advanced, and Eskimo roll classes), then take a tour of the islands and old fort. The intro class, which includes all equipment, transportation, and tour of the Fortín San Pablo, costs $34 a person and lasts three hours. Special bird-watching paddles run $20–30.

Accommodations

Hotel Isleta La Ceiba has 10 rooms with a/c, fan, private bath, pool, hot water, and your own desert island. They've got a whole fleet of boats to play around in, plus plenty of games—volleyball, billiards, *futbolín* —and boat and fishing trips. The price of $55 a person includes your room, three meals, transportation to and from Granada (15-minute boat ride), and taxes. Contact Nicarao Lake Resort in its Managua office in tel. 266-1694 or 266-1237, fax 266-0704, email: nlr@nicaraolake.com.ni.

rapid transport in the Isletas of Granada

PARQUE NACIONAL ARCHIPIÉLAGO ZAPATERA

Officially declared a national park by the Sandinistas in 1983, the Zapatera Archipelago is still struggling for the financial resources to protect and manage its many riches. About 34 kilometers south of Granada, Zapatera is an extinct volcano surrounded by Isla el Muerto and other islets, all of which comprise 45 square kilometers of land, and are home to some 500 residents. These islands were of enormous importance to indigenous peoples, who used them primarily as a vast burial ground and sacrifice spot. The sites of La Punta de las Figuras and Zonzapote are particularly rich in artifacts and have a network of caves that have never been researched. Also seek out the petroglyphs carved into the bedrock beaches of Isla el Muerto. An impressive selection of Zapatera's formidable stone idols is on display in the Convento San Francisco, but the islands' remaining archaeological treasures remain relatively unstudied and unprotected—and continue to disappear.

Zapatera is a natural wonder, rising 629 meters above sea level and boasting virgin forest and a great deal of wildlife on its upper slopes. The archipelago is home to parrots, toucans, herons and other waterfowl, plus white-tailed deer, an alleged population of jaguars, and a rich fishery off its shores.

However, despite a 1,000-page MARENA document describing its management, protection of Zapatera's treasures has been completely ineffective. With only one park ranger who visits the islands a couple times per month, inhabitants and visitors continually violate regulations by littering, robbing archaeological pieces, and illegally hunting the islands' wildlife. Its forests are being illegally harvested at an unprecedented rate.

Access the park from Granada's Puerto Asese, or if you can swing it, from the lakeshore in a borrowed dugout canoe. If you've got a tent, this is a great place to put it to use; just be sure you're not on the land of anyone who cares. There are no facilities on Zapatera, so be well prepared.

Southwestern Nicaragua:
Rivas, Ometepe, and San Juan del Sur

The hiker, volcano climber, bird-watcher, surfer, sailor, swimmer, and naturalist, not to mention the rum drinker, sunset watcher, and fresh fish–eater, will all find themselves quite content in Nicaragua's southwestern corner. The land was considered enchanted by the Nicarao, and it hasn't lost its charm—or magic—over the centuries.

There are few major towns along the isthmus that links southern Nicaragua. Rivas is the largest, a peaceful colonial city of traders and farmers set around a stately white cathedral. You'll most likely pass through it on your way to the bays, beaches, and rocky points that form the Pacific coast. The historic crescent bay of San Juan del Sur is the

the beach at Bahía Majagual

© JOSHUA BERMAN

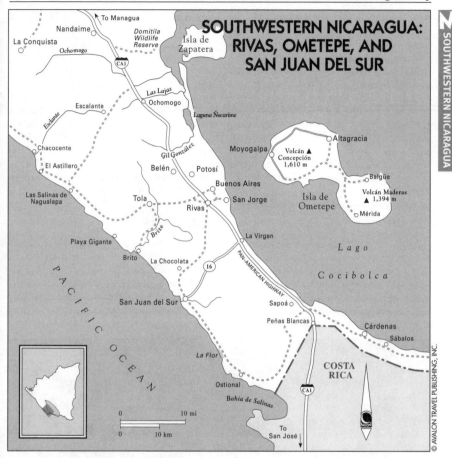

most popular of the beaches, and it sees its share of foreign travelers—just as it did during the gold rush 150 years ago. But in this century, instead of boarding sailing ships for San Francisco, travelers stick around San Juan del Sur and its neighboring bays to enjoy the surf and relax in beach bars over bottles of dark rum and plates of fresh snapper.

Across the isthmus, deep in the waters of Lake Cocibolca, sits mighty Ometepe, the twin-peaked emerald isle of Central America. An intensely volcanic island still steeped in tradition and mystery, Ometepe is the ancestral home of the Nahuatl people and the birthplace of modern Nicaragua. Legend has it the warrior chief

Nicarao still lies buried somewhere along Ometepe's tree-lined coast.

The Land and History

South of Managua, the land crumples suddenly into the impressive and windblown peak of Las Nubes (934 meters) and then falls slowly to the south until it spills into the verdant and lush plains that form the southern part of Nicaragua. Here Lake Cocibolca presses the land into a narrow belt that barely separates the lake from the Pacific Ocean. It's possible that, millions of years ago, it didn't separate them at all: there is geological evidence that suggests Lake Cocibolca once flowed across this slim margin of land to the west, emptying into the Pacific near the fishing community of Brito, instead of the Atlantic Ocean as it does today.

Noticeably lacking in the area south of Managua is the intense, grinding poverty so obvious in the parched lands of the north and west. It rains more in the south, and the rivers flow nearly year-round. The western shores of Lake Cocibolca are made of rich, productive, and deep volcanic soils. Nevertheless, cattle is king here, grazing lazily in immense lucrative ranches of improved breed stock and handsome haciendas. There are fields of sugarcane too, spreading from the rocky foot of Mombacho, one of Nicaragua's most picturesque volcano peaks.

The isthmus of Rivas is laden with history and ghosts. Although known as the land of Nicarao, the area was first inhabited by the Kiribisis tribe, who were pushed aside by the more powerful Chorotegas. The Nicaraos came afterwards, and had lived in the area only seven or eight generations when the Spanish arrived. During the gold rush, hundreds of thousands of passengers sailing between New York and California touched terra firma for the only time in their 30-day passage here, traveling in horse-drawn carts between San Jorge and San Juan del Sur before boarding ships for California. About the same time, William Walker tasted defeat at the hands of armed locals around the colonial farm of El Mesón, now a historical and archaeological museum in the city of Rivas. Nearly a hundred years later, many of the battles in 1978 and 1979 were fought on the wealthy lands south of the capital, and young Sandinista troops suffered a major setback in Nandaime before they were to eventually claim their victory.

NANDAIME

Just south of where the highways from Granada and Carazo join to continue on to Rivas and the border, you'll pass by the midsize city of Nandaime, located on the Pan-American Highway in the shadow of Volcán Mombacho. This is a humble, unassuming pueblo with the most basic of traveler's amenities, a small town tran-

mural in Rivas depicting when Nicaro met the Spanish

Usually more crowded, the rancho at Domitila is frequented by scientists and tourists alike.

quillity, and a passion for music. Nandaime's most famous son is Camilo Zapata, a key founder of the Nicaraguan folk style who composed the song, "El Nandaimeño." Nandaime is also home to three "philharmonic orchestras"; before you run out to rent a tux, though, you should probably know that this is merely the politically correct term for *chichera* groups, which are ragtag bands found in parades and bullrings. *Chichera* music is happy, loud, and scrappy, composed of a bass drum, a snare, cymbals, a sousaphone, and loud, clashing brass.

Domitila Wildlife Reserve

Just south of Nandaime on the coast of Lake Cocibolca and looking out on the island of Zapatera is a private wildlife reserve that is part of Nicaragua's system of protected lands and is reportedly one of the best places in the country to glimpse mammals and other wildlife in their natural habitat. Domitila sits on 230 hectares of private land encompassing tropical dry forest

and the coastline of Lake Cocibolca, with tree nurseries, hiking trails, and a ton of wildlife. The reserve is run like an eco-camp: composting toilets, wastewater treatment facility, a zero-trash policy, and specific rules about what you can and can't do on the reserve. Camping is prohibited. Domitila also offers comfortable, private cabins built on the premises, complete restaurant service, and facilities for groups of up to 25 researchers, scientists, or travelers.

The entrance is located five kilometers south of Nandaime (km 72) on the road south to Rivas; turn off the highway onto a dusty dirt road that will lead you 10 kilometers past the Lagunas de Mecatepe to Domitila. Well-built cabins cost $25 per person, which includes three meals per day. Call tel. 881-1786 at least 24 hours in advance to make reservations or email: mjbarme@ibw.com.ni. Several guided tours are available, including luxury tours to the island of Zapatera, where hot meals are prepared and served to you on-site.

Rivas

SOUTHWESTERN NICARAGUA

The bastion city of southern Nicaragua, Rivas has the distinction of being an important center of commerce and trade without having lost the Old-World charm that makes it such an agreeable place to live or visit. For travelers crossing the border and traveling north from Costa Rica, Rivas makes a pleasant first stop to take a taste of the relaxed Nicaraguan culture. For the beach crew enjoying San Juan del Sur, Rivas is the place to visit a doctor or pharmacy, check email, and buy groceries or bus tickets to points north or south—Rivas is even home to a Costa Rican consulate, in case you have immigration issues.

Rivas, with its 44,000 inhabitants, is just big enough to be fun, and just small enough to be friendly. It's often hot because of its low altitude, but just as often a cool lake breeze sweeps through town from nearby Lake Cocibolca. Rivas's population climbs well over 44,000 if you include all the *chocoyos* (parakeets) that have chosen the town park as their home. At sundown the park is alive with the sound of them as they return from a hard day's work in the trees along the lakeshore and surrounding woods. Rivas is known as Ciudad de los Mangos (the City of Mangos) due to the abnormally high number of mango trees in and around the city, and the *chocoyos* are big aficionados of the fruit.

Rivas was known as Valle de la Ermita de San Sebastión until 1717, when a delegation of villagers traveled to Guatemala, the capital of the republic at that time, to request their little town be declared a villa with the name of La Pura y Limpia Concepción de Nuestra Señora la Virgen María. The villagers were given an audience by Capitán General del Reino Francisco Rodríguez de Rivas, who agreed to make the change. To thank him, the villagers decided to modify the name to La Villa de la Pura y Limpia Concepción de Rivas de Nicaragua. Thankfully for travelers and mapmakers, that name was considerably shortened.

A LOVE STORY—THE LEGEND OF OMETEPE AND ZAPATERA

It is said that long ago, neither Lake Cocibolca nor the islands existed. In their place was a broad green valley called Caopol, inhabited by animals that lived in thick forest. Not a single human lived in the forested valley, but the Chorotega, Chontales, Nagrandando, and Niquirano tribes all inhabited the edges of the valley, where they fought battles between tribes.

In the Niquirano tribe there was a lovely Indian maiden by the name of Ometepetl, who caught the eye of the young Nagrandan warrior named Nagrando. He fell deeply in love with her, and she with him. Their love remained a secret because the Niquiranos and Nagrandans were sworn enemies. The day Ometepetl's father learned of the illicit romance he grew furious and swore he would chase Nagrando to his death, rather than see his daughter marry a Nagrandan. Ometepetl and Nagrando fled to the valley where they hid in the forest to escape the fury of Ometepetl's father. There they decided the only way they'd ever be able to have peace would be to die together. Ometepetl and Nagrando slit their wrists with a sharp blade and died in each others' arms.

Ometeptl, as death overcame her, leaned backwards, and her breasts swelled. The sadness that overwhelmed the valley caused the sky to darken and an intense rain to fall. The valley began to flood, and her breasts became the twin peaks of Concepción and Maderas. Nagrando grew into an island as well, the volcanic island of Zapatera, located halfway between the lands of the Nagrandan people and his love Ometepetl. Ometepetl's father and the men who accompanied him in the search to kill Nagrando all perished in the flood. They became the Isletas de Granada and the Solentiname archipelago.

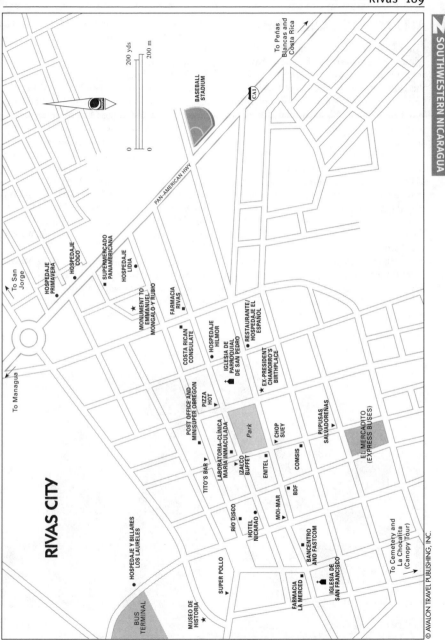

RIVAS CITY

To San Jorge

To Managua

To Peñas Blancas and Costa Rica

PAN-AMERICAN HWY

200 yds
200 m

BASEBALL STADIUM

CAI

HOSPEDAJE PRIMAVERA

HOSPEDAJE COCO

SUPERMERCADO PANAMERICANA

HOSPEDAJE LIDIA

MONUMENT TO EMMANUEL MONGALO Y RUBIO

FARMACIA RIVAS

COSTA RICAN CONSULATE

HOSPEDAJE HILMOR

RESTAURANTE/ HOSPEDAJE EL ESPAÑOL

IGLESIA DE PARROQUIAL DE SAN PEDRO

EX-PRESIDENT CHAMORRO'S BIRTHPLACE

POST OFFICE AND MINISUPER OBREGÓN

PIZZA HOT

LABORATORIA-CLINICA MARIA INMACULADA

Park

TITO'S BAR

IZALCO BUFFET

CHOP SUEY

ENITEL

COMSIS

PUPUSAS SALVADOREÑAS

EL MERCADITO (EXPRESS BUSES)

RIO DISCO

HOTEL NICARAO

MOI-MAR

BDF

BANCENTRO AND FASTCOM

To Cemetery and La Chocalita (Canopy Tour)

HOSPEDAJE Y BILLARES LOS LAURELES

SUPER POLLO

FARMACIA LA MERCED

IGLESIA DE SAN FRANCISCO

MUSEO DE HISTORIA

BUS TERMINAL

ATTRACTIONS AND SIGHTS

Considered the fourth most important church in Nicaragua, the **Iglesia Parroquial de San Pedro** sits at the center of town like a keystone. Built in the 18th century, the Church of San Pedro has been witness to the gold rush, William Walker, and the revolution. It is today, as always, a peaceful place to seek refuge; mass is held evenings around 6 P.M.

Four blocks west of the park at the town's center, the **Iglesia de San Francisco** was built in 1778 and was the first convent of the Franciscan friars. A beautiful statue out front commemorates the devotion of the friars, to both God and their work. When they began construction of the nearby Bancentro, an **underground tunnel** was discovered that linked the Iglesia San Francisco with the plaza (the open area adjacent to the north side of the central park); the tunnel passes beneath the library (one door east of Bancentro). Little is known of the tunnel, except it was probably dug at the same time the church was,

meaning it was in place and probably used during the Battle of Rivas, when the plaza was the site of a military barracks.

The Rivenses claim "nationalism began in Rivas." Though the expression makes reference to Rivas's defeat of William Walker, Rivas was also the birthplace of several former presidents of Nicaragua, including Máximo Jérez (Liberal, governed from June 8, 1818 to August 12, 1881), Adén Cárdenas (Conservative, governed from March 1, 1883 to March 1, 1887), and most recently, Violeta Barrios de Chamorro (Coalition, governed from April 25, 1990 to January 10, 1997). Chamorro's childhood home is located across the street from the south side of the Iglesia de San Pedro. There are also several direct descendants of William Walker living in Rivas.

Rivas has its own history museum: the **Museo de Historia y Antropología de Rivas,** set on the western side of town in a 200-year-old house that was once part of a cacao and indigo plantation. The Casa Hacienda Santa Úrsula, as the

Rivas' cathedral witnessed the Gold Rush.

© RANDY WOOD

building was known in its former incarnation, was the scene of a heroic battle on June 29, 1855, against William Walker, in which Walker and his men were defeated. The Battle of Rivas, as it became known, was one of the first manifestations of Nicaragua's growing sense of nationalism in the late 19th century. The museum has a healthy collection of pre-Columbian pottery and domestic utensils like kerosene lamps, silverware, and tools from the mid-19th century. Several old maps of the region are also on display, and of course the entire building itself is a museum piece, in the style of mid-17th century Mediterranean farmhouses. The museum is open rather irregular hours but generally follows an 8 A.M.–4:30 P.M. schedule. Foreign travelers pay $1 to enter; the museum sells several books.

The **Monument to Emmanuel Mongalo y Rubio** marks the final resting place of a young Rivas teacher who lived here in the mid-1800s. Mongalo y Rubio gained his fame during the Battle of Rivas by setting fire to the Mesón (the museum building) where Walker and his men had sought refuge; as they abandoned the blazing building they were captured or shot.

Another museum piece in its own right, the **Biblioteca Pública de Rivas,** next to Bancentro, is considered one of the oldest buildings in Nicaragua still standing. It is estimated to date back to at least the early 17th century. Among its various incarnations, the *biblioteca* was a secondary school founded in 1872 by Máximo Jérez, and El Colegio de la Inmaculada Concepción. Still easily visible in the building is a hole caused by a stray shot during the Battle of Rivas.

At the southeast end of town not far from the road to La Chocolata, the **Rivas Cemetery** is set on a little hill with a nice view of town and the surrounding hillsides. It's worth visiting in the late afternoon, as Rivas sunsets are often blazing washes of red and orange, thanks to the humidity in the air from Lake Cocibolca.

ENTERTAINMENT AND EVENTS

Rivas has one of Nicaragua's better discos, complete with light show, falling soap bubbles, dry ice, and fast, thumping merengue through heavy speakers—**Disco Río** rages on the weekends, especially Saturday nights; Thursday is Ladies' Night. There is an occasional cover charge, never more than $2.50.

Alternate Saturday nights in the town plaza (across from the park) are **Noches Rivenses,** typically presentations of dance, music, and theater. The combination of dance and the awesome backdrop of the cathedral and park make for an evocative experience.

Rivas is home to a handful of corner bars and clubs where you can tip a cold Victoria and relax. **Moi-Mar** is where Rivas's in-crowd goes to drink at tables set in an indoor-outdoor garden atmosphere; clientele generally have cell phones and great hair. Service with a snarl, but everyone knows the bartender, Marcia, and nobody minds. The "Moi" refers to Moises, the owner, but the "Mar" is a mystery. **Tito's Bar** is another option; casual and friendly, and the beer is ice cold. Tito's has a small dance floor and a couple of pool tables. If shooting pool is your bag, there are better tables at **Hospedaje y Billares Los Laureles** where games cost about $1 each. At the Fastcom Internet café you can play video games for about $4.25 an hour on one of five machines.

SPORTS AND RECREATION

No one enjoys baseball as much as they do in Rivas, which, as of 2001, had 138 officially registered baseball teams and over 3,900 registered players. Attending a Sunday afternoon game in the town's impressive stadium on the highway is a great way to experience Rivas and the energy of its people; tickets are $1, and in lieu of chili dogs there is plenty of *vigorón* and enchiladas in the grandstand. Ironically, even with all the community support, Rivas's pro team had to drop out of the 2002 national championship race for lack of funds.

Nicaragua's first **Canopy Tour** was built on the outskirts of Rivas, three kilometers along the road to La Chocolata. Nicarao Canopy Tour (tel. 266-1018 or 886-7548) has seven zip lines and eight platforms for a total length of 800 meters of high-speed canopy madness. It's a professional operation that puts safety first, and all the staff have been well trained. The whole "canopy tour" thing is a misnomer—you're not so much touring the canopy as you are zipping through it on high-tension steel cables stretched 16–30 meters off the ground; still, it's an awful lot of fun. The tour lasts about an hour and costs $10 per person. The area is a magnificent piece of dry tropical forest inhabited by monkeys, sloths, and brightly colored birds.

There are four buses a day to La Chocolata that pass by the Nicarao Canopy Tour. The buses leave the market in Rivas at 8 A.M., 11 A.M., 2 P.M., and 4 P.M., pass by the International Agriculture School, and get to the Canopy Tour about 20 minutes later. Other times of the day you're better off taking a taxi from town, which should cost no more than $2.50 for two travelers (and another $2.50 to return). The tour operators can arrange transportation to and from the site for larger groups, if you call ahead for a reservation.

If you're feeling adventurous, the road through La Chocolata eventually ends in San Juan del Sur, and makes a good bike ride or an ambitious hike (20–25 km).

Just south of the intersection of the Pan-American Highway with the road that leads to San Juan del Sur is CIBALSA, a hotel turned military base, turned hotel again. Their **swimming pool** is well liked by Rivenses who don't want to traipse all the way down to the ocean. Even if you don't want to swim, it's a pleasant place to relax and enjoy the unequaled view of the twin Ometepe volcanoes.

ACCOMMODATIONS
Under $10
For budget travelers, **Hospedaje Lidia** seems to be the most popular. Lidia has a dozen clean rooms; $5 a night per person for shared bath, $9.50 per couple. The only rooms with private bath are geared toward groups of three or four travelers and cost $14. Down by the market, **Hospedaje y Billares Los Laureles** sounds sketchy: near the market, pool hall, not expensive, etc., but travelers who have stayed there, as well as Peace Corps volunteers who work in Rivas, report it's safe and not scary at all. Take a look and make

your own decision. Eleven rooms with private or shared bath cost $2–4.50. It has nice box-spring beds and fans.

In town at the northeast and southeast corners of the church are two more options. **Hospedaje Hilmor:** walk through its living room and kitchen, across the clotheslines and the drying laundry, and find a small room or two at the back of the house that cost $3.50 per person. **Restaurante/Hospedaje El Español** is a pleasant corner place with a mellow bar and smoking room in the front *sala*. In the back are four very nice, modern rooms. Each pair of rooms shares a bath. Doubles are $18 per room.

$25–50
Hotel Cacique Nicarao is an upscale, modern hotel complete with front desk, and plush rooms with cable TV, a/c, a guarded parking lot, and great service. Singles cost $32, doubles $42, and triples $52, plus tax, tel. 454-3234.

Along the Highway
Not exactly in the thick of things, several hotels along the Pan-American provide additional alternatives for travelers to Rivas, particularly those driving their own vehicles. **Hospedaje Coco** looks like something out of a Mexican cowboy movie: 12 rooms in two stories set around a concrete courtyard; just add horse. Clean, safe, and $8.50 for rooms with private bath. Next door to Coco is **Hotel Primavera,** a family-run, friendly place with parking for your vehicle inside a gated compound in the back; $8.50 for a room with private bath. Across the street, **Hospedaje El Viajero** does a lively trade with truckers looking for a place to take a nap before moving on, as well as lovebirds from town who need somewhere to go for an hour or two; $2 per person if that's what you're looking for.

FOOD
Nearest to the park is the clean and orderly **Izalco Buffet,** open for lunches and dinner. It truly is a buffet, with steaming trays of food under heat lamps and behind glass, and it's first-come, first-serve, so get there early before the hordes clean it

out. A decent lunch will run you about $2.75, plus Internet in the back. Across the street from the Iglesia San Pedro is Rivas's take on a well-known pizza chain, **Pizza Hot.** The pizza is actually quite good (unless you're from New York), and the outdoor tables are a nice place to catch up on your journal and people-watch.

On the southwest corner of the park is **Chop Suey,** a Chinese food place that isn't far off the mark, though all the dishes have been subtly adapted to suit the Nicaraguan palate; $4–6 a plate. Fried, baked, broiled, breaded, and roasted chicken are found in **Pollo Dorado** (closest to the center of town) and **Super Pollo,** near the market.

Possibly the lowest-price alternative in town is **Pupusas Salvadoreñas,** where tasty, authentic Salvadoran meat, cheese, or bean *pupusas* (greasy, stuffed pancakes) are served hot off the grill with salad, $2, only open evenings, located across from El Mercadito. Also open only in the evenings, there are several *fritangas* in the plaza, notably **La Gitana** (the gypsy), who shows up in her pickup truck around 11 P.M. and serves the meanest *gallo pinto* in town—a lifesaver when you stumble out of the disco at 3 A.M. and want some grease.

The best upscale restaurant is in the **Hotel Cacique Nicarao,** which—besides its traditional menu of well-prepared foods—is one of the only places in Nicaragua where you can get buffalo wings with hot sauce.

Along the Highway

Near the southern limits of the city of Rivas there are several high-priced options that do a good business with truckers, travelers, and businesspeople heading through on their way to the border. Highly recommended is **La Estancia** on the east side of the highway, with a sort of "farm ranch meets barn" feel to it; well-prepared chicken or beef dishes go for $6, and fresh shrimp dishes $10 and up. Happily, they take credit cards. Almost directly across the highway is **El Mariscazo,** a word that is difficult to translate directly, but means something like "A huge slap in the face with seafood." It's a good option for fish, shrimp, and lobster, all of which run in the $10–13 range.

SHOPPING

There's a small shop that sells handicrafts on the west end of town by the International Agriculture School. The Hotel Cacique Nicarao also sells postcards, handicrafts, and souvenirs.

SERVICES

There are several good pharmacies in town if you're looking for suntan lotion, aloe, painkillers, or medication. The biggest and best is right across from the park on the side of the plaza, Laboratorio-Clínica María Inmaculada; in addition to the pharmacy, a well-respected doctor is available for consults Monday–Friday 2–4 P.M. They've also got professional massage therapists (the pharmacy is open Mon.–Fri. 8 A.M.–4:30 P.M. and Sat. until noon). Another well-stocked pharmacy is the Farmacia Rivas, two blocks east of the park at the intersection of the boulevard, tel. 453-4292.

Rivas's market

© RANDY WOOD

The ENITEL office is a block west of the park, open 7 A.M.–9:40 P.M. every day of the week. The post office is north and west of the park, has fax service, and is open Monday–Friday 7:30 A.M.–4:30 P.M. and Saturday 7:30 A.M.–noon.

Internet

Comsis, located one block south and one block west of the park, is open Monday–Friday 8:30 A.M.–10 P.M., Saturday 8:30 A.M.–6 P.M., $3 an hour. Tucked in the back of Izalco Buffet, the Centro Cyber has three machines that cost $4.25 per hour (open Mon.–Sat. 8 A.M.–10 P.M., Sun. 10 A.M.–10 P.M.). Next to the Bancentro, Fastcom has five machines, open from 8 A.M. to 6 or 7 P.M. depending on demand; they cost $4.25 per hour.

Money

There are several banks in town including BDF, Bancentro, Banpro, and BAC, all of which operate essentially on a schedule of Monday–Friday 8:30 A.M.–4:30 P.M., Saturday 8:30 A.M.–noon. Because BAC owns the credit card company Credomatic, you can take advances against your credit cards there, for—amazingly—no fee.

The Costa Rican Consulate in Rivas offers help with immigration issues for Costa Rica–bound travelers. It's located a block east and north of the cathedral, open Monday–Friday 7 A.M.–5 P.M. and Saturday 7 A.M.–noon.

GETTING THERE AND AWAY

Buses leave Managua's Mercado Huembes terminal for Rivas every 30 minutes. There are several express buses per day, especially in the early morning before 8 A.M. Express buses to Peñas Blancas will let you off on the highway at Rivas. They leave Huembes at 5 A.M., 8 A.M., 9:30 A.M., and 3:30 P.M.

Regular buses leave from the market on the northwest side of Rivas. Express buses, usually sleek little minibuses, leave from El Mercadito on the other end of town about once every hour.

From the market, buses leave every hour for Jinotepe, Granada, every 25 minutes for Nandaime, Diriomo, Diriá, Catarina, Masaya, and Managua. The last bus for Managua leaves from the Texaco station on the highway at 6 P.M. Four daily buses go to Belén (7 A.M., 10:30 A.M., 12:30 P.M., and 4 P.M.), and six for Salinas and Tola (9 A.M., 11 A.M., 12:40 P.M., 2:25 P.M., 4 P.M., and 4:30 P.M.). Service to Peñas Blancas and the border every 30–45 minutes. Last bus leaves Rivas at 6 P.M.

To and from Costa Rica

On the highway in the Supermercado Panamericana (next to the Texaco station) you can buy tickets for the TicaBus, which passes by Rivas each morning bound for Costa Rica between 7 and 8 A.M., and between 3 and 4 P.M. every afternoon bound for Managua. Buy your tickets the day before ($10–12 to San José, Costa Rica).

Taxis to San Jorge and San Juan del Sur

Taxis to San Jorge should cost you no more than $.80 per person whether you take them from the traffic circle or from Rivas. Ignore any taxi driver that tries to charge your foreign-looking self $2 or more. Taxis from Rivas to San Juan del Sur cost around $8 per person, or $1 if it's a *colectivo,* but you'll have to share.

Tola and Pacific Beaches

An easy 10 kilometers from Rivas is the agricultural community of Tola, gateway to a horrendous dirt shore road and a string of lonely, beautiful beaches that make up 30 kilometers of Pacific shoreline. Most everywhere along this stretch you can expect to be the only foreigner on the beach. Unlike San Juan del Sur, there are few tourist facilities.

TOLA

Tola is famous in Nicaragua as the subject of a common expression: *"Te dejó esperando como la novia de Tola."* (He left you waiting like the bride of Tola.) It refers to the real-life soap opera story of a young woman named Hillary, who on the day of her wedding, was left standing at the altar at Belén while the groom, Salvador Cruz, married his former lover, Juanita.

There is a great hike in the Tola area up a hill called **El Cielo** (heaven); it is not an easy hike, primarily because the trail isn't clearly marked, but for the effort you will be rewarded with a first-class view of the town of Tola, Lake Cocibolca, and the island of Ometepe to the east, Volcán Masaya blowing smoke to the north and the Pacific Ocean to the west. To hike El Cielo, walk straight out of town past the cemetery (don't turn left); follow the path as best you can until you get to a big hill with three coconut trees on top; climb straight up and don't let the wind blow you over while marveling at the views.

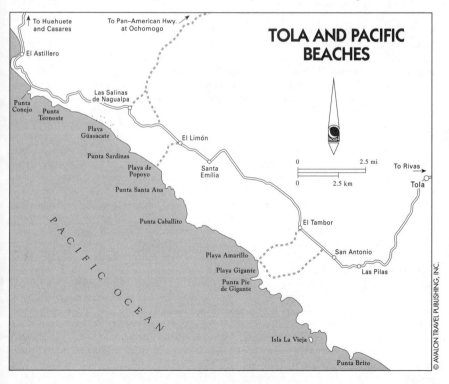

TOLA AND PACIFIC BEACHES

To Huehuete and Casares

To Pan–American Hwy. at Ochomogo

El Astillero

Punta Conejo

Punta Teonoste

Las Salinas de Nagualpa

Playa Güasacate

El Limón

Punta Sardinas

Playa de Popoyo

Santa Emilia

Punta Santa Ana

0   2.5 mi

0   2.5 km

To Rivas

Tola

Punta Caballito

El Tambor

San Antonio

Playa Amarillo

Playa Gigante

Las Pilas

Punta Pie de Gigante

PACIFIC OCEAN

Isla La Vieja

Punta Brito

© AVALON TRAVEL PUBLISHING, INC.

Volunteer Opportunities

Operating since September 2001, **Esperanza del Futuro,** a community-development program run by Doña Loida (an influential Sandinista leader) aims to provide better education to people in rural areas. There is a library, a set of classrooms, a sewing co-op, and planted crops. They give classes in guitar, agriculture, herbal medicine, sewing, and computers. Many travelers have stayed and worked with Doña Loida, from a week or two to as long as six months. You may need to pay rent while you're there, but she is involved in many inspired community projects and would be glad for your help. Esperanza del Futuro is located on the road that leads from the park to the baseball field/basketball court, about 100 meters past the baseball field.

Accommodations

One Tola family rents rooms in their house—**a bright pink place** you can't miss, one block south and a half-block west of Restaurante El Naranjito. They are a kind family, the beds are comfortable, and the rooms are clean; $2.25 a night, ask for Mauricio. El Naranjito used to have rooms but the family grew and decided to use the rooms themselves. Things may have changed, so it can't hurt to ask.

Food

There are four decent restaurants in town and several *fritangas.* In the park is **Soda El Recreo,** a nice place to relax over a soda or beer and a light dinner. During the day, the owners, Yanette and Erving, serve a different *comida corriente* each day. If you go around noon you can dine with all the workers from the mayor's office, where Erving works. At night they serve up chicken, *tajadas,* and tacos.

El Naranjito consists of dozens of tables around a sort of central courtyard; its claim to fame is a jukebox. It has a bar atmosphere and appetizers to help wash down all that booze; they sell beer by the bottle or pitcher and, naturally, lots of rum (discount on food if you buy a bottle). **La Esquina** is more commonly referred to by its owner's name, Marta Palma. It usually hosts a rowdier crowd, and the *fritanga* is yummy. If

you'd rather leave the bar brawls behind, have your dinner at **Lumby's,** a block toward the school on the same street as La Esquina; you can super-size that enchilada by ordering *doble carne* (double meat) for $.35 more—feel your arteries clogging as you chew. For a cold beer in a more out-of-the-way place with a mellow atmosphere, walk straight out of the park toward the ball field and take your first right. Three young women run a small bar out of their home there. **Esperanza del Futuro**, the social project and school, serves great food as well—the same dishes as everywhere else, but more expertly prepared and a fraction more expensive.

PLAYA GIGANTE

Gigante is the first beach you come to after Tola, and is named after the Punta Pie de Gigante (The Giant's Foot). This is a beautiful, crescent beach rather off the beaten track and slowly being developed into summer homes by Nicaragua's wealthy. At the beach there are a handful of basic, traditional restaurants (and one place to play pool), usually owned by folks from Tola. The restaurants are friendly, but may not have much on the menu during the rainy season. From February through May (especially on Sundays), you have a great chance of buying fresh whole fish right off the boat, which the local restaurants will cook up just for you with rice, salad, and plantains for under $3. During Semana Santa the food gets even better, and more plentiful; poke around.

To get to Gigante, take the La Salinas bus from Tola or Rivas and get off at either of the two entrances to the beach (the second one is a bit easier to follow). If you are not traveling by car you'll need to walk or bike about seven kilometers to the beach on a hilly dirt road. Look for Rivas–Tola–Gigante buses, leaving around 8 A.M. and returning late in the afternoon to Tola and Rivas. Travelers pay one price and go on the same bus both ways (under $1). During Semana Santa the buses run daily and the beach gets crowded with people from all over Rivas. At this time, many locals set up camp under the trees and spend the week at the beach sleeping in hammocks or under black plastic tarps. Also during Semana Santa, expect to see daily cockfights, and a lot of phenomenally drunk Nicaraguan men, every year several of whom overestimate their swimming prowess and drown.

PLAYA AMARILLO

Once at Gigante you can get to two or three other beaches by hiking along the water's edge. Head north and cross over the rocks (make sure you time your trip with the tide) to reach Amarillo, a beautiful white-sand beach. Because the waves are bigger, the beach will likely be empty. Farther to the north on the other side of another rock outcropping—if the tide is low you can cut in front of the rocks to get around them—is yet another gorgeous, secret cove, very similar to Amarillo, completely deserted and with even bigger surf.

RANCHO SANTANA AND LA ROSADA

Limón is the next bus stop after Playa Gigante. From there you can walk down the dirt road that leads to Playa Rosada (five km). La Rosada's beach is small pebbles, not sand; the waves are bigger than in Gigante and hide a strong undertow. Another, barely longer route begins at a big, peachy-orange colored arch with a guard outside, just before Limón. This is Rancho Santana, a real estate venture on about five kilometers of undeveloped beach. If you're interested in owning a piece of the beach, they'll be glad to talk to you, even put you up in their fancy guesthouse with a pool. Otherwise they probably won't even sell you a Coke—enjoy this beach before the condominiums go up.

POPOYO

North of Playa La Rosada is one of former president Arnoldo Alemán's farms, located as always on a prime piece of real estate. Past the farm and down a small hill is a sizable *pulpería* that sells dry goods, bicycles, housewares, and a lot more— the first sign of civilization in the area and a good place to ask for directions if you're lost. Just past the *pulpería*, take the first left (30 meters past a small, fenced-in house) and follow that to Popoyo.

LAS SALINAS DE NAGUALAPA

A quiet and poor beachfront community, Las Salinas has a lovely beach with several waves popular among surfers, and a place to stay. Check out **La Tica,** a simple and pleasant restaurant/ *hospedaje* where the owners are friendly and helpful; rooms cost about $2 per person.

Las Salinas has a few hot springs worth exploring if you get sick of the beach. Ask at La Tica for directions or take the road next to the school east (away from the water) about four kilometers past cow fields. The hot springs are natural but have been cemented in. There's one pool for swimming in, for which you pay around $.10. The local women are big fans of the hot springs for scrubbing clothes and have washboards set up.

GÜASACATE

Güasacate is one of Nicaragua's better beaches but remains virtually unvisited and undeveloped. It's a huge stretch of sand with nice waves and several wealthy homes—which may complicate the development and use of the beach for the public. The entrance to Güasacate is located 5–8 kilometers down the first left-hand road after crossing a bridge in Las Salinas. Güasacate is home to a surf camp run by a Florida native known throughout Las Salinas only as "J.J." Upon arriving at Güasacate, look for the tents and campers.

The easiest way to get to **J.J.'s Surf Camp** is from the Ochomogo road to facilitate access to the beaches of Las Salinas and El Astillero. There is at least one bus a day leaving Roberto Huembes in Managua bound for El Astillero via Ochomogo (not Tola). If you don't take a direct bus, it's an easy trip from Rivas, where buses leave about every hour. The road to the beach will take you past several beautiful salt flats, from which the nearby town of Las Salinas gets its name.

EL ASTILLERO AND BEACHES TO THE NORTH

There are lots of little deserted beaches in the 10-kilometer strip between Las Salinas and Astillero, many of which don't even have names. El Astillero itself is a fishing village full of small boats. North of El Astillero the road turns inland away from the coast. Accessing the beach anywhere along this area requires a boat and a lot of dedication. Ask around in El Astillero. There are plenty of underemployed sailors and fishermen that would be glad to strike a deal with you if you're interested in exploring the coastline.

San Jorge

The tiny lakeside port of San Jorge is the most popular access point to the island of Ometepe, and as such, most travelers breeze straight through it on the way to catch a boat to the island. If you have time to kill before your ferry departs, there's no reason to spend it dockside sitting on your luggage and waiting. A traditional village with a strong Catholic spirit, San Jorge is primarily a town that survives on the cultivation of plantains, its principal crop. Nearby Popoyuapa, true to its Nahuatl-sounding name, cultivates cacao, the tree whose seed is used to produce cocoa and eventually chocolate, and which was once used by the Nicarao people as a form of currency.

SIGHTS AND ATTRACTIONS

Most interesting is the **Cruz de España,** a graceful concrete arch that suspends a stone cross directly over San Jorge's main drag, which runs through town down to the water's edge and the docks. The monument commemorates October 12, 1523, the day Spanish conquistador Gil González Dávila and indigenous cacique Nicarao-

Cruz de España

Calli first met and exchanged words. The cross is supposedly built over the very point where the meeting took place.

Across the street from the base of the arch is a **mural** commemorating the same event, with the words attributed to Nicarao, "Saben los Españoles del diluvio, quien movía las estrellas el sol y la luna. Dónde estaba el alma. Cómo Jesús siendo hombre es Dios y su madre virgen pariendo y para qué tan pocos hombres querían tanto oro." ("The Spanish know about the flood, who moved the stars, the sun, and the moon. Where the soul was found. How Jesus, a man, is God and his virgin mother giving birth, and why so few men wanted so much gold.") Many believe that the Spanish went on to refer to Nicaragua as "The Land of Nicarao," which over time evolved into the modern word "Nicaragua."

Even if you simply cruise through San Jorge in a taxi, you can't help but notice the squat **Iglesia de las Mercedes,** one of Central America's earliest churches. Built around the year 1575, it was renovated and repainted in 2001.

Most tourists keep their bathing suits packed until they get to Ometepe, but San Jorge's beach is hugely popular among Nicaraguans, who flock there during Semana Santa to cool their heels in the lake's surf. The beach is a broad sandy crescent over one kilometer long, with a view of Ometepe's twin peaks. At certain, unpredictable times though, plagues of small white flies called *chayules* swarm the lakeside. They don't bite or sting, they're just relentless and always seem to wind up in your mouth, making the beach less than enjoyable.

San Jorge celebrates its *fiestas patronales* in honor of Saint George (San Jorge) every year April 19–23 (the date changes to accommodate Semana Santa when necessary). Expect the beach to be packed. San Jorge usually has a parade or two during the celebrations, and there are performances of traditional dances, including Las Yeguitas (the dance of the little mares) and Los Enmascarados (the dance of the masked ones).

ACCOMMODATIONS

Try **Hotel Mar Dulce,** whose owners are trying to make San Jorge a legitimate tourist attraction of its own; six clean rooms for $20 a night, breakfast included, tel. 453-3262.

FOOD

The menus of the numerous food-and-drink joints lining the beachfront of San Jorge are similar: chicken, beef, fish, French fries, and maybe a burger or simple sandwich. Wander the beachfront until something strikes your fancy and ask to see a menu. If you're visiting on weekdays (excluding holidays), the service can be slow.

GETTING THERE AND AWAY

Take any southbound bus from Managua's Huembes Terminal to Rivas and get off at the traffic circle on the highway at Rivas. From there to the dock at San Jorge is four kilometers, accessible by Rivas buses once an hour ($.25); they pass the traffic circle approximately 20 minutes after the hour. Unless you happen to be there right at that moment, however (or are traveling on an extraordinarily tight budget), you're better off taking a taxi from to San Jorge for $1 per person; ignore the ones looking to rip you off.

A more direct way is to take the Managua–San Jorge express, departing Huembes at 9 A.M., arriving in San Jorge at 10:50 A.M. The same bus departs San Jorge evenings at 5 P.M., arriving in Managua at 10:50 P.M.

Isla de Ometepe

The island of Ometepe is Nicaragüense to the core and yet completely insulated from the rest of the country (and the rest of the world) by the choppy waters of Lake Cocibolca. Singer-songwriter Luis Enrique Mejía Godoy called this "an oasis of peace," and the name has stuck. Not even the violence of the 1970s and 1980s reached the island, where the proud locals refer to the rest of Nicaragua as "over there." Story has it that in 1957, as Volcán Concepción rumbled and threatened to erupt, the government ordered the islanders to evacuate Ometepe; they soundly refused, claiming they preferred to die on their island than live anywhere else.

Ometepe is awash in myths and legends, some of which date back to the days of the Nahuatl. Long before the Spanish arrived, the islanders considered Ometepe sacred ground, inhabited by gods of great power, and today a palpable sense of mystery and magic permeates day-to-day life.

Ometepe's allure attracts Nicaraguans from other regions of the country in addition to foreign stragglers, and a visit here is a sensory experience unlike any other. At night the slopes of the volcanoes echo with the deep roar of howler monkeys, and by day the air is filled with the sharp cry of the thousands of parakeets and *hurracas* (bright blue jays that scold you from the treetops). Retaining much of its original forest, Ometepe represents what Nicaragua may have been like in 1522 when Gil González Dávila first set eyes on it: broadleaf trees, clean lake water, and fresh air, all under the towering presence of Concepción and Maderas, two immense volcanoes that make up the bulk of the island. Maderas's north flank is strewn with petroglyphs carved into rocks that local guides can take you over the mountain paths to find. Not far away is a 19th-century coffee hacienda where you can sleep on wooden bunks and watch the moon rise over the silhouette of Concepción. If you strike a deal with a local boat-

the Port at Moyogalpa, Ometepe

© RANDY WOOD

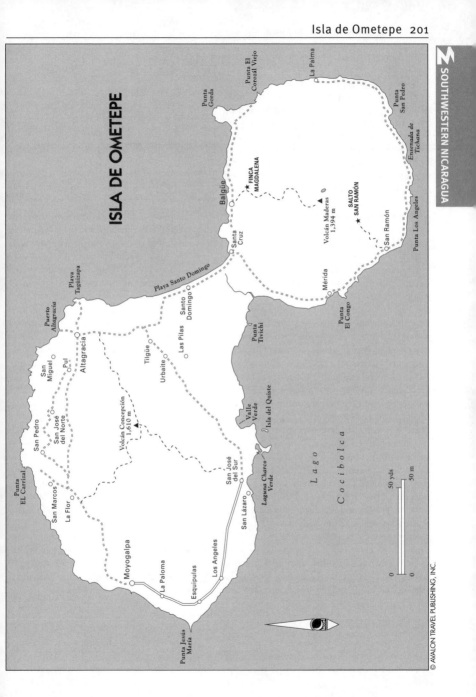

ISLA DE OMETEPE

SOUTHWESTERN NICARAGUA

© AVALON TRAVEL PUBLISHING, INC.

man you can arrange to be taken out to an even smaller island to camp.

Nicaragua's pre-Columbian history may have begun on and around Ometepe. It is theorized that the original Nahuatl settlers abandoned their lands in modern-day Mexico and followed the Central American isthmus southward in search of a new home, guided by a vision of two volcanoes in the middle of a broad lake. When they saw Ometepe (Nahuatl for two hills), they knew their exodus had come to an end. Today, Ometepe is a mosaic of small farms that produce plantains, avocados, beef, milk, coffee, and honey on the rich volcanic soils. Its two principal towns, Moyogalpa and Altagracia, function as ports, lazy commercial centers, and transportation hubs.

Centerpieces of the island are the twin Cenozoic volcanic peaks of Volcán Concepción and Volcán Maderas. The island of Ometepe has been called the edge of the tropics, and the dividing line between tropical and dry falls right between the two volcanoes. Maderas is an extinct volcano whose crater has long been filled with a beautiful lake. The slopes of Maderas are lined with more tropical and humid species, including cloud forest at the top. Concepción is an active volcano whose slopes are covered with tropical dry forest species like *guacimo* and *guanacaste*. In 1880, Concepción began to tremble, each day more violently until December 8, when it erupted with such force that lava and smoke flowed out of the crater for nearly a year. It was this eruption that created some of its more distinctive features visible today, like the Lava de Urbaite, Peña Bruja (a broad cliff visible from Altagracia), and Peña de San Marcos. Concepción erupted again in 1883, launching large rocks from the crater, and again in 1889 and 1902. This last eruption produced so much ash that crops in Rivas were ruined. Concepción is still active, and has erupted in the past century in 1907, 1921, 1924, and most recently in 1957.

GETTING AROUND

There's enough public transportation on the island you shouldn't need your own vehicle; of course, having your own vehicle speeds things up,

OMETEPE BUS SCHEDULE

Moyogalpa–Altagracia:
8 A.M., 11 A.M., noon, 1:30 P.M., 6 P.M.
Altagracia–Moyogalpa:
5 A.M., 9:30 A.M., 10:30 A.M., noon, 3:10 P.M.
Altagracia–Balgüe:
7 A.M., 2 P.M.
Balgüe–Altagracia:
9 A.M., 4 P.M.

and it is possible to ship it across on the ferry. Rusty old buses are the standard in Ometepe and they are the only ones we have seen in Nicaragua with "No Pukin' on the Bus" signs *(No Vomitar en el Bus)*. There's no such thing as an *expreso* here, but what's your rush? You're on island time, mon.

Buses leave Moyogalpa from the port, pass through the town park at the top of the hill, then head counterclockwise around the island to Altagracia. From Altagracia, buses depart for Moyogalpa and for the small towns of Maderas (San Ramón, Merida, Balgüe, and Santo Domingo). If you board a bus in Moyogalpa that's heading to Maderas, remember you'll pass through Altagracia first, where you'll spend 30 minutes waiting for more passengers before continuing on to Maderas. Moyogalpa to Altagracia is approximately one hour, and Altagracia to Balgüe is another hour. If you're not going all the way to Balgüe but plan to go only as far as Santo Domingo, you can save some time by getting off the bus at Empalme El Quino and walking the three kilometers to Santo Domingo, instead of waiting for your bus to go through Altagracia.

On Sunday, the entire transportation system breaks down. Buses, which are scheduled infrequently anyway, may or may not run according to the whims of the driver. Ask a lot of questions if you want to travel by bus on Sundays.

Rental Cars

You can rent vehicles while on Ometepe, but it's not cheap. Both Hotel Ometepetl and Hotel Cari will rent you a vehicle, usually a late-model Toyota or Suzuki Samurai. At Ometepetl the price is $35 per 12 hours, and at Hotel Cari, $45 per day (24 hours) or $25 per eight hours.

Taxis

Another way of avoiding the painfully slow bus routes is to hire a taxi in Moyogalpa. The representatives of taxi cooperatives usually linger at the port to drum up business as each boat arrives—don't worry, they'll find you. A taxi from Moyogalpa to the beach resort of Santo Domingo is around $15. Bargain hard—you have more leverage if you're traveling in a group.

ORGANIZED TOURS

The concept of the "organized tour" is a nascent one that is gathering strength on Ometepe. You can either independently get around and look for your own local guides, or you can bring in the pros: **Ometepe Tours,** located across from the ferry terminal in San Jorge, arranges complete package tours of the island, including tour guides, vehicle rental, and hotel reservations. By the time your boat crosses the waters of Cocibolca the arrangements will be made, and an Ometepe

HIKING THE VOLCANOES OF OMETEPE

The volcanoes that form the island of Ometepe are an irresistible temptation for travelers to the island, many of whom climb one or both while visiting. The two peaks, while nearly the same height, are radically different in personality.

Climbing **Volcán Concepción** (1,610 meters) is popular among travelers who like physical duress—it's not an easy climb, particularly the last third of the way, which is treeless and rocky. However, those who reach the summit are rewarded with the unique thrill of knowing they're perched at the razor's edge of the maw of an active volcano (in the middle of an island in the middle of a lake in the middle of Central America). You will be buffeted by a cold lake wind all the way up the slope until the moment you reach the crater lip, when the blast of hot sulfurous air rushing out of the bowels of the earth will strike your face. It's that mixing of hot and cold air that forms the almost permanent cloud cover at the top of the volcano, but should you reach the top during one of the few days a year when the clouds clear, you will be rewarded with an unparalleled view of the island, the lake, and the volcano's stony interior. Keep in mind Volcán Concepción is an active volcano that nearly erupted in 1957.

There are several guides in Moyogalpa and Altagracia, and almost all the hotels have their own guides as well. Berman Gómez at the Hotel Ometepetl is highly recommended (he was trained in Costa Rica in guide services and travels with first aid supplies and a radio). You can hire a guide for $10–20 per group of five people. Most travelers hike Concepción by way of the towns La Concha or La Flor, and there is an eastern approach from Altagracia that takes you through an impressive amount of monkey-inhabited forest before hitting the exposed section.

The hike is not to be underestimated—you'll get an idea of the severity of the volcano's surface just by admiring its steep cone shape as you cross the lake. (Concepción is one of the most perfectly cone-shaped volcanoes in Central America, Momotombo is another.) Allow a full day for the hike, five hours up and four hours down. Take plenty of water, sun protection, and good shoes and socks to protect your feet.

Volcán Maderas (1,394 meters) is the more frequently hiked of the two Ometepe volcanoes. There's a trail starting at the Finca Magdalena that leads to the crater lip, then down into the crater to a mist-swept turquoise lake straight out of Tolkien. You can hike it yourself without much difficulty, but both Magdalena and the other hotels offer guide service, which can be quite worthwhile, especially for the final descent down to the crater lake, which requires a rope descent. The trail, unfortunately, has seen better days. Lack of appropriate maintenance has made a mud pit out of much of the upper stretch of the trail. Allow four hours to go up and two or three to come back down, and count on spending an hour at the crater lake (59 minutes of which you'll spend deciding whether or not to jump in the icy water). If you're not staying at the Finca Magdalena you must pay a trail fee to enter and pass through the coffee plantations. You'll pass a petroglyph or two on the way up.

Tour vehicle will pick you up at the dock. It doesn't get much easier than that (they also have an Internet connection in the office). Stop in at the office in San Jorge or call 453-4779; in Moyogalpa call 459-4242.

Most hotels will help to arrange tours as well, including Central and Castillo in Altagracia, Ometepetl and Ali in Moyogalpa, and Villa Paraiso and Istiam in the Santo Domingo area. The Finca Magdalena offers its own tours of the petroglyphs, which are primarily located on the property of the Finca, and up to the crater of Maderas.

Provided you're traveling in a group of 3–4 people, in general you can expect to pay the following for tours: $20 per person to the top of Maderas, $20 to the waterfalls at San Ramón, and $20 to the top of Volcán Concepción.

MOYOGALPA

Moyogalpa (Nahuatl for Place of the Mosquitoes) is Ometepe's principal port town and major commercial center. While many tourists pass straight through Moyogalpa on their way to the beach towns, Moyogalpa makes a good base for your travels; there are several restaurants and a variety of places to stay.

Sights and Attractions

A good place to start your exploring is the **Fundación Entre Volcanes,** located across the street from the Moyogalpa ENITEL office. This small NGO is involved in several community projects across the island and may be able to help you find ways to volunteer your time while on the island. They also have some representative handicrafts of the region for display.

At the top of the hill, Moyogalpa's Catholic church is a charming place to visit, with a bell tower just high enough over the tree line to afford you a great view of the town, coastline, and lake. In front of the church is a park with two statues: a Native American with a spear, and a boy urinating—the islanders definitely maintain a sense of humor.

La Sala de Artesanía, located toward the top of main street, has a small but interesting collection of pre-Columbian artifacts found on the island over the years. Owner and amateur historian Herman García and his wife Ligia are very knowledgeable about the island history and lore, and *artesanía* in general, including which communities on Ometepe you can visit to see the artisans at work. Naturally, much of what you see on display is for sale.

Ometepe farmers raise a lot of cattle and produce not a small amount of meat and cheese. Visit **COPROLAC** to arrange a tour of the cheese processing facilities; speak with Moises Ghittis or Lisimack Amador, located on the west side of the cemetery in La Quinta. Both Ghittis and Amador are friendly types who may show you around their own farms as well, if you're lucky.

Saúl Cuadra raises bees and harvests honey. Look him up (he lives in front of the mayor's office) if you're interested in apiculture and would like to visit the bee farm and arrange for a photo op in a beekeeper's uniform; he doesn't travel out to the farm every day, so be flexible and be sure to pay him fairly for his effort.

There's a small **pool hall** on main street, the J&M, where you can go to meet the locals. Next door, the **Rancho Viejo** is a popular place to drink and relax.

The town of Moyogalpa celebrates its patron saint, Santa Ana, June 23–26. The Baile de las Inditas is performed in much the same way as the indigenous dance it replaced, with traditional costumes and the resonant sound of the marimba.

Beaches and Hikes

Besides the challenging hike to the top of Volcán Concepción (see Hiking the Volcanoes of Ometepe special topic), there are many other treks you can take along the slopes of the volcano without actually climbing to the crater's edge. Take with you a healthy sense of curiosity and enough Spanish to talk your way from farm to farm. The people of Ometepe are friendly and welcoming enough to let you traipse through their land in search of adventure, but remember that how you behave while "trespassing" will determine how the travelers who follow you will be received.

From Moyogalpa to the north, travel along the beach to the community known as Barrio de los Pescadores. Señor Augusto Rodríguez will take you out on fishing and boat tours—talk to him about a trip around the south side of Ometepe to the tiny **Isla de Quiste,** where you can camp. In the same town, Carlos Loco is a local painter who has done some impressive paintings of Ometepe. From Barrio de los Pescadores, follow the path closest to the beach, which will lead you through hardwood forest, farms, and clusters of bamboo huts. Three kilometers past the little lagoon of Charco Pelota you'll find the farm of César Mora; ask for permission to cut through, them follow the path up to the main road and cross it; walk back down the road toward Moyogalpa. An interesting side trip is the farm of Oscar Mora, which you'll reach via a small path on your left as you head back to town. From his farm the view of the island is unforgettable, and his farm has other paths you can explore by asking his family for permission.

From Moyogalpa to the south you can get to a beachside trail by cutting behind the Hotel Cari and continuing through Barrio de La Paloma. You can work your way along the beach across farms and through forests until you get to Punta Jesús María. You can get there by following the main road out of Moyogalpa too, though the buses that pass might coat you with a film of red dust as they go by.

Accommodations

Moyogalpa certainly has the most accommodations on the island, through not the best (that honor goes to Santo Domingo beach); they are all reasonably priced and located on the main drag between the dock and the park.

Under $10: Hotelito Ali is probably the best option for budget travelers willing to forego the luxury of air-conditioning. Nine rooms set around an ample garden patio cost $3.50 per person with private bath, or $2.50 with shared bath, tel. 459-4196. There's a convenient pay phone out front on the sidewalk. Ali also has a decent restaurant that serves breakfast, lunch, and dinner.

At the water's edge, **Hotel Cari** has 19 basic rooms for $5 a person with private bath and fan, or $10 a person for private bath and a/c. The restaurant downstairs is decent, and its lakeside bar is one of the most pleasant places in town to throw down a couple cold ones.

Hotel Moyogalpa and **Hotel Ometepetl** are a joint operation. Moyogalpa (tel. 459-4276) has seven basic and dark accommodations for $2 per person with shared bath, and three rooms with private bath for under $3 a person. Moyogalpa and the **Pensión Chela** across the street are tied for the most economical places to stay. A worthwhile step up is the Hotel Ometepetl (tel. 459-4276), which offers fancier rooms—all with a/c—for about $20 a couple; service is professional and the staff is experienced at arranging tours, finding guides, and renting vehicles.

Hotel La Isla Ometepe is a steel warehouse with a modern, clean hotel building behind it—six quiet, clean rooms, $20 per room—which can sleep as many as four, making this an economical option. Otherwise, stay in sweltering cubicles of the steel warehouse, nestled in between the garden tools and the riding mower, for $4.25 per couple.

Hotel Restaurant La Bahía is a better place to eat than sleep—five small rooms in the back cost $2.50 per person with shared bath or $3 with private bath.

$10–25: Off the main drag just far enough to be peaceful, **Hotel El Pirata** is a nice place to relax around the garden or restaurant and bar on the first floor. Six rooms with a/c and private bath cost $15 per room, or $8.50 for a fan instead of the a/c. Solo travelers pay a bit less—just come to an agreement with the owner, tel. 459-4262.

Food

All hotels serve food, but travelers tend to agree that one of the best meals in town can be found at **La Casa Familiar,** which offers chicken, steak, fish, and fast foods like burgers and sandwiches. The restaurant at **Ometepetl** serves up the most elegant fare, including fresh fish, all in the $4–5 range; also sandwiches and fresh fruit juices. **Doña Esperanza Jimenez,** a half-block east of the park, serves huge, inexpensive meals.

Bananas and plantains are two of Ometepe's principal exports.

Moyogalpa–Altagracia: 6 A.M., 7:30 A.M., 9:30 A.M., 11:30 A.M., 12:30 P.M., 1:15 P.M., 5:30 P.M., 6 P.M.
Moyogalpa–Altagracia via San Marcos: 8:30 A.M., noon, 4:20 P.M.
Moyogalpa–Balgüe: 10:30 A.M., 3:30 P.M.
Moyogalpa–Merida: 2 P.M., 4 P.M.

NEAR MOYOGALPA

San Marcos

Just northeast of Moyogalpa along the "back way around the island" is the small community of San Marcos, home to a women's group that makes and sells ceramic pieces, including authentic replicas of pre-Columbian art. Ask around in town for the *taller de artesanía*. To get there, take one of the buses that travels between Moyogalpa and Altagracia via San Marcos, or take one of the buses from Moyogalpa that goes only to San Marcos without passing through. Buses to San Marcos leave Moyogalpa at 5 A.M., 7:30 A.M., 9:30 A.M., 11:40 A.M., 1:40 P.M., 3:40 P.M., and 6 P.M.

Punta Jesús María

Long and sandy, the narrow peninsula of Punta Jesús María is one of the most popular beaches in the Moyogalpa area for swimming and absorbing a bit of the tranquillity the entire island is steeped in. At the end of a narrow peninsula jutting into the lake and lined with cattle farms on both sides, there's a small recreational center complete with run-down playground and coolers of cold beer. This is a good place to catch a sunset or kill an afternoon relaxing and soaking your bones. Talk with the owner, Joaquín Salazar, about setting up your tent on the beach and spending the night with the crickets and the lapping of the lake washing up on the sandy shore. He's usually agreeable about camping if you've been buying beer or food from him.

San Lázaro

In the community of San Lázaro, just to the east of Punta Jesús María, is the Nuestros Pequeños Hermanos (NPH) orphanage, and organic gardens managed by the Brothers and

Shopping

In addition to over 200 museum pieces that represent the indigenous peoples of Ometepe, the Sala Arqueologica (one block west of the park) sells examples of local handicrafts, including something called the hickory fruit style. Many of the pieces were found by the owner of the museum, Ligia González de García, on her own farm. Closed on Saturday and Sunday.

Services

The ENITEL office is located 1.5 blocks east of the main street, closed on Sundays. The Moyogalpa hospital is three blocks east of the park along the highway out of town, tel. 459-4247.

Getting Away

Buses leave from the dock, go straight up the hill along the main street, stop at the park, then head east out of town. The bus schedule changes from week to week, but in general there's a bus to meet every boat, and (roughly) follows the schedule below:

Sisters of Charity. The gardens are part of a wider set of environmental, irrigation, health, and education programs that benefit the poorer farmers of the island. Both the orphanage and the Brothers and Sisters of Charity take volunteers willing to spend some time helping out with the projects, but you can also ask to just be given a tour of the facilities.

San José del Sur

The Quincho Barrilette program for disadvantaged street kids has a chapter in the town of San José del Sur and is known to accept volunteers. Many of the kids come from as far away as Managua.

Charco Verde and Playa Venecia

At Charco Verde you can swim in the lake to the call of monkeys in the trees and watch colorful birds whiz over your head. This is still a relatively wild area, with enough tall trees remaining to house some very exciting wildlife. The entire area has been cordoned off to prevent development, leaving this cove an oasis of peace to be shared by you and the monkeys (who, incidentally, do their own part by throwing excrement at intruders from the trees—seriously).

Rubén Riveras runs a family-style guesthouse on the beach of Playa Venecia; seven rooms cost $10 per night and hold three people, solo travelers pay $5. The restaurant serves well-prepared pasta, chicken, fish, and beef dishes. From his place it's an easy walk along the shore into the reserve of Charco Verde and to Playa Balcón. A voluntary contribution is requested to maintain the reserve—$1–2 is appropriate. Riveras also makes boat trips along the shoreline to fish or out to Isla de Quiste, and rents horses. His brothers have a cattle farm just up the beach. Ask him for a chance to visit the farm and milk some cows.

Isla de Quiste

An island off of an island, Quiste means cyst in Spanish, probably in reference to its small size. It's overgrown and vacant, and a scant 100 meters long—a perfect place to pitch a tent and camp. To get there, all you need to do is make

The beach at Charco Verde is one of Nicaragua's more beautiful.

arrangements with someone with a small boat. In Charco Verde, Rubén Riveras has a motorboat and will make trips out to the island. He'll drop you off on the island and pick you up again later (or the next day) for about $15, depending on the number of travelers. But you can also try to strike a deal with the locals in the small communities to the north of Moyogalpa, like Barrio de los Pescadores.

El Tesoro del Pirata

The pirate's treasure is, in this case, not pieces of eight, but cheap rum and a good swimming hole. Walk 500 meters from the highway to a small establishment with changing rooms, bathrooms, bar, and restaurant service. The beach is a tremendous crescent, and there are many monkeys about.

Valle Verde

Lush and forested, Valle Verde is one of the prettiest coves in all of Ometepe. There is a small, private guesthouse that may rent you a room here.

> ## THE LEGEND OF CHICO LARGO
>
> Over the years, this famous legend has taken two forms. In the first version, an old man by the name of Chico Largo lives in the wetlands of Charco Verde. There he appears to people at night and offers to make a deal with them: wealth and prosperity during the entirety of their lives, in exchange for their souls, which upon death, he converts into cattle. Many of the cows on the island, then, are the souls of Ometepe's previous generation, which opted for a life of decadence instead of hard work.
>
> In the second version, the cacique Nicarao is buried with his throne made of solid gold along the edge of the Charco Verde. In this version, Chico Largo is a descendant of Nicarao and roams the area guarding and protecting Nicarao's tomb. Chico Largo, since he is already guarding the tomb, has now taken it upon himself to guard the forest, animals, and fish as well, and is the primary protector of Ometepe's wildlife.

Getting to Valle Verde by hiking through the jungle eastward from Charco Verde is a pleasant way to spend an afternoon and enough of the hike is under the thick canopy of *chilamate* and *guacimo* trees that you don't have to worry about burning yourself in the tropical sun.

ALTAGRACIA

The second largest community on Ometepe, and home to another port, Altagracia is considered more picturesque than Moyogalpa, but a little harder to get to. In 2000, *National Geographic* filmed a documentary about vampire bats here—and while there are indeed many vampire bats, they are a threat only to the local chickens, which the bats like to suck dry by hanging from the chickens' nerveless feet.

Sights and Entertainment

Altagracia's *fiestas patronales,* in celebration of San Diego, are held November 12–18. In addition to the traditional festivities common to other Nicaraguan towns, the Baile de las Ramas (Dance of the Branches) is a major component of the celebration. The dancers tear off smaller branches of the *guanacaste* tree, and hold them to their heads while dancing to imitate the worker *zompopo* ants carrying leaves off to the ant hills. Though the Spanish colonials claimed it was in honor of their successful fight against the ants, the locals claim it is an ancient dance in honor of gods that long predated the Spanish.

El Museo Ometepe has a few exhibits of the flora, fauna, and archaeology of Ometepe, including statues and ceramic pieces unearthed around the island. Open every day, 9 A.M.–5 P.M. (including midday); travelers pay $1 to enter the museum.

Accommodations

All of the lodging facilities are located within a block of each other, so feel free to walk around and compare before settling in. Altagracia's two principal hotels, **Hotel Central** and **Hotel Castillo,** have basically equal services. Both offer basic rooms with shared bath (under $3 per person) or fancier rooms with private bath (around $4.25

NAHUATLS AND THE PETROGLYPHS OF OMETEPE

In the days of the Nahuatls, Volcán Maderas was called Coatlán, The Place Where the Sun Lives, and Concepción was known as Choncoteciguatepe, The Brother of the Moon (Concepción was alternately known as Mestliltepe, The Peak That Menstruates). In the lush forests of the lower slopes of the two volcanoes, the Nahuatls performed complicated rituals in honor of many different gods: Catligùe, the goddess of fertility, Ecatl, the god of air, Migtanteot, the god of death, Tlaloc, the god of soil, and Xochipillo, the goddess of happiness. The Nahuatl gods were all-powerful and vengeful, and spent their days in the land where the sun rises—feeding on human blood.

The concept of a soul was an important part of the Nahuatl belief system, as were the concepts of an afterlife and some form of reincarnation. Their calendar consisted of 18 months of 20 days each, for a total of a 360-day calendar year. They believed in a cycle of catastrophic events that recurred every 52 years, and according to that cycle the Nahuatls would store grains and water, in case the catastrophe were to occur.

Scattered around the island of Ometepe, but principally on the north and northeastern slopes of Volcán Maderas, are the carved statues and petroglyphs that paid homage to the Nahuatl gods. The petroglyphs are estimated to have been carved around the year A.D. 300. Spirals are a consistent theme, representing perhaps calendars or the Nahuatl concept of time and space. It has been suggested the spirals also may represent the islands themselves, or that the twin-spiral shape of Ometepe gave the island even more significance to the islanders, as it fit in with their ideas about the cosmos. More mundane images can also be identified in the carved rocks: monkeys, humans hunting deer, and a couple in coitus, suggesting the petroglyphs represented the Nahuatls' wishes for prosperity and fertility.

per person), a central common area with tables and chairs for reading, restaurant service, and small gardens. In addition, Hotel Central has small cabins out back for the ultimate in privacy ($6 per person, capacity 2–4 people). Hotel Central, 14 rooms, tel. 552-8770; Hotel Castillo, 14 rooms, tel. 552-8774. The owner of Central, Oscar Flores, is related to the owners of the two fancy hotels in Playa Santo Domingo and he'll be glad to drive you out there for a small fee.

Slightly newer to the scene is **Hotel Don Kencho,** which is a little more basic but has a pleasant wooden deck which overlooks the street; five rooms with shared bath go for $2.75, and three rooms with private bath $3.50 per person, tel. 552-8772.

A bit out of town is the still-developing **Bamboo-Bar,** which offers a place to camp. From the Hotel Central, walk eastward, following the signs.

Services

The ENITEL phone office and the post office are found diagonally across from the park on the same corner as the Museo Ometepe; both are closed on Sunday. The Casa Cural, located on the south side of the park, has six computers and Internet service from Monday to Friday. There's also one computer at Tienda Fashion, a block south of the park. You'll have no privacy there, as the computer is located in the middle of the store, but it's open late and weekends; about $1.10 per 15 minutes.

There's a small Centro de Salud on the southeast corner of the park, which can treat patients 24 hours a day, tel. 552-6089. For serious injuries you should find a way to get to the hospital at Moyogalpa (get the owner of your hotel to take you in a vehicle).

Getting Away
Buses leave from the north and east sides of the town park. As always, the bus schedule is highly variable, so ask around the park to confirm.
Altagracia–Moyogalpa: 4:40 A.M., 7:10 A.M., 9 A.M., 11 A.M., noon, 1:15 P.M., 3:10 P.M., 4:30 P.M.
Altagracia–Balgùe: 5:30 A.M., 9:30 A.M., 2:10 P.M., 4:30 P.M.
Altagracia–Moyogalpa via San Marcos: 9:50 A.M., 2:10 P.M., 5:30 P.M.

NEAR ALTAGRACIA
Puerto de Altagracia
Located three kilometers north of the town of Altagracia, the port has boat service between Granada and San Carlos (Río San Juan). The road that leads to the port is shady and makes a nice, short walk—allow about 45 minutes each way. On the way you'll pass Playa Paso Real, an out-of-the-way bathing beach you'll likely have all to yourself. If you're heading to the port to catch the boat to Granada or San Carlos, it's worth your while to speak with the owner of Hotel Central. They offer pickup truck service to the port, so you don't have to carry all your luggage that far. Be aware that when the water is too rough, the boat may not show up at Altagracia, preferring to hug the eastern shore of the lake.

Pul
Just three kilometers west of Altagracia is the community of Pul, home to several artisans'

groups with ceramics for sale. To get there from Altagracia, walk out of town to the cemetery, continue around it and then down the road to San Marcos about one kilometer.

Playa Tagùizapa
From the park, walk east down a sandy road about 30 minutes to the bay of Tagùizapa, a fine sandy beach for swimming. You can pick up supplies in town for a picnic, and make a lazy day of it.

VOLCÁN MADERAS
It's possible to walk to Volcán Maderas from the town of Altagracia, if you have a few hours and a bottle of water. The hike is mostly along tree-lined roads, and you can also walk along the water's edge and check out all the shore birds.

Isthmus Istian
The narrow wedge of land that connects the volcanoes of Concepción and Maderas is nothing more than rich volcanic soil that washed down from the slopes and made the two islands into one. The river that runs down the center of the isthmus is the Istian, and it is a popular local swimming hole. The town of Santa Cruz on the north shore has a very nice beach that easily rivals the beaches of Playa Santa Domingo, and is largely unvisited. You can stay in the **Casa Hotel Istian** near the beach for a fraction of what you would pay farther east at Playa Santo Domingo. Also in town is Fundación Entre Volcánes, which runs projects all over Maderas and may well be interested in your volunteer time, should you get tired of just snoozing on the beach. Contact Raúl Mayorga or Martín Juarez for details—Raúl works in Moyogalpa (two blocks south and one block east of the Shell station, 882-5562) and Martín is based out of the town of Los Angeles (Ometepe, not California).

Playa Santo Domingo
Playa Santo Domingo offers the finest accommodations on the island, in a resort setting. Credit cards are accepted at all three establishments. The beach itself is a windswept series of

© RANDY WOOD

Volcán Maderas

sandy coves separated by mangroves and forest, but it's well liked and a good place to relax. **Villa Paraíso** is considered the single nicest hotel on all of Ometepe; it offers charming stone cabins with private bath and a/c starting at $30 per double. Paraíso also has smaller, simpler rooms upstairs in the main lodge with shared bath for about $18 a room depending on the season. Call for reservations but know that rooms can be tough to book, especially in busy seasons like Semana Santa and Christmas, tel. 453-4675. Right next door, **Hotel Finca Santo Domingo** has similar rates and services.

Just two kilometers farther down the beach is the far more comfortably priced (and just as good) **Casa Hotel Istiam.** The Istiam actually has a cleaner beach and a broader horizon, including a spectacular view of Volcán Maderas; four large rooms and two private cabins are $5 per person—or camp out on the premises. Friendly service and a good restaurant cinch the deal. Make reservations while in Moyogalpa by stopping by the Hotel Ometepetl (they're owned by the same proprietress) or call 459-4276.

La Finca Magdalena

Balgüe is the end of the road on the north side of Maderas, and the beginning of the road for those who intend to spend time at the Finca Magdalena or climb the foot trail up Maderas to the crater lake.

The lower slopes of the volcano's north face are the property of the Finca Magdalena, a coffee cooperative established in the 1980s and now run as a private business by the cooperative's former members. The Finca Magdalena, besides being a working coffee plantation, also raises cattle for meat and milk, and for several years now, has been acting as a simple lodge and guesthouse for travelers who prefer a more rustic experience than that offered in Playa Santo Domingo. Scattered throughout the grounds of the Finca Magdalena are Ometepe's most accessible pre-Columbian petroglyphs, lying practically unnoticed among fields of corn or beans, tucked in the woodlands, and in the narrow valleys. Magdalena offers guides to take you around and show you the petroglyphs (you won't find them on your own).

The private rooms are rustic and wooden, partitioned out of the upper story of the hacienda, and include one open dormitory space. You'll pay around $2.50 a night to stay there and bathe in water piped directly from a spring up the slope (prepare to be wide awake!). At night you'll eat fresh farm cooking hot from the wood stove, and watch the moon rise over the silhouette of Concepción. As for souvenirs, take home some fresh honey or roasted coffee.

To get to the Finca Magdalena, take the bus to Balgùe (the end of the road), where you'll be met by a representative of the farm. From the road it's a 20-minute walk up the hill (try to arrive before dark to do this walk—it can be tricky).

Merida

Little-visited and at the end of one of Ometepe's bumpier roads, Merida was once home to a Somoza coffee hacienda before the revolution. It has since been abandoned. The beach at Merida is a worthwhile visit, with a fantastic view of Concepción. Should you decide to spend the

night, there are no formal accommodations available, but several families in the area are willing to rent you a room. You can also try hanging your hammock down by the beach; ask around and use your best judgment.

San Ramón

San Ramón is now home to a biological experiment station frequented by researchers from all over the world. If there's room, they might take you in as a guest—speak to owners Alvaro and René Molinas. The station also has kayaks and small boats researchers use to explore the Río Istian. If you're lucky, you might be able to swing a deal. Far more interesting is a set of gorgeous 150-meter-high waterfalls on the south slope of Maderas. It's worth having a guide (again, speak with the hotel owners in Altagracia or Moyogalpa; Berman Gómez has regularly scheduled trips to the falls), as the trail up to the falls is not easy to find, nor is there one single trail. The hike up to the falls through dry and transition forest is a particularly enjoyable one and not quite as taxing as the hikes

ferry to Ometepe

© RANDY WOOD

OMETEPE FERRIES FROM SAN JORGE

San Jorge–Moyogalpa

9 A.M.	*Sor María Romero*
10:30 A.M	*Ferry Ometepe*
11:30 A.M.	*Señora del Lago*
12:30 P.M.	*Santa María*
1:30 P.M.	*Reina del Sur*
2:30 P.M.	*Ferry Ometepe*
4:30 P.M.	*Señora del Lago*
5:30 P.M.	*Ferry Ometepe*

Moyogalpa–San Jorge

5:30 A.M.	*Sor María Romero*
6 A.M.	*Señora del Lago*
6:30 A.M.	*Santa María*
6:45 A.M.	*Ferry Ometepe*
11 A.M.	*Sor María Romero*
12:30 P.M.	*Ferry Ometepe*
1:30 P.M.	*Señora del Lago*
3 P.M.	*Sor María Romero*
4 P.M.	*Ferry Ometepe*

to the peaks of both volcanoes. This area is known to be a good place to spot monkeys and tropical birds. From the falls, another, even more faint trail, leads up to the lip of the volcano. This one is a serious endeavor and you should not attempt it unless you start early in the morning and take along some basic precautions like a compass, water, matches, first aid kit, and machete.

The East Coast of Maderas

The lonely east coast of Maderas is one of the most isolated spots in Nicaragua, connected tentatively by a poor excuse of a road only during the dry season. During the rainy season, you're better off traveling by boat. There is never bus service to these towns, and the locals are not used to receiving guests. This is good territory for a hike, as you circumnavigate the volcano. Supposedly

along the coast of Tichana there are caves that contain paintings, as well as some petroglyphs near Corozal.

GETTING THERE AND AWAY

There are several different ways to get to Ometepe, and being an island, all those ways involve different kinds of boats, which you may share with boxes, bananas, cattle, and other travelers. Lake Cocibolca can get rough when the wind is high. At those times, choosing a larger vessel may make all the difference between a leisurely sail and a tumultuous barf-fest. Avoid the high seas by traveling early morning and late evening, when the seas are calmer. If you are prone to motion sickness, try to get a seat toward the center of the ship, where the pendulum motion of the ship will be less noticeable, and when the nausea comes on, fix your sight on the horizon.

From San Jorge

Most travelers travel from the Port of San Jorge, near Rivas. San Jorge has the most frequent boat service, and the majority of the cargo and cattle that gets shipped to and from Ometepe goes through here. There's quite a variety of vessels on the route between San Jorge and the island; unfortunately none of the companies will offer you information about the others, so if you're told "the next boat doesn't leave for four hours" keep asking around. Another company may very well have a boat leaving in 30 minutes.

The ***Ferry Ometepe*** is a modern steel boat with radar and life jackets. The other ships are heavy wooden craft—take a look, you'll probably see them docked at Moyogalpa. One-way passenger fare on the *Ferry Ometepe* is $1.50; on all other boats the fare is $1.

The *Ferry Ometepe* is the only vessel that accepts vehicles, though space is extremely limited. If you're interested in taking your vehicle across with you, call 459-4284 at least 72 hours in advance, and then again the day before your trip to remind them of your reservation (more than one reservation has gotten lost). The price for transport of your vehicle will be $28 including all taxes, plus your passenger fare.

From Granada

Though Granada was once the principal link with Ometepe, San Jorge has now surpassed it in importance. What remains of the once regular boat service across the lake is a single EPN (Empresa Portuario de Nicaragua) ship that leaves Granada on Mondays and Thursdays at 1 P.M. It's a slow, slow ride—nearly three hours—to Altagracia. The ship continues onward to San Miguelito and San Carlos before returning to Altagracia and Granada. On the return trip, the boat stops at Altagracia on Tuesdays and Fridays at 11 P.M., arriving in Granada at 4 A.M. The price for a one-way passage between Granada and Ometepe is $2.50. If the waves are *bravo* (rough), the ship will skip the Altagracia stop altogether, preferring to hold tight to the lee shore of the lake. The EPN also offers a weekend boat to Ometepe for vacationing Granada folk. The boat leaves Granada at 11 A.M. on Saturday, and returns at 10 A.M. Sunday.

There's another, more romantic way to get to Ometepe from Granada, via a group whose intent is to preserve the tradition of the small wooden sailing ships that once plied the waves between Ometepe and Granada. The M/N *Mozorola* makes the four-hour cruise (depending on the wind) twice a week, leaving Ometepe (Altagracia) every Tuesday and Friday at 11 A.M., and leaving Granada every Wednesday and Saturday at 11 A.M. Adverse weather conditions cause the cancellation of the trip, but it's otherwise a great sail past the Isletas and along the coast of the island of Zapatera, tel. 552-8764.

The *Crucero Solentiname* offers first-class and coach options between Granada, Ometepe, Solentiname, and San Carlos. The boat only leaves Granada on Fridays at 7 A.M., makes a port call in Moyogalpa 10–11 A.M., then contines on to arrive in Solentiname at 5:30 P.M. and San Carlos at 8 P.M. The weekly return trip leaves San Carlos on Sunday at 6 A.M., hitting Moyogalpa at 3 P.M., arriving in Granada at 6:30 P.M. From Granada to Ometepe costs $9 first-class, $3 coach, to Solentiname $12 first-class, $5 coach, each way. Call the EPN in Granada for reservations, tel. 552-4313, or Solentiname Tours, tel. 265-2716. (Note: as of press time, due to lack of demand, the *Crucero* was running every 15 days, sometimes less—you should definitely contact them beforehand to make reservations and be sure that it is operating.)

San Juan del Sur

Some call it a beach town, others call it a port, a fishing village, or lately, a backpacker's heaven. Indeed, San Juan del Sur has turned toward tourism as its principal economy during the last 12 years, earning it the status of Nicaragua's primary Pacific coast destination—for both Nicas and international tourists. But despite the increased number of visitors (including hundreds of cruise-ship passengers every other week), San Juan has not experienced the recent boom enjoyed by Granada, only a couple hours away.

Many residents still make a go at fishing, but most are putting their money on the ever-impending tourism explosion—the steady stream of big-spending visitors that has been just around the corner for a decade. Things are leisurely moving forward here, as far as tourism development goes, and it seems like everyone is working on some new shuttle service, surf camp, or fishing boat project—not to mention all the Euros and gringos buzzing around with the word "real estate" on their lips.

San Juan's principal resource is its perfect bay and crescent beach, opening to the setting sun and protected by black, rocky cliffs and El Indio (The Indian), whose silhouetted face hides in the vertical stone. Foreign investment is up, and so is the surf. In San Juan del Sur, you count your days by the sunsets—plan on being tempted to stay for more of them than you planned.

ORIENTATION AND GETTING AROUND

There are two principal streets; your bus or taxi will let you off on the one with the market, which runs perpendicular to the beach and is lined with a half-dozen *hospedajes*. The beachfront road has a few nicer hotels and nearly all of San Juan's restaurants and bars. The sole disco is at the northern terminus of the beach road, and the industrial dock anchors the opposite end of the road. There's no need for taxis to get around town (you'll only see them trolling for passengers to Rivas), and ciclo-taxis (three-wheeled bicycle taxis) and their drivers are imported from Rivas during the cruise ship arrivals and holidays.

To travel up and down the coast, you'll need a sturdy car, sturdy legs, or a decent mountain bike. You can rent bikes in town at Elizabeth's, Joxi, or Fogata. An increasing number of hotels and *hospedajes* offer daily shuttle services, and there are a handful of full-time taxi businesses with daily trips to Bahía Majagual ($2, leaves at 10 A.M. from Iguana Bar, day-trippers welcome), or custom trips to the turtle beaches, jungles, or anywhere else you want to go. Jorge's taxi can carry up to 10 people for $11–15, email: baloy28@hotmail.com.

SIGHTS AND SPORTS

The main show in town is the sunset, sometimes lasting for hours; make sure you're on the beach with a cocktail in hand, or else bobbing in the surf, watching the silhouetted fishing boats and waiting for the next set to roll in.

Hikes from Town

As the land around San Juan del Sur gets chopped up, bought, and sold, the new influx of property owners may have mixed reactions to hikers cutting across their plots. Be sensitive to this and always ask permission when possible.

The **lighthouse** is easily reachable (two hours round-trip) and offers fantastic views up the coast and south to Costa Rica. Walk south to the town port, go through the main gate, then through a smaller one next to the new building. Follow the trail up the hill, past an angry herd of goats, and through one of the last local pelican nesting areas (tread lightly); fork right and continue to the lighthouse—turning left brings you to the ruins of the old fort.

SAN JUAN'S PEAK SEASONS

Nearly all of San Juan del Sur's hotel, *hospedaje,* and restaurant owners significantly vary their prices with the changes in demand throughout the year. Prices skyrocket, primarily around September 15, Christmas, New Year's, parts of January and February, and always during Semana Santa. Expect rates to be multiplied by an extraordinary factor; unless you are traveling with a group and are able to strike a great deal, you'll pay a minimum of $15–20 a person to spend a night in San Juan during these times. Some hotels even vary their rates over weekends during the rest of the year, or whenever an unexpected spike of visitors arrive; making reservations during peak weeks is recommended. **All prices given here are the *corriente,* off-season base rates.**

For a viewpoint from the antennas, take a bus toward Rivas and ask the driver to let you off at **Bocas de las Montañas.** From there, head up through the trees and pastures to the breezy and beautiful mirador—an hour each way.

There are some 1,700-year-old **petroglyphs** accessible via a 1.5-hour countryside walk beginning east of the Texaco station. Take a left (north), pass the school, and walk right through a gate after about 500 meters; find the farmhouse and ask permission to cut through. Consider asking for a local guide. If not, follow the water pipes and the river until you find the stone. Continue upstream to reach the waterfalls, impressive only during the rainy season—wear good shoes and long pants to avoid being stung by the nettlelike *pica-pica* plant.

Some of the closer beaches, north and south of town, make for good day hikes as well, as does rock-hopping the northern curve of the bay and around the point—mind the tides.

Surfing and Boat Shuttles

Most of the beaches listed in this section have surf breaks. The bay in town is usually calm, but when a swell comes in, it makes for a perfect, waist-high training ground. For more

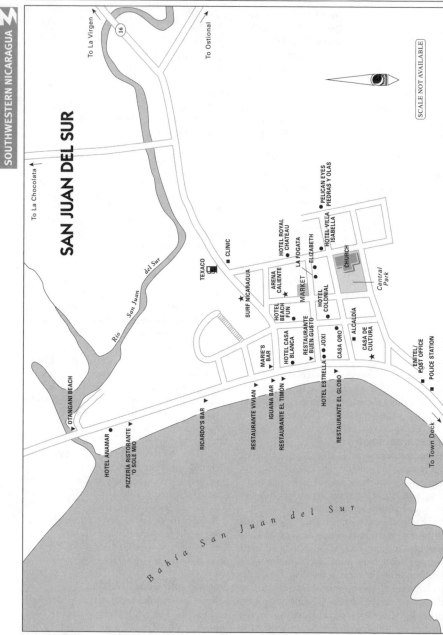

SAN JUAN DEL SUR

To La Virgen

16

To Ostional

To La Chocolata

SCALE NOT AVAILABLE

Río San Juan del Sur

CLINIC

TEXACO

★ SURF NICARAGUA

HOTEL ROYAL CHATEAU

ARENA CALIENTE

LA FOGATA

ELIZABETH

MARKET

HOTEL COLONIAL

PELICAN EYES PIEDRAS Y OLAS

HOTEL VILLA ISABELLA

HOTEL BEACH FUN

RESTAURANTE BUEN GUSTO

JOXI

CASA ORO

CASA DE CULTURA

ALCALDIA

CHURCH

Central Park

OTANGANI BEACH

HOTEL ANAMAR

PIZZERIA RISTORANTE 'O SOLE MIO

MARIE'S BAR

HOTEL CASA BLANCA

RICARDO'S BAR

RESTAURANTE VIVIAN

IGUANA BAR

RESTAURANTE EL TIMÓN

HOTEL ESTRELLA

RESTAURANTE EL GLOBO

ENTEL/ POST OFFICE

POLICE STATION

To Town Dock

Bahía San Juan del Sur

© AVALON TRAVEL PUBLISHING INC

detailed information, consult the *Surf Report,* or seek out local knowledge. Dale Dagger has been scouting breaks for nearly a decade and can be found in his home/boat shop on the east end of town. Ask about booking a surf trip on his boat, *La Masayita.* It's not a speed demon, but it's shaded, casual, and very familiar with the southern Nicaraguan coast. For rates, visit his website, www.nicasurf.com, or contact him at tel. 458-2492, email: ddagger@ibw.com.ni.

See local shredders Byron and Kevin López in their surf shop, **Arena Caliente,** next to the market. They run trips for as little as $15 a person, and rent and sell boards. Ricardo's also rents boards. Standard board rentals are about $7 a day.

Nica Sport is an ever-expanding service, with an office next to the Iguana Bar. Find Robert and ask about *panga* rides to "known and unknown" surf spots; fishing trips too; rates start at $25 a person, tel. 458-2418, email: robert@getglobal.net. Also, track down the local character known as **El Rana** (The Frog), a.k.a. Alberto Granada, for beach tours.

Fishing

Andreas Seeger will take you out on *Ivette* for sailfish, shark, snappers, tuna, or anything else that takes a bite; a six-hour trip for six people costs $240, tel. 458-2555. Go fishing with Jake for $35 an hour (four-hour minimum) on the 25-foot boat at Hotel El Pacifico, tel. 458-2557. Gabriel is a local fisherman who charges $125 for a six-hour trip, drinks and lunch included; book him through Chris Berry or Ricardo's Bar. Once you hook your monster, many of the restaurants will grill it up for you—the cook at Ricardo's is especially skilled.

Sailing

Take Chris Berry's *Pelican Eyes* for an all-day jaunt; lunch on a deserted beach, open bar all day; $45 a person ($450 minimum, plus deposit), or sunset cruises for $25 a person. Find him in his hotel, Piedras y Olas, or tel. 458-2110, email: pelican@ibw.com.ni.

ENTERTAINMENT AND EVENTS

Like any tropical beach town, San Juan del Sur is pretty much a continuous mellow party year-round, but with a huge spike in activity during Christmas, New Year's, and Semana Santa. During these times, the town is flooded with visitors, many of them young, well-off Nicaraguans looking to get their dance on. During the rest of the year, the town's sole disco, **Otangani Beach,** is open Thursday–Sunday; featuring an open porch backing the river as it flows into the bay, and a restaurant (meals from $5), owned by a French couple, tel. 862-1501. Ricardo's sets up a screen and shows movies Mondays and Thursdays.

The *fiestas patronales* takes place June 16–24, but you may find the events of July 17 even more interesting—the **Procesión de la Virgen del Carmen** is a celebration of the Patron Saint of Fishermen. The icon is paraded through town, and finally to the docks where waiting boats take her (and most of the townspeople) for a lap around the bay. September 2 is the commemoration of the tidal wave of 1992.

ACCOMMODATIONS

San Juan covers the entire spectrum, from grungy *hospedajes* to luxury hotels. Nearly all the cheapest *hospedajes* are on the main street, are Nicaraguan-owned, and are usually extensions of someone's home.

Under $10

Starting at the east end of the market street, **Elizabeth's** is a tucked-away two-story affair, with 19 rooms starting at $5. Elizabeth is a sweetheart, and the atmosphere is usually pretty quiet, tel. 458-2270.

Next door, **Hospedaje Eleonora,** tel. 458-2191, has a street-side balcony and four second-story, cement floor rooms for $4. After that, **Nina's** has five sparkling clean rooms, starting at $4, tel. 458-2302. Next up is one of San Juan's originals—**Hospedaje La Fogata,** which has been around for 40 years and has the biggest open-air common space of them all. The 14 rooms and three toilet stalls are nothing special, and the space is gloomy when the lights aren't on, but the *dueña,* Jennifer, is a native San Juaneña and a wealth of local knowledge and history. Rooms with shared bath go for $4, and the three with private bath and double beds cost $5 a person. There's a restaurant and bar, a garage (actually, you park right in the lobby), bike rental ($5 a day), and car/driver service for about $35 a day—design your own trip.

Across the street is **Hotel Almendros,** another basic, $3–4 per person family affair, with five rooms, tel. 458-2388. Turn right at the next corner for **Hotel Beach Fun** (formerly Casa 28), an 18-year-old *hospedaje* in a 90-year-old building. The 16 rooms are a bit run-down, but the open courtyard is nice and so are the owners; $3 a night, tel. 458-2441. Where the market street reaches the sea, you'll find **Hotel Estrella** on your left, reportedly the first hotel in San Juan del Sur. It's a little less glamorous than in its glory years, but this is the only place in town where you get an oceanfront balcony for $4 a person. Drawbacks are having to walk downstairs to use the bathroom—and the bats, unless you're into that sort of thing, tel. 458-2210.

Casa Oro is a dorm-style youth hostel in a big, old, wooden building just west of the central park; $4 a night gets you a bunk bed, access to the kitchen, and a hammock by the garden; email: rockettom@hotmail.com.

$10–25

Nearly all of the nicer hotels (and restaurants) accept all major credit cards. **Casa Internacional Joxi,** a Norwegian-owned hotel with 11 rooms starting at $10 (a/c, TV, shared bath; $18 s, $29 d with private bath). The small space is efficiently developed into two floors, with a great balcony. Joxi also has a miniapartment, with a fridge, bathroom, and master bedroom, which can accommodate seven people for $10 a person, tel. 458-2483, email: casajoxi@ibm.tmx.com.ni. **Hotel Anamar** is on the north end of the beach (near the disco), and has private apartments starting at $25 a couple, tel. 458-2589, website: www.anamar.com.ni.

$25–50

On your left as you roll into town (before turning right onto the market street toward the ocean), the **Hotel Royal Chateau** has 20 rooms starting at $30 with fan, $35 with a/c, private bath, parking; no credit cards, tel. 458-2551. Right across from the beach, the **Hotel Casa Blanca** is first-rate, with all kinds of perks, including a pool, parking, laundry, breakfast, and 24-hour security. Rooms are $46 s, $50 d, second-floor suite for $70 (plus tax), tel. 458-2135, email: casablanca@ibw.com.ni.

Hotel El Pacifico is located across the river, in the Barrio El Talanguera, accessible via the Chocolata road turnoff (at the gas station before entering San Juan). Rooms have a/c, private bath, parking, pool, restaurant and bar, starting at $36 s, $46 d, including breakfast; also offers car rental and fishing/beach trips, tel. 458-2557, email: pacifico@ibw.com.ni. **Hotel Colonia,** just off the park, has a minivillage feeling, with 12 rooms, $40 s, $46 d, $58 t, $69 for a suite with two single beds and a queen size; private bath, TV, breakfast, bar, tel. 458-2227. The **Aramar Lodge** is a basic bed-and-breakfast, a stone's throw from the beach, with a/c, TV, private bath, and a tiny pool, starting at $40 a person, more expensive on weekends, tel. 458-2259.

Pelican Eyes Piedras y Olas, built into the hillside on the east end of town, has singles starting at $45, suites $60, tel. 458-2511, email: pelican@ibw.com.ni.

Over $50

Hotel Villa Isabella offers four-star services, starting at $55 for a queen bed with private bath, a/c, and TV/VCR; also breakfast, business services, handicapped access, and plenty of info on what to do while in town, tel. 458-2568, email: villaisabella@aol.com, website: www.sanjuandelsur.org.ni/isabella. Or make reservations toll-free in the U.S. and Canada, tel. 888/508-1778.

FOOD AND BARS

If you are short on funds and unable to resist the splurging pull of the beach, eat three *corriente* meals a day at one of the counters inside the municipal market—about $1 a meal; but if you've got those Rice 'n' Beans Blues after traveling in the campo for a couple of weeks, San Juan del Sur is a great place to throw down some coin in exchange for good, hearty, food.

Nearly every *hospedaje,* hotel, and some of the beach restaurants make a variety of breakfasts, usually for $2–3. Start with the **Iguana,** which serves a solid, bacon-and-egg breakfast all day long from 7:30 A.M. Iguana also has Internet service, bar, restaurant, and boogie board rental. **Joxi** has good breakfasts as well, and opens early. For veggie breakfasts, lunches, and dinners, try the soy at **Comedor Soya,** behind the train station ruins; this place is also a *hospedaje* with cheap, clean rooms, and all the soysage you can eat, tel. 458-2572.

A typical row of identical thatched-roof Nicaraguan ranchos lines the middle part of the beach. In most parts of the country, this means fluorescent lights, bad music, and lots of naked beer chick posters, but San Juan's Nica strip is a bit more toned down. Most of these restaurants have legitimately excellent seafood—a basic fish plate costs $4, shrimp and lobster get up to $12.

As a welcome change of pace, San Juan del Sur's restaurant row is blessed with variety, thanks in large part to a handful of creative foreign entrepreneurs. **Marie's,** in particular, maintains a reputation for its cuisine, with wonderful pasta and veggie dishes, in addition to seafood. This is a fun, cozy bar as well (open Tues.–Sun. from 5:30 P.M., tel. 458-2555, email: mariebar@ibw.com.ni).

Ricardo's has European chow, burgers, and a tasty appetizer list. Come for the food, stay for the drinks—or vice-versa. Ricardo's bar scene is already renowned in traveler and expat circles, no doubt helped by its location—an open-air bar, looking out over a shaded patio, the beach, and the bobbing ships, snug in their harbor. Ricardo's also has Internet (two computers), a book exchange, beach chairs, rents surf and boogie boards, and owns the only "horizontal bungee" on the continent. Its proprietress, Marie, is a wealth of knowledge if you are looking for something to do besides damage to your credit card (and liver) by swilling tequila sunrises all after-

noon, tel. 458-2502, email: ricardo@ibw.com.ni, website: www.sanjuandelsur.org.ni/ricardos-bar/gue.html

Up the road, the **Pizzería Ristorante O Sole Mio** has just what you'd expect: real pizza, Italian food, and wine, and a seafood pasta to die for; meals, including pizza, start at $5 (open Tues.–Sun., 5–9:30 P.M., weekends 11 A.M.–9:30 P.M., tel. 458-2101).

SHOPPING

During weekends, holidays, and cruise ship arrivals, there are numerous street vendors from all over Nicaragua and Central America selling clothes, hammocks, jewelry, and other *artesanía.* **El Papagaya Artesanía** is a French-owned shop with goods from around the world, open 9 A.M.–7 P.M. Ask Regis if he's completed his surf camp at Playa Maderas yet.

INFORMATION AND TOURS

There is no one official point for tourism information in San Juan del Sur (the nearest INTUR office is in Rivas), but there are many local efforts to stay on top of the quickly developing scene—Marie at Ricardo's bar has even put together her own local guide and map, or check the bulletin board at the Casa de Cultura and at various *hospedajes.*

SERVICES

Try to take care of all your business, shopping, communication, and banking needs before you get to San Juan del Sur. There are some basic services available, especially at some of the nicer hotels, but there is still no bank in town. The

ON THE WEB

New businesses are arriving and rates are changing all the time in San Juan del Sur. Stay on top of things at **www.sanjuandelsur .org.ni,** also the site of many of San Juan's hotel and restaurant homepages.

THE *CRUCERO* QUESTION

In 1998, the Holland America Line added San Juan del Sur as a port call on several of their cruises. The announcement sparked hope in the people of San Juan del Sur, who began preparing their sleepy town to receive the thousands of cruise ship passengers scheduled to disembark.

Now, after several years of regular biweekly stops (during the cruise season), whether or not *los cruceros* have benefited San Juan del Sur depends entirely on whom you ask. The well-to-do Careli Tour company isn't complaining, owning a monopoly on the buses and guides who whisk most of the passengers straight from the dock in San Juan to day trips in Granada or Masaya. These passengers never set foot in San Juan proper, and the few hundred who decide to remain in town do not spend money in restaurants or hotels. A few

bars have made a good business catering to partying crewmembers, but the passengers themselves don't do much drinking. The ciclo-taxis and their drivers that cart passengers to and from the dock are all imported from Rivas and most of the crafts vendors that display along the tree-lined beachfront strip are Guatemalan. In fact, the majority of San Juaneños have not gained a dime from the arrival of the cruise ships and would only notice their absence by the lack of tinted-window bus convoys rumbling past their doors every two weeks.

Holland America passengers would do well to make an attempt to leave some dollars behind for someone other than their tour guides, whether in San Juan del Sur, or in other Nicaraguan cities they visit.

post office is located on the south end of the beach road, sharing a building with ENITEL.

Health Care

The couple of pharmacies in town are open from about 8 A.M.–9 P.M., and the Centro de Salud provides free consults Monday–Saturday 8 A.M.–7 P.M., Sunday 8 A.M.–noon; the dentist is there Thursday mornings, the gynecologist Saturdays. However, for any serious medical concerns, plan a trip to Rivas, as the Centro is typically under-staffed and crowded.

Internet

San Juan's handful of Internet cafés are all dial-up and twice as expensive as most other places in Nicaragua. Capt'n Eric's charges $5.50 an hour and is open 8:30 A.M.–8 P.M. every day. The Internet Café behind the Casa de Cultura is air-conditioned and charges $5 an hour (open Mon.–Fri. 7:30 A.M.–8 P.M., Sat. 8 A.M.–7 P.M.).

GETTING THERE AND AWAY

Expresses from Managua leave the Roberto Huembes terminal at 10 A.M., 5 P.M., 6 P.M., and 7 P.M.; the ride takes 2.5 hours and costs about $3. Otherwise, take any bus to Rivas, where reg-

ular buses leave every half-hour 5 A.M.–5 P.M. A better bet from Rivas is to hop in a *colectivo* taxi, which will pack in as many passengers as it can, but only charges $.75 for the 26-kilometer ride; private taxis can be rented for $7.

From the Costa Rican border at Peñas Blancas, buses for Rivas leave every half-hour. Get off at Empalme la Virgen and flag a bus, taxi, or ride going to San Juan from Rivas. The beach is 18 kilometers due west of the Empalme; taxis from the border to San Juan charge $11–20.

Express buses from San Juan del Sur to Managua leave from the corner in front of the market at 4 A.M., 5 A.M., and 6 A.M. *Ordinarios* to Rivas and Managua begin leaving at 5 A.M. and run through the afternoon. The last bus to Managua leaves San Juan del Sur at 5:30 P.M. You can also catch a *colectivo* taxi to Rivas out of town on its return trip. To the border at Peñas Blancas, get a ride to La Virgen, then catch a lift south; the first Rivas–Peñas Blancas bus passes at 7:30 A.M.

BEACHES TO THE SOUTH

A number of fabulous beaches are accessible by driving (or walking or biking) the south-pointing road east of the Texaco station, or along the bus route to Ostional. To reach the first group of beaches, do not follow signs to La Flor at the turnoff about five kilometers in; instead, go right and walk another couple clicks to the beach. There are no services here, so be prepared with water and food. **Playa Remanso,** in addition to its consistent but mediocre beach break for surfing, has a long, interesting shore that is fascinating to explore at low tide—look for bat caves, tid pools, blow holes, and plenty of wildlife.

Walking 30 minutes farther south, you'll hit **Playa Tamarindo** (also accessible by getting off the bus at El Coyol). **Playa Hermosa** is either an hour beach hike from the parking lot at Remanso or another walk from the bus stop at El Carrizol. There is a *pulpería* at El Carrizol—stock up on water and snacks, then cross the river and look for the sign that announces **Yankee Beach;** climb the fence and get the key from the friendly gatekeepers.

Playa Coco

The road deteriorates farther south and during the rainy season; four-wheel drive is recommended. Playa Coco is a jewel of a beach, great for swimming and fishing, and easy access to the turtles at La Flor. **Parque Marítimo El Coco** (18 kilometers south of San Juan) has a restaurant called Puesta de Sol (open 8 A.M.–9 P.M. every day), and a collection of bungalows, apartments, and houses for rent; prices range from $45 a night into the hundreds of dollars—reasonable with a group of people. Fully equipped houses have a/c, satellite TV, hot water, kitchen, and sleep up to eight people for $150 a day. Tel. 458-2512 (in Managua, tel. 249-1192), email: parquemaritimo@playaelcoco.com.ni, website: www.playaelcoco.com.ni.

La Flor Wildlife Refuge

One of the two Pacific turtle nesting beaches in Nicaragua. The park is being managed by Fundación Cocibolca, an NGO that is attempting to involve the local community in decision-making processes. There is a small fee to enter, plenty of beach on which to camp, park guards to protect the eggs, and adequate transport from San Juan del Sur (about 45 minutes away).

Ostional

This is a picturesque bay and community at the extreme southwestern tip of Nicaragua where the citizens still fish traditionally with nets. Accessed by buses from both Rivas and San Juan del Sur.

BEACHES TO THE NORTH

By land, these beaches are all accessed via the road to Chocolata, just east of the Texaco station (much of this road served as the old railroad

BEACHES SOUTH OF SAN JUAN DEL SUR

To La Virgen

16

Bahía San Juan del Sur

San Juan del Sur

El Carrizol

Playa Remanso
Playa Tamarindo
Playa Hermosa

Playa Escamequita
Yankee Beach

Playa Coco

Playa La Flor

La Flor Wildlife Refuge

Ostional

PACIFIC OCEAN

0   50 yds
0   50 m

© AVALON TRAVEL PUBLISHING, INC.

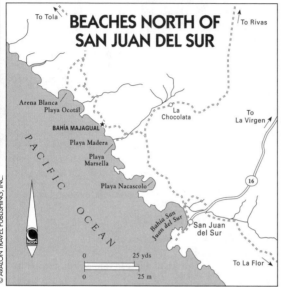

BEACHES NORTH OF SAN JUAN DEL SUR

To Tola

To Rivas

Arena Blanca
Playa Ocotál

La Chocolata

To La Virgen

BAHÍA MAJAGUAL

Playa Madera

Playa Marsella

Playa Nacascolo

16

Bahía San Juan del Sur

San Juan del Sur

To La Flor

PACIFIC OCEAN

0   25 yds

0   25 m

© AVALON TRAVEL PUBLISHING, INC.

of San Juan del Sur on one of the most beautiful beaches on the left coast of Nicaragua—no joke. The scene varies from a mellow campfire to an all-out beach disco; very short walk from the surf at **Playa Madera** (fast, hollow beach break, best on incoming tides). Off-season camping costs $2 per person per night, dormitory beds $4, private rooms $6 (peak prices reach $25–35, but backpackers are always accommodated). The menu has a range of options, including a fat $3 burger. Current capacity is 24, with 36 more dorm beds in the plans. Most of the services you need for the beach are here: surf and boogie rentals ($10 a day for surfboards), snorkeling gear, horseback rides, book exchange, games, and laundry service—they make it tough to find an excuse to return to civilization. Bring plenty of cash and keep an eye on your tab—it's easy to spend more than you planned on. Majagual accepts cordobas, dollars, and traveler's checks (credit cards on the way). Contact Paul, the Aussie owner, at tel. 886-0469, email: majagual@ibw.com.ni.

Getting There and Away: Look for a sign-up list for the shuttle that leaves daily from the Iguana Bar; the $5 round-trip fee will be added to your tab; day trips available from 10 A.M. to after sunset. There are plenty of other taxi services as well, for $2 per person each way. By bus, Bahía Majagual is a five-kilometer walk west of the *empalme* at Chocolata, a tiny community located 19 kilometers from Rivas, and seven kilometers from San Juan del Sur. Several daily buses run between Rivas and Chocolata.

grade back in the day). **Playa Nacascolo** (a.k.a. Navy Beach) and **El Torre** are only reachable by walking through fields and asking directions. Seven kilometers in, turn left at Chocolata to a fork in the road: left goes to Marsella and Madera, right to Majagual.

Playa Marsella

A pleasant, breezy beach, with good snorkeling around the rocks (watch the currents). The resort at Marsella has large cliff-top cabins with incredible views, which go for $40 a couple. The real treat here though is the kitchen—world-class food prepared to perfection by a South African chef. If you'd rather not stay, organize a dinner or lunch trip with one of the shuttles (one leaves at 6 A.M. from the Texaco, returning 1 P.M. or 10 P.M.), tel. 458-2563, email: resort@ibw.com.ni, website: www.nicaragualand.com.

Bahía Majagual

The source of all those cryptic "If you never ever go, you'll never ever know" posters in Managua *hospedajes,* the **Bahía Majagual Eco-Lodge** is a backpacker resort and former getaway for high-ranking Sandinista officals, 12 kilometers north

North of Majagual

Continuing north along the coast, you'll find **Playa Ocotál** and **Arena Blanca,** both accessible by turning right off the road to Majagual, just past the yellow and black gate—continue straight until you find another gate on your left. Both are beautiful beaches with individual charms.

Panga Drops, a powerful break over treacherous rocks, is surfable with considerable swell, and is accessible only by boat.

PEÑAS BLANCAS AND THE BORDER WITH COSTA RICA

Peñas Blancas is the official border crossing into Costa Rica, and south of Rivas it's pretty safe to assume everyone you meet on the highway is either headed to, or coming from the border. Since 1999 the border post has undergone massive construction and renovation, making it a nicer—and better organized—post than even Costa Rica's (although the Ticos have a cafeteria on their side, something still lacking on the Nica side of the border).

A major effort is underway, with financing from the United States, to make the border crossing a bottleneck and entrapment point for drug traffickers headed north. Many of the buildings you see in the compound are drug inspection points for the dozens of tractor-trailers that cross the border every day. Needless to say, this is one place you don't want to be smuggling furs. The bottleneck has been generally successful. In a recent incident, U.S. drug enforcement agents giving a training to the local inspectors on how to drill through the ceilings and floors of tractor-trailers to search for stashed cocaine were surprised to find several hundred kilos of cocaine stashed in the truck they'd chosen randomly as the guinea pig for their demonstration.

The large perimeter wall that forms the border was constructed in early 2001, to much criticism from the Nicaraguans, who claimed the Ticos were building a Wall of China to keep them out. The border remains easily penetrated on both sides along the largely unpatrolled border.

Hours

The border post works on "normal" and "overtime" hours. The only difference is how much you can expect to pay to have your paperwork processed. Normal hours are Monday–Friday 8 A.M.–5 P.M. and Saturday 8 A.M.–noon; overtime hours are Monday–Friday 6–8 A.M. and 6–8 P.M., Saturdays noon–8 P.M., and Sunday 6 A.M.–8 P.M.

Fees

Travelers exiting Nicaragua pay $2 at the border during normal hours and $4 during overtime hours. Travelers entering Nicaragua pay $7 during normal hours and $9 during overtime hours. Everyone traveling to the border on an international bus service like TicaBus or TransNica will be forced to pay $1 to the town government of Cárdenas before reaching the border. (Nicas consider Cárdenas to be the local version of Gabriel García Márquez's Maconda, the Latin American village that time forgot. It's an almost completely undeveloped area on the south shore of Lake Cocibolca that lacks even basic infrastructure, so the $1 is hopefully going toward a good cause.) Travelers using other means of transportation are, for the present, exempt from this charge.

Inside the Customs and Immigration building is a branch of Bancentro, which can help you change money if necessary. It's open 8 A.M.–8 P.M., i.e., whenever the border is open.

Travelers driving their own vehicles north from the border will be forced to pass their vehicles through a dubious "sterilization process" in which the exterior of the vehicle is sprayed with some mystery liquid that kills certain porcine and bovine diseases; it costs $1 and takes five minutes unless the line is long.

Paperwork

Just a passport and some cash is all that's required of North American and European travelers. To enter Costa Rica, Nicaraguan citizens must have acquired a Costa Rican visa from the consulate either in Rivas or Managua. Upon entering Nicaragua, most North American and European travelers are granted a 90-day visa, with the exception of Canadian and Japanese citizens, who for some reason are only given 30 days.

Crossing the Border with Your Vehicle

If you are driving your own vehicle, the process to enter Nicaragua is lengthy, but usually not difficult. You must present the vehicle's title, as well as your own driver's license and passport. You will be given a temporary (30-day) permit to drive in

Nicaragua that will cost you $10—should you lose the permit, you will be fined $100.

Getting There and Away

International bus services like TicaBus, TransNica, and NicaBus are popular ways to get across the border easily and comfortably. In many cases, the bus has a "helper" who collects your passports and money and waits on line for you. The disadvantage is that the bus won't pull away from the border post until every single traveler has had their papers processed, which can be time-consuming in some cases (waits up to four hours are not unheard of). Some travelers like to take a Nicaraguan bus to the border, walk across to Costa Rica, and take a Costa Rican bus to San José. For confident travelers, this is often faster. There are express buses from Managua to Peñas Blancas that depart Mercado Huembes at 5 A.M., 8 A.M., 9:30 A.M., and 3:30 P.M. Buses and microbuses leave the market in Rivas every 30–45 minutes. On the Costa Rican side, the last bus leaves the border bound for San José at 10 P.M. (about a six-hour ride).

León, Chinandega, and the Northwest Pacific Coast

Chinandega, León, and the northwest coast of Nicaragua as far as the Cosigüina Peninsula, comprise the most populated, agriculturally fertile, and swelteringly hot corner of Nicaragua. The centerpiece of the landscape—a massive chain of active volcanoes that extends northwest from Lago de Managua all the way into the Gulf of Fonseca—is nothing short of majestic. The long coastline boasts white- and black-sand beaches, mangrove swamps, and hundreds of kilometers of bird-filled estuary.

The region's two major cities include proud, colonial León, whose narrow cobbled streets are lined with cathedrals and universities, and whose coffee shops and cafés are filled with the buzz of politics. The horizon's towering and omnipresent volcanoes offer a menacing feel to the region, but danger has as often come at the hands of mankind as it has from Mother Nature. León's political history is as long as Nicaragua's itself, punctuated throughout the centuries with the staccato call of uprising and revolution.

The tension seeps out of the very land itself in the form of hot-springs, boiling geothermal vents, and the occasional trembling of a volcano. The Leoneses and Chinandeganos know very well

Chinandega

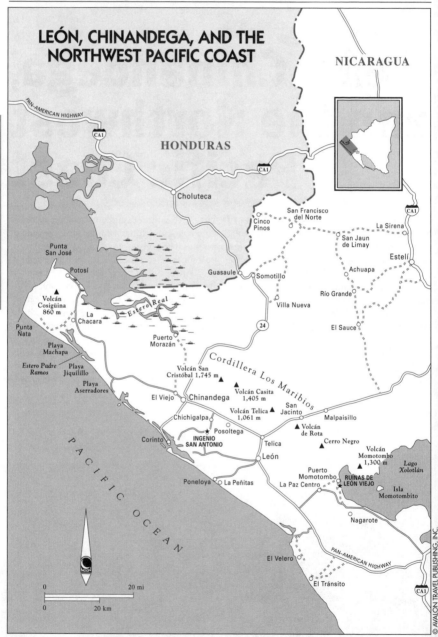

LEÓN, CHINANDEGA, AND THE NORTHWEST PACIFIC COAST

NICARAGUA

PAN-AMERICAN HIGHWAY

CA1

HONDURAS

CA1

CA1

Choluteca

San Francisco del Norte

Cinco Pinos

La Sirena

San Jaun de Limay

Estelí

Punta San José

Potosí

Guasaule

Somotillo

Achuapa

Volcán Cosigüina 860 m

La Chacara

Estero Real

Villa Nueva

Río Grande

Punta Ñata

24

El Sauce

Playa Machapa

Puerto Morazán

Estero Padre Ramos

Playa Jiquilillo

Volcán San Cristóbal 1,745 m

Cordillera Los Maribios

Playa Aserradores

El Viejo

Chinandega

Volcán Casita 1,405 m

Chichigalpa

Volcán Telica 1,061 m

San Jacinto

Malpaisillo

Corinto

Posoltega

INGENIO SAN ANTONIO

Volcán de Rota

Cerro Negro

Telica

Volcán Momotombo 1,300 m

Lago Xolotlán

PACIFIC OCEAN

León

Poneloya

La Peñitas

Puerto Momotombo

La Paz Centro

RUÍNAS DE LEÓN VIEJO

Isla Momotombito

Nagarote

PAN-AMERICAN HIGHWAY

El Velero

El Tránsito

CA1

MOON

0   20 mi

0   20 km

HIKING THE MARIBIO VOLCANOES

Nicaragua has been called "a violent expanse of volcanic strength," and there is nowhere better to feel that force than on the hot, baked slopes of its mountains of fire. Start early and bring a minimum of three liters of water per person.

Momotombo, 1,300 m, eight hours round-trip
The quintessential cone-shaped volcano, Momotombo rises up from the shores of Lago Xolotlán in a particularly menacing posture—and history has proven that the menace is real. Momotombo is climbable, but it's not easy, especially when you hit the loose volcanic gravel that comprises the upper half of the cone. Your triumphant reward will be one of the best views possible of Lago Xolotlán without use of an airplane. From the Ruínas de León Viejo, head out of town to the main highway and turn right (north) along the highway. Follow that to the geothermal plant where you'll have to convince the guard to let you through to hike. They're sensitive about people traipsing across their installation, so honor whatever promises you make.

Telica, 1,061 m, 4–5 hours round-trip
Despite its tendency to spew ash over its namesake town, Volcán Telica makes for a good climb. Take a bus from León to Telica, then follow the road to the community of La Quimera and keep going until the road disappears beneath your feet and becomes the volcano. Alternatively, access the volcano from Santa Clara, the town adjacent to the Hervideros de San Jacinto.

Cerro Negro, 450 m, five hours round-trip
This is the most frequently active volcano in the chain (its last eruption was August 1999). The lowest and youngest of the Maribios, Cerro Negro is easily the most disagreeable climb. Completely treeless and covered with loose, black, hot volcanic sand, ascending Cerro Negro means scrambling two steps up and sliding back one—for three hours. Going down is easy—bring a beater snowboard for the quickest and most stylish descent. Your jumping-off point is the Telica–San Isidro highway from wherever looks good. Or, an alternative route (with a longer but easier approach) involves walking northeast from the city of León to the community of San José. Leave as early in the morning as humanly possible.

La Casita, 1,405 m, eight hours round-trip
See San Cristóbal below for access information. Near the top of the climb, the guides will lead you into the saddle between La Casita and Cristóbal and then to the peak of La Casita itself. There are some radio towers here, and the terminus of an access road damaged during the landslide. Though it's also possible to hike to the top along the slide itself, it's a treeless, sun-baked hike, not to mention possibly disrespectful to the thousands who remain buried beneath it. Although not as tall, La Casita offers a better view of Managua and the lake than Cristóbal does.

San Cristóbal, 1,745 m, eight hours round-trip
This is the granddaddy of volcano hikes in the Pacific region. You'll need a guide to help you wend your way through the myriad fields, farms, and fences that obstruct the path upward (and which change every planting season). Find your guide in Chichigalpa. Enrique Reyes and his brothers are experienced at leading trips up San Cristóbal, and are found in the Barrio Pellisco Occidental, across from the Escuela Hector García (tel. 885-9154). If they're not around, finding a guide in Chichigalpa is easy. Horses cost $2 a day, and you should pay the guides at least $8 per group.

Cosigüina, 860 m, six hours round-trip to edge of crater, 11 hours round-trip to crater lake
Start walking from Potosi, or rent horses ($2 per day). Head back along the road toward the community of La Chacara, where the slope of Cosigüina is most amenable for climbing. From the edge of the crater you can see across the Gulf of Fonseca into El Salvador. There are competing claims about whether one can descend to the crater lake without the use of ropes. If you intend to descend the approximately 300 meters down to the crater lake you should take 30 meters of good rope with you (you can purchase it in El Viejo or Chinandega) and consider a guide from La Chacara. Luís Mejía Castro in El Viejo knows the Reserva Natural and its volcano intimately (from the Cine Imperial, two blocks west, tel. 886-5477).

that life can be short and violent, and it should thus be lived intensely. León and Chinandega suffered more than most during Hurricane Mitch, during which more than two meters of rain fell in three days. Nowhere else in Nicaragua was the destruction as intense, and the still-visible landslide at Las Casitas is a silent reminder of the worst of it. As you ride from Managua to Chinandega, bear in mind that every single bridge along that route was washed away in October 1998, and some weren't rebuilt until years after Mitch had passed.

City of León

León's principal attraction is the exotic feel one gets by walking the cobbled streets of a colonial city replete with churches and cathedrals, indigenous neighborhoods, and green parks. You'd do well to allow your stay in León to serve as a brief glimpse of what it's like to live in a colonial city. Instead of one of the cheap *hospedajes* on the edge of town, stay in a colonial hotel with a bit more atmosphere; go to Catholic mass; sit in the park and watch the college students buzz around; or wake up early to watch the birds on the power lines and the Leoneses sweeping the streets in front of their doorsteps.

HISTORY

Today's León is the city's second incarnation. The short-lived first attempt was the Spanish settlement that Francisco Hernández de Córdoba founded next to the indigenous village of Imabite on the shore of Lake Xolotlán in 1524. The Spanish were less than hospitable to the neighboring natives, whom they forced into slavery and often punished with death at the jaws of attack dogs. The old city was abandoned in 1610 when Volcán Momotombo erupted. The Spanish relocated their city to León's present location alongside the already existing indigenous village of Subtiava. As the centuries passed and both populations expanded, Subtiava found itself—for better or worse—a barrio of Spanish León.

Before 1852, León was the capital of Nicaragua several times, always under the leadership of Liberal governments. León has also, since colonial times, been both a university town and a hotbed of leftist thought. That predisposition for radical ideas proved to be fertile ground for Sandinista

support. The Leoneses contributed greatly to the revolution from its earliest days in the 1960s, and as a result, Somoza punished them dearly, in one case by torching the central market.

In September 1978, Sandinista forces attacked key locations in León, including the installations of the National Guard at the famous "XXI," and were soundly beaten. Somoza retaliated with fury, using the air force to bomb the populations of both León and Chinandega. He also tortured and executed anyone suspected of sympathizing with the Sandinistas. León lost not a few sons and brothers, and the bullet holes still adorn many buildings today.

By mid-1979, a weakened and militarily strained Somoza was unable to stop Sandinista troops as they entered León on June 2 and "liberated" it two days later. By the 17th, Somoza's last bastion of support in the city, the barracks of the National Guard, had been abandoned. The city of León has been largely Sandinista ever since, voting for the FSLN in the last three presidential elections.

ORIENTATION AND GETTING AROUND

León is laid out in the traditional colonial grid system centered around the central park and cathedral. The main bus station and market are located nearly a kilometer northeast of the park, and Barrio Subtiava is 12 blocks due west. Within the city, taxis charge $.50 during the day and $1 at night. León is also crisscrossed by small city buses and converted pickup trucks that charge about $.15; ask about your destination before getting on.

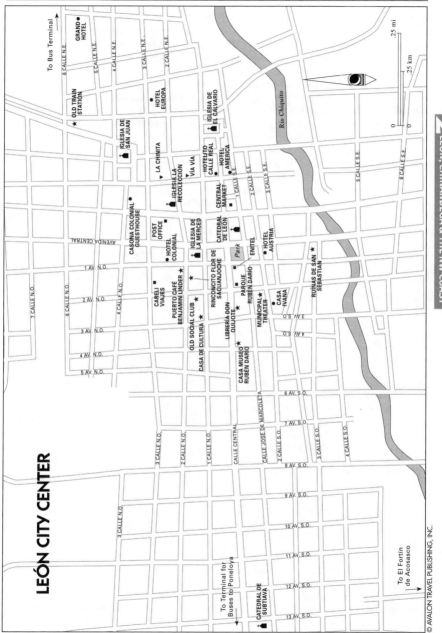

LEÓN CITY CENTER

To Bus Terminal

GRAND HOTEL

OLD TRAIN STATION

6 CALLE N.E.
5 CALLE N.E.
4 CALLE N.E.
3 CALLE N.E.
2 CALLE N.E.

HOTEL EUROPA

IGLESIA DE SAN JUAN

LA CHINITA

IGLESIA DE EL CALVARIO

IGLESIA LA RECOLECCIÓN

VIA VIA

HOTELITO CALLE REAL

HOTEL AMERICA

CENTRAL MARKET

1 CALLE S.E.
2 CALLE S.E.
3 CALLE S.E.

AVENIDA CENTRAL

CASONA COLONIAL GUESTHOUSE

POST OFFICE

HOTEL COLONIAL

IGLESIA DE LA MERCED

CATEDRAL DE LEÓN

Park

HOTEL AUSTRIA

ENITEL

RUINAS DE SAN SEBASTIÁN

Río Chiquito

7 CALLE N.O.
1 AV. N.O.
6 CALLE N.O.
2 AV. N.O.
4 CALLE N.O.
3 AV. N.O.
3 CALLE N.O.
4 AV. N.O.
2 CALLE N.O.
5 AV. N.O.
1 CALLE N.O.

CARELI VIAJES

PUERTO CAFÉ BENJAMIN LINDER

OLD SOCIAL CLUB

CASA DE CULTURA

RINCONCITO FLOR DE SACUANJOCHE

LIBRERÍA DON QUIJOTE

PARQUE RUBÉN DARÍO

MUNICIPAL THEATER

CASA IVANA

CASA MUSEO RUBÉN DARÍO

3 AV. S.O.
4 AV. S.O.
6 AV. S.O.
7 AV. S.O.
8 AV. S.O.
9 AV. S.O.
10 AV. S.O.
11 AV. S.O.
12 AV. S.O.
13 AV. S.O.

CALLE CENTRAL

CALLE JOSÉ DE MARCOLETA

1 CALLE S.O.
2 CALLE S.O.
3 CALLE S.O.
4 CALLE S.O.

5 CALLE S.E.
6 CALLE S.E.

To Terminal for Buses to Poneloya

CATEDRAL DE SUBTIAVA

To El Fortín de Acosasco

N

LEÓN, CHINANDEGA & THE NW COAST

0 .25 mi
0 .25 km

© AVALON TRAVEL PUBLISHING, INC.

SIGHTS

The **Parque Rubén Darío,** a block west of the central park, is a tribute to four famous Nicaraguan writers, all sons of León: Azarías H. Pallais (1884–1954), Salomon de la Selva (1893–1959), Alfonzo Cortéz (1893–1969), and of course the beloved Rubén Darío (1867–1916).

León's **Old Train Station,** built in 1884, was Nicaragua's first and most majestic. It survived a fire in 1956 that left only the outer walls standing, and was subsequently rebuilt. A rowdy market has taken over the old building now, but the grandeur of days gone past still resonates in the rafters.

El Fortín de Acosasco sits on a low grassy hill just south of the city. It was built in 1889 by Conservative president Sacasa to keep an eye on the Liberals that would overthrow him four years later. The fort was later abandoned until Anastasio Somoza took interest and rehabilitated it. El Fortín has since served as both a military base and jail, and is presently abandoned once again. From the Subtiava church, it's an easy 45-minute walk: go one block east and head due south out of town and up the hill along the shady dirt road. The view of the city from the fort is worth the walk.

On September 21, 1956, the poet-student Rigoberto López Pérez disguised himself as a waiter to gain access to the ballroom of León's **Old Social Club.** There he fatally shot Anastasio Somoza García, marking what some say was the beginning of the long end of the dictatorship.

A WALKING TOUR OF CHURCHES AND RUINS IN LEÓN

La **Catedral de León** is the largest cathedral in Central America and the modern anchor for the city. One (probably apocryphal) story claims the architect accidentally switched two sets of plans while on the ship from Spain, and the larger of the two cathedrals, originally intended for Lima, Peru, was built in Nicaragua. The cathedral was constructed in 1747 at the request of Archbishop Isidoro Bullón y Figueroa, and inaugurated in 1860 as a basilica by Pope Pius XI. It's an imposing and majestic baroque structure whose grandeur is magnified by the open space of the park in front of it. Late Gothic and neoclassic architecture is observable, primarily inside. Check out the paintings of the stations of the cross and the 12 apostles. The **Tomb of Rubén Darío** is a notable element of the cathedral—look for the golden statue of a lion. The cathedral is also home to the mortal remains of the musician José de la Cruz Mena and several religious figures. Look for the famous "Cristo de Pedrarias," a painting that once hung in the cathedral of León Viejo. A particularly beautiful part of the cathedral is found in the back, called the **Patio de los Príncipes,** a small courtyard of Andalusian design, with a fountain in the center and beds of flowers. Ask in the INTUR office about **rooftop tours.** The roof of the Catedral de León is fascinating in its own right—a conglomerate of white towers and domes and a stunning view of the city and nearby volcanoes.

North and East from the Central Park
Just north of the main cathedral (1.5 blocks) is **Iglesia de la Merced,** the church considered most representative of León in the 1700s. It was originally built in 1762 by the Mercedarian monks, the first order of monks to arrive in Nicaragua during the years of the conquest. It is essentially baroque in style but has neoclassical elements in the front, and colonial on the south, facing a small but lovely park popular amongst León's skate rats. Particularly attractive is the church's side bell tower.

Passing the Iglesia de la Merced and walking two blocks east along 2 Calle NE, you'll find the yellow **Iglesia de la Recolección** on the north side. This church has the most perfect baroque style of the León churches and a massive functional bell tower. It was built in 1786 by Bishop Juan Félix de Villegas and is the only church in León constructed using carved stone.

From the Iglesia de la Recolección, continue one more block and turn north. Walk two blocks until you reach the picturesque **Iglesia de San Juan.** The old train station is a block farther north

The National Guard killed López immediately, but he died a much-revered martyr to the cause of the revolution. This event is portrayed by the black-and-white tiled floor and pistol in the mural found in the **Park of Heroes and Martyrs,** a block north of the cathedral.

Murals

León is home to several noteworthy murals, most of them products of the 1980s. A block north of the cathedral is a long, horizontal work, painted with help from a German organization and telling the history of a proud and turbulent nation. Starting on the left with the arrival of the Nahuatl people, the mural traces the planned interoceanic canal, the exploits of William Walker, Sandino's battle with the U.S. Marines, the revolution of 1979, and the happy ending of a fertile, peaceful Nicaragua; flanking a doorway across the street, Sandino steps on Uncle Sam's and Somoza's heads.

One block to the west is another pointedly political mural: the CIA, in the form of a thick serpent, coils through the Sandinistas' agrarian reform, literacy campaign, and construction efforts, to strike at a Nicaraguan hand at the ballot box.

Museums

Nowhere else in Central America will you find such an eclectic assortment of museums than in León. Covering the political, natural, and all things cultural, we promise you'll be intrigued.

The **Museo Insurreccional Luís Manuel Toruño** is one man's personal contribution to

from the east side of the church. Built from 1625 to 1650 and rebuilt in the 1700s, the Iglesia de San Juan's architecture is a modern interpretation of neoclassicalism. This neighborhood of León will give you a good feel for what León was like in the 1700s: church, park, small houses of adobe and *taquezal,* and the nearby market.

Walking four blocks south down the same road, you'll find the **Iglesia del Calvario** on your left side. It is set at the top of broad steps on a small hill overlooking one of León's narrow streets. Renovated in the late 1990s, El Calvario was built 200 years previous in a generally baroque style, but with neoclassical ornamentation in the front that reflects the increasing French influence in Spain in the 18th century. Inside are two famous statues known as **El Buen y el Mal Ladrón** (the good and the bad thief).

South and West from the Central Park

La Iglesia y Convento de San Francisco, three blocks west of the park on the north side, and across the street from the Casa Museo Rubén Darío, is home to two of the most beautiful altars of colonial Nicaragua. The church was built in 1639 by Fray Pedro de Zuñiga and rebuilt and modified several times afterwards, notably in the mid-1980s to restore the damage done to it during the revolution. Its small, tree-lined courtyard is a pleasant place to escape from the hot sun and relax.

Turning and walking a block south you come to the unassuming **Iglesia de San Juan de Dios,** built in 1620 as a chapel for León's first hospital (now gone). Its simplicity and colonial style reflect the wishes of Felipe II when he designed it in 1573.

Two blocks farther south and one short block to the west is the **Iglesia del Laborío,** a graceful, rural-feeling church in the old mixed neighborhood of El Laborío. This church, one of León's earliest, formed the nucleus of the working-class neighborhood that provided labor to León's wealthy class in the 17th century. The street from Laborío east to the Ruínas de la Ermita de San Sebastián is known as **Calle la Españolita** and was one of the first streets built in León.

The **Ruínas de la Ermita de San Sebastián** consist of the shattered remnants of the outer walls, and inexplicably, the intact bell tower. The Ermita was built in 1742 on a site long used by the indigenous people for worship of their own gods. It suffered major damage in 1979 during Somoza's bombardment of León. El Museo de Tradiciones y Leyendas is across the street.

RUBÉN DARÍO (1867–1916)

Poet, journalist, diplomat, and favorite son of Nicaragua, Rubén Darío has become the icon for all that's artistic or cultural in Nicaragua. Born Félix Rubén Garcia Sarmiento in 1867 in the quiet agricultural town of San Pedro de Metapa (now Ciudad Darío), Darío hardly knew his parents and was raised instead by an aunt and uncle, Colonel Félix Ramírez Madregil and Bernarda Sarmiento, in the colonial city of León. Darío was a fast learner who was already able to read at the age of three. He studied in the Jesuit school Iglesia de la Recollección in León and began composing poetry at the age of 11. In 1882 he was sent to El Salvador by friends who wanted to dissuade him from marrying Rosario Murillo. There he met and was inspired by his new friend, the renowned poet Francisco Gavidia. In 1884 he returned to Nicaragua to work in the National Library of Managua.

Darío departed for Chile in 1886, where he worked as a journalist for the newspaper *La Nación*.

His epic poem about the glories of Chile won first prize in a contest sponsored by a Chilean millionaire. His breakthrough came with the publication of *Azul* in 1888, in which Darío introduced a profound change in the aesthetic conception of Spanish American literature. The stories in *Azul* revealed Darío's encounter with Prussian literature and exotic themes of a fantastic world: fauns, gnomes, fairies, nymphs, swans, azure lakes, and grand parks and castles. He was influenced by many, but his style was unique, playing off elements of the naturalism and symbolism movements of the era.

In 1893 he was named ambassador of Colombia to Argentina. He moved to Buenos Aires, a cosmopolitan city that suited him well. His friends there were the educated and elite, and he continued to publish his writings while the Latin American modernist literature movement began to organize under his influence.

In 1898 Darío resumed writing for *La Nación* in

the patrimony of Nicaragua. "El Chanclazo," as the owner and curator is locally known, has amassed an incredibly cluttered collection of Sandinista revolution memorabilia, and then some. Located in a former building of the Guardia Nacional on the southwest corner of the central park, the museum boasts a disorganized collection of black-and-white photographs of the war, books describing the Sandinistas' sensational literacy campaign, and mementos of Che Guevara, Ho Chi Minh, and Fidel Castro. More impressive than the toe-ringed Chanclazo himself is his collection of newspapers that encompasses every day the Sandinistas were in power; $1 contribution appreciated. The museum has no fixed schedule but is generally open daylight hours when El Chanclazo is making his living as a cobbler.

Inside a 200-year-old building across from the Parque Rubén Darío, the **Museo Alfonso Cortéz** houses many of the personal belongings of Nicaragua's beloved metaphysical poet, including some of his poems as originally written in the margins of newspapers. Generally open Monday–Friday 8 A.M.–5 P.M.; donations accepted.

Of Nicaragua's estimated 250,000 insect species, only 1 percent have been labeled or studied; that's still a lot of bugs. The **Museo Entomológico** is related to the UNAN and houses the best collection of national insect life in the country. The museum is generally not open to the public, but if you've got some kind of insect credentials, special visits can be arranged by calling tel. 311-6586, email: jmmaes@ibw.com.ni.

La Casa de Rubén Darío is a glimpse into León in the 19th century. Nicaragua's favorite son lived here with the aunt and uncle who raised him until the age of 14. Fellow poet Alfonso Cortéz later inhabited the same house at a time when he went insane (the room he inhabited still has the iron bars he bent in an effort to escape his confinement). Darío's bed and the rest of the furnishings of the museum are typical of middle-class León in the late 19th century, as is the building itself, built from adobe with a clay-tile and cane roof. On display are original copies of his most famous works translated into several languages, and copies of a magazine he published in Paris. The silver crucifix given him by Mexican poet Amado Nervos, correspondence from when

Europe. In 1910 he published what is largely considered to be his finest work: "Poema de Otoño." He was director and founder of the international publication, *Magazine,* while in France. In 1905 Darío published one of his best, and last, works: "Cantos de Vida y Desesperación," in which he introspectively re-embraces his Latin roots and examines themes of the passage of time, the suffering of a youth gone by, the pain of the loss of physical pleasure, the tiredness of life, man and his inevitable destiny, and the North American advance into Latin America during that period.

Shortly thereafter he became ambassador of Nicaragua to Spain in 1908. He remained in Europe until 1916, when, with his health failing, he returned to Nicaragua where he received a hero's welcome. Darío passed away in León on February 16th. One of his most quoted phrases is: *"Si la patria es pequeña, uno grande la sueña"* ("If one's nation is small, one makes it large through dreams").

Darío was the consul to Argentina and ambassador to Spain, and period coins and currency are also displayed; open Tuesday–Saturday 9 A.M.–noon and 2–5 P.M., Sunday 9 A.M.–noon; donations of $1–2 are accepted for the upkeep of the building.

A block north of La Casa de Rubén Darío is the **Museo de Arte Fundación Ortiz-Gurdián,** a museum said to have the best collection of international artwork in Nicaragua, with an emphasis on images of colonial America; open Monday–Friday 8:30 A.M.–5 P.M., Saturday 8:30 A.M.–noon.

El Museo de Tradiciones y Leyendas is the result of one strong-willed woman's wish to maintain Nicaragua's precious legends in the generations that followed her. Inside are figures she sewed herself, representing Nicaragua's favorite folk tales: the golden crab, La Carreta Nagua, the pig-witch, and La Mocuana (open Tues.–Sun. 8:30 A.M.–noon, 2–5:30 P.M., admission is $.50). Equally interesting is the building itself: the former **XXI jail** and base of the 12th Company of Somoza's National Guard. Built in 1921, the XXI saw nearly 60 years of brutal torture. The mango tree that now shades this museum was planted by a prisoner and watered from the same well that was used for electric shock and head-dunking sessions.

La Casa de Cultura is a must-see while in León. It is an old colonial home complete with swimming pool, and home to a collection of artwork that includes an inglorious painting of Ronald Reagan and Henry Kissinger. They serve light lunches and snacks here. Or try your hand at chess against León's local club (open Mon.–Fri. 8 A.M.–noon, 2–5 P.M. and the occasional Sat. and Sun., tel. 311-2116).

El Barrio Subtiava

Subtiava (Maribio for Land of the Big Men), though now a neighborhood of León, was once an indigenous settlement of its own, and to some degree, it still is. Subtiava retains its cultural identity and has a small local government, although it is presided over by the León municipality. Leoneses claim they can recognize who's from Subtiava by their facial features and skin tone, but to the casual traveler it may be impossible to tell the difference. There are several things of interest here, besides the thrill of walking through the streets of a village predating Columbus; notably, several ruins. Just about any of the microbuses that circulate through León will take you to Subtiava if you're not up for the 12-block walk.

La Catedral de Subtiava is second only to the Catedral de León in size and is the keystone of the community. Construction began in 1698 and finished 12 years later. The cathedral is beautiful in its aged simplicity and has many stories to tell. In one, the indigenous inhabitants of Subtiava were uninterested in the Spanish attempts to convert them to Christianity and kept worshiping their own gods. In an effort to at least get the locals into the church, the Spanish carved a wooden image of the sun, representing the local god, and mounted it on the ceiling of the church. This persuaded the locals to attend, but not to worship the god of the Spanish. It was a compromise that left everyone satisfied, even if during a church service the Spanish and the locals were simultaneously worshiping different gods. The sun is still there, beautifully crafted and mounted on the high interior ceiling of the cathedral. The cathedral's immense wooden columns bear testament to the kind of forest that surrounded León 300 years ago; think about that while you sweat. Next to the cathedral to the southwest is the Casa Cural, home to the local Catholic priest. The building predates the Cathedral of Subtiava by 160 years (though it was rebuilt in 1743).

Across the street from the cathedral on the north side is the **Museo Adiact,** a run-down but captivating museum that houses much of the area's archaeological treasures. Sadly, some of the better idols and statues were stolen in the late 1980s and sold to foreign museums (open Mon.–Fri. 8 A.M.–noon, 2–5 P.M., Sat. 8 A.M.–noon; pay a voluntary donation on your way in; $1 or $2 is appropriate).

Five blocks east of the southern side of the cathedral is a small park dedicated to the last cacique of Subtiava, Adiact, and his daughter Xochilt Acalt. From the Cathedral of Subtiava, three blocks south and two blocks west is **El Tamarindón,** an enormous tamarind tree where the Spanish hung Adiact from its branches. Now a small park has been made around the base of the old tree.

There are two sets of ruins in Subtiava, **Las Ruínas de Veracruz** and **Las Ruínas de Santiago.** Both are easily found and unguarded (i.e., no fee). The church at Veracruz was Subtiava's first, built sometime around 1560 and abandoned due to its small size in the late 1700s. The eruption of Volcán Cosigüina in 1835 caused its subsequent collapse. The church at Santiago, constructed in the early 1600s, is significant because its small square bell tower is still intact. Veracruz is located one block west of the cathedral, set in high weeds; Santiago is one block north of the cathedral on the other side of Calle Central (look for a small sign).

THE LEGEND OF ADIACT AND THE TAMARIND TREE

Several competing versions of this tale have been passed down over three centuries of Nicaraguan history. When Subtiava was still a rebellious Native American village and the Spanish were trying to subdue its inhabitants, victory appeared in the form of a young woman named Xochilt Acalt (Flower of the Sugar Cane). Her father was Adiact, the cacique of the Subtiava people and a ferocious warrior renowned for his victories in battle with the Spanish. But legend goes Xochilt fell in love with a young Spanish soldier. Some say the Spanish took advantage of the love affair to capture and hang Adiact; others say that when he learned of the illicit relationship he hung himself in shame. Xochilt Acalt disappeared from town, and legend has it she too committed suicide (though some say she banished herself to Poneloya, where another tribe took her in). Either way, everyone agrees that the 300-year-old tamarind tree that still stands proudly in the center of Subtiava is where Adiact was hanged. To modern Subtiavans the tree still represents the rebelliousness of the indigenous people and is a source of much community pride.

© TOMÁS STARGARDTER

sawdust paintings during Semana Santa in León

SPORTS AND RECREATION

León has earned more baseball championship documents than any other city in Nicaragua; catch a game during the season (January–May). Go swimming at the Hotel San Cristóbal pool (on the bypass highway) for the price of lunch and drinks (on the expensive side). Find the MetroSpa in Reparto Fatima and play some racquetball.

ENTERTAINMENT AND EVENTS

Cinemas, Bars, and Discos

León's cinema is in the **Plaza Siglo Nuevo** (from the cathedral, one block north, one block east). Look for the *cartelera* (schedule) at shops around the city for show times, or call tel. 311-7080; tickets cost $3.

Las Ruinas (Calle Central, one block west of the park) is a cavernous disco popular among the young crowd, tel. 311-4767. **Dilectus** is the fanciest and most expensive disco in town, with a fun crowd and well-mixed music; it's also an up-scale and attractive restaurant with occasional live music and karaoke. Thursday is mariachi night, Friday is teen night; entrance fee is $2, but budget in for a taxi ride home at the end of the night. Located south of the city center on

the highway, tel. 311-5439. Across from Parque La Merced, **Don Señor** is the favorite hangout of the college crowd and internationals. Saturdays is the best night for dancing.

Theater, Dance

Municipal Theater José de la Cruz Mena is the cultural heart of the city, open to the public 8 A.M.–12:30 P.M. and 1:30–5 P.M. The real action is at night, though; stop by to find out what's playing, as some big-name performers prefer a gig in León to Managua.

Special Events

In 2000 the Ministry of Tourism began Saturday evening presentations of dance and music called *tertulias* in the central park, but budget trouble has caused them to be irregular. Ask the INTUR office in León about events during the time you plan to be in town.

June 1st is the celebration of Somoza's defeat in León and August 14th is La Gritería Chiquita, when devout Catholics celebrate being spared from Cerro Negro's frequent eruptions. León celebrates its *fiestas patronales* on September 24th and the weeks surrounding it.

León's Semana Santa celebrations are acclaimed throughout Nicaragua as the nation's most lively.

In addition to tons of food and drink (and the best *nacatamales* in the country), beds of sawdust are laid out in the streets and ornately painted to show brightly colored religious scenes; when the festivities end, they are swept away. Semana Santa is a week of Catholic masses, parties, and lots of trips to the beach (see the section below on Poneloya).

ACCOMMODATIONS

Under $10

Vía Vía, León's newcomer hostel, is the most centrally located backpacker option, located from the Servicio Agrícola Gurdián, 75 meters south. Dorm beds go for $3.50, hammocks and mattresses a bit less, and two private rooms for $10 a couple, tel. 311-6142.

Casa Ivana has clean, quiet, safe rooms with private bath along a long garden in a family house. Conveniently close to the city center, $3.50 per person. A nearby lot offers overnight parking for your vehicle. Located across from the south side of the municipal theater, tel. 311-4423. **Hotel Avenida** is one of the cheapest sleeps in town and popular among backpackers, but it's not in the best area and not the cleanest facility either; 25 rooms available starting at $4 per person; simple breakfasts are available for $1; one block north of the old train station, tel. 311-2068.

Hotelito Calle Real has spartan rooms on the second floor of an old colonial home starting at $5.50 per couple, shared bath; a good place to meet other backpackers. Located from the cathedral, two blocks east and a half-block north, tel. 311-1120. **Hotelito California** has eight small rooms at $4 each. Guests are given cooking privileges in a shared kitchen. Cramped and hot, this is a good place to stay if you're on a severe budget and want to catch the first bus out of town in the morning; located directly across from the south side of the bus station, tel. 311-5074.

Just a few blocks away from the old train station, the **Casona Colonial Guesthouse** is a charming colonial home on a quiet street, complete with high ceilings, flower-filled courtyard,

and beautiful wooden furniture; rooms start at $7.50 with a private bath, hot water, and a fan. They give you a key so you can come and go at any hour, and there's a TV in the courtyard. Breakfast available for $2, or try the *cafetín* next door. There's Internet across the street for $2 per hour. Located from the park next to La Iglesia de San Juan one block west, tel. 311-3178.

Hotel America is an old hotel whose black-and-white tiled floors date back to the days of Somoza. Large and airy, nine rooms with private bath and a fan start at $8.50 a person. Breakfast is available for around $2.50 or try the bakery across the street for cheap fresh pastries; located one block east of the market, tel. 311-5533.

$10–25

Grand Hotel is not nearly as regal as its name implies, but it is clean, safe, and located on a bustling market street; rooms have TV and private bath and start at $18 s ($25 d without a/c or $28 s, $34 d with a/c); from the southwest side of the bus terminal, half-block south, tel. 311-1327.

$25–50

Hotel Colonial is a gorgeous building; 10 rooms with private bath, hot water, and TV start at $35. Breakfast available (not included); located 75 meters north of the Paraninfo de la Universidad, tel. 311-2279. **Hotel Europa,** on the northern side of town, has been around since the 1960s when it catered to the train crowd. Recently remodeled, it is clean, modern and has over 30 rooms, which start at $20 a room without a/c, $32 with TV, hot water, and a/c. It has restaurant and lounge areas and guarded parking for your vehicle; located one block south of the old train station, tel. 311-0016 or 311-6040.

Hotel Austria is probably the best bang for your buck in León: 17 clean, modern rooms with a/c, TV, and hot water. Prices start at $34 s, $48 d. Free guarded parking for your vehicle. A full breakfast menu is available mornings, but is not included. Located from the cathedral, one block south and a half-block west, tel. 311-1206 or 311-7178, email: haustria@ibw.com.ni, website: www.hotelaustria.com.ni.

FOOD

León is certainly not known for exotic or elegant cuisine. What you'll find here caters to a largely student crowd—i.e., burgers, pizza, Chinese, and plenty of traditional chicken, steak, and seafood dishes. For finer dining, try any of the nicer hotels listed above.

Comida Típica

A great Nicaraguan breakfast in a picturesque setting is found in the **Hotel Colonial** for about $2.50. **Restaurante Taquezal** is located across from the theater and serves the after-theater crowd in a pleasant atmosphere and with a varied menu; typical dishes cost $5–9; try the "Nicaccino": cappuccino with a shot of Nicaraguan rum. **Jala la Jarra** is located by the Teatro Municipal and has good Mexican fare.

Rinconcito Flor de Sacuanjoche has an excellent vegetarian menu, including salads, veggie burgers, and soy-based sausage and chicken, in addition to the standard beef and chicken dishes. They also do a good business in liquor; meals run $3–4.

Cafés

Right in front of the cathedral, **El Sesteo** is a trendy corner shop and the international crowd's favorite place to sip coffee and fresh juice drinks. **Puerto Café Benjamin Linder** has a traditional menu plus fresh cappuccino (not a common item in Nicaragua). The profits help support a local group of disabled children. The coffee shop is named after the only U.S. citizen killed in the Contra war (see Matagalpa and Jinotega chapter); a beautiful indoor mural depicts his life in Nicaragua.

Simple Dishes, Chinese, Gringo Food

Payita's offers burgers, hot dogs, or *comida corriente* from $2 and up; a pleasant corner outdoor café. The specialty at **Café Oasis** is hot soup, served Nica style at a reasonable price (five blocks north of the cathedral). **La Buena Cuchara** (two blocks south of the cathedral) is a small place offering a buffet lunch or dinner of typical food, sandwiches, hot dogs, and ice cream (Mon.–Fri. 10 A.M.–8 P.M., Sun. 10 A.M.–3 P.M.,

closed Saturdays). There's a smorgasbord of pizza, tacos, chicken, shish kebabs, and snacks in the **Plaza Siglo Nuevo** (from the cathedral, one block north, one block east).

Chinese food with a Nicaraguan twist plus traditional Nicaraguan dishes are found at **La Chinita.** Get your pizza fix at any number of options, including **Hollywood Pizza, Restaurante Italian Pizza**, and **Pizza Roma.**

SHOPPING

The market east of the cathedral is León's central clearinghouse for fruits and vegetables, but you won't find much in the way of *artesanía*. It's a good place to escape the sun, drink a bag of fruit juice, and chat up the locals. Being a university town, León has many interesting bookstores; the best is **Librería Don Quijote** (two blocks west of the park) with an interesting selection of new and used books including many old Sandinista titles (open Mon.–Fri. 8 A.M.–7 P.M., Sat. until 5 P.M., Sun. until noon). **La Galería,** 1.5 blocks west of the central park, calls itself a "Bazaar de Artesanía," and sells various types of art.

SERVICES

Banks

The most convenient option is Bancentro, a block north of the cathedral, open Monday–Friday 8 A.M.–4:30 P.M., Saturday 8 A.M.–noon.

Mail and Phones

The Correos is located three blocks north of the back side of the main cathedral (open Mon.–Fri. 8 A.M.–5 P.M., Sat. 8 A.M.–noon). It has fax service as well. Agencia de Viajes Premier is the authorized UPS agent in León, located across from the Rubén Darío park, tel. 311-5535. ENITEL is located on the west side of the central park; open daily 8 A.M.–9 P.M.

Internet

The place next to the park may be the most obvious email joint, but León has at least another four options. None are worth writing home about and nobody charges more than $2 per hour: M&M Internet (four blocks north of the cathedral on the right) is notable for its longer hours (Mon.–Fri. 8:30 A.M.–7 P.M., Sat. until 1:30 P.M.); La Oficina (two blocks north of the cathedral) is only open until 5 P.M., noon on Saturday; Espacio 3D (two blocks north, 1.5 west of the cathedral) is open until 6 P.M., Sat. until 4 P.M. Also, directly next door to restaurant Rinconcito Flor de Sacuanjoche is a small place, open 8 A.M.–5:30 P.M.

Travel Agents and Tickets

Viajes Mundiales (from the cathedral, three blocks north, half block east) can service your plane ticket and take passport photos; open Monday–Friday 8 A.M.–12:30 P.M., 2–5:30 P.M., Saturday until 12:30 P.M., tel. 311-6263 or 311-5920. Careli Viajes, in addition to organized tours and other travel services, is an authorized TransNica agency (bus service to Costa Rica); open Monday–Friday 8 A.M.–12:30 P.M., 2:30–6 P.M., Saturday until 12:30 P.M., tel. 311-2192. Agencia de Viajes Premier, in the north part of town by the Iglesia San Juan, is the authorized agent for La Costeña airline tickets, to plan your flight to the Atlantic coast, tel. 311-5535.

Organized Tours

Most of Nicaragua's tour operators (listed in the On the Road chapter) offer varying guided tours of the city, local farms, and the ruins of León Viejo. Contact each company for more details.

Opportunities to Study

If you're going to be in León for more than a brief visit, taking a course is a profitable way to get to know this city. The Casa de Cultura offers classes in guitar, pastry-cooking, drawing and painting, karate, and dance (folk and modern), tel. 311-2116. At Modas Carolina (two blocks east of the cathedral), Marlene Sánchez gives sewing and clothes-making classes; two hours per day, mornings, afternoons, or Saturdays, tel. 311-1462.

GETTING THERE AND AWAY

The bus terminal in the northeast corner of town is where all intercity transport is found, with the exception of buses to Poneloya, which depart from their own terminal on the west side of town. Buses depart regularly for Managua, Chinandega, and points along the Telica–San Isidro highway. There are also four express buses to Estelí, which leave daily at 6 A.M., 10 A.M., 2 P.M., and 3:30 P.M.

Hitchhiking to Managua is best accomplished at the StarMart parking lot at the *salida*. There you can corner drivers stopping to fill up on gas and hot dogs. Across the intersection is the road north to Chinandega and the border, but if you want to go east to Estelí or Matagalpa, you'll have to make it a couple kilometers north to the *empalme* just north of Telica, and strike out toward San Isidro.

Near León

LAS RUÍNAS DE LEÓN VIEJO

The ruins of Spain's first settlement in Nicaragua, found in Puerto Momotombo, make an easy and worthwhile day trip out of León. The ruins remain only partially excavated and restored, while grassy lumps around the excavations tell of still-unfound treasures. The settlement was founded in 1524 by Francisco Hernández de Córdoba; its first governor was Pedrarias Dávila, who had Hernández de Córdoba decapitated in the town square two years later. In 1610, Volcán Momotombo erupted, burying the site under ash. However, it is thought that by that time, León had already been abandoned, after a series of earthquakes convinced the settlers to look elsewhere for a place to call home. (Momotombo has erupted several times since then, most recently in 1905.) The ruins were first uncovered in 1966 by Dr. Carlos Tùnnerman and a team from the National University (UNAN). León Viejo was later declared a World Heritage Site and made international headlines in 2000 when the remains of both Córdoba and Dávila were discovered there and placed in an on-site mausoleum.

The site is open seven days a week with tour guides from 8 A.M.–5 P.M., entrance is $1. Buses leave several times a day from León and La Paz Centro. Also worth a visit is the old mansion of President Zelaya. From the center of town, walk to the lakeshore and head to the left about two blocks; get there soon, before it collapses entirely.

VOLCÁN MOMOTOMBO AND MOMOTOMBITO ISLAND

Volcán Momotombo is the most challenging Pacific volcano to climb (see Hiking the Maribio Volcanoes special topic). Its little brother, the

the ruins of León Viejo

island of Momotombito, is additionally an excellent adventure in the waiting. This long-extinct volcano was home to a religious sanctuary in the days before Columbus, when the islet was called Cocobolo. It is uninhabited today and considered a natural reserve of tropical dry forest, but getting there isn't easy. Your best bet is to pay someone with a small boat in the town of Puerto Momotombo to row you the 25 kilometers along the north shore of Lake Managua to the island (better yet—take turns and work off some of that *gallo pinto*). While the small town of El Cardón, on the other side of Volcán Momotombo, is closer, the town itself is difficult to get to from the highway. Should you decide to camp on the island, bring your own water and supplies to last you at least two days, and don't pay your boatman until he returns to take you off the island.

LOS HERVIDEROS DE SAN JACINTO

On the southeast flank of 1,060-meter Volcán Telica, **Los Hervideros de San Jacinto** are a collection of boiling mud-pits and thermal vents fueled by the underground geothermal activity. They make a great day trip from León. To get there, take a bus bound for Estelí, San Isidro, or Malpaisillo and get off at the town of San Jacinto (approximately 26 km from León). The entrance is marked by an enormous arch and a posse of women and children selling "artifacts" from the hot springs. The young boys will offer to guide you around for $.20, a good deal considering the danger of falling into a scalding mud bath.

NAGAROTE

About halfway between Managua and León, the historic village of Nagarote (Chorutega for the road of the Nagarands) is representative of the small agricultural and cattle villages of Nicaragua. Its claim to fame is an enormous old *genícero* tree said to date back to the time of Columbus, under whose branches the native markets were held. The *genícero* and a statue of Diriangén are found two blocks north and one block west from the central park. A Casa de Cultura is located

one block south of the tree. Nagarote is also renowned for its *quesillos,* a snack of mozzarella-like string cheese, sour cream, and onions, wrapped in a hot tortilla.

Nagarote also makes a good jumping-off point for some interesting hikes through the Cordillera del Pacífico, the range of mountains that runs alongside the highway to León. Walk southeast out of town and pass the Colonía Agrícola Presidente Schick. The road will take you up into a relatively wooded and uninhabited area of pretty mountain valleys, and eventually to a good view of the lake. From there, start your descent to the highway and catch a bus to León or Managua. Use INETER quad maps Nagarote and Mateare.

LA PAZ CENTRO

The small town of La Paz Centro is a pueblo of artisans who regularly turn out handicrafts based on the locally found clay (they also turn out great *quesillos* to rival their neighbors). *Fiestas patronales* are September 10th (San Nicolás de Tolentino). Near the center of town is a small Casa de Cultura that sells local artwork.

EL SAUCE

In the foothills of the Segovia Mountains, to the north and east of León, El Sauce (rhymes with wow-say) was once the eastern terminus of the railroad that carried Nicaraguan coffee down to Corinto. In the 1800s caravans of mules lumbered into town, laden with thousands of pounds of coffee beans. El Sauce has since faded into a sleepy cowboy village. Its pride is a breathtaking colonial church built in 1750 in tribute to the patron saint, el Cristo Negro de Esquipulas **(the Black Christ).** Its *fiestas patronales* are celebrated January 18th and are marked by a massive pilgrimage from all over Nicaragua to view the Black Christ icon. El Sauce made news in 2001 when the incumbent mayor lost the municipal elections... to his wife.

Sauce is off the beaten track and makes a good first stop on forays into the wilds of Achuapa, San Juan de Limay, and Estelí. There are a couple

THE SAUCE–CORINTO RAILROAD LINE

Perhaps the fame of El Sauce's Cristo Negro is due in part to access provided the town by the Sauce–León–Corinto branch of the Nicaragua National Railroad, which carried cattle, coffee, and passengers between 1932 and 1993. The Sauce branch was one of five that split off the principal line, which ran from Corinto to Momotombo, then shipped freight across the lake to the Managua–Granada line. The other branches were Chinandega–Puerto Morazón, Masaya–Jinotepe, Rivas, and San Carlos–Granada.

Sauce's economy boomed when the line was completed, as did that of the Segovia mountains, which used the train as an exclusive channel for its goods. Imagine thousands of mules parading into town, weighed down under sacks of coffee beans; or easy-riding vaqueros pushing gigantic herds of beef down the wide, green valleys. Most of the cattle carted to Corinto was shipped to Peru.

The railroad grew another 13 kilometers to Río Grande, en route to Estelí, but never made it farther. When the United States constructed the Pan-American Highway after World War II, the El Sauce line (and the rest of the railroad) was doomed to lose a race with the new system of highways and trucks.

El Sauce resident Noel Montenegro sold tickets at the depot down the block from his current home for 34 years. He blames the railroad's failure on bad management in addition to the new highways, especially during the 1980s when the railroad operation turned chaotic under heavy Sandinista subsidization.

"When they took the railroad away," Señor Montenegro said, "the town felt it. The rails were sent to Venezuela and El Salvador, and the cars were chopped up for scrap wood. There was a great sadness and the people suddenly felt isolated and depressed. They felt it." He tried recently to seek support for a small, local museum honoring the railroad, but found none. Some of his photographs from the railroad age are on display in the library.

Other reminders of this part of El Sauce's heritage are found by walking two blocks south of the Alcaldía and two blocks east. You'll be standing on the old grade and looking at the ruins of the offices which are now roofless, crumbling shelters for poor squatters. The former station is currently occupied by the firefighters, and the green building with the columns was the post office, now a private home.

---

places to eat, and several *hospedajes*: try Hotel El Viajero, $3 per night, tel. 319-2325.

BEACHES: PONELOYA AND LAS PEÑITAS

Only a 20-minute drive from León, **Poneloya** is the most popular beach in the area, and has been a playground of the wealthy for generations. Good food, good beds, and good surf. Nearby, **Las Peñitas** beach is less visited and more pristine. This is also your base camp for the Wildlife Reserve of Isla Juan Venado (below). Hotels in Poneloya fill up fast prior to Semana Santa so be sure to make reservations at least a month in advance.

Accommodations and Food

Cheap rooms on the second floor of the old wooden structure of **Hotel Lacayo** may remind you of a barn loft, but the sea breeze is refreshing; $3.50 per person, shared bath. **Hotel La Posada** has 19 simple rooms with private bath in a motel-like configuration, $20 with a/c or fan (sleeps up to three), tel. 317-377 or 317-378. **Hotel Suyapa Beach** in Las Peñitas is a modern hotel/restaurant that does a good trade in hosting conferences. Rooms with a/c and private bath start at $29, tel. 885-8345.

There's no lack of seafood in Poneloya, including fresh lobster for under $10. Restaurants abound, but of note is the **Restaurante Mediterraneo,** a charming Italian place in Las Peñitas, about a 20-minute walk from Poneloya. The owner, Marcello, imports many ingredients from Italy, and the prices are reasonable, starting at $6 for a plate of spaghetti and meat sauce, tel. 881-0631 or 779-4312.

Getting There

Buses for Poneloya leave every half-hour from the Mercado Félix Pedro Carrillo (in Subtiava), until 6 P.M. They stop first in Las Peñitas. If you have your own vehicle, you'll pay $1 to enter the town.

ISLA JUAN VENADO NATURE RESERVE

The tropical dry forest, mangroves, and inland estuary south of Las Peñitas make up the habitat of many migratory birds and wetland creatures, and are also an important nesting beach for sea turtles. The park is named for a man who, in colonial times, made his living hunting deer on the island and selling the meat in the market of Subtiava.

To get there, visit the **COMANEJO** office in Las Peñitas to meet the park rangers and get information. They'll help you strike a deal with one of the many boatmen in Las Peñitas to explore the endless riverine channels. Marcello at the Mediterraneo can arrange a picnic lunch and tour of the reserve for around $18 a person. The earlier you can get into the reserve the better chance you'll have of seeing wildlife, especially elusive bird species. Take sun protection and lots of water. Consider making a deal with your guide the previous evening to strike out by 5 A.M. You won't regret the couple hours of lost sleep.

EL VELERO

El Velero (the Sailboat) consists mostly of the summer homes of wealthy Leoneses along a gorgeous two-kilometer stretch of white-sand beach. There is lodging for travelers, but it's not cheap. Buses for Puerto Sandino and El Velero leave from the station at León.

Upon entering the hamlet, look for the administration office, where you can rent one of a half-dozen state-run cabins. Prices run from $25 a night for bunk beds and a fan, to $50 for an air-conditioned cabin with two double beds. To make it worth your while, bring several friends and a cooler full of food, as each cabin contains a fridge and gas stove. Or if you are traveling in a group, consider camping on the shoreline. The few restaurants that exist in El Velero are sketchy and not always open.

A little-used road, about 10 km long, runs down the coast to El Transito and can be hiked in a few hours. Consider this option if you've got time and want to end up catching a bus to Managua.

EL TRANSITO

El Transito is a quiet fishing community 60 kilometers from Managua along the old highway to León. Nearly devastated during the tidal wave of 1991, the town was rebuilt shortly afterward with extensive help from the Spanish; you can see the new town on the hills above the old one, which was at the shoreline.

There are no lodging facilities at El Transito, though pitching a tent on the beach is an attractive possibility. **El Ranchón** is a decent *pulpería* that will supply you with some foodstuffs, but consider purchasing a freshly caught red snapper at El Acopio, the fishermen's warehouse, and

volcanic rock formations on the beach at El Transito

roasting it over the coals of your campfire. If you'd rather have it served to you, **Primavera** is a basic restaurant with cheap, cold beer and fresh fish.

The swimming here can be a bit tricky, as there's a strong undertow that will pull you north along the cove. A safer bet is walking south along the shoreline to see the rock formations and popular swimming holes behind them. These rocks are parallel to the coast like a buttress, and take the full blow of waves as they come in from the sea. If you're swimming in one of the several pools there, you can count on an occasional salt-water shower, often with no warning at all. Ten minutes' walk north along the shoreline takes you to the wreckage of El Balneario, an old vacation spot in the Somoza years that has long since been abandoned to the elements.

Buses leave Managua every afternoon from Israel Lewites at 11:15 A.M., 12:40 P.M., and 2 P.M. Buses leave El Transito every day at 5 A.M., 6 A.M., and 7 A.M. A microbus leaves every afternoon at 3 P.M. If you've hiked here from El Velero, consider spending the night under the stars and catching an early bus to Managua.

Chinandega

Besides the full-grown alligators in the central park, there are not many tourist attractions per se in the city of Chinandega. Nevertheless, this regional capital makes a perfect base camp for volcano and beach expeditions, and provides a chance to see Nicaraguans coping with the hottest, driest part of their country.

The same threatening volcanoes looming over the city of Chinandega and its surrounding plains are also responsible for the high fertility of the soil. This attracted the first humans migrating through the area, the Nahuatl, who called their new home Chinamilt, (close to cane).

Poverty is rampant here, as it is in all of Nicaragua, but Chinandega also boasts a prosperous community of old and new money, based primarily in sugar, bananas, peanuts, sesame, soy, and shrimp. Cotton used to be the number one cash crop, especially during the Somoza dynasty, but the deforestation and agro-chemicals associated with its production had disastrous environmental effects still being felt today. The agriculture activity of the region and proximity to the northern borders and Port of Corinto make Chinandega Nicaragua's most important agribusiness center.

Did we mention that it's hot in Chinandega? It's so hot in Chinandega, that even when it's not hot, it's still bloody hot. You'd be wise to drink at least a liter of water on the ride up, because you'll sweat it all out before you can walk to the park to see the alligators.

ORIENTATION AND GETTING AROUND

Chinandega consists of two basic hubs of activity: the area surrounding the **Mercado Bisne** (from the English "business"), and the town center, or simply, *el centro*. The **Mercadito** is located two blocks north of the central park, and the Central Market a few blocks east of the park, along the Calle Central. La Rotonda los Encuentros and the Texaco StarMart are both important reference points you'll pass on your way into town. Everything is walkable, but *ay caramba* is it hot! Taxis are plentiful and cost $.40 within city limits; *ruta* buses are $.10.

SIGHTS AND RECREATION

To explore central Chinandega by foot, you may as well begin with the alligators and turtles in the park. They are impressive beasts, for sure, but their captivity is utterly depressing (unless of course, you're into the whole Developing World zoo thing). Pick your spirits up with a self-guided tour of Chinandega's colonial churches and central market, and then find an air-conditioned spot to eat some ice cream.

If you really enjoy sweating, join in a pickup basketball game at the courts by the park. If watching baseball is more your style, catch Team Chinandega in season (the stadium is located west across the river, on the road to El Viejo). You'll find a clean

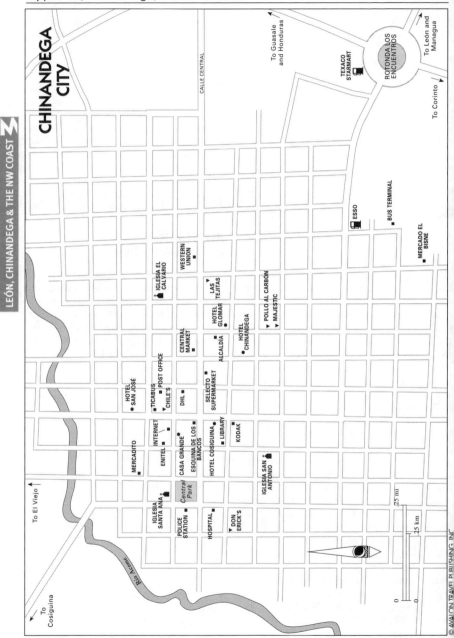

CHINANDEGA CITY

To El Viejo

To Cosigüina

Río Acome

To Guasale
and Honduras

To León and
Managua

To Corinto

ROTONDA LOS
ENCUENTROS

TEXACO
STARMART

CALLE CENTRAL

IGLESIA EL
CALVARIO

WESTERN
UNION

LAS
TEJITAS

HOTEL
GLOMAR

POLLO AL CARBÓN
MAJESTIC

HOTEL
CHINANDEGA

CENTRAL
MARKET

ALCALDÍA

ESSO

BUS TERMINAL

MERCADO EL
BISNE

HOTEL
SAN JOSÉ

TICABUS
POST OFFICE
CHILE'S

DHL

SELECTO
SUPERMARKET

MERCADITO

INTERNET

ENITEL

CASA GRANDE
ESQUINA DE LOS
BANCOS

HOTEL COSIGÜINA
LIBRARY

KODAK

IGLESIA SAN
ANTONIO

IGLESIA
SANTA ANA

Central
Park

POLICE
STATION

HOSPITAL

DON
ERICK'S

0   .25 mi

0   .25 km

© AVALON TRAVEL PUBLISHING, INC.

public swimming pool at the Instituto San Luis on the east end of town; complete with high dive, cheap beer, and a hot dog and burger stand (open Fri.–Sun., $1.50 for the whole day).

Deep pockets can splurge on a trip aboard the 43-foot luxury yacht, *Cosigüina II;* choose from one-day and sunset cruises to multiday fishing and snorkeling trips, tel. 341-3636, prices begin at $200.

There are also plenty of waves to surf up and down the entire coast, and zero surfers. This means equipment and logistics are in your own hands.

ENTERTAINMENT AND EVENTS

For a classy dancing experience, the **Dilectus** disco is at the top of the heap, located just east of town on the road to León. If you prefer a looser, younger crowd and still want air-conditioning, try **Montserat** on the highway to Guasale. Your next step down is an outdoor rancho-style disco called **El Bosque,** also located on the highway north, or give your feet a break and drink $2 pitchers of Victoria in the outdoor **central park kiosk.** **Casino Imperial,** next door to Hotel Cosigüina, offers a packed room of slots and blackjack.

ACCOMMODATIONS
Under $10
Hotel Chinandega, at less than $4 a night, is the best dump in town. Centrally located, 15 rooms, relatively clean, and only slightly depressing and dingy.

$10–25
Hotel Glomar, tel. 341-2562, across from the *alcaldía,* has 13 rooms, $10 for a simple single with a fan and shared bath, $13 d. Private bath and a/c cost $17 s, $22 d. Similar accommodations in the **Casa Grande,** 8 rooms, $15 with fan, s or d; $25 with TV and a/c, tel. 341-0325.

$25–50
The **Hotel San José** has beautifully decorated rooms (private bath, TV, a/c) in a spacious, converted home; $25 s, $35 d, $45, tel. 341-2723.

Hostal Las Mañanitas is near the Texaco station on Carretera Managua–Chinandega; rooms with private bath and a/c starting at $40 a night. It's more bed-and-breakfast than "Hostal" though. Internet connection available for guests, tel. 341-0522.

$50 and Above
The plushest digs in the city center are at **Hotel Cosigüina,** with 24 fiercely air-conditioned rooms; $46 s, $52 d, $58 t; also has Avis car rental, Internet, hot water, bar, restaurant, phones in rooms, and a tourist information desk. Located half a block south of *esquina de los bancos;* (bank corner) *tel.* 341-1663, email: hotelcosiguina@tec.com.ni, website: www.tec .com.ni/~hotelcosiguina.

Hotel Los Volcanes, on the highway to León km 129, has 46 rooms, priced from $46 to $100; a/c, TV, phones, room service, hot water, and Internet, tel. 341-1000, email: hotellosvolcanes@tec.com.ni.

FOOD

There is no shortage of options here, from the *comida corriente* in any of the markets (meals for less than $2), to a host of expensive restaurants. Located on the Calle Central, seven blocks east of the park, **Las Tejitas** may be the best *fritanga* in Nicaragua; so say the stream of regular clients, including several generations of locally placed Peace Corps volunteers. Sit outside on the sidewalk and enjoy a heaping plate of juicy roasted chicken, *gallo pinto, tajadas,* and any number of deep-fried delicacies, all for under $3, drink included; open evenings.

For just a couple cordobas more, eat in the air-conditioned comfort of **Don Erick's** buffet and bar, three blocks west of the Kodak, with fantastic food and service. Also reasonably priced is **Chile's Mexican Food,** two blocks north of the *esquina de los bancos.* If you are starving when you get off the bus at Bisne Market, walk three blocks west from the Esso station, then north to find the **Majestic "Bar y Snacks"** (a/c and excellent service, meals $4–10). It is next door to **Pollo al Carbón,** slightly cheaper. Hotel

Cosiguina has a quaint *rancho* in the back called **El Crater,** with meals from $8.

Many fancier restaurants abound along the highways in and out of town, and gringo fare is plentiful, including a Jerry's Subs and Pizza in the StarMart.

SHOPPING

The three markets (Bisne, Central, and the Mercadito) are dark and deep and are all surrounded by several square blocks of additional retail action—whip out some moist cordobas and go nuts. The Kodak store has an impressive stock of photo and computer supplies (and extreme air-conditioning), two blocks east and one south of the central park. Chinandega has two fully stocked supermarkets: El Palí in front of the park, and El Selecto, 3.5 blocks farther east.

INFORMATION AND SERVICES

INTUR maintains an office in the Hotel Cosigüina lobby that caters primarily to big spenders, and INETER sells detailed area maps and topo maps out of its office west of town, across the river.

The police take up the entire block along the west side of the central park, and the hospital is right across the street to the south. Money changers work the streets near the central market, and most of Chinandega's banks are clustered on *la esquina de los bancos,* two blocks east of the park.

The post office is three blocks east of the park, and 1.5 north. It is near the DHL Worldwide Express. Also, the TicaBus agent will send FedEx packages via their Managua office. ENITEL is one block east of the park and easy to find with its giant red and white tower.

Internet

Chinandega has at least four options, for about $2–3 an hour. The Hotel Cosiguira and Kiosko AEB, across from the Mercadito, charge $2, but only have a handful of computers each. There are two more Internet places along the Calle Central between the park and main market.

TEC, 1.5 blocks east of the *esquina de los bancos,* has the most computers.

Consulates

El Salvador, two blocks north of *la esquina de los bancos,* tel. 341-2049 (open Mon.–Fri. 8 A.M.–2 P.M.; when applying for a visa, leave your passport before 11 A.M.). Honduras, across from ENITEL, tel. 341-0949 (open Mon.–Fri. 8:30 A.M.–4:30 P.M.). Costa Rica, BANPRO half a block north, tel. 341-1584 (Mon.–Fri., 8:30 A.M.–5 P.M., Sat. until noon).

GETTING THERE AND AWAY

The main bus station is at Bisne Market, just past Rotonda los Encuentros. From La Rotonda, highways run north to Somotillo and the border with Honduras at Guasale (this is easily the most deteriorated stretch of the entire Nicaraguan highway system, a real bone-crusher), east to León and Managua, south to Corinto, and west into Chinandega. A second bus station located at the Mercadito (just north of the central park) provides service to El Viejo, Jiquilillo, Potosi, Cosigüina, and Puerto Morazán.

Car rentals starting at $35 a day are available at the Avis office in the Hotel Cosigüina and Budget in Hostal Las Mañanitas. Local buses, expresses ($1.85), and microbuses ($2.20) run regularly between Chinandega and Managua's Israel (Boer) Market, beginning at 4:30 A.M. and ending around 8 P.M. Service to and from León is even more frequent and hitching in any direction from La Rotonda is a cinch.

Those traveling north into Honduras or El Salvador can buy tickets in the TicaBus office. Prices are the same as from Managua, and you'll need to be in front of the StarMart no later than 6 A.M. to catch your ride, although "sometimes the bus comes later." The first TicaBus that passes (en route from Managua) will take you to Tegucigalpa and the second to San Salvador and Guatemala. Be advised: any foreigner who enters El Salvador must be carrying a visa, which can be purchased at the Salvadoran Consulate (across the street from TicaBus) for $30.

El Guasaule

Located about 1.5 hours north of Chinandega on the Pan-American Highway, El Guasaule is the principal Pacific side border crossing with Honduras. It is six kilometers from the town of Somotillo, where you'll find a large number of trucker and traveler services. At the actual border, there is a Bancentro branch and some basic food services. The migration office at Guasaule can be reached at tel. 346-2208.

Hours and Fees

El Guasaule is open every day 6 A.M.–10 P.M. It costs $2 to leave Nicaragua and $7 to enter the country. Just a passport and some cash is all that's required of North American and European travelers, with the notable exception of El Salvador— United States citizens must purchase a visa for $30 (available at the consulate in Chinandega), even if you are only passing through the tiny country on your way to Guatemala.

Crossing the Border with Your Vehicle

If you are driving your own vehicle, the process to enter Nicaragua is lengthy, but usually not difficult. You must present the vehicle's title, as well as your own driver's license and passport. You will be given a temporary (30-day) permit to drive in Nicaragua which will cost you $10—should you lose the permit, you will be fined $100.

Getting There and Away

There are numerous and regular buses traveling between the Bisne Terminal and El Guasaule, and the main international bus lines (TicaBus, etc.) heading to Honduras and El Salvador pass through Chinandega on their way to the border.

Near Chinandega

EL VIEJO

Only a few kilometers west of Chinandega, El Viejo is a cheerful farming town of some 35,000 El Viejanos, as they like to be called. Less service-oriented than its big neighbor, El Viejo still has enough basics to launch you on your next adventure.

El Viejo is much older than Chinandega. Originally an indigenous community called Texoatega, for the fierce cacique who once ruled it, the town was renamed for the old Spaniard who arrived in 1562 carrying a sacred image of the Virgin Mary. According to legend, when he tried to sail back to Spain, the Virgin created a hurricane so that she would be returned to her new home in Nicaragua. The old man complied, and she soon became the most important Virgin Mary in the country. Her fame lasted through the centuries, and in 1996 she was recognized by the pope himself, who came to declare El Viejo's church a Basilica Minor. The church is beautiful and worth your time.

Buses arrive half a block north of the basilica, across the street from the market where you'll find the cheapest eats. Buses back to Chinandega (called *interlocales*) leave from behind the basilica and run until about 11 P.M.

Entertainment

Nightlife in El Viejo is exciting and sometimes downright rowdy. Local volunteers say it's all "beer and bark" though, and everyone makes up and shakes hands the next day. Just south of the basilica is **Texoatega,** a nightclub whose fame spreads as far as León. Clean, good food and service, with a huge variety of music (check out mariachi night on Thursdays). **Los Coquitos,** on the same block, is home to boxing matches and super cheap pitchers of beer.

La Piscina, two blocks north of the basilica and half a block east, has great meals and appetizers, dancing Thursday–Saturday, and yes, a *piscina* (swimming pool), which is reportedly drained and cleaned once a week and costs $.75 to use all day. Half a block west of the *portón del instituto* (doorway of the institute) you'll find **Hemingway's Centro Recreativo y Cafetín,**

THE TRAGEDY OF VOLCÁN CASITAS

On October 30, 1998, the quiet municipality of Posoltega (whose Nahuatl name, Posoli-tecatl, means, roughly, "neighbor of the boiling place") was catapulted into a horrendous sort of fame as the site of one of the worst naturally caused disasters in Nicaragua's history. After Hurricane Mitch dropped two meters of rain in just three days, the southwest flank of Volcán Casitas transformed into a gigantic wave of mud and rock more than three meters high and nearly 1.5 kilometers wide. The communities of El Porvenir and Rolando Rodríguez were instantly consumed by the very soil on which they were built. Some 2,500 people immediately lost their lives.

Those that were not buried lived through the horror of losing nearly everything and everyone in their lives. Immediate relief efforts were held up by the politics of President Alemán, who stalled help to the Sandinista leadership of Posoltega.

One Witness for Peace volunteer was told by a survivor, "You should have seen how the children, the little ones, fought to survive. People were pulling themselves up out of the mud naked, completely covered in mud. They looked like monsters in a horror movie. All you could see were their eyes. Children didn't even recognize their own parents. For days we could hear the ones who were still half-buried crying for help."

Today, the slide is clearly visible from the León–Chinandega highway. International efforts helped construct several new communities for survivors, despite reports of disappearing relief funds reminiscent of Somoza's post-earthquake "emergency committee." The new suburban communities, however, provided no means of production for a people accustomed to living off the land. Many were psychologically devastated and eventually made their way illegally to search for work in Costa Rica.

The entire slide area has been declared a national monument, and a memorial plaque personally delivered by U.S. president Bill Clinton can be visited in the Peace Park on the highway, near the turnoff for Posoltega.

monument to the victims of the mudslide at Las Casitas

© RANDY WOOD

with fast food, Ping-Pong, chess, and dominoes (open Mon.–Fri. 9 A.M.–7 P.M.).

An outdoor movie theater, one block south of ENITEL and behind the *ferretería,* shows a daily double feature for under $.50. The first flick is for the whole family and the second is straight-up porn. El Viejo's *fiestas patronales* fall the week of December 6, with firework-spitting bulls every night, culminating in the Lava la Plata, when the nation's president often shows up to help "wash the church silver."

Accommodations

Until recently, the only places to stay were in "hotels of love." Now, **Casa de Huesped La Estancia,** two blocks north of the basilica (look for the McDonald's sign), has six simple rooms with shared bath for $3.75 a night.

CHICHIGALPA

Set in the middle of hundreds of square kilometers of sugarcane, Chichigalpa is home to the Ingenio San Antonio, Nicaragua's largest and most powerful sugar refinery, and more importantly, the Compañía Licorera, Nicaragua's alcohol monopoly and source of all the Toña, Victoria, Flor de Caña, and Ron Plata you've been drinking. The two companies belong to the wealthy Pellas family, which founded the sugar refinery in 1890 and has produced sugar and liquor ever since, (except between 1988 and 1992, when the business was briefly expropriated by the Sandinista government, then returned under the government of Violeta Chamorro).

As alcohol is a mainstay of Nicaraguan culture and legend, so the refineries and distilleries have been important parts of Nicaraguan life for over a century. If you're interested in seeing how the cane is crushed, processed, and distilled, arrange for a tour of the Flor de Caña distillery by calling the plant in advance (try asking for Simón Pedro Peréira) and requesting a guided tour, tel. 343-2344. At the moment, there is no charge for the tour, but neither are there free samples.

CORINTO

The barrier island of Corinto, with its port town of the same name, lies 20 kilometers southwest of Chinandega. Because of its shipping activity and beaches (one of which boasts a giant *Planet of the Apes*–reminiscent shipwreck), Corinto is fairly developed for tourists with a small range of simple hotels and seaside restaurants. Its long history of economic importance has ensured Corinto is well populated, with over 20,000 people living on 49 square kilometers of island, connected to the rest of Nicaragua by two small bridges.

The harbor was first used by the Spanish in the 1500s, but wasn't physically conquered until 1633, when an armada of 26 ships, 500 Spaniards, 227 horses, and 2,000 slaves arrived, swiftly defeating Texoatega's troops and taking many of them as additional slaves. The original port, placed at El Realejo (which still exists as a faint shadow of its former self), was transferred closer to the ocean at Corinto in 1858 after mangroves and sediment had choked the waterways.

Even when Corinto's first dock was built in 1875—consisting of nothing more than a wooden pier jutting into the harbor—Corinto was a vital link in Nicaragua's transport and shipping facilities. Nicaragua's coffee was transported by railroad from El Sauce to Corinto; from there it was shipped to the United States and European markets. A railroad constructed during Zelaya's presidency further expanded the port and its strategic significance.

In 1912, nearly 3,000 U.S. Marines landed in Corinto in response to Benjamin Zeledón's revolution, beginning what would be a 20-year occupation of Nicaragua. The gringos returned to Corinto in October 1983—this time in CIA cigarette boats as part of the counterrevolution to destabilize the Sandinista government. When U.S. agents and their hired South American accomplices (called UCLAs for Unilaterally Controlled Latin Assets) mined the harbor and blew up several oil tanks on the docks, they succeeded in producing an extraordinary amount of physical and economic damage. However, the "covert" operation was soon discovered, earning the Reagan administration international condemnation, and enraging U.S. citizens who, before Corinto, had not known what their government was up to in Nicaragua.

Much work went into Corinto in the years 2000–2001 to revitalize the port, dredge the harbor, and stimulate transport and shipping of goods through Nicaragua. Today, Corinto remains what it has been since the days the Spanish landed with their horses and slaves: a vibrant coastal community with all the headaches and spice of a port town.

Sights and Entertainment

Besides soaking up the sun and rum at **Playa Paso Caballo,** the curious traveler will want to check out the **beached oil tanker,** a short walk up the coast. The ship washed up here sometime in the 1980s after it caught fire (nothing to do with the war) and its owners decided to salvage what they could and let the rest drift to shore and burn. You'll have to swim across the mouth of the Río Aloya to reach the massive remains, and you should make sure you have about 27 tetanus shots before approaching or climbing the rusting hulk. Both the beach and the tanker are located on the northern tip of the island, and all buses from Chinandega pass by here before continuing to the center of town. Be careful, as the rip currents are notoriously strong. Paso Caballo fills up on Sundays and holidays, during which times you should keep a good eye on your stuff. Several ranchos on the beach provide shade, food, and alcohol.

In town, what was once the **Old Railroad Terminal and Customs House** is now a museum in tribute to the old train, well worth a visit. Three discos, **Ali Baba, Centauro,** and **Zam's Place,** are on the road between town and the northern beaches.

Festivals

If you are in the neighborhood around the weekend that falls closest to May 3, don't miss the **Féria Gastronómica del Mar** (Seafood Festival); try more than 100 different Corinteña recipes in the central park, Saturday and Sunday 10 A.M.–3

P.M. A fresh, varied, and cheap selection of fish, shrimp, and other local creatures.

Accommodations

Located about a block west of the Texaco station where buses arrive, the family-run **Hospedaje Vargas,** tel. 882-0187, has 10 simple rooms with fans; $4.50 for shared bath, $6 private bath. **Hospedaje Luvy,** tel. 342-2637, is 1.5 blocks west of the central park and offers 11 rooms ($5 s, $6 d, fan, shared bath). Stepping things up a notch, the **Hotel Central,** tel. 342-2637, offers a/c, private bath, cable TV, and a view of the industrial container loaders of Corinto's docks; 10 rooms, $30 s, $40 d.

Food and Services

As always, your best bargain is the *comida corriente* in the town market. Otherwise, numerous *cafetíns* dot the town, and a row of restaurants flank the town beach. **Restaurante Costa Azul,** and **El Peruano** have typical plates and seafood, starting at $5. They are both very pleasant, breezy, open-air ranchos with a view of the harbor and islands. The best restaurant in town got nudged out of the main plaza and can now be found toward Playa Paso Caballo on the main road to Chinandega, located near the bridge (from which you can jump into the water)—it's called **El Español** and the owner makes a mean sangria. Corinto Online, half a block north of the park, has Internet for $2.50 per hour. Getting to and from Corinto is a snap from Chinandega's Bisne Market, or hitching from the Rotonda.

PUERTO MORAZÁN

Accessed by bus from Chinandega, Puerto Morazán is the gateway to the magnificent and sinuous Estero Real, whose mangrove estuary provides habitat for countless marine species and birds. Morazán was built at water level, so it's no surprise that during Hurricane Mitch it flooded so severely only the church steeple appeared over the surface of the water. Shortly after Mitch, the community rebuilt itself on its original site, in spite of plans to relocate the community to higher ground.

Morazán is extraordinarily poor, but this was not always the case. During World War II, Morazán was home to a port and railway terminus, including a customs office that saw the movement of tons of cargo bound for European and North American destinations. When the war ended, so did Morazán's brief period of prosperity, and when Volcán Chonco erupted, damaging the railroad tracks, the final nail was put in Morazán's coffin.

The estuary itself is gorgeous, even if its "protected" status has been largely ignored by MARENA officials and the shrimp industry. Take a bus from El Viejo and pay someone to take you out into the estuary to bird-watch. You won't be disappointed by the extraordinary variety of wildlife, nor by the amazing view of Volcán Cosigüina.

COSIGÜINA PENINSULA AND BEACHES

The northwest corner of Nicaragua is a magnificent volcanic knuckle jutting out into the Golfo de Fonseca. The scenery is stunning, the beaches isolated, and the people strongly rooted in their indigenous past. All buses to the area leave from Chinandega's Mercadito and make stops in El Viejo before continuing on. Many of the following spots only have bus service once a day, which means you'll be making an overnight trip if you don't have your own wheels. Bring a hammock, flashlight, food, and plenty of water. El Viejo's *monjas* (nuns) know the area well—find them for additional information on any of the following.

Reserva Natural Volcán Cosigüina

Not only does this nationally protected reserve have incredible views from the volcano's rim, but the inside of the crater is densely vegetated and home to the only scarlet macaw population this side of the Segovia Mountains. Hiking or horseback riding to the rim is not to be missed (see Hiking the Maribio Volcanoes special topic). Your journey begins in the poverty-stricken town of Potosi, former trading port with El Salvador until it was blown up by the

Contras (the El Salvador–Nicaragua ferry was nearly reconstructed in Potosi recently, but plans shifted the project to Corinto). Of note is the three-day festival around May 19 on Meanguera, an El Salvadoran island that allows for unchecked passport access during the fiesta. Potosi is reachable by a 3.5-hour bus ride on "the crappiest road ever." Six buses leave daily and cost $1.50 each way.

Hiking the Cliffs at Punta Ñata

One bus a day leaves Chinandega at 12:10 P.M. for the 3.5-hour ride to the town of Punta Ñata. It is worth the time and hassle! Five-hundred-meter cliffs rule over the Pacific Ocean and the Farallones Islands (formed by Cosigüina's last eruption). Find a guide in Punta to show you the hike and how to climb down the cliffs.

Beaches

Los Aserradores is quiet and desolate, and the waves are calmer than elsewhere on the coast. Santa Maria del Mar seems to be the favored spot. The bus leaves Chinandega at 12:30 P.M. and returns the next day at 5 A.M.

Mechapa is one of the longest, shallowest stretches of pure beach in Nicaragua, rumored to be 20 kilometers in length. Buses leave Chinandega at 1:40 P.M. and return at 4 P.M. Buses to Punta San Jose, on the tippy tip of the peninsula, depart at 9:30 A.M. and 1:10 P.M., returning for Chinandega at 2:30 P.M. and 5 P.M.

Less than a one-hour bus ride out of El Viejo, Jiquilillo Beach makes for a beautiful, ultra-*tranquilo* day trip (except during Semana Santa when the place is a madhouse). Its uniqueness lies in the fact that it is relatively deserted, undeveloped, and absolutely beautiful. There used to be a town here but it was wiped out by a tidal wave. Six buses make the daily round-trip, starting at 6 A.M. If you miss the last bus back at 3 P.M., you can book a simple room at **Hospedaje Los Zorros** and keep partying. Four or five ranchos can be rented for about $3 each a day, and also serve decent food and rum and Cokes. In between hammock naps, check out the fishermen harvesting larvae for nearby shrimp farms.

Padre Ramos Wetlands Reserve

The bus to Jiquilillo continues up the coast, past Hospedaje Los Zorros, and arrives at the end of the road in the community of Padre Ramos. A simple fishing village of some 150 dispersed families, Padre Ramos is the gateway to the neighboring protected wetlands, and consequently the site of several grassroots tourism projects. The *estero* (estuary) is a decidedly mellower place to swim than the ocean and is home to all the wildlife—especially birds—you could hope for. Check out the visitor's center when you arrive to ask about fishing and boat trips into the wetlands. Of the plans currently in the works is an epic four-hour paddle to a community at the base of Volcán Cosigüina, from which point you can begin the three-hour hike to the crater; most likely an overnight trip, involving campesino guides, horses, and sleeping in a hammock under the stars. In Padre Ramos, you'll want to pay a visit to Doña Patrona (next to the visitor's center) to sample one of her massive fish dishes for under $4 a plate; alternately, there's a traditional rancho restaurant on the water's edge. You can get a quick *lancha* ride to the community of Venecia across the estuary, where you'll find long stretches of utterly deserted beach. The entire area is a breeding ground for sea turtles, who come to lay and hatch between November and January.

Estelí and the Segovias

O, the beauty of the mountains at Estelí. They sprang from the earth in improbable contorted forms, in shapes "plenty of fantasy," as the old tobacco map had put it.

Salman Rushdie

Have no doubt—the north country will inspire you. The ride from Managua begins by lifting you out of the Pacific lowlands and into the Sébaco Valley, lush with rice and sorghum fields. From there, the twisting, green climb to the Segovia Mountains is striking. In addition to the city of Estelí (a.k.a. the Diamond of the Segovias), you'll find mountains and valleys dotted with innumerable peaceful rural villages whose inhabitants are proud to call themselves *Norteños* and are additionally eager to brag about the beauty of their women, waterfalls, and music. Most get along by subsistence farming and ranching, but this is also tobacco and coffee country, and some communities have become famous for their crafts, such as pottery, stone carving, and leather work. Many of these pueblos have basic food and lodging services as well, and the curious and unrushed traveler will not regret breaking away from the Pan-American Highway and going deep into the countryside.

countryside surrounding Estelí

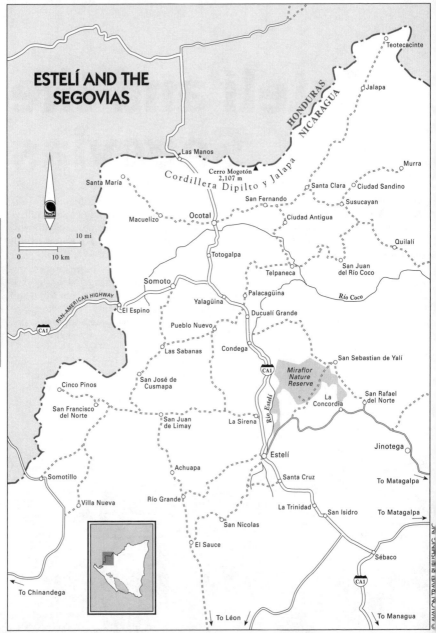

ESTELÍ AND THE SEGOVIAS

ESTELÍ & THE SEGOVIAS

Teotecacinte

HONDURAS

NICARAGUA

Jalapa

Las Manos

Murra

Cerro Mogotón
2,107 m

Cordillera Dipilto y Jalapa

Santa María

Santa Clara   Ciudad Sandino

San Fernando

Susucayan

Macuelizo   Ocotal

Ciudad Antigua

0   10 mi

0   10 km

Totogalpa

Quilalí

Somoto

Telpaneca

San Juan
del Río Coco

PAN-AMERICAN HIGHWAY

Yalagüina

Palacagüina

Río Coco

El Espino

Ducualí Grande

Pueblo Nuevo

CA1

Las Sabanas   Condega

San Sebastian de Yalí

CA1

Miraflor
Nature
Reserve

Cinco Pinos

San José de
Cusmapa

San Rafael
del Norte

La
Concordia

San Francisco
del Norte

San Juan
de Limay   La Sirena

Río Estelí

Jinotega

Achuapa

Estelí

Somotillo

Santa Cruz

To Matagalpa

Villa Nueva

Río Grande

La Trinidad   San Isidro

To Matagalpa

San Nicolas

El Sauce

Sébaco

CA1

To Chinandega

To Léon

To Managua

© AVALON TRAVEL PUBLISHING, INC.

HISTORY

When the Spanish first arrived, the people of the Segovias were ruled by the Nahuatl cacique Mixcoatl, or "Snake of the Clouds." The colonialists formed several settlements near the current border with Honduras. A hundred years later, in 1654, the English pirate Henry Morgan and friends made their way up the Río Coco from the Caribbean, terrorizing entire populations of both indigenous and Spanish settlers, who subsequently descended southward where they formed the communities that would grow into today's pueblos.

The sun shines hot on the Segovias, but the nights cool off deliciously. Perhaps this is why it is so hard to imagine the intensity of the history that happened here. After all, northern Nicaragua is Sandino country—the hills where General Augusto César Sandino and his "crazy little army" made their seven-year stand against the U.S. Marines. In the 1950s and 1960s, the Segovias served as the training ground for a new generation of warriors, this time Sandinistas mounting an insurrection against Tacho, and in the 1980s, the region once again became a bloody battleground as the new FSLN government struggled against the military aggression of the Contras.

City of Estelí

Spread across a broad, flat valley 800 meters above sea level, Estelí is an unassuming city with much to offer to the curious traveler. Its 110,000 merchants, ranchers, artists, and cigar rollers are furiously proud of their city, probably because they have endured so much together. As a Sandinista stronghold since the first guerrilla rebels were deployed in the surrounding mountains, Estelianos attracted plenty of attention from Somoza, who in the year leading up to his loss of power, punished them with constant aerial bombardment and National Guard aggressions.

ORIENTATION AND GETTING AROUND

Most buses to Estelí end up at the COTRAN Norte, located on the eastern side of the Pan-American Highway, about eight blocks south and five east of the city center. Depending on where you started your trip, some buses from the south arrive at the COTRAN Sur, one block south of the main market (14 blocks south of the park, and about the same distance from the other bus terminal, located to the east). The city is based on a grid divided into east-west *calles* and north-south *avenidas*, all named according to their respective quadrant: Nor-Este, Sur-Este, Sur-Oeste, and Nor-Oeste. However, even with street names and numbers, the town is unable to surmount the Nicaraguan penchant for giving directions in terms of landmarks and number of blocks.

The **central park** is bordered on the east by the cathedral and on the west by Avenida Principal, which runs more or less parallel to and five blocks to the west of the Pan-American Highway. The Avenida Principal runs from the COTRAN Sur north to the park, and is home to a large number of stores, sidewalk markets, hotels, and services. One block to the west is Ave. 1 S.O., also an important commercial road. Taxis are numerous and cost roughly $.30 to go anywhere within the city limits. *Urbano* buses run a big loop around the city, including up and down the main avenues.

SIGHTS
El Parque Central

Estelí's central plaza serves up everything you could want in a town park: a grand, white cathedral, a statue dedicated to Nicaraguan mothers, and a constant parade of local characters and mellow activity. Buy an ice cream cone, kick back on a bench, and watch it all swirl by.

Estelí's Cathedral has many stories to tell. Originally built in 1823, it was nothing more extravagant than a humble adobe chapel with a

ESTELÍ & THE SEGOVIAS

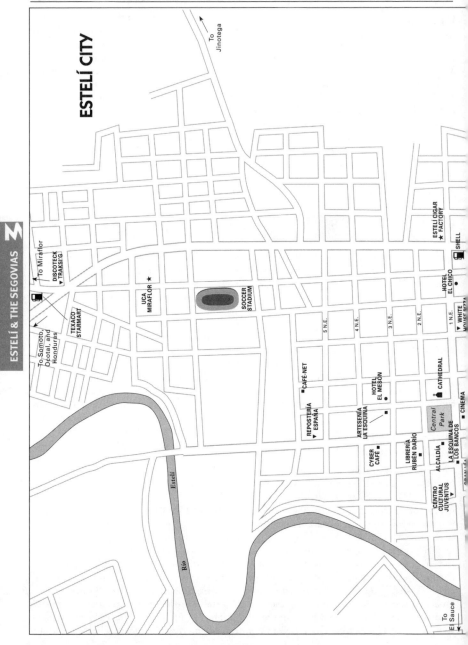

ESTELÍ CITY

To Jinotega

To Miraflor

DISCOTECK
TRAKSI'G

To Somoto,
Ocotal, and
Honduras

TEXACO
STARMART

UCA
MIRAFLOR

SOCCER
STADIUM

ESTELÍ CIGAR
FACTORY

SHELL

HOTEL
EL CHICO

WHITE
HOUSE PIZZA

5 N.E.

4 N.E.

3 N.E.

2 N.E.

1 N.E.

CATHEDRAL

CAFÉ-NET

HOTEL
EL MESÓN

REPOSTERÍA
ESPAÑA

ARTESENÍA
LA ESQUINA

LIBRERÍA
RUBÉN DARÍO

CYBER
CAFÉ

Central
Park

ALCALDÍA

LA ESQUINA DE
LOS BANCOS

CINEMA

CENTRO
CULTURAL
JUVENTUS

Río Estelí

To
El Sauce

ESTELÍ & THE SEGOVIAS

200 yds
200 m

HOTEL ALAMEDA

SHELL ESQUIPULAS

COTRAN NORTE

To Hospital and Managua

PAN-AMERICAN HIGHWAY

CALLE TRANSVERSAL

1 S.E.
2 S.E.
3 S.E.
4 S.E.
5 S.E.
6 S.E.
7 S.E.
8 S.E.
9 S.E.
10 S.E.
11 S.E.

HOTEL PANORAMA

To COTRAN Sur

QUICK BURGER

HOTEL MODERNO

HOTEL SACUANJOCHE

ARTESENIA NICARAGUENSE

BUFFET LAS DONAS

HOSPEDAJE SAN FRANCISCO

Parque Infantil

HOSPEDAJE CHEPITO

ROSTICERIA ESPECIAL

AVENIDA PRINCIPAL

PENSIÓN JUAREZ

SUPER EL HOGAR

POST OFFICE

LIBRARY

COMEDOR PINAREÑO

CASA HOTEL NICARAO

CAFETIN EL RECANTO

LECHE AGRIA

BANCENTRO

SUPER ECONOMICO

AVENIDA 1 S.O.

HOTEL ESTELI

HOSPEDAJE FAMILIAR

SUPER LAS SEGOVIAS

NICA CIGARS

MARKET

To Baseball Stadium

© AVALON TRAVEL PUBLISHING, INC.

© JOSHUA BERMAN

Boy Scout parade in Estelí

straw roof. It was rebuilt in 1889 to a grander scale and given a roof of clay tiles. Its facade was built in the baroque style and partially resembled today's structure. Still nowhere near as grandiose as the cathedrals in León and Granada, the cathedral was redesigned along bolder lines, resulting in a more modern building, with stately columns, a neoclassic facade, and twin bell towers topped with crosses.

La Galería de Héroes y Mártires

Just a half-block south of the cathedral, **La Galería** is only one accomplishment of the Association of Mothers of Heroes and Martyrs of Estelí, a support group of some 300 women who lost children during the battle against Somoza's National Guard. The gallery itself is a single room, filled with memorabilia from the days of the revolution—photos of Estelí as an urban battleground, quotes from Sandino and Che Guevara, and displays of weaponry and shell casings. Most touching are the portraits of young men and women killed in action, sometimes accompanied by uniforms and other personal effects.

The women also maintain a small kitchen, office, and classroom, and have regular community meetings. The highlight of this visit is talking with the mothers and tapping into their wealth of experience. See if you can get someone to show you the treasure trove of books, photos, and documents that didn't make it into the museum for lack of space. They are stored in unorganized boxes and piles in a back room.

La Galería (and the neighboring **Casa de Cultura**) is located in what was once a National Guard command post and jail, and is usually open Monday–Saturday 9 A.M.–4 P.M.; entrance fee is a voluntary donation, tel. 713-3753, email: emayorga70@yahoo.com. They also organize local tours, homestays, and a Spanish school.

Connected to the Galería, you'll find the less powerful, but still interesting **Museo de Historia y Arqueología,** with a small display of petroglyphs, artifacts, and the requisite photos and items from the revolution (open Mon.–Fri. 9 A.M.–noon, closed weekends and Wed.). For entrance on the weekends, call Felix Mendoza in the Casa de Cultura at tel. 713-3021.

THE CHILDREN'S MURALISM WORKSHOP

In 1987, in response to a request for help from community leaders in the struggling Barrio Batahola in Managua, three former art students began teaching mural painting workshops to children. The program was a success and two years later, the three muralists passed their roles onto other youth in Managua and moved to Estelí to continue their program. The idea was to empower the people while at the same time reclaiming Nicaraguan culture and promoting the participation of children in society. Under this new movement they found that painting murals was an empowering achievement for the participants, and the creation of the murals was invariably tied to further community activities and social work.

Of the 130 murals painted since 1989 by the children who attended the workshops, 20 (all on the walls of public schools) were erased by the post-Sandinista government between the years 1990–1991. The majority of the murals however, still remain, and more are being painted every year.

Today, the mural project is going strong as the Fundación de Apoyo al Arte Creador Infantíl (FUNARTE), a nonprofit, nongovernmental organization run by a group of youth who grew up through the original mural workshops. The foundation works primarily to contribute to the integral development of children, adolescents, and youth, promoting and facilitating the development of creativity, identity, self-esteem, and leadership. They offer weekly painting workshops to more than 550 Esteliano children and youth for free, and give special workshops for imprisoned teenagers and children with disabilities. The murals depict their history, culture, and the daily reality in which they live. Their artwork is an expression of their feelings, ideas, and dreams of building a more just society.

There are currently over 100 murals in Estelí, the majority of which were painted by participants of FUNARTE's workshops. The murals are best viewed and photographed in the late afternoon sun, as many of the best are on west-facing walls. The paintings are everywhere, but take special note of those on the *Alcaldía* (mayor's office), Casa de Cultura, and in and around the Parque Infantíl (nine blocks south of the main plaza). Also, be sure to get a good look at the long, horizontal mural on the wall of the army base along the Pan-American Highway, just south of the main bus station.

To visit FUNARTE's headquarters, walk three blocks south from the southwest corner of the plaza, then two west to reach the main workshop, itself covered in powerful paintings; continue another block west, turn right past the mural depicting the book *The Little Prince,* and make your next left to arrive at the offices and classroom. Contact FUNARTE at tel. 713-6100, email: muralism @ibw.com.ni.

SLIDE COURTESY JOSHUA BERMAN

ESTELÍ & THE SEGOVIAS

La Casa de Cultura

Still in the same building, but on the south side, the **Casa de Cultura** is easily recognized by its giant vertical murals announcing the activities within: Dance, Painting, Music. Offering a series of classes to the general public, the Casa often has a display of local artists in its spacious lobby.

Estelí Cigar Factory

Don Kiki, a.k.a. Henry Berger, is the president and master roller of **Estelí Cigar Factory**, a private label factory that produces some 60 brands of *puros* (cigars) for export to the United States and Europe, the most popular of which are *Cinco Vegas, Cupido,* and *Badge of Honor.* Don Kiki, of Cuban and Eastern European descent (a *"Jew-bano,"* he says), is a portly, amiable craftsman proud to give any cigar-lover a personally guided tour of his rolling factories and/or tobacco fields. He speaks perfect Miami English and doesn't charge for the tour, although you may want to let him know in advance if you are showing up with a busload of people. On a good day, he'll give you coffee and a rolling lesson—and don't be surprised if he hands you some fresh samples to take home and puff with your friends. "It's free advertising," he says casually. The Estelí Cigar Factory is located five blocks due east of the cathedral, on the east side of the Pan-American Highway, tel. 713-5688, email: etelici@ibw.com.ni.

Empresa Nica Cigars, is another non–free trade company, which means they are permitted to sell to local markets as well. They will also allow curious visitors to come inside and take pictures of their rollers. Located around the corner from the COTRAN Sur, you'll smell the tobacco from blocks away, tel. 713-2230.

SMOKING NICARAGUA

There is history in that cigar you're smoking—stories hidden among the tightly packed folds of tobacco and along the delicate veins of the wrapper leaf. As you light the *puro* in your hand and watch it turn into ash and then smoke, take a sip of rum and ponder the unique legacy of the Estelí cigar industry.

It all began with the 1959 Cuban revolution, when capitalist Cuban cigar lords found their businesses liquidated into the new socialism. These artisans of the finest cigars in the world quickly gathered together secret caches of the precious tobacco seeds their families had been cultivating for centuries and fled to Miami. From there it was only a couple of years before they discovered Nicaragua. One grower told *Cigar Aficionado* magazine that Cuba and Nicaragua "have the most fertile dirt in the world for tobacco. It's almost like God said, 'I'm going to pick these two countries and I'm going to use them for tobacco.'"

And so the core of the old Cuban cigar aristocracy moved to Estelí and, with their precious seeds from the homeland, began turning out world-renowned cigars once again. They endured another popular revolution in 1979, the ensuing civil war and land redistribution, and then survived the cigar boom and bust of the 1990s, followed by the waters of Hurricane Mitch that tore through their fields in 1998. But the business is sunk deep into the rich soil, and the handful of familial cigar dynasties that first came to Nicaragua 30 years ago are still here, and still rolling world-class cigars.

Most of the tobacco fields and giant wooden drying barns are found all across the Estelí valley as it runs north away from the city, as well as in many upper reaches all the way to Jalapa. In Estelí there are about 10 serious cigar producers, a few of which will let any traveler in their doors for an informal tour and perhaps a taste test. Most businesses are *zona franca* (free trade zone) though, which prohibits them from selling their product within Nicaragua. Don Orlando Padrón, head of Cubanica Cigars, keeps the doors to his Estelí factory shut for another reason: to protect the secrets that produce one of the most internationally acclaimed brands in the world, the Padrón.

Some of the other heavy hitters are Latin Tobacco, Estelí Cigar, Tabacalera Perdomo (formerly Nick's Cigars), Plasencia, and Nicaraguan American Tobacco (NATSA). Their facilities are scat-

ENTERTAINMENT AND EVENTS

Cinemas

Estelí's **old movie theater** on the main plaza is back in business showing mostly trashy American movies for $1.50 Thursday–Sunday. The seats are packed in pretty tight, but look for the "Gringo Row" if you've got long legs.

Bars and Discos

Reportedly the most flavorful and culturally minded bar in town is the **Rincón Legal,** on the north side of the park. Frankie Legal used to be a self-proclaimed *vago* (bum), traveling all over Central America. When he returned, he realized that Estelí lacked a meeting place where people could both express themselves and celebrate their common culture of revolution, music, and Nicaragua's historical relationship with Cuba.

Located near the park, but you've got to ask around to find it. El Rincón is open every night except Monday and Wednesday, 7 P.M.–1 A.M. (but if the joint is still jumpin' at the city-imposed closing time, Frankie will close the doors, turn the music down a touch, and keep the beer and good vibes flowin').

Discoteck Traksi'g, on the highway just short of the StarMart and northern edge of town, is the in-town favorite. Thursday is ladies' night; says one local resident: "Lots of pretty young women, lots of ugly old men," tel. 713-2961. Also very popular is **El Rancho de Pancho**, a few kilometers north of Estelí on the Pan-American Highway. The pricey taxi ride (over $1 a person) is offset by the lack of cover charge and excellent music mix. Saturday is the night of choice, but get there early, as El Rancho is jam-packed by 10 P.M.

tered across Estelí, and their degree of hospitality varies. Don Kiki, of Estelí Cigars, is the most inviting, offering casual tours and conversation, maybe even a cup of Cuban coffee and a smoke (see Estelí Cigar Factory for more information).

Cigar making is a proud family tradition here and elsewhere in the world, and there's no denying the craftsmanship of a fine cigar. But as the blunt you're smoking burns lower, and the heat of the cherry seeps into the leaf between your fingers, consider the yang side. Organic tobacco is grown in Nicaragua, but barely; most production employs massive quantities of chemicals, which invariably find their way into the earth, the water, or the lungs, hands, and feet of the workers. Tobacco handlers often absorb the toxic elements of the leaf, and although at least several of Estelí's factories have impressive, airy environments for their workers, conditions for the rollers are often no better than the worst sweatshops. And the history burns on.

© TOMÁS STARGARDTER

Much of Nicaragua's tobacco was brought to the Estelí Valley from Cuba.

ESTELÍ & THE SEGOVIAS

LA CASITA

The menu is simple at La Casita (The Little House), and it's also healthy and homegrown: yogurt, wheat bread, Brie and Swiss cheese, fresh tomatoes, granola, juices, and coffee. Beyond the food, La Casita is one of the most pleasant places in town to kill a couple of hours. It is located on the Pan-American Highway, a few kilometers south of the city. Take an *urbana* bus to the new hospital, then walk south around the bend in the road; or hail a taxi for about $.75—it's well worth the trip. In addition to wonderful food and mellow music, La Casita sells local crafts and has a handful of wooden tables surrounded by beautiful flowers alongside a babbling brook. There is also a small park and playground for the kids, an organic garden, composting outhouse, and a *vivero* (plant nursery) with all kinds of ornamentals and herbs for sale.

The owner is a Scotsman named David Thomsen who, after many years of experience in development work in Nicaragua, has made some insightful conclusions on the topic; namely, that imposing new technology on a people is for naught. The alternative, he explains, is to be a passive model of how one can choose to manage natural resources. Thus, when he was asked by a Danish NGO to travel to the village of Siuna to demonstrate his unique bread oven, he politely refused. But when a women's organization from that remote town displayed the interest to organize a trip to his *finca* in Estelí, he was more than happy to show them how to construct such an oven in their own pueblo.

La Casita, Finca Las Nubes, is located across from *La Barranca,* south entrance, and is open Tuesday–Saturday 7 A.M. to 7 P.M., Sunday 9 A.M.–7 P.M., and Monday 1–7 P.M. (closed some Mondays), tel. 713-4917, email: casita@ibw.com.ni.

© JOSHUA BERMAN

Estelí's *fiestas patronales* take place around October 12, and most years include a famous *hípica* (show-horse) parade.

Coffee Shops

There are exactly two places in Estelí that serve up both cappuccino and an environment relaxing and beautiful enough to pass hours just sitting and enjoying the afternoon. **Juventus Centro Cultural,** two blocks west of the southwest corner of the central park, is situated on top of the hill that drops down to the river, making for a spectacular vista of the mountains to the west; Juventus is open Monday–Saturday, 9 A.M.–6 P.M., tel. 713-3756, email: sltc@ibw.com.ni. The *dueño,* Walter Delgado, is planning on opening a Spanish school, tour service, and Internet café on the same spot. The menu includes *licuados* (fruit shakes), granola, open-face Swiss and Brie sandwiches on fresh wheat bread, and hot drinks, all for very reasonable prices. La Casita—located along the highway, just south of the hospital—is the other place to scratch your caffeine itch (also see La Casita special topic).

ACCOMMODATIONS

Under $10

Estelí's most inexpensive accommodations are the three *hospedajes* located within half a block of the Parque Infantíl, two blocks north of the market. **Hospedaje San Francisco** has nine cramped rooms, shared bath; $3 s, $4 d, $5 t, tel. 713-3787. **Pensión Juarez**, tel. 713-2740, half a block to the west, and **Hospedaje Chepito**, tel. 713-6388, half a block south, both have rooms for $4 s or d, shared bath, no fan. There are also a number of cheap *hospedajes* along the Pan-American Highway that are popular among the trucker set.

A better bet is to walk north to the **Casa Hotel Nicarao,** on the Ave. Principal, just south of the central park. Nicarao has 10 rooms surrounding a mellow, open-air, sheltered patio. Rooms start at $6 with shared bath and fan, $10 s and d with private bath. Excellent and friendly meal and beer service, tel. 713-2490.

Hospedaje Familiar, half a block north of the Supermercado Las Segovias, has seven rooms with similar prices to Nicarao, and a smaller courtyard. The owner, Edith Valenzuela Lopez, has 33 years of experience hosting *internacionalistas* and keeps her guests clean, safe, and healthy. She is also vegetarian, Sandinista to the core, and knowledgeable about natural medicine and yoga. If you were planning on getting sick anyway, this is a good place to do so, as she will set up a consult with a local Eastern medicine doctor, and will serve you herbal tea. Doña Edith also offers monthly rates ($150) with a very reasonable (and healthy) meal plan, and natural food, tel. 713-3666.

Hotel Sacuanjoche is a family-run establishment with a reputation for being clean, quiet, and safe. Thirteen rooms with bath, $4 – 12. Located 2.5 blocks south of ENITEL, tel. 713-2862.

$10–25

A few doors north of Hospedaje Familiar, **Hotel Estelí** has seven rooms on two stories, including several nice, furnished doubles and matrimonials for $18 with private bath, TV, and parking, tel. 713-2902. Also with rooms for $7 s or d with shared bath.

Hotel El Mesón, one block north of the cathedral, has eight rooms for $9 s, $11 d, $15 t; all with private bath, hot water, and fan. Mesón offers parking, a bar and restaurant, travel agency, car rental, and will change traveler's checks, tel. 713-2655, fax 713-4029.

The nicest accommodations in the city center are no doubt found in **Hotel Moderno,** (located one block east of the park and two south, tel. 713-2378, fax 713-4315). Eleven rooms surrounding a shaded courtyard, conference room, bar, and restaurant, all with private bath, hot water, TV, and fan; a good a deal at $17 s, $24 d.

Hotel Panorama No. 1, across from Quiabú army base on the highway, has 34 rooms with private bath, hot water, a/c, TV, plus a conference room and parking. Rooms are $35 s, $30 d, tel. 713-3147, fax 713-3148. **Panorama 2** has singles for $15, one block south of the plaza, tel. 713-5023.

Hotel Alameda boasts its own mini-complex with a bar, restaurant, swimming pool, and two conference rooms. Alameda has 15 rooms with private bath, TV, and a/c for $40 s, $45 d; its only disadvantage is its location on the eastern side of the Pan-American, behind the Shell Esquipulas, but it's only a short cab ride into the city center (tel. 713-6292, fax 713-5219, email: alameda@ibw.com.ni, website: www.alameda.com.ni).

Long-Term Housing

All of the **Spanish schools** have networks of families accustomed to housing foreigners for a weekly or monthly rate, and Doña Edith at the **Hospedaje Familiar** offers extended room and board deals, starting at $150 a month. For house and apartment rentals, call Bienes Raices Gomez, tel. 713-3835.

FOOD

Although elegant dining experiences are few and far between, Estelí has an excellent selection of cheap, safe, quality food. **Cafetín el Recanto** is a prime example, located right around the corner from Hotel Nicarao, and offering some of the tastiest local eats and quality service in the area. A plate of *salpicón* (minced meat with lime juice), rice, beans, salad, tortilla, and one of many fresh juices costs $2–3 (also serves breakfast), open 7 A.M.–6 P.M., tel. 713-7630.

One block east of El Recanto is the varied and cheap **Buffet Las Doñas.** A typical *fritanga* sets up on the sidewalk every evening in front of the pool hall next to the firehouse, just south of the cathedral.

On Ave. Principal, two blocks south of the Super Economico, you'll find a delicious plate of roast chicken for less than $3 with cold beers for $.75 at the **Rosticeria Especial.** The **Comedor Cándida** is famous for its chicken soup and is located just north of the main bus station on the Pan-American, across from Shell Esquipulas. Nicaraguan men enjoy their hot soup served with a few shots of rum on the side, and Cándida offers a half-liter of Flor de Caña with all the fixin's for only $4; open 5 A.M.–10 P.M.

Bakeries

There is an excellent Spanish bakery, **Repostería España,** 3.5 blocks north of the central park, and a German one, **Repostería Alemán,** behind the cathedral.

Vegetarian

Leche Agria, located 2.5 blocks south of *la esquina de los bancos,* serves excellent *quesillos,* juices, and cheeses. Another block south is the *cafetín* at the **Hospedaje Familiar** with homemade yogurt, fresh fruit, pancakes, salads, and herbal teas, all impeccably clean and safe. **Comedor Popular La Soya** is on the Ave. Principal, 2.5 blocks south of the park, and true to its name, serves soy-based meals and soy milk drinks. (More veggie food is listed under Coffee Shops, above.)

Cuban

Comedor Pinareño has a full Cuban menu, plus a selection of local and Cuban cigars. Located one block south of the park, meals cost $2–7, tel. 713-4369.

Chinese

La Gran Vía has meals from $4, tel. 713-5465, closed Sundays, located just south of the *esquinas de los bancos.*

Gringo Food

White House Pizza, one block east of the park, will deliver to your hotel, tel. 713-7575; **Quickburger,** a block away, lives up to its name, and the 24-hour **StarMart** at the northern exit out of town has a Jerry's Subs and Pizza.

SHOPPING

The main outdoor market of Estelí is just north of COTRAN Sur and mostly sells meats and produce. A more pleasant place to shop for fruits and vegetables is the *mercado municipal,* less than a block north of the central park. For plain old window shopping, the entire length of Ave. Principal is full of fun stuff in little boutiques. The shops are often choked with activity and when they're not you can expect the shop girls to whistle at you to entice you into the store.

The southern half of Avenida 1 S.O. is the place to go if you are looking for handmade leatherwork, like belts, saddles, or **cowboy boots.** A pair of quality cowhide boots (or deerskin or snakeskin, the latter of which might get confiscated at your home customs office) goes for about $45 and takes a week when custom fit to your foot. Order a pair on your way north and pick 'em up on the way back to Managua. Also found throughout Estelí are an uncountable number of used U.S. clothing shops full of polyester treasures.

Supermarkets

There are three supers in Estelí, all of about the same size and quality. Las Segovias is on Ave. 1 S.O., five blocks south of the park. El Economico and El Hogar are both on Ave. Principal, 3.5 and 12 blocks south of the park, respectively.

Musical Instruments

Guitarras y Requintas el Arte (tel. 713-7555) sells handmade guitars, mandolins, and *guitarrones* (the bass guitar used by mariachis) out of a tiny barber shop; the floor is littered with wood shavings and hair clippings. The musical instruments go for $90–120 and the shop is located adjacent to the INISER building. Imported, more expensive instruments are sold in the **Colegio Musica de Estelí,** two blocks north of the park.

Artesanía

Two shops—**Artesanía La Esquina,** one block north of the cathedral, tel. 713-2229, and **Artesanía Nicaragüense,** one block south of the cathedral, tel. 713-4456—each have a huge selection of Nicaraguan arts and crafts from all over. In general, prices are cheaper in the Managua and Masaya markets, but for locally produced items like soapstone carvings and Ducualí pottery, these are good places to shop. Plans are in the works for a government-sponsored crafts market in the Hospital Viejo building on Ave. Principal.

Bookstores

There are many bookstores in Estelí, but the hands-down winner is **Librería Rubén Darío,** one block west of the park. For a more sentimental experience, check out the tiny **Librería Leonel Rugama,** on the Ave. Principal, across from the Kodak, run by the famous poet-martyr's parents. Rugama's dramatic death at the hands of the *Guardia* is legendary: cornered in a building in Managua with Carlos Fonseca (who escaped through the sewers), Rugama held off a contingent of guardsmen, who finally ordered him to his knees; *"¡Rindase, Sandinista!"* ("Surrender, Sandinista!") they shouted. *"¡Que se rinda tu madre!"* ("Your mother!") were Rugama's now-famous last words.

INFORMATION

INTUR has a tiny, tucked-away office in the back of the Hospital Viejo (open Mon.–Fri. 7 A.M.–2 P.M., tel. 713-6799). Although they don't offer any services, they may be able to point you in the right direction if you have a specific question. The public library, a corner building covered with murals, is one block west and one south of the park. Open Monday–Friday 8 A.M.–noon, 2–5 P.M., tel. 713-7021.

Guide Services

Most of Estelí's Spanish schools offer ecotours and day trips to surrounding sites in addition to, or as part of, their language classes. UCA Miraflor has transportation and tours of Miraflor, and access to a network of local guides.

Emergencies

El Hospital Regional de Estelí, tel. 713-6300, was donated by the Spanish government in the

NATURAL MEDICINE IN ESTELÍ

Knowledge of folk medicine and the use of natural plants and herbs in curing all types of ailments is common throughout all of Nicaragua, especially in rural areas where natural meds are cheaper and more available than modern drugs. However, nowhere in the country is the use of natural medicine as well institutionalized as it is in Estelí.

There are several organizations devoted solely to the production, marketing, and selling of natural medicines. The two most prominent are CECALLI and ISNAYA. The former maintains a nursery and nature museum at their gardens south of Estelí, right next door to the La Casita café. They sell their herbs, teas, and other natural products in a store on the Ave. Principal, 1.5 blocks north of the plaza.

Managed by the Centro Nacional de la Medicina Popular Tradicional, ISNAYA maintains a beautiful farm called El Cortijo, located near La Sirena, eight kilometers north of Estelí on the Pan-American Highway. They also run several stores and a lab and packaging plant in the city of Estelí. Check with ISNAYA's offices (from the park, three blocks south, 1.5 to the west) if you are interested in living and working on the farm for an extended period, tel. 713-4841, email: CNMPT@ibw.com.ni.

ESTELÍ & THE SEGOVIAS

mid-1990s and is located just south of the city. Ave. Principal has many private clinics and consultations—both Western and Eastern medicine. La Policía Nacional, tel. 713-2615, is located on the main highway, toward the northern exit.

SERVICES

Banks and Exchange

La esquina de los bancos is one block west of the park; Bancentro, tel. 713-6549 or 713-6550, is 2.5 blocks south on Ave. Principal, open Monday–Friday 8 A.M.–5 P.M., Saturday 8 A.M.–12:30 P.M. Street money changers can be found on Ave. Principal, just south of the Super Economico, and also on Ave. 1 S.O., two blocks south of *la esquina de los bancos*. The travel agency in Hotel Mesón changes traveler's checks, as do most of the banks, and there is a cash machine in the StarMart.

Mail and Phones

El Correo, tel. 713-2085, is open 7 A.M.–8 P.M. The Farmacia Corea, a block north of the main market, offers mail and package service, as well as money transfers, tel. 713-2609. DHL Worldwide Express is one block west of the park, and a half-block north, in the same office as Careli Viajes, tel. 713-7077. ENITEL, tel. 713-2222, is located one block south of the cathedral and half a block east, open 7:15 A.M.–9 P.M.

Travel Services and Car Rental

A multitude of travel agencies line the streets of Estelí, but the most impressive operation is Agencia de Viajes Tisey, in Hotel El Mesón, with a fully staffed and modern office, international travel services, as well as booking on national airlines. It also has a Budget car rental desk, starting at $19 a day (plus tax and insurance), tel. 713-3099, fax 713-4029, email: barlan@ibw.com.ni. Careli Viajes, a full-service travel agency, also with a Budget car rental, shares an office with DHL; open Monday–Friday 8 A.M.–noon, 1:30–5:30 P.M., Saturday 8 A.M.–noon, tel. 713-7077, email: info@carelitours.com.

Internet

Cyber Café, 1.5 blocks north of the park on Ave. Principal, charges $4 per hour, and serves cheap beer and soft drinks; open 8 A.M.–8 P.M., tel. 713-2475. Café-Net also has its act together, and continues to grow and obtain the latest technology. It has an attractive sandwich menu, and generous hours. Rates from $3 per hour (15 percent discount with international student ID), open all week, 8 A.M.–10 P.M., tel. 713-4056, located four blocks north of the back of the cathedral, but if you are taking a taxi, say "frente al portón principal del Instituto San Francisco." There is also one computer available in the library for $3 an hour.

Laundry

The most economical service is to ask your *hospedaje* to have your clothes washed by hand, but if you've got the cordobas, go to the Super Steam Dry Cleaning Lavandería, next door to the DHL, open Monday–Saturday 8 A.M.–5 P.M., tel. 713-7681.

Special Courses

For anyone spending more than a few weeks in Estelí, there are considerable opportunities to do some learning. La Casa de Cultura offers daily classes in *baile folklórico* (folk dancing), theater, guitar, keyboard, and painting, all for next to nothing, tel. 713-3021. Right next door, the Association of Mothers of Heroes and Martyrs will school you in piñata and pastry making, also for incredibly cheap fees. The Colegio Musica de Estelí, two blocks north of the park, offers classes in guitar and keyboard. It is also rumored that classes in yoga, tae kwon do, and judo can be found; ask Doña Edith in the Hospedaje Familiar.

Escuela Horizonte can sponsor conferences with historical, cultural, educational, health, political, and economic themes for organizations, professionals, and students.

GETTING THERE AND AWAY

Estelí is located on the Pan-American Highway, 150 kilometers north of Managua, and 90 kilometers south of the Honduran border. All buses from Managua to Estelí leave from the Mayoreo Terminal, located in the northeast corner of the capital. Express buses leave Managua roughly every hour; the nicest, luxury buses leave at 1:15 P.M. and 3:15 P.M. The express ride takes about 2.5 hours and costs $2.25. *Ordinarios* cost $1.50 but may take up to an hour longer. For more information, contact Expresos del Norte at tel. 233-4729.

With the 2001 construction of two new bus terminals in Estelí, schedules have been inconsistent. It would be wise to double check all bus information in this chapter—both your bus's time and from which COTRAN it leaves. The Ministerio de Transporte is located one block north and west of the main market, and can answer most questions about bus schedules; open 9

A.M.–2 P.M., tel. 713-2357. Another direct source of bus information is the *cooperativa* office, tel. 713-2529.

The COTRAN Norte (also called "Interbusa") is the biggest and most modern of the two stations, and (in general) services all points north and east, as well as many of the standard routes to the south (i.e., Managua, Matagalpa, and León). León *expresos* leave at 7:45 A.M. and 3:10 P.M., and three microbus *expresos* leave whenever they fill up, starting around 7 A.M. There is one daily bus at 2 P.M. that goes straight to Masaya, bypassing Managua by turning at Tipitapa; it runs every day except Wednesday and Sunday.

The COTRAN Sur runs *ordinario* service to Managua every half-hour, 3:30 A.M.–5 P.M., *expresos* 4:45 A.M.–3:15 P.M. Service to Matagalpa every half-hour 5:20 A.M.–5:50 P.M.

The large amount of long-distance traffic running up and down the Pan-American Highway makes hitchhiking from Estelí a breeze. To go south to Managua (or to the turnoff in Sébaco for Matagalpa or the San Isidro junction for León), take an *urbano* bus or taxi to the southern exit. Across the street from the PetroNic gas station is a good spot because vehicles have to slow down to climb the small hill. To points north, go to the StarMart parking lot.

Near Estelí to the South

EL SALTO ESTANZUELA WATERFALL HIKE

El Salto Estanzuela is hidden in a deep, gouged-out ravine in the countryside west of Estelí. Here you'll find a cold, shady swimming hole, a rock beach, and a beautiful cascade, all smothered in colorful native flora and fauna.

The road to Estanzuela leaves the Pan-American just south of the new hospital and is sandwiched between two *pulperías* where you can stock up on fruit, crackers, and *gaseosa*-in-a-bag (soft drinks) for your journey. This is the terminus of the *urbano* bus routes, or take a taxi from the city center. The walk is about five kilometers and should take between 60 and 90 minutes each way. It's an easy hike, but with lots of ups-and-downs.

Before you reach the *pueblito* of Estanzuela for which the waterfall is named (a cluster of houses and a school that you'll see from the road), look for a gated road on your right; it's at the bottom of a hill, just after the first two slapped-together wooden homes of the village (you might want to ask a lingering child for confirmation). Walk down this road-less-traveled for about 10 minutes until it veers steeply down to the left. Before it turns to the right again, take the path in front of you straight down to the falls, which you should now be able to hear.

Make sure you swim behind the falls for a refreshingly cool perspective on Nicaragua. Before you know it, you'll be sweating the hike back—unless, of course, you're able to hop an afternoon pickup on its way to sell beans and tomatoes in the market in Estelí.

LA TRINIDAD

Just as the Pan-American Highway begins its curvy climb north into Nicaragua's mountains, a mid-size pueblo straddles the road and monitors your entrance into the north country. It would be easy to stay on the bus as you pass through La Trinidad toward Estelí, only 22 kilometers farther north, but it would be just as easy to get off at the Texaco station, and wander up to the park, where few tourists have ever set foot.

La Trinidad, named for the three hills that cradle it gently in their arms, is a festive town of bakers, bus drivers, musicians, and cowboys. Its unhurried and friendly populace can often be found hanging out in the lush park, a well-tended and utilized central plaza—green even in the height of the dry season—and home to Kameleón, La Trinidad's pet tree sloth who lives untethered in the park's canopy. The Catholic Church, although decidedly ugly and noncolonial, may be worth a visit during mass to hear the dueling mariachi choirs.

"La Trini" is also famous (or infamous, depending on who you're talking to) for being an island of anti-Sandinismo in a zone of strong FSLN support. This fact stems from the handful of resident landowning families that used to control much of the Sébaco Valley to the south before losing the land in massive confiscations in the early 1980s. The Contras mounted a major military offensive in 1986 to take a stretch of the Pan-American Highway through La Trinidad. They were outgunned by Sandinista military in helicopter gunships. The failed maneuver was instrumental in making clear the Contras had the support of many local citizens, who in La Trinidad kept the guerrilla soldiers well fed with coffee and *rosquillas* during the battles.

The rip-roaring *fiestas patronales,* celebrating La Virgen de Candelaria and Jésus de Caridad, occurs during the last week of January and rolls raucously into the first week of February, with a famous *hípica* (show horse) parade that attracts riders from all over Central America.

Hikes

Walk one block south and two west of the park to begin a half-hour climb up to the old Spanish wooden cross and stunning views of La Trinidad, the Sébaco Valley, and the rising hills in all other directions. Another beautiful countryside hike can be had by walking westward up the river valley road to the shady Rosario shrine—allow about an hour each way. The hill to the east of the highway is the legendary Mocuana, with its caves of witches, gold, snakes, and a tunnel to Sébaco, if you believe everything you hear. La Trinidad's homegrown fiesta band, Los Mokuanes, have been playing their *embrujo musical* (musical witchcraft) all over Central America (and occasionally in the United States) for over 30 years.

Food and Accommodations

Having never been a tourist destination, La Trinidad offers delicious, typical, and cheap food without the hype. Don Juan's **Las Sopas,** on the south outskirts of town, is a popular stopover

La Trinidad, Estelí

© JOSHUA BERMAN

THE LEGEND OF THE MOCUANA

When the Spanish conquistadores at the command of Gabriel de Rojas arrived at the Chontaleña settlement of Cihuacoatl, the cacique who governed there presented the Spanish with a small gift of gold from his immense collection of riches from the mountains of Matagalpa and the east. The cacique also gave Rojas several golden pieces in the form of the fruit of the tamarind tree. The conquistador was intrigued by the gold, and left the community politely while he schemed of ways to return and abscond the riches for himself. The cacique was no fool, however, and realizing the Spanish would soon return and demand his riches, hid them in a secret location known only to him and his daughter.

The Spanish returned to Cihuacoatl, and fought many battles with the Chontal people there, suffering greatly to the well-armed warriors of the area, and never learning where the treasure had been hidden. Meanwhile, the cacique's daughter fell deeply in love with one of the Spanish soldiers. The two ran off together, and the girl showed the soldier where the treasure was hidden. He betrayed her immediately, and before carrying away the riches of her father, locked her up in a cave so she wouldn't escape to tell the tale of his ruse.

The girl did manage to escape, but she lost her mind due to the ravages of the betrayal, the immensity of her own naïveté, and the punishment she knew awaited her if she ever found her way back to town.

Many modern Nicaraguans living in the countryside claim to have seen the Mocuana. She appears at night to men traveling alone. She never lets them see her face, because she'd die of shame for what had happened to her. Instead she lets them get a glimpse of her smooth and lovely back and shoulders, and her long and gorgeous hair, all of which are quite obviously the features of a young woman. Some say the Mocuana is vengeful, and tries to get the young men to accompany her to where the treasure is, so she can kill them and avenge her own betrayal; others claim she's just a poor, suffering girl who has gone crazy for love, a love she knows she can never recapture.

The tall hill on the east side of the highway at La Trinidad is called La Mocuana, in her honor. Some believe that's the hill where the cacique had once hidden the treasure.

for Pan-American commuters and truck drivers, with an open-air patio, a pathetic attempt at a zoo, and a fantastic menu of local soups—including *huevos de toro* (Rocky Mountain oysters), ox tail, and chicken soup. Squeeze in plenty of lime and, to fit in with your fellow lunchers, down a shot of Extra Lite rum after every couple of bites (tell the bus driver to let you off here, or take a taxi from the town's center). Also, diagonally across from the Texaco, the **Rinconcito Familiar** has great lunches and *fritanga*.

There is a cheap *hospedaje* across from the hospital on the south end of town, but La Trini works well as a half-day stopover on your way to or from Estelí if you'd rather not spend the night. La Trinidad is too small for a town market, but it has most other services, including a Western Union and Internet.

Near Estelí to the North

MIRAFLOR NATURE RESERVE

It is difficult to find words to describe the experience at Miraflor, mostly because there is not much with which to compare it. Perhaps this is what Costa Rica's Monteverde was like 40 years ago when residents first conceived the idea of inviting visitors to come and experience the natural beauty of their home. Miraflor was declared a protected natural reserve by the government in 1990 and in 1999 its denizens began developing the basic infrastructure to host curious guests. The results, while still in progress, are enchanting.

Miraflor as an entity is totally unique (and a little confusing). The total population of Mirafloreños is about 5,000, dispersed throughout the 206 square kilometers of the reserve. In some areas, the people live close enough to one another to be called a community, but as for a central "town," there isn't any. The Miraflor Reserve is privately owned, cooperatively managed in many parts, and receives very minimal help from MARENA.

Much of the development effort has come from, or been channeled through, one of several associations of small-scale producers. Most notable among these is the UCA Miraflor (or in its full, bulky

MIRAFLOR NATURE RESERVE

ESTELÍ & THE SEGOVIAS

© AVALON TRAVEL PUBLISHING, INC.

LEGENDS OF THE LAGUNA

La Laguna de Miraflor is not exactly spectacular. Sure, the surrounding dense cloud forest that crowds its marshy banks and is filled with singing birds is admirable, and one feels a remote peacefulness sitting by the still water of this hidden crater lake, but compared to other Nicaraguan *lagunas,* this is a mere puddle. The fame of the Laguna de Miraflor lies not in its grandeur, but in its myth. There are at least five legends surrounding the lagoon, stories passed down over the years that have enveloped the 10-hectare body of water in a shroud of mystery as thick as the white clouds sweeping through the trees and over its surface.

The most famous of these legends is the **Ramo de Flores:** Every Thursday of Semana Santa, a cluster of beautiful flowers rises to the surface of the lagoon, and circulates around and around. The flowers, say some, are bringing a message to the people that they should unite. The name Miraflor (flower view) comes from this legend, and variations tell of a tiny dancing prince in the middle of the flowers and dwarfs bearing the flowers to give to local girls.

Also well known is the story of the **Ciudad Perdida** (The Lost City). Only the oldest of Mirafloreños knows of the secret entrance, but everyone knows of the vast fields of exotic fruit-bearing trees in the city at the bottom of the lagoon (which, by

the way, has been measured at 27 meters deep, plus three meters of sediment). One can eat all they want when in the city, but if they try bringing the fruit back to the surface world, they will not be allowed to pass.

Every now and then the water of the lagoon turns jet black; evidence, say some, of the giant black serpent that lives in the water and occasionally stirs up the sediment on the bottom. The snake may or may not have something to do with the lagoon's vengeful nature, punishing anyone who speaks disrespectfully of it or their disbelief in its power. One unfortunate young man did so "recently" while swimming in the middle—he had barely spoken his blasphemy when a whirlpool formed, sucked him under, and then spit him back up, whereupon he apologized profusely and pledged his eternal respect for the enchanted waters.

Just across the road, the **Laguna de Lodo,** or Lagoon of Mud, has its share of legends as well. The mud pond is half the size of its counterpart, and lies above the subterranean river that feeds the main lagoon. One day, a local *leñador* (lumberjack) was working near the Laguna de Lodo and dropped his axe into the mud, which promptly swallowed it up. He cried and cried and cried, until his axe finally rose to the surface. . . with a head and blade of shining gold.

ESTELÍ & THE SEGOVIAS

form: the Union de Cooperativas Agropecuarias Héroes y Mártires de Miraflor—not to be confused with the University of Central America), an association of 14 small farmer cooperatives made up of 120 families living within the protected area. Although they have accomplished a great deal promoting tourism, this is not UCA Miraflor's number-one priority. They are primarily seen as a credit-providing institution, but have also worked on issues such as community health and education, organic agriculture and diversification of crops, cooperative coffee production, gender and youth groups, and conflict resolution.

Sights and Attractions

Miraflor has something for everyone—nature lovers, hikers, social justice workers, organic farm-

ers, artists, horse lovers, orchid fanatics, birders, and entomologists—each of whom will find their own personal heaven here. You can certainly see parts of Miraflor in a day trip from Estelí, but read on and consider experiencing the unique housing opportunities.

It should be noted that every attraction in Miraflor is privately owned, often by poor campesinos. A fee system is being developed, and should be worked out soon, but be aware that this is a perfect opportunity to support the preservation of the remaining forests here by paying an entrance to enjoy them.

Birding: UCA Miraflor president and chief birder, Francisco "Chico Períco" Muñoz, has identified 236 bird species so far (60 of which are migratory, traveling south between October and April), belonging to 46 different families. If Chico's data are correct, then 37 percent of the identified bird species in all of Nicaragua are observable in the 206 square kilometers of Miraflor! This includes four species of the elusive quetzal *(Pharomachrus mocinno),* toucans, the *ranchero (Procnias tricaruntulata)* with its three dangling chins, and the Nicaraguan national bird, the *guardabarranco.*

Other Fauna: Illegal hunting still persists and most of Miraflor's animals are much more elusive, say, than the birds and orchids. Nevertheless, if you spend enough time with the right guide, you may see coyotes, sloths, deer, howler monkeys, or one of six different feline species, in addition to various raccoons, skunks, armadillos, and exotic rodents.

Orchids: With more than 300 identified species, Miraflor is one of the richest and most unexplored orchid viewing regions anywhere. Of note is an enormous colony of *Cattleya skinniri* (the national flower of Costa Rica). Miraflor also boasts many bromeliads and an *Orquídeario* (orchid museum) of replanted fallen orchids from throughout the reserve.

Hikes and Waterfalls: Short hikes are possible in any of the hundreds of clumps of forest, but ask your guide to take you on one of the more adventurous trips. Although difficult to access, La Chorrera is one of the wildest spots in the reserve, with a 60-meter waterfall (only impressive in the rainy season), prime bird viewing, and the chance to glimpse monkeys and maybe even a puma.

The Caves of Apaguis are located 1,000 meters off the road, and were created by indigenous peoples mining gems. Surrounded by robles and pines, the site offers beautiful views toward Estelí and the legend of the *duendes* (dwarfs).

Bosque Los Volcancitos is a mature cloud forest and home to the quetzal and several families of howler monkeys. It also contains the highest point in Miraflor (1,484 meters). When the clouds break, there are extensive views from any of a number of overlooks, including El Tayacán, Cerro Yeluca, Cerro El Aguila, La Coyotera, and Ocote Calzado.

Ruins: Indiana Jones types take note: there is still a great deal of archaeological work to be done here, as only a few of the sites have actually been excavated. Included in these is the *casa antigua,* a 1,200-year-old foundation in the Tayacán area, surrounded by dozens of other unearthed *montículos* (mounds).

Progressive Agriculture: Anyone interested in observing one of many alternative farming techniques will get an eyeful in Miraflor. Compared to the rest of the country, where slashing and burning is de rigueur, the campesinos of Miraflor are advanced in the use of organic compost, natural pest management (including a fungal insecticide lab in Puertas Azules), watershed protection, live fences, crop diversification, soil management, reforestation, worm farming, and environmental education. In addition, Miraflor boasts a number of small-scale, fair trade, organic coffee cooperatives, and a cupping lab (in Cebollál). The people are proud of their accomplishments and ready and willing to show them off. They'll even let you get some dirt under your fingernails if you so desire.

Accommodations and Food

Have no doubt: this is a rustic experience. There are no traditional hotels nor restaurants in Miraflor, but there are sufficient places to stay and eat. The majority of those involved in the tourism project are experienced and trained in taking care of foreigners, and their accommodations are clean (it's all relative), safe, and comfortable. There are two ways to spend the night in Miraflor: staying with a campesino family in their home or renting a room in the more developed *cabañas.* Choosing the former option means slightly less privacy, but the experience will be unforgettable.

Campesino Homes: A number of campesinos have adapted their homes to receive guests, and some are definitively more earthy than the others. In Cebollál, there are eight such families, and larger groups can arrange homestays in several of these houses at the same time. One of the most isolated is the home of José Ernesto in Cebollál Abajo, reached by driving down a nonroad, then hiking through his bean fields and across a creek with several shaded swimming holes. Of the more visited homes is that of Juan

Antonio Rodriguez, who, in addition to accepting guests, maintains a model farm with 100 percent organic broccoli, coffee, citrus, and carrots. The community of Sontule has 10 homes with capacity for housing 30 visitors. These accommodations cost roughly $4 for the first night, $2.20 the second night, three meals for $5.

Cabañas Turísticas: Posada la Soñada is tucked behind a field of organic cabbage in the community of Cebollál and is a wonderful bed-and-breakfast. The owner, Doña Corina Picado, knows what she's doing and runs a professional, immaculate business. She has three rooms, each with two bunk beds, and capacity for 12 guests, with an outside latrine. The key phrase here is "peace and quiet," best experienced with a hot cup of locally grown *manzanilla* (chamomile) tea, sitting on the porch and watching the clouds roll through the forest in her backyard.

But let's talk about the food: Doña Corina is surprisingly talented. She's traveled the world, always on the lookout for new recipes, and while her food is definitely Nicaragüense, she will direct her menu and ingredients to suit the nationality of her visitors. She has studied cooking and nutrition and has much experience teaching what she has learned to her neighbors. The inclination must run in the family—her grandmother was a camp cook for Sandino. Speaking of the general, Doña Corina's uncle, who lives out back and is in his nineties, remembers encounters with Sandino and has stories to share. Doña Corina claims she was "born Sandinista" and was very active in the first literacy and preschool brigades of the revolution. Ask her about her experiences over that cup of tea. She charges $4 a night for a bed, and $2 per meal—it's hard to imagine a better deal. Contact her through the UCA, or call her at home in Estelí during the week, tel. 713-6333.

Just down the road, and hidden in its own clump of cloud forest and coffee, is the **Finca Lindos Ojos.** You'll find two cabins with capacity for 16 guests, including two queen-size beds for couples. The farm produces organic coffee and vegetables, and has a solar panel and generator for the water pump and lights. Lindos Ojos is affiliated with the UCA, but maintains a certain

independence, handling its own publicity and promotion. Run by a German couple in Estelí, it offers package trips that include meals, guided hikes, and organic agriculture demonstrations; $25 per person per weekend, $10 day trips, extra charge for horse rental, tel. 713-4041, email: kahrin@ibw.com.ni.

La Casita has comparable facilities, but is located on the other side of the reserve, in San Jose del Terrero, run by Everardo Moreno, with two rooms and four beds. Contact through UCA Miraflor.

Information and Services
Your main source of information is the UCA Miraflor office in Estelí, located from the Esso station, two blocks north, one west, half north. The building faces the Pan-American and has a well-marked corner store of natural agricultural supplies, but the office entrance is located on the other side, facing away from the highway (open Mon.–Fri. 8 A.M.–12:30 P.M. and 2–5 P.M., tel. 713-2971, email: miraflor@ibw.com.ni, website: www.arrakis.es/~barneo).

As for services in Miraflor, there aren't any. There is no electricity (except for the solar panels at Lindos Ojos and Casitas), no telephones, no running water, no banks—*nada*. Your meals will be taken care of where you stay, but if you want anything special, pack it in, or arrange it with your host beforehand. There are a couple of ramshackle *pulperías* scattered around, but that's about it.

What to Bring
Miraflor is situated 1,400 wonderful meters above sea level. It is a paradise, but because of the altitude and frequent precipitation, it can be a cold, wet, and muddy paradise. If you don't have one, pick up a sweatshirt at one of Estelí's millions of used clothing stores. The *cabañas* usually have a supply of purified water, but you'd be wise to carry a couple of gallons in with you, or else some way to treat the local water.

Getting There and Away
Driving may be tricky, as there are still no signs on any of the turnoffs. Start by forking right at the StarMart near Estelí's northern *salida,* and

stay right as you cross the flat tobacco fields. After the first major climb (stop to climb the unmanned, birdcage-looking fire tower), you'll wind across a flat, dry mesa and come to another fork in the road (about 13 km from Estelí), in the middle of which is the **Miraflor Visitor Reception Center,** currently under construction. The right branch goes to La Concordia, so turn left and continue across the plain and up into the clouds. This is where the magic begins: oak forests draped with Spanish moss (called *barba de viejo,* old man's beard). About 12 kilometers past the visitor center, you'll come to another fork, called "La Rampla" bus stop. The left road goes to Cebollál and the accommodations there; the right continues toward the lagoon, Puertas Azules, and eventually San Sebastian de Yalí.

There are three daily buses for Yalí that leave Estelí's main COTRAN at 6 A.M., noon, and 4 P.M. They all turn off the highway at the Texaco StarMart (where they'll stop to pick up passengers; you can quickly stock up before the trip here if you're lucky) and head northeast on a dirt road out of town. Buses back to Estelí pass La Rampla at 7 A.M., 11 A.M., and 4 P.M. The UCA Miraflor may be able to arrange a ride for you, but if you decide to take your chances hitchhiking (not many vehicles travel this road, and those that do may not be heading exactly where you want to go), then put yourself on the road to Yalí next to the StarMart.

CONDEGA

Quiet and slow, like many sleepy agrarian towns in northern Nicaragua, Condega is nicknamed Tierra de los Alfareros (Land of the Potters), has about 9,000 inhabitants, and is a centuries-old commercial center for area farmers, most of whom eke out a living raising cattle or corn and beans. The word "Condega" refers to the large quantity of pre-Columbian pottery that has been dug out of area cornfields. This same potters' tradition lives on today with a women's cooperative in Ducualí Grande that produces pottery in much the same way as their ancestors did.

Because Condegans supported the Sandin-istas in the 1970s, Somoza's National Guard knocked on a lot of doors looking for trouble, and Sandinista Omar Cabezas (see Suggested Reading) hid out for months with his troops in those same mountains, reportedly in a cave near El Naranjo.

Upon gaining power in 1979, the Sandinistas confiscated lands around town from the few *terretenientes* (landowners)—only three men owned all the land from Condega east to Yalí—and distributed it to the poor. The people remain largely Sandinista to this day. When Contra soldiers began roaming the area after the revolution, they found easy pickings in the unprotected, subsistence farms east of Condega. Several major skirmishes occurred in the Canta Gallo Mountains 20 kilometers east of the city, and the locals are full of horror stories from the events of the 1980s.

During Hurricane Mitch, Condega was cut off completely from the rest of Nicaragua due to washed away bridges north of the city and a major rockslide that blocked the highway to the south. Over 200 homes were washed away, as was a major cigar box producing workshop. The waters of the Río Estelí rose to a point only two blocks east of the park. Stand at that point and look east toward the river to get an appreciation for what happened.

Sights

"In Condega, we don't have an airport, but we've got a plane," locals will tell you, referring to the famous **airplane park.** Toward the end of his grip on power, Somoza took to strafing the northern hillsides with his air force. When, on April 7, 1979, the Sandinistas downed one of his planes, it was considered a major victory and huge morale booster. Patriotic Nicaraguans from all around come to visit the plane's wreckage, which is visible from the highway and surrounded by a quasi-park. Follow the dirt road behind the cemetery up the hill 100 meters to the top.

Founded in 1977, the **Casa de Cultura** resides in the former command post of the National Guard. One of its elements, a public library, enjoyed widespread community support during the Sandinista years, when each family donated a book to the room. The Casa offers classes in sewing and guitar playing. Among other things, the museum, named after the town's first archaeologist, has a fascinating collection of pre-Columbian ceramic work that has been unearthed in the cornfields around town (open weekdays 9 A.M.–5 P.M., reading room open weekdays from 1–5 P.M.).

Condega boasts its own **baseball stadium,** where the home team competes with surrounding towns like Ducualí and Estelí. Check out authentic grassroots games on weekends—especially Sundays during the dry season.

Condega has not one but two public **swimming pools.** The Linda Vista ($1.50) is along the highway just south of the cemetery, and the Piscina La Granja ($1) is about one kilometer west along the road to Pire. The second, farther away from town, is set in the middle of a very pretty flower garden.

Town meetings are held at the **Centro Recreativo Xilonem** and most afternoons, children swarm in to play games and sing. During Hurricane Mitch, hundreds of refugees from the surrounding communities huddled in the Recreativo while the river swept through their homes. The *fiestas patronales* occur in the weeks surrounding May 15th and celebrate San Isidro Labrador.

Crafts and Workshops

To reach the **Taller de Cerámica Ducualí Grande,** take a bus north about two kilometers and get off where a large concrete sign points west to the workshop. Follow that road one full kilometer across the bridge and through the community of Ducualí Grande. Turn left when you see the small church and look for the white sign on the right side. The workshop was founded in the 1980s with the help of a Spanish volunteer, and the 13 workers still proudly turn out charming ceramic pieces, using the simplest of wheels and firing the pieces in a wood stove; prices are from $1–7.

Tenería Expisa, an offshoot of the old slaughterhouse (once owned by one of Somoza's wealthy cronies, then confiscated by the Sandinista government, which ran it into bankruptcy), this leather processing plant exports several different types of raw products to other Central American countries and the United States. Hurricane Mitch left the already-struggling company unable to pick up the pieces of what remained of the flooded factory. It was subsequently purchased by a Costa Rican investor and the leather processing continues. Ask the manager, David Silva, to see the photo album from Mitch.

One of the most famous musical instrument workshops in the north is located behind the Casa de Cultura and makes quality guitars, violins, and *guitarrones.*

A Sandinista cooperative of women carpenters, the **Taller de Carpinteras Mujeres** makes good furniture to this day and has managed to remain financially solvent. **Taller de Candelas de Condega** is a small candle workshop, whose wares are found in shops all over Nicaragua; the designs are simple and colorful, and you can pick one up for under $2.

Hikes near Condega

Plaicí Loop: From Condega, walk or bus one kilometer to the baseball stadium. Hike 8.5 kilometers east along the road to Yalí, then turn south toward Plaicí (Nahuatl for Valley of Fear). You can also catch a Yalí bus (one leaves approximately every hour from the park at Condega). Hiking south through Plaicí, ask for directions to get to San Ramón, which is located along the highway (total distance 20 kilometers).

Venecia: From Condega take the early morning bus (5 A.M.) east to the coffee cooperative of Venecia (45 minutes). There are several small trails starting in Venecia that wind down and around the hillside through pine trees and coffee fields. The view is fantastic and the air is cool compared to Condega. There are neither lodging facilities nor restaurants in Venecia, so travel prepared (last bus from Venecia back to Condega leaves at 5 P.M.). Venecia is a relatively new town, created to house the local coffee workers when the land was made a coffee cooperative. As a stand-out Sandinista position, the Contras attacked it brutally, even burning it mostly to the ground in the mid-1980s.

San Andrés: From Condega take any of the buses heading to Yalí/La Rica, and get off at Empalme El Hato (12 kilometers, 45 minutes). Follow that dirt road straight through El Hato and

Sialcuna northwest to the small cattle town of San Andrés. The road will take you through a pine forest down to the edge of the Río Coco; total distance 25 kilometers. The hilltop of Cerro Sialcuna is a good spot to sleep on a pine needle bed if you've got a tent, and the view of the valley and the steep green hills to the east is well worth spending the night. To get to the spot, walk past Sialcuna and look for a trail on your right side as you begin to descend.

Accommodations

Pensión Baldovinos has been a mainstay in the community for decades. This old, wooden boardinghouse is worth a visit even if you stay elsewhere; 20 small, private rooms with shared bath go for $3 a night; each room is a little different, so ask to see several. The kitchen, run by a trio of mothers, serves traditional meals and coffee, tel. 752-2393. **Hospedaje Framar** is new and clean, and right in front of the park with single and double rooms and one large room for groups. Eight impeccably clean, simple rooms with shared bath, set around a small patio, $4; doors close at 10 P.M., so be prompt or get locked out. The owner scrupulously weeds out the shady elements, so be presentable, tel. 752-2222.

The newest of Condega's lodging facilities, **Rincón Criollo La Gualca,** is owned by a Belgian-Nicaraguan couple. It's a bar/restaurant/disco with a half-dozen clean, small rooms downstairs for $4. The shared baths have the only hot water in town. The rooms can be noisy on Friday or Saturday nights, or damn convenient if you get lucky on the dance floor. The restaurant offers Nicaraguan and European breakfasts.

Food

Possibly your best option for a typical beef or chicken dish, **Comedor Herrera** sells a plate with *fresco* for $2. A clean and well-run place, **Lekamar** (a word composed of three daughters' names) will cost a little more but is generally worth it; plates of chicken, beef, or fish run $3–5. Quiet and discreet, **Bar Café Carolina** offers a chance to eat a meal well off the street in tables set alongside a quiet garden. Good tacos, chicken, juice drinks and beer, and a little privacy if you need to get away. **Comedor Rosamelia** serves heart-stopping deep-fried chicken for $2 a plate.

Restaurante El Típico serves up the best *mondongo* in town—if you've got a yen for a bowl of tripe soup. Pricey but with a nice atmosphere; give it a try while you're waiting for a Sunday afternoon bus. On the north end of town, **Restaurante El Higinio** is your best chance of getting serenaded by roving mariachi bands while you kick back with a cold beer and eat from a decent menu, too ($1.50–5). The party lasts all night long, or until the boys get too rowdy.

Services

There are several pharmacies in town, but Ramón Zavala, owner of the Farmacia Santa Martha one block east of the park, is worth visiting regardless of whether you need medicine. He runs a lively business in traditional and herbal medicines, homemade stogies, and farm goods. His stories of the Contra attacks east of Condega are riveting.

Getting There and Away

Any bus that travels between Ocotal, Somoto, or Jalapa and Managua or Estelí can drop you off on the highway in front of Condega, a two-block walk from the center of town. Or take the Yalí/La Rica buses from Estelí (5 A.M.–4:10 P.M.). Make sure to ask if the bus goes through Condega, as there are two routes to Yalí. Express buses will let you off on the highway by the cemetery; *ordinarios* will let you off in front of the park.

PALACAGÜINA AND COFFEE COOP

The town of Palacagüina is widely known as the setting for Carlos Mejía Godoy's revolutionary and religious anthem, "Cristo de Palacagüina," in which Jesus is born "*en el cerro de la iguana, montaña dentro de la Segovia*" ("in the iguana hill, deep within the mountains of Segovia"). In the song, the Christ child's campesino parents, Jose and María, are dismayed when, instead of becoming a carpenter like his father, he wants to be a guerrilla fighter. Located a few kilometers off the main highway, Palacagüina is reached by most *ordinario* buses traveling between Estelí and Somoto or Ocotal, which make a detour through the city center.

There is one place to stay in Palacagüina proper, **Hospedaje Arón,** but the main attraction is one of Nicaragua's largest **fair trade coffee cooperatives,** PRODECOOP, on its own compound between Palacagüina and the northern exit to the highway. Made up of some 2,000 grower families, PRODECOOP exports as much as 30,000 *quintales* (100-pound bags) a year. PRODECOOP can house and feed up to six

guests in brand new accommodations atop the cupping lab and overlooking the vast drying beds, which bustle with activity during the harvest. There is also a swimming pool, and a 360-degree view of the surrounding hills. Cost is about $20 per person per night, but be sure to make arrangements in advance; their office in Estelí is 75 meters west of the *esquina de los bancos,* tel. 713-3268, email: prodecoop@ibw.com.ni, website: www.prodecoop.com.

Near Estelí to the North and West

West of the Pan-American Highway is found a series of pueblos nestled in the mountains, all connected by rustic and rutted country roads, and each with its own peaceful flavor.

PUEBLO NUEVO

First inhabited in 1652, Pueblo Nuevo is one of the few northern towns that was not affected much by the Contra war. There are about 3,000 urban inhabitants and some 19,000 living off the land in the surrounding countryside. **Doña Selina** will rent you a room in her house, feed you, and should be able to help you find a local guide to go hiking in the surrounding hills or to view some of the organic agriculture by the river. One nice hike is up to the community of Pencal, across the river and about 1.5 hours each way. You can also stay in the farmhouse/hospedaje **Finca La Virgen.** While in Pueblo Nuevo, take a look at the infrequently visited **Museo Arqueologico** in the Casa de Cultura, showing pottery, old farm implements, and archaeological pieces found in the area. Located next to the phone office, open Monday–Friday 8 A.M.–noon and 2–5 P.M., tel. 719-2512.

Twelve kilometers west of town on the road to Limay, you'll find **El Bosque,** an archaeological dig site where the bones of several mastodons, glyptodons (predecessors to modern armadillos), and early ancestors of the horse species have been uncovered. At 18,000–32,000 years old, the bones are considered one of the oldest archaeo-

logical sites in the Americas. While digging for bones, remnants of Paleolithic hunting weapons were discovered on an upper stratum of soil, from an age when our human ancestors roamed the continent hunting mastodons. No conclusions have been drawn from the site yet.

Pueblo Nuevo honors San Rafael Arcángel during the week leading up to October 24. Buses leave Estelí twice a day at 11:45 A.M. and 3:10 P.M., leaving Pueblo Nuevo at 6:30 A.M. and 8:30 A.M.; ask in the park about transportation that continues farther west into the country.

SAN JUAN DE LIMAY

Limay's claim to fame is its abundance of *marmolina* (soapstone) reserves and local artists who have been working the stone since 1972, when a priest named Eduardo Mejía arrived to see how he could help the population improve their lot. Padre Mejía helped the new artists mine the soapstone from nearby Mt. Tipiscayán (Ulúa-Matagalpa for mountain of the toucan), develop their talent, and market the figurines they created. They made beautifully polished long-necked birds, kissing swans, iguanas, and rounded, womanly shapes. After the revolution, the minister of culture, Ernesto Cardenal, came to Limay to help the stoneworkers create an artists' cooperative. The coop enjoyed a brief success, but has since disbanded, its members scattering far and wide. A core of local carvers still live and work in Limay, and they all have open workshops where

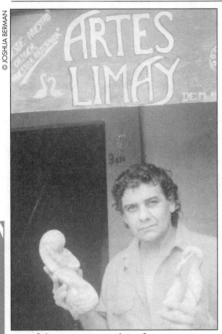

© JOSHUA BERMAN

ESTELÍ & THE SEGOVIAS

one of the soapstone artists of
San Juan de Limay

you can watch them at work and buy their products (to find them, just ask for the *artesanos de piedra*). To enjoy the surrounding nature, hike the Río Los Quesos, which wanders around outside of town and is home to the Poza La Bruja, with its swimming hole and age-old petroglyphs.

Accommodations and Food

El Pensión Guerrero (warrior), a pink corner building located one block north of the Catholic church, has 15 beds, a row of pit latrines, and a place to shower (or take a bucket bath), all for $2 a night. El Guerrero also has a smoke-blackened kitchen that offers typical Nicaraguan breakfast, lunch, and dinner for $1 a plate. Next door to the Guerrero is Antonio Vindell's bookstore/hardware/music/smoke shop. The produce of his tobacco field out back goes into handmade and hand-rolled cigars for export. At his shop you'll find fresh *puros* for the prepackaging, pretax price of less than $.50 each.

Getting There and Away

San Juan de Limay is 40 kilometers from Estelí and reached via a gorgeous (but painfully slow) bus ride over a cool, coffee-producing mountain pass over a kilometer high. Buses follow two routes to Limay *(por la Shell y por El Pino),* and leave Estelí at 8:45 A.M., 9:15 A.M., 12:15 P.M., and 2 P.M. By car or hitching, travel to the Empalme La Sirena north of Estelí. Soon after turning left, you'll hit a fork—turn right and continue up into the clouds. At the next division, fork left. After you've dropped down into the flat valley, you'll come to a T; a right turn will take you to Pueblo Nuevo, a left to Limay. About 10–15 minutes after the T, look for a well-used right turn opposite an enormous billboard. Turn right and continue into town.

Ocotal

This is a true frontier town, the last major settlement before the end of the road at Jalapa and the enormous wilderness that stretches to the Caribbean. Only a couple of streets are paved, and rugged mountains stand guard in every direction.

The Departamento of Nueva Segovia is a jewel, concealing from the rest of Nicaragua pine tree–carpeted hills with hikes, waterfalls, hot springs, colonial ruins, and indigenous communities.

History

The Spaniards who came to settle in the remote Segovia Mountains in the early 16th century did not have an easy go of it. Constantly threatened and attacked by the Xicaque tribes and marauding English pirates traveling up the Río Coco, they were forced numerous times to move their settlement in search of safety. Ocotal is the fourth and final Spanish settlement of Nueva Segovia, formed in 1780 and named after the thick pine forests of *Pinus oocarpa,* or *ocote* in Spanish.

More recent history is evident in the disintegrating guard tower just south of the bus station. Located only 22 kilometers from the Honduran border at Las Manos, Ocotal, and the surrounding communities were extremely hot and strategic points during the Contra war. For a detailed, personal history, just talk to anyone older than 15. Ocotal's new battle is currently against the pine bark beetle that is killing off the pine forests quicker than the people have been able to with their machetes and axes. Several thousand hectares of Nicaragua's precious few remaining pine reserves have been destroyed by the beetle, and poor legislation means it's cheaper for the locals to let the fallen wood rot on the ground than try to harvest it, a tragedy on top of tragedy.

ORIENTATION AND GETTING AROUND

Buses drop you at the COTRAN, about 10 blocks south of the main plaza. Two main *entradas* (entrances) to the city, one from the south, and another from the highway to the west, lead straight into the town center. Climb the *monumento* stairs near the western entrance to look around and get a lay of the land. Most of the commercial activity occurs between the park, the market, and around the Shell station on the highway. Ocotal is walkable but has numerous taxis anyway, plus a recently acquired fleet of ciclo-taxi rickshaws.

SIGHTS AND ATTRACTIONS

Many people consider Ocotal's **park** to be one of the finest in Nicaragua. In the evenings it's a magnet for the townspeople, who all come out to gossip and relax. While you're there, pop into the church, whose **bell tower** allegedly still bears the names of gringo marines where they carved them with their bayonets. The marines had plenty of time on their hands as they patrolled the hillsides for Sandino and crew.

NEARBY HIKES

Cerro Mogotón is the highest point in Nicaragua at 2,107 meters and is climbable as a day trip from Ocotal. Las Tres Señoritas and their two swimming holes (known as *Las Pozas la Ladosa y Salterín*) can be reached by walking west (or grabbing a taxi) on El Nuevo Almanecer road, and then crossing the river. Explore on your own, or ask locals for more specific directions, but be careful—the rivers here are said to be *encantada* (enchanted). To the south of Ocotal is El Cerro Picudo, an inviting mountain with plenty of trails and allegedly containing a hidden lagoon on top, as well as the "Caves of the Dwarf."

ENTERTAINMENT

A half-block west of the park, Ocotal's **movie theater** costs $1. Both of the city's discos are open Saturday and Sunday (and sometimes Friday), and cost $2 or so to enter. **Discoteca Infinito,** a few blocks north of the cathedral, is

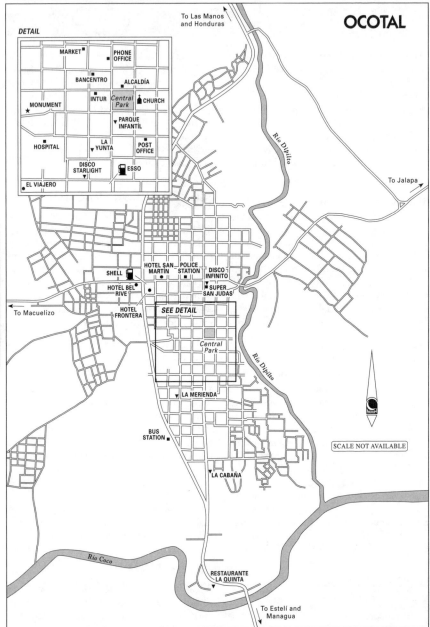

OCOTAL

To Las Manos
and Honduras

Río Dipilto

To Jalapa

DETAIL

MARKET

PHONE
OFFICE

BANCENTRO

ALCALDÍA

MONUMENT

INTUR

Central
Park

CHURCH

PARQUE
INFANTÍL

HOSPITAL

LA
YUNTA

POST
OFFICE

DISCO
STARLIGHT

ESSO

EL VIAJERO

SHELL

HOTEL SAN
MARTÍN

POLICE
STATION

DISCO
INFINITO

HOTEL BEL
RIVE

SUPER
SAN JUDAS

To Macuelizo

HOTEL
FRONTERA

SEE DETAIL

Central
Park

Río Dipilto

LA MERIENDA

SCALE NOT AVAILABLE

BUS
STATION

LA CABAÑA

Río Coco

RESTAURANTE
LA QUINTA

To Estelí and
Managua

home to a more low-key crowd than the **Starlight** (one block west of the Esso) where the occasional fight breaks out.

ACCOMMODATIONS

Under $10

Ocotal boasts at least five *hospedajes* that charge under $2 for a bed, all located within two blocks of the central park. Most are family-run and probably safe, but the good news stops there. Alternatively, **El Viajero,** 3.5 blocks west of the Esso, has 18 simple rooms ($4 s, $7 d, and $11 t, tel. 732-2954). **Hotel San Martín** is a good budget call, offering "matrimonial" beds in clean rooms with private bath and fan ($6 s, $11 d, one block east of the Shell, tel. 732-2788). Although still in the low cost category, **Hotel Bel Rive** is a big step up, located on the west side of the highway across from the Shell; its 27 rooms are clean and modern, with private bath, phone, TV, and fan for only $7 s, $11 d, and $18 t, parking available, tel. 732-2146 or 732-3249.

$10–25

Ocotal's finest is **Hotel Frontera,** on the highway right behind the Shell station. Poolside bar, conference room, parking, Internet, and restaurant; 25 rooms and growing, $35 s, $45 d, $55 t, private bath, phone, TV, and wonderful airy porches overlooking the city and mountains, tel. 732-2668.

FOOD

Start with a lunch at the **Llamarada del Bosque,** a delicious and cheap eatery facing the south side of the park. Also, simple fare and well-prepared *licuados* and juice drinks can be found at the **Cafetín Parque Infantíl,** a half-block south of the southwest corner of the park.

La Cabaña, eight blocks south of the park, has a beautiful open dining patio, with thick vegetation and shady tables, and an accompanying midrange hotel. Meals are on the pricey side ($5–12 a plate), and you should probably be wary of so much seafood on the menu, but there is plenty of meat too, tel. 732-2415. A similar menu is offered at **La Merienda,** three blocks west and six south of the park; also a great drinking spot, tel. 732-2633. **La Yunta,** one block west and three south of the park, is another moderately priced steak restaurant, tel. 732-2180. Another favorite is **La Quinta,** on the highway south of town, which boasts the most varied menu in town.

SHOPPING

The municipal market is one block north and one west of the park. Ocotal's only supermarket, San Judas, is 3.5 blocks north of the cathedral. Limited selection of local *artesanía* is sold in the INTUR office and **Ayuda en Acción,** an NGO just north and west of the park. Find photo supplies in the Kodak Express. Located two blocks north of the cathedral, it has a good stock of supplies and one-hour developing (open Mon.–Fri. 8 A.M.–6 P.M., Sat. until 2 P.M., tel. 732-2126).

INFORMATION AND SERVICES

For whatever reason, Ocotal is blessed with impressive access to tourist information. The INTUR office, located half a block west of the northwest corner of the park, is years ahead of its counterparts around the country. Not only is it friendly, helpful, and stocked with its own local tourist guide, but it also works locally training waiters and hoteliers, and organizes cultural exchanges with other parts of Nicaragua (open Mon.–Fri. 8 A.M.–noon, 2–5 P.M., tel. 732-3429). Equally impressive is the Alcaldía's Center of Documentation on the northwest corner of the park, offering a full library of local maps, histories, and photocopy services, as well as workspace in which to study.

Basic Services

There are four banks in Ocotal; Bancentro is one block west and one north of the park, tel. 732-3367. The post office is one block south of the cathedral and one east (open Mon.–Sat. 8

A.M.–noon, 2–5 P.M., tel. 732-3021 or 732-2018). ENITEL is two blocks north of the park (open 7 A.M.–8:45 P.M., tel. 732-2221). Careli Viajes maintains a travel agency a half-block north of the cathedral, tel. 732-2649.

Internet

The Cyber Café, across from the Instituto Nacional, may or may not be functioning. Internet access is also available at the Hotel Frontera, though its prices may be a little higher than elsewhere.

Immigration

The office is located in a shiny blue and white building two blocks south of the COTRAN, open Monday–Friday 8 A.M.–5 P.M., tel. 732-3084 or 732-3038.

GETTING THERE AND AWAY

Nine *expreso* buses leave daily from the CO-TRAN for the four-hour ride to Managua, the first at 4 A.M. and the last at 3:15 P.M. The last *ordinario* bus for the capital leaves at 6 P.M. Buses north to the border at Las Manos leave regularly from 5 A.M.–4 P.M.

Crossing the Border at Las Manos

The Honduran border is 24 kilometers north of Ocotal, or a 45-minute bus ride. It is open 8 A.M.–5 P.M. every day. You will be charged $2 to leave Nicaragua and $7 to enter, according to Ocotal immigration officials. This is the least used of all the northern border stations and services on either side are scarce. Make sure you have dollars or lempiras, as there is no place to change money. The nearest town in Honduras is El Paraíso, 12 kilometers from the border. From there, the bus ride to Tegucigalpa is about three hours.

NEAR OCOTAL

With a little poking around, you'll find plenty to explore throughout Nueva Segovia. Plan on a few day trips out of Ocotal to the hot springs, swimming holes, artisan communities, and colonial remnants, then go deep with an overnight in frontier-town Jalapa or the Contra community of Quilalí, birthplace of every warrior movement in the last century.

If sitting in a completely undeveloped, natural hot spring appeals to you, grab a *camión* for the Macuelizo Termales at the Shell station and settle in for the 90-minute ride. Find a guide in town. There is nowhere to stay in Macuelizo, so count on it being a day trip.

Ciudad Antigua

Built in 1610 after the sacking of the first settlement by the Jicaque people, Ciudad Antigua was the second Spanish attempt to settle Nueva Segovia (the remnants of the first settlement, built in 1543 at the bequest of then-governor Rodrigo de Contreras, are called Ciudad Vieja, and can still be seen near Quilalí at the junction of the Jícaro and Coco Rivers). Many of the colonial structures withstood the various sackings by pirates and indigenous peoples (traces of which are still visible in the scorch marks on the wooden church doors). Ciudad Antigua has an interesting museum of well-loved religious pieces and a few historic documents that survived the onslaughts of the 19th century. Check out the **Museo Religioso de Ciudad Antigua** next to the Iglesia Señor de los Milagros, open Monday–Friday 8 A.M.–4 P.M.

Mozonte

Only about an hour away from Ocotal, the largely indigenous-descendant community of Mozonte is most notable for its workshops of potters that produce pieces made of a particularly fine clay. You can spend the better part of a morning in Mozonte admiring the craftsmanship of these potters. Start with William Gomez, across from the central park, and then the workshop **Tierra Fertil**.

San Fernando

San Fernando's 7,000 inhabitants live on over 200 individual coffee farms and produce an estimated 25,000 *quintales* of coffee annually. More famous than its coffee, however, are its inhabitants, who since the colonial days have been a little lighter-skinned and a little more Spanish-looking. Many have blue or light brown eyes. How do they do it? Well, just don't ask about those last name combinations: Herrera-Herrera, Urbina-Urbina, and Ortez-Ortez, though many attribute the blue eyes to the town's occupation by the U.S. Marines from 1927 to 1931. Life revolves around coffee in San Fernando, and many homes double as coffee processing plants and even *beneficios.* San Fernando is a notably picturesque village of thick adobe–walled homes set around the town park and **Templo Parroquial.**

You can stage a hike to Pico Mogotón, Nicaragua's highest point (2,106 meters) from San Fernando, but even from there Mogotón is 20 kilometers away. A better hike is to the **Salto San José,** where water rushing off the Dipilto mountain range cascades into a small pool. Take a bus to the community of Santa Clara and get off across from the ball field, turn left (north), and walk the 6–8 kilometers to the river. To be sure of the trail, hire a local kid to take you for some food and a couple cordobas. They all know the way, and might even jump in for a swim with you.

JALAPA

Tucked back in one of Nicaragua's farthest corners, fertile, moist Jalapa enjoys a microclimate suitable for the production of tobacco and vegetables its drought-stricken neighbors could only hope for. Jalapa is practically a country apart, only four kilometers from the border and separated from the rest of Nicaragua by 60 kilometers of rutted, disintegrating, nearly impassible road. Surrounded on three sides by Honduras and only surpassed in its remoteness by border outpost Teotecacinte, Jalapa struggles to remain integrated with the rest of Nicaragua.

Throughout the 1980s that isolation made it prime stalking ground for Contra incursions from three nearby bases in Honduran territory—Pino-I, Ariel, and Yamales. The city of Jalapa was flooded with refugees from farming communities farther afield in response to Contra

attacks like that of November 16, 1982, when a Contra unit kidnapped 60 campesinos at Río Arriba. Jalapa is a peaceful and laid-back place these days, most concerned with good tobacco harvests and the repair of the road that connects it to Ocotal. The whole town comes to life every year at the end of September for the **Festival de Maíz** (the Corn Festival).

Another form of *artesanía* appeared in the mid-1990s: baskets and small containers made of coiled and lashed pine needles. The folks from the Ocotal area and the folks from the Atlantic coast battle it out for who had the idea first. **Grupo Pinar del Norte** has lots of fine examples of this unique craft.

QUILALÍ

Quilalí has seen many of the battles fought in Nicaragua, starting in the 1930s when Sandino dug into the area of El Chipote and held off the U.S. Marines. Many battles of the Contra years were fought in the Quilalí area as well and you won't find a family in town that didn't lose a loved one to the war. The town remains steadfastly Contra to this day and is home to both El Chacál (José Angel Talavera) and El Chacalín (Alex Talavera), the heads of the Resistance Party (made up of ex-Contras).

Upon entering town you'll notice Quilalí is surprisingly well developed, courtesy of international aid money destined to support the Sandinista government's opponents. Rumor has it Quilalí's main street was often used as a secret airstrip during the 1980s. Many of the Contras here were trained for battle in the United States or in secret bases with locations unknown even to the participants. Their mementos from the U.S. military are treasured today: look for U.S. Army tin cups, knives, and mosquito nets—not to mention secret stashes of large weaponry that weren't turned in to Doña Violeta's government. The area is also well known for its marijuana production.

The road to Colina La Gloría offers beautiful views of surrounding mountains, and there are at least two swimming holes, one each in the Río Jícaro and Río Coco.

Accommodations and Food

Hospedaje Tere on main street costs $3 a night and is the cleanest place in town. **Hospedaje El Sol** is $2 and less desirable. Several informal, family establishments, including **Comedor Jackson** and **Sholla,** serve typical food for about $3 a plate.

Services

Quilalí has a very good hospital supported by Médicos sin Fronteras, and standard services like ENITEL and Correos.

Getting There and Away

Five buses leave daily from Estelí (5:45 A.M. – 1:40 P.M.). The five-hour trip goes through San Juan del Río Coco and continues on to Wiwilí. The road from Estelí is worse than the one from Ocotal; four buses a day travel from Ocotal to Quilalí via Santa Clara.

Somoto

Located on the south side of the Pan-American Highway as it veers westward toward the Honduran border at El Espino, Somoto is a middle-sized city of 15,000 and capital of the Department of Madriz. A branch of the Río Coco runs through the city, which, tucked into the hills at 700 meters above the sea, maintains a fresh climate most of the year. Somoto resides in the Cordillera de Somoto, the highest point of which is Cerro Tépec-Xomotl at 1,730 meters.

Originally named Tépec-Xomotl, or "Valley of the Turkeys," Somoto is known today more for its donkeys, *rosquillas* (baked corn cookies), and blowout carnival in November of every year. Although the *Ciudad de Burros,* as it is nicknamed, has less-obvious attractions than nearby Ocotal, spending a quiet evening in its quaint and friendly park, admiring the church, and enjoying the warmth of the townsfolk can be a pleasant option. The nearby airstrip that was built by U.S. Marines in the 1930s is reportedly the first runway ever built in Central America. It was subsequently used to launch the world's first aerial bombardment against Sandino and his troops.

Somoto and its surrounding communities have had a rough go of it lately, most recently in the droughts of 2000 and 2001. The poverty is obvious and the number of beggars truly sad. Your business will be appreciated. Note the *caites* sandals on the campesinos' feet—a resourceful use of old tires and, for some reason, totally unique to the area.

ORIENTATION AND GETTING AROUND

The new COTRAN bus terminal should be open, located on the north side of the highway, five blocks north of the church. The various taxis and ciclo-taxis (three-wheeled bicycle taxis) probably aren't necessary, as Somoto is pretty small.

SIGHTS AND EVENTS

The church, **La Parroquia Santiago de Somoto,** is one of Nicaragua's oldest monuments. Construction began in 1661, some 86 years before León's great cathedral.

If you're around Somoto on the eighth of any month, consider joining the religious masses on their pilgrimage to the tiny community of Cacaulí, all hoping for a glimpse of the Virgin Mary. Ever since she appeared to a young muchacho named Francisco in the late 1980s, thousands of people have arrived to try to repeat the miracle. They each carry a clear bottle of holy water, which they hold up to the sun at exactly 4 P.M. The Virgin should appear in the glass. If the eighth falls on a Sunday, be prepared for a massive event.

Somoto's *fiestas patronales* take place July 15–25, but the town is more famous for the Carnival of November 11 (or the second Saturday of the month), when it celebrates the creation of the Department of Madriz in 1936. All of Nicaragua's best party bands make the trip north, each setting up on one of seven

ROSQUILLAS SOMOTEÑAS

Although *rosquillas* are baked all over Nicaragua, the ones from Somoto's main street are particularly renowned throughout the country. The *rosquilla* is a simple, baked-corn snack that comes in various forms, sometimes with molasses or cheese baked into them, and always eaten alongside a cup of steaming black cof-

fee. The two main producers in town are La Rosquilla Somoteña Betty Espinoza and Rosquilla Garcia (tel. 722-2009), across the street from each other and two blocks west of the CO-TRAN. If you're traveling anywhere else in the country, Somoteñas make a cheap, simple gift, greatly appreciated by any Nicaraguan.

stages—plus mariachis, dance parties, and the standard bull- and cockfighting. As for everyday nightlife, try the **Bar Sueña La Luna,** on the highway just east of the CO-TRAN.

Time to make the *rosquillas* ... Somoto is famous for its baked corn treats.

ACCOMMODATIONS

If you're only traveling through and need a quick, simple bed on the side of the highway, the **Hospedaje Solentiname** has 13 rooms barely bigger than the beds in them ($3 shared bath, $8 private bath, tel. 722-2100).

The **Hotel Panaméricano,** on the north side of the park, has a variety of rooms and services, a small zoo, lots of room, and (best of all) cold cans of Milwaukee's Best beer for $.70: it doesn't get any better than this. Single room with shared bath is $4; $6 gets you a private bath and fan; add hot water, TV, and a fridge for $11 s, $15 d. There are 21 rooms, with an additional 12-room annex two blocks away, tel. 722-2355.

The nicest accommodation in Somoto is no doubt the **Hotel Colonial,** located a half-block south of the church. Its 10 rooms have private bath and TV, and cost $11 s, $22 d, $30 matrimonial. Parking and laundry services, typical breakfasts and lunch, tel. 722-2040.

FOOD

Comedor Soya, on the plaza, serves soy milk, soy tacos, and soy enchiladas. The *dueña's* bark is worse than her bite, and occasionally the menu is limited. For excellent *frescos* and fries, check out **Café Santiaguito,** 1.5 blocks south of the church. There are numerous typical *comedors* around the market, all *más o menos.* Try the **Rostiería El Buen Pollo,** next to the market entrance, for standard roast chicken.

The Almendro (across from the Colonial) has nicer meals from $4 (open 10 A.M.–9 P.M., closed Mon., tel. 722-2152). Similar menu at **Tepecxomth,** tel. 722-2667, accepts credit cards, located two blocks south of the church and half-block east.

INFORMATION AND SERVICES

INTUR has an office hidden away in a two-story government building, 2.5 blocks south of the church, but it is practically useless as a resource; call or stop by to see if it's gotten its act together (open 7 A.M.–2 P.M., tel. 722-2777). The Alcaldía, one block south of the church and one west, may be more helpful.

There is a Banco de Finanzas across the street from the Alcaldía. The Correos is across from the Hotel Colonial, and ENITEL is behind the church. The hospital is on the highway toward the border.

GETTING THERE AND AWAY

Buses to Somoto from Estelí run every hour 5:30 A.M.–5:20 P.M. *Expresos* to Managua run 5 A.M.–3:45 P.M. (Sun. only 2 P.M. and 3:45 P.M.), and *ordinarios* 4 A.M.–7:20 P.M. When hitching from Estelí, be sure you stay left at the turnoff to Ocotal. From there, it's a short 15-minute ride to Somoto, but you may have lots of competition.

Border Crossing at El Espino

Buses leave from COTRAN for La Frontera between 5 A.M. and 5 P.M. daily. It's a 40-minute ride, or quicker in a taxi, which costs about $4.

Matagalpa and Jinotega

Nicaragua's cool, central highlands are made up of endless rows of blue-green mountains speckled with small farms, clay-tiled adobe houses, and shady forest streams. It gets chilly in Nicaragua's mountains, and with the clouds blowing through as your exploration leads you from one enchanted valley to another, it can seem like a lost land. This is a country of caves, legends, myths, and above all, fresh produce and coffee.

Matagalpa and Jinotega were, for too long, places of tremendous violence and warfare, where thousands of wet guerrilla soldiers marched muddily through its forests, staging ambushes up and down its valleys. One of the earliest to raise arms was Augusto César Sandino, who fought against the U.S. Marines and the National Guard. Forty years later, many of the battles that led up to the revolution of 1979 took place in the same region, particularly between San José de Bocay, Matiguás, and Bilampi. Far more devastating than either of those conflicts, however, were the 1980s, when Matagalpa, Jinotega, and the RAAN (*Region Autónoma Atlantica del Norte* or North Atlantic Autonomous Region, one of Nicaragua's departments) experienced the worst of the incessant violence between the Sandinista military and Contra troops, and farmers in fear of ambush tended their crops with rifles slung over their shoulders.

harvest time in Matagalpa

The war is long over and today's northern campesinos live without fear but have been hardened by war, poverty, and, most recently, a drought and a depressed coffee market. They work hard harvesting coffee, corn, beans, flowers, and vegetables, and their warmth and friendliness will astonish you as much as the fresh beauty of the rolling, rocky countryside.

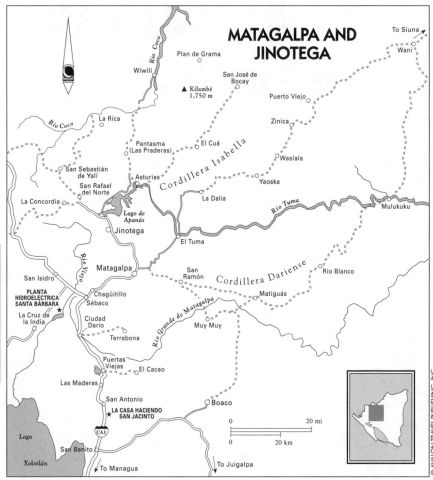

MATAGALPA AND JINOTEGA

To Siuna
Wani
Plan de Grama
Wiwilí
Río Coco
San José de Bocay
▲ Kilambé 1,750 m
Puerto Viejo
Zinica
La Rica
Río Coco
Pantasma (Las Praderas)
El Cuá
Cordillera Isabella
Waslala
San Sebastián de Yalí
Asturias
Yaoska
San Rafael del Norte
La Concordia
La Dalia
Río Tuma
Mulukuku
Lago de Apanás
Jinotega
El Tuma
Matagalpa
San Ramón
Cordillera Dariense
Río Blanco
San Isidro
Río Viejo
PLANTA HIDROELECTRICA SANTA BÁRBARA
Chagüitillo
Sébaco
Matiguás
La Cruz de la India
Ciudad Darío
Muy Muy
Río Grande de Matagalpa
Terrabona
Puertas Viejas
El Cacao
Las Maderas
San Antonio
Boaco
LA CASA HACIENDO SAN JACINTO
CA1
Lago
Xolotlán
San Benito
To Managua
To Juigalpa

0   20 mi
0   20 km

© AVALON TRAVEL PUBLISHING, INC.

The Matagalpa Lowlands

The phrase "lowlands" is relative, of course. Matagalpa is considered a mountainous department cherished for its rugged horizon and winding country roads. But it is also composed of the humid lowlands north of Managua, starting at 300 meters of elevation and climbing upward as you travel farther north. The ride from Managua is a visual experience, as one climbs from the sugarcane plains, rising in a series of abrupt plateaus, until finally reaching the long mountain valleys. If you've got the time, there is plenty to explore and do before you actually reach the city—and altitude—of the city of Matagalpa.

LA CASA–HACIENDA SAN JACINTO

A must-see on the high school curriculum of all Nicaraguan history students, the Casa–Hacienda San Jacinto, located about 35 kilometers north of Managua along the Pan-American Highway, is considered important enough to merit its own roadside statue. Guarding the turnoff to the battlefield of San Jacinto is a striking statue of a defiant Andrés Castro standing atop a pile of rocks. This is the site where, in 1856, the Liberals and Conservatives were battling each other fiercely—the Liberals supported by Tennessee native William Walker and his band of filibusters. Conservative Andrés Castro, out of ammunition, picked up a rock and hurled it at his aggressors, allegedly striking a Yankee in the head and killing him. Today, Castro represents the fighting spirit of Nicaraguan nationalism that refuses to bow to foreign authorities. The name Andrés Castro is now more often associated with the band of rebels calling itself the Frente Unido Andrés Castro (FUAC, the United Andrés Castro Front), which roams the mountains of northeastern Jinotega and the RAAN. FUAC is less interested in fighting U.S. imperialist aggression than it is in stealing and kidnapping for an easy buck.

The museum at San Jacinto is run-down and little visited except by occasional hordes of high school students, and probably carries less impact than the impoverished area homes. It's an easy 20-minute walk from the highway if you're interested in a look at a piece of 19th-century history. You might have to pay $1 to get past the gate, but more often than not even the ticket window is abandoned.

LAS MADERAS

Located at the foot of the first mountains of the north, Las Maderas is an interesting place to hike around and get a feel for the countryside. There are two interesting, short walks you can take in two hours' time, one on each side of the Pan-American Highway. Get off the bus in town and head eastward at the road just before the bridge. There's a broad bowl of mountains set behind town that will afford you a tremendous view of the pueblo and the small fields behind it. On the west side of the highway, a 45-minute climb will get you to the top of a gorgeous stone mesa. Back in town, have a tall glass of cacao at the refresquería while you wait for your next bus.

ARTESANÍA EL CAMINANTE IN EL MADROÑO

You'll know you're there when you come to a bend in the Pan-American Highway and see rows of large wooden figures, particularly herons and egrets, all guarded by a two-meter-tall green crocodile (or is it a dinosaur?). This is the fresh air gallery of Asención Zeledón, self-taught woodcarver and sculptor. He's been carving his creations for nearly 25 years and selling them at the side of the highway, attracting crowds from around the country. The hillsides of El Madroño and north to the Sébaco Valley were once lined with valuable trees like brazilwood, the majority of which were harvested and sold over the past 150 years, leaving the hillsides mostly deforested except for low-value species like *escobillo, guacimo,* and *miligüiste.* These are what Zeledón uses for his art, binding their branches with strong vines to form original furniture and sculpture.

COFFEE: NICARAGUA'S BLACK GOLD

In 1852, Germans Ludwig Elster and his wife Katherina Braun were passing through Nicaragua on their way to the California gold rush. They never made it to California, but they did find gold. Rather, Katherina did. While crossing Nicaragua, Ludwig met many travelers returning home, hopes shattered after failure in California. He and Katherina decided to cut their journey short and look for gold in the mines of San Ramón, Matagalpa. While Ludwig worked the taxed gold deposits of Matagalpa, Katherina Braun established a home garden and planted some of the coffee beans they'd picked up the last time they'd bought provisions in Managua. Katherina's discovery—that Matagalpa's climate and soils were just right for the cultivation of the bitter but full-bodied arabica coffee bean—dwarfed the importance of San Ramón's gold mines and changed the course of Nicaragua's history. Katherina had discovered black gold.

Coffee fever gripped Matagalpa in the 1880s, and the Nicaraguan government, eager to capitalize on the crop that neighbor-states Costa Rica and Guatemala had already been growing for 40 years, threw its weight behind the Germans. Laws were passed encouraging young Germans to immigrate to Nicaragua. Provided they were young and interested in growing coffee, they were given land on which to grow it. The farms this program spawned included Alemania (established by Otto Zeyss), Hammonia (Otto Kùhl), Sajonia (Bruno Mierisch), and Milwaukee (Niels Hawkins et al.).

At first, coffee was shipped in bean (parchment) form through the port of Corinto, around the Cape Horn to Europe importers in Bremen and Hamburg, but by 1912 the Nicaraguan German community had established their own processing plants where they milled and processed the coffee beans. Otto Kùhl is considered by many to be the inventor of the wet coffee processing method that strips the beans of their pulp over grated steel cylinders. Today Nicaragua is home to over 40 wet cof-

He's a civil war veteran with the shrapnel scars to prove it, fighting now to earn a decent living after having been economically abandoned by the army at the end of the 1980s. El Madroño is located about 75 kilometers north of Managua and about 40 kilometers south of Sébaco, just south of the Laguna de Moyoá, which makes a good landmark.

LA LAGUNA DE MOYOÁ AND LAS PLAYITAS

After conquering the first big climb on the highway from Managua (known as Cuesta del Coyol), you'll officially enter Matagalpa's highlands and be greeted by the Laguna Moyoá, on the west side of the highway and the swampy Laguna Tecomapa to the east. Both lagoons are considered the remnants of the ancient Lake of Sébaco, a giant reservoir that helped formed the heavy clay soils of today's Sébaco Valley. The lake ceased to be when a tectonic shift forced the Río Grande de Matagalpa to flow eastward toward the Atlantic instead of into Lake Xolotlán

through Moyoá. Moyoá (Nahuatl for place of the small mosquitoes) is known to dry up from time to time, reestablishing itself in years of big rains. During Hurricane Mitch the waters rose to the edge of the highway, and the swampy Tecomapa became a legitimate lake, through which cattle waded to graze.

Countless rumors abound regarding Moyoá, many of which are unfounded and others simply unconfirmed. It is widely believed that Moyoá is the site of a forgotten colonial city and an ancient Chontaleña community that worshiped Cihuacoatl—the serpent woman—possibly on the small island found in the northern part of the lake. Another says that at the turn of the 20th century when the lake dried up, a farmer dug a hole near its edge to see if he could make a well; he was astonished to find not water, but the remains of stone pillars from a church, and small amounts of silver coins from the colonial period. No archaeological work has taken place at Moyoá to confirm or disprove the theory. Better known is that Moyoá was once home to the Chontaleña people, whether they had a fixed

fee mills. This, however does not include the thousands of micro-mills on individual farms. The fact that so many individual, small-scale farmers take part in processing the beans they grow is one of the unique aspects of Nicaraguan coffee.

Coffee processors and mills in Matagalpa have evolved and modernized since the first haciendas were built at the end of the 19th century, but the basic process of coffee production remains largely unchanged. Coffee is a labor-intensive crop which requires many workers to pick, de-pulp, and sort the beans. Today's challenges include the appropriate disposal of coffee waste, including the pulp, mucilage, and shell, and the appropriate use and recycling of the water used during the processing of the beans. In the far north, much coffee pulp is simply dumped into the nearest stream, causing severe temporary water pollution.

The *Terrocarril*

An interesting episode in Matagalpa's history of coffee production was the *terrocarril,* a steam engine train that ran without tracks. In 1903, a group of immigrants and coffee growers formed the Matagalpa Transportation Company with the goal of getting harvested coffee to the port of Corinto. After repairing the old road from La Paz Centro to Matagalpa, they imported an old German steam locomotive, that they adapted with wide iron wheels. The steam engine traveled over land without the benefit of steel rails. In La Paz Centro, the coffee harvest was transferred to the traditional railroad and transported to the harbor. The first successful run from Matagalpa to Corinto was in 1905 and was celebrated like a holiday under the flags of Nicaragua, Germany, England, and the United States. The *terrocarril* was short-lived, however, sinking deeply into the muddy roads. By 1907 the steel giant had been retired. One of its wheels, and a collection of historic photos, remain at the Hotel Selva Negra.

settlement on the island in the lake or not. Some clay pottery has been uncovered that seems to be from the period from A.D. 500 to 1500 that would indicate they at least frequented the site, probably to fish and hunt.

La Laguna de Moyoá is good for birding, and a peaceful place to pitch a tent, camp, and hike around. If you're interested in something a little more sedentary, the locals do a good business catching fish out of Moyoá—mostly *mojarra* and *guapote*—both very good for eating. To visit the lake or to camp, stop in at **Comedor Treminio** and ask for Anita Vega or Humberto Treminio, the owners of the land that borders the lake. You can eat your meals at their establishment, and strike a deal with them for the right to camp out on their land. Try the shady grove down at the end of the road that leads to the lake. Birds you might see at Moyoá include *playeritos, piches, zambullidores,* and several types of heron.

You can hike around the lake in a day, but you might have to cross some swampy sections on the north and west side. From Treminio's place, start by hiking the two hills that form the northern edge of the lake: Chichigua and San Cristóbal. There are small country roads along the west side of the lake that eventually wind their way back to the Pan-American Highway at a small community just south of the lake called San Agustín, for a total distance of around 16 kilometers; use the Laguna Moyoá INETER quad.

CIUDAD DARÍO

Named after the prized poet of Castilian literature, Ciudad Darío was known by the indigenous name of Metapa in 1867 when Rubén Darío was born. Today at the southern entrance to the city stands a handsome brass statue of Darío.

Sights and Entertainment

The primary attraction is the **Casa Natal Rubén Darío,** located along the main street in front of the ENITEL building. Darío was born in this small rural house, though he moved to the city of León shortly afterward to live with relatives. The house is open Monday–Friday 8 A.M.–12:30 P.M.

and 2–5 P.M. The east part of the house has been converted into a small amphitheater for the presentation of cultural shows.

A popular entertainment spot is the merengue party/pool/restaurant **El Pantanal.** Have some lunch (the *quesillos* are recommended), go for a swim in a crowded pool, and relax a while before continuing your journey. Entrance is $1, or just grab one of the several hammocks hanging around the perimeter and watch the Nicas enjoying themselves. Summertime Saturdays and Sundays are the liveliest time to go.

If you're in Darío on the weekend, stop by the baseball stadium Estadio Carlos Santí to see if there's a game. If so, you'll have a chance to rub elbows with almost the whole town. Darío's park is nothing special to look at, but weekend evenings, it's the best place to see and be seen.

Food

The market near the bus stop and bridge is a good place to fill your belly with meat, beans, and tortilla meals; you'll share a table with local campesinos. Start up a conversation by asking them how high the water came during Hurricane Mitch (hint: it's higher than you think). **Comedor Clementina** (from the mayor's office, two blocks north and half a block west) serves a solid meal; Doña Clementina provides a rustically upscale atmosphere. She whips up a mean beef soup, and her chicken and *ayote* (a type of squash) is well recommended. Plenty of fresh fruit juices to sip while you wait for your meal and try to talk with her pet parrot, who speaks Italian (so she claims!). A half a block east from Clementina's is a big *fritanga* that opens up around 6 P.M. and serves all that deep-fried Nica goodness, $1–2 a plate.

El Coctel likes to serve upscale crowds coming out of the museum, and specializes in *carne a la plancha;* a bit pricier than the other options in town—you can pay over $7.50 for some things— but it's one of few restaurants with a real ceiling overhead, so you get what you pay for. To get there, find the Pulpería Masaya, go west one block and north a half block.

The favorite restaurant among the NGO and businessperson crowd is **Doña Conchi's,** a relatively upscale place with a full menu ranging from $1.50–7.50 per dish (located a block north of the Shell station toward the north end of town). In addition to the pool, **El Pantanal** has a full menu of chicken, beef, and fish dishes. At **La Embajada,** Don Pablo makes a decent living by peddling cheap grain alcohol in plastic bags to the local drunks, while his wife sells the best *gallo pinto* in town—plus beef soup and other favorites (located from the mayor's office, three blocks north and one block east); when you go back home, tell all your friends you bought moonshine at "the embassy."

Services

The ENITEL phone office is located across from the Casa Natal Rubén Darío, open 7 A.M.– 10 P.M. daily.

Getting There and Away

Express buses between Managua and points north save an hour off the trip by not entering Ciudad Darío, so if you're headed there, make sure to take an *ordinario.* Any local bus leaving Matagalpa or Estelí headed to Managua will go by way of Darío.

Near Ciudad Darío

Anyone between the ages of seven and 15 will know exactly how to get to the following destinations and can be hired for cheap. The Darío neighborhood of **Santa Clara,** located about one kilometer east from the town's park (not far from the Carlos Santí baseball stadium) is home to several historical and geological places of interest for the hiker and explorer, including rock paintings. To get to the rock paintings, start at Darío's mayor's office in the park and head east toward the stadium at the top of a hill (0.5 km). On the other side of the stadium is a school for deaf children. Beyond that, the paved road will turn to dirt as you enter Barrio España. There is a *pulpería* on the corner where one can get directions to the paintings, which are less than a half-hour walk away. There are actually several large rocks with petroglyphs painted on them, and a small trail that meanders through them.

La Posa de Las Yeguas (The Mare's Pool) is a deep spot in the creek where the legend goes that women who weren't faithful to their husbands were turned into mares and went to live. There are several rocks that have been inscribed with petroglyphs, as well as with more modern graffiti. It is said the friars of old would go to meditate at **La Cueva del Fraile** (The Friar's Cave), not far from La Posa de Las Yeguas.

SÉBACO

No matter where you travel in the north of Nicaragua, at some point you'll probably find yourself in Sébaco, whether passing through or waiting for a bus or a ride. Located right where the highway splits to take travelers to either Estelí and the Segovias (fork left) or Matagalpa, Jinotega, and the northeast (go right), Sébaco, or La Ciudad de Cebollas (City of Onions) does a lively business in roadside commerce. If you're traveling at night, Sébaco is a sudden blast of street lights and bustle.

Not only are there clean restrooms at the Texaco station, but Sébaco is also a good place to pick up fresh produce, especially carrots, beets, and of course, onions—all of which can be done without leaving your bus. The aggressive roadside vendors will scale the side of the bus and display their goods through your window—Nicaragua's version of a drive-thru. If you have a long bus ride ahead of you, this is a good place to pick up bags of fruit juice or snacks.

If you need to get out and stretch your legs, or have urgent errands, Sébaco also has several banks, a telephone office, and a well-equipped private health clinic.

History

The name Sébaco comes from the Nahuatl "Cihuacoatl," the snake-woman. In 1527 the Spanish founded the city they called Santiago de Cihuacoatl on the banks of the Río Viejo alongside the Native American settlement of Cihuacoatl, capital of the Chontales people. But when a major flood put the town under water in 1833, Sébaco was moved to the hill just east of town, where the remnants of Sébaco Viejo can still be

found. When they moved, the residents of Sébaco picked up their buildings piece by piece and nail by nail and transported the materials to the new location, where they reconstructed the buildings to approximately their original form. Since then, the houses have slowly crept down the hill and back to the water's edge, waiting for history to repeat itself.

And that's exactly what happened. In 1998, Sébaco was hit so hard by Hurricane Mitch it became one of the primary obstacles separating Managua from the north. The large bridge at the south

THE LEGEND OF CIHUACOATL

At the edge of the Río Viejo, there was once a powerful community ruled by a mighty cacique. His wife was considered the most beautiful woman in the country, but she made regular suspicious trips down to the river with great quantities of carefully prepared foods: beverages of seeds and berries, and birds prepared with spices and grains. One day, one of the cacique's men decided to follow the woman down to the river to see what she did. There, he watched as the woman sat calmly on a rock at the river's edge, and struck the palm of her hand against the water's surface several times with a sharp smacking sound. From out of the ripples on the water's surface emerged a giant snake, which rose halfway out of the water and placed its head on the woman's beautiful smooth thighs. She fed the snake, its head resting on her lap, and afterwards the two made love at the water's edge. Then the serpent slithered back into the river, down to its underwater cave, and the woman gathered her things to leave.

The cacique's servant ran quickly back to tell the story, trembling as he related the infidelity to the cacique. When the woman returned home, her husband, in a jealous rage, killed the woman with a single stroke of his knife. The snake, upon realizing his lover had been slain, agitated the river with its tail, causing it to rise up violently and destroy the entire community. The goddess Cihuacoatl—the Snake Woman—has been worshiped ever since by the Nahuatl people in the area.

end of town resisted the floods of the Río Grande de Matagalpa, but the river overflowed its banks just south of the bridge and sliced a new channel through the road several hundred meters wide. Some of the flood waters wound up flowing into the watershed of the Río Viejo (which flows south from Jinotega). The combined torrent ripped through Ciudad Darío in an incredibly destructive wall of water. When the floods finally subsided, buses transiting Sébaco between Managua and the north were obliged to ford the new river valley for months afterward, and the reconstruction of that stretch of highway lasted until 2001.

Attractions

Of primary interest in Sébaco is the wreckage of **Sébaco Viejo,** located on the hill just east of town. Take a look at the Templo Viejo, the old church, which in 1996 was officially declared a part of the cultural patrimony of Nicaragua. Inside the church is a simple collection of archaeological artifacts, including pieces of pottery and ceramics, some small statues, and a wooden carving of the deity Cihuacoatl.

Just south of Comedor Mariela, the no-name office supply store run by Doña Hilda Moreno has displayed some of her photography, notably a photo-montage of what Sébaco looked like during Hurricane Mitch. Looking at the sheer amount of water that flowed through Sébaco at the peak of the hurricane will give you more respect for that bridge at the south end of town.

For an adventure, track down the house of Carlos Miranda, known popularly as Borbollón. On his property is an ancient tamarind tree that's the pride of the city—they call it **El Tamarindo de Oro** in memory of the golden gifts given to Spanish conquistador Gabriel de Rojas. Said to be 500 years old, its powerful branches arch down to the ground, then turn upward again, forming a verdant leafy cave inside. Borbollón himself is an ebullient character who will tell you stories and raunchy jokes as he shows you the tree and his beautiful farm—as well as a stone known as the Piedra de la Mocuana.

Accommodations and Food

If for some reason you're forced to stay in Sébaco,

there are two *hospedajes* in town—**Hospedaje Plaza** in front of the park and **Hospedaje Rosario** alongside the highway about 50 meters north of the bridge. You're better off in other towns, however, as these two dingy establishments cater largely to a seedy, trucker crowd. Try to catch the last bus to Matagalpa (around 7 P.M.) or hitch—Matagalpa and Estelí are both no more than an hour away.

There are dozens of decent roadside restaurants, all with similar menus of chicken, tacos, beef, hot dogs, and sandwiches. **El Sesteo** is the best sit-down lunch in town, with uniformed waiters, an air-conditioned *sala,* and the nod of the expat community, which has been enjoying lunches there since it opened. Cheaper and closer to the highway, two standouts among the many capable eating establishments are **Sorbetería Macet,** serving sandwiches, hot dogs, light lunches, fruit juices, and ice cream (on the east side of the intersection across from the triangle), and **Comedor Mariela,** with a menu of traditional fare, soft drinks, and beer (located on the east side of highway just south of the intersection).

Services

There are several banks in Sébaco, including BAMER, Banic, BDF, and Bancentro, all with standard hours. There's also a very good health clinic—Profamilia, constructed in 2001. It's located just outside of town within easy walking distance (assuming you feel well enough to walk), along the road that leads to Matagalpa (open Mon.–Fri. 8 A.M.–noon and 1:30–5 P.M.). The ENITEL phone office is located just south of the triangle on the west side of the street, open 7:30 A.M.–9 P.M..

Near Sébaco
Chagüitillo

About two kilometers north of Sébaco along the highway to Matagalpa, Chagüitillo is a small community with a surprising amount of history. At the turn of the 19th century, Carlos Mántica recorded something the locals had known about for ages: the presence of dozens of pre-Columbian petroglyphs scratched into the stone walls of a canyon just outside the village. He named the site **Apamico,** Nahuatl for Place of the Monkeys. Additional petroglyphs were discovered along the banks of **Aranca Burba** stream. The petroglyphs are well organized between the two—while the petroglyphs in the canyon mostly depict monkeys and frightening shamans carrying human heads, the petroglyphs that line the second streambed typically depict deer and humans hunting.

The locals can easily help you find the two streambeds and show you the petroglyphs; both sites are an easy walk from the center of town. Particularly good guides with a renowned interest in the petroglyphs are Orlando Dávila (tel. 622-2149) and Melvin Rizo, who speaks some English (tel. 622-2546). Dávila lives in front of the school (the school has a tall green wall painted with representations of the petroglyphs); Rizo lives a block or two closer to the highway.

In town, find the *pulpería* run by Bernabe Rayo. Chagüitillo is the source of a water project for the city of Matagalpa, and in digging the trenches for the pipelines, many artifacts have turned up. Some are scattered amongst the many houses of the community, but Rayo has done an admirable job of collecting some of them and trying to form a small community museum out of the pieces. You can support him by purchasing something from his store. He's got an interesting collection of old ceramic pots, cups, and small statues, plus some larger pieces he's reconstructed from the shards. His place is located on a side street off the main road through town.

Seven kilometers along the road between Sébaco and Molino Sur is a small waterfall and plunge pool called **El Salto de Sébaco.** It's a pleasant way to spend an afternoon if you're in the area, but ask around first: in recent years it has been known to occasionally dry up.

PLANTA HIDROELECTRICA SANTA BÁRBARA

Located south of a long and battered highway that leads between San Isidro and Telica, León, the hydropower plant and dam at Santa Bárbara makes a decent hike if you're willing to sweat. The better part of the lowlands just north of Lake Xolotlán are arid and treeless and you can expect to experience high temperatures the entire walk from the highway to the dam (stick your thumb out for a ride if you can't bear it anymore). The hydropower plant at Santa Bárbara— one of three in Nicaragua—is the only one you can get near. It produces about 15 percent of Nicaragua's hydroelectric power and came within an inch of being destroyed as millions of cubic meters of water rushed over it during Hurricane Mitch. The damage has been repaired and the power plant chugs on, but the immense valley carved out by the storm flows warrant a look. To get there, get off any bus at the Empalme León, where the road from Telica intersects with the Pan-American toward Estelí. Then hitch or bus westward toward Telica and get off at the big sign that says Planta Hidroelectrica Santa Bárbara. Follow that road 10 kilometers south to the dam. The locals lie low at midday in this part of Nicaragua and so should you—do your hiking in the early morning or late evening.

MATAGALPA & JINOTEGA

Matagalpa City

The department of Matagalpa is the most mountainous in Nicaragua, and its capital city remains true to form. As you walk up and down the steep streets you'll realize the city is draped over the rolling valley floor like a blanket over the land beneath it. Nicknamed "La Perla del Septentrión" (The Pearl of the North), Matagalpa would be more aptly associated with a ripe, red coffee bean, which is the true precious stone here. Matagalpa is blessed with clean air, but the water, whose sources have been greatly affected by deforestation and human contamination, is another story. During the driest times, water is severely rationed, as city officials cope with the problem. The surrounding mountains are sadly scraped clean of trees, but during the wet season, they turn emerald green and remain so throughout the Christmas season, when the coffee harvest turns the city of Matagalpa into a lively center of coffee pickers, prospectors, packers, and processors.

Matagalpa has a strong Nahuatl presence to this day, even in day-to-day language. The Nahuatl word *chùisle,* for example, is used instead of *quebrada* for stream. The city has a central office for the region's indigenous community, where land disputes and other issues are settled. Modern-day Nicaraguan politicians prize Matagalpa because its high population can often swing the vote. Tourists will prize Matagalpa as a welcome respite from the heat of the lowlands, plus a chance to sip the best coffee in the world while plotting their forays deeper into the mountains.

HISTORY

Matagalpa has been settled for as long as anyone can remember. The beautiful valley where the city of Matagalpa now sits was already a cluster of Nahuatl communities—including Solingalpa and Molagùina, which still exist today—when the Spanish first set eyes on it. Interestingly, Nahuatl traditional histories don't include any stories of their people having arrived in this valley—as if they have always been here. Long before

it was called the Pearl of the North, Matagalpa was known as the City of Ten in Nahuatl, in reference to the ten small settlements that made up the valley. The name is also attributed to the powerful cacique Atahualpa who governed the area during the time of colonization (Solingalpa was his wife).

The Spanish established a camp alongside the Nahuatls around 1680. Some powerful Spanish families made up the first settlers; their last names are still common in the region: Alvarado, Castañeda, Reyes, Rizo, Escoto. They set up extensive cattle ranches and planted fields before coffee was even a dream. In 1838 the area was named Departamento del Septentrión and later in 1862, Matagalpa was elevated to the status of city. But even as recently as the mid-1800s the city of Matagalpa was of far less economic importance to the nation than Sébaco.

That changed in the second half of the 19th century when Matagalpa became the focus of a sizeable immigration of Germans. They had not arrived in Nicaragua to plant coffee, as is commonly believed, but to develop the gold mines in the east. Once established in Nicaragua, however, they quickly realized how perfect the climate was for the cultivation of coffee and their interest switched to the crop that would define Nicaragua's economy for over 100 years. Matagalpa had developed a new reason for being, and coffee has been the focus of Matagalpa ever since.

Today Matagalpa is faced with several problems it must overcome before it can continue to grow and enjoy the prosperity it had in the 19th century. Foremost among them is a critical lack of potable water. A major water project began in 2000 to bring water up from the town of Chagùitillo, near Sébaco, but some scientists believe even that water will only be a viable source for 10 years. Other important projects include the construction of good roads to facilitate the extraction of the region's harvest of coffee and vegetables, and a method of dealing with the increasingly urgent problem of solid waste.

QUALITY COFFEE COOPERATIVE TOURS

Ten percent of Nicaragua's annual coffee production is grown by 6,000 small-scale campesino producers working as members of nine cooperatives in the country's northlands. Many agree that this—as opposed to the traditional plantation-style haciendas where growers and pickers are merely paid laborers—is the future of coffee, and that cooperative-grown coffee may grow to as much as 50 percent of Nicaragua's harvest in the next five years.

One reason is the focus on quality—not only because specialty, or "gourmet," coffee brings a higher price, and is a way out of the current worldwide coffee glut, but because the quality of coffee is inextricably tied to the quality of life of those that produce it, as well as the quality of the environment in which they live. This translates into shade, organic, and fair trade certified coffee, all important new trends that can be further researched at the following websites: www.globalexchange.org/economy/coffee and www.transfairusa.org.

In the meantime, many of these cooperatives—and the cloud

Matagalpan coffee schleppers

forest producers that comprise them—invite you to come see what all the excitement is about. Call it "Coffee Tourism" or the "Ruta de Café"; you'll find that there are entire worlds of real live people behind every sip you have ever taken in your life, and this is your chance to visit them. To experience the most activity, be sure to arrange your visit during the peak of the harvest, usually from mid-December through February.

Start at CECOCAFEN, the Center of Northern Coffee Cooperatives, whose main office in Matagalpa city is located 1.5 blocks east of ENEL. They can arrange anything from an afternoon coffee cupping at their Sol Café *beneficio* to a day trip to visit some of their farmers to a multiple-night excursion, staying in campesino homes and touring their farms (or even putting some work in during the harvest). Trips include transportation and food, and hikes (with pick-ups) can be arranged between towns. Prices fully depend on the trip, which should be arranged in advance, tel. 612-6353, fax 612-3386, email: cecocafe @ibw.com.ni.

Another Matagalpa option is the Beneficio La Esperanza, an example of estate-grown coffee (i.e., not a cooperative), based in a stately yellow building on the south side the highway toward Sébaco (km 120). The three English-speaking and warm-hearted brothers are constructing a bed-and-breakfast with balcony views over the coffee-drying courts for about $22 a couple. You're a little isolated from Matagalpa, but you're right smack in the middle of the coffee processing (tel./fax 612-2719, email: esperanzacoffee@tmx.com.ni, website: www.esperanza.com.ni).

In Jinotega, SOPPEXCA (Society of Small Coffee Producers, Exporters, and Buyers) is eager to serve as your tour guide of the region, arranging any number of hikes, trips, and homestays among its growers in the surrounding hills. Located one block west of the Ferretería Blandón (tel./fax 632-2617, email: soppexcc@tmx.com.ni).

© JOSHUA BERMAN

MATAGALPA & JINOTEGA

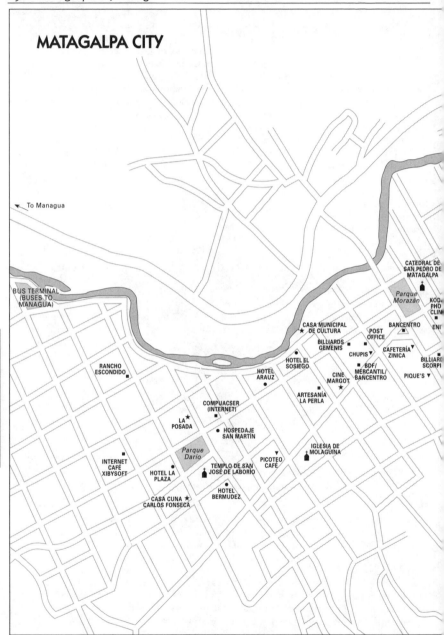

MATAGALPA CITY

To Managua

BUS TERMINAL
(BUSES TO
MANAGUA)

CATEDRAL DE
SAN PEDRO DE
MATAGALPA

Parque
Morazán

KOD
PHO
CLIN

CASA MUNICIPAL
DE CULTURA

POST
OFFICE

BANCENTRO

ENI

BILLIARDS
GEMENIS

CHUPIS

CAFETERÍA
ZINICA

RANCHO
ESCONDIDO

HOTEL EL
SOSIEGO

BDF/
MERCANTIL/
BANCENTRO

BILLIARI
SCORPI

HOTEL
ARAUZ

CINE
MARGOT

PIQUE'S

ARTESANÍA
LA PERLA

COMPUACSER
(INTERNET)

LA
POSADA

HOSPEDAJE
SAN MARTÍN

IGLESIA DE
MOLAGUINA

INTERNET
CAFÉ
XIBYSOFT

Parque
Dario

PICOTEO
CAFÉ

HOTEL LA
PLAZA

TEMPLO DE SAN
JOSÉ DE LABORIO

CASA CUNA
CARLOS FONSECA

HOTEL
BERMUDEZ

MATAGALPA & JINOTEGA

To Jinotega

HOTEL
FOUNTAIN
BLUE

Río Grande de Matagalpa

TEL
EAL

To San
Ramón

FLAMINGO
PUB ▼

INTERNET EXPRESS
CYBER CAFÉ ■

ERÁMICA
NEGRA

HOTEL
GLASÓN

LA VITA
E BELLA ▼

HOSPEDAJES ZELAYA
AND MOLINA

HAMBURLOOCA
AND PIZZA ▼

GRUPO
VENANCIA ★

BUS TERMINAL
GUANUCA

HOTEL LOMAS
DE GUADALUPE

SCALE NOT AVAILABLE

ORIENTATION AND GETTING AROUND

Matagalpa can be confusing, but it doesn't have to be. There are two parks: the Parque Darío at the south end of the city, and Parque Morazán at the north end. To the west is the highway that runs between Sébaco and Jinotega, and to the east, a bare mountain ridge. Much of Matagalpa's commercial center is contained along the two streets that run roughly parallel to each other between the two parks. The principal bus terminal is located at the southern tip of town, just six blocks from the Parque Darío, and with service to points north, west, and south. At the other extreme end, the northern bus terminal has buses heading east on the highway to Muy Muy and the interior of the department.

Matagalpa is a perfectly good city for walking, except for the damn hills; taxi fare across town is $.50. Matagalpa is also served by city buses that ply three different routes back and forth across town, and cost about $.10.

SIGHTS

You shouldn't pass through Matagalpa without spending some time in **Parque Darío.** Buy a crushed ice *raspado* and spend some time people-watching. There are probably more trees jammed into the park's tiny confines than any other park in Nicaragua, and come sunset the branches fill with the chatter of thousands of birds—kind of like a mini-jungle. A permanent fixture in the park is a vendor with rows and rows of hand-made ceramic piggy-banks for sale, none of which costs more than $1.

El Templo de San José de Laborío sits at the edge of the Parque Darío at the south end of town. It's probably as old as the colonial presence in Matagalpa, but no one is quite sure exactly when it was built. It was rebuilt in 1917 on top of its old foundation, but underneath

MATAGALPA, WATER, AND THE LEGEND OF THE SERPENT

Matagalpa is a water-stressed city. In some neighborhoods the water pressure is only turned on once a day; in others, Matagalpinos are forced to walk to distribution points to fill up containers from tanker trucks. You may see these trucks along the city streets in the early mornings, when everyone comes out with buckets and pans to get what water they can.

At the same time, there's more water in Matagalpa than some people know what to do with. Time and time again, shallow excavations in the city for routine projects have turned up a moist layer of earth just several meters below the surface. When a well-loved priest died in the 1990s his tomb was dug underneath the floor of the cathedral. Before they had finished digging, the hole had begun to flood. Studies have determined the water under the city of Matagalpa isn't exploitable in quantities great enough to supply the city, and so other alternatives are being developed.

Much of Matagalpa's limited water supply comes from the forested hillsides that surround the city, hillsides that are rapidly being stripped of their timber. Matagalpinos speak of an old legend: the hill known as Apante, just southeast of the city, was said to be an enormous upwelling of water trapped within a pocket of soil and rock. Within the water lived a great snake. One day the snake began to shake, and the hillside began to crumble, threatening to unleash a massive landslide upon the residents of the city. In despair they turned to the Virgin Mary for protection. Mary fought the snake and subdued it by planting its tail underneath the foundation of the church of Molagùina in the center of the city.

But the snake grows stronger each day… when it finally has enough strength to break free it will shake its tail again, causing the hills to crumble and collapse upon the city. If the deforestation of the hillsides that surround Matagalpa continue, that prophecy may very well become true.

that foundation are the ruins of another that date to at least 1751, and possibly a bit earlier. In 1881 an indigenous uprising used the church as its garrison.

Matagalpa was the birthplace of the founder of the FSLN, Carlos Fonseca. The house he was born in has been converted into a museum. Known as **La Casa Cuna Carlos Fonseca,** it's located one block east of the south side of Parque Darío (open Mon.–Fri. 2–5 P.M., tel. 612-3665).

La Iglesia de Molagùina, found in the center of the city, is another church whose history has been lost over the centuries. It was probably constructed between 1751 and 1873, though those dates have been questioned by historians. Simple and monastic, it is a well-used and well-loved church: Molagùina is home to a Catholic order of nuns and the College of San José.

At the northeastern end of town, **La Catedral de San Pedro de Matagalpa** was a disproportionately large cathedral—the third largest in the nation—when it was built in 1874, reflecting the opulence of Matagalpa at the time. The cathedral is built in the baroque style, with heavy bell towers set at both sides and an airy, spacious interior. It's the most prominent building in town and easily visible from the hillsides north of town on the road to Jinotega. The cathedral's interior is crisp and cool, tastefully adorned with bas- and medium-relief sculpture, carved wood, and paintings. Mass is held nightly at 6 P.M.

There are two adjacent **cemeteries** on the hillside east of the city. One is for locals, and one is for foreigners, a rare arrangement in Nicaragua. Both contain headstones hand carved from dark rock, something seen only in Matagalpa. Buried in the foreigners' cemetery is one of the most famous casualties of the 1980s war: Benjamin Linder. Linder was an avid juggler and unicyclist, and his headstone reflects those passions, along with some doves, the symbol of the peace he never lived to see. The cemetery is about a 30-minute walk from town.

Cerro Apante (1,442 meters)

Green, forested Cerro Apante, located just east from the city, has been declared a natural reserve. It has several good, short hikes, all of which can easily be hiked in an afternoon. Apante is a well-preserved piece of tropical humid forest that still contains decent stands of oak and pine, as well as several hundred types of wildflowers, and serves to protect an important source of water for the city (apante is Nahuatl for running water). It is crisscrossed with many small trails that lead to its streams and lagoons. There are cattle farms as well, some of which are beginning to get on the ecotourism train and organize hikes, day trips, and horseback rides.

Your best bet until the farms formally get their act together is to walk to the base of the hill from Parque Darío and go about it on your own. Start with a sunset hike to the antennas. From Matagalpa, walk south out of town along the main street that links Parque Morazán and Parque Darío. As the road leaves town it quickly hooks a left and begins to wind its way along a spectacular series of mountain ridges and valleys. Some say it's one of the best mountain roads in the country in terms of scenery. The road winds up and past a gate with a huge star on the left. Follow that road up to the antennas.

ENTERTAINMENT AND NIGHTLIFE

Matagalpans celebrate their *fiestas patronales* on September 24th, and the anniversary of their becoming a city on February 14th. Every September there is a rowdy country fair that brings in the crowds from the north and east, and cattle traders from all over the country. This is the best time of year to catch Matagalpa's traditional music of polkas, mazurkas, and *jamaquelos,* performed by the roving street bands that play at restaurants. **Noches Matagalpinas** are held the last weekend of every month in Parque Darío; the weekend typically involves a street stage with live music and stands set up by the local restaurants. Once in a while they get rowdy, but more often than not they're just a good time.

In 2001, a new dance academy started up, under the able direction of Marcos Valle, who studied modern dance in Spain. The **Academía de la Danza de Matagalpa** puts on dance presentations several times a year. If there's going to be a show, they advertise it at the **Casa Municipal de Cultura,** next to the fire station. More regular events are to be found at **Grupo Venancia,** a women's center, which has a presentation almost every Saturday night by musicians and theater groups from all over Nicaragua; trendy among Matagalpa's upper crust (tel. 612-3562, email: venancia@ibw.com.ni).

Matagalpa's movie theater, **Cine Margot,** shows films just a few months after they're shown in the United States, and just a month or so after they're shown in Managua. It's clean, modern, and cheap; tickets cost $2.

As for dancing, the cosmopolitan set (and especially those with their own vehicles) enjoy shaking their cowboy boots at **Luz de Luna,** even if it's a southbound taxi ride out of town; open Wednesdays–Sundays from 8 P.M. until the cows come home, tel. 612-4774. A mellower option is **El Rancho Escondido.** In town, just a half-block west of the northwest corner of the Parque Darío, is the hugely popular **La Posada,** across the street from Radio Stereo Yes; usually no cover charge. Also in town and catching on in popularity among the under-20 crowd is **Equinoxio,** located on the highway out of town toward San Ramón, tel. 612-6223; happy hour from 6–8 P.M., and Friday is ladies' night. One last place is more bar than disco, but Matagalpans are known to dance there too: **Flamingo Pub** on Santa Ana St., tel. 612-4022.

There are several pool halls in town, including the popular **Club de Billares Gemenis,** which fills up on lazy afternoons and weekends.

ACCOMMODATIONS

Under $10

Not recommended is one of the easiest *hospedajes* to find: Hospedaje Colonial, located right on the northeast face of Parque Darío. They do a brisk business in couples looking for an hour-or-so romantic getaway. Hard-core travelers eager to catch a crack-of-dawn bus to the east may decide to stay in one of the spartan, dirt-cheap options at the north end of town, all on the grungy side of things. From the Terminal de Norte, turn left and walk down the street to just over the

first hill where the road makes a sharp S curve. There are two places there where you can stay for under $2: **Hospedaje Zelaya** and **Hospedaje Molina,** both of which do a fair business with campesinos traveling in from Muy Muy and Mulukuku. A better option than either of those two is **Hospedaje Glasón,** tel. 612-4258, which is brighter and cleaner, $2–3.

Not far from the Parque Darío is **Hotel Bermúdez,** a run-down but clean family establishment and probably the cheapest safe sleep in town (excluding the untouristed establishments in the north by the bus terminal), $2.50–3 for small rooms with shared bath.

Hotel Matagalpa is just a few doors down and is a better deal for the money; five rooms with private bath cost $7 per person, eight rooms with shared bath cost $4 each (discounts for groups of three or more). Near the Parque Darío, **Hospedaje San Martín** has 16 clean rooms with shared bath for $2.50 each. It's in a convenient location, and the rooms are set far enough off the street they're quiet. Door closes at 10:30 P.M., after which time you need to knock loudly to be let in.

Hotel Plaza is found at the southwest side of Parque Darío and has been a stalwart in the Matagalpa lodging scene for decades; eight rooms with private bath $4.50 each, and 10 rooms with shared bath $2.50 each, tel. 612-2380.

You'll probably find **Hotel Arauz** easily enough; it's directly adjacent to Supermercado La Matagalpa. It's a unique hotel: on the direct opposite side of the city block is **Hotel Soza,** and in 2001 the two hotels knocked out the back wall that separated them and combined businesses to form one long, narrow hotel. It's a clean and pleasant place, with 23 rooms for $5.50 per person or $9.50 per couple, private bath and fan. They have a large water tank so your shower doesn't run dry, and serve three meals in the small *cafetín,* tel. 612-3030 or 612-7200. There's one computer with Internet connection in the owner's room you can borrow to check email—ask the front desk for permission. Directly across from the supermarket is the spacious but dark **Hotel del Centro,** with 11 rooms from $2.50–3.50 with shared bath, or $7 private bath, tel. 612-2913.

SELVA NEGRA

A trip to Selva Negra is a visit to another world—perhaps something like Germany's Black Forest, for which the area and the mountain resort are named. Selva Negra has been a solid anchor in Nicaragua's tourism network for a long time, and it remains so, extremely popular for people looking to hike, dine, monkey watch, or tie the knot.

Selva Negra is, at its heart, a coffee farm by the name of La Hammonia, owned and run by Eddy Kùhl and Mausi Hayn, third and fourth generation German immigrants to Nicaragua and members of the founding families of the Nicaraguan coffee industry. The farm—considered one of the most diversified in Central America—has been built up into an enchanting resort. In the German tradition, the resort boasts wooden chalets set around a peaceful mountain lake with access to hiking trails in a nearly virgin forest, and hearty meals of farm-fresh food raised on the premises. Needless to say, the coffee—internationally renowned—is superb and served fresh.

You can easily spend two or three days at Selva Negra, relaxing and exploring. It's one of the more pleasant places in Nicaragua to read books and sip fresh java on the porch overlooking the lake. But if you enjoy hiking, this is one of the best places in the north to do so. There are 14 forest trails of varied difficulty on 120 hectares of forest, considered one of the last remaining examples of what Nicaragua's forests looked like in the 15th century. Birders can search for more than 200 species of birds that have been identified here. There are facilities for horseback riding, and tours of the coffee farm, the flower plantations, and the cattle and livestock.

Should you decide you want to spend your time at Selva Negra getting hitched, you can do that too. In 2000 the Kùhls built a gorgeous stone chapel for the wedding of their daughter, and they now rent out the facilities—chapel, horse-drawn carriage, and fresh-cut flowers.

Expect to have a chat with the owners while you're there—Eddy is a wealth of knowledge, a prolific writer, and many of the family's ideas have come from the suggestions and talent of the guests that visit them. Prices run from $10 for a spot in the youth hostel to $30 for a double overlooking the lake, to $50 for a private bungalow. Selva Negra is located at kilometer 140 on the highway between Matagalpa and Jinotega. Take any bus from Matagalpa heading to Jinotega. It'll let you off at the entrance to the hotel, where you'll see an old ruined military tank.,tel. 612-3883, email: resort@selvanegra.com, website: www.selvanegra.com.

© JOSHUA BERMAN

This tank still marks the entrance to Selva Negra.

Hospedaje El Sosiego is a little off the main drag, which makes it quieter than most places (*sosiego* means peaceful); family-run, five rooms cost $6.50 per couple or single. Doors close after 11 P.M.

$10–25

Hotel Fountain Blue (Fuente Azul) has eight rooms with private bath, hot water, and a small guarded parking area for your vehicle, $10–14 each. Quiet and comfortable; there's also a convenient pay phone on the premises. Located at the third entrance to Matagalpa, just west of the bridge, or from Salomón López 1.5 blocks west, tel. 612-2733.

Hotel Ideal has 19 rooms in two categories: $8.50 for small basic rooms with shared bath, or $23.50 for fancier rooms with a/c, and private bath with hot water. The hotel offers enclosed parking for your vehicle near the third entrance to Matagalpa, from Repuestos Brenes one block west, tel. 612-2483.

$25–50

Hotel Lomas de Guadalupe, set on a breezy hill just east of town, is the fanciest establishment in the city of Matagalpa. It gears itself for business conventions and the NGO crew: secretarial services, huge conference rooms, fax, and Internet. You might enjoy it just for the sense of peace and the breathtaking view of the city, especially at night under a full moon. To get there, leave the highway at the third entrance to Matagalpa and pass straight through town following the signs (about 800 meters from the highway). At the eastern edge of town, turn left and climb the hill on a cobblestone road to the hotel, tel. 612-7505, email: hlghotel@ibw.com.ni. **Hotel de Montaña Selva Negra** is located 10 kilometers outside of town on the highway to Jinotega (see Selva Negra special topic), tel. 612-5713, email: selvanegra@tmx.com.ni.

FOOD

As always, there's food in both parks, and as always, it's *vigorón* or *chancho con yuca*. If that's not what you had in mind, don't fret; Matagalpa has several good options for dining.

Picoteo Café is a place much-visited by travelers who stay in the south end of town. It serves chicken, burgers, pizza, and lots of beer, and the walls are covered with platitudes painted on wooden plaques. Have a beer and some chicken wings and make yourself a better person by reading the walls; most dishes run around $1.50.

Pique's, not far the Parque Morazán, is a stylish Mexican joint, with dishes in the $2.75–4 range. Their *chalupas* and mole are especially good, and the atmosphere is relaxing. **La Casona** offers a variety of chicken, salads, burgers, and some decent soups for $3–4, plus lots of munchies to accompany your beer. Look for the big 7-Up sign outside. **Cafetería Zinica:** in the words of the proprietress herself, "We don't have a menu. We just serve hamburgers—the best damn hamburgers in the country." Actually, they do have a menu and serve several other things, including fresh fruit juices. Super-clean, the place is named after the Matagalpa town where Carlos Fonseca, founder of the FSLN, was killed by Somoza's National Guard.

There are several other small eateries where you can get sandwiches, burgers, and light meals, including **Pollo Loco** for chicken and ice cream. A favorite among travelers is **Chupis,** and **Sub-Pizza-Pan** (a block from the ENITEL office) and **White House Pizza** have more fast food.

A most welcome addition to the Matagalpa dining scene is **La Vita e Bella,** tucked just far enough off the beaten path you'll have to hunt for it, but with a menu of Italian and vegetarian dishes, and desserts that will make you glad you found the place. This is possibly the best restaurant in the city for non-chicken-and-beef dishes—only open for dinner, from 6 P.M. Located at Callejón de la Colonia Laines.

Out on the highway, **El Pullazo** just might serve you the best piece of beef tenderloin you'll taste in Nicaragua, but they won't tell you what their secret recipe is. They have a few other beef dishes too, but no one orders the... Your *pullazo* of meat (a vulgar reference to the word for injection) is accompanied by a sweet *guilira* pancake and hunk of *cuajada* cheese. Wash it down with some beer and you're still only $4 in the hole. Located just west of the city about 2 kilometers out of town, open for lunch and dinner.

SHOPPING

Both Matagalpa and Jinotega are famous for a particular brand of black pottery produced in the area, though it's by no means a prolific industry. Black pottery—made black by a particular firing technique—is unique in Nicaragua, where most ceramic work is left a natural reddish-orange color. There are several places where it can be found for sale. Try the aptly named **Cerámica Negra,** near the Parque Darío, **Artesanía La Perla,** located next to the mayor's office, **La Casa de la Cerámica Negra,** or the other **Cerámica Negra** located two blocks due east of the north side of Parque Morazán.

If you plan to do some adventuring out east, it's worth your while to stock up at one of Matagalpa's two grocery stores. A block north of the cathedral is an enormous Palí, open 8 A.M.–8 P.M. all week. The Supermercado La Matagalpa is 2.5 blocks north of Parque Darío, open Monday–Saturday 8 A.M.–9 P.M., and Sunday 8 A.M.–8 P.M. The *supermercado* is higher priced but has a better selection. For a more colorful experience, check out the municipal market across from the Terminal Guanuca at the north end of town.

INFORMATION

There's a small INTUR office on the southeast side of town. It can give you some up-to-date brochures on the better-quality hotels in the area and discuss the upcoming festivals. It's particularly worth visiting the INTUR offices in September, when the *fiestas patronales* are underway. INTUR will steer you to where the action is.

Radio Stations

Local stations include Radio Norteña, FM 94.1; Radio Stereo Apante, FM 94.9; and Radio Yes, FM 90.1. The latter has several programs for a rural audience, including impersonations, jokes, and news commentary. Their morning news pro-

gram is worth a listen in the early hours of the day while you're taking a cold water mountain shower.

Opportunities to Volunteer

Matagalpa is home to at least 16 organizations that occasionally accept volunteer help, if you'd like to make Matagalpa your home for a few weeks. The Movimiento Comunal deals with indigenous issues, tel. 612-3200, and rumor has it they sometimes provide Spanish lessons. La Casa de la Mujer Nora Hawkins promotes social programs that benefit women, tel. 612-3047. Also try the Comunidad Indígena, which is rather disorganized but well-intentioned, tel. 612-2692. You may well find a way to make yourself useful.

SERVICES

Banks

There are a half-dozen banks in Matagalpa—BAC, Banpro, Banexpo, Banco Caley Dagnall, Bancentro, and Banco Mercantíl—and a fistful of money changers that hang out in front of the Banpro. Fortunately, the banks are mostly clustered in a three-block area along the main drag, halfway between the two parks. A few others are within a block of Parque Morazán, and both the Esso and Shell gas stations near the first entrance to the city have ATM machines.

Post Office and Fax

Correos de Nicaragua is located a few blocks south of Parque Morazán. It's open from 8 A.M.–4:30 P.M. and offers fax service too.

Internet

Located just a few blocks from Parque Darío is Internet Café XibySoft, open 8 A.M.–9 P.M. every day of the week (and it doesn't shut down at midday); 10 computers cost about $2.50 per hour, but they have a fast connection so you'll save money by not having to wait for slow downloads, tel. 612-3998. A few blocks from the Parque Morazán is Internet Express Cyber Café, renting five machines for about $3.50 per hour. They have a scanner and CD burners. Open 8 A.M.–8 P.M. every day of the week, tel. 612-2933. Located between the two parks but a bit closer to Parque Darío, Compuacser offers a half-dozen machines for $3.50 per hour, open Monday–Friday 8 A.M.–9 P.M. but closed for lunch 12:30–2 P.M., open Saturdays 8 A.M.–5 P.M. with no break for lunch, tel. 612-5546.

Phone Office

The ENITEL building is located to the east of Parque Morazán; just look for the tower antenna jutting out from the city skyline; open 7 A.M.–9 P.M.

Photo Processing

The Fotocentro de Matagalpa is located 20 meters west of ENITEL, tel. 612-4810. Photos are developed on-site.

GETTING THERE AND AWAY

Matagalpa has two bus terminals located at the far south and far north ends of town— which one you head to depends on your destination. At the south end of town, the Terminal del Sur services Managua, Estelí, and León to the south, and Jinotega to the north. There's a public bathroom there ($.10) and several small eateries. Express buses to Estelí leave at 10 A.M. and 4:30 P.M. Regular buses leave every half-hour until 5:45 P.M. To Managua, there are express buses every hour 5:20 A.M.–4:20 P.M. Regular buses leave every half-hour from 3:35 A.M.–6 P.M. There are four express buses that go to León via San Isidro and Telica. They leave at 6 A.M., 2 P.M., 3 P.M., and 4 P.M. Another option is to take any bus bound for Estelí and get off at the Empalme León in San Isidro. From there you can catch buses to León just about every 20 to 30 minutes. To Jinotega, buses leave every half-hour for Jinotega until 5:30 P.M.

At the north end of town, the Terminal de Guanuca is the home to buses departing for the interior of Matagalpa, including El Tuma–La Dália, San Ramón, Río Blanco, Muy Muy, and Bocana de Paíwas. These cities are not served by the nation's best roads, so bus service slackens in the rainy season. Buses to points east depart approximately every 45 minutes to an hour until around 4:30 P.M.

WEST OF MATAGALPA

Looking at a map, you'll notice the city of Matagalpa is perched precariously at the western end of a very long and well-populated department. Most of the rest of Matagalpa lies to your east, along bumpy country roads that ensure your exploration will be slow and unforgettable. Matagalpa is the nation's most mountainous department, and the constantly changing scenery of green hillsides and valleys is beautiful.

La Parada Larga

About 10 kilometers west of the city of Matagalpa, La Parada Larga is a popular rest stop for travelers bound for Matagalpa, and a popular day trip for Matagalpinos looking for a relaxing afternoon outside of the city. The cozy traditional-style roadside restaurant sits at the top of a steep hill, and there's a narrow walkway along a mountain ridge out to a grass-roof overlook. The view of the valley below is unforgettable, especially in the late afternoon when the valley ridges fill with shadow. Any bus between Matagalpa and Managua, León, or Estelí can let you off here for a leisurely meal and a walk down to the overlook for some picture-taking. The food is traditional Nicaraguan fare, and a typical dish of beef, pork, or chicken will set you back around $4.50.

El Atajo de Guayacán

About 25 kilometers west of the city of Matagalpa is a dirt road known as El Atajo de Guayacán (the Guayacán Shortcut). The road leads north along the west side of a pretty mountain valley to the city of Jinotega. Drivers headed from Sébaco to Jinotega can bypass the city of Matagalpa completely and save an hour's drive. It's the road to several great hikes too, all of which make good day trips from Matagalpa city. To get there from the city of Matagalpa, take any bus heading west, toward Managua or any other city, and get off at El Atajo de Guayacán. Walk or hitch north along the road about seven kilometers and then break off the road to the northeast. Use the Matagalpa, Sébaco, and Jinotega INETER quad maps. Your first hike should be Cerro Los Chiles, a peak that forms a half-basin along the side of the Atajo de Guayacán.

EAST OF MATAGALPA

For intrepid explorers anxious to leave behind the security of the urban life and head into the rising sun east of Matagalpa, there is adventure waiting. As you head into the geographic heart of the nation you cross through stunning scenery: broad hillsides of shiny coffee bushes or vegetables, plots of corn and beans, and small communities of tile-roofed adobe houses that sit along the edges of rivers and at the base of the rugged mountains making the eastern reaches of the Cordillera Dariense. The campesinos in the folds of these mountains live much the way they have for centuries, as governments, revolutions, and natural disasters have swirled violently around them.

The major communities of the east, Río Blanco, Matiguás, and Muy Muy, serve as commercial and transportation centers for the region, and offer rudimentary accommodations for the traveler. But don't expect any luxury rides here: the roads east of Matagalpa are some of the most neglected in the country, notably the stretch between Siuna and Mulukuku, which is practically impassable during the wettest months of the year. That said, enjoy the ride. You will be traveling through some of the most beautiful—and little visited—areas of an already undertouristed nation. This is as off the beaten path as you can get without forsaking the "convenience" of a bus.

Santa Emilia and Salto El Cebollál

The farming community of Santa Emilia is located between San Ramón and La Dália, and is frequently visited by Matagalpinos who want to cool their heels in the waterfall known as Salto El Cebollál. It's located an easy 200 meters from the highway along a well-marked trail. Ask the bus driver to let you off at *el camino para el salto.* There was at one time a small shrine set up at the falls, but it is now in disrepair.

Piedra Luna

About 10 kilometers (15 minutes) southwest of the mountain town of La Dália is a top-notch **swimming hole** called Piedra Luna by the locals. This makes a great day trip from Matagalpa and will give you a chance to appreciate some of the remaining monster trees in the area. Ask your bus driver to let you off at Piedra Luna and descend the steep hillside down to the river's edge. The swimming hole was formed by the waters of the Río Tuma as they swirled around a several-ton rock sitting in midstream. The swimming hole is easily seven meters deep, and local kids come from all over to dive off the rock into the pool. How did the rock get there? Ask the locals, so you can hear for yourself the fantastic legend of the spirits that carried it there from someplace far away. To get there, take any bus from the north terminal at Matagalpa bound for Waslala or El Tuma–La Dália and ask to be let off at Piedra Luna (approximately a one-hour trip from Matagalpa).

San Ramón

San Ramón is the first town east of Matagalpa and is nestled in a lovely valley at the base of massive Mt. Wabule (1,305 meters). Founded in the late 1800s, San Ramón got its start due to the gold mine La Leonesa, but its claim to fame these days is as the destination of one of the best walks in Matagalpa. When you get to San Ramón, the place to stay is **Finca Esperanza Verde,** a private and quite unique farm that is quickly making its name known in the ecotourism world. Up to 16 people can stay in newly built brick cabins for $13 a night and eat traditional Nicaraguan meals for $4 a day; camping sites are also available. Spend your days hiking and horseback riding through the cloud forest and waterfalls, picking coffee on the plantations,

FROM BEAN TO BEVERAGE:
HOW NICARAGUAN COFFEE IS PROCESSED

One of the unique aspects of the Nicaraguan coffee process is how many of the following steps are performed on the farm, *before* the product is shipped elsewhere. This is a significant difference from Costa Rican coffee growers, most of whom send off their harvest after only the second step.

1. Coffee berries are picked during the harvest months from December to February. The berries are red and fleshy and called *café en uva* (grape, or cherry coffee).

2. The berries are de-pulped, i.e., the fleshy covering is removed. This is done the same day they're picked to prevent fermenting, which would affect the flavor. This is either done dry, or while suspended in water ("wet processing").

3. The coffee beans at this stage still have a mucilaginous coating on them. The beans are allowed to sit for 24 hours to allow the coating to ferment, facilitating the removal of the mucilage.

4. After 24 hours, the beans are soaked in water and stirred with wooden paddles. The mucilaginous coating dissolves. During this stage the good beans sink to the bottom of the vessel, and the bad beans float to the surface, where they're removed.

5. The beans are now called *café en pergamino* (parchment coffee). Small growers sell their beans to the coffee cooperatives at this point. They still have a hard shell around them.

6. The beans are laid out in the sun on broad concrete slabs to dry and raked continuously to prevent burning.

7. When the beans reach 12 percent humidity, they are stored for around one month in a cool, semi-dark building. During this time the coffee beans' flavor is enhanced.

8. When ready for shipping, the beans are milled to remove the hard shell. What is left after milling is the familiar coffee bean, in two halves. At this stage the coffee is considered *café oro* (gold, or green coffee).

9. The beans are sorted. All broken, burned, or blackened beans are removed by hand.

10. The beans are packed in 150-pound burlap sacks and shipped to the port of Corinto for shipments to the western United States and Asia, or Puerto Cortéz, Honduras, for shipments to the eastern United States and Europe.

11. The green coffee beans are roasted, ground, and brewed into the beverage so many people can't wake up without. Repeat step 11 as often as necessary.

harvest time in Jinotega

or checking out one of Nicaragua's only butterfly farms; the scenery is breathtaking, tel. 612-5003, Internet available. From the Finca it's easy to catch a bus back to Matagalpa. Buses to and from San Ramón are extremely frequent, leaving every hour 6 A.M.–7 P.M., in addition to the many other eastbound buses that pass through San Ramón on their way elsewhere. A cab from Matagalpa can cost $2.50–4.50 per person if you're interested in day tripping from the city of Matagalpa.

Mulukuku

Mulukuku is a city on the edge of the mighty Tuma River, far enough downstream that the river is quite wide and unforgettable. Best known these days for the political controversy that surrounded Doña Dorotea, a 70-year-old nurse who's lived and worked in the community for over 11 years, Mulukuku is an otherwise quiet mountain town. As part of what was later perceived to be nothing more than political mischief and blind personal vengeance, ex-president

Alemán accused Doña Dorotea of favoring Sandinista patients in her clinic, proselytizing Sandinista propaganda, and performing abortions; he ordered her deported. Over a period of several weeks in 2001, Dorotea's fellow townspeople rallied behind her even as Alemán continued threatening to throw her out of Nicaragua and she pleaded she had nowhere else to go. Though she was never deported, she suddenly found it impossible to renew her residency permit and was forced to leave the country without having ever been formally tried. Ashamed Nicaraguans are trying to forget the whole fiasco ever happened and Alemán was never asked to explain.

Río Blanco

In Río Blanco, you can stay at the **Hotel and Restaurant Musun 2,** located at the edge of town on the road to Mulukuku; tel. 284-0103 restaurant, 284-0216 hotel. There are no less than seven waterfalls you can get to on Cerro Musun in a full day's hike (there and back)—find a guide at the FUNDENIC office in town.

Bocana de Paíwas

Bocana de Paíwas has a *hospedaje* and several restaurants, including the well-liked **Restaurante Mirador,** located on a long peninsula overlooking the Río Grande de Matagalpa. This is also the site of some pre-Columbian petroglyphs, located alongside the Río Grande de Matagalpa.

THE MATAGALPA–JINOTEGA HIGHWAY

The sinuous mountain road between Matagalpa and Jinotega is considered one of the most scenic roads in all of Nicaragua. The road was first opened around 1920 by the English immigrant and coffee farmer Charles Potter for use by mules and wagons taking coffee from his farm to Matagalpa. No small feat of engineering, Potter had to negotiate over 100 curves, the worst of which was the still-legendary Disparate de Potter (see below). A stubborn old man, Potter built his road even when he was told it was impossible, and it's said he used the road to carry a piano—strung atop two mules—all the way to his farm.

WHAT MAKES A COFFEE GOURMET?

As much as 80 percent of Nicaraguan cooperative produced coffee can be considered "quality coffee," because it fills the following internationally recognized requirements:

- Arabica beans, not robusta, grown at an altitude of 900 meters.
- Big beans, aromatic, well sorted, and free from broken or burned beans and small stones.
- Beans are given one month to sit during processing and are not de-hulled until just before shipping.
- Beans are transported in sealed containers.
- Beans are adequately stored by the purchaser.
- Upon toasting, the beans are sealed immediately in special one-pound vacuum-packed bags that prevent the introduction of light, air, and moisture, but permit carbon dioxide to escape.
- The consumer can buy the coffee in whole bean form, not ground.

the falls at Peñas Blancas

The long, valley views are awesome, with Momotombo and the Maribio Volcanoes visible on a clear day. You'll pass neatly arranged coffee plantations, shaded by windrows of cedar and pine, banana trees, and canopies of precious hardwoods. There is also an endless succession of vegetable (and recently, flower) fields and roadside stands. Should you take the express bus, you'll miss the opportunity to stop and take photographs, buy fresh vegetables, and hike into the coffee plantations. But if you drive, you may need to concentrate on the road so much you miss the scenery. The best alternative is to take it easy; hop on and off passing buses and offered rides over the course of an afternoon, enjoying the following sights until you get to Jinotega.

Mirador de La Chispa (kilometer 133)

Just three kilometers outside of the city of Matagalpa, there's a great overlook on the right side of the highway, with a view of the city.

Hotel Selva Negra (kilometer 140)

The entrance to Selva Negra is marked by an old tank on the side of the road, a relic from the revolution and since painted over with the rainbows of Doña Violeta's UNO coalition in the early 1990s.

Disparate de Potter (kilometer 143)

This was the worst, rockiest curve of all the obstacles that Charles Potter faced when building the road between Matagalpa and his farm La Fundadora. There was no way around the rock that made up that part of the mountain, so he stubbornly blasted his way straight through it. The hill in two pieces remains exactly the way he left it, with the single addition of a lookout platform on the needle of rock left standing on the outside of the curve. At the side of the road is a well-liked restaurant serving traditional Nicaraguan food.

Santa Lastenia (kilometer 148)

At 1,555 meters above sea level, Santa Lastenia is the highest point along the road, after which one drops rather precipitously into the valley of Jinotega.

Vegetable Stands (kilometer 152)

Jinotega and Matagalpa are the two most copious producers of vegetables in Nicaragua, and a set of small farm stands along the road are evidence of the rich harvests of this area. Whether you want to eat them or just photograph them, the stacks of fresh cabbage, carrots, broccoli, radishes, beets, lettuce, squash, and greens are a culinary feast for the eyes. The stands are typically run by the older children of the family who might just sweet-talk you into making a purchase.

PEÑAS BLANCAS (1,445 METERS)

Located on the road that leads between El Tuma–La Dália and El Cuá, the cliffs of Peñas Blancas are several hundred meters high and carved out of the top of a massive hillside; this is unquestionably one of the most stunning natural sights in northern Nicaragua. At the top of the cliff is a copious waterfall, gorgeous and little known, even by Nicaraguans who live outside of the immediate area. The cliffs and waterfall are easily visible from the highway, on property owned by Alan Ball. He's currently developing hikes and tours to the waterfall, but you can be proactive and get there yourself by asking around.

Getting there requires some effort, more so if you're using public transportation. By bus, leave Matagalpa on a Waslala bus, and pass through El Tuma–La Dália on the road to Waslala. Ask to be let off at the *empalme* of the road to El Cuá–Bocay. Ask for "Isla de Peñas Blancas." From the intersection walk 15 minutes north to where you will find a sign that says Centro de Entendimiento con la Naturaleza. From there, ask for the best route to the falls. The hike is only possible in the dry season, and there is no well-established trail to the falls. The walk is worth it, as you'll pass through a series of humid forest ecosystems of orchids and mossy trees. Near the falls the wind is full of spray. The hike up and down can be done in two hours but expect to get extremely muddy and wet.

Jinotega City

When walking the cobbled streets of Jinotega, you can't help but feel you're at the edge of the world, with all kinds of unknowns in the hills to the north and east. Medieval mapmakers would have emblazoned the valley of Jinotega with Beyond Here Lie Dragons, referring to the hundreds of kilometers of wild, lush mountain country. East of the city the pavement stops, and the roads turn rutted and bumpy, bus service is less frequent, and the accommodations dwindle—at least the kind where they leave a mint on your pillow and fold the edge of the toilet paper into a little triangle. But the immense department of Jinotega is home to hundreds of small communities and thousands of farmers who make their livelihood in the hills around them—including many who have barely ever traveled beyond this land in their lives. Jinotega is lined with fragrant valleys of orange groves, white corn, plantains, and sweet vegetables, not to mention countless head of cattle. But in between the small farms, Jinotega is open space—virgin forest, small freshwater lagoons, stately mountain ranges, and some of the loveliest rivers in Nicaragua, including the mighty Río Coco (which forms the northern border of the Jinotega department) and the Río Bocay, one of the Coco's most important tributaries. Jinotega is open sky country, and the nights are filled with stars.

Jinotega, or La Ciudad de las Brumas (The City of Mists), is the watering hole and commercial center for the department of the same name. Farmers from the north and east inevitably find their way here to do their business and trading, and Jinotega City has built itself into a clean, prosperous community around the business needs of those farmers. It's a working town whose streets are lined with cobblers, tailors, barbers, blacksmiths, watch repairmen, and merchants that deal in housewares, veterinary supplies, saddles, cowboy hats, firearms, auto parts, and an endless stock of farming tools. It's a town very much in tune with the rugged and self-sufficient life of the Nicaragua campesino, and you will learn much just by wandering its streets among such hardy characters. Jinotega is at once charming and thrilling, and your gateway to the wide open expanses of the east. As late as the mid-1960s, it wasn't uncommon to find wild monkeys in the old-growth park canopy of *lechito* trees.

Travelers enjoy Jinotega because its high elevation (a full kilometer above sea level) gives it a pleasant climate, especially nice in the picturesque setting. Jinoteganos themselves are at once friendly and aloof—they might leave you to your own, but if you make the effort to talk to them you'll find them warm, open, and full of country hospitality.

HISTORY

The name Jinotega is said to come from the Nahuatl *Xilotl-Tecatl*, (Place of the Jiñocuao Trees), but it has also been translated as The Place of the

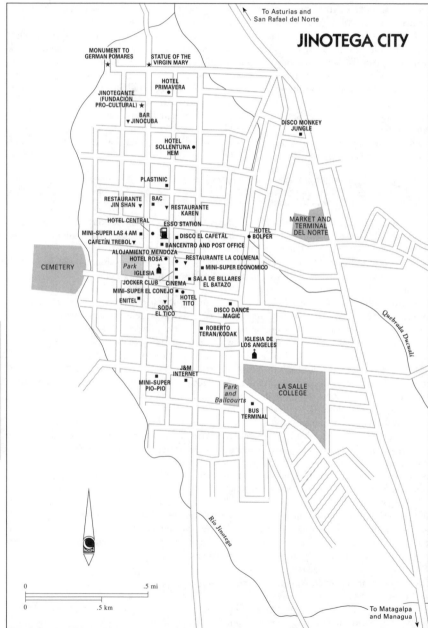

JINOTEGA CITY

To Asturias and
San Rafael del Norte

MONUMENT TO
GERMAN POMARES ★

STATUE OF THE
VIRGIN MARY ★

HOTEL
PRIMAVERA ●

JINOTEGANTE
(FUNDACIÓN
PRO-CULTURAL) ★

BAR
▼ JINOCUBA

DISCO MONKEY
JUNGLE ■

HOTEL
SOLLENTUNA ●
HEM

PLASTINIC ■

RESTAURANTE
JIN SHAN ▼

BAC ■

RESTAURANTE
KAREN

HOTEL CENTRAL ●

ESSO STATION

MINI-SUPER LAS 4 AM ■

CAFETÍN TREBOL ▼

DISCO EL CAFETAL ■

BANCENTRO AND POST OFFICE ■

HOTEL
● BOLPER

MARKET AND
TERMINAL
DEL NORTE

ALOJAMIENTO MENDOZA ■

HOTEL ROSA ●

Park

IGLESIA ♦

RESTAURANTE LA COLMENA ■

MINI-SUPER ECONOMICO ■

CEMETERY

JOCKER CLUB ■

CINEMA ■

SALA DE BILLARES
EL BATAZO ■

MINI-SUPER EL CONEJO ■

ENITEL ■

HOTEL ●
TITO

SODA
EL TICO ▼

DISCO DANCE
MAGIC ■

ROBERTO ■
TERAN/KODAK

IGLESIA DE
LOS ANGELES ♦

J&M ■
INTERNET

MINI-SUPER ■
PIO-PIO

Park
and
Ballcourts

LA SALLE
COLLEGE

BUS
TERMINAL ■

Quebrada Ducualí

Río Jinotega

MOON

0   .5 mi

0   .5 km

To Matagalpa
and Managua

© AVALON TRAVEL PUBLISHING, INC.

MATAGALPA & JINOTEGA

Eternal Men and Women. Indeed, the natives who lived in this peaceful valley enjoyed healthy and prosperous existences and were known to live to more than 100 years of age. Today's department of Jinotega was in those days the border between two diverse indigenous peoples: to the north, in the Bocay region, lived the Chontales (Kiribie) people, and near the present-day city of Jinotega, the Chorotega. They were an agricultural people who lived off of small plots of corn, beans, cacao, roots, tubers, and fruit orchards. Their clothing was woven from wood fiber and cotton, as well as animal skins tinted with plant extracts. When the Spanish arrived in the late 18th century, they chose to inhabit the southern part of the Jinotega, forcing the indigenous peoples to the north. The community of Jinotega was officially recategorized as The Valley of Jinotega in 1851, and as a city in 1883.

For better or for worse, nearly every major armed uprising in recent Nicaraguan history began in the Jinotega department. The young Sandinistas first took to the hills here to battle squadrons of the National Guard in the 1960s, and when the Sandinistas took power, the first groups of Contras took to the hills, again in Jinotega. At the end of the Contra war, the two groups that refused to lay down their weapons and accept the peace treaty (the Recompas and Recontras) fled back into the mountains of Jinotega to keep up their fight.

Today, remnants of fighting groups like FUAC plague certain wilder areas of northeastern Jinotega. It may be indicative of the warrior spirit still present in Nicaragua's hinterlands, but it's been taxing on the peace-loving Jinotegan farmers trying to raise crops and their families at the same time. Jinotega was possibly the worst affected department in Nicaragua during the 1980s, as Contras and Sandinistas fought each other on the mountain roads and the deep valleys. In those days, there was only one bus per day between the city of Jinotega and Managua (as compared to one every hour now), and travelers intent on driving their own vehicles ran the daily risk of being ambushed, robbed, raped, or killed. Since the 1980s Jinotega has voted

steadfastly against the Sandinistas, who they claim are responsible for 10 years of devastation. The survivors of the generation that was marched off to the mountains as machine gun fodder are resentful and frustrated now, robbed of their adolescence, and desperately trying to make a decent, honest living off the land.

ORIENTATION AND GETTING AROUND

Jinotega sits in the bottom of the steep-walled bowl formed by the mountains that surround Jinotega on all sides. The highway passes along its east side, and the cemetery is at the western edge. It's a city with a pleasant, cool climate and not too much vehicular traffic, both of which make it a pleasurable city for walking. There are no city buses, nor is there need for them.

There are several taxi cooperatives that roam the streets of Jinotega. You can get from one side of town to the other for $0.80. But Jinotega isn't a big place, and the temperature never gets hot enough to be unpleasant. You should be able to walk anywhere you need to go.

SIGHTS AND ATTRACTIONS

Jinotega was the scene of a few ferocious battles during the revolution years, and it was down by the riverside in Jinotega where much-loved Sandinista commander German Pomares (a.k.a. El Danto) was killed in battle. Pomares and his troops had fought many battles against Somoza's National Guard and had been instrumental in the operation that led to political prisoner Daniel Ortega's release from jail. His sacrifice has not been forgotten, and a very carefully maintained red-and-black memorial marks the spot where he was killed.

Don Pilo is a second generation medicine man who lives in an unknown location in the mountains west of Jinotega city. Twice weekly he climbs down out of the mountains with his bags of herbs and potions and sets up camp at the cemetery to sell. He's a well-loved town character who some put off as a charlatan, and other consider a true magician and physician; regardless, both rich and poor wait for him Tuesdays and Fridays to see if he can cure their ills, from intestinal parasites and coughs to bad marriages, naughty children, and spurned lovers. And you don't need a prescription, just a strong stomach. The cures are all natural and brewed out of the stronger medicinal plants of the region, plus bark, moss, and sometimes even soil.

The town cemetery is an interesting place to wander. The graves started at the entrance to the cemetery and have worked their way south over time. The victims of the war in the 1980s are located at the south end of the plot. Some of the older gravestones are particularly ornate and well crafted in stone.

Festivals and Celebrations

Jinotega's *fiestas patronales* begin on May 1 and continue through May 15. You can expect to see folks from all over the north of Nicaragua show up for the occasion. The *fiestas patronales* of San Juan de Jinotega are June 24th. In addition (perhaps just to round out the year with parties), the Aniversario de la Creación del Departamento de Jinotega is celebrated on October 15.

ENTERTAINMENT AND NIGHTLIFE

There's a small movie theater that opens up just before the show and closes down just after—a good place to lick your wounds if you need a rest from walking and/or hiking. There are two small discos in town, but Jinotegans do even less dancing than Matagalpans do. Nonetheless, they're both enjoyable places to spend a Saturday evening. Check out the tried-and-true **Dance Magic,** not far from the center of town. It was formerly a house but was converted into a dance floor, so it's got a cozy feel to it. Newer and more modern, and making an attempt to throw a little style into the Nicaraguan disco scene, is **Monkey Jungle,** out on the highway across the street from the Coca-Cola distributor (just north of the market and north bus terminal). Look for the bamboo walls on the outside and the stuffed animal monkeys on the inside.

Sports and Recreation

Basketball is the game of choice in Jinotega, and there are pickup games most evenings on the *cancha* (town court). Jinotega has an active youth league and both women's and men's teams; the players are better than you'd expect, if you're thinking about getting in a game.

HIKES FROM THE CITY OF JINOTEGA

The western wall of the valley of Jinotega makes a popular climb for a Saturday morning. Start at the cemetery and work your way upward to Peña de la Cruz where the cross is planted. Depending on how ambitious you are, the hike is from 30 to 90 minutes, and you'll be rewarded by an impressive view of the city and the verdant valley of Jinotega. The cross isn't the original—its predecessor was bigger and "better" according to the locals. But the current is illuminated, thanks to an electric cable that climbs the same steep hillside you did. Look for the shining beacon of Christianity at night from the city. During misty nights it's particularly eerie, emitting a diffuse white glow through the mists.

The eastern wall of the valley is steeper and longer, and there are no trails. That doesn't stop many locals from making their way to the top for a look around. Plan on two hours for this one. The easiest way to do it is the steep, windy dirt road that climbs abruptly out of the city and snakes its way to the top of the ridge. By road it's around an hour on foot, but it's still not an easy walk, as the road is exceptionally steep; watch your step on loose gravel.

ACCOMMODATIONS

Keep in mind Jinotega's chief clientele are the small-scale farmers of the east who come in for weekends at a time to see a dentist, sell some corn, and have their boots fixed. They don't require many luxuries and don't want to waste too many cordobas while they're in town. Accommodations in Jinotega are simple but clean, and not too expensive. Start by asking yourself if you'll want hot water in the morning to wash with. Odds are you will—Jinotega is chilly.

Under $10

Hotel El Tico is next to the restaurant of the same name: four small and basic rooms with private bath for about $4, tel. 632-4530. **Hotel Rosa** is the oldest gig in town, and a hundred years ago when it first opened its doors, the only gig in town. Its 19th-century charm is still apparent in massive wooden beams, simple rustic rooms, and a laid-back atmosphere. While clean and charming, there are no amenities you wouldn't have found a hundred years ago, with the exception of the one television in the central parlor, which is usually turned to the latest Mexican soap opera; 30 rooms cost $2 per person, tel. 632-2472.

Hotel Tito is in town, with seven rooms with shared bath for $5 s, $8.50 d; clean, modern and popular with travelers. It closes its doors at 10 P.M.; knock to be let in after-hours. Downstairs there's a small dining room that serves three meals a day. **Hotel Central** is indeed central, only a block from the park, with two kinds of facilities: 17 small rooms not much larger than the bed, $2.50 each for a shared bath with no hot water. Also three nice rooms upstairs with cable TV, private bath, and hot water, $10–13; meals are available at the dining room for around $2 each. Both the hotel and restaurant are closed Sundays.

Toward the north end of town, but still in a quiet residential area, **Hotel Primavera** is run by a family that expects you to behave; 19 small rooms set around a courtyard are nothing special, but they're clean, simple, and cheap—$2.50 per person. There's an additional room with its own private bath for a relatively steep $8.50. Inside the family's living room there's a pay phone available; the doors close at 10 P.M. and don't open until morning—make sure you're on the right side of the door.

$10–25

There are two places in town with hot water. At the north end of town, convenient to the bus terminal, **Hotel Bolper** is the most upscale and modern hotel in town. The owner tries very hard

(there's even a suggestion box in the hallway!) and offers 13 clean rooms that cost $13 per night, with hot water and cable TV, located on the south side of the El Carmen Shell station, tel. 632-2966.

Hotel Sollentuna Hem is owned by a Swedish woman, and the hotel's meticulous Scandinavian style reflects it (the name is Swedish for Home of the Green Valley). In business since 1988, the hotel has 12 rooms with private bath and hot water starting at $10, plus eight rooms with shared bath for a bit more. Complete laundry service is available, as are tours of her farm on the outskirts of town. If you plan on staying in Jinotega for a while, Sollentuna Hem also has one fully furnished apartment that you can rent out for $24 a day, tel. 632-2334. **Hotel Café,** two blocks east of the park, is a new, reportedly luxury hotel aimed at the business class. **Restaurante La Colmena** has six rooms upstairs above the restaurant.

FOOD

Street Food

If you don't want to spend a lot of money on dinner, Jinotega is a good place to eat cheap. After dark the streets fill with *fritangas,* and families open their front doors and set up shop in their living rooms and front parlors. You can eat your way to greasy happiness for under $2 with no effort at all. Start at the southeast corner of the park and troll the two main streets through a sea of enchiladas, *papas rellenas,* and *gallo pinto.* There's a pizza truck that sets up shop at the park. A slice of pizza (à la frozen pizzas of the 1970s) will cost you about $.80. There are also several kiosks in the park that sell crackers, cookies, fruit drinks, and soft drinks.

Restaurants

Soda El Tico appears on the map twice. The original is next to the bus station across from La Salle school, serving mostly ice cream and light meals like sandwiches. A more complete affair (i.e., they serve chicken and burgers, too) is in town just north of the park. Clean and inexpensive. *Comida corriente* for $1.50 or $2, or lighter stuff. **Cafetería Trebol** is popular with travelers for a charming, almost European feel. Located on the north side of the park, Trebol has a simple menu of burgers, chicken, and sandwiches, but it's the best place in town to drink a hot chocolate or *café con leche* and remarkably, it serves French toast. Opens for breakfast at 8:30 A.M., 11 A.M. on Sundays. **Restaurante La Colmena** is arguably the nicest restaurant in town, though there are many who argue on behalf of **Restaurante El Tico;** both have similar menus of beef, chicken, and fish, good service, and a pleasant, mid- to upscale atmosphere.

SHOPPING

Jinotega is not geared to foreign tourism yet. You won't find postcards or handicrafts for sale here. Instead, Jinotega is a town well prepared to equip you for your adventures north and east of the city. There are several mini-supers with a wide variety of canned goods, breads, and staples to take on the road with you. Mini-super Pio-Pio (named after the sound hungry little chicks make) has the best selection of wine in town, or you can also do your shopping at Mini-Super Las 4 A.M., which is big enough to have outgrown the moniker "mini." Mini-Super El Conejo, located more centrally, is smaller but still has more canned and dried foods than you'll ever be able to eat.

Jinotega is also your last chance to load up on car parts if you happen to be driving into the mountains. Elsewhere we wouldn't mention this, but travelers heading north and east of the city should travel prepared with everything necessary to repair their vehicles if necessary (and be prepared for at least two flat tires). On some of the beat-up roads that lead out from Jinotega, being prepared can mean the difference between adventure and disaster (Or at least a long wait. Maybe you should stock up on reading material, too). Stop by Repuestos El Pistón for supplies.

INFORMATION
Guide Services

Not only does Luis Lautaro Ruiz seemingly know all there is to know about his native Jinotega and the surrounding mountains, he speaks some Eng-

lish and is a professional writer, film producer, musician, and clown. He is a flexible freelance tour guide and will charge comparable prices to guides in Managua ($15–20 a day). He also claims his house, located a half-block north of the Escuela Mistral, is a museum, tel. 632-4460, email: lautaror@ibw.com.ni.

Radio

The radio programs of Jinotega are particularly delightful, as their audience, the hardworking campesinos of the north, likes their news spicy and their jokes raunchy. Check out Radio La Dinámica (FM 103.7), Radio Estereo Libre (FM 95.3), and Radio Family Estereo (FM 90.7).

SERVICES
Banks

There's a bank on practically every corner in Jinotega. All the major players are present—Banpro, Bancentro, Banexpo, Banic, BAC, and more. Bank hours are standard; check your firearm at the door, please.

Internet

J&M Internet Café opened in October 2001 and has five machines for $3 per hour. Scanner and CD burner also available, and soft drinks and snacks.

Phone Office and Mail

The ENITEL office is located just north of the park along the main street. It's open every day from 7 A.M.–9 P.M. The post office is a bit hard to find. It's tucked into a business complex behind Bancentro. As you're facing the front door of the bank, look for a sidewalk that leads behind the building to the offices that are part of the same complex. Open 8 A.M.–4 P.M. Fax machine available.

OPPORTUNITIES TO VOLUNTEER

One of the most active organizations in Jinotega is Habitat for Humanity. To work with them you'll have to have arranged the trip before coming down. Still, if you'd like to be useful and plan to spend some time in Jinotega, consider stopping by the following organizations to volunteer your time and services: Club Infantíl de Niños Trabajadores de Jinotega (tel. 632-3435) offers classes and workshops in trades like carpentry to disadvantaged children and orphans of Jinotega. Associación de Voluntarios para el Desarrollo Comunitario—AVODEC (tel. 632-2885) works with campesino groups in several areas, including agriculture and social development.

GETTING THERE AND AWAY

Buses at the Terminal del Sur head south to Matagalpa and Managua, including several express buses that make one stop along the highway at Matagalpa without entering the city itself, then continue straight on to Managua. Express buses to Managua ($3) leave every hour, and more express buses are being put into service every day, so ask ahead of time to find out what your options are. These buses may or may not make a brief stop along the highway and Matagalpa before continuing straight on to Managua (three to four hours).

To Points South

The bus terminal (actually, just a parking lot) is located across from La Salle. The main road behind the bus station is lined with several eateries where you can relax and wait for the bus to leave, as the terminal doesn't have any facilities for passengers. Buses to Matagalpa leave every half-hour from 4 A.M. to 6 P.M. (the trip takes one hour). Buses to Estelí are in "trial stage" at present. There's a direct bus to Estelí every two hours, and if there's enough demand, more will be put in service to run this route. Getting to Estelí is easy even if you don't take one of these *expresos* however. Simply take any Managua bus to Sébaco, and transfer to a northbound bus heading to Estelí, Ocotal, Somoto, or Jalapa.

To Points North and East

Buses at the Terminal del Norte go to points inland in Jinotega and beyond, including El Cuá, San José de Bocay, San Rafael del Norte, and Wiwilí. This is where the adventures start, and the rugged conditions at the terminal should prepare you mentally for what awaits you inland: mud, livestock, and a lot of friendly people moving sacks of produce, selling grains and cheap merchandise, and laughing. There is one *expreso* to Wiwilí each day (five hours), but regular buses leave about every hour (seven hours). There are two expresses per day to El Cuá–Bocay (three hours), and regular service about once per hour (four hours). Two expresses to Pantasma (three hours) and regular service about once per hour (4.5 hours). Pantasma buses go past Asturias and the dam at Lago Apanás.

The north terminal also has regular bus service to San Sebastián de Yalí and La Rica, via San Rafael del Norte and La Concordia, from where you can get back-road bus service to Estelí—a fun way to make a loop through some really beautiful country.

NORTH AND EAST OF JINOTEGA

El Valle de Tomatoya

Located just north of the city of Jinotega on the road to San Rafael del Norte, this is the home of a women's cooperative that produces the famous **black pottery** of the region. Although few like to admit it, the cities of Matagalpa and Jinotega vie with each other for recognition as home of the black pottery. Check in at Grupo de Mujeres de Las Cureñas to see their work. The production of black pottery is a little more intricate than other types of ceramic arts, and these women have produced some very beautiful pieces of art, including faithful replicas of some pre-Columbian designs.

Right along the highway is **El Centro Recreativo de Tomatoya,** a bathing area made by damming up the San Gabriel stream. The owner, Blanca Dalla Torre, has gotten special permission from the Ministry of Health to run the swimming hole, on the condition she regularly empties out the pool and lets it refill with fresh water. Drinks and snacks are available too, as well as a complete selection of beer.

Lago de Apanás and the Mancotal Dam

Lake Apanás is the largest body of water in Nicaragua after the two natural lakes. Luís Somoza Debayle's administration created it in 1964 by damming up the waters of Río El Tuma and flooding the broad valley just north of the city of Jinotega, which until that time had been home to pasture, small farms, and an airstrip that serviced the north of Nicaragua. Today, Lake Apanás is a long, irregularly shaped lake that feeds the twin turbines at the Planta Hidroeléctrica Centroamérica, which produces 15 percent of the nation's hydropower (downstream along the Río Viejo, the same water passes through the turbines at Santa Bárbara and Lago La Virgen, where an additional 15 percent of the nation's hydropower is produced). Apanás is not a typical reservoir; unlike many hydropower plants that are located at the dam itself, the Planta Centroamérica is located at the upstream end of the lake, so keeping the lake full is essential. The water is taken underneath the highway through massive steel pipes, where it drops and passes through the turbines. The hydropower project actually forces the water to change watersheds: water from the Río El Tuma watershed is discharged into the tributaries of the Río Viejo, where it flows south to Lake Xolotlán (Managua) instead of the Atlantic coast.

The Mancotal dam was nearly destroyed by Hurricane Mitch in 1998, when waters overtopping the round Morning Glory Spillway (the concrete structure that looks like a flying saucer on its head in the middle of the lake), flowed through the secondary spillway channel, under the bridge, and down a long stair-step energy dissipater. The volume of water rushing through the channel quickly eroded it away along with all of its concrete, nearly destroying the dam itself and nearly causing a tidal wave that would have raged for hundreds of kilometers downstream. The loss of the lake would have been economically catastrophic, considering the loss of water for irrigation, fishing, and hydropower production, not to mention the loss of life and property downstream on the Río El Tuma. The government has been negotiating since 1999 to find a

the Morning Glory Spillway, Lago de Apanás

© RANDY WOOD

way to repair the spillway and return the dam's safety structures to normal.

To get to the dam, take any bus headed toward Pantasma and get off at Asturias (60–90 minutes from Jinotega). The highway crosses the dam, so you'll know when you've arrived. The lake itself is picturesque, but equally impressive are the remains of the damaged spillway. On the lake side of the road are the remains of an old military base built in the 1980s to prevent Contra troops from destroying the dam. (The Planta Centroamérica was a highly sought Contra target in the 1980s and was similarly tightly guarded to prevent its destruction. Some land mines still litter the hills around the hydropower plant.)

Swimming and Fishing at Apanás: Don't miss the opportunity to cast a line and do some fishing (Apanás is full of giant tilapia and *guapote*) or swimming. There are several grassy areas at the lake's edge where you can jump in for a refreshing dip in the surprisingly cold waters of Apanás. From the dam, walk along the highway in either direction and choose your place. The lake is safe—there are no underwater structures or water intakes to be afraid of, and the water is quite deep and refreshing.

Lago Asturias and the El Dorado Dam

The El Dorado dam was completed in 1984 and filled in 1985 as a supplement to the Mancotal Dam. Water is captured in Asturias and pumped up to Apanás, where it flows through the turbines for energy production. Fishermen in the know realize that Asturias is home to some monster freshwater fish. To get there from the Mancotal Dam, walk back toward the city of Jinotega about one kilometer to the first major intersection. That road descends quickly past a few coffee farms and small farming communities to the El Dorado Dam. El Dorado also experienced severe damage during Hurricane Mitch. As you look at the lake, imagine that the same massive deluge that destroyed Mancotal's spillway also flowed through that placid little lake and out the other side — then appreciate how fortunate it is to have withstood the hurricane.

Fishing at Asturias: There's a little grassy hill on the upstream side of the dam where you can pitch a tent and do some fishing. Occasional vehicles transit this road—mostly old IFAs and pickup trucks—bound for the communities east of El Dorado, if you'd like to try to hitch a ride with all your catch.

San Rafael del Norte

This is a beautifully green and misty mountain town, often rainy and downright cold. Being at the top of the watershed, the country around San Rafael is thick with clean swimming holes. The easiest to access are in the two creeks that meet at the **Los Encuentros** restaurant, located a 10-minute walk out of town on the road toward Yalí. The more adventurous should hike down into the gorge that runs on the north edge of town; descend from the Hospedaje Rolinmar and then start upstream. Cold water rushes through a narrow canyon, shady and thick with green vegetation.

To know San Rafael is to know history. A visit to the General Augusto César Sandino museum (right off the park) gives you a sample of the small town's pride at having served as the proving grounds for the general's legendary battles with the U.S. Marines in the 1930s. Sandino's wife was a San Rafaelina, and Nicaraguan folk musician Carlos Mejía Godoy wrote moving lyrics about love and war in Sandino's hills there. The marines, incidentally, (who Sandino once referred to as "the enemies of all humanity") just returned to the pueblo to help doctors perform special surgeries in the local health clinic.

La Iglesia de San Rafael del Norte is a surprisingly large and impressive church for such an out-of-the-way town; some call it the most beautiful church in all of Nicaragua. Pastel-colored windows admit a calming light in which to view the many bright murals, reliefs, and shrines (despite Sandino, one artist took a pot shot at Ortega; look closely at the interior mural, you'll spot a portrait of Satan painted with the face of Daniel Ortega, implying that he has betrayed the ideals of Sandino).

The community has the Italian priest Odorico d'Andrea to thank for their church—and a whole lot more. From his arrival in 1953 to his death in 1996, Father Odorico achieved virtual

BEN LINDER

As the only reported incident in which a United States citizen was killed by Contra soldiers, Benjamin Linder's death had enormous repercussions, stemming primarily from the fact that he was shot with guns and bullets purchased by his own government, and by soldiers carrying out a hotly contested policy of violence supported by the same government. Linder's death was elevated to the status of martyrdom by those that shared his values. He was one individual in a huge wave of international supporters of the Sandinista revolution, leftists from Europe and North America who saw a chance to take part in the real-world political laboratory of Nicaragua. Some came to make a stand against the policies of the Reagan administration, some to physically help as development workers, teachers, and coffee pickers, and some came simply to experience the new world order at ground level.

Oregon native Ben Linder, like thousands of other *internacionalistas,* believed in the revolution and came to Nicaragua to contribute to its success in order to help the country's poor. Linder graduated from the University of Washington in 1983 with a degree in mechanical engineering. He moved to Nicaragua, where he shared a small apartment in the capital and worked for the electric company. In his free time he would dress up in a clown suit and rubber nose, and pedal around on a unicycle, to the delight of the Nicaraguan children.

In mid-1985 he moved to Jinotega to help install a mini-hydroelectric plant in the town of El Cuá. This was an area overrun with raiding Contra, and the danger in the region was real, a fact not lost on Linder. Rather than avoid the danger, his engineer's passion for solving problems led him further into the bush, to San José de Bocay, to repeat the success he'd had at El Cuá. Bocay was even farther out of Sandinista control than El Cuá, and the Contra were everywhere. On April 28, 1987, Linder and a crew of Nicaraguans went into the field to build a small concrete weir that would measure the flow in a stream Linder thought would be a good site for a hydroelectric plant. His crew crossed paths with a squadron of Contra. Shots were exchanged, and Linder was killed.

The political repercussions were enormous and blame flew in all directions—between the Sandinistas, the Contras, and the U.S. government. The Sandinistas claimed Linder was killed by a bullet in the back of the head, execution style; the Contras claimed that Linder had been dressed in combat uniform, was carrying a weapon, and that Linder's team had fired the first shots. It was eventually determined that Linder had indeed been carrying a rifle, and that he was mistaken for a Cuban military advisor.

Linder was buried in a small, neat grave in the foreigner's section of the Matagalpa cemetery. Today, his legend and inspiration live on; if you wander through the peaceful community of San José de Bocay, you'll notice the town has been electrified, courtesy of the "Benjamin Linder Mini-Hydroelectric Power Plant," constructed after his death. The Benjamin Linder School is down the road, and one of Bocay's more newly settled neighborhoods was christened Barrio Benjamin Linder.

In the early 1990s, when the Sandinistas handed power over to Doña Violeta's administration and it became obvious the great socialist revolution of the 1980s was not to be, most of the international crowd packed up and returned home, but what Ben Linder set out to do—bring progress and hope to the people whose lives are the most difficult—is an ideal that did not die with the revolution.

Today, the Asociación de Trabajadores de Desarrollo Rural Benjamin Linder (The Benjamin Linder Association of Development Workers) continues to do what Linder was doing the day he was killed: build small-scale hydroelectric plants to promote rural development. The association is located 25 meters south of the Hotel Bermúdez in Matagalpa, tel. 612-2030, managed by Rebecca Leaf.

sainthood among the people of San Rafael and the surrounding communities. His image, a smiling, warm, obviously kind man in plain brown robes, can be seen in nearly every home, business, and vehicle in the town. Among his achievements are a formidable health clinic, a library, several neighborhoods for the poor, and the beautifying of the church. Mention the padre's name to any local and you will immediately gain his or her friendship.

As time passes, the people of San Rafael speak even more greatly of Father Odorico; many believe he performed miracles and that his body has not decomposed. You can check for yourself at its resting place, called the **Tepeac,** located on the hill overlooking the town. Ascending the stairs, you'll pass the 12 stations of the cross until you reach the shrine on top where the tomb lays. The top of the hill offers shade from an impressively diverse grouping of old trees, as well as gorgeous views of the town and surrounding hills. Virgin pine forests still speckle the countryside, although they were once much thicker.

There are great eats at **Doña Chepita's,** and there are two places to stay: **Rolinmar** (near the gas station and the nicer of the two) and **Comedor y Hospedaje Aura.** Buses pass through San Rafael del Norte regularly on the route between Jinotega and San Sebastián de Yalí/La Rica. There is also one express bus to Managua that leaves at 4:30 A.M., passes through Jinotega at 5:30 A.M., and continues south through Matagalpa to Managua. The same bus leaves Managua at 3 P.M., and retraces the route to San Rafael del Norte, arriving sometime after 7 P.M.

El Cuá and San José de Bocay

El Cuá is best known for Benjamin Linder, the only known American casualty of the Contra war. Both towns are now illuminated by mini-hydroelectric power plants he helped design and implement. Both towns were completely in the thick of the nastiness during the 1980s, overrun first by Contras and then by the FSLN. El Cuá has three *hospedajes,* a gas station, and several places to eat. There's one *hospedaje* in Bocay, a few small eateries, and a gas station.

Ayapal

Ayapal is a small community on the banks of

© RANDY WOOD

boat traffic on the Río Bocay

the Río Bocay. From here you can hire boats to take you downstream to several Miskito communities (not cheap).

Wiwilí

Wiwilí is the upstream capital of the Río Coco region. It's a mestizo town, meaning it's of Spanish origin as opposed to the indigenous capital of the Río Coco, 550 kilometers downstream at Waspám. Wiwilí, a town on both sides of the Río Coco, was devastated by Hurricane Mitch. The Río Coco swelled to several times its normal size during the hurricane, as an unfathomable quantity of water came rushing down from the mountains of the Segovias. Several hundred inhabitants of Wiwilí lost their lives to the river, and the town has never been the same since. Post-Mitch, the two sides of the community went their own separate ways to find international aid, and subsequently decided to become independent. While they retained the same name, Wiwilí on the north side of the river is now part of the department of Madriz, while Wiwilí on the south bank remains part of Jinotega. Wiwilí is an important port town with access to the deep waters of the Río Coco. This is where you would want to put in to ride the Río Coco east to Waspám to brave the crocodiles, armed bandits, and drug smugglers.

Wamblán

Wamblán saw some ferocious battles during the 1980s. The last part of the drive to Wamblán is notable for a stunning descent to the city along a mountain ridge. If your trip happens to coincide with the end of the day, the long mountain shadows falling into the ridges will ensure you never forget the moment you entered Wamblán. There's one unpleasant *hospedaje* in town.

Boaco, Chontales, and the Road to El Rama

As you fork east out of Managua at the roadside community of San Benito and rumble into Nicaragua's interior, a world very much unlike Nicaragua's other regions unfolds before you. Less volcanic than León, drier than the south, and more open and accessible than the deep mountains of Jinotega and Matagalpa, the cattle-dominated landscape of Boaco and Chontales has a flavor all of its own.

That flavor is cheese. Over 60 percent of Nicaragua's dairy products originate here, mostly along the east side of Lake Cocibolca. Of course there's much more to Nicaragua's cowboy country, but above all else, there is cheese—dozens of varieties of it, not to mention millions of gallons of fresh milk.

Broad cattle farms make up the bulk of Boaco and Chontales, divided into ranches of

© JOSHUA BERMAN

cowboy country

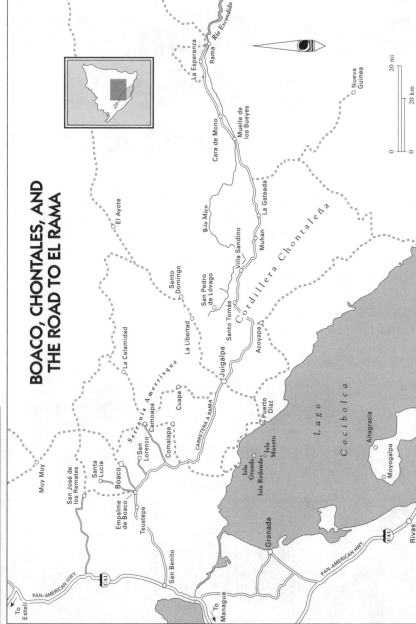

BOACO, CHONTALES, AND THE ROAD TO EL RAMA

sometimes thousands of hectares of land. Towns are fewer and farther between than they are on the other side of Lake Cocibolca and, in spite of the lengthy coastline, Boaco and Chontales have few fishing communities—there are only a few, accessed at the end of tortuous dirt roads. The emphasis here is on the land.

The cattle ranchers of the east are often well-to-do by Nicaraguan standards, and their wealth is apparent in towns like Juigalpa, a clean and well laid out city. Juigalpa's patron saint celebrations are among the best in Nicaragua, involving elaborate bull riding competitions, horsemanship contests, and festivals. But in true Nicaraguan spirit, even the disadvantaged communities haven't lost their sense of humor. The Boaco town of La Calamidad (The Calamity) retains its name in spite of two government attempts to rename it something less frightful. The locals insist that with poor land, little fresh water, and few opportunities for productive farming, their little town is a calamity and should be named accordingly.

The Land and History

The lands now known as Boaco and Chontales were first settled by the Chontal people, whose name in Nahuatl means "savages" or "foreigners." They were responsible for many of the statuary and stone monuments unearthed in the Amerrisque mountain range.

In their infancy, the first Spanish settlements of what was then called El Corregimiento de Chontales suffered greatly at the hands of aggressive Miskitos and Zambos, whose frequent attacks devastated seven of 12 Spanish settlements. In 1749, Camoapa, Boaco (today known as Boaco Viejo), and Juigalpa were attacked; the towns

were nearly destroyed and the churches burned to the ground. Boaco's then-governor, Alonso Fernández de Heredia, returned the aggression, leading an excursion that returned with over a hundred Miskito prisoners. The settlers reestablished their communities eight kilometers to the south, and nothing remains of Boaco Viejo to this day. From 1750 to 1760, the same indigenous groups attacked Juigalpa, Camoapa, Lóvago, Loviguisca, Yasica, Guabale, Santa Rosa, and nine other communities. In 1762 Boaco was reestablished by Father Cáceres, who was killed shortly thereafter by yet another Miskito attack. In 1782 the church in Juigalpa was—you guessed it—burned to the ground.

When the threat of attack from indigenous peoples diminished, the lands east of Lake Cocibolca were developed into extensive cattle ranches. Coffee was introduced around the Boaco area, but before long its production had been pushed up into the better lands in northern Boaco and southern Matagalpa. Cattle ranching soon became the economic mainstay of the area, followed by the extraction of gold from the mines at La Libertad and Santo Domingo.

The social and economic reorganization of the Sandinista years earned the unbridled antipathy of the people of Chontales and Boaco, who were generally frontier-minded people uninterested in government regulation. As their lands were confiscated from them and reorganized, they naturally had more sympathy for the Contra forces, whom they clandestinely supported throughout much of the 1980s. Much of the violence of the 1980s occurred in the towns that border both sides of the highway and inland. In the 1990s both departments have voted against the Sandinista party with overwhelming margins.

Boaco

The modern city of Boaco began on a hilltop in the fertile mountains of central Nicaragua and as it grew, crept down the hillside into a valley, earning it the nickname "The City of Two Floors." But the two levels are rapidly multiplying into more as Boaco—once a cattle town of nine families—expands up and over the adjacent hilltops.

Boaco is a paradox: a departmental capital, yet set back in the hillsides like a common country villa, an agriculture center whose hillsides are now struggling to produce cattle and corn, and a commercial center beset with poverty.

Regardless of Boaco's challenges, it's been an inspiration to several notable Nicaraguan authors and scholars, four of whom have won the Nicaraguan Rubén Darío prize for literature. Diego Sequeira, Antonio Barquero, Hernan Robleto, and Julian N. Guerrero. There is a monument in their honor, just east and north of the park, set in a sort of balcony that overlooks some of the lower streets of Boaco.

Most travelers visit Boaco after a dip in the hot springs of Agua Clara and are surprised to find they need a day or two more to check out the area. The hills and valleys around the city are home to charming country towns and small communities of farmers and ranchers who like to claim their hills are made of cheese and their rivers of milk. They're home as well to lots of mystery: petroglyphs, waterfalls, and hilltops for climbing.

THE LAND AND HISTORY

Boaco is nestled in a notch in the Amerrisque mountain range, 379 meters above sea level. It was built along the edge of the Río Boaco (now Río Fonseca). Boaco gets its name from a combination of Aztec and Sumu words that mean

painting of 16th–century Boaco

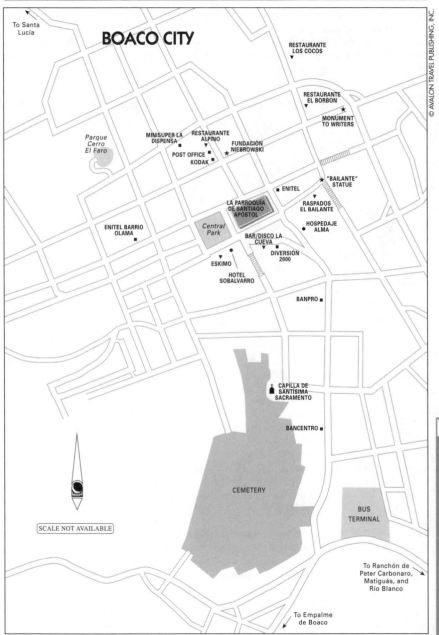

BOACO CITY

To Santa Lucía

RESTAURANTE LOS COCOS

RESTAURANTE EL BORBON

MONUMENT TO WRITERS

Parque Cerro El Faro

MINISUPER LA DISPENSA

RESTAURANTE ALPINO

FUNDACIÓN NIEBROWSKI

POST OFFICE KODAK

"BAILANTE" STATUE

ENITEL

LA PARROQUÍA DE SANTIAGO APÓSTOL

RASPADOS EL BAILANTE

ENITEL BARRIO OLAMA

Central Park

HOSPEDAJE ALMA

BAR/DISCO LA CUEVA

DIVERSIÓN 2000

ESKIMO

HOTEL SOBALVARRO

BANPRO

CAPILLA DE SANTISIMA SACRAMENTO

BANCENTRO

SCALE NOT AVAILABLE

CEMETERY

BUS TERMINAL

To Ranchón de Peter Carbonaro, Matiguás, and Río Blanco

To Empalme de Boaco

Land of the Sorcerers. The city of Boaco is currently in its third incarnation, two previous cities by the same name having been built and destroyed in the 18th and 19th centuries. In 1749, an expedition of Zumos, Miskitos, and Zambos armed with English rifles attacked Boaco, sacking it completely, killing the priest, taking several females hostage, and later burning the town to the ground. The settlers started over along the edge of the Río Malacatoya in what's now the town of Boaquito, and in 1763, due to a brutal outbreak of cholera and the difficulties the land presented for agriculture, moved to the present site of Boaco.

Boaco in the 19th century was already a cow town, though several other crops (such as *cabuya*, for making rope) were raised for sale in the markets of Masaya, a four-day trip with mules and wagons. William Walker and his men passed through in the 1860s, confiscating haciendas and cattle. Boaco was elevated to the status of villa in 1873 and city in 1895. In the early 20th century, Boaco was considered part of Chontales.

Far more instrumental in the development of modern Boaco than any mayor was a man of the cloth, Father Niebrowski of Poland, who upon his arrival in 1916, helped bring Boaco into the modern world. Niebrowski built a cinema, a brick factory used to rebuild the church, and a small hydropower plant on the Río Fonseca that provided electric light to the city for the first time. Niebrowski also established the first hospital, community music band, and countless other things that contributed to Boaco's social welfare. To this day the Niebrowski Foundation provides for small programs in the Boaco area.

During the Contra war, Boaco was spared from direct battles, but in the hillsides that surrounded the city, Contras and Sandinistas fought numerous skirmishes in Muy Muy, San José de los Remates, and San Francisco. The violence dislodged countless campesinos, all of whom eventually found their way to the city of Boaco seeking refuge. Many decided to stay, and Boaco has swelled over the past 20 years, faster than it can provide for its new inhabitants, most of whom occupy neighborhoods of small concrete homes around the outskirts of the city.

SIGHTS AND ATTRACTIONS

Boaco's patron saint is Santiago Apóstol, and the *fiestas patronales* in his honor are a particularly interesting event to experience. The festival lasts the entire month of July, during which time the saint's statue is paraded daily from one neighborhood to the next. The crux of the ceremony falls around the 23rd to 25th, when the procession is accompanied by dancers whose performance tells an elaborate tale of the expulsion of the Moors from Spain.

A statue located one block east of the church represents a dancer complete with snake stick in one hand and brass knuckles in the other (he's been repainted several times in order to get the skin tone just right—from 1999 to 2001 he went from pink to brown to an off shade of yellow).

Boaco's two churches neatly serve the residents of Boaco's two levels without their having to traipse up and down the hill. In the lower half, the unmistakable **Capilla de la Santísima Sacramento** is an elaborate and untraditional church whose architecture is nearly Greek Orthodox. A statue of the Virgin Mary stands and keeps watch over the earth from its starched white rooftop. Inside, statues of Jesus and the Virgin Mary line up side by side with the carved stone statuary of Boaco's Chontal and Sumu ancestors, an intriguing compromise between the religions of new and old.

La Parroquia de Santiago Apóstol, located at the top of the hill, is a Boaco landmark unchanged since the mid-1800s when it was designed and built. There is a mass every day, and several on the weekends, when the ringing of the church bells fills the town square and scatters the pigeons.

Boaco's highest point is occupied by **Cerro El Faro,** home to the lighthouse without a sea. A concrete pedestal and tower, the Faro offers a good view of the city and the valley of the Río Mayales. Technically the tower is open all week, but the caretaker closes it when he pleases. Underneath is the town convention center, and a popular gymnasium. Evenings the Faro is one of Boaco's more popular places to steal a few kisses.

ENTERTAINMENT AND NIGHTLIFE

Boaco has two discos, and a very different crowd in each one. In town, just 10 meters down the hill from the park, **La Cueva** is popular among a younger crowd that just wants to dance to modern music: Backstreet Boys, Britney Spears, and the like. Newer and more popular, **Ranchón de Peter Carbonaro** is a kilometer or two out of town along the highway to Muy Muy, just far enough to weed out the teens. It's more of a relaxing atmosphere to drink to the sound of more traditional Latin music: salsa, *cumbia,* and merengue (and the occasional ranchero) but by 10 P.M. its dance floor is just as packed as La Cueva's, especially when there's live music—even Dimensión Costeña has played there. Take a taxi there for about $1 per couple.

You can kill an hour or two while you wait for buses at **Diversión 2000,** a video game hall of Sony PlayStations and Nintendos and usually mobbed with 10-year-olds waiting to play Mario Brothers. Games are priced for the budget of a 10-year-old, so you'll be hard-pressed to spend $2 while you're there. Same goes for the ENITEL is Barrio Olama, which has a few Nintendo machines of its own.

ACCOMMODATIONS

There are really only two places to stay in the city of Boaco. Located at the south edge of the park, **Hotel Sobalvarro** has 10 rooms for $5 each, tel. 842-2515. The Sobalvarro is a remnant of Boaco's history, a once grandiose building of wooden rooms set around a courtyard with a balcony overlooking the lower half of Boaco. It's none too fancy, but it's clean and well cared for. Just where the already steep road turns nearly vertical, **Hospedaje Alma** is even more unassuming, with a half-dozen rooms with shared bath for $4 each.

The lower half of Boaco has several *pensiónes* along the main road and near the terminal that do a brisk trade in prostitution and quick romantic getaways for young couples; not recommended for travelers.

FOOD

The top floor of Boaco has several good restaurants that serve Nicaraguan traditional dishes, burgers, sandwiches, and other foods. One of the least expensive places to have a meal is **Restaurante Maraíta,** which doubles as a popular drinking hole. A little pricier than the others but still well within the budget of economizing travelers, **Restaurante Alpino** is considered the best (the name is a result of the owner's former business selling Christmas trees in Tipitapa). Its burgers are good, but the beef *churrasco* is the bomb and costs $4.50. The locals and NGO workers like **Restaurante Borbon,** which is known for its *pollo al vino* and pork chops, among other classics, for around $2.50 a dish, plus huge glasses of *fresco* served on a breezy balcony overlooking the hills. A block farther north on the same street, having a meal at **Restaurante Los Cocos** is like eating lunch in someone's living room, and the food is quite good.

Pastries and snacks are for sale in the park; wash 'em down with ice cream at **Eskimo,** adjacent to Hotel Sobalvarro—it's also got shakes, sandwiches, and burgers, served on the best front porch in the city. A popular place to people-watch. A block east of the park near the statue of the dancer is **Raspados El Bailante,** selling crushed-ices in a half-dozen flavors at $.35 each.

SHOPPING

The best supermarket in town is the well-stocked and well-run **Minisuper La Dispensa,** which has a selection of breads, cheeses, canned and dry goods, wines, and liquors. In the daytime, a woman sets up shop on the sidewalk outside La Dispensa to sell fresh fruits and vegetables. Of course no one can beat the prices in the **market** in the lower half of town.

SERVICES

Banks

In the lower part of Boaco along the main strip are two banks: Banpro, and 1.5 blocks

THE PITA HATS OF CAMOAPA

Pita, a thick-leaved succulent plant in the *amarilidácea* family, is originally from Mexico. Its leaves can reach one meter in length and gather at the center of the plant around yellow flowers. In the Americas, pita is known by various names: *toquilla* in Ecuador, *cogollo* in Venezuela, and jipijapa or pita in Nicaragua.

The plant is grown primarily in the Masigue area, just north of Camoapa, and is the natural base for a mini-economy of area hatmakers. Weaving a pita hat is a time-consuming process that can last as long as three

months if the fiber and weaving are fine. The quality and the price of a hat are determined by the smoothness of the fabric, as well as the number of weaves per inch.

One door up the hill from **Restaurante Camfel** is the home of a family that works with pita, where they can show you, in addition to hats, several kinds of baskets, bags, and other products they weave by hand in their home. Other artisans take up their work in the Camoapa neighborhoods of Mombachito, Las Lajas, Laguna Negra, and several others.

farther south, Bancentro. Western Union is near the market, open Monday– Saturday 8 A.M.– 4:30 P.M.

Internet
Check your email at the rather slow connection in the ENITEL office in Barrio Olama, 1.5 blocks west of the park. It charges $8.50 per hour, and is open 8 A.M.–10 P.M. seven days a week.

Mail, Phone, and Film
The post office is 1.5 blocks north of the church on the left side. There's a pay phone out front (open Mon.–Fri. 8 A.M.–5 P.M., Sat. until noon). ENITEL is located across from the northeast corner of the cathedral (open Mon.–Fri. 8 A.M.–9 P.M.). Kodak Express is one block north of the church (open Mon.–Sat. 8 A.M.–6 P.M.)

GETTING THERE AND AWAY

Buses to Boaco leave every 30–40 minutes from Managua. From Boaco, the most comfortable way to travel to Managua is by microbus. Two leave each day from the terminal, at 6:30 A.M. and 12:30 P.M. ($2). Regular buses leave every 30

minutes for Managua until 5:40 P.M.

Five buses leave each day for Santa Lucía, 10:30 A.M. –5 P.M. (one hour). Buses leave from 5:50 A.M. until 5 P.M. bound for Río Blanco (three hours) and Muy Muy. Or for the travel masochist, there's the 12-hour Boaco to Siuna kidney-bruiser over some of the worst dirt roads in the nation.

NEAR BOACO
Hot Springs of Aguas Claras
The Aguas Termales (Hot Waters) located seven kilometers west of the Empalme de Boaco are one of the best reasons to visit the Boaco area. The area is called **Aguas Claras,** where out of a crack in the ground there bubbles a hot spring heated by an uninvestigated geothermal source (the locals will tell you it's an underground volcano, which probably isn't too far from the truth). Around 2000, the hot spring was collected into pipes and channeled into a series of pools protected by palm-thatch roofs to form a hotel and resort complex.

There are three large pools and two small ones

for children. All five are spotlessly clean and more professionally maintained than you'd expect. The water isn't boiling hot the way you find in similar establishments in Scandinavia, but it's extraordinarily warm, and you can try all the pools until you find one whose temperature suits you. While you lounge in the pool you can order food from an extensive menu of traditional Nicaraguan food (chicken, fish, beef) and a wide selection of alcohol. Under the palm thatch are several soft hammocks, and in the lobby of the hotel are a pair of good billiards tables.

There's a high-class hotel on the premises with 17 rooms—six inside the main building and 11 more in private cabins set around the back. Fancy, modern rooms with air-conditioning and hot water baths (they're not quite hot tubs, but that was the idea) cost $25 each. Two simple rooms upstairs have a shared bath (no hot tub), fan instead of a/c, and cost $15. It's well worth the extra money to go for the better-quality accommodation. Day-use fees vary during the week, but are never more than $1.50, cheaper for kids;

credit cards accepted for hotel and restaurant expenses, not the entrance fee.

During Semana Santa and weekends in the dry season, the hotel can fill up quickly. Call the office in Managua to make reservations, tel. 244-2916. There is no phone on the premises, but the Managua office communicates via a radio.

The Baseball Field at Empalme de Boaco

Years ago, a North American traveler named Jake Scheideman fell ill during an ambitious bicycle tour of Central America and was taken in by a family at Empalme Boaco. Over several days they nursed him—a complete stranger—back to health. In 1998 after Hurricane Mitch, Scheideman returned to Nicaragua after many years of having been away, wanting to do something for the community that had taken care of him when he was ill. He asked what they would like, and they chose a ballpark. Now located in Empalme Boaco (the intersection of the road to Boaco), it was constructed over two years and is the best

© RANDY WOOD

Aguas Claras hot springs

of its kind east of Lake Cocibolca; games are Saturday and Sunday afternoons in season.

La Cebadilla

Around the turn of the 20th century, a farmer from the mountain town of Cebadilla was surprised to see the Virgin Mary appear before him amongst the rocks where he was tending his cattle. The site has been treasured by the locals ever since.

La Cebadilla is no easier to get to than it ever was, and if you're interested in a hike through an out-of-the-way corner of Nicaragua, try walking up the mountain to La Cebadilla. At one time a small chapel was erected in honor of the Virgin, and there was a small well where it was said the water was blessed. Today the chapel has mostly fallen to bits.

The hike starts 1.6 kilometers east of Empalme Boaco, where on the south side of the highway there's a dirt road leading south to the community of Asedades, and a steel sign with a picture of the Virgin Mary and the words La Cebadilla. The road leads south one kilometer to Asedades, a poor community of adobe houses, flower gardens, and awful, rocky fields. Asedades is surprisingly clean in spite of its poverty and is an interesting look at how resourceful campesinos can eke out an existence even when the land is more rock than soil. It's imperative that you find a guide in Asedades to take you up the mountain to La Cebadilla. There are many small footpaths that lead up the hill, but they intertwine and none is well-enough used to be more obvious than the others. The walk up the hill will take you between three and four hours—take water and food along with you and make sure you have something to share with your guide. The walk back to Asedades can take two to three hours. Your guide will recommend that you stay at the top of the hill through midday and do your walking in the cool of the afternoon.

At La Cebadilla, you may or may not have visions of the Virgin Mary, but you will certainly have a fantastic view of the valley below and the hills of Boaco to the east, sometimes all the way to the big lake.

Santa Lucía and Petroglyphs

The town of Santa Lucía was created in 1904 by the decree of president José Santos Zelaya in an effort to concentrate the disperse and poorly administrated farming communities of the hillsides north of Boaco. Its well-planned and organized beginning boded well for Santa Lucía, which, a century later, remains a picturesque and enchanting mountain village in a valley ringed with green mountains.

Santa Lucía itself doesn't have hotel rooms or fancy restaurants. Nevertheless, travelers should consider a trip to Santa Lucía for three reasons: the beautiful scenery, marked by **Cerro Santo Domingo,** the long rocky precipice of **Peña La Brada,** and the indigenous artifacts along the road. The various petroglyphs and other remnants of past cultures are still out in the wilds, including stones just 20 meters off the highway, and a hidden sight along the Río Fonseca, called Las Máscaras. We couldn't find anyone who knows where the site is, only the rumor. Another area in those hillsides north of Boaco with **Paso Las Lajas** with petroglyphs showing indigenous peoples sitting with the Spanish and their dogs. These carvings were seen several times earlier in the century, but were subsequently lost and passed into the lore of the people of Boaco. Sharpen your machete; they're waiting to be rediscovered.

Two additional hikes in the Santa Lucía area include a gorgeous waterfall, called the **Salto de los Americas;** either ask your bus driver to let you off near the waterfall as you travel between Boaco and Santa Lucía, or from Santa Lucía, hike five kilometers (one hour) back down the road south toward Boaco. Look for a *gancho* opening in the wooden fence on the east (left-hand) side. This is a V-shaped tree branch through which you can step to avoid the barbed wire. Hike through the fence, down the hill to the Río Fonseca. Hike up the river five minutes to a seven-meter waterfall. The pool beneath the falls is deep enough to swan dive off the top, and you can crawl to the cave behind it. There are also several families of monkeys that live in the area.

To get to **Peña La Brada,** hike up the road past the Instituto out of town for an hour along the steep path that leads to the top of the ridge. When you get to the road, walk to your right along it until you reach a little wood shack; just past the shack is a small trail that leads away from the road. Follow it through the forest and across the fields until you reach a big open pasture with a big farmhouse (as a courtesy you should introduce yourself before proceeding). The residents will tell you how to find the cliff from there. It's a simple matter of crossing several barbed-wire fences to get to the cliff edge, where the view from the top is amazing. In addition to a panoramic view of Boaco you'll be able to see all the way out to the highway, and the mountains that rise on its south side.

On the direct road from the highway to Santa Lucía (not the road that leads from Boaco) keep your eyes peeled for **La Roca del Tigre,** a rock emblazoned with a petroglyph of a tiger, located practically at roadside.

For any hikes in the Santa Lucía area, Osmin is the right gentleman to ask to accompany you. He can be found in the ENITEL office, where he works—he's a fun tour guide and trip leader for expeditions into the wild hillsides.

Technically there are no lodging establishments in Santa Lucía, but should you find yourself stuck there, the **Comedor Santa Lucía** will put you up and feed you. More good food can be found in the *comedor* in the park, which specializes in grilled meat. A direct bus leaves from Managua for Santa Lucía at 10:30 A.M. ($1.50), bypassing Boaco entirely. The same bus leaves Santa Lucía for Managua at 4 A.M. and 5 A.M.

Camoapa

A cow town of 13,000 people set in the mountains east of Boaco, Camoapa got its name from a Nahuatl phrase that can be translated as either Place of the Parrots, Place of the Dark Rocks, or Place of the Yams. It was once an indigenous community ruled by the cacique Taisiwa, and was later absorbed by the Spanish settlers and incorporated under the name San Francisco de Camoapán.

Today, besides the abundant commerce in dairy products, Camoapa is best known to Nicaraguans for its production of woven straw hats. In the 1960s a school for promoting the art of weaving was formed, and the art was passed through several generations; there are reportedly several hundred weavers in Camoapa. The hats they are known best for are created from intricately and tightly woven strips of fibrous white pita and are sold all over Nicaragua's craft markets.

Camoapa's economy is largely tied to three dairy cooperatives, the workers of which like to have a good time on the weekends, when they return from their farms and ranches outside of town to party and relax. Camoapa's *fiestas patronales* begin on October 2 in honor of San Francisco de Asís, with bull riding, cattle contests, and the like. Camoapans boast they have the toughest bulls and best horses around. Other weekends, the disco at **Atenas** is the place to be, unless you're a hat-wearing cowboy, in which case the party is at **La Asociación (Asogacam)** out by the ball field. Beer, mariachi music, and the occasional brawl—just like the old days.

In Camoapa, stay at **Hotel Las Estrellas** (tel. 849-2240); a former auto-hotel turned honest; 15 rooms for $7 or $10 for singles or doubles without a/c, or $10 or $13 for luxury rooms with a/c and TV, credit cards accepted. Las Estrellas is located seven blocks east of the north side of the church (six paved blocks and one more along the dirt road). Smaller but closer to town along the main road, **Hotel Taisiwa** (tel. 849-2304), named after the former cacique, has 11 rooms at $4.25 per person shared bath, $5 private bath.

Camoapa has several good restaurants, including **Atenas** (one block east of the south side of the church), which turns into the town's best disco after hours on weekends; **Camfel** (one block west of the north side of the church), a clean place run by seven women who will gladly prepare special orders like chicken salad if you get tired of steak and fried foods; also **Bosquecito,** a restaurant filled with potted plants and flowers, just down the road that leads to Comalapa. A few blocks farther west of Camfel is **Chupi,** with sandwiches, chicken, and ice cream.

Services

The ENITEL phone office is easily located by the imposing tower planted on the premises. The post office is on the south side of the church. The Miscelanea Urbina located one block north of the northeast corner of the park is a good place to pick up snacks or supplies, especially if you're gearing up to hike Cuisaltepe.

If you bust your head climbing Cuisaltepe, check in at Camoapa's Centro de Salud, where a doctor is always on call, or the Clínica San Francisco de Asís, located a half-block east and a half-block north from the Colegio San Francisco.

Getting There and Away

Buses from Managua to Camoapa depart Mayoreo Monday–Saturday, starting at 4:30 A.M., and running through 4:10 P.M. Reduced schedule on Sundays, but still adequate transportation.

Buses to Managua depart from the shady side of the church (whichever side that is as the day progresses), Monday–Saturday beginning at 6:25 A.M. and running through 5 P.M. The reduced Sunday schedule begins at 5:25 A.M., leaving roughly every two hours until 5 P.M. There is a minibus that shuttles between the Empalme del Camoapa (San Francisco) and Camoapa, but it's irregular. A ride between the two points will cost you $.50.

Hiking Cuisaltepe

Unless you breezed by it on the midnight bus to Rama, Cuisaltepe inevitably caught your eye: a massive, rocky promontory that juts out of the hillside between San Lorenzo and the entrance to Camoapa. Approaching it from the west, its silhouette resembles the tip of an upturned thumb, pointing in the direction of the highway. In Nahuatl, Cuisaltepe means place of the grinding stone because it was a good source of the volcanic rock the indigenous peoples used for making long, round stone implements with which to grind corn into dough. Cuisaltepe was the home of the last cacique of the region, Taisigüe.

Hiking Cuisaltepe is no casual endeavor. Over 300 meters high, much of the south side of the rock is a series of vertical crevasses and overhangs and much of the rest of it is prohibitively steep. However, there is one summit approach—from the north side of the rock—which you can reach

from Camoapa. Hike with much caution—this rock is an easy place to hurt yourself. The climb takes around six hours round-trip, but adjust that estimate according to your own climbing ability. You should have good shoes, as much of the route is loose and slippery gravel.

Your point of entrance is the road to Camoapa. Any bus traveling between Managua or Boaco and the east will take you there, leaving you at Empalme de Camoapa (also called San Francisco) along the highway. A better option is to take a direct bus to Camoapa, 10 of which leave per day from Managua (five on Sundays). From the highway, the road that leads to Camoapa climbs 25 kilometers to the city. Get off the bus before you reach Camoapa at kilometer 99, where a small turnoff to the west leads to the community of Barrio Cebollín with a little red bus stop at the entrance. Walk down that road and watch to your left where you'll see a turnoff that goes south, over the hills to the base of Cuisaltepe. It would be far wiser to pick up a guide in Cebollín, though, as the access to the top of the rock is neither obvious nor easy, and involves climbing partway up, crossing the small forest located in a notch in the hillside, then climbing the ridge to the summit. There's a crevasse or two to avoid en route. You can find guides in Barrio Cebollín in the first house on the left after you pass the school, the house nearest the utility pole. Euclídes and brothers know the mountain well and climb it periodically and would make good guides for those who want to climb.

A good alternative to messing around with early morning buses from elsewhere is to arrive the previous evening and spend the night in Camoapa, leaving on an early morning bus that can leave you at Barrio Cebollín on its way out of town.

Hiking Mombacho

In the early 1900s, Nicaraguans from the Granada area transferred their homes and possessions to the Camoapa area to try growing coffee on the area's hillsides. They chose the slopes of one mountain in particular because of its rich soils, and named the peak Mombacho, in memory of

Cuisaltepe

their Granada homeland. Camoapa's Mombacho is a forested mountain with a rocky protuberance jutting out of the top. It is home to several coffee plantations and a handful of radio towers and makes a pleasant day hike from Camoapa. Long ago, Mombacho was the site of a moonshine distillery, the products of which were sold under the name Mombachito.

Hiking the hill is significantly easier than the Cuisaltepe and offers a beautiful bird's-eye view of Camoapa's open ranges. From Camoapa, the road to Mombacho can be accessed by the Salida de Sangre de Cristo (Sangre de Cristo is the name of a church found along the first part of that road). From ENITEL in the center of Camoapa, walk approximately six blocks west, crossing over a small bridge and arriving at the public school. Turn right at the school and head north until you see the Iglesia de Sangre de Cristo. Continue on that road until you reach Mombacho. The hike from town takes between three and four hours. There's a dirt road that leads up Mombacho from Camoapa to the radio towers. In Nahuatl, *mombacho* means steep, so be prepared.

Hiking Peña la Jarquína

At the entrance to Camoapa on the southeast side of the highway (to your right as you head toward Camoapa) is a broad, rocky cliff face with a hardwood forest nestled at its base. This is Peña la Jarquína, named after the Jarquíns, a prominent local family. It's an easy 90-minute hike from the entrance to Camoapa, around the back side of the hill to the top. Skilled climbers might find it makes a suitable technical ascent; the rock is solid and has plenty of cracks—and is almost assuredly unclimbed.

Comalapa

Over the hill from Camoapa, the even tinier village of Comalapa has remained almost completely unchanged through the passing centuries and is worth a look if you're interested in seeing what Central American villages of the 18th and 19th centuries looked like (just ignore the concrete slide in the center of the park). In 1752, Friar Morel de Santa Cruz visited Comalapa and described it as follows: "This is a town of Indians located in a land that's stony, mountainous, and fenced in by hills. Its church is of straw, reduced and indecent, lacking a vestry, but possessing an altar… 100 families and 484 persons both Indian and Ladino." Comalapa is largely the same 250 years later, though the church is now a quaint stone structure.

Access to Comalapa is through Camoapa. There is one bus per day, leaving Camoapa at 6:30 A.M. The same bus leaves Comalapa at 4 P.M. At other times of the day, hitch a ride with pickups traveling between the communities, or try hiking a piece of the road. From Camoapa to Comalapa is over 20 kilometers, too far to walk from end to end, but the entire road is shady and has some vantage points for good panoramic views of the surrounding hillsides.

Juigalpa

The last big settlement on the road southeast to Rama, Juigalpa is a prosperous city of cattle ranchers and farmers whose *fiestas patronales* are considered some of the best in the country, drawing visitors from all over Nicaragua and elsewhere. Juigalpa still strongly bears the traces of its indigenous roots in elaborate statuary and other archaeological pieces still being discovered in the mountains east of town.

THE LAND AND HISTORY

Juigalpan in the languages of Aztec origin means Great City or Spawning grounds of the black snails. Its first inhabitants were likely the Chontal people, who had been displaced in the Rivas area by the stronger Nicaraos. They resisted the Spanish occupation fiercely in the 16th century, rising up no fewer than 14 times to attack the installations of the colonial government.

Upon Nicaragua's independence, the land that comprised Chontales and Boaco was controlled by Granada. In 1858 the Department of Chontales was formed, of which Boaco and part of the Río San Juan remained a part. Juigalpa and the now desolate Acoyapa were the departmental head at different times. In the 18th and 19th centuries, travelers bound for the gold mines of Santo Domingo and La Libertad crossed Lake Cocibolca, landed in Puerto Díaz, and spent a night in Juigalpa before proceeding.

GETTING AROUND

Juigalpa is an easily walked city that you can traverse in under a half hour. There are no city buses but plenty of taxis; you can get from one end of town to the other for between $.35 and $.70 per person, even out to Restaurante El Tonga at the outskirts of town.

SIGHTS AND ATTRACTIONS

Juigalpa's most interesting attraction is the **Museo Arqueológico Gregorio Aguilar Barea,** an airplane–hangar-like building housing a collection of over a hundred examples of pre-Columbian statuary uncovered in the folds of the Amerrisque mountain range. Ranging from one meter to seven meters tall, the pieces are reminiscent of totem poles, elaborately carved in high- and low-relief, with representations of zoomorphic figures and humans (the latter often clutching knives or axes in their hands, or presenting their arms folded across their chests). The statues, thought to be 1,000 years old, were the work of the Chontal people, driven to the east side of Lake Cocibolca by the more powerful Nicaraos some 1,500 years ago.

In contrast to the indigenous cultures of the Pacific region, relatively little is known about the Chontal culture and its statues, more of which are continually being discovered in the Amerrisque range. The museum was built in 1952 by the well-loved former mayor of Juigalpa, Gregorio Aguilar Barea. It also exhibits Nicaraguan coins from across two centuries, gold figurines, original paintings by the museum's namesake, and several historical paintings and photographs. Although supposedly open Monday–Friday,

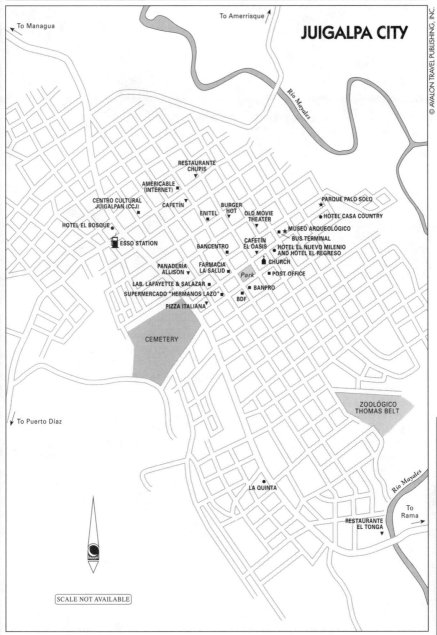

JUIGALPA CITY

To Managua

To Amerrisque

© AVALON TRAVEL PUBLISHING, INC.

Río Mayales

RESTAURANTE CHUPIS

AMERICABLE (INTERNET)

CENTRO CULTURAL JUIGALPAN (CCJ)

CAFETÍN

ENITEL

BURGER HOT

PARQUE PALO SOLO

HOTEL CASA COUNTRY

HOTEL EL BOSQUE

OLD MOVIE THEATER

MUSEO ARQUEOLÓGICO

BUS TERMINAL

ESSO STATION

BANCENTRO

CAFETÍN EL OASIS

HOTEL EL NUEVO MILENIO AND HOTEL EL REGRESO

CHURCH

PANADERÍA ALLISON

FARMACIA LA SALUD

Park

POST OFFICE

LAB. LAFAYETTE & SALAZAR

SUPERMERCADO "HERMANOS LAZO"

BANPRO

BDF

PIZZA ITALIANA

CEMETERY

To Puerto Díaz

ZOOLÓGICO THOMAS BELT

Río Mayales

To Rama

LA QUINTA

RESTAURANTE EL TONGA

MooN

SCALE NOT AVAILABLE

BOACO, CHONTALES, & THE ROAD TO EL RAMA

© RANDY WOOD

the bull ring in Juigalpa

9 A.M.–noon and 2–5 P.M., the museum's hours more frequently follow the whims of the caretaker. The building has an open front, so even if the gate to the museum is locked, all the statues can be seen from the street.

The view from the park, **Parque Palo Solo,** at the north end of town, is unforgettable and unsurpassed elsewhere in the region. To the north the Amerrisque range sits at the far end of several kilometers of broad tropical savanna. The park is elevated above the surrounding streets, located at the very edge of the hill Juigalpa was built on, and giving the impression of looking over the bulwark of a fortress. The fortress feeling isn't entirely accidental: Juigalpa was built at the top of the hill to offer it some means of defense from the Miskito and Zambo peoples who once raided it from those same mountains 200 years ago.

The park was built by Mayor Aguilar Barea in the 1960s and named after the one tall tree that dominated its center. The tree has since been replaced by a fountain adorned with images of the mainstays of the Chontales economy: corn and

cattle. A restaurant at the edge of the park serves fancy lunches and dinners.

The park in the center of Juigalpa is an orderly and clean place, whose statue of a boy shining shoes is unique in Nicaragua; made by a former mayor who spent his early years earning money as a shoe-shine boy, the inscription reads, "Hard work dignifies a man." Toward the center of the park is **El Templo de la Cultura,** built in 1995 with the express purpose of hosting concerts and performances.

Juigalpa is well known among Nicaraguans for its zoo, the **Zoológico Thomas Belt,** named for the British mining engineer and naturalist who surveyed parts of Santo Domingo, Chontales between 1868 and 1872. Like most zoos in developing countries, however, the Thomas Belt is a depressing collection of large animals—monkeys, snakes, even a few African species—in small cages. Located seven blocks south of the southwest corner of the church, the zoo can also be reached from the highway by following signs for the Profamilia clinic and then continuing another block past Profamilia (open 8 A.M.–6 P.M. seven days a week, entrance fee is $.25).

Juigalpa's *fiestas patronales* from August 11to August 18 attract visitors from the entire nation and even Honduras and Costa Rica. Much of the festivities takes place on the north side of town, in Juigalpa's Plaza de Toros, but you'll find parties all over. It's a rowdy cowboy festival of bull riding, rodeo competitions, and horseback games. In one of these, called the *carrera de cinta,* mounted riders gallop underneath a wire from which is suspended a small ring; if the riders successfully put a pencil through the ring at full gallop, he can present it—and a kiss—to the woman of his choice from among the contestants vying to be queen of the festival; the woman who receives the most rings is crowned the queen.

Even when the *fiestas patronales* are a long way off, you can test your merit as a cowboy on Nicaragua's only **mechanical bull** at La Quinta for $1.50. It's not always available for public use, so you should stop in and ask while you have a meal.

NIGHTLIFE AND ENTERTAINMENT

The best disco in town is **La Quinta** out on the highway; weekend nights, and particularly Saturdays, the dance floor tends to collect the young people of the city (entrance $1 most nights, $1.75 Saturday night). Second best is **Caracoles Negros,** which picks up the slack on Sunday night and appeals to the cowboy crowd more than La Quinta does. Located a half-block south of the PetroNic station along the highway. Toward the center of town, **Casa Bravo Club** is an upscale pool hall where you can sink some balls behind the obscurity of tinted glass and in the comfort of an air-conditioned hall. The baseball field is located down by the river at the south end of town in Barrio Paimuca, and games are played Sundays.

ACCOMMODATIONS
In Town

Lacking sufficient auto-hotels, Juigalpans looking for romance employ the town's plethora of *hospedajes.* The city is littered with inexpensive accommodations, but the trouble is many of those rooms are intended to be occupied for one hour at a time. Two otherwise obvious places to the west of the park, Hospedaje Angelita and Hospedaje Central, fall into that category and should be avoided.

Stay to the east (rear) side of the church instead. **Hotel El Regreso** (the one-story establishment) has 14 clean rooms with shared bath for $3.50 each or $5.75 per couple, tel. 812-2068. Immediately next door is **Hotel El Nuevo Milenio,** with 16 rooms, shared bath $3.50, private bath $7 s, $10 d, tel. 812-0646.

For a bit more coin, **Hotel Casa Country,** located a block from the Parque Palo Solo at the north end of town, has five luxury rooms on the second story of a gorgeous colonial-style house. With private bath and cable TV, rooms with two beds cost $10.75 without a/c, $14.25 with; the views are easily worth the extra money (across the street is the sometimes-functioning **La Casita Country,** a dining establishment related to the hotel).

Along the Highway

There are two hotels along the highway that cater to Nicaraguan businesspeople more interested in getting an early start on the day than having fun in town: **La Quinta** and **El Bosque.** La Quinta, farther east along the highway (almost directly across from the hospital) is considered the better of the two and is home to the town's best disco and restaurant. El Bosque is a step below in quality but still one of Juigalpa's better accommodations. It has neither restaurant nor disco, so it may a bit quieter. Though most rooms share bathrooms, they're clean, modern, tiled affairs; several rooms have private baths. La Quinta has 38 rooms ($8.50 s, $10 d with fan or $12 s, $14 d with a/c). El Bosque has 10 rooms, from $6.50 s/d with fan, to $16 with a/c and private bath, tel. 812-2205.

As you face La Quinta, the first road on the right side is where you'll find **Hotel Mery.** It's a half-block down the road on the right side, with 12 concrete block rooms with private bath at $3 each. The rooms are set around an ample parking area for your car, tel. 812-2902.

FOOD

Juigalpa has a variety of food, often at reasonable prices, naturally, with massive quantities of beef and dairy on the menu. You can start in the park, where three small places serve up light lunches and drinks. **Restaurante Arco Iris** in the northwest corner of the park is popular among the locals. Also near the park, **Cafetín El Oasis** has a similar menu and adds heartier fare like chicken and pork dishes, all in the $1.50–4.50 range.

For good, fresh bread and pastries, stop by **Panadería Allison,** which makes fresh baked goods daily. Open 5 A.M.–7 P.M. all week, and they have a refrigerator full of cold milk to wash it down with.

Restaurante Chupis offers traditional Nica foods, ice cream, sandwiches, and burgers in a pleasant atmosphere with windows along two walls for people-watching. Two other *comedores* have no names but good menus of well-prepared Nicaraguan favorites: one is diagonally across from Americable, and the other a little

café adjacent to the Wild Boulevard boutique. The first place serves lunch and dinner only, while Wild Boulevard opens in time for a late breakfast. Also serving inexpensive Nicaraguan breakfasts is **Comedor La Quintanilla** on the highway 1.5 blocks south of the cemetery (about a block north of Hotel La Quinta). Service is usually fast here, as they do a good business with folks in a hurry to continue driving. Less expensive and fancy is the **Comedor La Asunción** in front of Hotel La Quinta; lots of fried meat, 'nuff said.

On the highway in front of the Esso station, **Restaurante Tacho** has great chicken and steak at moderate prices ($2–3.50) in a pleasant atmosphere. Roving bands of mariachis frequent the place, which is a mostly masculine crowd. For more upscale dining, try **Restaurante La Tonga**, with plates from $5 and up, and of course Juigalpa's favorite, **La Quinta**, with a juicy *churrasco*.

Gringo Food

A restaurant popular among Juigalpa's expat community is in the building that once housed the

Fruit juices served the old-fashioned way: in a *jicaro* mug.

town's cinema. It is set up in the atrium of the theater; look behind one of the doors to see the dark, empty cinema. Besides the sandwiches, chicken wings, and burgers, they've actually got chicken burritos prepared in flour tortillas. **Burger Hot** serves you-know-what from 11 A.M. onward. If you can't do without pizza, try **Pizza Italiana,** two blocks west of the park.

SERVICES

Juigalpa has one well-stocked supermarket, the Supermercado Herman Lazo (open Mon.–Sat. 8 A.M.–7 P.M., closed Sundays).

Internet
The local cable company, Americable, has machines for $3 an hour (open Mon.–Fri. 8 A.M.–7 P.M.). The Centro Cultural Juigalpan (CCJ) is a bit cheaper, with seven machines for $1.75 per hour, open Monday–Saturday 8 A.M.–8 P.M., located near the highway a block from the Esso station.

Money
Two of Juigalpa's three banks are located conveniently across the street from each other at the southeast corner of the park. Banpro and BDF are both open Monday–Friday 8:30 A.M.–4 P.M. and Saturday until noon. Two blocks north of the park, Bancentro keeps the same hours. There is an ATM machine in the Esso station on the highway where you can make withdrawals from your credit card, and the Ferretería Reinaldo Hernandez doubles as a Western Union office (open Mon.–Fri. 8:30 A.M.–5 P.M., Sat. until noon). There's an additional Western Union office a block north of ENITEL.

Post Office and Phone
The post office is located around the corner from the church (open Mon.–Fri. 8 A.M.–5 P.M., Sat. 8 A.M.–noon). ENITEL is four blocks north of the park, open Monday–Saturday 8 A.M.–noon, and 1:30–5:30 P.M., closed Sundays. There are several pay phones scattered around town, the most convenient of which is located in front of the Robert Teran building on the north side of the park.

Medical
There are several pharmacies in town. One of the better ones is Farmacia La Salud, at the northwest corner of the park (open Mon.–Fri. 8 A.M.–10 P.M., Sat. 8 A.M.–8 P.M., tel. 812-0932). Hospital La Asunción is located on the southeast side of town along the highway but doesn't have very good facilities by international standards. A better option for travelers is the Lab Lafayette & Salazar, a private clinic and doctor's office two blocks west of the park, tel. 812-2292.

Film Processing
Roberto Teran's Kodak facility is located across from the park, open Monday–Friday 8 A.M.–6 P.M., Saturday 8 A.M.–2 P.M. Another option is Laboratorio Nuevo Imagen, an independent facility that takes and processes photos in its own lab (open Mon.–Fri. 7:30 A.M.–6 P.M., Sat. 7:30 A.M.–5 P.M.).

GETTING THERE AND AWAY

With the exception of express microbuses to Managua, which depart from the north or east side of the church, all buses depart Juigalpa from the cramped bus terminal in the market, and follow the following schedule:

Rama: nearly every hour, 4:30 A.M.–1:30 P.M.

Managua: every 30 minutes, 4 A.M.–5 P.M.

Nueva Guinea: approximately one every hour, 4:15 A.M.–3:20 P.M.

Boaco via Camoapa and Comalapa: 7:15 A.M. and 8:45 A.M.

El Ayote via La Libertad and Santo Domingo: one every hour, 3 A.M.–5:30 P.M.

In addition, two express microbuses depart for Managua each day from the north side of the church, one at 6 A.M. and one at 1:40 P.M. The trip between Managua and Juigalpa by express bus takes 2.5 hours.

NEAR JUIGALPA
Balneario el Salto
Juigalpa's favorite swimming hole is located an easy two kilometers out of town on the highway to Managua. Look for the big blue sign on the

Balneario el Salto

northeast side of the highway; the falls are located a scant 100 meters from the highway. El Salto is formed by a concrete dam that causes water to pool up in a natural reservoir. In the dry season there's no waterfall at all, though the swimming hole remains quite deep. In the rainy season the water from the Río Mayales tumbles first over the concrete dam and then through a gorge of enormous boulders carved into fantastic shapes by the flowing water. The near shore gets littered with the remains of old picnics after major holidays (like Semana Santa, when the place is packed), but the far shore is tree-lined and grassy. Consider swimming across to the far side and watching the local kids turn somersaults off the wooden plank diving boards. There is supposedly a $1 fee to get in, but the locals have skirted the fee for so long by entering downstream and walking up the streambed that no one seems to try to charge any more (except during Semana Santa).

Puerto Díaz

It's a short and uncomfortable ride from Juigalpa down to the village of Puerto Díaz, a sleepy lakeside town of fishing families that pretty much live off what they catch. Puerto Díaz doesn't have any facilities for travelers but is worth a day trip on a lazy Saturday to see how the "far" side of the lake (i.e., the world across the lake from Granada) lives. Buses leave from Juigalpa three times a day at 5 A.M., 2 P.M., and 5 P.M. From the bus terminal they cross the highway at the Esso station before working their way slowly down to the shoreline.

Cuapa and El Monolito de Cuapa

Tiny, isolated, lonely Cuapa, once just another anonymous farming town in the foothills of the Amerrisque mountain range, gained an awful sort of notoriety during the 1980s, when it came to represent the worst of what the Contra war had become.

In 1985 Contras attacked and took control of Cuapa, holding it for several hours. They captured the Sandinista mayor Hollman Martínez but later released him when the townspeople pleaded for his life. Twelve other Sandinista activists, sent from the capital to work in Cuapa, weren't so fortunate: the Contras marched them out of town and executed them at the roadside. When the Sandinista military got wind that Contras occupied the town of Cuapa, they dispatched a truckload of 40 soldiers to defend the town. Contras ambushed the vehicle along the road to Cuapa, killing nearly all of them. A small roadside monument bearing the Sandinista flag commemorates both the civil servants and the soldiers killed during the war.

Cuapa is also famous among devout Catholics. In late 1980 and early 1981 the Virgin Mary appeared several times—bathed in radiant light and dressed in pure white—to local farmer Bernardo Martínez. She told Martínez she had a message for the world and for Nicaragua: "Don't preach the kingdom of God unless you are building it on earth. The world is threatened by great danger." She later asked for prayers for unbelievers and for peace on earth. Devout Catholics were overjoyed at the appearance of the Virgin, but even that moment became rapidly politicized in the toxic climate of the 1980s. Some claimed her message was a coded recrimination of the Sandinista government, and the Sandinistas responded by clamping down on all press coverage of miracles not previously accepted by the Vatican. An elaborate and well-maintained statue and sign greet you at the entrance to Cuapa with *Bienvenido a la Tierra de María*—Welcome to Mary's Land. Believers from all over eastern Nicaragua flock to Cuapa on May 8, the anniversary of the day the Virgin first appeared.

El Monolito de Cuapa (the Cuapa Monolith) is a 75-meter-high chunk of granite that projects like a giant needle out of a field, as though it dropped from the sky and pierced the ground; it's first visible on the bus ride to Cuapa.

Hiking El Monolito isn't easy, but it isn't impossible either. The locals in Cuapa know all the trails that lead there, and any young campesino will be glad to show you the way to the top to see the cross. From the town of Cuapa it's a 2.5-hour hike to the top, including several extremely steep sections. Hike with good shoes; locals recommend not climbing it on particularly windy days. Ask around for Nicolas, an English-speaking resident of Cuapa (originally from Bluefields) who can be a guide. He runs a tire repair shop next to Parque Zapera.

Whether you've come to see the shrine to Mary or to climb the monolith, Cuapa isn't a bad place to spend the night. One option for the climb is to arrive in the evening, spend the night at Cuapa and set off to climb the monolith the following morning. You can find accommodations and meals at **Restaurante Hospedaje La Maravilla,** with rooms in the $1.50–3.50 range. The menu is traditional Nicaraguan food. The hotel fills up the week of June 19–27, when Cuapa celebrates its patron saint, San José.

Six buses leave Juigalpa for Cuapa every day, starting at 6 A.M. and the last departing at 6 P.M. Buses from Cuapa to Juigalpa leave from the town center every day, 6 A.M.–4:30 P.M.

Serranía Amerrisque

A powerful backdrop to the city, the Amerrisque mountain range forms a rocky backbone to the history of the city. Most of the archaeological pieces in the Juigalpa museum were unearthed in the Amerrisques, and countless other sites have yet to be discovered and explored. Although the area is undeveloped for tourists, the rocky peaks make a tempting hike and the locals claim the east side of the range contains several caves.

Your starting point is the road called the Camino de la Vaticana, built by Rome and Holland in the late 1990s. It will lead you nine kilometers east toward the range and the tiny farming community of Piedra Grande. From there you can strike into the hills to explore. You can try hitching a ride out there to trim down the flat, boring part of the hike, but it won't be easy, as traffic along the road is sparse at best since there are few communities along its length. Consider hiring a pickup truck in town; a group of five travelers offering $15–20 might be able to convince someone to drive them out there. Try to swing a deal for the ride back while you're at it.

Daniel Molina can serve as a guide, tel. 812-2940; he is a young man who speaks English and can help you arrange a trip out to the mountains, where he'll help you find a local guide to show you the trails.

Thermal Vents at Agua Caliente

When they're hot they're hot, but when they're

Amerrisque mountains

© RANDY WOOD

not they're not—a trip out to the hot springs at Agua Caliente is a gamble because their activity is cyclical. On the down side of the cycle they're nothing more than a trickle of hot water seeping out of the side of the creek bed. When they're active, however, expect to see torrents of bubbles gushing out of the creek bed in water too hot to touch. While eastern Nicaragua lacks the volcanoes of the Pacific horizon, it too was formed volcanically and the hot springs are evidence that under the surface, even quiet old Chontales is bubbling and tectonically active.

To get there, take the Camino de la Vaticana as though you were going to the Amerrisque mountains, but take the first major left-hand turn instead; Aguas Calientes is 4.8 kilometers down the road. You'll know you've reached the site when you get to a relatively new school building followed immediately by a streambed. The hot springs are located about 100 meters upstream from where the road crosses the stream.

La Libertad and Santo Domingo

These two pueblos have been the site of small-scale gold mining for well over a hundred years. British mining engineer Thomas Belt was surveying in the Santo Domingo area when he wrote his famous book, *A Naturalist in Nicaragua,* in 1874. The mines were, until recently, run by a Canadian organization that ceased activities around 2000. The curious may be interested in poking around either town, both of which, though run-down and slightly decrepit, still very distinctly bear the traces of a gold rush boomtown atmosphere. La Libertad is the birthplace of former president Daniel Ortega as well as Nicaragua's outspoken and politicized Catholic archbishop Miguel Obando y Bravo.

The Road to Rama

During the 1980s, the highway from San Benito (Managua) to Rama, known as the Rama Highway, was a hotly contested military prize. At stake was control of the port at Rama, through which Managua received much of its oil and supplies from the Baltic states and the Soviet Union. The town of **La Gateada** (The Crawl) was the site of several major battles and is perched on a steep hillside on the Rama Highway. After five years of failed attempts, the Contras finally succeeded in capturing the highway in 1987. In a massive offensive 2,500 Contras captured four towns, including **Santo Tomás** and **San Pedro de Lóvago**. In all four, they burned down Sandinista government buildings, the phone office, the courts, fuel depots, and military garrisons. The Contras also demolished five bridges, all but the crown jewel—the bridge at **Muelle de los Bueyes** which, standing 150 meters high over the Río Mico, was easily the most irreplaceable bridge

in the nation. The Sandinista military successfully defended the bridge with 400 troops, and it stands today, still one of the highest bridges in Nicaragua.

By the year 2000, the Rama Highway was in bad shape, due not to war but to old age and neglect. Its thin veneer of asphalt was pocked with axle-breaking holes along its entire length. A bus trip between Managua and Rama could easily take 12 hours as traffic lurched along in first gear, swerving madly to avoid the worst of the craters. The project to pave the highway was one of the changes the Nicaraguan public was most pleased to receive from the Alemán administration, although, inevitably, it was rocked by scandal, granting bloated contracts to several of the president's cronies. Today, the highway as far as Juigalpa is much improved, but the remaining stretch to Rama is still a nightmare. The trip takes about eight hours by bus.

Nueva Guinea

Nueva Guinea was founded as part of U.S. president John F. Kennedy's Alliance for Progress, a program meant to defuse demands for land reform across Latin America in the wake of the Cuban revolution and the postcolonial struggles in the rest of the world. Original settlers were given one *manzana* of land (about one hectare) in the urban center, and 60 in the countryside. The same program was applied to help victims of natural disasters—victims of both the Managua earthquake of 1972 and the eruption of Cerro Negro near León in 1973 were shipped out to Nueva Guinea. In the 1980s the area was a hot spot of Contra activity under the command of Edén Pastora's group, ARDE, based across the Costa Rica border.

Technically, Nueva Guinea is part of the RAAS (*Región Autónoma Atlántica del Sur* or the Southern Atlantic Autonomous Region), but it is more easily accessed from the Rama Highway and

Juigalpa than Bluefields and the Río Escondido. A full 293 kilometers southeast of Managua, Nueva Guinea lies in the tropical, humid, rolling lowlands that stretch toward the Caribbean. It's one of the rainiest corners of Nicaragua, receiving an average of 8,000 millimeters (yes, that's eight meters) of rainfall each year, but that varies from town to town, based on the forest cover of the area. In terms of population it is the second largest municipality in Nicaragua, with a de facto population of 120,000 people, many of whom technically live in the municipality of Bluefields, but whose transport and public services come from Nueva Guinea.

In the 1960s, Nueva Guinea was a rich, dense, tropical rainforest with a wide variety of animal life, but since then, due to poor public policy, misguided development projects, and inadequate agricultural practices, much of the territory has been transformed into barren, useless pasture.

Forested areas include the land that borders the Reserva Indio-Maíz and the Reserva Natural Punta Gorda. Even that land is in the process of being slowly and illegally colonized and exploited, and poor farmers in desperate need of land overwhelm the capacity of the Nicaraguan government to prevent their homesteading.

These days, farmers in the area of Nueva Guinea live in some 140 colonies and neighborhoods and dedicate their labor to the production of basic grains—corn, beans, and rice—as well as ginger. Nueva Guinea is a wild place, a town that could easily have been part of the western United States, with horses parked outside of bars and people walking their pigs or herding cattle down main street. The town of Nueva Guinea has few facilities that lend themselves to travelers, but the truly adventurous or curious may appreciate visiting a place so out of the way and so full of history and emotion.

ACCOMMODATIONS

There are three options in Nueva Guinea. **Hotel Nueva Guinea,** located on the main street in front of the Casa de Cultura, is the nicest place to stay in Nueva Guinea. Rooms with TV and bath start at $8.50, or $3 for simpler rooms with neither bath nor TV, tel. 285-0090, email: katerine@ibw.com.ni. At **Las 24 Horas Hospedaje,** located across from the police station, pay $2.50 each for spartan rooms with *mosquiteros.* More than one foreign volunteer working in the area has liked the rooms enough to stay there longterm. At **Hospedaje Central,** located from the municipal market 1.5 blocks north, basic rooms cost $2.50 per person.

FOOD

The best food in town is allegedly found at **Llamas del Bosque,** next to the Esso station. Fish, chicken, or beef for around $5. You can get a decent meal at **Ranchón Kristofer,** located three blocks north of the park. It's also got the best dance floor in town. Or for cheaper fare, the least expensive *comedor* in town is located in front of the mayor's office, **Comedería Tamara,** with hot, greasy goodies for less than a buck.

SIGHTS AND ATTRACTIONS

At **Finca La Esperanzita** you can get a glimpse of a good organic agriculture project where small farmers are growing cacao, vanilla, pepper, and several species of tropical hardwoods. They'll gladly provide you with a tour of the facilities, where ecological agriculture was first formally experimented with. There is also a **coffee, cacao, and cinnamon processing plant** run by World Relief. Find it one block south and one block east of the hospital. Technically, the Nueva Guinea community of Fonseca is the gateway to the Indio-Maíz Reserve, but the road from Fonseca south into the reserve is trafficked by well-armed people with their own interests in lumber, forest products, and more. A guide is crucial to anyone contemplating a hike into the reserve. The mayor's office can help you find one.

GETTING THERE AND AWAY

Buses leave for Nueva Guinea from Managua's Mayoreo terminal approximately every hour (eight-hour trip) until 10 A.M.

The Atlantic Coast

[The Atlantic Coast] is perhaps best understood if one imagines it as a Caribbean island that, by some geological catastrophe, drifted toward Central America and found itself part of a foreign nation.

Stephen Kinzer

To be sure, Nicaragua's right side has its islands of paradise—the kind of white sand, coral reef, and coconut palm images usually associated with the Caribbean. But the experience of Nicaragua's "Reggae Coast" is more than a beach getaway; it is a swim through a cultural ocean unlike any other in the world, a fascinating conglomeration of history in the very blood, skin, and language of the people here, like some tropical New York neighborhood—with an island attitude.

As far as the tourist is concerned, the vast majority of Nicaragua's 450 kilometers of Atlantic coastline are unexplored, undeveloped, and unapproachable. Edward Marriot calls it "Nicaragua's jungle coast. Not the 'Caribbean'—despite cartographers' insistences—but, deliberately,

Corn Island

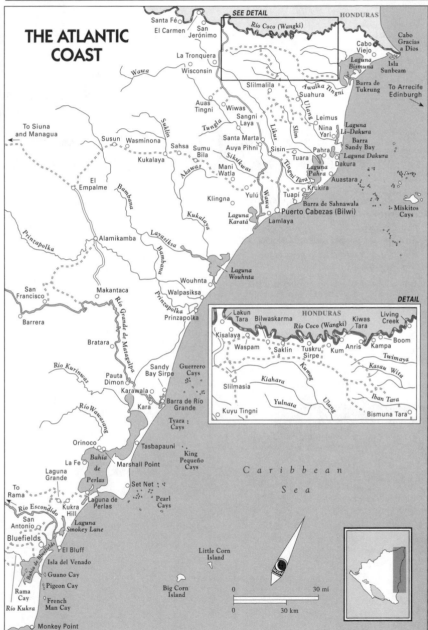

THE ATLANTIC COAST

© AVALON TRAVEL PUBLISHING, INC.

the 'Atlantic.' No one here spoke of this ocean, with its broken, unlovely shoreline, as the Caribbean: that would have been too misleading, too obvious a misrepresentation. No, this was the Atlantic Coast, with its mangrove swamps and alligators, hurricanes and stiff westers that washed up bales of high-grade cocaine, shrink-wrapped for export."

"The Other Nicaragua" (as the tourism board likes to call this side of the country) can be rough at times, but, more often than not, it is languid, lazy, and relaxing. Walking the noisy streets of Bluefields, riding a *panga* up a twisting, jungle river, or sunning yourself on Corn Island, you may start to wonder if the rest of Nicaragua even exists. Welcome to La Costa, where residents have lived this isolation for their entire history. Fill your belly with fresh fish and rum, your ears with reggae (and country) music, and your journal with a new collection of rich adventures.

Sometimes called the Mosquito Coast (a corruption of the Native American *Miskito*), the region is composed of both the shoreline and the broad expanses of swamp, savanna, and rainforest that push inland from its many bays.

HISTORY

The region is divided into two departments known as the Región Autónoma Atlantica del Sur (RAAS) and the Región Autónoma Atlantica del Norte (RAAN), which comprise nearly half of Nicaragua's landmass. Before 1988 they were one enormous department called Zelaya. The Atlantic coast of Nicaragua was originally populated primarily by the native Miskito, Mayangna (Sumu), and Rama people, who made their settlements along the rivers and coastline, living on fishing and small-scale agriculture. Europe gained its first impression of Nicaragua when Columbus cruised the coast in 1502. Throughout the 16th century, little was known of the area except its reputation for being totally inhospitable—unbearably rainy, insect-drenched jungles, and home to aggressive and warring Native American tribes.

WHEN TO VISIT

Meteorologically, the Atlantic coast's main distinction from the rest of the country is the amount of rain it receives—between 3,000 and 6,000 millimeters annually (with the higher levels falling in southern RAAS), making it among the wettest places in the world. The rainy season is punctuated by hurricanes in September and October, and can extend well into December, sometimes longer. The end of December is marked by cool, "Christmas" winds, and the period between late January and April is generally dry, sunny, and ideal. The biggest crowds arrive for Christmas, Semana Santa, and during various regional fiestas, when making reservations in advance is a good idea.

The Spanish made two exploratory forays into the Atlantic coastline, one by Esteban Verdelete, who tried to convert the Mayangna and Tawaka (a subtribe) along the Río Coco to Christianity, the other by Cristóbal Martínez, who tried to convert the Miskito (Guanae) peoples living in the Caratasca and Wani (Bismuna) lagoons. Both missionaries were killed, and the Spanish subsequently lost interest in the Caribbean coast. It remained largely unexplored and became the sailing grounds of English and Dutch pirates, who hid in the labyrinthine bays and channels from where they preyed on Spanish ships traveling to and from the European mainland. One of these was the Dutch pirate Abraham Blauveldt, whose name in English, "Bluefields," was later given to the bay he made his haunt in the 1630s.

In the same century, a number of escaped and shipwrecked African slaves mixed with the natives, serving as the first of many ingredients to be thrown into the area's singular cultural melting pot over the next several hundred years. The offspring of this original mix were known as "Sambos," a word which became a derogatory expression for African Americans in the United States.

In the 1700s, the English organized the Atlantic coast into a protectorate, giving the British Crown its first "legal" colonial presence along the Caribbean coast. The protectorate established "Miskito Kings" who were educated, supported, and kept in power by the British. Under the pretext of protecting the rights of indigenous peoples, England armed the Miskito and Sambo people, encouraging them to raid the lands of nearby tribes, in search of prisoners of war to be spirited off for slave labor on Jamaican sugar plantations. The English also encouraged their armed companions to make aggressive forays into Spanish territories of Nicaragua. The Miskito war raids reached as far inland as Nueva Segovia and Chontales. Sparring between England and Spain didn't conclude until 1790, when a peace accord was drawn up between nations. The accord, which the Nicaraguan government had no part in, created a Miskito Reserve between the Ulang River and Punta Gorda.

When the British departed in 1860, the void they left behind was filled by big businesses from the United States, which established timber and banana company camps all along the Atlantic coast. Bluefields became a thriving commercial center with a brass band, small industry, an English-language daily newspaper, and regular steamship connections to New Orleans, Baltimore, Philadelphia, and New York.

Such was the state of Bluefields and the Atlantic coast when President José Santos Zelaya ordered its military occupation in 1894. The maneuver was carried out by Zelaya's most trusted general, Rigoberto Cabezas, whose troops

MAYANGNA LEGENDS

The Origin of the Sun and Moon

In the beginning of time there were, in addition to the humans, two great gods: Uhubaput, the creator of the world, and his companion Udo. One day the two gods came down to earth disguised as humans suffering from a horrid skin disease that caused blemishes and oozing sores. All the humans who came across Uhubaput and Udo insulted them. The men tried to run them out of town, while the women scolded Uhubaput and Udo, and refused to offer them glasses of *chicha* or *wasbul* to drink. Finally the townspeople captured the two and "killed" them. Of course, they had no idea Uhubaput and Udo were gods, and of course the two gods came back to life immediately.

Uhubaput and Udo returned to town and the first thing they did was to steal all the *wasbul* and drink it. They then began to attack the town. Cutting small saplings they made a great quantity of arrows. As they shot each arrow they called out the name of an animal. The arrow, in midflight, was converted into the animal, and ran through the town causing great damage. Uhubaput and Udo then transformed themselves into strong, handsome humans, and reentered the town. This time they were received gladly by the women of the town, who were attracted to Uhubaput's and Udo's good looks, and who offered to become their wives.

Uhubaput and Udo were enraged the women who had been so unfriendly to them when had appeared sickly were now so eager to marry them. In their fury they cast divine spells on the women of the town, turning them into different types of small animals. Only two women were spared—the most beautiful and light-skinned. These Uhubaput and Udo took to be their wives.

When they were done, Uhubaput and Udo danced on the campfire like *Sukias* (priests), raising their arms and fingertips upwards to rise into heaven. Udo began first, but had no luck in rising. Uhubaput then tried. He rose slowly into the heavens where he became the sun. When Udo tried again he too rose upwards into the heavens, where he became the moon.

The Origin of the Rocks of Kiawa

The god Papangh sent his servant Alwana (Thunder) to earth to teach the people how to be farmers and create baskets and pots with their hands, as well as other things humans would need to prosper. One day when Alwana wasn't home a *walasa* (evil spirit) by the name of Kiawa entered Alwana's home and stole his wife.

But a parrot had seen what happened, and flew to Alwana to tell what had happened in his absence. Alwana was in the fields at the time, plant-

sailed down then Río Escondido in February, deposed the Miskito government, and officially united Nicaragua from Atlantic to Pacific. "Integrating" the Atlantic coast was more a show of strength than an effort to include the Atlantic in Nicaragua's more populous and powerful Spanish-influenced regions. Little respect was shown for Miskito customs, and taxes collected along the Atlantic coast were siphoned off to Managua instead of being invested in Atlantic coast infrastructure as promised. Spanish was made the official language, and lumber concessions that extended deep into tribal territories were granted to foreign companies for exploitation.

As the inland mineral deposits grew depleted and the soils of the banana plantations were impoverished, the foreign companies began to withdraw from Bluefields and the Atlantic coast, hastened by anti-imperialist guerrilla attacks on foreign settlements. During the 20th century, the Atlantic coast government and economy decayed into a state of corruption and financial mismanagement and ruin.

The 1980s

When the Sandinistas rolled into the Atlantic coast and announced the region's "liberation," they were surprised to find that the Costeños weren't very interested. Somoza had largely left the Atlantic coast to its own devices and Costeños generally viewed the goings-on in Managua as they would news from a foreign country. The

ing pine trees in a rocky area known as *Alwana kumani umhna*, a place that really exists: it's found on the Kiwaska River and is a rocky area covered in pine trees. Alwana immediately stopped what he was doing to search for his wife and recapture her. After much searching he found Kiawa and the woman far upstream in a tributary of the Río Tuma called Río Iyas. But even though Kiawa was drunk, he was an immense and powerful giant, and Alwana was unable to defeat him.

As they fought, Kiawa transformed himself into a giant boa constrictor and devoured the woman so she wouldn't run to Alwana. Alwana grew bigger to try to topple Kiawa, but Kiawa continued growing. The two grew larger and larger until finally Alwana was taller than the clouds. Hidden by the clouds, he took out his machete and cut Kiawa into many pieces. As the pieces fell to earth, the many people Kiawa had devoured were released and returned to life. The pieces of Kiawa became rocks, which can be seen today at the headwaters of the Río Iyas in an area now known as Kiawa. The locals say these rocks are known to bleed from time to time, and certain pieces of Kiawa's body, like his navel and his head, can be spotted very easily.

The Great Flood
Two brothers by the names of Suku and Kuru

went out fishing on the Kwahliwah creek, a small tributary of the Río Ukungwas. They caught many fish, especially the *Sirik*. But suddenly a huge fish by the name of Susum took the hook and Suku reeled it in. Suku wanted to roast and eat the fish immediately, but Kuru was opposed to the idea, thinking suspiciously Susum was really an evil demon. But Suku stubbornly cut a piece of the fish, roasted it and ate it. Immediately Suku was consumed by a terrible thirst. He had eaten quite a bit and felt too full to get up to get water so he asked his brother Kuru to bring him water from the river to drink. But no matter how much water Kuru brought him, Suku couldn't slake his thirst. Finally Kuru grew tired of making so many trips to the river for water and helped drag Suku to the river's edge so he could drink his fill. But as Suku bent down to drink from the river's edge his body lengthened and grew slippery and he began to change into an anaconda with a human face. Kuru grew frightened and ran alone back to town, where he told people Suku had stayed behind to fish. But people were suspicious and finally everyone went down to the river's edge to find Suku—now an immense anaconda—at the top of a ceiba tree. As everyone looked up at Suku in the tree, a massive wave rose out of the river, drowning the entire nation with the exception of Suku and his offspring.

Moravian Church's teaching that "the kingdom of God is pure and the kingdom of politics is profane" also contributed to the Atlantic coast's apolitical tendencies. What followed was arguably one of the Sandinista regime's greatest misjudgments and internationally condemned disgraces.

The revolution coincided with a growing sense of Native American autonomy worldwide, which included Nicaragua's Atlantic coast. Miskito and Creole leaders up and down the coast formed a political group called MISURASATA, a union of the words Miskito, Sumu, Rama, Sandinista, and the Miskito word for together. The group's original intent was to work with the new government in Managua, but it soon found itself at odds with the Sandinistas, and subsequently disputed their authority to rule the Atlantic coast.

In 1981, Sandinista authorities, pushed to their breaking point by indigenous resistance in the Atlantic—and especially along the Río Coco—ordered the forced relocation of entire Miskito communities. The empty villages were burned, cattle machine-gunned, and orchards razed, presumably to deny support to Contra soldiers operating in the area. Ten thousand Miskito villagers were resettled to refugee camps, while over 40,000 Miskitos and Mayangna escaped over the Río Coco to Honduras.

Throughout the early 1980s, while the Miskito refugees huddled in the camps, the Sandinista military devastated the entire Río Coco region in search of rebel groups antipathetic to their revolution. The U.S. government capitalized on the discontent to win Miskito converts to the Contras, and the Contras (including Miskito members, who were subsequently known as Yatama) were equally responsible for death and destruction in the region. In 1985, Minister of the Interior Tomás Borge came to a compromise with the Miskito people: in exchange for laying down their arms, they would be permitted to return to the sites of their original villages along the Río Coco to rebuild and begin anew. Many accepted, and since the mid-1980s the Río Coco communities have slowly rebuilt in the delicate autonomy now granted to the two departments of the Atlantic coast.

Political disasters aside, the Atlantic coast has always been vulnerable to natural catastrophes, es-

pecially hurricanes. Like most Nicaraguans, Costeños have a particularly violent event around which the region's history is measured. In 1988, Hurricane Joan leveled and drowned Bluefields and other Atlantic coast communities. It killed 148 people and caused $1 billion worth of damage, including the destruction of Big Corn Island's prosperous coconut industry and much of its coral reef system. In addition, over 100,000 hectares of tropical swamp forest were killed, all of which burned disastrously during the following dry season. Today, when locals speak of "the hurricane," they are referring to Joan, not Mitch.

LANGUAGE AND RELIGION

The Atlantic coast is a part of Nicaragua only geographically. Culturally, socially, and linguistically, it is another world. Due to the rugged wilderness separating it from the rest of Nicaragua, its residents have always looked eastward for their connection with the rest of the world.

The southern part of the Atlantic coast has a largely English-speaking Creole population, though Spanish is pretty much universal as well. Puerto Cabezas and the Río Coco are composed of more Miskitos, who speak their native tongue. In Puerto Cabezas Spanish is widely spoken, but there are some places along the Río Coco where only Miskito is understood.

Beginning in the mid-1800s, German Moravian missionaries began proselytizing their version of Lutheranism on the Atlantic coast. They persuaded the people to wear clothing, abandon polygamy, and adopt Western-style work habits, attempting to hammer the Miskito people into good, German form. In addition to constructing a series of simple, elegant churches, the Moravians improved material conditions admirably, introducing new schools, hospitals, and sanitation systems, plus the first attempt to record the Miskito language.

Today most Costeños are Protestant rather than Catholic. On the Atlantic Coast, the evangelical groups (fundamentalist Protestants) have a lesser presence than they do in other parts of Nicaragua. The most common professed religion is Moravian Protestantism. The missionary influence is strong, and groups from the United States find fertile ground in the English-speaking Atlantic population.

In recent years, a large immigration of Pacific-side (and mostly Catholic) Nicaraguans has tipped the demographics of most major Atlantic coast communities, putting the black and indigenous populations in the minority for the first time in their history. Considering their long-held isolation and resistance to the Managuan government, this is no small change. For the most part, everybody gets along, but there are undoubtedly rising tensions as the "Spaniards" (as Costeños have always referred to mestizos) seek housing and employment, and at the same time, attempt to import their language, music, food, and other cultural aspects to their new home.

El Rama

At the far end of the highway from Managua, El Rama straddles the frontier between Atlantic and Pacific more perceptibly than any other Nicaraguan town in the country's wild lowlands. A longtime riverine port and trader town, El Rama is a melting pot where mestizo cattle traders meet Caribbean steamer captains, and dark-skinned Creoles meet Nicaraguan "Spaniards" from the Pacific.

The name "Rama" is a tribute to the Rama people who once inhabited the shores of the Siquia, Rama, Escondido, and Mico Rivers. The inhabitants of today's El Rama, however, are the progeny of immigrants from Chontales, Boaco, and Granada, all of whom swarmed here in the late 18th century to take advantage of the boom in the wood, rubber, and banana trade. The original city of El Rama was located on the southwest shore of the Río Siquia before 1880, but was relocated to the present location due to the unbearable mud, floods, and swamps that characterized the original location.

© RANDY WOOD

Rama's international port

While Nicaraguans from all over the country resented the stringent rationing of food and basic goods during the war years of the 1980s, no one was more indignant than the people of El Rama, whose international port was where the millions of metric tons of military hardware were brought on shore from Eastern-bloc freighters to be shipped up the Rama Highway to military bases around the nation. In the 1980s, while locals were forming lines to receive a half-bar of soap and one pound of rice, they watched armored-steel convoys of tanks, fighter planes, and trucks full of rifles, grenades, and antipersonnel land mines pass through their town bound for the battle lines. Short of the trenches of the front line, nowhere was the military buildup—and the irony of the shortage of basic goods—more obvious.

El Rama, though wholly dependent on the river, is also at the mercy of it. El Rama has been under water several times, including during Hurricane Joan, when for three days the only thing seen above the surface of the boiling, muddy waters of the swollen Río Escondido was the church steeple. Deforestation upstream means the river floods more and more frequently these days, and with less advance warning. An electronic system of flood warning devices installed along the river in 2000 will hopefully give residents a chance to evacuate.

The typical traveler spends no more than 15 minutes in Rama between the time he gets off the bus and onto a boat to Bluefields. But should you find yourself stuck here (because let's face it, few travelers will brave the nine-hour bus ride just to go to Rama), you may find El Rama to be worth a second look, and even useful as the base for an expedition or two.

ACCOMMODATIONS

Not recommended are the two sketchy places down by the port, **Hotel Amy** and **Hotel Mantial,** where for $7 you get nasty bathroom facilities, questionable security, and probably prostitutes and their company for your neighbors. The locals direct foreign travelers to **Hotel Johana,** which is simple and safe; they have over 30 rooms in a large wooden building ($2 a person, tel. 817-0066). A bit cleaner and far quieter is **Hospedaje García,** with singles for $2.75, double beds for $5, and fancier rooms on the 2nd floor with a/c and a view of the river for $10.50.

FOOD

Without a doubt, the best place in town for a meal is **Restaurante El Expreso,** whose name has no relation to the speed of the service; lots of seafood, soups, chicken, and steak. Across from the market, **Antojitos Mexicanos** is popular with the locals for Mexican dishes and beer. The **Eskimo** sells sandwiches in addition to ice cream. A good **fritanga** sets up shop evenings near the market (approximately across from Antojitos Mexicanos).

SERVICES

The ENITEL and post office are located across the street from each other. ENITEL is open Monday–Saturday 7 A.M.–9 P.M. For late night phone calls, try the Pepsi booth on the street that leads to the municipal pier (i.e., the pier with boats for Bluefields). There's a phone there the owner will let you use. Farmacia El Carmen, open Monday–Saturday 8 A.M.–1 P.M. and 2–6:30 P.M. is well stocked with medicines, sanitary supplies, and more.

GETTING THERE AND AWAY

The trip between Managua and El Rama can take up to nine hours, not because of distance but because of the vast expanses of ruined road which buses are forced to traverse at a crawl. Once the pavement gives way to dirt it deteriorates rapidly into fields of rainwater-filled potholes that carpet the road from one side to the other; Rama is approximately six hours from Juigalpa. Buses from Managua's Mayoreo terminal depart at 5 A.M., 6 A.M., and 7:30 A.M. From Juigalpa, buses leave from the market every hour until 1:30 P.M.

Many travelers choose to travel by overnight bus, both to experience the early morning *panga* ride, and so as not to arrive in Bluefields in the dark. Night buses to El Rama are owned by two companies. The first is Transporte Vargas Peñas (tel. 280-4561 in Managua, tel. 822-1510 on the dock in Bluefields), leaving from the bus terminal Ivan Montenegro in Managua at 9 P.M., arriving in El Rama around 7 A.M. The same company owns the fleet of Rama–Bluefields *pangas* and can sell you the boat ticket in Managua, ensuring you don't get stranded on the dock. The second company, Transporte Aguilar (tel. 248-3005 or 244-2255), leaves Managua's Mayoreo at 9 P.M. and 10 P.M., arriving in El Rama at 5 A.M. and 6 A.M. It's a quicker ride, but you'll have to fend for yourself to get a place on a departing *panga*. With both companies, the ride costs $6. The return journey begins at 5:30 A.M. on the docks of Bluefields, putting you in Managua about 12 hours later.

By Bus to Managua

Five buses for Managua leave from the market from 3–9 A.M.; an express bus leaves from the wharf road (approximately a block east of Hotel Amy) at noon, 7 P.M., and 10 P.M. Saturday, Sunday, and Tuesday. Express buses don't linger in Juigalpa or stop along the road, saving approximately two hours off the trip.

By Boat to Bluefields

All transportation is found at the municipal wharf: *pangas* cast off from the dock as they fill up, from 6 A.M. to 4 P.M. (1.5-hour trip to Bluefields, approximately $10 per person). There's a bigger ship that carries freight and passengers but is much slower than the nimble *pangas*. It leaves every Tuesday and Saturday at 11 A.M. (five hours, approximately $5 per person).

NEAR EL RAMA

The folks at El Rama are interested in developing their ecotourism infrastructure; they just don't know how to do it yet. Any adventuring you do in the region will require ingenuity and patience. Divided by rivers and swamps, the lands around El Rama are teeming with places to explore and look for wildlife. **Los Humedales de Mahogany** is a wetlands reserve important for the reproduction of local species. It's a 4–5 hour trip by boat downstream in the direction of Bluefields along the Mahogany River near the entrance to the Caño Negro (Black Creek). **Cerro Silva** was declared protected in 1997; it's located 2.5 hours along the Río Rama in the direction of San Jerónimo. Once you disembark from your boat, it's a 2.5-hour hike from the river's edge to the park; find a guide in San Jerónimo to lead you there.

The falls at **Salto Mataka** are found along the Río Siquia, 2.5 hours from La Esperanza (the town with the big bridge, just west of El Rama). Also located near La Esperanza is **El Recreo,** a popular swimming hole three kilometers north of town.

Bluefields

A rich waterfront melting pot of nearly 50,000, Bluefields has never been connected to Nicaragua's highway system and is reached only by water or air. Its large, protected harbor made it a favorite hideout for European pirates hundreds of years ago and today, Bluefields Bay, polluted as it is, ensures the city's place as Nicaragua's primary Atlantic port and capital of the RAAS. Bluefields is also the capital of the Palo de Mayo (Maypole), an exuberant and erotic calypso-tinted dance and music, unique to the city and celebrated fervently throughout the month of May.

While fascinating culturally, there's not much for the traveler to do in Bluefields except eat huge quantities of seafood and dance the "hug-up" at one of its dark reggae bars (unless of course, one of the famous festivals is going on, where you can eat huge quantities of seafood

and dance the... uh, oh yeah). Still, Bluefields merits a stopover and serves as a jumping-off point for trips to Pearl Lagoon, various river villages and cays, and of course, the Corn Islands.

ECONOMY

Bluefields's commercial activity is, not surprisingly, based largely on lobster, fish, shrimp, oysters, and several species of endangered turtles (sharks used to be a staple for the Asian fin soup market, but have since been fished into oblivion). Logging generates significant income as well, at the expense of the Atlantic coast's tremendous hardwood forests. In recent years, a significant number of Bluefields residents have found work in the cruise ship industry, where they are prized for their ability to speak English (and exploited for their willingness to accept

floating into Bluefields

© JOSHUA BERMAN

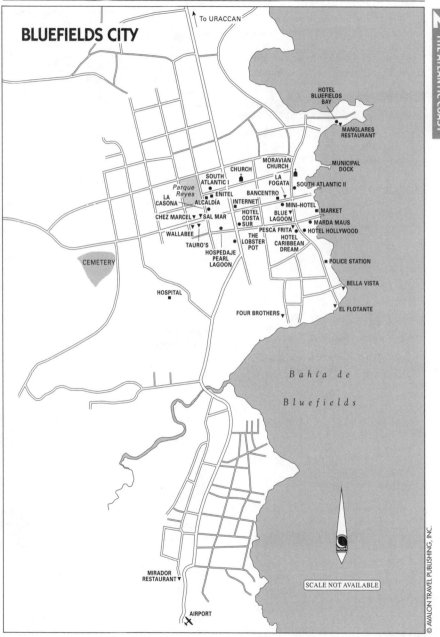

BLUEFIELDS CITY

To URACCAN

HOTEL BLUEFIELDS BAY

MANGLARES RESTAURANT

MUNICIPAL DOCK

MORAVIAN CHURCH

CHURCH

SOUTH ATLANTIC I

LA FOGATA

SOUTH ATLANTIC II

Parque Reyes

ENITEL

BANCENTRO

LA CASONA

ALCALDÍA

INTERNET

MINI-HOTEL

MARKET

CHEZ MARCEL

SAL MAR

HOTEL COSTA SUR

BLUE LAGOON

MARDA MAUS

HOTEL HOLLYWOOD

WALLABEE

PESCA FRITA

TAURO'S

THE LOBSTER POT

HOTEL CARIBBEAN DREAM

POLICE STATION

HOSPEDAJE PEARL LAGOON

CEMETERY

BELLA VISTA

HOSPITAL

FOUR BROTHERS

EL FLOTANTE

Bahía de

Bluefields

MIRADOR RESTAURANT

AIRPORT

SCALE NOT AVAILABLE

© AVALON TRAVEL PUBLISHING, INC.

low wages). The income these seasonal workers send home is an important asset to the coastal economy.

Bluefields is also an important educational center for the Atlantic coast. In addition to host-

CREOLE EXPRESSIONS

Put your Spanish dictionary away while in Bluefields — you're in Creole country! While Spanish will get you by, the following expressions will make you understood, and probably earn you a couple of laughs:

"How you mean?"
"Explain that."

"No feel, no way."
"Don't worry."

"I no vex."
"I'm not angry."

"Do you manage what time…"
"Do you know what time…"

"That ain't nothing."
"Thank you."

"Check you then."
"Goodbye."

"Drop yo booka to da bench."
"Sit down."

"Make I get tree o dem."
"Give me three of those."

"She feelin to eat some."
"She was in the mood to eat some."

"He own"
"His."

"It molest we."
"It bothers us."

"She done reach Raitipura."
"She arrived at Raitpura."

POLICE CHECKS

Because of drug trafficking crackdowns, you can expect police to thoroughly inspect your bags at every dock and airport on the Atlantic coast.

ing the largest chapter of the University of the Autonomous Regions of the Atlantic Coast of Nicaragua (URACCAN; the other campuses are in Puerto Cabezas, Siuna, and Nueva Guinea), this is also the home of the Bluefields Indian and Caribbean University (BICU).

Despite all the activity, Bluefields suffers chronic and massive unemployment, with levels of up to 85 percent. The social ills that accompany such a crisis, combined with the increased presence of drugs—including crack—have made life a daily struggle for many residents (maybe one of the only things Bluefields has in common with the rest of Nicaragua).

ORIENTATION AND GETTING AROUND

From the Bluefields airport, it's a walk of several kilometers north into town; taxis will take you for under $1. If you are arriving by *panga* from El Rama at the municipal docks, walking half a block puts you on the main waterfront drag and within a stone's throw of most of Bluefields's hotels. The central park, also known as Parque Reyes, is located three blocks west of the waterfront road. Once in town (called Barrio Central), taxis have a cheap fixed rate, charging just a little extra to reach the airport or the URACCAN campus. There are two bus routes (which differ very little) that run from 6 A.M.–7:30 P.M. Get on and off where you like for $.10.

SIGHTS AND ATTRACTIONS

The **Moravian Church** was the first of its kind on the Central American Atlantic coast. It was built in 1848 with a combination of English and French design elements—and a touch of Caribbean; the cut wood is reminiscent of New

Orleans in the 1800s. CEDEHCA is a human rights organization with a photography display in its lobby, including shots of the destruction caused by Hurricane Joan (open Mon.–Fri. 8 A.M.–6 P.M., closed during lunch).

You can walk up to the water tower with a local tour guide. The hike through town to the north end near the URACCAN will reward you with a good view of the harbor; take a bottle of rum and pretend you're an English pirate. Blue-fields is also a good place to take in an amateur game of baseball, soccer, or volleyball. Ask at the fields or b-ball courts (in the central park) for game times.

FESTIVALS

Known alternately as the *¡Mayo Ya!* and **Palo de Mayo** (Maypole) Festivals, Bluefields's May Day celebration is unique in Central America. In North America, this pagan-rooted party is about springtime, fertility, and the reawakening of the earth after a long winter; in Bluefields, May falls on the cusp of the rainy season, and the entire month is a bright burst of colors, parades, costumes, feasting, and, most importantly, dancing and chest-shimmying mayhem around the May-pole. Every night is a party, and the festival comes to a rip-roaring peak at the end of the month.

Not able to endure a whole year without a party, Bluefields exuberantly honors its patron saint, San Jerónimo, on September 30, and then rolls right into its birthday celebrations throughout the month of October.

NIGHTLIFE AND ENTERTAINMENT

Four Brothers is more than a bar and reggae hall—it's also ground zero for the Creole social scene in Bluefields. Milling with the crowd outside is just as entertaining as sweating in the packed, dark heat of the wooden-plank dance floor. Once inside, there's not much room in which to move,

THE PALO DE MAYO

The Palo de Mayo, or Maypole dance, is the most well known and colorful feature of Nicaragua's vibrant Caribbean culture, the result of a mixture of several cultures in the 1800s. In English and Nordic tradition of that century, on the first of May young men and women would collect freshly cut flowers. This was known as "going-a-maying." A long, straight pole was set in the center of town and decorated with the fresh flowers, and colored ribbons anchored to the top of the pole. The celebration ushered in the spring and expressed hopes for happiness and a good harvest.

How the Palo de Mayo got to Bluefields and the Atlantic coast of Nicaragua remains a mystery, though it was very probably brought directly from England during the years the Atlantic coast was a protectorate of that country. Another theory suggests it was brought indirectly by way of Jamaica, where it evolved into something more Caribbean and erotic. To date, the Palo de Mayo is celebrated,

due to English influence, in such disparate locales as Austria, Spain, and amongst the Wenda and Galla people of Africa.

The Palo de Mayo refers to two things: a massive celebration and outpouring of joy held the first of May every year in Bluefields, Pearl Lagoon, and the Corn Islands, and it is also the name of a dance and style of music. The dance has gotten progressively more sensual in recent decades—sometimes appearing as simulated sex on the dance floor—and the more conservative Costeños have started a movement to return the dance to its more respectable origins.

Most cultural presentations on the Atlantic coast and elsewhere in Nicaragua include a version of the Palo de Mayo that you should make an effort to see, if possible. Set typically to the tropical rhythms of Dimensión Costeña, the popular Bluefields band, dancers in brightly colored satin costumes go through a series of provocative routines of gyrating hips and shimmying chests.

but when you learn to dance the "hug-up" you'll discover you don't need the space, since the only movement is a sensual grind from the hips down. Watch out for scam artists and shady drug deals. Located about six blocks south of city center and known by all. Take a cab at night. **Blue Lagoon** is right on the main drag, and **Caimitos** is located south toward Four Brothers—both specialize in island *soka* and reggae music.

Disco Bacchus, half a block south of the central park, and **Wallabees** (one block south and one west) are more typical of what you'd find on the Pacific side of Nicaragua—i.e., *puro* salsa and merengue.

ACCOMMODATIONS

There are a wide range of options in Bluefields; for safe and clean, expect to pay more than what you would on the other side of the country. If you do decide to go for one of the budget hotels, you'd be wise to check several out and carefully assess their security measures before booking a room, including paying attention to the kind of people hanging around.

Under $10

Hotel Claudia has 10 rooms near the market for $6–11, tel. 822-2376. Around the corner, **Hotel Hollywood** has more services than Claudia with comparable prices, and with a few high-end rooms as well (with private bath, TV, a/c), tel. 822-2282.

Moving away from the water, **Hospedaje Pearl Lagoon** has nine semi-sketchy rooms starting at $5, with private bath, laundry, and a strongbox, tel. 822-2411. **Lobster Pot** has a restaurant and a row of rooms with fan and private bath, also for $5. **Dorado,** on the same block, has 15 rooms with TV, private bath, fan, and a big bed for $7–11, tel. 822-2365. A block north, across from the Lotería building, **Hotel Costa Sur** has 13 second-story, bare-bones rooms with private bath and access to a nice balcony for $6 s, $10 d, tel. 822-2452.

$10–25

Across from Bancentro, **Mini-Hotel** is central and clean, and run by great people; 10 rooms at

$10 per person, TV and a/c, tel. 822-2362. **Hotel Caribbean Dream** is an excellent midrange option, right on the main drag (across from Hotel Hollywood). In addition to 22 secure (and surprisingly quiet) rooms, Caribbean Dream has a breezy balcony with a view of both the street activity and the bay; rooms with private bath, fan, a/c, TV, start at $12, tel. 817-0107. On the street to the dockside municipal market, **Marda Maus** charges $11 s or d for its 12 rooms (fan, laundry, TV, bar, restaurant), tel. 822-2429.

$25–50

Hotel Bluefields Bay is an elegant bed-and-breakfast, right next to the water in Barrio Pointeen with 10 rooms ranging for $27–50; TV, telephone in room, a/c, and (expensive) Internet access, tel. 822-0120, email: kriol@ibw.com.ni.

Just east of the park (near the ENITEL tower), **South Atlantic I** has 24 rooms for $26 s, $45 d, $55 t; bar/restaurant, laundry, private bath, a/c, fax, and TV, tel. 822-2242. Its sister hotel is just south of the Moravian Church: **South Atlantic II** has 18 rooms, $32–58, with private bath, a/c, TV, phone/fax, and laundry service, tel. 822-2265. **La Casona,** located across from Disco Bacchus, has nine rooms for $22 s, $40 d; includes breakfast, private bath, TV, and a/c, tel. 822-2436. Restaurant downstairs.

FOOD

This is one of Bluefields's fortes, and you'd be a fool not to take advantage of being in seafood central. While fish is more common than meat in most restaurants, there are still abundant and cheap options for the hardcore carnivore, including the ever-present chicken chop suey. Many of these places also sell *comida corriente* (which can be made for vegetarians) for under $3, like the **Glorieta Peach Pit** in Parque Reyes, also specializing in tacos and *frito* for $1. **Kati,** in Barrio Central across from Miscelánea Eddi, serves up steak, chicken, and pork dishes for $1.50; check across from the Lotería building for a nightly no-name *fritanga*.

La Fogata, next to Bancentro, serves up breakfast, chicken, tons of seafood, and in November, a "Thanksgiven Dinner"; most meals under $4. Across the street, the **Mini-hotel Cafetín** has great breakfasts, burgers, a big menu, and ice cream to top it off. Breakfast, fresh cake and bread, and ice cream can be had at **Los Pipitos,** open 7:30 A.M.–9 P.M.

There are three options for waterside dining, the nicest of which is found at the **Manglares Restaurant,** located beneath the Hotel Bluefields Bay and extending over the water on its own dock. Watch the sunset as you enjoy the breeze and lobster from $5, tel. 822-2143. On the opposite side of the waterfront, you'll find the **Bella Vista,** tel. 822-2385, just south of the police station, and **El Flotante,** which also has a dance floor, tel. 822-2988.

Pesca Frita has a dimly lit, pleasantly convivial atmosphere. It's located on the corner next to Caribbean Dream and has reasonable seafood prices. If you feel like getting out of the downtown area, grab a cab to **Restaurante Loma Rancho,** atop the hill behind INATEC (Instituto Nacional Tecnológico). There's a great view from the balcony of the **Mirador Restaurant,** looking out over the greenery south of town; serving seafood, pork, beef, and chicken, tel. 822-1781. There's also a nice restaurant at the airport, if you're waiting for a flight, tel. 822-2862.

Walk one block south from the *Alcaldía* and turn right for a cluster of three well-known local restaurants, starting with **Sal Mar,** open 4 P.M.–midnight, and specializing in chicken, seafood, and soups, tel. 822-2988 or 822-2128. Across the street, **Tauro's** is a good choice to sample the famous *rondon* (or "rundown") soup, tel. 822-2492. Finally, on the same block, the highfalutin' **Chez Marcel** is, and for decades

MUSIC AND RADIO

Bluefields likes its music loud. You'll hear the reggae bumping wherever you go, and in all its different versions: dance hall, roots, *soka, punta,* Palo de Mayo, *reggae romantica,* and of course, long sets of the eternal king, Mr. Marley. Interestingly enough, the Atlantic coast's second favorite is country music from the United States. We're talking roots country like George Jones, Tammy Wynette, and Merle Haggard—real "tear in yer beer" twangers that residents proudly claim as their own "coastal music."

Bluefields is home to nine (count 'em) radio stations! Check out programs like "Roots Rap Reggae" (9 A.M. on Radio Zinica, 95.9 FM), "Energía Volumen" (4–6 P.M. on Radio La Morenita, 102.1 FM), and "Caribbean Breeze" (1 P.M. on Radio Punto Tres, 90.7 FM). The Voice of America is heard daily at 6 A.M. on Radio Bluefields Estereo (96.5 FM), followed by a country music show.

has been, the most exquisite dining experience in Bluefields; this means impeccable service, folded cloth napkins, and credit card service; fresh fish and lobster run around $9–12 in air-conditioned splendor (open noon–3 P.M. and 6–10 P.M., tel. 822-2347).

SHOPPING

The municipal market is an enclosed building connected to its own dock, where, every morning, dugout canoes paddle up to unload heaps of fruit and fish. The bustling *barrio central* is lined with stores selling most food and other items you may need. As for *artesanía,* there's an extremely talented woodcarver named Julio Lopez who has made a good name for himself and who sells his goods out of the store in the Hotel South Atlantic.

INFORMATION

Long ignored by the central government's tourism institute, Bluefields has finally been graced with its very own inefficient INTUR office, tel. 822-1111. The delegate there has very limited information about taking area trips and may know if there are any new tourism operators in the area. The *Alcaldía*, across from the southeast corner of the park, occasionally has a bulletin board listing upcoming cultural events. Also, check out the photos, articles, and listings on www.bluefieldspulse.com.

SERVICES
Phones and Mail
The original ENITEL building is found at the

bottom of the giant red-and-white antennae; the new one is across the street and a half-block toward the park. The post office is a half-block west of the Lotería building, tel. 822-1784, and there is at least one Western Union in town.

Banks
Banco Caley Dagnall is the older of the two banks on the Atlantic coast, located in front of the Moravian Church, tel. 822-2775 or 822-2261. Bancentro is around the corner on Calle Cabezas, tel. 822-0227. Both are open Monday–Friday 8:30

ATLANTIC COAST FLIGHT SCHEDULE

Convenient and regular flights are provided every day by two carriers with a fleet of single- and twin-prop puddle jumpers. All flights between Managua and Corn Island land briefly in Bluefields to transfer passengers and cargo. Because of the steady schedule, it's easy to buy an open return ticket, giving you flexibility on how long you decide to stay. This could be a risky strategy during the high season though, especially if you absolutely must be back in Managua on a certain day.

Airlines
Atlantic Airlines

Managua:	tel. 222-5787 or 222-3037, fax 228-5614
Bluefields:	tel. 822-1299 or 822-0259
Corn Island:	tel. 285-5055 or 285-5151
Email:	reservaciones@atlanticairlines.com

La Costeña

Managua:	tel. 263-1228 or 263-2142, fax 263-1281
Bluefields:	tel. 822-2500
Corn Island:	tel. 285-5131/2

Flights
Managua–Bluefields

La Costeña	6:30 A.M., 10 A.M. (except Sun.)
Atlantic	6:45 A.M., 10:30 A.M., 2:10 P.M.

Bluefields–Managua

La Costeña	7:40 A.M., 8:40 A.M., 11:20 A.M. (except Sun.), 4:10 P.M.
Atlantic	9:10 A.M., 11:45 A.M., 4:35 P.M.

Corn Island Flights
Managua–Corn Island

La Costeña	6:30 A.M., 2 P.M.
Atlantic	6:45 A.M., 10:30 A.M., 2:10 P.M.

Corn Island–Managua

La Costeña	8:10 A.M., 3:40 P.M.
Atlantic	8:35 A.M., 4 P.M.

Managua–Puerto Cabezas

La Costeña	6:30 A.M., 10:30 A.M., 2:30 P.M.
Atlantic	6:30 A.M., 10:30 A.M.

Bluefields–Puerto Cabezas

La Costeña	12:10 P.M.

Puerto Cabezas–Bluefields

La Costeña	11:10 A.M.

BLUEFIELDS EMERGENCY NUMBERS

The fire department is just north of the Moravian church, tel. 822-2050; the police are on the same side of the street, three blocks south, tel. 822-2333 or 822-2432; and the Red Cross can be found in Barrio Fatima at tel. 822-2582. Bluefields's Hospital Ernesto Sequeira is located about five blocks south and west of the park, tel. 822-2391 or 822-2621.

A.M.–4:30 P.M., Saturday 8 A.M.–noon. Look for money changers on the corner opposite Bancentro.

Internet
Bluefields has its own server and relatively quick service at several places. URACCAN's Ciber Blue Café is the cheapest, with the breeziest and best view to boot—but it's the most out of the way, on campus north of town; $2 per hour, open Monday–Friday 8 A.M.–5:30 P.M. (closed noon–1:30), Saturday until noon only. Caribbean Coast Cyber Cafe is connected to the human rights offices of CEDECHA, across from Los Pipitos, open on a complex, part-time basis. Costs nearly $5 an hour. Probably the most professional operation, the Ocampos and Mejia Internet Café, a block south of the big ENITEL antenna, charges $3 an hour and is open Monday–Friday 8 A.M.–7:30 P.M., closed for lunch; Saturday until noon.

Film
The Kodak store is located in the Barrio Central, open Monday–Friday 8 A.M.–6 P.M., Saturday 8 A.M.–2 P.M., tel. 822-2050.

GETTING THERE AND AWAY
By Land
The legendary overland route is the true stuff of travel stories. Leave Managua at night, endure a nine-hour, dusty, rutted-out bus ride from hell to the river port of El Rama; then, in your sleep-deprived dream-state, board an early morning *panga* and soak up two hours of fresh air, sunrise,

and a beautiful trip down the Río Escondido to Bluefields. Choosing this route saves some money, it's true, but its real appeal is that—more than the easy flight—it will allow you to appreciate both Nicaragua's massive girth, and the historically important geographical isolation of the Atlantic coast (see El Rama section for more bus information).

By Air
Both La Costeña and Atlantic Airlines offer regular, daily flights between Bluefields, Managua, and Corn Island. The trip to and from Managua takes about one hour and costs $45 each way. It is entirely possible to buy a Managua–Corn Island ticket with a couple days' stopover in Bluefields to explore the area. This will save you a few bucks, and they can be flexible if your plans change. Once in Bluefields, make ticket arrangements with either of the two airlines by calling or visiting the airport, or by dealing with one of their many ticket brokers around town—look for the Costeña and Atlantic signs at numerous hotels. See Atlantic Coast Flight Schedule special topic for flight times and contact information.

By Boat
Most passenger boat traffic passes through the main municipal dock where Transporte Vargas Peñas operates a fleet of 24 *pangas*. In addition to regular service to El Rama, Pearl Lagoon, Bluff, and other nearby communities,

BOAT VOCABULARY

Although there are as many different kinds of watercraft as there are Atlantic coast cultures, they are generally grouped into a few categories that are important for the traveler to know. *Pangas* refer to the water taxis used to shuttle passengers around the area. In general, they are powered by motors, are 23 feet in length, made of fiberglass with wooden benches, and seat 16–20 people. *Lanchas* usually refer to smaller motorboats and fishing vessels. *Canoas* are wooden dugout canoes. *Barcos* are bigger, slower ships for fishing, cargo, and sometimes passengers.

they can arrange special trips to any of the cays, or more distant points to the south, like Monkey Point and even San Juan del Norte (gasoline costs $3 a gallon, and the hazardous, open-water journey to San Juan del Norte would run at least $200).

To Corn Island, it's a long, rough, diesel-belching ride, but only costs $4, which is more than 10 times less than a plane ticket. Leaves Bluefields Wednesday at 8 A.M. and returns the following day. Take lots of water, sun protection, and your sense of humor.

Near Bluefields

EL BLUFF

Swimming in the waters of Bluefields Bay will get you a quick trip to the fungus farm, but a short $2 *panga* ride to El Bluff grants you access to the clean Caribbean. El Bluff is set on the spit of land that separates Bluefields Bay from the ocean, and before Hurricane Joan breached the bar, it was connected to Bluefields by land. Nearly all of Bluefields's major port and fish packing facilities are located on the inland side of El Bluff in a harbor built by Bulgarian engineers in the 1980s with hopes of creating a supertanker port. Wander around the docks and check out the enormous steel ships of Nicaragua's Atlantic fishing fleet.

Pangas leave for El Bluff all day from the municipal dock in Bluefields, setting sail as soon as they fill up with passengers. The last return boat is 4 P.M.—miss it, and you'll have to stay in **Hospedaje El Bluff,** eat in one of several restaurants, and dance in the community's sole disco.

RAMA CAY

Ten kilometers south of Bluefields, in the middle

Moravian church in Pearl Lagoon

© JOSHUA BERMAN

COMMON FISH FOUND ALONG THE ATLANTIC COAST

Queen triggerfish	Pejepuerco cachuo	Balistes vetula
Blue tang surgeonfish	Navajón azul	Acanthurus coerelus
Squirrelfish	Candil gallito	Holocentrus ascensionis
Atlantic spadefish	Paguara	Chaetodipterus faber
Yellowtail snapper	Rabirrubia	Ocyurus chrisurus
Puddingwife wrasse	Doncella arco iris	Halichoeres radiatus
Blue parrotfish	Pez loro	Scarus coeruleus
Chub mackerel	Estornino	Scomber japonicus
Bar jack	Cojinua carbonera	Caranz rubber
Hogfish	Doncella de pluma	Lachnolaimus maximus
Caesar grunt	Ronco carbonero	Haemulon carbonarium
Red grouper	Mero rojo	Epinephelus morio
Great barracuda	Picuda barracuda	Sphyraena barracuda
French angelfish	Cachama negra	Pomacanthus arcuatus

of the bay, is Rama Cay, the ancestral home of the Rama people. From an unknown tribal origin, the Ramas came to inhabit Rama Cay centuries ago, where they remained largely unaffected by the political turbulence that surrounded them. Then, in July of 1984, Sandinista troops hunting down indigenous supporters of the Contras strafed the island in a vicious air attack. Inhabitants had gotten word of the impending assault and had all escaped to Bluefields, leaving the Sandinistas to devastate an island on which not a single person was to be found. The Ramas returned to their island shortly afterwards, going back to their lifestyle of fishing and harvesting oysters. Today, the population is around 1,000, and visitors are welcome. Getting to Rama Cay is an easy, $4 *panga* ride from Bluefields and about an hour crossing the bay. You'll find a tropical haven of fruit trees and grasslands, crisscrossed by footpaths paved with oyster shells. The pastor's family, the McReas, live across from the Moravian Church and may rent you a room for the night.

GREENFIELDS NATURE RESERVE

Located some 30 kilometers up the river toward Pearl Lagoon (and eight kilometers inland from the sea), Greenfields is a publicly protected wildland, privately managed as an ecotourism business by a Swiss couple who have been living in Nicaragua for 20 years. The prices are steep, but they include lodging, meals, and guided tours over 25 kilometers of trails, and three kilometers of canoe routes through the mangroves. You will be isolated in a silent wilderness, surrounded by wildlife and lush vegetation. There is a three-night minimum stay that costs $235 for one person, $330 a couple, and $520 for four people, which, at present, is the maximum capacity. To arrange a visit, call the office in Managua at tel. 268-1897, email: vero@ibw.com.ni.

PEARL LAGOON

If you dig that isolated, end-of-the-road feeling, hop a boat to Pearl Lagoon, 50 kilometers to the north. Pearl Lagoon is a quiet, clean, and safe Caribbean community, especially compared to Bluefields. Signs posted along the sandy streets exhort citizens to "clean up your own mess" and "bury dead animals before they stink." If nothing else, Pearl Lagoon is a pleasant place to experience, with access to a wonderful Caribbean beach and day trips to indigenous river communities and the enchanting Pearl Cays.

Pearl Lagoon's economy is taken from the water—you'll see the wooden fishing *pangas* and

MISKITO VOCABULARY

The Miskito language doesn't use the vowel sounds "e" (as in bread) or "o" (as in boat), which makes it a flowing, rhythmic language of "a," "i," and "u," as in the following sentence, which exhorts the locals not to let the Yellow Coconut Virus infect the coconut plantations: *Coco lalahni taki pruiba sikniska alki takaskayasa.*

Here are a couple of words you might come across during your travels in the northeast:

Hello	*Naksa*
Goodbye	*Aisabi*
What is your name?	*Ninan dia?*
How are you?	*Nakisma?*
Fine	*Pain*
Bad	*Saura*
Sick	*Siknes*
Bye-bye	*Aisabe*
Thank you	*Dingke pali*
Food	*Plum*
Toilet	*Tailet*
Water	*Li*
Help	*Help*
Dirty	*Taski*
Clean	*Klin*
Meat	*Wina*
Chicken	*Kalila*
Rice and Beans	*Rais n bins*
Fish	*Inska*
Small boat	*Duri*
Lagoon	*Kabu*
River	*Awala*
Birds	*Natnawira nani*
Parrot	*Rahwa*

dugout canoes down by the water's edge, and the larger fiberglass craft that venture to deeper waters of the ocean. There are five companies in Pearl Lagoon that have to do with fishing and seafood processing. Denmark and Norway have been very active in the economic development of the region, constructing the municipal piers in Pearl Lagoon, Haulover, Tasbapauni, Kakabila, Brown Bank, and Marshall Point with the goal of helping fishermen get their catch to market.

Of interest in town is the iron cannon parked in front of the ENITEL building, referred to as the "great gun" by locals. It is embossed with the seal of the lion and unicorn, symbol of the British empire, and an engraved date: 1803. There is also a whitewashed Moravian church with its typically clean architectural lines. Attending an evening service there is a memorable experience (dress appropriately), reminiscent of oil-lantern and prayer book churchgoers in the 1800s in the United States. To the south of town is a small branch of URACCAN. If you are in Pearl Lagoon on the weekend, don't miss a night of reggae at the **Bucket,** a dirt-floor, thatch-roofed Caribbean disco. The area's four baseball teams—Sweet Pearly, First Stop, The Young Brave, and the Haulover Tigers—battle it out on Sundays during the dry season.

Accommodations and Food

For a cheap street snack, buy some proudly advertised "meat on a stick" in the evenings across from the ENITEL; mmm... soft strips of marinated, Caribbean beef—on a stick. Also, as you lazily walk the streets, always sniff the air for freshly baked coconut bread; act quickly and decisively when you pick up the scent and buy as much as possible.

Pearl Lagoon's first, nicest, and most successful tourist operation is the **Casa Blanca Hotelito y Restaurante,** owned and run by Danish immigrant Svend Friberg and his Nica wife Dell. The success of their business inspired no less than six *hospedajes* to spring up in recent years (all owned by native Pearl Lagoon families), glutting the weak market and resulting in rock-bottom prices all over town. The Casa Blanca is set several hundred meters back from the dock and has seven very nice rooms for $7–20. Svend runs a clean shop and, with the gaze of an ancient Nordic mariner, will look you straight in the eye and claim that his restaurant serves the best food on the Atlantic coast, pointing out the many non-fried seafood options he offers. He and Dell can arrange fishing and snorkeling trips, and boat or horseback excursions to nearby communities, tel. 822-0508.

Right on the main drag in front of the dock, **Sweet Pearly's** *hospedaje* and restaurant is another standby, with 11 small, clean rooms, $7 for fan, shared bath, $11 for a double bed and private bath.

The restaurant is excellent and serves a massive bowl of seafood soup for under $8, tel. 822-0512.

The **Bella Vista,** right across from the dock, has six rooms, private and shared bath, fan, and mosquito nets ($7–10, tel. 822-0512). Up the block is the **Green Lodge,** with eight rooms, run by the amiable Wesley and Arlene Williams; prices from $4 s, tel. 822-0507. Across the street and set back between the river and a noisy woodshop, **Hospedaje Estrella** has small, clean rooms, each with a fan and desk, shared bath, $5 s, $7 d. Thirty meters away and right on the water is a cluster of sagging wooden shacks for $5 a night, accompanied by Cherry Leño's smoke-stained kitchen.

A two-minute walk north from the dock will take you to the **Hotel and Restaurant Moonlight View,** on its own stilts atop the river. Marva Thyne offers 10 rooms for $7 a night and an open-air restaurant/disco with a beautiful view up the river.

Services

"Downtown" Pearl Lagoon is a toss-up between the lazy activity of the docks, and that at the iron cannon intersection, where you'll find the ENI-TEL office (tel. 822-2355, open Mon.–Fri. 8 A.M.–noon, 2–6 P.M.) and a police post. The health clinic is a few blocks south, to the right of the church. There is a computer project in town, and possibly Internet service; ask around.

Getting There and Away

The *panga* trip up the Río Escondido and then north through a complex network of waterways is a thrilling, beautiful ride that takes under an hour and costs $5 each way. On the way, you'll pass several shipwrecks, and also the active dock at Kukra Hill, named after a cannibalistic indigenous tribe once common in the area. Go to the municipal dock in Bluefields and sign up for the Pearl Lagoon *panga*. Only a couple boats make the trip, leaving Bluefields daily 7–9 A.M., depending on how fast they fill up. The last boat back from Pearl Lagoon leaves between noon and 3 P.M. If you really need to get back, be sure to make friends with your *panga* driver and get signed up on his list a few hours before he leaves.

Near Pearl Lagoon

The town of Pearl Lagoon actually sits on the

MODERN PIRATES AND THE PEARL CAYS

According to Nicaragua's autonomy laws, all 18 Pearl Cays off the coast north of Pearl Lagoon belong, in perpetuity, to the Nicaraguan government for the collective use of indigenous peoples of the region. Local residents and indigenous leaders have found it curious, then, as to how seven of these islands ended up "belonging" to a Greek-American real estate investor named Peter Tsoskos, who is selling them off at extraordinary (we're talking tens of millions of dollars) markups on the Internet.

The Pearl Cays possess important turtle nesting beaches, unspoiled coral reef systems, and drinking water supplies used by the Miskitos in the nearby mainland village of Set Net for hundreds of years. The islands are also important base camps for local fishermen. With the alleged sale, however, locals have been prevented from landing on some of the islands by armed squads of Nicaraguan police officers, allegedly hired as private guards by the new "owners." Official suits against Tsoskos, the Bluefields police chief, and the Pearl Lagoon municipal chief by leaders of indigenous groups have resulted in the national government's environment branch, MARENA, stepping in. In April 2001, MARENA ordered the sales and resales reversed and all development activity stopped immediately. They acted too late though, and to date, have not backed up their mandate.

Tsoskos, who claims that all the sales have been declared legal by the Bluefields court system, is also reportedly erecting buildings on the traditional Rama lands at Eagle Point, 60 kilometers south of Bluefields, and part of the Cerro Silva Nature Reserve, one of the last areas of virtually intact rainforest in Central America. Investigate for yourself at Tsoskos's website: www.tropical-islands.com.

© RANDY WOOD

the Pearl Cays

southeast side of a small prominence jutting out into the bay. Walk west from the town to get to the broad, shallow Caribbean beach community of **Awas.** It's reportedly no more than a half-hour walk down a flat, sandy road that crosses a saltwater estuary and a small footbridge. When you get to the Miskito community of Raitipura (Miskito for on top of the cemetery), turn left and follow the road to Awas. Rent a small palm-thatch hut from one of the locals for $2–4, kick back, and relax. You can also take a *panga* ride up into the Laguna de Perlas (the water body, not the town), and visit the communities of Orinoco and Marshall Point.

Farther up the coast, on the Caribbean side of the land, are the communities of Tasbapauni (two hours from Pearl Lagoon, no lodging) and the Man of War Cays. For your own adventure, investigate reports of a five-hour *panga* ride to **Sandy Bay Sirpe** (for $15 a person), just past the mouth of the Río Grande, where there are supposedly two $4-a-night places to stay and a local, ancient version of surfing. Let us know what you find.

The Pearl Cays

Despite the current controversy over their "ownership" and development by outside investors, most of the 18 utopian desert islands that make up the Pearl Cays are still untouched and accessible (for now). They are located six kilometers east of the small Miskito village of Set Net. Hire a boat from Pearl Lagoon and enjoy the ride through the harbor into the open Caribbean, then up the empty coastline to the cays.

The cays have zero tourist facilities (except for one high-priced, fully serviced "eco-lodge," wrapped up in the scandal). Be sure to bring drinking water, basic first aid supplies, and snorkel gear, plus a hammock if you plan on spending the night. Make a deal with your boatman—but pay the bill when he picks you up, not when he drops you off. A round-trip *panga* ride to the Pearl Cays can cost $150, so the more people chipping in the cheaper it'll be. If you find yourself sharing one of the islets with local fishermen, you may find them cutting down coconuts and telling fishing stories over a beach fire kitchen; strike up a deal for some fresh fish.

The Corn Islands

Eighty-three kilometers due east of Bluefields Bay's brackish, brown water, the Corn Islands are a pair of Tertiary period volcanic basalt bumps in a rainbow-blue Caribbean Sea, tempting you to take a taste of Eden. Indeed, tourism is the hope for the islands' sustainability, say many. Ever since local fish and lobster populations began to be stressed by the steadily growing human populations on both islands, poverty has risen. Of course, Hurricane Joan didn't help matters when she flattened the islands' thriving coconut industry in 1988, forcing a greater portion of Isleños to attempt to pull a living from the sea (or from Colombia, whose nearby San Andrés Islands are part of a major drug route). Today, the Corn Islands' seasoned batch of hotels and restaurants are hunkered down and awaiting your arrival.

BIG CORN ISLAND

Pirates on their way to maraud the coast of Central America and Nicaragua's Río San Juan first visited here in the 16th century, sometimes not by their own choice after running their ships up on the reefs. Corn Island was inhabited way before that though, by Kukra Indians, a subtribe of the Mayangnas. Their habit of consuming the bodies of their enemies (in a light coconut sauce, we're sure) inspired the first English visitors to call these the Skeleton Islands. The Kukra were soon exterminated at the hands of pirates and Miskitos.

The current population of nearly 8,000 is increasingly mestizo, now in the majority. The native islanders trace their roots to any of a number of points in the island's history. There are direct descendants from several of the more infamous European pirates, as well as that of English royalty and plantation owners—don't be surprised if you meet people with names like Kennington.

Corn Island is 10 square kilometers of forested hills, mangrove swamps, and stretches of white coral beaches. Several attempts by foreign investors to drain swamps critical to the island's freshwater system have been thwarted and even punished by community groups and the local government, but it's an ongoing battle. The highest points are Queen Hill, Little Hill (55 and 57 meters above sea level, respectively), and Mount Pleasant (97 meters).

The north side of the island is guarded by three distinct layers of reef, composed of more than 40 species of coral. The snorkeling is still impressive, but the reefs are considerably deteriorated, a result of overfishing, damaging algae (which grow as a result of increased nutrient levels in the water from sewage runoff), and sedimentation from the poorly managed hillsides of the island (not to mention the worldwide coral die-off due to global warming). Of the six sea turtle species swimming off Nicaragua's shores, four live in Caribbean waters. On land, Corn Island boasts three endemic species of reptiles and amphibians, all threatened by the continued swamp draining.

Orientation and Getting Around

From the airport, it's a five-minute westward walk to the waterfront, town park (a thin strip of grass and benches), and municipal docks with *panga* service to Little Corn. This "downtown" area is known as Brig Bay. The road is only paved for a short section through town, and for the rest of its circumnavigation around the island, it is in horrible condition, completely rutted and filled with messy puddles during the wet season (10 months of the year). The road is not quite a complete circle, with some funky offshoots near town. One of these leads to Southwest Bay, or Picnic Center, a 15-minute walk south of town, the widest, shallowest, and calmest beach on the island; it's also the most popular and gets downright crowded during peak seasons. The eastern side of the island is called Sally Peaches, and the community surrounding Long Beach is known as South End. Taxis cost under $1 to go anywhere on the island, prices double at night. Walking around the entire island would probably take about three hours.

THE ATLANTIC COAST

BIG CORN ISLAND

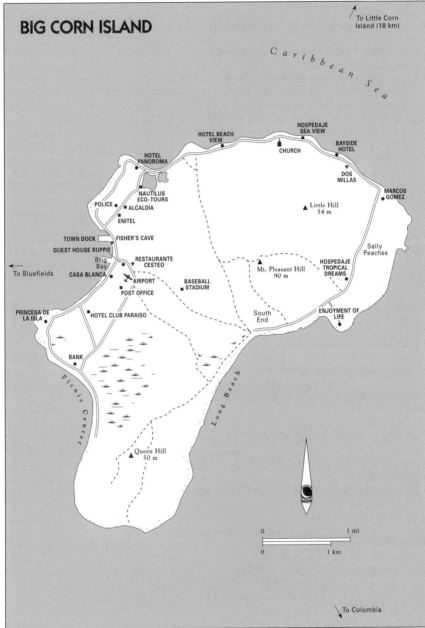

Caribbean Sea

To Little Corn
Island (18 km)

HOTEL BEACH
VIEW

HOSPEDAJE
SEA VIEW

CHURCH

BAYSIDE
HOTEL

HOTEL
PANOROMA

DOS
MILLAS

NAUTILUS
ECO-TOURS

Little Hill
54 m

MARCOS
GOMEZ

POLICE

ALCALDÍA

ENITEL

Sally
Peaches

TOWN DOCK

FISHER'S CAVE

GUEST HOUSE RUPPIE

Mt. Pleasant Hill
90 m

HOSPEDAJE
TROPICAL
DREAMS

Brig
Bay

RESTAURANTE
CESTEO

To Bluefields

CASA BLANCA

AIRPORT

BASEBALL
STADIUM

POST OFFICE

South
End

ENJOYMENT OF
LIFE

PRINCESA DE
LA ISLA

HOTEL CLUB PARAISO

BANK

Picnic Center

Long Beach

Queen Hill
50 m

0   1 mi

0   1 km

To Colombia

© AVALON TRAVEL PUBLISHING, INC.

Sights and Entertainment

There are no museums, but that's not why you came. **Picnic Center** is the most popular beach, followed by **Long Beach.** Also, walking the point between Enjoyment of Life and Sally Peaches is a gorgeous expedition. A sweatier affair is to hike up to the island's high points—ask at Nautilus for details. As for nightlife, hang loose in **Morgan's** in Brig Bay. Corn Islanders are serious about their baseball, with a huge stadium and a league of eight teams (including two from the Little Island).

Be here at the end of August for the ages-old **Crab Soup Festival.** This is a happy remembrance of the islanders' emancipation from British slavery in 1841 and the freed slaves' spontaneous celebration around a big pot of crab soup on the beach. Be sure to catch the crowning of Miss Corn Island, Miss Coconut, and Miss Photogenic.

Nautilus Eco-Tours

The island's only dive shop offers weathered equipment and the divemaster services of "Chema" Ruiz, a jolly Guatemalan with a wall full of framed scuba diplomas and an air compressor in his living room; he offers various dive packages and PADI courses for all levels, $15 for an introduction, $45 for a two-tank dive, $250 for open water certification. Chema also rents snorkel gear, bicycles, and can get you a guide to hike or bike the island's high points. Most importantly, his wife, Regina, makes the best cup of coffee on the entire Atlantic coast (no kidding), not to mention a mean lemonade, pizza, and wheat bread upon request. Nautilus also has a fully equipped house for rent, with a porch, kitchen, and seven beds for $50 a night, tel. 285-5077.

Accommodations

Unless you've got your own yacht parked in Brig Bay, you'll be dropping quite a few bones for your bed, at least compared to the rest of the country. The only rooms for under $10 are in **Hospedaje Brisas del Mar,** located across from the town park; you're taking your chances to save a cou-

ple of bucks at this grimy *pensióne* ($7 a person) with a rowdy country music cantina underneath its 11 rooms, tel. 285-5173. There are a couple of other *hospedajes* located in Brig Bay for $10 a person. They are **Guest House Ruppie,** near the airport, with six rooms, tel. 285-5162, and the **Casa Blanca** (painted blue), a couple hundred meters past the fish plant and along the beach, with eight rooms right near the water.

The **Enjoyment of Life Bungalows,** the most pleasant budget option, are on the opposite end of the island on their own isolated, sunrise-facing beach. Your taxi driver will know all about Ira's place at the end of a 200-meter spur road. Ira (who grew up on this land) has built six nice cabins with private bath and double beds which go for $20 a night. He also has a bar and simple restaurant, and camping in the dry season, tel. 285-5005.

The *hospedaje* at **Picnic Center** is the only place to stay on this beach; 11 rooms with private bath, fan, and big beds for $15 a night (per room). There's also a restaurant right there. It's a nice spot on the popular beach, but it wouldn't be the most intimate place among the crowds during peak seasons.

Traveling clockwise around the island from the dock at Brig Bay, you'll come across a handful of widely dispersed and more expensive hotels, most right on the water, but also right on the road. Just past the Catholic church, **Hotel Panorama** has a *cafetín* and 10 rooms with private bath, a/c, and TV; $30 s, $35 d, tel. 285-5065. Next up is **Hotel Beach View,** with a beautiful balcony, and a new group of annex rooms being built across the street with a/c and a restaurant for guests. Prices run $10–25 a room, depending on its position in the building, tel. 285-5062. **Hospedaje Sea View,** a 10-minute walk past the Baptist church, has seven rooms, $25, tel. 285-5021; another 10 minutes brings you to the Little Hill community and the **Bayside Hotel,** with 20 rooms starting at $35 (private bath, a/c, laundry service, bar-restaurant, TV, tel. 285-5001).

Up the road in Sally Peaches territory, **Dorsey Campbell** will rent you a house for $15 and has snorkeling gear for rent. Additionally, **Marcos and Jeanette Gomez** have many years' experience renting five rooms in their own house, two additional houses out back, facing the beach and reefs. Rooms run $11–$15, tel. 285-5187. Marcos is a founder of Corn Island's small business association (he also runs a kiosk in the park where he sells local crafts) and is extremely knowledgeable about his island.

Continuing around the island, **Hospedaje Tropical Dreams** on your right is actually two full houses for rent with 11 rooms total for $20–35 a room. It's a six-minute walk to get to the beach, but the rooms have fans or a/c (depending on price), private bath, and TV. Contact Irod Earlin Ruiz Lam at tel. 285-5056.

Alex and Catarina, a transplanted Italian couple from Rome, recently opened their hotel, the **Princesa de la Isla,** on the southern tip (Waola Point) of Brig Bay. Their three large, unique, and stylish furnished rooms go for $40 a night, which includes private bath, fan, and queen-size beds. They've got a beautiful, intimate Italian restaurant and kitchen—for guests only.

Hotel Club Paraíso, tucked away on its own grounds in Barrio Brig Bay, has 13 *cabaña*-style rooms for $33–55; private bath, fan or a/c, laundry service, and snorkel gear. The restaurant here is not cheap, but the variety and food are all right; from $4 breakfasts and $5 burgers, all the way up to the $17 surf and turf. Snorkel rental and a short walk to the beach, tel. 285-5111.

Food

The trick is finding hot-out-of-the-oven coconut bread, which usually comes out around midday. Sandra, 50 meters past the airport, has the best bakery and a number of cheap *comedores* grace the streets of Brig Bay. If you're waiting for a flight, the tiny blue house on the corner, **Restaurante Cesteo,** is a great place to hole up and eat lobster and fish for only $4.

There are only a couple of real restaurants outside the hotels. The most obvious is **Fisher's Cave,** right next to the dock, with a breezy deck over the turquoise water of the bay. The service is atrocious, and you're forced to listen to slot machine ruckus, but they prepare a good meal and

the view of the activity on the docks makes the long wait interesting. **Dos Millas,** toward Sally Peaches, is a classier option.

Shopping

There are a few *pulperías* in Brig Bay, plus some "commercial center" mini-supermarkets scattered around the island. For local crafts, your best bet is to try to seek out the local craftsmen and see what they have to offer. Marcos Gomez has a little kiosk in the park (across from the Good Time Comedor) where he sells local shell work and black coral. Plenty of people sell beautiful pieces out of abalone, tortoise shell, conch, etc. There is also a shop of Guatemalan goods on the porch of Nautilus.

Information and Services

An INTUR shack greets you as you try to walk away from the airport. The woman there may make you sign your name, after which she'll hand you a hand-drawn, totally inaccurate map of the island. Her walls are a useful bulletin board though; open Monday–Friday 8 A.M.–noon, 2–5 P.M., tel. 285-5160.

The post office is 50 meters south of the airport. There is no Internet on the island, but there is a fax machine at the Acopio across from Fisher's Cave for a steep fee. The cute little ENITEL building is on the road past the docks, right before the *Alcaldía* and across from the police (there are only four officers on the island, and they don't inspire much confidence). Corn Island has one bank, a Caley Dagnall over by the turnoff for Picnic Center. You need a passport to exchange cash or traveler's checks, and there are no credit card cash advances.

Getting There and Away

For air service, see the Atlantic Coast Flight Schedule special topic.

By Sea: The old ship that makes the five-hour run from the mainland leaves Bluefields Wednesday morning, and returns from Big Corn the following day. Contact the Emusepci office just inside the gates of the municipal dock for current ship schedules (tel. 285-5193); it's open 7 A.M.–5:30 P.M., and someone may be able to tell you more about the direct ship to and from El Rama, leaving here Monday, "sometimes Tuesday," and taking around seven hours. It apparently leaves El Rama on Thursdays. When asked what time it leaves and how much it costs, the answer was a deep, "I can't tell you dat one, boy," accompanied by laughter.

LITTLE CORN ISLAND

This is the humble, wilderness version of its big brother, a mere three square kilometers of roadless desert island, surrounded on three sides by nine kilometers of thriving coral reef schooling with wildlife. "La Islita" or "Little Island," as it is called by locals, is indeed a delicate paradise, visited by an ever-increasing number of travelers. Although there are accommodations for several ranges of travel budgets here, the rough ride across 30 kilometers of open ocean should serve to hold destructively large crowds of tourists at bay.

Orientation and Getting Around

Unless you make special arrangements with your *panga* driver to take you elsewhere, you will be let off to wade up to the southwestern-facing beach, where you'll find a cement sidewalk that runs the length of the village. This is also called the "front side" by islanders and is the center of most social activity. Walking north on the sidewalk takes you up to the school, baseball field, and telephone office, as well as the dirt path that leads through the heart of the island and out to the other side. Walking the other way takes you to another cross-island (shorter) path to the "breezy side" of Little Corn. Circumnavigating the island on the beach is not possible, interrupted by the rocky points near Goat Beach and on the southern tip of the island, passable during low tide, but difficult; still, there are long, isolated stretches of beach to explore.

Sights and Entertainment

There is actually plenty to do on La Islita. In between meals, plan for beach hikes, snorkel excursions, and maybe a couple of reading-in-your-hammock sessions for good measure. The Casa Iguana offers fishing, snorkeling, and picnic trips, and most of the beachfront hotels have snorkel gear for rent. There is also a hike up to the lighthouse for a view of the surrounding horizon (go past the school and ask for directions).

The fishing remains extraordinary around Little Corn. Fish with a rod, spear, speargun, or even with your bare hands. There are lobster and sea urchin everywhere, and within a couple kilometers of shore, you'll find schools of kingfish, dolphin, amber jack, red snapper, and barracuda. Fly fishermen can catch tarpon and bonefish right from the beach, or hire Grant at Casa Iguana to take you out for $35 a person. Boat trips can also be arranged with a number of locals, or at the Hotel Delfines—ask around on the front side for a good deal.

As for dancing, check out the **Happy Hut** (a reggae-colored building on the front side) for a grinding good time on weekends. Or get your fight on at the "Bucket of Blood" Pool Hall, up near the school.

Dive Little Corn

This is Nicaragua's first, biggest, and most professional dive shop, right on the beach next to the Happy Hut. Services include daily morning and afternoon dives for novice through advanced divers, night dives by appointment, hourly and all-day snorkel trips, PADI certification courses, and kayak rentals. Most dives around the island are shallow (under 60 feet), but there are a few deeper dives that are over 100 feet. Little Corn's reef system is unique not only for its healthy abundance of wildlife, but also for its coral formations that include overhangs, swim-thrus, and the infamous shark cave. For up-to-date prices and more details, visit the website at www.divelittlecorn.com or email: info@divelittlecorn.com.

Accommodations

There are a handful of places to stay and eat on La Islita, each one catering to a different niche of traveler. **Derek's** offers a cluster of beach huts to the backpacker crowd, providing the most natural and difficult-to-reach accommodations on the island. Find him by taking the footpath past the

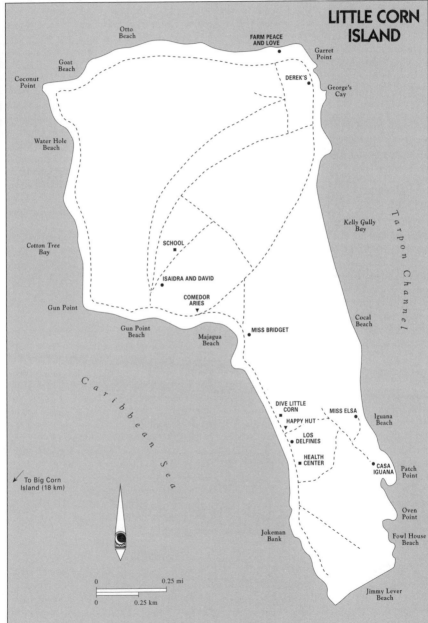

LITTLE CORN ISLAND

Otto Beach

FARM PEACE AND LOVE

Garret Point

Goat Beach

DEREK'S

George's Cay

Coconut Point

Water Hole Beach

Kelly Gully Bay

Tarpon Channel

Cotton Tree Bay

SCHOOL

ISAIDRA AND DAVID

COMEDOR ARIES

Gun Point

Gun Point Beach

Majagua Beach

MISS BRIDGET

Cocal Beach

Caribbean Sea

DIVE LITTLE CORN

MISS ELSA

Iguana Beach

HAPPY HUT

LOS DELFINES

HEALTH CENTER

CASA IGUANA

Patch Point

To Big Corn Island (18 km)

Oven Point

Jokeman Bank

Fowl House Beach

0   0.25 mi

0   0.25 km

Jimmy Lever Beach

© AVALON TRAVEL PUBLISHING, INC.

Little Corn Island: the view from Casa Iguana

school and into the woods, then by asking everyone you pass if you are on the right trail. Or, cross the island on the path to Casa Iguana, and walk north up the beach for 20 minutes or so, until you see a small blue structure and solar panel (the beach route is the most pleasant trip during the rainy season, when the inland path turns into pure mud). Alternatively, you can pay your *panga* driver a little extra to take you around and drop you right on Derek's beach. Derek's is constructed of coconut fronds, wild cane, and bamboo poles, and he is continually working toward his ever-organic vision of paradise; dorm-style bunks cost $5 a person, and private huts a couple dollars more; campsites available. Veggie and fish meals are $4–6 a plate. The beach here is beautiful, and Derek rents snorkel gear to explore the nearby reef—come live out all your *Gilligan's Island* fantasies.

If you'd rather have a more traditional structure between you and the elements, but are still on a budget, try one of three locally owned *hospedajes* on the front side, each charging $10 a room, single or double. **Miss Bridgett** is in the center of "town," and has 11 rooms; **Isaidra and David** rent rooms up near the school; and **Miss Elsa** has a house a couple hundred yards past Los Delfines.

Casa Iguana is a cluster of *cabañas* on the southeast, breezy side of the island, and is a long-time favorite among travelers. In addition to its private cabins, Iguana also has a communal, hilltop lodge where guests gather to eat, drink, and listen to the waves. The compound is run by two southerners from the United States, Grant and Cathy Peeples, who have brought their native hospitality and an effort to live harmoniously with their adopted environment. They have an organic fruit and vegetable garden, solar and wind power, and structures that feel very much a part of the landscape.

The two budget cabins go for $17 a room for a double bed (or two twins); there are five luxury rooms for $40 a night; one deluxe cabin for $75 a night, great for families or people who want a better-equipped little house. Reservations are encouraged, but cost a couple dollars extra—worth it if you don't want to risk being turned away after the long voyage out. There are no camping facilities, nor is the kitchen open for guest use.

Casa Iguana provides a host of services, such as snorkel gear rental, snorkel and picnic excursions to Goat Beach, fishing trips ($35 a person, "Guaranteed Catch"), and free satellite email for guests. Breakfast and dinner are offered, as is a cooler full of beverages—it all goes on your tab. Pay with dollars, cordobas, traveler's checks, or credit card. Grant and Cathy know the island well—above and below the waterline—and are always willing to help you plan your days. Email: casaiguana@mindspring.com, website: www.casaiguana.net.

Hotel Los Delfines is the only traditional hotel on the island; 14 rooms (a/c, private bath, laundry service), featuring a pink beachside porch with a western view of the water. Rooms start at $40, tel. 892-0186 or 285-5239, email: hotellosdelfines@hotmail.com. Inquire about various trips, including sportfishing and horseback riding.

Food

Nearly every accommodation offers meals, but feel free to get out and about to discover some other options. **Elsa's Great Food, Drinks,** offers just that, in a beachside barbecue setting on the east side of the island, just north of Casa Iguana. Give her plenty of advance notice; fish and lobster for $5 a plate, plus beers, hammocks, and natural shade. On the front side, find local food at the **Comedor Aries** or **Bridgett's First Stop Comedor.** Fresh coconut bread and buns are baked behind a hedge, near the church, or in the blue house past the school.

Arrange for a genuine Italian meal at the **Farm Peace and Love** (on the north side of the island, just past Derek's). Paola Carminiani will set you up with the real deal for about $8 a person; drinks are extra and include wine from the home country. She aims for quality over quantity and can accommodate up to 12 people for lunch, but plan your visit with her well in advance. Contact Paola by radio from Casa Iguana or the dive shop, and make a day of it swimming and snorkeling at her beach. Paola also has a guest room for $40 a

couple (plus breakfast), and a $20-a-night tent during the dry season, email: farmpeacelove@hotmail.com.

Services

There is an ENITEL on the front side near the school, and a limited service health clinic on the other end of the beach, down past Los Delfines. That's about it. Little Corn Island falls within Big Corn's municipal powers, but for the most part, is as ungoverned as it was during the days of the pirates. There are no police, no firemen, and electricity only when the generators for the fish plant ice-makers are on (or your solar panel is charged). Bring a flashlight.

Getting There and Away

Panga service to and from the Little Island costs $5 each way, takes about 40 minutes, and is coordinated with the departure and arrival of the two rounds of daily flights. The two *panga* runners are named Hilario and Tattoo, and both originate their service from Little Corn, staggering their schedules when demand necessitates. They begin their day with a 7 A.M. run from Little to Big Corn, returning to La Islita at 10 A.M. The next trip back to Big Corn is around 2 P.M., returning between 4 P.M. and 5 P.M.

The majority of the time, the ride to Little Corn is into the wind and very rough, especially when the seas are up. A smoother, safer ride is had by sitting toward the stern and by choosing to travel with Tattoo, who has a bigger, deeper boat and is much more sensitive to his passengers' comfort (just don't ask him to shout "Da plane! Da plane!," as tempting as it may be). Hilario hasn't lost a passenger yet, but he's been known to drive drunk, race his friends, and try to catch mad air. Another option is to rent your own boat and driver, which runs $60–80 each way. Charlie, on Little Corn, provides this service; he can be contacted through any of the hoteliers on the island.

No matter what the weather, it's a good idea to plan on you and all your belongings getting wet during the voyage—prepare by wearing rubber flip-flops and a bathing suit, and protecting your bags. The *pulperías* across from the dock on Big

Corn sell heavy, blue plastic bags that fit over a backpack for under $1—an excellent investment.

A number of larger fishing boats travel between the islands, and these may agree to take on a paying passenger. See Miss Bridgett for the day's schedule. Also, coming soon: boat service for up to 50 passengers between Bluefields and the Corn Islands on Captain Emíldo's ship, *The Adventurer.*

Puerto Cabezas (Bilwi)

Far away from everything, in the northeastern corner of Nicaragua, Puerto Cabezas (or just "Puerto," as it is affectionately known) is hard enough to get to that it may just as well be an island. Marginally connected to the rest of Pacific Nicaragua by semi-passable roads that turn marshy and unusable during most of the rainy season, most travelers prefer to fly to this outpost city. Puerto is connected to Bluefields by common heritage and history, but nothing more; no roads have ever linked the two major communities of the Atlantic coast.

Travelers searching for sleepy, isolated Caribbean settlements will find them here. In Puerto, the streets are nothing more than streaks of bare red earth connecting neighborhoods of humble wooden homes set on stilts. It's a glimpse of many worlds, with Miskitos sailing wooden canoes that share the old dock with steel fishing boats. Puerto is homely and accessible, and it's an easy walk from anywhere in town to the water's edge for a swim in the Caribbean. In spite of all the talk about drugs, you'd have to look hard to see any evidence. You can feel safe in Puerto and even walk around at night—it hasn't lost its innocence yet.

This is one of the most important economic centers for the Miskito communities of the northern Atlantic coast and the Río Coco. Outside of Waspám and the communities of the Río Coco, it's one of very few places in Nicaragua where you're less likely to hear Spanish than Miskito—or even Mayangna—spoken on the street.

THE LAND AND HISTORY

The Mayangna inhabitants that settled in Puerto Cabezas gave it the name "Bilwi," in reference to the great quantity of leaves ("wi") and the equally great number of snakes hidden in the foliage ("Bil"). Renamed after the general that President Zelaya sent out to the Atlantic coast to unify the nation, Puerto Cabezas—like much of Nicaragua's Atlantic coast—has seen more glorious days. Its zenith was probably at the start of the 20th century, when Puerto Cabezas was the center for exportation of Atlantic coast lumber and mineral products, especially gold. Its airstrip was, in 1964, the longest in Central America. Testimony to the wealth of Puerto Cabezas during the lumber boom is the enormous wooden dock that juts into the Atlantic, built in the mid-1940s out of locally cut hardwoods.

Somoza was well liked in Puerto and the northeast because he largely left the area alone. Puerto locals fondly recall the times Tacho would arrive on the Atlantic coast in his private plane, barbecuing with the locals and telling jokes. Their fondness for Somoza made the Sandinista

HOW THE MAYANGNA COUNTED THEIR DAYS

As told by Captain William Jackson in the 17th century

The Mayangna Indians of Cabo Gracias a Dios, when undertaking a lengthy journey or expedition, would find two lengths of rope. Tying one knot in each rope for each day they expected to be away from home, they would take one rope with them and leave the other one behind with friends or loved ones. Throughout the journey, they would loosen one knot for each day they traveled. Their family back home did the same and knew, if the traveler didn't return before all the knots had been untied, that something had happened.

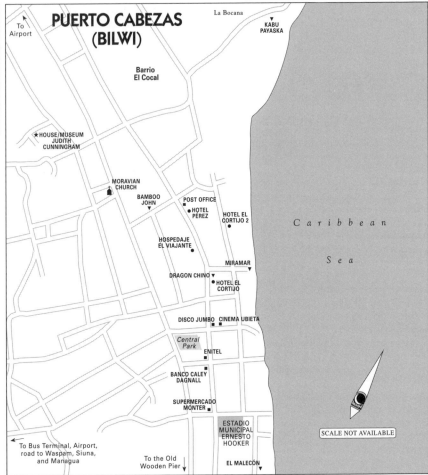

PUERTO CABEZAS (BILWI)

To Airport

La Bocana

KABU PAYASKA

Barrio El Cocal

★ HOUSE/MUSEUM JUDITH CUNNINGHAM

MORAVIAN CHURCH

BAMBOO JOHN ▼

POST OFFICE

● HOTEL PÉREZ

HOTEL EL CORTIJO 2

HOSPEDAJE EL VIAJANTE ●

Caribbean

Sea

MIRAMAR ▼

DRAGON CHINO ▼
● HOTEL EL CORTIJO

DISCO JUMBO CINEMA UBIETA

Central Park

ENITEL ■

BANCO CALEY DAGNALL ■

SUPERMERCADO MONTER ■

ESTADIO MUNICIPAL ERNESTO HOOKER

← To Bus Terminal, Airport, road to Waspam, Siuna, and Managua

To the Old Wooden Pier ↓

EL MALECÓN ▼

SCALE NOT AVAILABLE

© AVALON TRAVEL PUBLISHING, INC.

years even more bitter for the Miskito people. During the 1980s, Puerto absorbed the brunt of the refugee flow out of the Río Coco area when Contra and Sandinista incursions made day-to-day existence miserable and impossible for the Miskitos.

Today, with the war behind them and the people back in their ancestral homes, Puerto Cabezas is largely a coastal backwater of snapper and mackerel fishermen, and the commercial stronghold for the northeast. Its small economy is based on commerce—particularly of wood, fish, and transport. Puerto is the main hub for northeastern Nicaragua, including the mining triangle. The Nicaraguan military maintains a naval base here, from which it patrols the northern Atlantic coast and Miskito Cays. There are scattered jobs in the timber and fishing industries, and a lot of people looking for a legitimate way to earn a living. While a significant number of Puerteños work in government jobs—Puerto is not only the departmental capital, but also the center of the indigenous community's government as well—several thousand workers were laid off when the Chamorro government replaced the FSLN, and the city has never quite recovered.

Tankers from Venezuela and Curaçao periodically pull up at the dock to replenish the town's supply of petroleum products, and *pangas* line up along the lee side of the dock for passenger transport to the communities of the Atlantic coast. The town's future may drastically change in 2004, when a Louisiana-based engineering company's plan to revitalize the port is implemented. The revitalization involves replacing the old wooden dock with a modern port complex, complete with grain silos, a power plant, container storage, industrial cargo cranes, and facilities for deepwater tankers. If it comes to be, Puerto Cabezas will come back to life as Nicaragua's most vital Atlantic port. In the meantime, Puerto Cabezas is experiencing a wave of immigration from two sides: poor Miskito families from the Río Coco area in search of a better life, and wealthy families from Managua and the rest of the Pacific region who are starting businesses and buying beachfront properties.

GETTING AROUND

Puerto Cabezas has no bus system, though the mayor's office is trying to put a couple of local city buses in place. In the meanwhile, Puerto has—no joke—500 licensed taxis cruising the streets in search of fares. The price is fixed at about $.35 per person to go anywhere in town, with two exceptions: if you go from the airport all the way to the pier or all the way to the bus terminal you'll pay double.

SIGHTS AND ATTRACTIONS

The **Old Wooden Pier** is the mainstay of the town and certainly worth a look. Built in the 1940s of precious woods culled from the nearby forest, the pier is now on its last legs due to extensive hurricane damage, saltwater, and old age. Tied up there are usually a motley crew of old fishing freighters, Miskito double-ended sailboats, and small fiberglass *pangas*. The pier is beautiful during the day, but dangerous at night.

Near the center of town is an interesting **house/museum** commemorating the life and work of Judith Kain Cunningham, a local painter who left behind many works of art when she passed away in 2001 (entrance $1). A prolific artist and artisan, her subject matter was the Río Coco and the Miskito communities of the Waspám region, her passion for which shows through in many of her paintings; also on display are other works of macramé, sculpture, and more.

At the north end of town just past Kabu Payaska restaurant is **La Bocana,** a sandy Atlantic coast beach. Enjoy a swim or a splash in the surf, or walk north along the beach to explore **shipwreck** of an old fishing boat that wandered in too close to shore.

In Barrio El Cocal, in the northern part of town, the **Moravian church** has services in Miskito every Sunday morning. Puerto has several other pretty churches: the **Moravian church and school** in the center of town, the **Catholic church** with its stained glass, and the remnants of the former Catholic church behind it.

the old Catholic church in Puerto Cabezas

© RANDY WOOD

Located a few kilometers away on the road out of town is the local **URACCAN** campus. What's interesting about the Puerto branch is that during the 1980s it was a military base from which soldiers patrolled the northeast corner of the country. These days, its transformation to an institution of higher learning has been so complete you'd never guess its former incarnation. There's a good library, as well as people with a wealth of information about the area.

ATLANTIC COAST PLACE-NAMES

The names given to the land, the rivers, and the communities of the Atlantic coast celebrate the ethnic history of the region. Many names are of Mayangna origin, some are Miskito, and a few are Mayangna with a Miskito suffix thrown on the end. Also in the forests of the Atlantic coast are the communities of Chicago and Wisconsin! Besides the places of English or Creole origin, here are a few places of pre-Columbian origin:

Bilwi (Puerto Cabezas) "Bil" serpent, "wi" leaves. Refers to the great quantity of water plants from which the Mayangna extracted fiber and fabric, plus the serpents that inhabited those plants.

Karma "The source of water."

Matiguás "Mati" mouse, "was" water; "the river of mice."

Kurinwas "Kurin" a small wooden boat, "was" water; "the navigable river."

Kama "Iguana"

Kukalaya "Kuka" grandmother, "Laya" river.

Lamlaya "Lam" a large fish, like the dolphin, "Laya" river.

Wangki "The great river."

Orinoco Garífuna corruption of "Urunugu."

Tasbapauni "Tasba" land, "pauni" red.

Raitipura "On top of the cemetery."

Kakabila "The mouth of the kaka plant" (the kaka is a long, spiny palm).

ENTERTAINMENT AND EVENTS

Just east of the park is a brand-new movie theater, the **Cinema Ubieta,** built in 2001. It show films as soon as a week or two after the Managua theaters; admission is about $2, and it shows around two movies per week. In light of the sudden stiff competition, Puerto's original theater, on the corner facing the park, has taken to showing only after-hours adult films.

Disco Jumbo, on the east side of the park, is an old classic with a Caribbean feel that hasn't changed in years. Dance to the throbbing beat of *soka* and salsa; Tuesdays and Wednesdays are ladies' nights. A better atmosphere is found at **Miramar,** but the crowd is definitely a bit younger than at Jumbo. Tuesdays, Wednesdays, and Thursdays are ladies' nights. At both clubs, the entrance fee Tuesday through Friday is $.75, Saturday $1.50, and $2.25 for special events. Two other discos in town are rumored to be sketchy and/or unsavory: **Atlantico,** a bar, and the **Midnight,** located right across from the park and the favorite hangout of Puerto's late-night underworld.

Semana Santa in Puerto Cabezas is an unforgettable event that all overseas Puerteños try to come home for. The town sets up dozens of thatched-hut *ranchos* at La Bocana beach, and the party lasts all day and night for at least a week. Food, drink, music, and of course lots of Caribbean-style dancing—it's all here. Stumble back to your hotel room once in a while to rest and rehydrate.

SPORTS AND RECREATION

Baseball rules in the northeast and passions can run high during the height of the season. Check out games almost every weekend in **El Estadio Municipal Ernesto Hooker,** two blocks south of the park. A good homer can just about land in the Caribbean.

ACCOMMODATIONS
Under $10
Hospedaje El Viajante is the cheapest sleep in town, but you don't have to sacrifice your comfort

or safety. Nicer than it looks from the street, El Viajante has 30 rooms; with shared bath for $7, $21 for double-occupancy rooms with private bath, a/c, and cable TV. Three meals a day are served in the restaurant; Barrio Revolución, tel. 282-2263.

$10–25

El Cortijo has six rooms starting at $17, with a/c, cable TV, laundry service, parking, and phone/fax; Barrio San Pedro, Calle Comercio, tel. 282-2223 or 282-2340. **El Cortijo 2** is a second-generation affair, built and run by the son of the owner of the original. It's classy and elegant with stained hardwood interiors; it also has the best deck of any hotel in town, with a great view of the ocean from twin hammocks. Six rooms cost $21 per room for a double with private bath, a/c, and cable TV. It serves breakfast and light lunches.

Hotel Pérez (tel. 282-2362) has three classes of rooms, all set in a fancy old wooden house built in a style reminiscent of an old U.S. farmhouse. All rooms have their own bathroom, and several have a/c; $15, $20, and $25, depending on how fancy a room you choose, and even the cheap ones are nice.

FOOD

There are three excellent restaurants in Puerto Cabezas evenly distributed through town, all offering essentially the same menu of shellfish, fresh fish, soups, beef, and chicken. At the north end of town, the single best meal in the city can be had at **Restaurante Kabu Payaska** (Sea Breeze), serving seafood on a beautiful grassy lawn overlooking the ocean; $6–8 for lobster, shrimp, or fresh fish. More toward the center of town, **Miramar** is a fraction cheaper and has a view just about as good. Meals at night here can be unforgettable, as the moon rises out of the Atlantic in front of you. There's also dancing on weekends—in fact, some people think of it only as a disco. At the south end of town near the dock is **El Malecón,** with very much the same type of environment and menu.

If for some reason you get tired of fresh, cheap, delicious seafood, you can give your palate a

© RANDY WOOD

the "Be on Time" Diner

break at the **Dragon Chino,** which serves Nicaraguan-influenced versions of chow mein, egg rolls, and stir-fries. The fried wontons are a town favorite (of course you can get seafood here as well).

INFORMATION

For a taste of life in Puerto and Nicaragua's northeast, tune in one of the local radio stations for news and commentary—even more interesting if you speak Miskito. Radio Miskut (104.1 FM) has lots of Miskito music and other programming; they also present the Voice of America. Radio Van (90.3 FM) presents itself as "The Voice of the North Atlantic," but it throws in a cheesy *ranchera* song now and again just for good measure.

SHOPPING

Supermercado Monter is a surprisingly good store, offering a full selection of canned and dry goods, fresh foods, and basic housewares. A good place to stock up if you're headed north toward the Río Coco.

SERVICES

The post office is located northeast of the park (open Mon.–Fri. 8 A.M.–noon, 1:30–5 P.M., Sat. until noon). ENITEL is located a block southeast of the park, open Monday–Friday, 7 A.M.–9:30 P.M. Banco Caley Dagnall is located next to ENITEL, tel. 282-2211; being the only bank in town, the lines can be horrendous—you may easily have to wait 60 minutes to change money. Your best bet is at noon, when everyone else in town goes home for lunch; otherwise, bring a book. To date there is no Internet in Puerto Cabezas, but it's just a matter of time. Look for your first Internet café sometime in 2004.

There's a run-down municipal hospital a block from the bus terminal. It has well-trained staff but struggles to keep on hand even the most basic supplies, so, while it's adequate for basic treatment, you should probably leave the complicated procedures for elsewhere, preferably Managua.

GETTING THERE AND AWAY
By Air

A quick flight from Managua or Bluefields is the only practical way to get to Puerto Cabezas. From Managua, Atlantic Airlines has flights to Puerto departing at 6:30 A.M. and 10:30 A.M., and La Costeña has flights departing at 6:30 A.M., 10:30 A.M., and 2:30 P.M. (no 2:30 flight on Sunday). Atlantic Airlines has flights to Managua from Monday through Sunday at 8:15 A.M. and 12:15 P.M. (no 8:15 A.M. flight on Sunday). La Costeña has flights to Managua Monday through Saturday at 8 A.M., noon, and 3:30 P.M. and at 8 A.M. and

SPECIAL SAFETY CONCERNS FOR THE RÍO COCO AREA

The Río Coco area requires some special travel precautions to be safe. This is an area particularly prone to malaria and dengue fever outbreaks, due to its lowland and wet geography. All travelers to the Río Coco area should ensure they're taking chloroquine to prevent malaria, and take standard precautions to prevent being bitten by mosquitoes: keep your skin covered, try to stay indoors around 5 P.M., and use repellent. A major issue is the availability (or lack) of medical facilities and supplies in the region.

At the same time the Río Coco is venerated, it is also the public toilet for most of the communities that line its shores. Don't be surprised to see someone scooping a bucket of river water out for cooking just downstream of someone defecating. Although the water is usually treated with chlorine, you should pay extra attention to the food and beverages you ingest, and especially all water and water-based drinks. Treat all water with iodine pills or a portable water filter before drinking. That goes double any time you are downstream of Waspám. If you are not carrying bottled water

from Managua, it is recommended that you use a good water filter. While it is possible to purchase bottled water in Waspám, the supply is not always guaranteed, so don't rely on it.

Remember the Río Coco was a heavily mined area in the 1980s. Though the land mines have largely been cleared away, known mined areas still exist and have been cordoned off with ribbon or wire. Ask the locals before you go wandering—this is *not* a good place to go exploring. Additionally, the locals took care of some land mine clearing operations themselves, to speed the process of returning to their homes, by scooping up the mines and throwing them into the river. Some of them probably settled down into the mud, and others were carried downstream. Be wary at all times.

Finally, the entire Atlantic coast is experiencing the effect of drug trafficking from Colombia, and the Río Coco area is no exception. The delta at Cabo Gracias a Dios is a known point of entry for small smugglers who take advantage of the almost total lack of police vigilance there. Watch your back.

You can catch boats northbound from Puerto Cabezas.

noon on Sunday. The flight from Managua takes 90 minutes.

One flight per day (every day except Sunday) leaves Bluefields at 12:10 P.M., arriving in Puerto at 1 P.M. From Puerto to Bluefields, La Costeña has one flight per day every day except Sunday leaving at 11 A.M. In Puerto Cabezas, the Atlantic Airlines phone numbers are 282-2586, 282-2255, or 282-2523; La Costeña can be reached at 282-2255 and 282-2586.

By Land

The municipal bus terminal in Puerto Cabezas is located a bit west of town just past the Puente Nipco along the road that leads out of Puerto (the one with the statue at its terminus). From here catch the morning buses to Waspám, and many of the communities that border Puerto Cabezas (commonly called *Las Comunidades*).

The overland trip between the Pacific region and Puerto is one of Nicaragua's most promising and, of late, most dangerous adventures. It consists of two to three days of run-down chicken buses, traversing the most poorly maintained roads in the country. But the potholes are the least of your worries—the trip takes you through the mining triangle (Siuna, Bonanza, and Rosita), all frequently visited by armed bandits looking for trouble and hostages. The police and army are currently dealing with the problem, and in the meantime, all foreign embassies in Nicaragua discourage travel to or through the mining triangle. When the situation mellows out, the trip starts at Jinotega's north terminal on a bus bound for Waslala; from there, you board a second bus to Siuna, and then another to Puerto Cabezas. There's an alternate road from Matagalpa to Siuna by way of Río Blanco and Mulukuku. Both roads are largely impassable during the wet season.

NEAR PUERTO CABEZAS

In **Tuapí,** just 10 kilometers north of Puerto, there's a popular swimming hole on the banks of the river by the same name. Buses leave for

Tuapí several times a day from the terminal in Puerto. It's also possible to travel by boat north or south along the Atlantic coast to visit Miskito communities. For points north make arrangements with a boat owner at the old dock in Puerto Cabezas. You'll have better luck in the early mornings when the boats are setting out for a day's fishing. Someday, travelers will have interesting adventures in the gorgeous beach-front community of Sandy Bay (two hours from Puerto Cabezas) and the Miskito Cays (two hours across the open sea from Sandy Bay), but as of press time, both locations are known rendezvous points for drug runners and other dangerous types.

For points south take a bus or taxi ($5 per person) to the community of Lamlaya. From there, you can hire a boat to take you to Haulover, Karatá at the mouth of the Río Wawa, and Prinzapolka, quite possibly the single hardest destination to reach in Nicaragua. Prinzapolka is also statistically the poorest town in the nation. You should have a basic command of Miskito to visit these communities on your own, to avoid suspicion as well as to be able to communicate.

Tours to the Miskito Communities of the Atlantic Coast

A more controlled way of visiting the communities is through **AMICA** (Asociación de Mujeres Indígenas de la Costa Atlántica), an organization making an effort to promote the empowerment and development of women along the northern Atlantic coast. AMICA gives training in gender development, reproductive health, leadership, and AIDS, plus the laws that affect indigenous women.

AMICA is developing tours to the Miskito communities of the Atlantic coast, with home-stays in some communities, and dance or cultural presentations in others. The accommodations aren't nearly as rustic as you'd think—the beds even have box spring mattresses, and the organization provides towels and so on. Prices vary depending on how many people travel and what you'd like to experience on the trip. In all cases, it's crucial to call ahead at least three days in advance so the dancers can limber up and the boatmen can tune up the outboards, tel. 282-2219. The office is located 2.5 blocks south of the baseball stadium.

Waspám and the Río Coco

Waspám, in the far northern reaches of the Miskito pine savanna and at the edge of the mightiest river in Nicaragua, is the gateway, principal port, and economic heart of the Miskito communities that line the banks of the Río Coco. It is, in itself, a difficult place to get to, yet it is really the first step of the voyage to places even farther away still. The communities here would prefer to be left to their own ways, but this has not been the case, and the Miskito peoples of the Río Coco suffered more than most during the 1980s, including a massive relocation that is still cause for resentment.

Adventures along the Río Coco are neither easy nor cheap, and accommodations and travelers' facilities in the traditional sense of the word are practically nonexistent. The chance to visit this frontier—and it is truly frontier, to live and travel amongst the Miskito people, and to feel the spiritual power of the mighty Río Coco should

not be missed. For a successful journey, travelers in this region absolutely must speak decent Spanish and make an effort to learn and use at least some rudimentary Miskito.

THE LAND AND THE PEOPLE

The Miskito people are reserved but friendly—once you've broken the ice you'll find them helpful and inquisitive. They like to be left alone but they will certainly greet you with a smile if you approach them. They're also more conservative than other Nicaraguans, so leave the short shorts and bikini tops back home. The Miskito people speak Spanish as a second language, and practically no English at all (even though some English words have been assimilated into Miskito, like rice and beans). Foreigners who speak languages other than Spanish or Miskito will inevitably be called *Miriki* (American). Even Nicaraguans from the Pacific region are considered foreigners and are referred to as mestizos. The Miskito people live largely off the river, fishing for small freshwater species, and off their small, neatly tended fields of corn, beans, and even upland rice. Their version of the ubiquitous tortilla is a thick, wheat flour cake which is fried in coconut oil. Starch makes up the rest of the diet along the Río Coco, including tubers like *quiquisque* and yuca. *Rondon* is a fish stew (and along the Río Coco it will be made of fish, not turtle, like on the coast), and the *gallo pinto* is cooked in coconut milk—there's no tastier way to clog your arteries. Wild game also finds its way onto the menu; don't be surprised to find boar, deer, and armadillo.

ENTERTAINMENT

Waspám has one small movie theater—if you call a video recorder projected onto a large screen a theater. Shows cost $1. There are two discos in town. **Ko Fu** is the liveliest, and plays variety of music, including Bryan Adams, the theme song from *Titanic,* and Palo de Mayo—cut a rug, Miskito style.

ACCOMMODATIONS

There are several lodging establishments, mostly offering shared baths consisting of bucket baths and pit latrines. Remember the Río Coco area is particularly prone to malaria and dengue fever. Make sure your *hospedaje* provides you with a mosquito net, or use your own. You can't rely on a fan to keep the mosquitoes away, as the electricity often fails or is cut off during the night. **Las Cabañas** is the most popular among foreign travelers, where you can sleep in a bamboo hut for around $3.50. **Hospedaje Vanessa** offers more modern rooms in a two-story cement building for around $7.

FOOD

There are several small eateries in town, most serving rice and beans accompanied by a hunk of meat, sometimes fish. You can ensure fish—or

TAKING PICTURES IN THE MOSQUITIA

In the lands around the Río Coco, you should always ask before taking pictures. Some people do not understand cameras and may have developed their own theories as to they are good or evil. Don't be afraid to snap pictures, however. In general, the Miskito people enjoy having their picture taken and, if you have a digital camera, enjoy seeing themselves. It's nice to make an attempt to send a copy of pictures to any special friends you meet, although using the Nicaraguan postal service to Waspám is a gamble. Don't make any promises you do not intend to keep, as it can foster bad feelings and leaves a bad reputation for future visitors.

shrimp—for dinner by arranging beforehand with a restaurant you intend to eat at later that day. Vegetables are scarce and any salad usually consists of cabbage and some tomatoes in vinegar; eggs are usually available as well. Ask to try some *wabul*, a thick, warm, green banana drink which has many variations. Coconut bread can usually be found at the market during the evening, when it's still warm from the oven, or early mornings. The restaurant **Funes** is well recommended and has a phenomenal view of the river. Traditional fare plus several dishes cooked with *chile cabro,* a spicy bonnet chili pepper grown only along the Atlantic coast.

SHOPPING

There are four larger stores besides the *pulperías* where one can pick up food supplies for trips up or down the river: El Chino, William White, Ruben Suho, and Chessman. The owners are friendly and can usually provide dependable information about the region.

INFORMATION AND SERVICES

Besides the people on the street, the current mayor and owner of the only gas station is a dependable source of information. Waspám finally has an

YATAMA AND THE STRUGGLE FOR INDIGENOUS SELF-DETERMINATION

Fraught with frequent reversals and setbacks, the struggle of Nicaragua's indigenous people for human rights, electoral privileges, and autonomy has never been easy. The Somoza government was popular in the Atlantic coast largely because Anastasio and his sons largely ignored non-Spanish speaking Nicaragua. The Miskito people of Puerto Cabezas fondly recall the days when Tacho would fly into the northeast for a visit, accompanied by tons of fresh meat he would distribute. To this day, Tacho is popularly associated with summer barbecues and relative isolation. The Sandinistas, however, paid quite a bit of attention to the Atlantic coast.

The FSLN came to power just when a sense of unity and independence was growing among the Miskito people. The new government gave the native peoples a unique opportunity to press for their own interests and historic demands. The Sandinistas moved quickly to attempt to incorporate the indigenous movement into their own organizational structure, but soon learned the Miskito people were not even remotely interested in being a part of any group led from Managua. The indigenous peoples of the Atlantic coast instead organized themselves into the political group Misurasata and renewed their fight for self-determination. The Sandinistas blundered badly in their early years on the Atlantic coast. Attempts to break up indigenous patterns of life and form state-sponsored cooperatives, mandates on which crops were to be planted and for how much they would be sold, and expropriations of foreign-owned companies alienated the indigenous peoples of the Atlantic coast from the start.

The Sandinistas met the growing resistance with violence and repression. Labor strikes and other organized disruptions led to a massive increase in government military presence, and in 1981 more than 30 Miskito leaders were rounded up and arrested on the grounds that they were inciting the indigenous peoples to rise up against the Nicaraguan state. Whether the charges were true or not, the arrests cemented the Miskito's mistrust of the new

government into hatred and many communities packed up and moved across the Río Coco to Honduras, where the Contras tried to win them over. The rancor was mutual: the Sandinista government broke ties with Misurasata, forcefully relocated the remaining Miskito villages to refugee camps outside of Puerto Cabezas, and burned the old villages to make sure roving bands of Contras couldn't make use of them.

Against insurmountable odds, Misurasata leaders like the controversial Brooklyn Rivera hoped to convert the entire Atlantic region into an autonomous, self-governing reserve for indigenous peoples. Sandinista minister of state Tomás Borge offered them instead a few concessions that, when accepted, eventually helped to restabilize the region: a limited form of autonomy and self-policing, and the chance to return to their ancient homelands. In 1987, after two and a half years of consulting with the Atlantic coast communities, the government went a step further in reaching out to the indigenous peoples of the coast, signing into law an Autonomy Statute.

The statute reshaped the Atlantic coast like nothing else had since the days of the British. It guaranteed self-rule and first-class citizenship for all minority groups on the Atlantic coast without sacrificing their cultural roots or identities. The statute permitted them to use their own languages, common land, and have a say in the development of the Atlantic coast's natural resources. The statute called for two 45-member coastal governments to be formed, one each for the northern and southern regions, responsible for governing trade, the distribution of goods, and the administration of health and education. The statute's one weakness was its flexibility, which opened the door for internecine feuds and leadership rivalries among Atlantic peoples.

The Miskitos who eventually found their way into the ranks of the Contras during the 1980s organized themselves into a group called Yatama (*Yapti Tasba Masraka Nanih Aslatakanka,* or Sons of the Mother Earth). With the advent of the Chamorro government, the Yatama Contras gen-

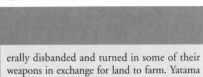

erally disbanded and turned in some of their weapons in exchange for land to farm. Yatama made the conversion from armed movement to political party. Chamorro's effort to stabilize the region, plus her government's respect for the newly created Autonomous Regions earned her the respect of the indigenous peoples.

In contrast, the government of Arnoldo Alemán has apparently tried to set the indigenous movement back a hundred years, causing the entire political climate in Puerto Cabezas and the Atlantic to become more tense as a result. Not lost on the indigenous peoples of the Atlantic coast is the auspicious fact that Alemán is of the same political party as Zelaya, who integrated the Atlantic coast at gunpoint a century ago. The now infamous Sandinista-Liberal "Pact" (see Introduction chapter) in which the Sandinista and Liberal parties essentially divided the government between themselves, imposed election criteria that makes it nearly impossible for small or new parties to get a foothold in the elections.

During the departmental elections of 2000, violence erupted when Yatama was completely excluded from appearing on the ballot or taking part in the elections. Representatives of Yatama vowed that unless they were permitted to participate in the municipal elections, there would be no elections. The military was sent to Puerto Cabezas and bullets flew in armed confrontations with protesters. Several people were killed. During the elections, there was significant Miskito abstention, resulting in the election of a Sandinista mayor.

Outspoken supporters of Yatama accused Alemán of trying to politically eradicate the indigenous community, leaving the Miskito, Mayangna, and Rama peoples to continued poverty and exploitation. Since many of the raw materials Nicaragua exports (such as wood, fish, and gold) are located in areas where the indigenous population has some claim to the land, the threat of political extinction is a real one. The struggle continues.

ENITEL phone office, after many years of struggle to have service installed (open most weekdays 8 A.M.–noon and 1–5 P.M., Sat. until noon). In a real emergency you might be able to look for the manager's house and ask for a favor. There is no Internet. The post office—really just a private home with a Correos de Nicaragua sign posted out front—is along the airstrip.

There is a local, under-equipped police station in town, and a health clinic with very basic services. The Catholic church has a private clinic with slightly better service and more resources; in case of an emergency go to the convent and tell the nuns. One of the attending doctors speaks good English. If traveling to the area, it is highly recommended that a preventative chloroquine dose be taken as recommended by your doctor because of the limited health services and the presence of endemic malaria.

GETTING THERE AND AWAY

Whether you get to Waspám by land or by air, remember there is a strong presence of drug dealers operating in the area. Under no conditions should you accept or agree to carry packages for someone else. The outcome of being a foreigner implicated in a drug-trafficking scandal would be drastic and horrendous, involving newspaper headlines and a jail stay in conditions you won't want to write home about.

By Air

La Costeña (tel. 263-2814) is the only airline that services the dusty little airstrip at Waspám. Upon approaching the runway, the pilot radios ahead to have someone shoo the cattle off the runway. Flights leave Managua Tuesdays, Thursdays, and Saturdays at 10:30 A.M. and Fridays at 9 A.M. The flight is about 90 minutes long over some of the most exotic scenery in Nicaragua: rugged mountains, tropical jungle that fades gradually into broad pine savanna. Upon landing at Waspám, the plane turns around immediately and returns to Managua, so flights from Waspám to Managua leave Tuesdays, Thursdays, and Saturdays at around noon, and Fridays at around 10:30 A.M. Be at the airstrip early to ensure you don't get left behind.

By Land from Puerto Cabezas

The trip to Waspám is a chance to experience scenery you won't find anywhere else in Nicaragua—the Miskito pine savanna. White pine species grow well in the poor soils of northeastern Nicaragua, and they're exploited commercially in pine farms along the road from Puerto. This area is about as flat as Nicaragua gets, and in many areas it is only a few meters above sea level. Spontaneous forest fires are not uncommon. Transportation to Waspám can be arranged in Puerto Cabezas. The grueling bus trip takes 3–4 hours when the road is in good condition and it isn't raining; in the rainy sea-

THE ATLANTIC COAST DRUG TRADE

Long the territory of pirates plying the waves in tall-sailed wooden vessels, Nicaragua's Atlantic coastline of sparsely populated rivers, cays, and hidden lagoons is now the haunt of drug merchants and traffickers transporting narcotics (primarily refined cocaine) from South America to the United States. Nicaragua is increasingly finding itself part of the shadowy and violent world of narco-trafficking that threatens to unravel the social fabric of the entire Atlantic coast.

During the 1980s, each Atlantic coast community had a Sandinista police force and a boat to patrol the coastal waters and estuaries. The governments that have succeeded the Sandinistas have done away with that police presence for lack of the resources to sustain it, and in the vacuum of power the Atlantic coast has become a lawless and virtually unpatrolled haven that plays easily into the hands of drug runners who land to reconsolidate, divide, or distribute their merchandise. The government and military's meager resources are no match for the well-equipped "Go-fast" boats sporting 250–500 horsepower engines with the latest in GPS, radar, and weaponry.

It's a well-known fact that many drug boats pass through the wilds of the Miskito Cays, an archipelago of islets, mangrove swamps, and trackless lagoons where the police have found stashes of gasoline used by drug boats headed north to the States. Other points of entry to Nicaragua include Cabo Gracias a Dios and the Río Coco, the city of Rama and the Río Escondido, the northern half of the Pearl Lagoon, and the community of Sandy Bay.

Other drugs come to shore when Colombian traffickers transiting Nicaraguan waters jettison their cargo into the sea when threatened with boarding or capture, either abandoning it or circling back later, using their ample knowledge of the Atlantic currents to predict where the packages will turn up on the beach.

Whether recovered off the beach by the locals or traded offshore by Nicaraguan traffickers, some of the Colombian cocaine inevitably makes it to the communities of the Atlantic coast, where its resale value is irresistible in a region with such rampant unemployment and a rapidly declining quality of life. No one knows for sure just how much coke is passing through Nicaragua's Atlantic coast, though the unofficial word on the street is that 10 kilos change hands every day in Puerto Cabezas alone.

At present, the issue of drug trafficking is far more serious than that of drug use. Even the local ministers have given up exhorting locals not to touch drugs, conceding it's all right to sell or transport drugs (but not use them) if it benefits the community. The reality of the area's poverty is too hard to overcome. But the situation is turning dangerous. In early 2001 three Colombians turned up dead in the coastal community of Sandy Bay, with no explanations; a popular rumor is they were killed by Yatama for trying to hook the locals on their product, which they were offering at ridiculously low prices. But even just aiding in the trafficking of drugs has deteriorated the coastal societies, which are suddenly caught in the kind of turf wars and gun battles that South Americans and the residents of inner cities of the United States know too well.

son the trip can take as long as six hours. Two or three daily Waspám-bound buses leave Puerto at the crack of dawn. The following day the same buses leave Waspám at the crack of dawn bound for Puerto Cabezas. Because all the buses leave their respective starting points in the morning, it's impossible to go and return in the same day.

Additionally, there's a truck that leaves Puerto Cabezas every morning between 5 and 6 A.M.— a lumbering, diesel-belching IFA—and many opt to travel with El Chino Kung Fu, a local character with a decent pickup truck that makes regular trips between Waspám and Puerto Cabezas. Ask around and try to form a group to share the costs. Bear in mind that hitchhiking runs the danger of being implicated as an accomplice to transporting narcotics.

RIVER TRIPS FROM WASPÁM

Waspám is your gateway to the Río Coco, and small boats—fiberglass *pangas* and dugout *batu* canoes—are your means of transport. Nothing is easy or cheap, by the standards of travelers accustomed to the prices of the Pacific side. In general, expect to pay $35–$100 per person per day for boat transportation along the Río Coco, which includes the boat, the gasoline, and the boatman. The price of fuel is the most critical factor. The dream adventure of course is a trip all the way to Wiwilí, the port at the upstream end of the river. El Bailarín makes the trip from time to time, but charges $1,000 round-trip per person for the extended voyage, which is over 550 kilometers each direction. Talk to local store owners or the mayor for pointers in selecting a good motorist.

Three small villages are located upriver between Waspám and Leimus. Visitors are not common and facilities are somewhere between limited and nonexistent. Don't plan on staying overnight or finding food for sale.

Waterfalls on the Río Yahuk and Río Waspuk

Two tributaries to the Río Coco, the Yahuk and the Waspuk, are both home to waterfalls the locals say are beautiful places to visit, but long trips. To visit the Yahuk, for example, you'd have to hire a boat for two days. The first day you can motor up the Río Coco to the Yahuk and continue upstream to the falls, then spend the night in San Carlos, and return the following day. The Waspuk falls are reportedly a site of religious significance to the Miskito people. The trip is just upwards of 130 kilometers in each direction.

Crossing into Honduras at Leimus

Though it's technically possible to cross the Nicaraguan–Honduran border at Leimus, it's a little-used corridor and a sketchy immigration process. You are sure to be stopped and questioned, especially as crossing involves at least two days of travel *after* you get your exit stamp from Nicaragua. Bear in mind that immigration issues get expensive fast. Get your exit stamp in Puerto Cabezas beforehand or you will not be permitted to cross. There is no immigration office in Waspám or along the Honduran border.

TRIPS BY LAND FROM WASPÁM

Travel is difficult, transportation infrequent, and food and lodging service nonexistent. If necessary, you can try arranging a meal with a local family, for which you'll pay. There are two local villages that are close to Waspám: Kisalaya (five kilometers) and Ulwas (three kilometers). Locals will point you in the right direction. There are two taxis in town which might be able to take you to Ulwas, where you might be able to find a small store to buy cookies, crackers, and maybe a warm soda. Bilwaskarma (10 kilometers) is a pleasant village with a small health center that was a world-famous nursing school before the conflict of the 1980s; approximately a 45-minute walk from Waspám.

Solentiname and the Río San Juan

The long watery arc connecting the Solentiname archipelago in southern Lake Cocibolca and San Juan del Norte, 200 kilometers down the Río San Juan, is being called Nicaragua's "Golden Route" of tourism, a hopeful and well-deserved label, and one whose development is still in the making. The Río San Juan and environs are—unlike any other part of the country—rich, green, hot, and lush, and comprise some of Nicaragua's most extensive nature and wildlife reserves. It is also a remote and challenging destination to reach. If you don't have the big bucks for a tour company or a private *panga* and driver, allow some time (at least a week) when visiting the Río San Juan; cheap boat transport is possible, but the schedules can be limiting.

The isolation of the region translates into a higher cost of living—both for residents and tourists, with goods and services costing 25 percent more than the rest of Nicaragua, and up to 35 percent more on Solentiname. When traveling in the region, remember that this is a border area and you should always have your passport accessible.

HISTORY

Remembering that their original idea was to get to Asia, it's no wonder that after New World explorers realized the immensity of the land mass blocking their way, the prospect of a passage across Central America took on enormous importance. They soon found that Nicaragua's Río San Juan—along with Lake Cocibolca and the 18-kilometer-wide strip of land separating it from the Pacific—offered the most plausible route. Since then, writers have searched relentlessly for a way to properly express the strategic significance of Nicaragua's famous waterway; the most successful remains Hernán Cortés, who in 1524, wrote a letter to

El Castillo

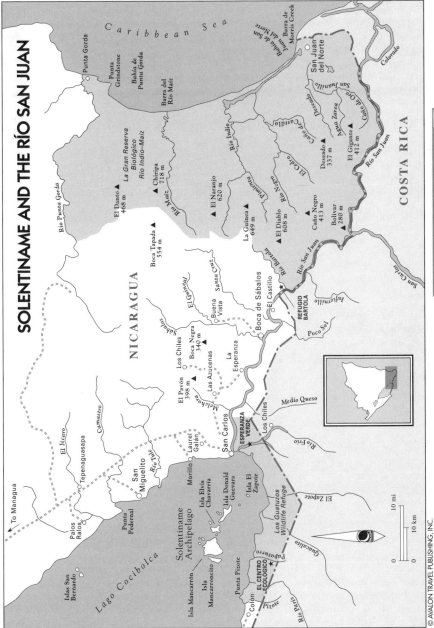

SOLENTINAME AND THE RÍO SAN JUAN

SOLENTINAME & THE RÍO SAN JUAN

CANAL DREAMS PAST AND PRESENT

By Tim Coone

After realizing the coveted natural water passage across America was nonexistent, geographers discovered that the lowest point along the entire north-south American divide—from Alaska to Tierra del Fuego—is found in Nicaragua. The fact that it is possible to go no higher than 40 meters above sea level in crossing from the Pacific to the Atlantic Ocean has maintained a fierce interest in the building of an interocean canal there since the early 1500s.

U.S. Army engineer Col. Orville Childs carried out the first systematic study of the canal route in 1852, at the invitation of U.S. millionaire Cornelius Vanderbilt, who, three years earlier, had set up a trans-isthmus transit route across Nicaragua to carry gold prospectors between California and New York.

The original Childs proposal, designed to move sailing ships from ocean to ocean, was followed by another half-dozen U.S. Army and Navy surveys over the next 100 years, with the greatest interest occurring at the turn of the century. At this time,

Panamá and Nicaragua were vying for the construction of a U.S.-controlled Pacific-Atlantic canal. After intense lobbying by promoters of both projects, the U.S. Congress finally opted to buy out the bankrupt French company that had already started building the Panama Canal.

The 1914 Bryan-Chamorro treaty, signed by the U.S. and Nicaragua in the year the Panama Canal opened, gave the U.S. exclusive rights—in perpetuity—to build a canal through Nicaragua. Two further U.S. Army studies for a Nicaraguan canal were commissioned by Congress during the 20th century, one in 1929–1931 for a deep-draft canal similar to that in Panamá, and another in 1939–1940 to build a shallow-draft barge canal. However, despite wartime fears of damage being caused to the Panama Canal, the U.S. Congress never saw sufficient economic merit in either variant to approve construction funds.

The Bryan-Chamorro treaty was abrogated in 1970, at around the same time as containerized cargo traffic began to grow exponentially in international maritime trade. These facts, together with the signing of the Carter-Torrijos treaty in 1979, which would hand over the Panama Canal to

King Carlos I of Spain, saying, "He who possesses the Río San Juan could be considered the owner of the World."

Granada was founded in the same year as Cortés's letter, becoming—via the Río San Juan—Spain's first Atlantic port in Central America. Thus began the river's 500-year history of blood and power, which commenced with the attempted genocide of thousands of indigenous people living in the wilderness along the river and on the islands of Solentiname.

At the time Granada was settled, southern Lake Cocibolca and the Río San Juan had still been little explored. Not until 1539 was a Spanish expedition sent out from Granada to travel downstream in search of the river's outlet to the Caribbean. The Río San Juan's mouth, completely hidden in labyrinthine estuaries, had eluded explorers for years, including Christopher Columbus, who failed to find it

when he sailed by in 1502 on his fourth and final voyage.

The first Spanish trade expedition between Granada and Panamá was attempted in 1567. The three ships laden with agricultural products were successful in reaching the Caribbean, but the trip ended there with an attack by English pirates who fed the surviving Spaniards to the sharks. For the next 300 years, tension and conflict between European nations across the Atlantic resulted in a virtual state of war between Spain's colonial holdings in Nicaragua and English, Dutch, and French pirates encouraged by their respective governments to give the Spanish hell. Most of their activity centered on attempts to plunder the riches of Granada. They were disastrously successful—until the Spanish improved their fortifications all along the Río San Juan: by 1724, antipirate fortresses had been constructed at San Carlos, Pocosol, El Castillo,

Panamá at the end of 1999, spurred renewed interest in the Nicaraguan canal.

During the Sandinista period, a proposal was made by a Japanese consortium to construct a canal that would accommodate ships four times the size of the largest that can squeeze through the locks at Panamá. The Sandinistas were busy fighting the Contra war, with their economy in tatters, and the proposal never prospered.

In the 1990s, two "dry canal" projects surfaced (CINN and SIT-Global) with proposals to build high-speed, trans-isthmus railways connecting ports on both oceans, which would transport containers on specialized railcars between ships berthed at either terminal of the railway. The routes are being proposed as a potential alternative to the Panama Canal and the U.S. transcontinental rail system, both of which are becoming increasingly congested for the east-west container trade between Asia and the East Coast of the United States. The construction cost has been estimated at $1–2 billion.

In 1999, Nicaragua's National Assembly approved a 30-year concession to a private company named EcoCanal for the construction of an inland waterway to permit the navigation of shallow-draft barge traffic along the Río San Juan from Lake Cocibolca to the Caribbean. Although not an interocean project as such, the $50-million waterway could be converted to one with the excavation of the 18-kilometer stretch of land between the Pacific Ocean and Lake Cocibolca—at an additional cost of some $300–400 million.

Politicians from the two leading parties, the Liberals and Sandinistas, have also revived variants of the 1980s Japanese proposal for building a huge, post-Panama canal, with a price tag in excess of $20 billion.

Until now, recent proposals have been paralyzed by a lack of venture capital to finance full feasibility studies, necessary to convert them into bankable projects for construction. Until such studies are completed, doubts will persist over their economic and environmental viability. Nonetheless, the EcoCanal waterway is generally considered as having the greatest possibility of being undertaken due to its low cost and smaller ecological footprint.

In the meantime, after five centuries, the canal in Nicaragua remains a dream.

Bartola, El Diamante, Machuca, Río San Carlos, Río San Francisco, Sarapiqui, Concepción Island, and San Juan del Norte.

Enter the Gringos: Boom and Bust

It wasn't long after the creation of the United States—and the capitalist system that has since driven it to attempt to conquer the hemisphere—that new interests arrived in San Juan del Norte with their eyes looking upstream. California gold was the main incentive, as entrepreneurs and adventurers looked for an alternative to the long and dangerous overland trip across the United States. Cornelius Vanderbilt and friends formed the first company providing passage between New York and San Francisco via Nicaragua. He made the first successful voyage in 1851, after 45 days of travel. The trip to California involved three separate ships to reach Lake Cocibolca, followed by a short overland trek to San Juan del Sur, where one boarded a ship to California.

By 1854, the British had pulled out and Vanderbilt's company had transported more than 23,000 passengers between New York and California. Business was booming along the route, which now included a short railway to avoid the rapids at El Castillo. San Juan del Norte became a rip-roaring port town with 127 foreign consulates and embassies, and a stream of adventuring gringos, foreign investors, and New Orleans whores, prompting U.S. envoy E. G. Squier to remark on the town's "general drunkenness and indiscriminate licentiousness." The party lasted another half a century, fueled after the end of the gold rush by the prospect of an interoceanic canal. The dream all but died when the bid went to Panamá in 1902, and communities up and down the Río San Juan began their long, neglected decline.

The Río San Juan Today

As a sensitive border area, the Río San Juan served as a southern front for Contra forces, most notably was the Alianza Revolucionaria Democrática (ARDE), under the leadership of Edén Pastora, a.k.a. Comandante Cero, who based out of Costa Rica for several years even after losing CIA support. The result, in many parts of the region, was the evacuation of entire communities, with residents fleeing across the border, or migrating elsewhere in Nicaragua. The population of the region dropped to under 40,000, and then, when the war ended, nearly doubled as people returned, many with new families. This quick expansion has had a noticeable effect on the area, especially in the impoverished rural communities which strain to support their inhabitants. Politically, the Río San Juan is split pretty evenly between Sandinista and anti-Sandinista sympathies.

Due to general governmental abandon, the lower reaches of the Río San Juan are neglected and isolated, and many thousands of desperate Nicaraguans still flee to Costa Rica, legally or otherwise, in search of work and better living conditions. (This will likely change as wealthy Nicaraguan legislators buy land along the river and have more reason to pay attention to the area.) Meanwhile, the immediate result is a general antipathy among Costa Ricans, who are occasionally straight-out racist toward their northern neighbors. Nevertheless, Nicaraguans up and down the Río San Juan receive Costa Rican news, radio, and television stations, and sometimes rely on Costa Rican schools and health services. In many towns—especially San Juan del Norte—the colón is used as widely as the cordoba.

CLIMATE AND SEASONS

Weather can be intense in Nicaragua's southern parts, with the long rainy season beginning in May and pushing well into January, the rain falling longer and harder the farther down the river you go, with annual levels around San Juan del Norte reaching 6,000 millimeters—one of the wettest spots in the hemisphere. Lake and river levels correspond to the season, swelling and sometimes flooding in June and November, or after a particularly long stretch of hard rain, when residents of El Castillo can be seen paddling canoes down main street. Remember that lots of rain plus not so much pavement equals a whole lot of mud. Take boots. When the sun comes out between rainstorms, and then more or less continuously in February, March, and April, it is violently strong, especially when reflected by the water; be prepared or risk getting burned. By April, expect low river levels and a whole lot of dust. At the end of January, an incredible amount of vegetation breaks into bloom, especially on Solentiname.

San Carlos

Nearly everyone traveling in the Río San Juan region will spend at least some time in San Carlos, whether they wish to or not. Some visitors are less than enchanted with the port town of 10,000 and try to make their stay here as short as possible. Edward Marriot called it "a place where the air smelled sour as old banknotes; where dead animals lay unremarked in the streets for days; where each day felt hotter than the last; where things of all kinds felt near their end." We think that's a little extreme. There's no denying that the town is filthy, but neither can one deny San Carlos's incredible tourism potential—easily as great as the strategic military importance that prompted its creation in the first place over four centuries ago.

San Carlos is surrounded on three sides by a watery horizon that makes for long, beautiful vistas, often colored with rainbows. It is a raucous and spirited hamlet of transients. Many of today's San Carleños were born elsewhere in the country, ending up here to service the large numbers of migrating Nicaraguans who pass through its streets. They are field hands on their way to Costa Rican harvests; border soldiers in town from remote posts to spend their meager paychecks; lake

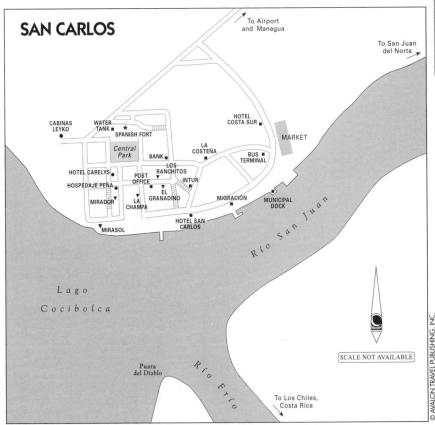

SAN CARLOS

To Airport and Managua

To San Juan del Norte

CABINAS LEYKO
WATER TANK
SPANISH FORT
Central Park
BANK
HOTEL CARELYS
POST OFFICE
HOSPEDAJE PEÑA
MIRADOR
LA CHAMPA
LOS RANCHITOS
EL GRANADINO
INTUR
MIRASOL
HOTEL SAN CARLOS

HOTEL COSTA SUR
MARKET
LA COSTEÑA
BUS TERMINAL
MIGRACIÓN
MUNICIPAL DOCK

Río San Juan

Lago Cocibolca

Punta del Diablo

Río Frío

SCALE NOT AVAILABLE

To Los Chiles, Costa Rica

and river merchants trading goods with Chontales cattlemen; and, of course, international travelers in search of a piece of history.

It's true that San Carlos has some work to do before it becomes an obviously desirable destination. Opening up the *malecón* (waterfront) by moving the filthy marketplace across town was a good start. Still, the runway needs paved and the highway between San Carlos and Acoyapa—nearly half of the journey to Managua—remains one of the worst roads in the country, effectively cutting locals off from the rest of Nicaragua and forcing them to turn to nearby Costa Rica for many services and trade.

Today's San Carleños are lively people; they will welcome and embrace you—and then ask you to treat them to a *cervecita* (beer). A careless welder started a market fire in 1984 that burned down a huge part of San Carlos, and its subsequent reconstruction was extremely… casual. Poverty abounds, but the economy pushes on: in addition to trade, transit, and fishing, it is buoyed by the 30-odd NGO offices in San Car-

los, each one with a noble mission—and a need for Nicaraguan *tecnicos,* secretaries, cleaning people, and a staff of foreign development workers who live, work, and spend money in town. Bring in tourism and see what happens.

ORIENTATION AND GETTING AROUND

If you are landing at the "airport" (actually a dirt runway and open-air waiting room), you'll want to grab one of the four-wheel-drive, taped-together taxis to take you the couple of kilometers into town—the five-minute ride costs $.75. The bus station is more or less in the town center, right across from the gas station and docks. Coming in by boat puts you right in the middle of the action. The main center of San Carlos is only about a dozen city blocks, all south of the central park on the flank of a hill looking south over the water. The waterfront can be a little confusing, especially if you find yourself in one of the narrow market aisles, but all in all, there's not

Solentiname islanders arrive in San Carlos to do some trading.

© JOSHUA BERMAN

much actual town in which to get lost. "Main Street" would be the one running from the market on the lakefront, curving to the south and west with the land until they reach the docks around the corner in the Río San Juan. The city sprawls northward along the "highway" to the hospital and airport.

SIGHTS AND ENTERTAINMENT

The **old Spanish fort** behind the park is presently getting a facelift, and will soon be San Carlos's only true "sight," per se. Then, of course, there are the cannons on the mirador lookout point—great for photo opportunities, especially during sunset.

As for entertainment, that's easy: **La Champa** is San Carlos's one and only disco (excepting the occasional town dance at the *recreativo*). Those in the know turn the name (which is slang for an army cot) into a verb, as in, *"¡Vamos a champear esta noche!"* (Let's go *champear* tonight!) Bars are abundant—the ones down by the market are the rowdiest (or most depressing, depending on the night), and the **Granadino** and **Ranchito** are popular hangs as well. Try to find the town's one roving mariachi band for some extra flavor. As for events, if you're around in September, ask about the annual sportfishing competition. The *fiesta patronales* is San Carlos Borromeo on November 4; La Purísima is celebrated December 2–8.

ACCOMMODATIONS
Under $10

San Carlos has about a half-dozen sleazy *hospedajes,* most on the main drag, and some charging as little as $1.50 for a bed. If you're short on cash, or just into slumming, try **Hospedaje Peña,** a block back from the water with 10 rooms and a wooden street-side balcony with a view of the Solentiname Islands; $2 a person, tel. 283-0298. **Hotel San Carlos,** built above a scummy pool of river water, is a small step up in price ($5 s, $7 d), but not much in terms of quality.

Hotel Costa Sur, found on the road past the bus station, is cheap, pretty clean (but musty),

and probably a lot quieter than its counterparts in town. Its 15 rooms start at $4 s, $6 d with shared bath, $7 for private bath, tel. 283-0224. A block south of the park, see what you think of the **Guest House Yure,** tel. 283-0348, with 10 rooms for $4–10.

Easily one of the most pleasant stays in San Carlos, **Hotel Carelys** (alternately found by asking for "Aquiles" or "Doña Coco") is a half-block south of the park, with 10 safe, super-clean rooms with private bath, fan, and complimentary soap, drinking water, and old magazines in Spanish— all for $9 a room, single or double (all queen beds), tel. 283-0389.

Another popular choice is the **Cabinas Leyko,** two blocks west of the church, tel. 283-0354. Its 18 rooms range from a single $6 no-frills cell to a $35 double with a/c and great views, and a range of options in between. You'd be wise to compare the rooms with Hotel Carelys before committing.

FOOD

There are two types of food in San Carlos: cheap Nica food and overpriced Nica food. For the former, try any of the dockside *comedores,* or market stalls, specifically, the **Soda la Amistad,** which makes delicious *gallo pinto,* and serves burgers and sandwiches in addition to the standard *corriente* fare. On the next street up, **Los Ranchitos** serves *corriente* plates from $2, fish dishes from $5. Across the street, the same basic food is served in **El Granadino,** with beautiful murals and a pleasant vibe. There is another *rancho* right on the water, past the Migración office, featuring a caged-in river-view dining room.

For a couple dollars more a plate, there are two options. The **Mirador** (up by the cannons) and **Mirasol** (just below, on the waterfront), both with sunset views of the big lake. Meals start around $5.

SHOPPING

There is no supermarket, but plenty of standard goods are available at the distributors along the waterside drag, and in the market. There is still very little *artesanía* sold in San Carlos; check around town, but you're better off buying directly from the artists on Solentiname.

INFORMATION AND SERVICES
Tourism Office

INTUR is across the street from the Clínica San Lucas, at the bottom of one of the staircases, tel. 283-0301 or 283-0363. It has basic info on the area and may be able to help you arrange for special transport.

Emergency

The police station, tel. 283-0350, is located three kilometers from the center of San Carlos on the road to Managua. Fire station, tel. 283-2149. Hospital Luis Felipe Moncada is north of town on the highway, tel. 283-0238 or 283-0244. The Centro de Salud, tel. 283-0361. San Carlos's medical services may be okay for minor problems, but for any real emergencies (including poisonous snakebites), you're better off chartering a boat south to the hospital in Los Chiles, Costa Rica (one hour or less by boat)—assuming the daily flight to Managua is not an option.

Phones and Mail

Phone service to San Carlos, in a word, sucks. The system is overloaded, and when too many people try to call Managua (or anywhere else), it shuts down, prompting the frequent declaration of *"No hay comunicación."* When there *is* communication, it is often faint, scratchy, and delayed. This is true all the way down the river as well, but this is slowly changing with the installation of a series of satellite phones, more expensive (a dollar a minute within Nicaragua, $3 to the United States) but more reliable, and often your only option; satellite numbers are recognized by the 892 exchange—do not dial zero first. The San Carlos post office, located a block south of the park, delivers mail via the daily La Costeña flight, has cheap phone service to and from Managua, tel. 283-0276, and can receive faxes: tel./fax 283-0000. Open Monday.–Friday. 8 A.M.–5 P.M., one hour break for lunch, Saturday until 1 P.M. You can also receive a fax in the house

of Don Carlos Reyes, fax 283-0090, near Hospedaje Peña. ENITEL is located up the road toward the hospital.

Internet

Sorry—get your fill in Granada and then enjoy being off-line for a while. Inevitably, the new satellite phones will get Internet access, so ask around if you're really desperate.

Banks

The sole bank, Banco de Finanzas, located one block east of the park, does not change traveler's checks or colones, nor does it offer any credit card cash advances (open Mon.–Fri. 8:30 A.M.–4 P.M., Sat. until noon, tel. 283-0144). There are plenty of *coyote* money changers down by the Migración office, trading cordobas, dollars, and colones. For quick bail money, there is a Western Union just west and south of the church.

Radio

Most stations come in from Costa Rica and feature Spanglish reggae and *soka*. Local entertainment is provided by Radio San Carlos at 94.9 FM and Radio Trópico Humedo at 590 AM.

GETTING THERE AND AWAY
By Land

Settle in and enjoy the ride; we're talkin' nine hours of rutted-out endurance—marked by severe mud or dust, depending on the season. Actually, the first 150 kilometers to Acoyapa are paved, but the remaining half of the highway is hellish. A half-dozen buses leave Managua's Mayoreo Market throughout the day, and the 300-kilometer trip costs $15. If driving on your own, be sure to have a spare tire and jack, plus water

BOAT NOTE

As the demand for transportation continues to grow and shift, so do boat schedules. Always check departure times at the docks well in advance, and be sure to get a second (and third) opinion.

and provisions. Buses leave San Carlos at the terminal across from the gas station. Buses bound for Managua leave at various random times, day and night, and those bound for Nueva Guinea leave in the afternoon. Ask the *chequeador* for an updated schedule.

By Boat

The old ferry departs Granada's municipal dock Monday and Thursday at 2 P.M., arriving in San Carlos around 3 A.M. The trip costs about $4 each way, and returns from San Carlos at 2 P.M. on Tuesday and Friday. The boat can get crowded at times, especially around Semana Santa, when the lake turns *bravo* (rough), the air is hot, and the ride turns into a 12-hour puke-fest. Get there early and be aggressive to stake your territory deckside. The ride is mellow more often than not, more so going from San Carlos to Granada. The other option is the *Crucero Solentiname,* leaving Granada at 7 A.M. on Fridays stopping at Ometepe and Solentiname, and arriving in San Carlos at 8 P.M. The weekly return trip leaves San Carlos on Sunday at 6 A.M., arriving Granada at 6:30 P.M. One-way trip is $6 coach, $20 first class (Note: as of press time, due to lack of demand, the *Crucero* was running every 15 days, sometimes less—you should definitely check beforehand to make reservations and be sure that it is traveling, tel. 265-2716, email: zerger@ibw.com.ni).

For trips down the Río San Juan, go to the **Venta de Boletos Transporte Acuático** on the main drag, toward the gas station. The little shack is staffed Monday–Saturday 7 A.M.–3 P.M. and has up-to-date schedules and advance ticket sales for its fleet of some two dozen *lanchas,* tel. 283-0200 or 892-0174.

Private *panga* trips can be arranged at the Venta, INTUR, or directly with one of a variety of private boat owners *(pangueros).* Ask around the docks or walk the streets looking for signs, such as Armando Ortiz's Viajes Turísticos, near the Western Union, tel. 283-0039. These trips are expensive because gas costs $3 a gallon, but they are much faster and more convenient than the *colectivos.*

RÍO SAN JUAN BOAT LINGO

Boats and the river are so central to the people of the Río San Juan they have their own vocabulary to describe boats and boat transport. This brief list will help you make yourself understood.

Lancha: long, skinny passenger or cargo boats; usually the cheapest public transportation between towns, used by locals to get around, carrying up to 60 passengers.

Pipante: a particularly long and skinny *lancha.*

Colectivo: public *lanchas.*

Panga: smaller, open-air fiberglass boats with outboard motors, capacity from six to 10 passengers; these are private boats that you rent, always more expensive.

Canoa: dugout canoes; also *botecita, cayuco,* or *bote de canalete.*

Plana: motorless, flat-bottom mini-barges, towed by *lanchas.*

Bote: a general word, but also used for the 50-passenger vessels with bathroom.

Barco: a bigger ship, as in the kind that comes from Granada.

Crucero: the weekend tour cruiser, *El Crucero Solentiname.*

By Air

The daily 50-minute flight from Managua leaves at 9 A.M. Monday, Tuesday, Wednesday, Thursday, and Saturday; at noon on Friday and Sunday. The return flight is 10 minutes shorter, departing San Carlos around 10 A.M. and 1 P.M., respectively, as per the schedule above. The round-trip cost is $80. Contact La Costeña in Managua, tel. 263-1228 or 263-2142. In San Carlos, the La Costeña office is run by Doña María Amelia Gross, one block north of the INTUR office, open waking hours (it's also her home), tel. 283-0271. Always reserve a spot a day or two in advance, if possible.

Crossing into Costa Rica

Crossing the border begins with a visit to the shabby, blue-and-white Migración office on Main

Street. It is easily recognized by the line of people that starts forming every day at 7 A.M. The office is open seven days, 8:30 A.M.–6 P.M. There are two lines: one where a very self-important official will curiously scrutinize your passport; the second where you'll pay $2 to be showered with seals, stamps, and signatures. Boats leave from the dock just past the passport window at 10:30 A.M., 12:30 P.M., 3 P.M., and 3:40 P.M. The hourlong chug up the Río Frío to Los Chiles, Costa Rica costs $5 each way.

In Los Chiles: Once in *"Ticalandia,"* there are two more lines: one to search your bags, another to stamp your passport (Costa Rica Migración is located 200 meters up the road from the dock—be sure to stop and get stamped). If you're entering Nicaragua from Costa Rica, you'll need to buy a Cruz Roja (Red Cross) stamp for less than $1, either across the street from Migración, or four blocks away in the Nicaraguan consulate, located a half-block north of the church, open Monday–Friday, 8:30 A.M.–noon, 2–4:30 P.M. Boats leave regularly for San Carlos through about 5 P.M. If continuing south, there are daily direct buses to San José; the trip takes six hours. (Note: be aware that there exists a Los Chiles, Nicaragua, located about two hours northeast of San Carlos, and when asking for information, you may need to distinguish between the two towns.)

Near San Carlos

SOLENTINAME

If you've only seen images of Solentiname as presented by the famous archipelago's primitivist artists, you'd think this was a lush, rainbow-colored fantasy land. You'd be right. The 36 volcanically formed islands in southern Lake Cocibolca have a long history of habitation, and the signs of its original inhabitants are abundant, including petroglyphs, cave paintings, and artifacts. The inviting name comes from *Celentinametl,* (Nahuatl for Place of Many Guests). Today's Solentiname is home to 750 people belonging to 129 families, as well as an amazing diversity of vegetation, birds, and other wildlife. In addition to its natural beauty and indigenous heritage, Solentiname's most unique and well-known attraction is its current inhabitants' internationally renowned artistic creativity, a talent "discovered" in 1966 by Padre Ernesto Cardenal when he gave brushes and paint to some of the local *jícaro* carvers.

The islands are of volcanic origin, and the soil, composed of compacted ash, is rich but rocky and thus difficult to farm. Nevertheless, campesinos are able to get some basic grains in the ground, and the bean harvest happens in January. Lately, islanders have put their money in avocados, and several plantations are making a go of it on several islands. The archipelago was all but completely denuded by Somoza's logging interests, and afterwards grazed to the ground by rich Boaco cattlemen. In the last three decades, however, much of the forest has been allowed to regenerate, which it has done marvelously. The natural rebirth has attracted artists and biologists from all over the world. Fishing, of course, has always been a mainstay of the islanders' diet, and still is.

Cardenal's arrival occurred shortly after he spent several years at a Trappist monastery in Kentucky, and he formed a Christian community in Solentiname in the late 1960s. He stayed on Isla Mancarrón to live, work, and write for the next 10 years. Under his guidance, the simple church at Solentiname served as the heart of Nicaragua's Liberation Theology movement, in which Christ was represented as the revolutionary savior of the poor, and which inspired Carlos Mejía Godoy to write *La Misa Campesina* after a visit in 1972. Masses were communal, participatory events, and Cardenal's book, *The Gospels of Solentiname,* is a written record of the phenomenon, with transcriptions of a series of campesino-led services throughout the 1970s.

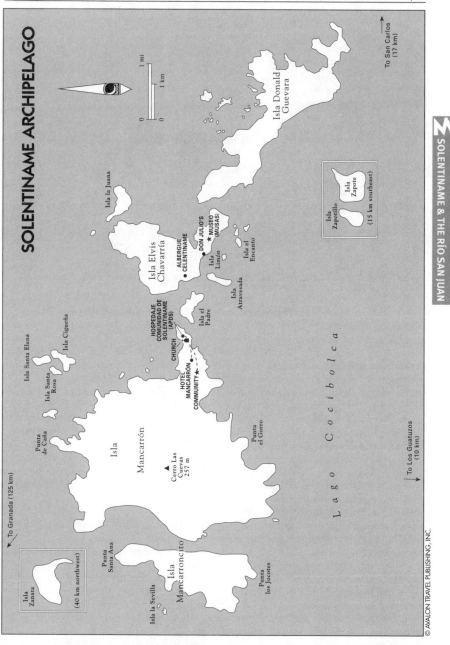

SOLENTINAME ARCHIPELAGO

To Granada (125 km)

Isla Zapate (40 km northwest)

Isla la Sevilla

Punta Santa Ana

Isla Mancarroncito

Punta los Jocotes

Punta de Caña

Isla Santa Elena

Isla Santa Rosa

Isla Cigüeña

Isla Mancarrón

▲ Cerro Las Cuevas 257 m

Punta el Gorro

Isla la Juana

Isla Elvis Chavarría

ALBERGUE CELENTINAME

HOSPEDAJE COMUNIDAD DE SOLENTINAME (APDS)

CHURCH

HOTEL MANCARRÓN

COMMUNITY ★

Isla el Padre

Isla Atravesada

DON JULIO'S

★ **MUSEO (MUSAS)**

Isla Limón

Isla el Encanto

Isla Donald Guevara

Isla Zapote (15 km southeast)

Isla Zapotillo

Lago Cocibolca

To Los Guatuzos (110 km)

To San Carlos (17 km)

SOLENTINAME & THE RÍO SAN JUAN

© AVALON TRAVEL PUBLISHING, INC.

0 1 mi
0 1 km

© JOSHUA BERMAN

There are 36 islands in the Solentiname Archipelago.

But Solentiname was politically involved long before Padre Cardenal. On October 13, 1977, a group of anti-Somoza islanders staged a daring and successful assault on the Guardia Nacional post in San Carlos. Somoza's vengeance was swift and violent, burning many of the islands' structures to the ground, and forcing the evacuation of a large number of their residents. After becoming the revolution's minister of culture in 1979, Cardenal formed the Asociación Para el Desarollo de Solentiname (Solentiname Development Association), or APDS (pronounced ah-pay-day-essay). Under APDS, much of what had been destroyed was rebuilt, and the arts continued to flourish and receive much attention from the rest of the world. Today, there are no less than 50 families who continue to produce Solentiname's unique art of balsa wood carvings and bright, scenic paintings of the landscape and community.

Interestingly, primitivist painting as a social movement is found in only two other places in the world, each of which was also begun and nourished by a single person: in Haiti it was a Protestant pastor, and in Yugoslavia, a painter and community leader who persuaded the people to paint on glass.

Orientation and Getting Around
Of the three dozen islands, four are significantly bigger than the rest and, with a few exceptions, the only inhabited islands. They are Isla Mancarrón, Isla Elvis Chavarría (a.k.a. Isla San Fernando), Isla Donald Guevara (a.k.a. Isla la Venada), and Isla Mancarroncito. Only the first two have services for tourists. If you are on a budget, getting around the islands will be your biggest challenge, especially considering that the *colectivos* only run twice a week, ensuring a minimum stay of three days. You can either catch a free or discounted ride in someone's *panga,* or you can rent a dugout canoe or rowboat and do some paddling.

The Islands and Their Attractions
Mancarrón
This is the biggest island (20 square kilometers), and the highest, with a peak (Cerro las Cuevas) of 257 meters above the lake, reachable by foot or horseback. The island is home to about 200 people, belonging to 34 families. Mancarrón was the birthplace of Ernesto Cardenal's project in the 1960s and home to the church whose reconstruction and design was one of his first en-

deavors on the island. It is unlike any house of worship you've ever seen, featuring children's paintings on the whitewashed adobe walls, a unique crucifix sculpted by Cardenal, and an altar decorated in pre-Columbian style. The nearby APDS compound boasts a wonderful library/museum/gallery, featuring a huge collection of indigenous artifacts, books in a variety of languages (including the complete works of Ernesto Cardenal, whom residents refer to simply as "El Poeta"), and the original "primitivist" painting by local resident Eduardo Arana that helped start the whole project.

The "town" of Mancarrón was all constructed during the 1980s and is nothing more than a cluster of houses, a health center, school, and *pulpería,* five minutes up the muddy path from the dock. Much of the island is off-limits and was recently bought and sold by a mysterious party acting through a group of wealthy Boaco cattlemen. Rumors abound.

Elvis Chavarría: "La Elvis," as the island is affectionately known, was named after one of its young residents who was captured and killed by the *Guardia* just two days after participating in the attack on their post in San Carlos in 1977. The island has a health center, a school (Escuela Mateo Wooten, named after the Peace Corps volunteer who promoted its construction in the mid-1990s), a museum, and a hiking trail.

El Museo Archipiélago de Solentiname (MUSAS) was built in September 2000 to preserve and display the natural and cultural heritage of the Solentiname Islands and its people. The museum costs $1 to enter and is located at the top of a steep path that is planted with flowers to attract butterflies and hummingbirds. After catching your breath from the climb and enjoying the view, step inside, where you'll find depictions of the island's history by local artists, as well as several interesting maps of the area, archaeological information, and a display of traditional fishing techniques and the balsa wood carving process. Behind the museum is an orchid display, natural medicine garden, arboretum of 42 tree species, and a model organic avocado and balsa wood plantation. Coming soon: a guided forest loop trail, weather station,

and community library. If that's not enough, the Fundación MUSAS (made up of six community leaders, the Italian NGO Asociación de Cooperación Rural en Africa y América Latina, or ACRA, and several other organizations) also organizes environmental education workshops in the island's school, and supports a number of research projects in the area. The museum is open every day 7 A.M.–noon, 2–5 P.M., but if you find it closed, speak with the cleaning woman at the bottom of the hill who will help you find Moncho, the local curator, caretaker, and key master. For more information, swing by the ACRA office near the hospital in San Carlos, tel. 283-0095, or in Managua tel. 249-6176, email: musasni@yahoo.com.

If you find yourself here at the peak of the dry season (March and April), be sure to ask whether or not **La Cueva del Duende** is accessible. The Dwarf Cave, underwater for most of the year, is an important archaeological site that the islands' past inhabitants believed to be the entrance to the underworld. They painted faces to represent their ancestors whom they believed to reside there, and left other markings as well, including a female fertility figure.

Donald Guevara: Also known as Isla la Venada, or simply, "La Donald," the island's martyred namesake was killed alongside his compañero Elvis Chavarría.

Mancarroncito: This is the most well preserved, wild, and least inhabited of the main islands, with its high point of 100 meters surrounded by steep, thickly vegetated hills.

Zapote and Zapotillo: These are the closest two islands to the mainland around San Carlos, and are both owned by APDS, which has decided to pretty much leave them alone. Zapote is a key nesting area for a variety of birds, and turns into a whitewashed, foul-smelling squawkfest in March and April when some 10,000 breeding pairs build nests there. Observe the reproductive mayhem from your boat only, as landing there disturbs the birds. The smaller island, Zapotillo, has less bird activity and a more sordid history involving a fruit farm, an orphanage for boys, and a pedophile Evangelist priest who was eventually chased into Costa Rica, barely escaping with his life.

Isla el Padre: Located just off the western tip of La Elvis, the island became a howler monkey sanctuary when someone introduced a single breeding pair in the 1980s, subsequently reproducing into a family of some 50 members. The population has never been studied, so write yourself a grant and come on down.

Isla la Atravesada: Just off La Elvis and to the east of Isla el Padre, the island is owned by a North American and is also home to one of Solentiname's densest crocodile populations.

Accommodations and Food

Note that all prices include three meals. Isla Mancarrón's **Hospedaje Communidad de Solentiname,** is APDS's guest compound, located up to your right and through the gate as you disembark on the island's concrete dock. The compound includes the guest cabins, *comedor* with a view, a library and reading room, and Ernesto's home up on the hill. The rooms were only recently opened to tourists, but they have been hosting visitors for decades, especially during the revolution, when artists, writers, and poets from all over the world came to witness the artistic and social experiment here. The list of famous minds who slept in these beds is endless, and inspiration is encouraged in the form of "Turismo Contemplativo," in which guests are offered space to read, write, or just sit and purify their souls. (Makes you wonder what they're doing with two Jet Skis for rent.) Staying in one of the three *cabañas* costs $25 a person, $30 with a fan (which operates on limited hours), three meals included. Backpackers are welcome and can set up a tent for next to nothing. Meals bought separately cost $3 breakfast, $5 lunch, and $4 dinner. Contact in Managua is tel. 278-3495 or 267-0304, fax 278-5781; in San Carlos, tel. 283-0083, email: escritor@ibw.com.ni.

Up on the hill, **Hotel Mancarrón** is a fenced-in mini-resort with 15 basic rooms, a bar, restaurant, and facilities for groups and conferences. Rooms go for $50 a person, including private bath, fan, three meals, and electricity between 5 and 11:30 P.M., tel./fax 265-2716 in Managua, email: zerger@ibw.com.ni, or contact Solentiname Tours. Hotel staff can arrange guided tours

of the islands, but be aware that due to a local property dispute and family feud, you may be discouraged from visiting certain people and attractions, including the museum on La Elvis Chavarría.

On La Elvis, Doña María Guevara has been running the **Albergue Celentiname** since 1984, on a beautiful point at the western edge of the island. She and many of her family members are painters, participating in Cardenal's project since its earliest days. The hotel has eight rooms and capacity for up to 25 people (group rates available), all with shared bath. There is a wonderful porch, a bar, *comedor,* kayaks, and a rowboat; guided fishing trips available. Price is $22 a person and includes three meals. Try to make reservations in advance if possible, and she can help arrange for your transportation as well (around $120 round-trip). Contact Doña María's mother, Olivia Silba, in Managua at tel. 276-1910, or Berta Rosa in San Carlos at tel. 283-0083.

Several hundred meters east, with his own dock on the southern shore of the island, check out **Don Julio's** rooms for rent. This is the simplest, most basic option in Solentiname, and also the most economical. The two rooms and kitchen are separate from his own house, with a waterfront porch, and cost $10 a person, three meals included. He's working to replace the latrine with a flush toilet, but expect simple, rustic, campesino living. It's a family affair: Don Julio Sequeira Pineda's brother, Chepe, runs transport to and from San Carlos, and can arrange any custom trip you desire. Contact their sister, Elena Pineda, at her art gallery in Managua: Galería Solentiname, tel. 277-0939.

Tour Packages

The same foundation that runs the museum on Isla Elvis Chavarría has also arranged a fully guided, four-day exploration of the entire Solentiname Archipelago and the **Río Papaturro** in Los Guatuzos, including all its natural, archaeological, and cultural attractions. With a group of five people, the price (which includes transportation from San Carlos and around the islands, guide, room, and board) is $134–188 a person, depending on which of the three *hospeda-*

jes you stay in (not available from Hotel Mancarrón). Price per person also goes down as the size of the group increases. Contact the Fundación MUSAS through ACRA (contact information listed above). Many of the bigger, Managua-based tour companies listed in On the Road also have packages to Solentiname.

Getting There and Away

From San Carlos, the two *colectivos* originate on La Elvis. Each boat makes one weekly trip, leaving the island at 3 A.M. Tuesday and Friday (driven by Chepe and Sylvio, respectively), passing by Mancarrón, and arriving in San Carlos by 6:30 A.M. Each boat leaves San Carlos the same day at 1 P.M. for the return trip to Solentiname. The trip costs only $2 each way. Renting a private *panga* in San Carlos costs anywhere from $85 to over $100 and takes half the time (45 minutes) to arrive; not a bad option if you are pressed for time and have a decent-sized group.

The days of the 3.5-hour hydrofoil ride from Granada have been over for some time now. However, *El Crucero Solentiname* leaves Granada every Friday (with some exceptions—always check beforehand) at 7 A.M., making a port call in Moyogalpa, Ometepe at 10 A.M., then departing an hour later, arriving at Mancarrón at 5:30 P.M., and continuing to San Carlos, arriving at 8 P.M. The return trip departs from San Carlos on Sunday at 6 A.M., hitting Solentiname at 8 A.M., arriving in Moyogalpa at 3 P.M. and Granada at 6:30 P.M. First-class tickets between Solentiname and Granada cost $17 each way, and include full bar and restaurant service; coach service for about $5. (As noted above, you should definitely contact them beforehand to make reservations and be sure that it is traveling, tel. 265-2716, email: zerger@ibw.com.ni).

LOS GUATUZOS WILDLIFE REFUGE

This is an extensive, 438-square-kilometer strip of protected wetlands and wildlife reserve, bordered on the south by Costa Rica and on the north by the extreme southern shore of Lake Cocibolca. In addition to the myriad species of animals, the area is inhabited by some 1,700 fishermen and subsistence farmers in 11 small communities, descendants of the Zapote and Guatuzo (or Maleku) peoples that originally settled here, as well as the mestizos who arrived in the late 19th century in search of rubber trees. These same *huleros* reverted to the slave trade when the world rubber market crashed, selling Guatuzo Indians for 50 pesos a head in San Carlos; from there, the slaves were taken to the gold mines of Chontales (today, only a handful of full-blooded Maleku exist, mostly in Costa Rica).

The history of the area continues with the formation of numerous cacao plantations in the 1930s. Because of the crop's need for shade, much of the area's original forest canopy was preserved until a combination of low world prices and a deadly fungus wiped out the industry in the 1970s. Some hardwood harvesting succeeded, but halted when border fighting during the 1980s drove nearly the entire population of Los Guatuzos to flee into Costa Rica. When families returned in the early 1990s, the area's ecosystem was still largely intact, and the new government quickly acted to protect it from destruction.

Today, residents count on the richness of their natural surroundings to attract curious folks like yourself. No less than 389 species of birds have been observed here, and between February and April some migratory species fly through in spectacular concentrations. Los Guatuzos contains dense populations of crocodiles, caimans, feral pigs, jaguars, and howler, white-faced, and spider monkeys. This is also home to a rare, ancient species of fish called the gaspar (*Actractoseus tropicus*), a living armored relic of the Jurassic age, with a snout and fangs that it uses to eat other fish, crabs, and small turtles.

El Centro Ecológico

The research center and guest facilities are located 40 kilometers from San Carlos, up the Río Papaturro, which drains the slopes of Costa Rica's northern volcano chain. The river is narrow, and the jungle—rife with wildlife—closes in above you as you approach the community of Papaturro. Research station, nature center, and an isolated backpacker's heaven, the Centro Ecológico offers a full list of activities, including photo/bird-watching safaris, fishing trips, horseback rides through the woods, boat trips in the wetlands and lake, excursions to Solentiname, alligator night hikes, and tours of local campesino villages (all of these activities cost extra—the most expensive are those tours that involve burning gasoline, i.e., boat trips). There is also an orchid display (92 species), butterfly farm, and a turtle nursery (for export to the pet industry).

There is an army post just upstream (where, 10 years ago, a young soldier lost his marbles and gunned down his entire platoon and then himself), and then another stretch of beautiful river before reaching the Costa Rican border. You need permission to travel beyond the army post, and on the return, you'll be asked to pay a $2 *zarpe* (fee) per boat. Do not attempt to cross the border. **Accommodations at Papaturro:** El Centro has two dorms with eight beds in each one, for $10 a night, plus campgrounds (tents and sleeping pads for rent). Food can be arranged in advance for less than $2 a meal. The center also boasts a conference room, workshop facilities, and support for anyone coming to do field research (GPS equipment, bird nets/traps, and field assistants). In the case of all lodging and services, discounts can be worked out for groups and students.

Your hosts and guides, Armando and Aiellen, offer some supplies like rubber boots for the mud, but it is strongly suggested that you bring quick-drying clothes and adequate protection from the sun, rain, and bugs. Contact the Amigos de la Tierra office in San Carlos, across from the Iglesia del Nazareno, tel. 283-0139, or FUNDAR in Managua (from the Vicky, two blocks south, one east, and one south, across from OXFAM), tel. 267-8267 or 270-5434, email: fundar@cablenet.com.ni, website: www.geocities.com/guatuzos/guatuzos.html.

Getting There and Away

From San Carlos, *colectivos* leave for Papaturro Tuesday, Thursday, and Saturday; the three-hour trip costs $2 a person. Or you can rent a *panga*—which costs $100, but can take up to 10 people to Guatuzos in only 1.5 hours. You can also arrange for an expensive pickup from Solentiname by calling 270-5434 or 267-8267, or by talking to any of the *pangueros* on Solentiname.

ESPERANZA VERDE

Also a part of the Guatuzos Reserve, this is a 5,000-hectare protected area, accessed by traveling 15 minutes up the Río Frío. The reserve is part of an effort to reforest and protect the overgrazed watershed of the Río Frío and the Río San Juan. At the dock on the river you'll find the Centro de Interpretación Ambiental Konrad Lorenz, and a row of six guest rooms with 20 beds. The cost to stay here is $10 a person, plus $12 for three meals (special rates for NGOs, students, and Nicas). The area immediately surrounding the guest facilities is more or less bare and not the most attractive of places. However, a 40-minute walk up the road brings you straight into the heart of the rainforest—monkeys, 200 species of birds, giant spiders, mosquitoes, pumas, you name it—and you can spend all day hiking and soaking in the jungle vibe. Take any of the Los Chiles–bound *colectivos,* or arrange for private transport. Contact Leonel Ubau with FUNDE-VERDE at tel. 283-0080, or in Hotel Cabinas Leyko in San Carlos.

NORTH OF SAN CARLOS

There are several small pueblos inland from San Carlos, and as you travel north along the eastern shore of Lake Cocibolca, you'll encounter a series of waterfront fishing villages, each one at the end of an unimproved spur road from the San Carlos–Managua highway, and each one completely and totally off of any normal tourist route. There are a lot of unknowns here, but one thing's for certain: bitchin' sunsets.

San Miguelito

A peaceful, lakeside community, San Miguelito boasts an interesting **Casa de Cultura,** women's bakery, and access to the island of El Boquete. You can also venture up various rivers, into local wetlands, or over yonder to Solentiname. There are accommodations in the hardwood, Italian-run **Hotel Cocibolca,** with 16 rooms for $6, shared bath, right on the lake with views of amazing sunsets behind Ometepe. One daily direct bus leaves Managua's Mayoreo at 7 A.M.; in San Car-los, ask at the bus station. You can also take the long ferry from Granada and get off in San Miguelito before it reaches San Carlos.

Down the Río San Juan

Shove off from the dock, say goodbye to scummy San Carlos, and revel in the excitement of your imminent expedition. Lake Cocibolca's *desaguadero* (outlet), as it was originally referred to by Spaniards in Granada, begins its 190-odd-kilometer journey to the sea as a broad, flat mass of brown water, bordered on both sides by bird-heavy greenery and cattle farms. As you float downstream, you'll have the opportunity to stop in several villages, isolated clusters of stilted homes, or in one of several river resorts and research stations. There are several minor *raudales* (rapids) where the channel suddenly narrows, including the infamous **Raudal el Diablo** in front of El Castillo. Monstrous *sábalos reales* (tarpon) are often seen rising just upstream from these fast waters, especially when the river is

high—their enormous silver hulks breaking the surface and then mysteriously disappearing. Beyond El Castillo, things become decidedly wilder, especially on the Nicaraguan side where the enormous Gran Reserva Río Indio-Maíz spills over the left bank. Finally, you'll reach San Juan del Norte, with all its ghosts, and a long sandbar, beyond which lies the Caribbean. (Note: in the following section, the terms "river right" and "river left" refer to a boater facing downstream).

BOCA DE SÁBALOS

A two-hour *lancha* ride brings you to Boca de Sábalos, a town long overshadowed by El Castillo and the famous fort just six kilometers downstream. Boca de Sábalos is a working town of

© JOSHUA BERMAN

panga ride on Río San Juan

about 1,200 souls, located at the mouth of one of Río San Juan's nearly 1,000 tributaries. Boca de Sábalos is not as solidly constructed or as fully developed as El Castillo, but it is more commercially active and has more bars, *hospedajes,* and places to eat than its neighbor. Sábalos is the de facto seat of the El Castillo municipality, which was transferred here temporarily during the war, and then never moved back. There is cheap lodging for the sawmill workers and government employees (many of whom commute each day from El Castillo), and there are facilities for the foreign and national aid workers as well, who work with the 11 NGOs in town.

Attractions

The casual tourist is a rarity in Boca de Sábalos, but absolutely welcome. Travelers interested in canoeing up a beautiful river and being surrounded by trees and animals are sure to be rewarded. To set out exploring, simply negotiate a deal with one of the *chavalos* (young boys) near the dock to rent his boat and paddle—feel free to take the kid along for the smiles and knowledge as well. If you don't go up the river, you should at least cross it and check out the other side, even if just for the quick trip. You have surely not lived until you have paid a barefoot five-year-old girl wearing a pink dress and cowboy hat to paddle you across the Río Sábalos in a crude dugout canoe. The trip costs one cordoba each way—or whatever you feel like paying. On the other side, you'll find an army post, riverfront bar, and Don Simeón's hotel.

If you prefer to stay on land, hire a vehicle to take you to the massive African palm plantation, about a half-hour away. The 2,000-hectare plantation is one of only two such operations in Nicaragua and is also accessed via the Río Santa Cruz. Until recently, the entire operation, including the palm oil processing factory, was entirely owned by the farmer cooperatives who worked it, employing hundreds of locals. The cooperatives had to sell the factory to the Chamorro family, thus losing control over the price they receive for the palm fruit, and they have consequently been struggling. The long, shady rows of palms are a beautiful background for a daytime walk—just watch out for the snakes.

Or hike down the Río San Juan on the road set back from the river to reach Yaro's frog and amphibian farm (he exports them to the pet industry in the United States), or the 100-year-old steamship wreck—a rusted hulk half-buried in sand. Ask around for a guide or more detailed directions.

To go tarpon fishing, get a permit from the town MARENA office (hook only, no spears), and then hire a guide and boat to take you to just above the Toro Rapids, less than five minutes down the Río San Juan.

Accommodations and Services

Walking up from the dock, you'll first come to **Hospedaje y Comedor Katiana** on your right, a beautiful hardwood building run by Doña Rosario Manzanares, who is also a great source of local knowledge and unofficial local tourism promoter. Her 14 rooms go for $4.50 for shared bath, $10 private bath. Next door is the **Hospedaje Clarica,** with eight rooms for $3 a person; mosquito net, fan, shared bath. Doña Clarica is a wonderful cook, and willing to make your favorite dish from home, provided the ingredients are available. Across the street, the **Hotel Central** is cheap and not bad, but not nearly as nice as the other two. Coming soon is **Don Simeón Parrales Ulloa's** hotel, currently under construction across the Río Sábalo, right where it meets the Río San Juan. Don Simeón is considered the town's historian (and its most successful merchant). The town's sole **satellite phone** is found in his store on main street, tel. 892-0176.

Montecristo River Resort

Six kilometers downstream from Sábalo, on river right (only 20 minutes before El Castillo), Montecristo is an "alternative tourism" complex, which offers sportfishing, hot tubs, ATVs, hiking trails, and tours (and tastes) of local shrimp and fish farms. Don Augustín's six *cabañas* are actually reasonably priced. They are equipped with TV, fridge, and kitchen for your use if you choose not to dine in the bar and restaurant (breakfast

NICARAGUA'S FAMOUS FRESHWATER SHARK

How *Carcharhinus leucas* became the only shark in the world able to pass between saltwater and freshwater is a fascinating story. After thousands of years of hunting in the brackish outflow of the Río San Juan, Nicaragua's freshwater sharks made their way up the river and formed a healthy population in Lago de Nicaragua. The tale continues with the arrival of humans and their role as both victims and hunters of Nicaragua's bull shark, told in full in Edward Marriott's 2001 book, *Savage Shore.* Indigenous tribes on Ometepe worshiped the shark, sometimes feeding their dead to it. This fear and reverence only faded when the Asian market for shark fin soup helped to create an industry around harvesting the famous fish, culminating in the late 1960s, when Somoza's processing plant in Granada butchered up to 20,000 sharks a year. Today, the only freshwater shark in the world is seldom seen, although it is still inadvisable to swim in the waters near San Juan del Norte.

$3.50, lunch and dinner $8). The cheapest room is a $35 double, going up to a family cabin for $150. The small fleet of fully equipped fishing boats, with guide, cost $45–85 a day, plus gas. Tel. 266-1694/1237/1018, or 276-1119, email: mca@cablenet.com.ni, website: www.montecristoriver.com.

Getting There and Away

It's possible to visit Boca de Sábalos (or Montecristo) as a day trip—simply leave San Carlos on the early boat, get off in Sábalos, and then continue to El Castillo when a boat passes in the afternoon (the last one is around 5 P.M.).

EL CASTILLO

El Castillo is a town of about 1,500 built into the bank of the Río San Juan and named after its principal attraction: **El Castillo de la Inmaculada Concepción de María.** The fortress, whose dark, moss-covered ruins still loom above town,

was strategically placed with a long view downriver, right in front of the shark- and crocodile-infested **Raudal el Diablo**—still one of the biggest challenges for upstream vessels. Although only partly successful in preventing English pirates from penetrating into Nicaragua, the Fortress of the Immaculate Conception is an impressive and sure bet as a tourist attraction.

The town of El Castillo is a happily isolated river community with no roads, no cars, and within earshot of the rapids. Its residents work on farms in the surrounding hills, fish the river, commute to the sawmill in Sábalos, the palm oil factory up the Río San Juan, or at one of the new resorts up and down the river. Then, of course, there are those who illegally cross into Costa Rica (only a 45-minute walk away) and send money home after the seasonal harvests.

History

The first fortification was placed here in 1602, in what was named "The House of the Devil" by the mayor of Granada, Ruy Díaz, on the first Spanish exploration of the river in 1525. Later, in 1673, Spain commissioned the building of a new fort, which, when completed two years later, was the largest fortress of its kind in Central America, with 32 cannons and 11,000 weapons. Granada, at long last, felt safe and its people celebrated in the streets.

In 1762, Spain and Britain began the Seven Year War, prompting the governor of Jamaica to order an invasion of Nicaragua. An expedition of 2,000 soldiers took all the fortifications until they reached El Castillo, where a massive battle commenced on July 29th. Rafaela Herrera, the 19-year-old daughter of the fort's fallen commander, Jose Herrera, seized command of her father's troops and succeeded in driving the British off, who retreated to San Juan del Norte on August 3rd.

Eighteen years later, 22-year-old Horatio Nelson entered the Río San Juan with a force of 3,500 men. He captured the fortification at Bartola on April 9th, and then, two days later, made a surprise attack on El Castillo by circling around on foot and storming it from the land. Nelson's attack was successful, and he took 270 Spanish prisoners. Alas, holding on to his new possession

SOLENTINAME & THE RÍO SAN JUAN

© JOSHUA BERMAN

the Río San Juan seen from the ruins of El Castillo

proved more difficult than the actual battle, and in 1781, after nine months in El Castillo without any reinforcement, the soon-to-be Lord Admiral Horatio Nelson and his handful of surviving soldiers—all rotting from sickness—pulled out of the Río San Juan.

Today, there's less blood on the castle and a lot more moss; and El Castillo is still a strategic place to visit.

Orientation and Getting Around

Pulling up to the dock on the south side of the river, you'll find a small cement square, guarded by twin cannons and a tourism office, and sitting on the main sidewalk that runs along the river's edge in both directions. The **Albergue** is above you at the top of the stairs, which also lead to a second walkway that passes the Castillo, the town school, and more homes.

Visiting the Fort

As part of its celebration of 500 years of influence in the Americas, the Spanish government launched a big project in El Castillo in which it cleaned up the ruins of the old fortress, installed a historical museum and library within the structure, and built the nearby school and Hotel Albergue. The museum costs $1 to enter and is a must-see if you've made it this far. Consider spending some downtime sitting in the surrounding grass fields and contemplating the river. Ask about the Centro de Interpretación and the alleged *mariposario* (butterfly farm).

Fishing

Abner Espinoza, better known as Cofal, and his organization, AMEC (see below under Information and Services) are busy arranging a regular service for travelers intent on snagging a *sábalo* bigger than themselves. Local boat rental goes for $10 an hour for two people, rods and lures for $5 a day ($10 to replace a lost lure). Cofal can also find you a more professional rig (probably one of Montecristo's boats) for up to $100 a day.

Hikes and River Tours

A number of half- or full-day river tours and hikes can be arranged, also through Cofal and the AMEC *caseta,* and involving upstream journeys on several of the area tributaries. For $5 a person, you can hire a local guide to take you on a four-hour hike through the hills and farms behind El Castillo, including visits to one or more of the seven rural communities; horses cost $10 per beast per day. All boat trips are for groups of six, and figure an additional cost of $15 a day for your guide. A four-hour hike in the Gran Reserva Indio-Maíz costs $32, a deeper jungle trip called **Sendero de Agua Fresca** costs $60, and a wildlife tour of the **Ríos Santa Cruz** (palm plantation), Romerito, and Poposól is $50. These packages and prices are most likely subject to change with increased or diminished demand, so be sure to ask around and know exactly what kind of deal you're striking.

Accommodations

There are several *hospedajes,* including **Aurora** and **Manantial,** on the main drag. They charge $2 a night and don't offer much. Walking downstream from the dock, look for El Chino's **Hospedaje Nena,** with 14 rooms and a street-side balcony for $4 a night.

Hotel Richarson [sic] can host 10 people in six rooms, with private bath and fan, $10 single, $15 couple, run by Danny Aragón, vice president of AMEC. It's set off on a side path from the main drag.

The **Hotel Albergue El Castillo** was built by the Spanish in 1992 as part of the same project that refurbished the fort. The Albergue is a two-story wooden lodge with a double balcony overlooking the thin strip of town, the river, and rapids beyond. It sleeps up to 30 people, with shared bath, and the $12 per person price includes a solid breakfast and bottomless cup of coffee (legitimate coffee, not instant—a rarity in these parts). There is also a roomy, elegant bar and restaurant. Sit on the porch with your journal and a thermos full of coffee as you watch the tarpons rise above the rapids, tel. 892-0174.

Food

Oddly enough, as of press time, there are only two restaurants in all of El Castillo. One is the

Hotel Albergue, with meals from about $4, river shrimp for $7. The **Bar y Restaurante Cofalito,** right on the water, specializes in *chorizo de sábalo.*

Information and Services

The tourist *caseta* in front of the dock is actually a group operation known as the Asociación Municipal Ecoturismo El Castillo (AMEC) and headed up by Cofal. AMEC is constantly working on an updated list of local guides, boat services, and has compiled a series of hikes and other things to do while in town; contact them via the phone at the Albergue. Speaking of which, the most reliable—and expensive—phone in town is the satellite phone at the Albergue ($1 a minute within Nicaragua, $3 out of country).

Getting There and Away

Lanchas colectivas depart San Carlos daily at 8 A.M., noon, 2 P.M., and 3 P.M. The 2.5-hour trip to El Castillo costs only $3. Alternatively, a private *panga* costs $110 each way for a group of 10 people and takes under two hours.

BARTOLA

This is your first access point into a vast, 3,618-square-kilometer virgin rainforest, set aside by the Nicaraguan government as the Gran Reserva Biológica Río Indio-Maíz. The western border of the reserve is made up by the Río Bartola at its confluence with the Río San Juan, just six kilometers down the river from El Castillo (or about three hours by boat from San Carlos). Hikes can be arranged through the local MARENA post, with AMEC in El Castillo, or at the **Gùises de Montaña y Refugio Bartola,** a self-described ecolodge and research station. The compound (soon to feature a natural history museum as well) has 11 rooms at the end of the world, with private bath and mosquito nets, all surrounded by rainforest and fueled by solar energy. **Hotel Refugio Bartola,** tel./fax 289-7924 or 289-4154, email: bartola@guises.org. (Bartola is difficult to contact and you may need to wait until you're in El Castillo.)

SAN JUAN DEL NORTE

About 100 winding kilometers beyond El Castillo, Nicaragua's extreme southeast corner is home to a motley mix of some 900 residents in the small, yet hugely historic, town of San Juan del Norte. Known as Greytown for much of its history as an English settlement (after the land was seized in 1848 by Sir Charles Grey, governor of Jamaica), this lonely cluster of eternally damp buildings is, perhaps more than anywhere else in the country, the end of the line. The town was completely reconstructed on a new foundation after the Contra war and Hurricane Joan leveled it in the 1980s, and now it lies hidden in the brackish swamps at the mouth of the Río San Juan. The site of the old San Juan and its interesting cemetery (where segregated burial plots and many English and U.S. graves attest to the town's rich history) is overgrown and spooky, accessible with the help of a local guide.

Of the backpackers who have journeyed to San Juan del Norte looking to continue north to Bluefields, most have found themselves stranded in a rat-infested room, with nothing to do but play dominoes, drink beer, swat mosquitoes, and sweat profusely. The few travelers we know who succeeded in reaching Bluefields universally reported near-death experiences and spending hundreds of dollars (except one, who found herself speeding north as a personal guest of Comandante Cero, the famous army commander with a legacy in both the revolution and the Contra war).

Nevertheless, most of those who have made the trip to San Juan del Norte reported it worth their while, if only for time spent drinking Costa Rican beer with reggae-loving fishermen and outlandish local characters. They also warn of impressive quantities of both rain and mosquitoes. As for getting around or arranging trips into the jungle, there are many local *pangueros*—talk to a few, find someone you trust, and compare prices.

Accommodations and Food

Tío Pum offers basic rooms for $3, shared bath, and an early curfew. Hedley Acton Thomas Barss, known more commonly as **Chalí,** also has a *hospedaje* for $3. Chalí is the person in charge of the cemetery and can help you get there. **Melvin** has clean rooms for $7 a night. For food, try **Doña Angela, Doña Fran,** or **El Ranchón,** and for dancing some *soka,* it's **Disco-Bar de Pulú Fantasía.**

Services

There aren't many. There are some newly installed satellite phones, including one in the mayor's office, tel. 273-3055. There is also a MARENA office, army and naval base, and police station.

The Río Indio Lodge

Just to keep things interesting, San Juan del Norte is the site of a $1.2 million, five-star, "ecotourism and sportfishing resort," on the riverbank one kilometer outside of town, right on the border of the Río Indio-Maíz Reserve. The Río Indio Lodge has already attracted various tour operators (including Solentiname Tours) to bring their clients here, and, despite the whopping price tag (rooms start at $225 a night!), the hotel is reportedly booked solid for its debut 2002 season. The operation includes a main lodge and restaurant complex, guest rooms, a swimming pool, and spa. Coming soon: a jungle survival camp with training by Nicaraguan special forces agents. Or so its literature says. For a list of the five-star prices (this is not for your average backpacker), go to www.bluwing.com, or email Dr. Lopez himself at: bluewing@racsa.co.cr., tel. 273-3082.

Getting There and Away

The easiest way to get to San Juan del Norte is to fork over some major dollars to a tour company; the most realistic is a long boat ride downriver from San Carlos. The boat leaves there Tuesday and Friday at 6 A.M. (buy tickets the day before), takes at least nine hours, and costs $11 each way. The same vessels leave San Juan Thursday and Sunday at 4 A.M.

The proposed air strip is still just that—proposed. Nevertheless, with big money investing in the area, regular flights to Managua can't be too far away.

Crossing into Costa Rica

Many of San Juan del Norte's residents commute the three-hour walk to work at the tourist facilities in Tortuguero, Costa Rica, which is also accessible by descending the Río Colorado. However, we have received conflicting reports about the feasibility of making this crossing as a tourist. There is reportedly only one dazed migration officer in town to take care of your paperwork, and he may insist on any amount of bureaucracy involving his superiors in San Carlos, which could take weeks. If you go illegally, you risk being gunned down by army patrols as a suspected smuggler. You're better off at the border crossing on the Río Frío.

SOLENTINAME & THE RÍO SAN JUAN

Resources

Glossary

alcaldía: mayor's office

arroyo: stream or gully

artesanía: crafts

ayudante: "helper"—the guy on the bus who collects your fee after you find a seat

barrio: neighborhood

bombero: firefighter

bravo: rough, strong, wild

cabo: cape

cafetín: light food eatery

calle: street

cama matrimonial: "marriage bed"—motels and hotels use this term to refer to a double, queen, or king-sized bed, a bed meant for two people.

campesino: country folk

campo: countryside

carretera: highway, road

cayo: cay

centro de salud: public MINSA-run health clinic; there's one in most towns

centro recreativo: public recreation center

cerro: hill or mountain

cerveza, cervecita: beer

chinelas: rubber flip-flops

ciudad: city

colectivo: a shared taxi or passenger boat

colonía: neighborhood

comedor: cheap lunch counter

comida corriente: plate of the day

complejo: complex (of buildings)

cooperitiva: cooperative

cordoba: Nicaraguan currency

cordillera: mountain range

corriente: standard, base

coyote: illegal immigrant smuggler; or profit-cutting middleman

cuajada: white, homemade, salty cheese

departamentos: subsection of Nicaragua, akin to states or counties

empalme: intersection of two roads

entrada: entrance

estero: estuary or marsh

expreso: express bus

farmacia: pharmacy, drugstore

fiestas patronales: Saint's Day Party, a yearly throw-down in every town and city

fritanga: street-side barbecue and fry-fest

gallo pinto: national mix of rice 'n' beans

gancho: gap in a fence

gaseosa: carbonated beverage

gringo: North American, or any foreigner

guaro: booze

guitarrón: mariachi bass guitar

hospedaje: hostel, budget hotel

iglesia: church

isla: island

laguna: lake

lancha: small passenger boat

lanchero: lancha driver

malecón: waterfront

manzana: besides an apple, this is also a measure of land equal to 100 square *varas*, or 1.74 acres

mar: sea or ocean

mariachi: Mexican country/polka music

mercado: market

mesa/meseta: geographical plateau

mosquitero: mosquito net

muelle: dock, wharf

museo: museum

ordinario: local bus (also *ruteado*)

panga: small passenger boat

panguero: *panga* driver

playa: beach

pueblo: small town or village

pulpería: corner store

puro: cigar

quintal: 100-lb. sack

rancheras: Mexican drinking songs

rancho: thatch-roofed restaurant or hut

rato: a short period of time

reserva: reserve or preserve

río: river

salida: exit, road out of town

salto: waterfall

sierra: mountain range

suave: soft, easy, quiet

vara: colonial unit of distance equal to roughly one meter

volcán: volcano

Spanish Phrasebook

Pronunciation Guide

Spanish pronunciation is much more regular than that of English, but there are still occasional variations.

Consonants

c — as 'c' in "cat," before 'a', 'o', or 'u'; like 's' before 'e' or 'i'

d — as 'd' in "dog," except between vowels, then like 'th' in "that"

g — before 'e' or 'i,' like the 'ch' in Scottish "loch"; elsewhere like 'g' in "get"

h — always silent

j — like the English 'h' in "hotel," but stronger

ll — like the 'y' in "yellow"

ñ — like the 'ni' in "onion"

r — always pronounced as strong 'r'

rr — trilled 'r'

v — similar to the 'b' in "boy" (not as English 'v')

y — similar to English, but with a slight "j" sound. When standing, alone it's pronounced like the 'e' in "me".

z — like 's' in "same"

b, f, k, l, m, n, p, q, s, t, w, x — as in English

Vowels

a — as in "father," but shorter

e — as in "hen"

i — as in "machine"

o — as in "phone"

u — usually as in "rule"; when it follows a 'q' the 'u' is silent; when it follows an 'h' or 'g', it's pronounced like 'w,' except when it comes between 'g' and 'e' or 'i', when it's also silent (unless it has an umlaut, when it again pronounced as English 'w'

Stress

Native English speakers frequently make errors of pronunciation by ignoring stress—all Spanish vowels—a, e, i, o and u—may carry accents that determine which syllable of a word gets emphasis. Often, stress seems unnatural to nonnative speakers—the surname Chávez, for instance, is stressed on the first syllable—but failure to observe this rule may mean that native speakers may not understand you.

Numbers

0 - cero
1 - uno (masculine)
1 - una (feminine)
2 - dos
3 - tres
4 - cuatro
5 - cinco
6 - seis
7 - siete
8 - ocho
9 - nueve
10 - diez
11 - once
12 - doce
13 - trece
14 - catorce
15 - quince
16 - dieciseis
17 - diecisiete
18 - dieciocho
19 - diecinueve
20 - veinte
21 - veintiuno
30 - treinta
40 - cuarenta
50 - cincuenta
60 - sesenta
70 - setenta
80 - ochenta
90 - noventa
100 - cien
101 - ciento y uno
200 - doscientos
1,000 - mil
10,000 - diez mil
1,000,000 - un millón

Days of the Week

Sunday - domingo
Monday - lunes
Tuesday - martes
Wednesday - miércoles
Thursday - jueves
Friday - viernes
Saturday - sábado

Time

While Nicaraguans mostly use the 12-hour clock, in some instances, usually associated with plane or bus schedules, they may use the 24-hour military clock. Under the 24-hour clock, for example, *las nueve de la noche* (9 P.M.) would be *las 21 horas* (2100 hours).

What time is it? - ¿Qué hora es?
It's one o'clock - Es la una.
It's two o'clock - Son las dos.
At two o'clock - A las dos.
It's ten to three - Son tres menos diez.
It's ten past three - Son tres y diez.
It's three fifteen - Son las tres y cuarto.
It's two forty five - Son tres menos cuarto.
It's two thirty - Son las dos y media.
It's six A.M. - Son las seis de la mañana.
It's six P.M. - Son las seis de la tarde.
It's ten P.M. - Son las diez de la noche.
Today - hoy
Tomorrow - mañana
Morning - la mañana
Tomorrow morning - mañana por la mañana
Yesterday - ayer
Week - la semana
Month - mes
Year - año
Last night - anoche
The next day - el día siguiente

Useful Words and Phrases

Nicaraguans and other Spanish-speaking people consider formalities important. Whenever approaching anyone for information or some other reason, do not forget the appropriate salutation—good morning, good evening, etc. Standing alone, the greeting *hola* (hello) can sound brusque.

Hello. - Hola.
Good morning. - Buenos días.
Good afternoon. - Buenas tardes.
Good evening. - Buenas noches.
How are you? - ¿Cómo está?
Fine. - Muy bien.
And you? - ¿Y usted?
So-so. - Más o menos.
Thank you. - Gracias.
Thank you very much. - Muchas gracias.
You're very kind. - Muy amable.
You're welcome - De nada (literally, "It's nothing.")
Yes - sí
No - no
I don't know. - No sé.
It's fine; okay - Está bien.
Good; okay - Bueno.
Please - por favor
Pleased to meet you. - Mucho gusto.
Excuse me (physical) - Perdóneme.
Excuse me (speech) - Discúlpeme.
I'm sorry. - Lo siento.
Goodbye - adiós
See you later - hasta luego (literally, "until later")
More - más
Less - menos
Better - mejor
Much, a lot - mucho
A little - un poco
Large - grande
Small - pequeño, chico
Quick, fast - rápido
Slowly - despacio
Bad - malo
Difficult - difícil
Easy - fácil
He/She/It is gone; as in "She left," "He's gone" - Ya se fue.
I don't speak Spanish well. - No hablo bien el español.
I don't understand. - No entiendo.

How do you say... in Spanish? - ¿Cómo se dice... en español?

Do you understand English? - ¿Entiende el inglés?

Is English spoken here? (Does anyone here speak English?) - ¿Se habla inglés aquí?

Terms of Address

When in doubt, use the formal *usted* (you) as a form of address. If you wish to dispense with formality and feel that the desire is mutual, you can say *Me puedes tutear* (you can call me "tu").

I - yo
You (formal) - usted
you (familiar) - tú
He/him - él
She/her - ella
We/us - nosotros
You (plural) - ustedes
They/them (all males or mixed gender) - ellos
They/them (all females) - ellas
Mr., sir - señor
Mrs., madam - señora
Miss, young lady - señorita
Wife - esposa
Husband - marido or esposo
Friend - amigo (male), amiga (female)
Sweetheart - novio (male), novia (female)
Son, daughter - hijo, hija
Brother, sister - hermano, hermana
Father, mother - padre, madre
Grandfather, grandmother - abuelo, abuela

Getting Around

Where is... ? - ¿Dónde está... ?
How far is it to... ? - ¿A cuanto está... ?
from... to... - de... a...
Highway - la carretera
Road - el camino
Street - la calle
Block - la cuadra
Kilometer - kilómetro
North - norte
South - sur

West - oeste; poniente
East - este; oriente
Straight ahead - al derecho; adelante
To the right - a la derecha
To the left - a la izquierda

Accommodations

¿Hay cuarto? - Is there a room?
May I (we) see it? - ¿Puedo (podemos) verlo?
What is the rate? - ¿Cuál es el precio?
Is that your best rate? - ¿Es su mejor precio?
Is there something cheaper? - ¿Hay algo más económico?
Single room - un sencillo
Double room - un doble
Room for a couple - matrimonial
Key - llave
With private bath - con baño
With shared bath - con baño general; con baño compartido
Hot water - agua caliente
Cold water - agua fría
Ducha - shower
Ducha eléctrica - electric shower
Towel - toalla
Soap - jabón
Toilet paper - papel higiénico
Air conditioning - aire acondicionado
Fan - abanico; ventilador
Blanket - frazada; manta
Sheets - sábanas

Public Transport

Bus stop - la parada
Bus terminal - terminal de buses
Airport - el aeropuerto
Launch - lancha; tiburonera
Dock - muelle
I want a ticket to... - Quiero un pasaje a...
I want to get off at... - Quiero bajar en...
Here, please. - Aquí, por favor.
Where is this bus going? - ¿Adónde va este autobús?
Round-trip - ida y vuelta
What do I owe - ¿Cuánto le debo?

Food

Menu - la carta, el menú
Glass - taza
Fork - tenedor
Knife - cuchillo
Spoon - cuchara
Napkin - servilleta
Soft drink - agua fresca
Coffee - café
Cream - crema
Tea - té
Sugar - azúcar
Drinking water - agua pura, agua potable
Bottled carbonated water - agua mineral con gas
Bottled uncarbonated water - agua sin gas
Beer - cerveza
Wine - vino
Milk - leche
Juice - jugo
Eggs - huevos
Bread - pan
Watermelon - sandía
Banana - banano
Plantain - plátano
Apple - manzana
Orange - naranja
Meat (without) - carne (sin)
Beef - carne de res
Chicken - pollo; gallina
Fish - pescado
Shellfish - mariscos
Shrimp - camarones
Fried - frito
Roasted - asado
Barbecued - a la parrilla
Breakfast - desayuno
Lunch - almuerzo
Dinner (often eaten in late afternoon) - comida
Dinner, or a late night snack - cena
The check, or bill - la cuenta

Making Purchases

I need... - Necesito...
I want... - Deseo... or Quiero...
I would like... (more polite) - Quisiera...
How much does it cost? - ¿Cuánto cuesta?
What's the exchange rate? - ¿Cuál es el tipo de cambio?
May I see... ? - ¿Puedo ver... ?
This one - ésta/ésto
Expensive - caro
Cheap - barato
Cheaper - más barato
Too much - demasiado

Health

Help me please. - Ayúdeme por favor.
I am ill. - Estoy enfermo.
Pain - dolor
Fever - fiebre
Stomach ache - dolor de estómago
Vomiting - vomitar
Diarrhea - diarrea
Drugstore - farmacia
Medicine - medicina
Pill, tablet - pastilla
Birth control pills - pastillas anticonceptivas
Condom - condón, preservativo

Suggested Reading

There are more out-of-print books about Nicaragua than there are currently on the shelves. If you can't find the following books in the library or online (www.dogbert.abebooks.com/abe and www.powells.com are both excellent sources, with hundreds of books about Nicaragua), go to a used bookstore and get lost in the Latin America section.

The Revolution

Probably 98 percent of all books ever written about Nicaragua deal with the Sandinista revolution and ensuing civil war. Of these, many were written by journalists assigned to the country in the 1980s— their books are often unique hybrids of history, novel, travelogue, ethnography, and political science text. Also, being the literary people they are, a great deal of books were written by participants in the revolution, and readers with some time on their hands can experience some fascinating inside perspectives on what has been called "one of the great contemporary events of the Western Hemisphere."

Barrios de Chamorro, Violeta. *Dreams of the Heart.* Simon & Schuster, 1996. A very readable and human history of Nicaragua from the Somoza years through Doña Violeta's electoral triumph in 1990.

Cabezas, Omar. *Fire from the Mountain (La Montaña es Algo Más que una Grán Estapa Verde).* Crown, 1985. A ribald, vernacular account of what it's like to be a guerrilla soldier in the mountains of Nicaragua; one of the few books about the early stages of the revolution.

Cardenal, Ernesto; Walsh, Donald D. (translator). *The Gospel in Solentiname.* Orbis Books, 1979. These are the transcripts of the masses on Solentiname that helped spawn the Liberation Theology movement.

Chomsky, Noam. *Turning the Tide: U.S. Intervention in Central America and the Struggle for Peace.* South End Press, 1985. Succinctly and powerfully shows how U.S. Central American policies implement broader U.S. economic, military, and social aims.

Cruz, Arturo, Jr. *Memoirs of a Counterrevolutionary: Life with the Contras, the Sandinistas, and the CIA.* Doubleday, 1989. Although the narrative jumps all over the place, Cruz offers interesting anecdotes to the reader who already knows something of the central characters, including an up-close portrait of Edén Pastora. Overall, Cruz is most successful in showing just how complex the situation actually was— with treachery and shifting alliances on both sides; at times, however, it is so complex that the reader is lost in a sea of names.

Davis, Peter. *Where is Nicaragua?* Simon & Schuster, 1987. Davis breaks down the revolution and Contra war, and ties it all into the country's history; he articulates the complexity of the situation in a graspable manner.

Dickey, Christopher. *With the Contras.* Simon & Schuster, 1985. Dickey was the *Washington Post* correspondent in Honduras and his book makes an excellent complement to Kinzer, who spent much more time with the Sandinistas.

Gentile, William Frank. *Nicaragua: Photographs by William Frank Gentile; Introduction by William M. LeoGrande; An Interview with Sergio Ramírez Mercado.* W. W. Norton & Company, 1989. These are some of the deepest, most powerful photos you'll ever see, with fantastic juxtapositions of Contra and FSLN soldiers.

Kinzer, Stephen. *Blood of Brothers: Life and War in Nicaragua.* G. P. Putnam's Sons, 1991. If you're only going to read one book, this is the one.

Kinzer, the *New York Times* Managua bureau chief during the war, sensed that Nicaragua was "a country with more to tell the world than it had been able to articulate, a country with a message both political and spiritual."

Kunzle, David. *The Murals of Revolutionary Nicaragua 1979–1992.* University of California Press, 1995. Many murals were strictly political, but most intertwined the revolutionary process with cultural, historical, and literary themes, all celebrated in Kunzle's book; 83-page introduction and 100 color plates.

Randall, Margaret. *Risking a Somersault in the Air.* Just as much about Nicaraguan literature as it is about the revolution, this is a fascinating series of interviews with Nicaraguan authors and poets, most of whom were part of the FSLN revolution and government.

Randall, Margaret. *Sandino's Daughters.* New Star Books, 1981. Written about the role of feminism in the Sandinista revolution, via a series of interviews with participants.

Rushdie, Salman. *The Jaguar Smile.* Elisabeth Sifton Books, 1987. A poetic, passionate jaunt with the Sandinistas and careful (if short) examination of their policies.

Sklar, Holly. *Washington's War on Nicaragua.* South End Press, 1988. Inspection of the Washington politics behind the Contra war.

Nicaraguans

Lancaster, Roger N. *Life Is Hard: Machismo, Danger, and the Intimacy of Power in Nicaragua.* University of California Press, 1992. Lancaster is an anthropologist and this is an ethnography studying not current events, but their effect on the Nicaraguan individual and family. It is intimate and offers details about Nicaraguan life that one can only get living with the people in their very homes. Also, Lancaster pays attention to issues often passed over, like homosexuality, domestic violence, broken families, and the roots of machismo.

Plunkett, Hazel. *In Focus Nicaragua: A Guide to the People, Politics and Culture.* Interlink Books, 1999. A 100-page overview to Nicaragua, including Nicaraguans in the 1990s.

Squier, Ephraim George. *Nicaragua; Its People, Scenery, Monuments, and the Proposed Interoceanic Canal.* D. Appleton, 1852. Squier remains one of Nicaragua's most prolific writers; this massive, multivolume tome is available for hundreds of dollars in rare bookstores. The discussion is divided into five parts in which he describes geography and topography; the events during the author's residence, including accounts of his explorations; observations on the proposed canal; notes on the indigenous of the country, including information regarding geographical distribution, languages, institutions, religions, and customs; and the political history of the country since its independence from Spain.

Poetry

Morelli, Marco. *Rubén's Orphans.* Painted Rooster Press, 2001. An anthology of contemporary Nicaraguan poets, with English translations.

White, Steven, translator. *Poets of Nicaragua: A Bilingual Anthology 1918–1970.* Unicorn Press, 1983.

Miscellaneous

Hulme, Krekel, and O'Reilly. *Not Just Another Nicaragua Travel Guide.* Mango Publications, 1990. Get it if you can find it.

Marriot, Edward. *Savage Shore: Life and Death with Nicaragua's Last Shark Hunters.* Owl Books, 2001. A curious and descriptive journey up the Río San Juan and beyond.

Norsworthy, Kent, with Tom Barry. *Nicaragua: A Country Guide.* The Inter-Hemispheric Education Resource Center, 1989.

Internet Resources

Moon Handbooks and the Authors
Moon Handbooks: www.moon.com
Joshua Berman: www.stonegrooves.net
Randy Wood: www.therandymon.com

Links
The Internet is loaded with pages concerning Nicaragua and long, eclectic lists of links abound. Following are a few central sites to get you started.

IBW Internet Gateway
www.ibw.com.ni
This is one of the most complete, most regularly updated portals to all things Nicaraguan, including services (tourism and otherwise), publications, organizations, and general information (mostly in Spanish).

University of Texas
www.lanic.utexas.edu/la/ca/nicaragua
A very complete list of links, including academic institutions and sites, more Nica portals, active nongovernmental organizations, and government ministries in Nicaragua.

Virginia Tech
www.cyber.vt.edu/wd3784nic/niclink.html
This is a long, very complete list of general Nicaragua links, notably with a focus on forestry and environmental issues.

General
U.S. State Department
www.state.gov
Seek out the U.S. government's background Nicaragua notes and travel warnings.

CIA World Factbook
www.cia.gov/cia/publications/factbook/geos/nu.html
More current U.S. government-sponsored information on Nicaraguan geography, people, government, economy, communications, transportation, and the military, courtesy of the folks who brought you the Contra war.

Current population data
www.population-statistics.com/fr/fr_ni.htm

Photos
www.agstar.com.ni
Tomás Stargardter is a Nicaragua-based photojournalist whose website features a wide range of Nicaraguan images, from the natural to the extreme to the political (several of which are featured in this book).

Travel logs
www.mrhalliday.com
This site features write-ups and photos of Mark Halliday's adventures in Nicaragua, including "You Won't Die," which has invaluable details on what to expect if traveling down the Río Coco.

Political/Solidarity
The Nicaragua Network
www.nicanet.org
For over 20 years the U.S.-based Nicaragua Network has been committed to social and economic justice for the people of Nicaragua.

Witness for Peace
www.witnessforpeace.org
This is a politically independent, grassroots organization whose mission is to support peace, justice, and sustainable economies in the Americas by changing U.S. policies and corporate practices that contribute to poverty and oppression in Latin America and the Caribbean.

Global Exchange
www.globalexchange.org

Global Exchange is a human rights organization dedicated to promoting environmental, political, and social justice around the world. It has long had a focus on Nicaraguan issues.

Moving to Nicaragua
Escape Artist
www.escapeartist.com/nicaragua/
nicaragua.htm

Practical information for expatriates.

Hurricane Mitch
Mitch's official homepage
www.ncdc.noaa.gov/ol/reports/mitch/
mitch.html

This is the U.S. National Oceanic Atmospheric Administration's fact page on one of the most destructive storms on record, with specific information on how it affected Nicaragua.

USA Today
www.usatoday.com/weather/
huricane/1998/wmitch.htm

The *USA Today* Hurricane Mitch story index with links to articles, satellite photos, and other Mitch paraphernalia.

BEACHES

FESTIVALS

HIKING

MUSEUMS

NATIONAL PARKS AND RESERVES

Acknowledgments

We are indebted to a tremendous number of people who were kind enough to share their knowledge, time, and artistry with us, enabling us to fill this book with as many hard facts (and subtle nods) as we were able to. The following folks are biologists, engineers, agronomists, historians, and poets; they are mothers, farmers, musicians, and professors; they are Nicaraguans and they are *internacionalistas* alike, each with a unique and passionate connection to this country.

With that, we thank Tomás Stargardter, who was incredibly generous to share his photography with us and our readers; his images appear throughout the book and can also be seen at www.agstar.com.ni. We are also grateful to Todd Berman for submitting his wonderful illustrations even though, because of evolving design paradigms, they did not get printed. Todd is a big-haired, politically active original artist in San Francisco, California, and can be reached via his website: www.whatdemocracy.org. We tip a steaming cup of black, shade-grown coffee to Byron Corrales, Paul Katzeff, Chris Bacon, Eddy Kuhl, Carlos Javier Mejía, and Beth Goodall; followed by a nod to Daniel Alegría (who has forgotten more about Nicaragua than we will ever know) and Juan Carlos Martinez, who tapped us into a golden network of contacts; Gianantonio Ricci and Jordi Pascual Sala were key in the Río San Juan, and Tim Coone graciously gave us "Canal Dreams" and a whole lot of history; *gracias* to David and Dorothy Ferber, Margaret Harrit, Maritza Rivera, Porfirio Zepeda, Josie Walker, Birgit Cory, Marco Morelli, and Jean Michel Maes. Don Noel Montenegro sat and discussed the El Sauce railroad in his home one evening, and Carlos Mejía Godoy served up a private lunch and lecture on Nicaraguan music; in Diriamba, thanks to Ing. Sylvio Echeverry, Jaime Cerano, and Pat Werner. Zoila Blandón helped flesh out the Managua chapter and Milena Popp helped get it all on the map, Arely Waldsam showed us some of

León's secrets, and Tommy Haskins helped with the early proofing.

A huge, beachfront hug to Marie Mendel in San Juan del Sur, and while we're down there, how 'bout a sloppy, soul-surfing kiss for Dale "Jale-la-Juja" Dagger; thanks to Paul Phelan, Chris Humphrey, Richard Tuck, Kaia K., Eric van der Berghe, Monica Drazba, Raúl Gavarrette, Jeffrey McCrary, Sergio Zepeda, Ligia María Vaughan, David Brooks, Gladys Morales, Prof. Josefa Emelina Delgado de Breves, Agustín Aguilar P., Carlos Danilo Vargas Gutierrez, Luis Lautaro Ruiz, Ruth Coles and Phoebe; Danny Boster and Laurindo Maranhao test drove some of the worst roads in the east, and Jairo y Maribet and Dr. Armando Incer Barquero spilled the beans in their hometowns of Jinotega and Boaco.

We'd like to acknowledge Stephen Kinzer, whose book, *Blood of Brothers,* was instrumental in our initial and continued understanding of Nicaragua. We must also mention Henry Morgan at Radio Pirata, who spun the soundtrack for much of our production process (but we *do not* thank his lame sidekick, Sancho Panchez).

Significant parts of this book would not have been possible without the affection, hospitality, and *gallo pinto* of the Escoto family in La Trinidad (Darwin, Karla, Darling, and Karling) and the Ortiz Gaitans in Pio XII (Mama Mercedes, Don Julio, Lastenia, Mardis, Neyda, and Edén). Thanks to the Zavala Zamora family (and especially Kenia, Marillita, and Maykeling) in San Diego, and Eugenio and Telma and family in El Hato for helping provide the inspiration for this book. Special thanks to Ericka Briceño, for countless additions to the text of the manuscript, for proofing the early chapters, and much much more. Without her love and good-humored patience, this book wouldn't have been possible. And of course, thanks to our parents, all four of whom are on Long Island and are finally starting to see some payback for those Ivy League educations (kind of).

We'd like to send out a heartfelt thanks to our Peace Corps volunteer (PCV) friends and coworkers, who responded to our nagging requests for info about their sites. This book was conceived while the authors were themselves volunteers, immersed in the enormous collective knowledge of the widely distributed PCV network. We firmly believe this book is a much more valuable resource because of their contributions. They include Chinandeganos Todd Buchanon, Matteo "El Diablo Rojo" Harper, Cynthia Medina, and Miguel Doran; Carley Lovern for Corinto lovin' and Olin Cohan in Padre Ramos. Thanks to Michael Kojis, Kathy Seppone, and Barbara Whitelaw in Somoto; Jaime Tong and Cara Forster in La Trinidad; Kristina Underdal and Chris Bacon in Pueblo Nuevo; Kara Beckman and Scott Hasselman in Miraflor, and, along with Eileen Dunne, for their Estelí disco article in ¡Va Pué! Frank Giglio and Dawa Romito for Jinotepe gold, Charlyn Preheim and Joanna "The Canadian" Yazer (PCV by association) for hospitality in Diriamba, and of course, the Diriamba Dame herself: Karen Fligger. The inside Granada poop was served up by Nathan Dolenc, Jesse Griffin, Matt Prezanno, Aaron Davis, and Donna Tabor. Mad props to the "Rivas Divas Jodidas," Jean Walsh and Kim Feinberg, and to Aleen Tierney for all the good suggestions. An Atlantic coast reggae hug-up to Ana Bilik, Melissa Schuette, Max Gomberg, Renée Nickerson, Cara Endyke, Laura McCarthy, David Hatch, James "Jota-Jota" Saul, Ana Mercedes, and Andrew Middleton. Thanks to Karen Lam in Masaya, Libby Hayes in Boca de Sábalos, and the Queen of El Castillo, Christina Marsigli. Back in the north country, shout-outs for Kip Panabianco, Summer O'Meara, Sae Phu in Boaco, Emily White in Camoapa, Casey Welch, Susan, and Gerald Schwartz in Juigalpa, Julie McLaughlin in San Ramón, and Jim Russell in Santa Lucia. Large agradecimientos to Ryan Lamberg for test-driving several chapters (and never while escondido). Also Walter "Pijudo" Perkel on Ometepe, Chris Broughton in Nueva Guinéa, Nica 15-ers the world over, and everyone else who helped out or offered slurred secrets at the Shannon Bar, but whose names regretfully slipped through the cracks. Back in Bolonia, abrazos for Georgia, Timoteo, Mimi (María-Eugenia), Ana, María-Antonia, Miguelito, Paul, and the printers in the sala; and, although he was shipped off to Bolivia before he could help directly with our book, we offer a silent cowboy nod to our eternal jefe, Howard T. Lyon.

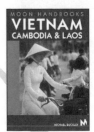

U.S. ~ Metric Conversion

1 inch	=	2.54 centimeters (cm)
1 foot	=	.304 meters (m)
1 yard	=	0.914 meters
1 mile	=	1.6093 kilometers (km)
1 km	=	.6214 miles
1 fathom	=	1.8288 m
1 chain	=	20.1168 m
1 furlong	=	201.168 m
1 acre	=	.4047 hectares
1 sq km	=	100 hectares
1 sq mile	=	2.59 square km
1 ounce	=	28.35 grams
1 pound	=	.4536 kilograms
1 short ton	=	.90718 metric ton
1 short ton	=	2000 pounds
1 long ton	=	1.016 metric tons
1 long ton	=	2240 pounds
1 metric ton	=	1000 kilograms
1 quart	=	.94635 liters
1 US gallon	=	3.7854 liters
1 Imperial gallon	=	4.5459 liters
1 nautical mile	=	1.852 km

To compute celsius temperatures, subtract 32 from Fahrenheit and divide by 1.8. To go the other way, multiply celsius by 1.8 and add 32.

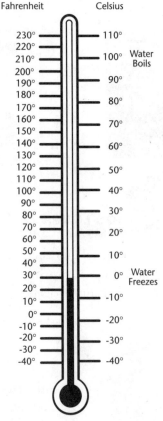

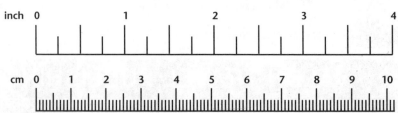